Police Interrogation and Confessions

Police Interrogation

and Confessions

Essays in Law and Policy

by Yale Kamisar

Ann Arbor The University of Michigan Press

Copyright © by The University of Michigan 1980

All rights reserved

Published in the United States of America by
The University of Michigan Press and simultaneously
in Rexdale, Canada, by John Wiley & Sons Canada, Limited

Manufactured in the United States of America

*Grateful acknowledgment is made to the following publishers for permission to reprint, with
alterations, the author's previously published articles:*

The Georgetown Law Journal for *Foreword:* Brewer v. Williams—*A Hard Look at a Discomfiting
Record*, 66 GEO. L.J. 209–43 (1977) and Brewer v. Williams, Massiah, *and* Miranda: *What Is
"Interrogation"? When Does It Matter?* 67 GEO. L.J. 1–101 (1978). Reprinted with permission
of the publisher; copyright © 1977 and © 1978 (respectively) by the Georgetown Law Journal.

Journal of Criminal Law and Criminology, Northwestern University School of Law, for *Fred E.
Inbau: "The Importance of Being Guilty,"* 68 J. CRIM. L. & CRIMINOLOGY 182–97 (1977).

The Michigan Law Review Association for *A Dissent from the* Miranda *Dissents: Some Comments
on the "New" Fifth Amendment and the Old "Voluntariness" Test,* 65 MICH. L. REV.
59–104 (1966) and *Kauper's "Judicial Examination of the Accused" Forty Years Later—
Some Comments on a Remarkable Article,* 73 MICH. L. REV. 15–38 (1974).

Rutgers Law Review, Rutgers University, for *What Is an "Involuntary" Confession? Some
Comments on Inbau and Reid's* Criminal Interrogation and Confessions, 17 RUTGERS L. REV.
728–59 (1963).

The University Press of Virginia for *Equal Justice in the Gatehouses and Mansions of American
Criminal Procedure,* in CRIMINAL JUSTICE IN OUR TIME 11–38 (A. Howard ed. 1965).

Library of Congress Cataloging in Publication Data

Kamisar, Yale.
  Police interrogation and confessions.

  Includes bibliographical references.
  1. Confession (Law)—United States—Addresses,
essays, lectures.   2.   Police questioning—United
States—Addresses, essays, lectures.   I.   Title.
KF9664.A75K35   345.73'052   80–10640
ISBN 0–472–09318–5

To My Mother and to the
Memory of My Father;
and to Christine, David,
Gordon, and Jon

Preface

I HAVE BEEN reading and thinking about police interrogation and confessions, and speaking, debating, and writing about the subject, for some two decades. In all that time many friends, colleagues, students, and former students have contributed significantly to my efforts. So have the many able lawyers, judges, professors, and law enforcement officials with whom I served on the *Model Code of Pre-Arraignment Procedure* and *Uniform Rules of Criminal Procedure* projects in the 1960s and 1970s. Although we did not always conduct our business dispassionately and in low voice (certainly *I* did not), today I have nothing but fond memories of the participants in those two major re-examinations of criminal law enforcement procedures.

My list of acknowledgments, then, is unusually long. Among those to whom I am indebted for contributing, directly or indirectly, to one or more of the essays that appear in this volume are: Frank Allen, Ron Allen, Bob Bartels, Elizabeth Bartholet, Steve Brodsky, Bill Bryant, Mitch Cheyette, Jesse Choper, Jack Cound, George Edwards, Ethan Falk, Ron Gould, Joe Grano, Alfred Hagan, Jim Hale, Bernie Hellring, Larry Herman, Mort Horwitz, Wayne LaFave, Ken Kirwin, Gary Kohlman, Peter Langrock, Jim Martin, Bert McElroy, Maynard Pirsig, Bob Pitler, Ken Pye, Jay Rabinowitz, Wally Rudolph, John Salmon, Herman Schwartz, Louis Schwartz, Claude Sowle, the late Harris Steinberg, Geoffrey Stone, the late Arthur Sutherland, Roger Traynor, Bernie Weisberg, Peter Westen, and Welsh White.

I am indebted most of all to my close friend and long-time colleague and collaborator, Jerold Israel. In the fifteen years we have been together at the University of Michigan Law School, Jerry and I have spent literally hundreds of hours discussing, and fighting about, the law and policies of confessions. My debt to him is huge, despite the fact (or should I say *because* of the fact) that more often than not we have disagreed.

Jerry Israel is only one of a goodly number who, hopefully, sharpened my thinking and improved my writing about the subject by forcing me to re-examine basic premises and underlying assumptions. I am indebted to this group, which includes: Ed Barrett, Paul Bator, Charles Breitel, Eugene Burdick, Frank Carrington, Arnie Enker, Charles Fried, Henry J. Friendly, Fred Inbau, John Keenan, Dick Kuh, J. Edward Lumbard, Frank Remington, Walter Schaefer, Dick Uviller, and Jim Vorenberg.

I wrote the essays collected in this volume while serving under six different deans. Each provided much encouragement and support. They are, in chronological order: William B. Lockhart, Erwin N. Griswold, Allan F.

Smith, the aforementioned Francis Allen, Theodore J. St. Antoine, and Terrance Sandalow. I thank them all.

Finally, I would like to express my gratitude to Alfred Sussman, Dean of the Rackham School of Graduate Studies at the University of Michigan at the time I dealt with the University of Michigan Press, and Walter Sears, Director of the University of Michigan Press, for their encouragement; to the members of the Michigan Press staff, who edited, produced, and promoted this collection with loving care; to Nadezhda Freedman, who prepared the tables of cases and authorities with speed, efficiency, and good cheer; and to my secretary, Anna Brylowski, who, as usual, performed admirably under trying conditions.

*

On a number of occasions I have updated the discussion of a point by calling attention to a case decided, or an article published, since the essay originally appeared. See bracketed portions of footnotes at pp. 92, 96-97, 133, and 177, and notes at pp. 236-37, 246, 249, and 282.

*

Footnotes in this volume are indicated in text by superior numbers; they appear at the bottom of relevant pages and are cross-referenced as *footnotes*. Notes are indicated in text by parenthetical superior numbers; they appear in a separate section following the last essay (p. 225) and are cross-referenced as *notes*.

—Y. K.

Contents

Introduction: "History never looks like history when
you are living through it," but the 1960s and 1970s
look like history now   xi

What Is an "Involuntary" Confession?   1

Equal Justice in the Gatehouses and Mansions
of American Criminal Procedure   27

A Dissent from the *Miranda* Dissents   41

Kauper's "Judicial Examination of the
Accused" Forty Years Later   77

Fred E. Inbau: "The Importance of Being Guilty"   95

Brewer v. Williams—A Hard Look at a
Discomfiting Record   113

Brewer v. Williams, Massiah and
Miranda: What Is "Interrogation"?
When Does It Matter?   139

Notes   225

Table of Cases   305

Table of Authorities   311

Introduction:

"History never looks like history when you are living through it," but the 1960s and 1970s look like history now

DESPITE APPEARANCES to the contrary, I never planned to write a series of articles on police interrogation and confessions. My first article on the subject, "What Is an 'Involuntary' Confession?", was not part of a grand design but merely a response to an invitation by the *Rutgers Law Review* to review a new edition of the Inbau-Reid interrogation manual. Until then, although I had written a number of articles on other criminal procedure issues, I had never wrestled in print with the police interrogation–confessions problem.

When, in 1963, I did finally get around to writing about confessions (the Inbau-Reid "book review" grew into an article and was published as such), it was later than I thought. Before I had finished the project, Winston Massiah (who had lost in the United States Court of Appeals for the Second Circuit) and Danny Escobedo (who had lost in the Supreme Court of Illinois), were seeking review in the United States Supreme Court, and one Ernesto Miranda—whose case would, in three years, push even the famous *Escobedo* and *Massiah* decisions off center stage—had been arrested for, and had confessed to, kidnapping and rape.

Thus, although I was unaware of these cases at the time, let alone the significant ways in which they would change our thinking about the law of confessions, my first confessions article turned out to be one of the last ever written about the "voluntariness"–"totality of the circumstances" test (at least until the 1980s).[1]

I had no intention of starting work on another piece about the subject so soon after the appearance of my Rutgers article, but a year later a member of the Magna Carta Commission of Virginia, Professor A.E. Dick Howard, persuaded me otherwise. For one thing, Professor Howard assured me that my remarks could be quite brief. For another, since my first article on the subject had been published, the Supreme Court had handed down two very interesting and highly controversial cases, *Massiah* and *Escobedo*. And after all, as Professor Howard reminded me, the 750th anniversary of Magna Carta does not come along every day.

So I agreed to give a talk at the College of William and Mary in February of 1965, contrasting the largely unregulated and unscrutinized practices in the

---

1. At this writing, Professor Joseph Grano is putting the finishing touches on an article urging a return to a *substantially modified* version of the "voluntariness" test. His article will appear in a forthcoming issue of the *Virginia Law Review*.

police station—the "gatehouse," where ideals are checked at the door and "realities" are faced—with the proceedings in the courtroom—the "mansion," where the defendant is "even dignified, the public invited, and a stirring ceremony in honor of individual freedom from law enforcement celebrated." How, I asked, can we reconcile the proceedings in the "mansion" with those in the "gatehouse"—through which most defendants journey and beyond which many never get? How can we explain why the Constitution requires so much in the "mansion," but means so little in the "gatehouse"?

When published some months later, along with essays by Professor Fred E. Inbau and Judge Thurman Arnold, in a handsome little paperback book, *Criminal Justice in Our Time*, my remarks, "Equal Justice in the Gatehouses and Mansions of American Criminal Procedure," were anything but brief. For I had spent months revising and expanding the original William and Mary speech. (A long section of the essay, one exploring the meaning and scope of *Escobedo*, has been omitted from the present volume because *Miranda* and other subsequent developments have rendered it largely obsolete.)[2]

As I trust the footnotes in my first two confessions essays reveal, a number of commentators who had arrived on the scene before me contributed much to my early writing on the subject: Professors Francis Allen, Albert Beisel, Charles McCormick, Bernard Meltzer, Monrad Paulsen, and Claude Sowle; and a young civil liberties lawyer (who was to file a splendid brief in the *Escobedo* case), Bernard Weisberg. But the root from which I drew the juices of indignation, I am convinced, was the tape recording of the six-hour interrogation in the 1962 *Biron* case.[3]

This was not simply a tape recording of a confession (they are not that rare), but of the interrogation itself—beginning with the first interrogator's opening remark (there were five interrogators in all) and the suspect's initial response. The decision to record the interrogation was not made with the intent to offer the tape in evidence or with any expectation that it would ever appear in the record. (Some of the interrogators didn't even realize that their remarks were being taped.) Most, if not all, of the detectives who interrogated Biron had been questioning murder suspects for years. There is no reason to think that the essential thrust and basic features of the Biron interrogation were any different from those that these same detectives had conducted in dozens of other cases. Indeed, if the various "how-you-do-it" and "how-we-did-it-ourselves" manuals are any indication, the "interrogation atmosphere" estab-

2. For a summary of the wide disagreement over the probable meaning of *Escobedo*—and over what it ought to mean—*see* p. 161 fn.26 *infra. See also* p. 217 fn. 94 *infra.*

3. Perhaps the Biron tape recording should be called the "secret root." For when I reread my first two confessions articles recently I discovered, to my surprise, that I had made no mention of the Biron recording in either one. The recording and its significance are discussed in my later writings. *See* pp. 98–99 *infra* and p. 134 fn.23 *infra. See also* the discussion in W. White, *Police Trickery in Inducing Confessions*, 127 U. PA. L. REV. 581, 615, 619, 624 (1979).

lished by Biron's interrogators and most of the tactics they employed were standard practice.[4] Yet, as far as I know, the *Biron* confession—the only one accompanied by a tape of the interrogation—was the only confession obtained by any of Biron's interrogators that a court ever excluded.

If the Biron interrogation had been an extraordinary instance of "wrenching from [an accused] evidence which would not be extorted in open court with all its safeguards,"[5] the tape recording would have been a good deal less troublesome. But it was not "an exhibit in a museum of third degree horrors."[6] For the most part, rather, it was a vivid illustration of the kinds of interrogation practices that at the time satisfied the best standards of professional police work and fell within the bounds of what the courts of that day called "fair and reasonable" questioning.[7] Even the state supreme court that struck down Biron's conviction (on the narrow ground that false legal advice by the police had vitiated the confession) repeatedly characterized the interrogation sessions as "interviews."[8]

"Interviews"? How can anyone who listens to the tapes call the interrogation sessions that?[9] How can anyone listen to the insistent questioning of Biron and to the many different ways his interrogators urged, cajoled, and nagged him to confess without feeling the relentless pressure, without sensing Biron's confusion and helplessness, without getting the message—confess now or it will be so much the worse for you later—and without wondering: what ever happened to the privilege against self-incrimination and the right to the assistance of counsel?

*

A year after the "gatehouses and mansions" essay appeared, the Supreme Court decided *Miranda*—the case that has come to symbolize the Warren Court's "revolution" in American criminal procedure. *Miranda,* especially the three *dissenting* opinions in the case, produced the only "self-initiated"

---

4. Some of the tactics utilized by Biron's interrogators (such as the misrepresentation that although Biron was slightly "over-age" he might be treated as a juvenile offender if he "cooperated" with the police) would be condemned by the writers of the interrogation manuals. But most of the interrogation techniques employed were those recommended by the manuals. *See* p. 98 fn.2, 3 *infra.*

5. Watts v. Indiana, 338 U.S. 49, 54 (1949) (Frankfurter, J.).

6. *Compare* the extracts from the ACLU brief in the *Escobedo* case (commenting on the widespread and "recommended" police interrogation techniques of the time) in Y. KAMISAR, W. LaFAVE & J. ISRAEL, MODERN CRIMINAL PROCEDURE 519 (4th ed. 1974).

7. *See id.* at 519–21.

8. *See* p. 99 fn. 3 *infra.*

9. When I was a Co-Reporter for the *Uniform Rules of Criminal Procedure* project in the early 1970s, some members of the project's Special Committee expressed reservations about a proposal, eventually adopted (*see* Rule 243), to record, whenever feasible, "the information of rights, and waivers thereof, and any questioning." I sent each of these committee members a

confessions article I have ever written, "A Dissent from the *Miranda* Dissents."

For some time I had been one of those who had applauded the direction in which the Warren Court was moving—catching heavy fire for doing so in various meetings of the Advisory Committee to the American Law Institute's *Model Code of Pre-Arraignment Procedure* project and in other professional gatherings. Thus I welcomed *Miranda*. But when, a short time after the decision had captured the headlines, I attended the annual meeting of the American Bar Association, it was plain that I was in the distinct minority. When I met with the Chief Justices of the States (whose annual meeting was held at about the same time) and participated in a series of confessions "workshop sessions" with them, I was struck by their overwhelming opposition to the recent confession ruling.

Even before the imperfections in Chief Justice Warren's opinion for the Court in *Miranda* were brought into sharp focus by the new prodding of the facts of subsequent confession cases, it could not be denied that various portions of the long opinion left something to be desired. But there would be no shortage of commentators to spotlight these warts and blemishes. I feared, however, that in the hue and cry over *Miranda,* few, if any, would dwell on the weaknesses in the *dissenting* opinions. (It is much easier, it has always seemed to me, to take pen in hand when one is distressed by a decision than when one is content with it.)

In my judgment—and this was the primary thrust of my article—the *Miranda* dissents were far more vulnerable to criticism than the majority opinion. Although the *Miranda* dissenters still proclaimed the virtues of the old "voluntariness" test, the old test had proved to be highly elusive, largely unworkable, and woefully ineffective. Although the *Miranda* dissenters expressed astonishment at how the Court had managed to bring the privilege against self-incrimination into the police station, more wondrous, I thought, was how the courts had managed to keep it out for so many years.

*

About a decade after I had said a few good words for *Miranda* (and many bad ones about the old "voluntariness" test), the death of my senior colleague, Paul G. Kauper (1974), and the retirement from teaching of my old adversary, Fred E. Inbau (1977), caused me to return to the confessions topic.

Kauper's proposed remedy for the third degree was written way back in

---

copy of the Biron recording and asked each to play it and to consider how, if at all, the nature and impact of the Biron interrogation could be grasped without such a recording. When the committee next met, all doubts about the need for the recording proposal seemed to have vanished.

Some years earlier, the Reporters for the American Law Institute's *Model Code of Pre-Arraignment Procedure* project had made a similar proposal. This, too, was eventually adopted. *See* § 130.4.

1932 (when he was still a third-year law student)—four years *before* the Supreme Court first imposed the "voluntariness" test on the states as a matter of fourteenth amendment due process. Although he was not the first to offer a judicially supervised interrogation procedure as the solution to the "confessions problem," he seems to have been the first to deal in any comprehensive way with the practical, policy, and constitutional considerations involved in such a proposal. When the editors of the *Michigan Law Review* asked me to reexamine Kauper's article in the light of forty years of subsequent developments, I could not resist the opportunity to do so.

Inbau had been an outstanding interrogator himself and had taught many hundreds of others how to practice the art. He was the leading police-prosecution spokesman in academe and a longtime critic of the Court. Not only had he joined with others in criticizing the Warren Court for handing down *Escobedo* and *Miranda*, but a generation earlier he had also reproached the Stone Court for deciding *McNabb* (1943) and *Ashcraft* (1944).

Moreover, although many had attacked the *Miranda* decision, none had done so with Inbau's gusto. *Miranda* was the case that Inbau had feared, and had tried to head off, for most of his professional career. Nor was it any comfort to him that the *Miranda* opinion had quoted from or cited his manuals no less than ten times—never with approval. "If *Miranda* is a monument to anyone," Judge George Edwards had observed at the time, "perhaps it is to Fred Inbau."[10]

I had, as the editors of the *Journal of Criminal Law* described it, "tilted swords with Inbau many times, both in print and face-to-face."[11] So when the *Journal* editors invited me to sum up and reflect upon Inbau's rich, colorful career, I could not refuse.

When I started writing my comments on Kauper's article, I did not know that I would end up finding a modernized version of his proposal, what I

10. Edwards, *Interrogation of Criminal Defendants—Some Views on* Miranda v. Arizona, 35 FORDHAM L. REV. 181, 186 (1966).

11. *See* the *Foreword* to the June 1977 issue of the *Journal of Criminal Law & Criminology* (In Honor of Fred Inbau).

Perhaps our most memorable debate took place nine months before *Miranda,* as part of a panel discussion on the Supreme Court's decisions on defendant's rights—with both Chief Justice Earl Warren and Justice William Brennan in attendance. *See* PROCEEDINGS OF THE TWENTY-EIGHTH ANNUAL CONFERENCE OF THE THIRD CIRCUIT OF THE UNITED STATES (Sept. 1965), in 39 F.R.D. 375, 423-62. On that occasion, Professor Inbau expressed unhappiness with "the trend of the last few years with respect to interrogation opportunities for the police," voiced fear that the Supreme Court might some day "outlaw" all interrogations, and maintained that "there is nothing in the Constitution that guarantees the right to counsel on the arrest level." *Id.* at 441-44.

A short time later, Chief Justice Warren commented that the panel discussion reminded him of "the old hillbilly from Arkansas who said, 'You know, no matter how thin you make the pancake there are always two sides to it.'" *Id.* at 474. I venture to say that nine months later Inbau, and he was hardly alone, had great difficulty finding the "other side of the pancake" in the *Miranda* opinion.

called the Kauper-Schaefer-Friendly model,[12] as attractive an alternative to the *Miranda* model as I did. Nor did I know that I would express as much disappointment in *Miranda* as I did. Similarly, when I started work on the piece about Inbau I did not think I would view him as sympathetically as I wound up doing. In a sense each article "wrote itself."

*

Perhaps the best examples of how articles can "write themselves" are the last two essays in this collection. No sooner had I finished the Inbau piece than the *Georgetown Law Journal* editors asked me to write a short preface to their "Circuits Note" (an annual survey of federal appellate decisions dealing with criminal procedure), reminding me that Justice William O. Douglas had written the preface the previous year.

I yielded. I had become quite interested in a new confessions case, *Brewer v. Williams* (the so-called Christian burial speech case),[13] and the Georgetown editors readily agreed that it was a case worth highlighting in a preface to the "Circuits Note." All that was expected of me, and all I promised myself I would do, was a three- or four-page comment on the *Williams* case. Surely I could do that in a few days. Besides, it would be nice to "succeed" Justice Douglas, if only in one respect.

The roots of the 1977 *Williams* decision were to be found in the 1964 *Massiah* case. Decided only a few weeks before the more famous *Escobedo* case, *Massiah* seemed to say that the filing of an indictment, or the initiation of other adversary judicial proceedings, marks an "absolute point" at which the sixth amendment right to counsel attaches. Until the recent decision in *Brewer v. Williams,* however, there was good reason to think that *Massiah* had only been a steppingstone to *Escobedo* and that both cases had been more or less displaced by *Miranda.* But *Brewer v. Williams* made plain that despite the Court's shift from a "right to counsel base" in *Escobedo* to a "compelled self-incrimination base" in *Miranda,* the *Massiah* doctrine was still very

12. In the late 1960s, first Justice Walter Schaefer and then Judge Henry Friendly, two of the most eminent critics of *Escobedo* and *Miranda,* had in effect returned to and built upon the old Kauper proposal. *See* pp. 83 and 94 *infra.*

13. Williams, suspected of murdering a young girl in Des Moines, Iowa, surrendered himself to the Davenport, Iowa, police. Captain Leaming and another Des Moines detective went to Davenport to pick up Williams and drive him back to Des Moines (some 160 miles away). By the time the two Des Moines officers arrived in Davenport, adversary judicial proceedings had already commenced against Williams, and he had already retained counsel. On the return trip, admittedly in an effort to induce Williams to reveal the location of the girl's body, Captain Leaming remarked to Williams: "[Y]ou yourself are the only person that knows where the little girl's body is. . . . I feel that [the parents] should be entitled to a Christian burial for [their] little girl [and that] we should stop and locate [the body] on the way [back to Des Moines]."

much "alive and well. "[14] It had emerged as the other major Warren Court confessions rule.

In the process of revivifying *Massiah,* however, the *Williams* case, I feared, had blurred the *Massiah* and *Miranda* rationales. Although this was not clear from the *Williams* opinion, the *Massiah* doctrine has nothing to do with "custody" or "interrogation," the key *Miranda* concepts.

When Massiah made incriminating statements, he was unaware that he was dealing with a government agent. He thought he was simply talking to a friend and codefendant. There is no indication that he was ever "interrogated" (as that term is normally used) or "compelled" to speak or "restrained" of his liberty in any way. But a government agent had "deliberately elicited" statements from him after he had been indicted and retained counsel and while he was out on bail. The government, *Massiah* held, cannot do this—*either* directly, by means of a uniformed officer, *or* indirectly, by means of a "secret agent"—once adversary judicial proceedings have been initiated. *Massiah* represents a "pure right-to-counsel" approach.

The suspect in the *Williams* case was plainly in "custody" when given the "Christian burial speech," and arguably the speech was a form of "interrogation." Thus, the incriminating disclosures *might have been* excluded on *Miranda* grounds. But the *Williams* Court chose to decide the case on the basis of *Massiah* rather than *Miranda*. Once it did so, once it chose to rest on "sixth amendment-*Massiah*" rather than "fifth amendment-*Miranda*" grounds, there was no longer any need to consider whether the Christian burial speech constituted police "interrogation." All that mattered was that a government agent, by means of the speech, had deliberately elicited incriminating statements from a person after adversary proceedings had commenced against him. (Moreover, although I do not think this is necessary to trigger the *Massiah* doctrine, Williams was also represented by counsel at the time.)

Nevertheless, the *Williams* majority evidently thought it important, if not crucial, to establish that the Christian burial speech did amount to "interrogation"—but all four dissenters insisted it was not. The Christian burial speech, I am convinced, did *happen to be* a form of *"Miranda* interrogation,"* but *it did not have to be* in order for the *Massiah* doctrine to have protected Williams.

What I have said above is pretty much all I wanted to say, and planned to say, about the *Williams* case in my preface to the "Circuits Note." Somehow, however, what began as a very modest project took on a life of its own. Before I was able to call a halt—more than a year, 130 printed pages, and 600 footnotes later—two separate articles had more or less "written themselves."

---

14. *See* Israel, *Criminal Procedure, the Burger Court, and the Legacy of the Warren Court,* 75 MICH. L. REV. 1319, 1380–82 (1977).

The three- or four-page preface had already grown into a fifteen-page foreword when I dipped into the *Williams* record to clarify a point. I had a great deal of difficulty ever getting back out. I found the record incomplete, contradictory, and confusing.

For one thing, although neither the Supreme Court nor other courts which had mulled over the Christian burial speech seem to have been aware of this, the police captain who had rendered the speech had given one version of it at a pretrial hearing and, in my view, a significantly different version at the trial itself.[15] Moreover, as I read the record, there was a distinct possibility that during the five-hour drive to Des Moines, the captain had delivered more than one Christian burial speech. But this point, along with many others, had never been adequately explored at the trial.

Williams sharply disputed the captain on many points but, as might be expected, no court paid any attention to what he had to say. Yet whenever the captain got into a "swearing contest" with Williams's lawyers, as he did on three occasions, he lost every time. Doesn't this raise serious questions about the swearing contest the captain won when he disputed Williams?

The woefully inadequate *Williams* record underscored the need, whenever feasible (and I think it was feasible in the *Williams* case), to record all police "interviews" or "conversations" with a suspect, and all warnings and "waiver transactions" as well.[16] Why, after all these years, were police interrogators still able to prevent objective recordation of the facts? A police interrogator, no less than the rest of us, is inclined to reconstruct and reinter-

---

15. The captain's second version was the only one quoted and discussed by the Supreme Court and lower federal courts.

16. For a powerful statement, by a British commentator, of the need to require "all interrogations in police stations in the large centres of population [to] be electronically recorded," *see* Glanville Williams's *The Authentication of Statements to the Police*, [1979] CRIM. L.R. (Brit.) 1. Unfortunately, since this article did not appear in print until after I had published my study of the *Williams* record, I was unable to make any use of it.

Professor Williams carefully considers and, in my judgment, effectively deflates various objections to tape-recording, *e.g.*, the danger of alteration of the tapes, the likelihood that the tapes would be full of inadmissible evidence (such as evidence about prior convictions), the possibility that the suspect would engage in "play-acting" (such as pretending that he was being physically abused), and the argument that "the suspect may be totally unwilling to speak while the recorder is running, but willing to speak without it." *See id.* at 15–22; *see also* p. 133 fn.22 *infra*.

"One cannot help wondering," observes Williams, "whether the real objection of the police to tape-recording (although it is never avowed) is their fear of the consequences of public inspection of what happens in the interviewing of suspects." Williams, *supra*, at 22. He points out, however, how a sound recording "can work to the advantage of the police as well as against them." *Id.* at 13.

"The time is not far distant," "suspect[s]" Professor Williams, "when we will totally exclude disputed evidence of verbals unless there are special circumstances indicating their truth, or unless they are electronically recorded." *Id.* at 15. I wish he were right, but I fear he is much too optimistic.

pret past events in a light most favorable to himself. As long as he is permitted to be "a judge of his own cause" in this sense, *any* confessions rule, I feared, would be "a house built upon sand."

What began as a textual footnote describing the unsatisfactory condition of the *Williams* record grew into a separate section—one that eventually became so large that it dwarfed the rest of the article. (Moreover, I had yet to complete the rest of the article.) There could be only one solution, and the Georgetown editors, growing frantic at my inability to finish the piece, quickly concurred: I had to pull out the analysis of the record from the unfinished manuscript and run it by itself as the foreword to the "Circuits Note." Thus emerged "Foreword: *Brewer v. Williams*—A Hard Look at a Discomfiting Record."

I agreed that at a later date I would return to and complete my appraisal of the various *Williams* opinions in light of *Miranda, Massiah*, and other cases and that I would publish this discussion as a separate second article. Eventually I did—but not before adding three major sections that I had never contemplated writing when I first took on the assignment.

In the course of presenting some hypotheticals designed to illustrate the differences between the *Miranda* and *Massiah* approaches, I discovered that the applicability of these doctrines to the use of "jail plants" and other "secret agents" was a good deal more complicated than I had suspected. This led to a twenty-five-page treatment of that subject. Although, as I have already indicated, I was convinced that "interrogation" was constitutionally irrelevant for *Massiah* purposes, I, too, could not resist the temptation to discuss whether, *in any event,* the Christian burial speech did amount to "interrogation." This led to a twenty-page discussion of the general problem.

At this point I had done all that I had originally set out to do, and considerably more. But I felt the article still needed an "ending." It had grown so large that it was no longer enough simply to compare and contrast how the *Miranda* and *Massiah* doctrines worked. I felt the need to appraise their relative strengths and weaknesses and to consider the merits of a third approach as well—New York's *Donovan-Arthur-Hobson* rule. Under the New York rule (a first cousin to *Massiah*), regardless of whether adversary proceedings have commenced or whether the suspect is willing to waive his *Miranda* rights, once an attorney "enters the picture" (a phone call to the police department central switchboard will suffice), the state is prohibited from "interfering with the attorney-client relationship" by questioning the suspect in the absence of counsel.

The *Massiah* doctrine and the New York rule each have a certain neat logic and a strong symbolic attractiveness, and it is not inconceivable that either or both will outlast *Miranda*. After thirty pages of "further thoughts," however, I concluded that there was less to be said for *Massiah* or the New York rule than for the basic *Miranda* approach. Whatever its shortcomings, *Miranda* tried to take the "police interrogation"–"confessions" problem by the throat. I did not see how the same could be said for either *Massiah* or the New York rule. Both, rather, turn on nice distinctions that seem unresponsive to either the government's need for evidence or a suspect's need for "a lawyer's help."

Thus emerged what is, by a wide margin, the longest confessions article I have ever written—"*Brewer v. Williams, Massiah*, and *Miranda:* What Is 'Interrogation'? When Does It Matter?"

*

The early and middle 1960s were exciting times for students of criminal procedure. The 1970s, if less exciting, were no less interesting. Nor were they without controversy. Depending upon one's viewpoint, they were a time of reexamination, correction, consolidation, erosion, or retreat.

History, it has well been said, "never looks like history when you are living through it. It always looks confusing and messy. . . ."[17] But the 1960s and 1970s look like history now. Hopefully the combination of these seven essays, written during a period of unprecedented change in American constitutional-criminal procedure, constitutes a useful historical overview of the Supreme Court's efforts to deal with a most troublesome and most controversial cluster of problems. Hopefully, too, these essays contribute significantly to an analysis of the constitutional and policy issues that confronted the Court along the way.

*

In the 1960s those who shared my outlook on the criminal justice system celebrated various victories.[18] But events in the 1970s reminded us that here, as elsewhere, "there is no final victory. However great the triumph, it is ephemeral. Without further struggle, it withers and dies."[19] In the 1980s we may have to remember what Allen, Paulsen, and other commentators of the 1950s never forgot—there is no final defeat, either.

YALE KAMISAR

Ann Arbor, Michigan
December, 1979

---

17. J. GARDNER, *Hazard and Hope*, in NO EASY VICTORIES 169 (H. Rowan ed. 1968).

18. *But see* Amsterdam, *The Supreme Court and the Rights of Suspects in Criminal Cases*, 45 N.Y.U.L. REV. 785 (1970).

19. F. ALLEN, *On Winning and Losing*, in LAW, INTELLECT, AND EDUCATION 16 (1979).

What Is an "Involuntary" Confession?

September, 1963

Of all the tools at Law's disposal, sure
That named Vigiliarum *is the best—*
That is, the worst—to who so has to bear:
Lasting, as it may do, from some seven hours
To ten, (beyond ten, we've no precedent;
Certain have touched their ten but, bah, they died!)
It does so efficaciously convince
That,—speaking by much observation here,—
Out of each hundred cases, by my count,
Never I knew of patients beyond four
Withstand its taste, or less then ninety-six
End by succumbing: only martyrs four,
Of obstinate silence, guilty or no,—against
Ninety-six full confessors, innocent
Or otherwise,—so shrewd a tool have we!

—Robert Browning

"To DISCUSS police questioning without knowing what such questioning is really like," it has been well said, "is playing Hamlet without the ghost."[1] One who reads the lively, absorbing *Criminal Interrogation and Confessions* (1962), a revision and expansion of an earlier work[(1)] by the same authors, Professor Fred Inbau and John Reid, learns much about police questioning. Whether he likes what he learns is another matter.

A number of manuals deal with this fascinating subject,[(2)] but Inbau and Reid's incisive, lucid, brisk, zestful treatment of the psychological tactics and techniques of "effective interrogation" is, I think, the best to be found.[2] Their

---

1. Weisberg, *Police Interrogation of Arrested Persons: A Skeptical View*, in POLICE POWER AND INDIVIDUAL FREEDOM 155 (C. Sowle ed. 1962).

2. Scores of prosecutors and police officers who have read the earlier works on interrogation by the same authors and/or attended one of Professor Inbau's "short courses" at Northwestern Law School tell me, with few exceptions, that the stuff works remarkably well.

I must confess that since commencing this commentary I have become so enthralled by the subject matter that, as the occasions arose, I found myself utilizing various recommended interrogation techniques against two babysitters, a newsboy, a trash collector (all suspected of various forms of negligence) and two used-car dealers. I have achieved notable success against all but the car dealers. No doubt they must be likened to hardened criminals.

section on the form, content, readability and understandability of a written confession (and the preparation of supplemental statements when physical evidence and photographs are available)[3] is outstanding.

This is not surprising. Both authors are top-rung interrogators and lie-detector examiners. In his time, each has gripped many a suspect's hand, executed many a well-timed pat on the shoulder, and let many a "female offender" cry on his.[4]

Back in the 1930s the senior author, Professor Inbau, instructed in police science at the country's first scientific crime detection laboratory and, when the Chicago Police Department took over the laboratory in 1938, he became its first director. In the course of obtaining confessions from murderers, Inbau has been known to spill over with such "sympathy" for his prisoner that he has had to "pause to wipe away a tear."[5] He may be just about the surest, craftiest interrogator around.

A policeman's lot may not be a happy one, but no reader of this book can escape the conclusion that a suspect's lot is a good deal unhappier still. To illustrate:

The interrogator should sit fairly close to the subject, and between the two there should be no table, desk, or other piece of furniture. Distance or the presence of an obstruction of any sort constitutes a serious psychological barrier and also affords the subject a certain degree of relief and confidence not otherwise attainable . . . .

. . . As to the psychological validity of the above suggested seating arrangement, reference may be made to the commonplace but yet meaningful expressions such as "getting next" to a person, or the "buttonholing" of a customer by a salesman.[6]

. . . .

. . . To facilitate matters with respect to an avoidance of smoking by a subject, it will be helpful if there are no ash trays present, for when present they represent a tacit invitation to smoke. Their absence may carry the opposite impression, as well as afford a basis, if necessary, for a suggestion by the interrogator that any smoking be postponed until the subject leaves the interrogation room.[7]

. . . .

. . . Once the subject's attention is called to a particular piece of incriminating evidence the interrogator must be on guard to cut off immediately any explanation the subject may start to offer at that time. . . . [T]o permit the subject to offer an explanation of the incriminating evidence will serve to bolster his confidence, for then he is putting the interrogator on the defensive and this should never be permitted to occur.[8]

. . . .

. . . Many subjects who are on the verge of confessing will start picking their fingernails, or scratching themselves, or dusting their clothing with hand movements, or they will begin fumbling with a tie clasp or other small object. As politely as the interrogator can, he should seek to terminate such conduct. He may do so by gently lifting the subject's hand or by removing the object from his hand, always avoiding any rudeness as he seeks to end such tension-relieving activities. . . .

. . . When a subject of the emotional offender type is being interrogated, it is advisable to remind the subject that he "doesn't feel very good inside," and that this peculiar feeling (as if "all his insides were tied in a knot") is the result of a troubled conscience.[9]

. . . .

. . . When the various techniques of sympathy and understanding have proved ineffective, the interrogator may resort to a so-called "friendly-unfriendly" act. . . .

. . . Although the friendly-unfriendly act is usually performed by two persons, one interrogator can play both roles. In fact, the authors are of the opinion that this is the more effective way to apply the technique. . . .

. . . [T]he interrogator may even apologize for his loss of patience by saying, "I'm sorry. That's the first time I've lost my head like that." The interrogator then starts all over with the reapplication of the sympathetic approach that formed the basis for his efforts prior to the above described outburst of impatience. Now, by reason of the contrast with which he has been presented, the subject finds the interrogator's sympathetic, understanding attitude to be much more appealing. This places him in a much more vulnerable position for a disclosure of the truth.[10]

. . . .

. . . Not only must the interrogator have patience, but he must also display it. It is well, therefore, to get the idea across, in most case situations, that the interrogator has "all the time in the world." He may even express himself in those exact words.[11]

What about the subject who refuses to discuss the matter under investigation at all? You know, the pesky sort who insists on his right to remain silent? An Inbau-Reid–trained interrogator will be ready for him. He will counter by pretending to concede him the right to remain silent (impressing him with his apparent fairness) and then, after some more "psychological conditioning,"[3] ask him "innocuous questions that have no bearing whatever on the matter under investigation. . . . As a rule the subject will answer such questions, and then gradually the examiner may start in with questions pertaining to the offense."[12]

What about that other troublesome type, the chap who expresses a desire to see a relative, friend, or lawyer? Once again, a police officer who has read this book is forearmed; advise him to "tell the truth" to the interrogator *first,* "rather than get anyone else involved."[13] And if the request is for a lawyer, "suggest that the subject save himself or his family the expense of any such professional service, particularly if he is innocent."[14] "Joe," the interrogator may add, "I'm only looking for the truth. . . . You can handle this by yourself."[15]

Commenting on an earlier work by Inbau and Reid, a British professor who

3. *E.g.,*

"Joe, you have a right to remain silent. That's your privilege. . . . But let me ask you this. Suppose you were in my shoes and I were in yours . . . and I told you, 'I don't want to answer any of your questions.' You'd think I had something to hide. . . ."

F. INBAU & J. REID, CRIMINAL INTERROGATION AND CONFESSIONS 111 (1962).

has taught at several American law schools observed: "An Englishman's reaction to these procedures is generally squeamish; the American lawyer's tougher reaction is: 'why not?' "[16]

Why not, indeed? Particularly, if, as Inbau and Reid suggest, all we are dealing with are *criminal offenders:* "From the *criminal's* point of view, *any* interrogation of him is objectionable. . . . Of necessity, criminal interrogators must deal with *criminal offenders* on a somewhat lower moral plane than that upon which ethical, law-abiding citizens are expected to conduct their everyday affairs. "[17]

I share the view that not many *innocent* men (at least those of average intelligence and educational background) are likely to succumb to these "methods of debatable propriety."[18] But how many *innocent* men are likely to be *subjected* to these methods? How "tough" would the American lawyer's reaction be if he had some notion of the price we pay in terms of human liberty and individual dignity?

Surely the nation's capital is blessed with one of the better police departments in the land. Undoubtedly its interrogators are familiar with the widely read earlier works of Messrs. Inbau and Reid, or at least with some of the other manuals espousing the same approach.[19] Yet, a distinguished citizens' committee, appointed by the Commissioners of the District of Columbia in 1961 "to inquire into the policy and practices of the Police Department that lead to arrests for 'investigation,' "[20] reported, *inter alia*—and these "findings" are uncontested—that:

[I]n about 17 out of each 18 cases in which an arrest for "investigation" is made, the prisoner is ultimately released.[21]

. . . .

. . . Approximately 55 per cent of the prisoners ["arrested for investigation"] in each year, were held for more than 4 hours. In 1960, 17.5 per cent—690 prisoners—were held for more than 12 hours, and 84 prisoners—2.1 per cent—were held for more than 24 hours.[22]

. . . .

. . . Of the 1,356 persons held for 8 hours or more in 1960, only 16, or 1.2 per cent, were charged. In 1961 the percentage was slightly higher—2.3. As the period of detention increases, the percentage of those charged generally declines. Of the 690 persons held for more than 12 hours in 1960 only 7—1 per cent—were charged.[23]

. . . .

. . . The data show that, almost without exception, the "investigation" proceeds without benefit of counsel to the prisoner, and indeed in the great majority of cases without knowledge on the part of anyone that the person arrested is in custody. . . . There is, in other words, more than a loss of liberty as such. There is a loss of liberty accompanied by a loss of contact with lawyers, friends or relatives.[24]

To question the propriety of some of the interrogation methods recommended by Inbau and Reid in 1953 and '63 is not to deny that we owe the senior author a great deal for antiquating the interrogation practices of 1923 and '33. When recent Tulane Law School graduate Fred Inbau arrived in Chicago in 1932, the prevailing "interrogation methods" there, and elsewhere, included:

The application of rubber hose to the back or the pit of the stomach, kicks in the shins, beating the shins with a club, blows struck with a telephone book on the side of the victim's head. The Chicago telephone book is a heavy one and a swinging blow with it may stun a man without leaving a mark. [25]

Young Inbau

objected to use of the rubber hose on moral as well as legal grounds. In law, no confession is valid if obtained through physical violence, threats of violence or even through promises of clemency. Third-degree methods could result in "confessions" by the innocent. Professor Inbau did not believe in these methods. He believed in psychology, which could trap the guilty, but not the innocent. *And it was legal.* [26]

Was it? More precisely, is it today?

In accordance with the "general rule that trickery or deceit will not nullify a confession," so long as the artifice involved is "not . . . of a type . . . apt to make an innocent person confess," [27] the authors maintain that "an investigator may pose . . . as a friend of the subject, and a confession obtained as a result of such trickery is admissible." [28] Tell that to the police lieutenant in *Spano v. New York* [4] who instructed Officer Bruno, a "childhood friend" of petitioner, to importune his friend to confess by playing on his sympathies. Bruno's pretense that Spano's phone call "had gotten him into trouble, that his job was in jeopardy, and that loss of his job would be disastrous to his three children, his wife, and his unborn child," [29] plainly militated against the admissibility of the resulting confession. [30]

Officer Bruno may have put a beautiful friendship on the line, but it is hard to see how even a man of Spano's background (a foreign-born person with only a junior high school education) would respond to such entreaties by confessing to a murder he did not commit.

Citing *Rogers v. Richmond,* [5] the authors point out that "a threat to merely bring in an invalided wife for questioning" has been held to nullify a confession. [31] Apparently they have no difficulty reconciling the ban against such a threat with their "general rule" that trickery is permissible so long as it is not likely to produce a false confession. I do not regard it evident that a man of average intelligence will confess to a murder he did not commit in order to

4. 360 U.S. 315 (1959).
5. 365 U.S. 534 (1961).

spare his wife (even one suffering from arthritis, as was Rogers's) the trouble of being transported to the scene of the interrogation.

Indeed, the *Rogers* trial judge found that this device "had no tendency to produce a confession that was not in accord with the truth."[32] The Supreme Court did not consider the finding *unwarranted*, but *irrelevant*. The Court did *not* rule—as the authors claim—that the pretense of calling Rogers's wife barred the resulting confessions, but it did "conclude that the question . . . [had been] answered [below] by reference to a legal standard which took into account the circumstance of probable truth or falsity"[33]—the Inbau-Reid test[34]—"and this is not a permissible standard under the Due Process Clause.[35] . . . Any consideration of this 'reliability' element was constitutionally precluded."[36]

But I am getting ahead of my commentary. I am appraising the authors' proposed standard for admitting confessions into evidence, a subject I dwell on later. It is time, however, to get into the second half of the book, the part entitled: "The Law Governing Criminal Interrogations and Confessions."

It should be said at the outset that anyone who attempts to set forth and analyze "the law" on these subjects in sixty-two pages—which is all the space the authors take—strives for the near impossible. Mr. Justice Frankfurter's opinion in *Culombe v. Connecticut*[6] alone runs longer than that. Nevertheless, others, operating under similar handicaps, have accomplished far more. Inbau and Reid do not approach the painstaking, penetrating analysis of the subject by Professor Beisel,[37] nor the issue-crammed, richly documented treatment afforded the area by Professor Maguire.[38] Nor do they manifest anything like the balance and breadth to be found in Professor Paulsen's selection of materials pertaining to the problem.[39]

"[T]he extorted confession is often the white flag of surrender, followed by a plea of guilty."[40] An estimated 75 to 90 percent of criminal cases are decided by such pleas,[41] but Inbau and Reid have nary a word to say about the derivative use of a prior coerced confession to obtain a plea. Although much sweeping language continues to appear in lower court opinions to the effect that a plea of guilty "constitutes a waiver of all non-jurisdictional defenses,"[42] and, once a plea has been made, any prior violation of defendant's rights is "removed from our consideration,"[43] the Supreme Court has indicated that an otherwise free and voluntary plea may be invalid if induced by an inadmissible confession.[44] Surely, a book designed to furnish guidance to police and prosecutors should have touched on this pervasive problem.[45]

The recent case of *Wong Sun v. United States*[7] underscores another omission in the authors' legal analysis. This decision jeopardizes the admissibility of any incriminating *statements* preceded by an illegal search or arrest—

6. 367 U.S. 568 (1961).
7. 371 U.S. 471 (1963).

especially statements obtained shortly after such police misconduct.[46] *Wong Sun* was a federal prosecution, of course, but when *Mapp v. Ohio*[47] is taken into account, *Wong Sun* may have a great impact on every police force in the land. For, if "the policies underlying the exclusionary rule" do not "invite any logical distinction between physical and verbal evidence"[48] in the federal courts, then "the danger in relaxing the exclusionary rules in the case of verbal evidence would seem too great to warrant introducing such a distinction"[49] at the state level, too.[50]

The authors can hardly be blamed for overlooking the Supreme Court's opinion in *Wong Sun*; it was handed down some time after their book was published. But they can be criticized for failing, even in their discussion of the principles governing confession admissibility in federal cases, to so much as raise the issue posed by the case.

Not only did this very issue split the Ninth Circuit when it decided *Wong Sun* below,[51] long before the book appeared, but the Supreme Court granted certiorari on this question some eight months before Inbau and Reid went to press.[52] Moreover, although no court prior to *Wong Sun* had regarded a wrongful arrest a sufficient reason in itself for excluding a subsequent confession, a substantial number of federal cases, some as far back as the 1940s, had barred verbal evidence preceded by unlawful searches or induced by illegally seized "real" evidence.[53]

The failure even to flag the growing problem of when "detention" for "investigation" or "questioning" ends and an "arrest" begins marks still another deficiency of the book.[54] Long before there was any direct authority for the view that a wrongful arrest was a *decisive* factor, such illegality was nevertheless considered *a factor* militating against the admissibility of any subsequent confession obtained by state or federal officials.[55] Furthermore, there is reason to think that federal officers have sought to avoid the effect of the requirement that an arrestee be brought before the nearest available magistrate "without unnecessary delay" by "detaining," "questioning," or arresting for "investigation," not for a specific crime.[56]

An important principle for prosecutors to keep in mind is "the rule of automatic reversal"—the rule that the use of a coerced confession necessitates reversal, regardless of how much other evidence remains to support the conviction.[57] Among other things, the rule is designed to deter the prosecution from supplementing other evidence by introducing a confession of questionable validity in order to guarantee a conviction.[58] The prosecutors have not always resisted this temptation may be seen from the fact that of the twenty-two state convictions overturned by the Supreme Court on "coerced confession" grounds, the defendants in exactly half of these cases were again convicted of the same (seven) or of a lesser included offense (four).[59]

The authors do not give "the rule of automatic reversal" the careful attention it merits. They claim that the rule was "repudiated" in *Stein v. New York*

(1953);[60] they suggest that the Court reversed and applied the rule in *Payne v. Arkansas* (1958)[61] either because *Stein* was overlooked or because the evidence of guilt, apart from the inadmissible confession, was not sufficiently convincing.[62] In the first place, as most commentators pointed out at the time,[63] *Stein* did not mark an abandonment of the "automatic reversal" principle. In the second place, whatever doubts *were* raised by *Stein* must be read in the light of the resounding reaffirmation and application of the principle, not only in *Payne,* but in the more recent decisions of *Spano v. New York*[64] and *Culombe v. Connecticut,*[65] neither of which were mentioned by the authors in their exposition of the rule. In short, the authors leave one with the impression that the future of the "automatic reversal" principle is very much in doubt, when one should be informed that no principle in this area is more secure.

The treatment of the "automatic reversal" rule evidences a pervasive shortcoming of the authors' exposition of "the law." They are torn between telling their readers (primarily law enforcement officials) what they would like to hear and what they ought to know. Consequently, numerous opportunities to *explain* what the Court is doing (rightly or wrongly), and why, are passed up in favor of: (i) forceful language from dissenting opinions *complaining* about what the Court has done, and (ii) an expression of the authors' own hostile reaction.[66]

Perhaps the best illustration of this is their treatment of the *McNabb-Mallory* rule.[8] Most of the space allocated to this problem is devoted to a showing that the *McNabb* case has met with "general disapproval";[67] a history of several bills designed to nullify the rule;[68] a discussion of the Court's apparent misconceptions about police interrogation practices which, say the authors, gave rise to the rule;[69] a criticism of the Court for "misinterpreting": (i) the intent of the statutory provisions pertaining to prompt commitment,[70] and (ii) the facts in the *McNabb* case itself;[71] and, finally, "an interesting sequel to the *Mallory* case": the defendant was later convicted of burglary and aggravated assault.[72]

The law enforcement official who reads this section is furnished with ample material for some rock 'em, sock 'em speeches at the local Elks or Rotary Club: "The Victims of Rapists and Murderers Have Some 'Rights,' Too;" "The Courts are 'Handcuffing' Your Police;" "The Rights of the Criminals: Has the Pendulum Swung Too Far to the Left?" Unfortunately, however, he learns next to nothing about what the Supreme Court is advocating and how the lower federal courts are implementing it. The authors are too busy cas-

---

8. McNabb v. United States, 318 U.S. 332 (1943), as reaffirmed by Mallory v. United States, 354 U.S. 449 (1957), operates to exclude from federal prosecutions all confessions or admissions elicited during prolonged pre-commitment detention, whether or not they appear to be voluntarily made.

tigating the Court to address themselves to such questions as: What significance attaches to the "inaccessibility" of a committing magistrate? Do drunkenness, recovery from wounds, verification of the accused's or victim's story or other "special circumstances" justify delay? Just how much interrogation is permissible in the absence of these collateral considerations?[73]

The *McNabb-Mallory* rule is really an outgrowth of the Court's awareness of the tremendous problems of proof raised by the "coerced confession" issue. Since "the use of third-degree tactics is . . . difficult to prove because there is always the word of the police against the word of the accused; and the prestige of police testimony usually carries the day,"[74] the safeguards upon which the traditional confessions rules rest have aptly been called "illusory."[75] The main thrust of the *McNabb-Mallory* rule—and the same goes, in spades, for the "inherently coercive" approach to protracted questioning in *Ashcraft v. Tennessee* (1944)[76]—is to bypass conflicts over the nature of the secret interrogation and to minimize both the "temptation" and the "opportunity" to obtain coerced confessions.[77] One searches in vain for any hint of this in the authors' analyses of *McNabb-Mallory* and *Ashcraft*.

The *McNabb-Mallory* rule has another set of functions to perform: the effectuation or implementation of various constitutional rights, such as the right to counsel and the right to be confronted with pending charges, the right against self-incrimination, and the protection against arbitrary arrest.[78] Again, the reader gets no inkling of any of this from Messrs. Inbau and Reid.

The "test of confession admissibility" put forth by the authors may reflect the extent to which they (and many police interrogators) are willing to be restrained, but not the extent to which the Court is prepared to impose restraints. Indeed, the intermeshing of the *is* and the *ought* in the authors' statement of the permissible limits of police interrogation is, I think, self-evident:

"Is what I am about to do, or say, apt to make an innocent person confess?"
If the answer to the above question is "No," the interrogator should go ahead . . . if the answer is "yes," the interrogator should refrain from doing or saying what he had in mind. . . .
In our judgment this is the only understandable test of confession admissibility. *It is also the only one of any practical value and utility. Moreover, it is also the only test that is fair both to the public and to the accused or suspected individual.*[9]

9. F. INBAU & J. REID, *supra* footnote 3, at 157 (emphasis added). Although they do not say so, the authors seem to have fallen back on the old Wigmore test. *Cf.* 3 J. WIGMORE, EVIDENCE § 824 (3d ed. 1940):

[W]ere the prospects attending confession . . . as weighted at the time against the prospects attending non-confession . . . such as to have created, in any considerable degree, a risk that a false confession would be made? Putting it more briefly and roughly, was the inducement such that there was any fair risk of a false confession? (emphasis in the original)

This, the authors tell us, is "about all we can suggest—until such time as the Supreme Court settles upon a clear-cut test of its own."[79] As I have already suggested,[80] it is not good enough. It cannot be squared with what the Court has done and, *as the authors themselves point out only two or three pages earlier,* with what the Court has said.

"The abhorrence of society to the use of involuntary confessions does not turn alone on their inherent untrustworthiness,"[81] observed the Chief Justice for the majority in *Spano v. New York.* "It also turns on the deeprooted feeling that the police must obey the law while enforcing the law; that in the end life and liberty can be as much endangered from illegal methods used to convict those thought to be criminals as from the actual criminals themselves."[82] The authors quote this language, but only for the proposition that in *Spano* "the Supreme Court appears to have brushed aside all that it had been saying and holding... during the preceding eight years."[83] They would have done much better to view the *Spano* language as a candid description of what the Court had been doing for the preceding fifteen years.[84]

Not only do the authors make short shrift of *Spano,* but they completely ignore *Blackburn v. Alabama,*[10] decided the following Term, where the Court, again speaking through the Chief Justice, pointed out:

It is also established that the Fourteenth Amendment forbids "fundamental unfairness in the use of evidence whether true or false." *Lisenba v. California,* 314 U.S. 219, 236 [1941]. Consequently, we have rejected the argument that introduction of an involuntary confession is immaterial where other evidence establishes guilt or corroborates the confession.... As important as it is that persons who have committed crimes be convicted, there are considerations which transcend the question of guilt or innocence.[85]

Surprisingly enough, the authors do consider *Rogers v. Richmond* "perhaps the clearest expression to come from the United States Supreme Court regarding a 'general test' of state court confession admissibility."[86] They do recognize that in *Rogers* the Court took the position that "a confession's admissibility in a state court should be determined... 'with complete disregard of whether or not [the accused] in fact spoke the truth.'"[87] But evidently they just *can't* believe it!

All I can conclude is that Justice Frankfurter's generous use of the "voluntariness" terminology in *Culombe v. Connecticut*[11] has thrown Inbau and Reid off course. Apparently, they view the "voluntariness" test as a *synonym*

10. 361 U.S. 199 (1960).
11. 367 U.S. 568 (1961). There was no majority opinion. Mr. Justice Frankfurter announced the judgment of the Court, an opinion in which Mr. Justice Stewart joined. The Chief Justice, Mr. Justice Douglas (joined by Mr. Justice Black), and Mr. Justice Brennan (joined by the Chief Justice and Justice Black) wrote three separate concurring opinions.

for the "trustworthiness" or "reliability" test. Thus, they analyze *Ashcraft* and other cases in terms of the "inherent coercion test" versus the "original voluntary-trustworthy test,"[88] and they report (with glee) that "a majority of the Court did revert to the voluntary-trustworthy test" in the early 1950s.[89]

Justice Frankfurter's warning in *Rogers* that the "reliability" element *cannot* be taken into account in determining the "voluntariness" of a confession[90] seems to have been disregarded in favor of the same Justice's reassurance in *Culombe* that "the ultimate test *remains* that which has been the only clearly established test in Anglo-American courts *for two hundred years:* the test of voluntariness."[91]

Only two years after the Court handed down its first fourteenth amendment confession case,[12] Dean McCormick defended the statement of the confession rule in terms of "voluntariness" on the ground that this "shorthand expression" might reflect a recognition that the rule not only protects against the danger of untrustworthiness, but advances other values as well.[13] "Can we not best understand the entire course of decisions in this field," he asked, "as an application to confessions *both* of a privilege against evidence illegally obtained . . . and of an overlapping rule of incompetency which excludes the confessions when untrustworthy?"[92] Many Supreme Court decisions later, the Chief Justice answered in the affirmative. He pointed out in *Spano,* as already noted, that the ban against "involuntary" confessions turns not only on their unreliability but on the notion that "the police must obey the law while enforcing the law."[93] And he acknowledged in *Blackburn* that "*a complex of values* underlies the structure against use by the state of confessions which, by way of *convenient shorthand,* this Court terms involuntary."[94]

However, whatever the *current* meaning of the elusive terms "voluntary" and "involuntary" confessions, *originally* the terminology was a *substitute* for the "trustworthiness" or "reliability" test. For *most* of the two hundred years within which this formulation had constituted "the ultimate test," it had been no more than an *alternative statement* of the rule that a confession was admissible so long as it was free of influences which made it "unreliable" or "probably untrue."[95]

Why, for most of this time, was a confession admissible if "freely and voluntarily made"? Because under such circumstances the "insistent and ever-present forces of self-interest" and "self-protection," as Dean McCor-

---

12. Brown v. Mississippi, 297 U.S. 278 (1936).

13. McCormick, *The Scope of Privilege in the Law of Evidence,* 16 Texas L. Rev. 447, 452–57 (1938). To the same effect is C. McCormick, Evidence 154–57 (1954) [hereinafter cited as C. McCormick]. Wigmore long condemned the use of "voluntary," in part for the reason that "the fundamental question for confessions is whether there is any danger that they may be untrue, . . . and that there is nothing in the mere circumstances of compulsion to speak in general . . . which creates any risk of untruth." 3 J. Wigmore, *supra* footnote 9, § 843.

mick had described them,[96] rendered the confession "reliable" or "probably true." *Why,* during most of this period, did "coercion" or "compulsion" or "inducement" bar the use of a confession so obtained? Because, when such pressures or influences were brought to bear, "the presumption . . . that one who [was] innocent [would] not imperil his safety or prejudice his interest by an untrue statement, ceases."[97]

Indeed, as late as 1941, when as much as 90 percent of the "voluntariness" test's two-century reign had elapsed, Justice Roberts, joined by six other members of the Court, including Justice Frankfurter, could still say:

The aim of the rule that a confession is inadmissible unless it was voluntarily made is to exclude false evidence. Tests are invoked to determine whether the inducement to speak was such that there is a fair risk the confession is false.[98]

The aforementioned misleading line in his *Culombe* opinion to the contrary notwithstanding, Justice Frankfurter struggles valiantly to make the "voluntariness" test clear and understandable. The authors entertain grave doubts (as do I) whether he succeeds. They suggest,[99] I think it fair to say, that "the explanations themselves often need more explanation than the term explained."[14] Bewildered, if not overwhelmed, by the torrent of words in the principal *Culombe* opinion, and further dismayed by the various concurring opinions in the case,[100] the authors beat a hasty retreat from the Supreme Court decision and "offer some guidance" of their own[101]—their "apt to make an innocent person confess" test.

If Messrs. Inbau and Reid are somewhat exasperated by Justice Frankfurter's long, involved opinion in the *Culombe* case, a good argument can be made that they have been amply provoked. One who plods through the sixty-seven-page *Culombe* "treatise,"[102] tripping over such stilted expressions as "persons who are suspected of crime will not always be unreluctant to answer questions,"[103] and bogging down in such rich terminology as "the external, 'phenomenological' occurrences and events surrounding the confession"[104] and "the imaginative recreation, largely inferential, of internal, 'psychological' fact,"[105] cannot help but wonder whether the struggle was worth it.

The "first pole" of the problem, *Culombe* tells us, is "the recognition that 'questioning suspects is indispensable in law enforcement.'"[106] Thus:

[I]f it is once admitted that questioning of suspects is permissible, whatever reasonable means are needed to make the questioning effective must also be conceded to the police. Often prolongation of the interrogation period will be essential, so that a suspect's story can be checked. . . . Often the place of questioning will have to be a police interrogation room. . . . Legal counsel for the suspect will generally prove a thor-

---

14. To borrow a phrase used by Dean McCormick in a different context, C. McCormick, *supra* footnote 13, at 682. This is my description of the authors' reaction, not theirs.

Evidently, an uncounselled, uninformed suspect all alone in an interrogation room is not deemed "helpless." Evidently, if he confesses under such circumstances, he has not been "exploited" or "overreached," although this is certainly debatable. At what point *is* he rendered "helpless" or "exploitable?"

There is much talk in *Culombe* of "involuntariness" and the "suction process";[114] of "draining" the "capacity for freedom of choice";[115] of "overreaching," "overbearing," or "breaking" the "will."[116] But are these words and phrases any more illuminating than, say, the talk of yesteryear about "affected with a public interest," "subject to the exercise of the police power," or "devoted to the public use?"[117] Is "involuntariness" or "coercion" or "breaking the will" (or its synonyms) little more than a fiction intended to vilify certain "effective" interrogation methods? Is "voluntariness" or "mental freedom" or "self-determination" (or its equivalents) little more than a fiction designed to beautify certain other interrogation techniques?[118]

The trouble with *Culombe* is not that it fails to achieve precision in the area—this is only a failure to do the impossible—but that it threatens to enhance existing uncertainty and confusion.

It is all very well to be told that "the notion of 'voluntariness' is itself an amphibian" which "purports at once to describe an internal psychic state and to characterize that state for legal purposes."[119] But not many clues are given, although frequent resort is made to the term and its many synonyms, as to *when* the "amphibian" is being used in *which* sense. A law professor may view these terms as "merely colorful substitute language for fairness [and unfairness]" and criticize "their intended use as analytical terms in this law" as "fanciful or fictitious."[16] But a police officer (and one resolute enough to read *Culombe* from beginning to end is likely to be a persistent interrogator indeed) will probably take this colorful substitute language much too seriously. Indeed, as I hope I have already shown, Professor Inbau and Mr. Reid, two long-time authorities on the subject, have been led astray.

The one misleading sentence about the two-hundred-year reign of the "voluntariness" test to the contrary notwithstanding, it is plain from a reading of the *Culombe* opinion in its entirety that "voluntariness" is not used as a substitute for "trustworthiness." If a suspect's "will has been overborne and his capacity for self-determination critically impaired, the use of his confession offends due process,"[120] quite apart from the reliability of the resulting confession. But Justice Frankfurter by no means makes it clear—as I think the Chief Justice did in *Spano* and *Blackburn*—that "voluntariness" is being employed as a term of art, not in its ordinary dictionary sense.

---

16. A. Beisel, Control over Illegal Enforcement of the Criminal Law: Role of the Supreme Court 78 (1955).

ough obstruction. Indeed, even to inform the suspect of his legal right to keep silent w
prove an obstruction. [107]

Consider too, Justice Frankfurter's observation later in the opinion, th
"neither extensive cross-questioning . . . nor failure to caution a pri
oner . . . nor refusal to permit communication with friends and legal counsel
is necessarily "constitutionally impermissible." [108]
  "*At the other pole* is a cluster of convictions . . ." that:

> [T]he terrible engine of the criminal law is not to be used to overreach individuals wh
> stand helpless against it. . . . Cardinal among them, also, is the conviction . . . tha
> *men are not to be exploited for the information necessary to condemn them before th*
> *law.* . . . Its essence is the requirement that the State which proposes to convict an
> punish an individual produce the evidence against him by the independent labor of it
> officers. . . . [109]

How can it be steadfastly maintained that a suspect must not be "over
reached" or "exploited," yet readily conceded that questioning is "indispens
able," permitting "reasonable means" to make it "effective," when these
means include interrogation in an "atmosphere of privacy and non-
distraction," [110] a failure to advise the suspect of his rights, and a refusal to
permit defense counsel, friends, or relatives to be present? How can these two
"poles" coexist?

As the *Culombe* opinion elsewhere recognizes, the mere knowledge that
"no friendly or disinterested witness is present . . . may itself induce
fear." [111] As it points out too, "questioning that is long continued . . . inevitably suggests that the questioner has a right to, and expects, an answer." [112]
But so does questioning for any substantial period when the suspect does not
know, and has never been told, that he may remain silent. The opinion also
reflects awareness that the subject of long questioning "has every reason to
believe that he will be held and interrogated until he speaks." [113] But need ten
or fifteen hours of questioning elapse before the suspect arrives at this conclusion? Isn't he likely to do so after, say, only two or three hours of steady
questioning? After all, isn't it standard procedure to "get the idea across" that
the interrogator has "all the time in the world?" [15]

If the police may tear suspects from their homes, friends, and neighbors,
put them in an "interrogation room" without informing them of their right to
keep silent, and shut out the "outside," they *can* "exploit" suspects for
information "necessary to condemn them," can they not? They *need not*
produce the evidence against a suspect by "independent labor" after all, need
they? Talk of two "poles" connotes end parts, differentiated areas, opposite
points. Aren't we really talking about intersecting circles?

15. *See* text *supra* at note 11.

If talk of "voluntariness," "coercion," and "breaking the will" demonstrates no more than that "the mere formulation of a relevant constitutional principle is the beginning of the solution of a problem, not its answer,"[121] these terms are not apt ones even for this beginning solution. For as Professor Paulsen has pointed out, they do not focus directly on either the risk of untrue confessions nor the offensiveness of police interrogation methods.[122]

If these terms do *something more* than restate the question, if they bear some resemblance to popular usage—and much of the *Culombe* opinion suggests that they do—then they are "at once too wide and too narrow."[123]

In one sense, in the sense of wanting to confess, or doing so in a completely spontaneous manner, "in the sense of a confession to a priest merely to rid one's soul of a sense of guilt,"[17] no criminal confession worth arguing about is "voluntary." Yet, in another sense, *all* criminal confessions are "voluntary."

The situation is always one of choice between two alternatives—either one disagreeable, to be sure, but still subject to a choice.... All conscious verbal utterances are and must be voluntary; and that which may impel us to distrust one is not the circumstance that it is involuntary, but the circumstance that the choice of false confession is a natural one under the conditions.[18]

To call the "voluntariness" terminology loose and unrevealing is not the worst that can be said for it. It can also be downright misleading.

To conjure up a horrible example, one suggested by the aforementioned criticism of the traditional "voluntary" formula, suppose a suspect acknowledges sin to a police officer impersonating a priest? I venture to say this would be branded a constitutionally impermissible tactic.[19] If so, why? Surely neither because the suspect's "mind" or "will" had been "broken" or "overborne," nor because his "powers of resistance and self-control" had been "sapped." Ridding one's soul of a sense of guilt is no less a rare, pure instance of a "voluntary" confession when, unbeknown to the confessor, a lawman sits in the confessional.

Consider, too, the following four-stage hypothetical, based on various factors deemed relevant in numerous cases:

(a) Mr. *X*, a twenty-one-year-old high-school graduate of average intelligence, is lawfully arrested for rape-murder, then quickly taken to an interrogation room in the county jail. He has no close friends, and his only living relative is his mother, whom he has not seen for five years. He has no hope or

---

17. Jackson, J., dissenting in Ashcraft v. Tennessee, 322 U.S. 143, 161 (1944). *See also* Justice Jackson, speaking for the majority, in Stein v. New York, 346 U.S. 156, 186 (1953).

18. 3 J. WIGMORE, *supra* footnote 9, § 824.

19. *Cf.* Leyra v. Denno, 347 U.S. 556, 559 (1954) (suspect in need of medical relief treated by psychiatrist "with considerable knowledge of hypnosis" posing as "general practitioner").

expectation that she will help him. He asks to see nobody, and no one asks to see him.

After thirty minutes of questioning, X is taken to the nearest town with a Justice Court for preliminary examination in compliance with state law, but the magistrate, also a bus driver, has already departed on an evening run.[124] The sheriff and one of his deputies then take X to the second-nearest town with a Justice Court, only to discover that this magistrate is seriously ill. X has no idea, nor is he told, why he is being transported from town to town (and intermittently questioned along the way). By now, three hours have elapsed since X's arrest and night has fallen. X is returned to the original interrogation room and questioned for another hour.

At this point, X is removed from the jailhouse and taken to a secluded place. He has no idea why. Again, he does not ask, nor is he told, but the primary reason is his captors' concern for his safety. An angry mob is gathering outside.[20] Within minutes after he arrives at the new interrogation site, X confesses.

(b) Same facts as situation (a) with these changes:

Mr. X has been unlawfully arrested (he is unaware of this) and within the next few hours a score of persons are also "arrested for investigation" of the same crime and questioned in other rooms of the same jailhouse and in other places.[125] (X has no reason to suspect any of this.) A magistrate sits less than 100 feet away from the very room in which X is being interrogated, but the suspect is not brought before him, as state law dictates. X is unaware of both the state requirement and the magistrate's proximity.

Unbeknown to X, his mother has learned of his plight and retained a lawyer for him; but, also unbeknown to X, this lawyer has twice been refused permission to see him. After four hours of intermittent questioning, X is removed from jail for questioning elsewhere. (No mob is gathering.) Although the magistrate is still in the building, no application is made to him for removal, as required by state law.[126] X does not know, does not ask, and is not informed why he is being transferred to another interrogation site, but the reasons are: (i) to frustrate his lawyer's efforts to see him, and (ii) to put some distance between him and the nearby magistrate.[127]

(c) Same facts as situation (b) except that before X is removed from the jail, the lawyer retained by his mother makes a dash for the interrogation room. But a burly deputy seizes him just before he can reach the door and blackjacks him into submission. Pursuant to the sheriff's orders, X's mother, who has

___

20. Removing a prisoner from jail to a distant place in order to thwart the efforts of friends or relatives to secure his release, or at least to contact him, militates heavily against the admissibility of any resulting confession. *Compare* Ward v. Texas, 316 U.S. 547, 552–54 (1942) *with* Fikes v. Alabama, 352 U.S. 191, 197 (1957). Where removal to a distant spot is motivated by a genuine concern for the prisoner's safety, it is still a factor to be considered but "not, as such, a predominant element in our decision." Culombe v. Connecticut, *supra* footnote 6, at 630.

witnessed this brutal incident, is quickly thrown into a cell on an "open charge." *X*, who by hypothesis is being questioned in precisely the same manner as in situations (a) and (b), has no inkling of any of this.

(d) Same facts as situation (c) with these changes:

The sheriff has a hunch that *X* "did it" and will soon "crack." Thus, minutes after *X*'s lawyer is blackjacked and his mother hustled off to a cell, the sheriff phones a newspaper reporter he knows and invites him to attend *X*'s interrogation. He also suggests that the reporter bring a photographer along.[21]

The reporter (who happens to be a casual friend of *X*) and a photographer arrive in time to catch the last half of the proceedings. *X* regards the reporter as a fearless newspaperman who will not hesitate to expose "third degree" tactics.

At the sheriff's urging, the photographer takes two pictures (no flash bulbs or lights) of the sheriff interrogating the suspect, one posed, the other un-

---

21. *Cf.* Haley v. Ohio, 332 U.S. 596, 600–01 (1948):

A photographer was admitted once this lad broke and confessed. But not even a gesture towards getting a lawyer for him was ever made. This disregard of the standards of decency is underlined by the fact that he was kept incommunicado for over three days during which the lawyer retained to represent him twice tried to see him and twice was refused admission. A photographer was admitted at once; but his closest friend—his mother—was not allowed to see him. . . . [Other factors, and] the callous attitude of the police toward his rights combine to convince us that this was a confession wrung from a child by means which the law should not sanction.

Since the aforementioned took place *after* Haley confessed, these offensive events were utilized to refute the police version of what occurred *earlier*. *See also* Haynes v. Washington, 373 U.S. 503, 511 n.8 (1963). Nevertheless, I think *Haley* manifests a determination to discourage resort to such methods without regard to their bearing on the "voluntariness" of the confession, as that term is generally used. That is to say, even if the police version of what happened inside the "interrogation room" had gone unchallenged by Haley, if the offensive events had *preceded* the confession, the Court would still have overturned the conviction.

It can be argued under this "police methods" rationale that the Court should carry its disciplinary power one step further and reverse convictions in order to deter police misconduct, even though such misconduct occurs *subsequent* to, or is *wholly unrelated* to, the acquisition of evidence by the state. But it is plain that in the field of constitutional-criminal procedure generally, the Court has drawn the line short of this point. Even in the *McNabb-Mallory* area where the "voluntariness" of a confession is irrelevant:

[T]he illegality of . . . detention does not retroactively change the circumstances under which [a suspect] made the disclosures. These . . . were not elicited through illegality. Their admission, therefore, would not be use by the Government of the fruits of wrong-doing by its officers.

United States v. Mitchell, 322 U.S. 65, 70 (1944). *See also* Hollman v. State, 235 Ark. 622, 361 S.W.2d 633 (1962), *cert. denied,* 373 U.S. 933 (1963). Even in the field of arrest, search and seizure, where the exclusionary rule bars admittedly trustworthy evidence, an unreasonable search or "seizure" *without more* is of no consequence, *e.g.,* wrongfully arrested persons are not

posed. Later on, when X confesses, the sheriff encourages the reporter to ask X further questions and permits the photographer to induce X to act out certain sadistic details of the crime.[128]

As I read the decided cases, it is evident that as we build on the first hypothetical situation, the resulting confessions become progressively more difficult to sustain. But it is equally evident, I trust, that *they do not become increasingly less "voluntary,"* in any fair sense of the term.[22]

What is happening outside the interrogation room in situations (b) and (c) may be offensive, but by hypothesis, X has no hint of any of this. If "voluntariness" is the test, *what is happening outside is irrelevant.* What X does not know, or even suspect, cannot hurt him, cannot "overbear" or affect his "mind" or "will" in any way.

The removal from jail in situation (b) is no doubt less defensible than the removal in (a),[129] but X doesn't know this. So far as he is concerned, neither nighttime removal is any more "terror-arousing" than the other.[130] The failure to bring X before a magistrate is plainly less excusable in (b) than in (a);[23] but again, so far as X is concerned, neither failure has any more effect on his "powers of resistance" than the other.

---

immunized from criminal prosecutions. Frisbie v. Collins, 342 U.S. 519 (1952); Mahon v. Justice, 127 U.S. 700 (1888); Ker v. Illinois, 119 U.S. 436 (1886); United States v. Sobell, 244 F.2d 520 (2d Cir.), *cert. denied,* 355 U.S. 873 (1957).

> It is one thing to say that officers shall gain no advantage from violating the individual's rights; it is quite another to declare that such a violation shall put [the accused] beyond the law's reach even if his guilt can be proved by evidence that has been obtained lawfully.

Sutton v. United States, 267 F.2d 271, 272 (4th Cir. 1959). *But see* City of St. Paul v. Webb, 256 Minn. 210, 97 N.W.2d 638 (1959); Allen, *Due Process and State Criminal Procedures: Another Look,* 48 Nw. U.L. REV. 16, 27–28 (1953); Broeder, *The Decline and Fall of* Wolf v. Colorado, 41 NEB. L. REV. 185, 199–200 (1961); Scott, *Criminal Jurisdiction of a State over a Defendant Based Upon Presence Secured by Force or Fraud,* 37 MINN. L. REV. 91, 97–98 (1953); Note, 100 U. PA. L. REV. 1182, 1215 (1952).

22. Of course, the Wigmore-Inbau-Reid test also breaks down; *i.e.,* as we build on the first hypothetical, the risk that an innocent person will confess does not increase one iota.

23. An unreasonable delay in bringing the prisoner before a magistrate does not necessarily render a resulting confession inadmissible in state courts, but it is certainly *a factor* operating against admissibility, apparently regardless of whether the prisoner is aware that his statutory right has been violated. *See* Culombe v. Connecticut, *supra* footnote 6, at 631–32; Payne v. Arkansas, 356 U.S. 560, 567 (1958); Fikes v. Alabama, *supra* footnote 20.

The reason this delay is a factor, Mr. Justice Frankfurter has opined, is that "the *ordinary motive* for such extended failure to arraign is not unrelated to the purpose of extracting confessions." Fikes v. Alabama, *id.* at 199 n.1 (concurring opinion) (emphasis added). Once they gain custody, isn't the "ordinary motive" for most things, if not everything the police do, "not unrelated" to this purpose? Besides, if we use the term "voluntariness" in anything like its dictionary meaning, how revelant is the interrogator's *motive* (assuming it is uncommunicated) to the question of a confession's "voluntariness?"

What *is* the factor, the extended delay, or the fact that it constitutes a statutory violation? As

Before *Mapp v. Ohio* and *Wong Sun*, even before "the security of one's privacy against arbitrary intrusion by the police" was deemed "implicit in 'the concept of ordered liberty' and as such enforceable against the States,"[131] the illegality of an arrest was considered a factor militating against the admissibility of a subsequent confession.[132] *Why?* An arrest—any arrest—may generate "unusual emotional tension,"[133] but can it really be said that an illegal arrest produces more tension than a lawful one? The average suspect is not likely to know whether the police are acting on "probable cause," or, if they have a warrant, whether it is a valid one. Moreover, if the suspect is savvy enough to draw these distinctions, he is likely to view an *illegal* arrest with *less* alarm, for he is also likely to be knowledgable enough to realize that the police will have to let him go or that any incriminating evidence found on his person or in his home cannot be used against him.

To sum up, if the confession obtained in situation (a) is far more likely to be admitted in evidence than are those secured in (b) and (c), and I am confident this is so, then to apply the "voluntariness" test is surely to pursue a false lead. For the changed circumstances of (b) and (c) are in no way more "irreconcilable with the possession of mental freedom by a lone suspect"[134] than the first fact situation. Moreover, if the "voluntariness" test does not fare well in situations (b) and (c), it fares still worse in (d).

X's "powers of resistance and self-control" are not merely undiminished, as in (b) and (c), but are, if anything, actually *enhanced* by the changed circumstances of (d). After all, the presence of the newspapermen furnishes some assurance that *X* will not be abused "through excess of zeal or aggressive impatience or flaring up of temper,"[135] some prospect that *X* will not be "faced with the task of overcoming, *by his lone testimony,* solemn official denials."[136]

Since, to some degree, the presence of the newspapermen tends to reinforce *X*'s will to resist and thus to render a resulting confession more "voluntary," if "voluntariness" were the true test, confession (d) would be *easier* to sustain than the one obtained in situation (c). But the newspapermen are significant in another way. The sheriff's invitation to them evidences an offensive "pandering to the morbid craving for the sensational and sadistic."[24] Their presence in

---

Professor LaFave has pointed out, some states have no provision covering police detention prior to initial appearance; a few others seem to permit delays as long as 20 or 48 hours. *See* LaFave, *Detention for Investigation by the Police: An Analysis of Current Practices,* 1962 WASH. U.L.Q. 331, 332-33. As a factor bearing on the admissibility of a confession, would a ten-hour delay in a jurisdiction permitting delays as long as twenty hours stand on the same footing as a ten-hour delay in a state whose laws require prompt commitment and make criminal a failure to comply? I think not. Yet the *motive* of the interrogator and the *effect* on the prisoner is precisely the same in both cases, is it not?

24. *Cf.* Fournier v. People of Puerto Rico, 281 F.2d 888, 892-93 (1st Cir. 1960):

Our sense of justice and fair play is offended by the spectacle of an accused being permitted,

the interrogation room and their freedom to ask questions and take pictures also accentuates the blunt, callous manner in which those who had a far greater claim to see X—his own lawyer and his own mother—were stymied in their desperate efforts. [25] Thus, the *net effect* of the newspapermen's presence, I submit, is to render confession (d) the most vulnerable of all.

Does *Rogers v. Richmond,* decided the same Term as the *Culombe* case, furnish the much-needed guidance in this area? Does it succeed where *Culombe* fails? I think not.

Rogers does tell us that the "reliability" element *cannot* be considered in determining the "voluntariness" of a confession, but it has too little to say about what *may* and *must* be taken into account. Apparently a trial judge "adequately define[s] the 'voluntariness' required by due process"[137] simply by tossing out a few "threadbare generalities" and "empty abstractions,"[138] *e.g.,* "freely and voluntarily made, made without punishment, intimidation or threat,"[139] or "made . . . freely and voluntarily and without fear of punishment or hope of reward."[140]

Such instructions, as Professor Meltzer pointed out almost a decade ago, "fail to advise the jury of factors, such as the legality of the defendant's detention, the length of his interrogation, his education and sophistication, his opportunity to consult counsel and friends, which the Supreme Court has declared to be relevant to the issue."[141] Moreover, they permit the trier of fact to use the terms "voluntary" and "involuntary" in their ordinary, every-day sense. Yet, portions of the *Culombe* opinion to the contrary notwithstanding, it is fairly clear that whatever the special meaning assigned to these elusive terms, the Supreme Court is employing them in *some* special sense. Is it evident that such unruly "voluntariness" instructions are preferable to those cast in terms of substantial danger of "unreliability"?

This question in turn evokes another one. What precisely do we mean by "untrustworthiness" or "unreliability?" It seems these terms, too, are "amphibians." A good deal turns on whether one means: (i) Is *this particular* defendant's confession "unreliable" or "untrustworthy?" or (ii) What is the likelihood, objectively considered, that the interrogation methods employed in this case create a substantial risk that a person subjected to them will falsely confess—*whether or not this particular defendant did?* [26]

---

if not actively encouraged, to act out his sadistic and brutal crime . . . before newspaper reporters and photographers who were invited to attend and allowed actively to participate in the whole sordid business. . . . We shall not encourage [trial by newspaper] further by sanctioning oral confessions for the benefit of those elements of the press which seek to profit by pandering to the morbid craving for the sensational and sadistic.

25. *See* sources cited footnote 21 *supra.*

26. *Cf.* Frankfurter, J., concurring in Sherman v. United States, 365 U.S. 368, 382–84 (1958) (entrapment test); MODEL PENAL CODE § 2.13(1) (Proposed Official Draft, 1962) (entrapment test). *See also* 3 J. WIGMORE, *supra* footnote 9, § 853.

Whether the Inbau-Reid "apt to make an innocent person confess" approach (*see* text accom-

It is fairly clear that the Supreme Court of Errors of Connecticut applied Reliability Test (i) *supra* in *Rogers v. Richmond,* [142] but it is far from clear that the trial judge did so. The reasoning which guided him in admitting the confessions for the jury's consideration was that the pretense of bringing petitioner's wife in for questioning "was not calculated to procure an untrue statement,"[143] and was a trick or device which "had no tendency to produce a confession . . . not in accord with the truth."[144] Whether or not he applied the test *correctly* and whether or not such a trick *does* create a substantial risk that a false confession will result, the trial judge seems to have invoked what I call Reliability Test (ii) *supra.*

Is utilization of the "voluntariness" formula, rather than Reliability Test (ii), likely to affect the result? If the trier of fact finds (as seems to have been the case in *Rogers*) that the *police methods* at issue raise *no risk* of a false confession, or have *no tendency* to produce one, is the confession likely to be barred if the "voluntariness" test is substituted? Is the same judge or jury which viewed the challenged police methods as creating no danger of a false confession likely to conclude that nevertheless these methods rendered the confession "involuntary" and that nevertheless they "broke" defendant's "will?" I think not in 99 cases out of 100.

No "reliability" test can satisfactorily explain why certain factors militate against the admissibility of confessions.[145] But these factors have yet to be isolated in a real case.[146] To date, they have always been intermeshed with other elements creating "credibility risks," at least in the Reliability Test (ii) sense.

I am convinced that were the appropriate case to arise, one with a sufficient degree of offensive or deliberate and systematic police misconduct, the Supreme Court would exclude the confession as a matter of due process even though neither the particular defendant *nor anybody else* were at all likely to confess falsely under the circumstances. But no such case has arisen. If we define "police misconduct" to exclude interrogation techniques creating a substantial risk that the average man, or many men, subjected to them will falsely confess, then no Supreme Court case clearly supports the pure "police misconduct" or "police methods" test.[147]

Although what the court is *prepared* to do cannot be adequately explained

---

panying footnote 9 *supra*) reflects Reliability Test (i) or (ii) is not free from doubt. Sometimes the authors focus on "the subject," and at other times on whether the interrogation methods are of such "a nature" or "type" as to induce a false confession. *See, e.g.,* F. INBAU & J. REID, *supra* footnote 3, at 184, 187–88. However, they criticize the Court for making in *Ashcraft* "what appears to be an abstract psychological appraisal of a thirty-six hour interrogation . . . regardless of the effect of the police practices upon the particular defendant. . . ." *Id.* at 150. And they applaud the decisions in *Gallegos, Stroble,* and *Stein* which revealed, as they saw it, that "the court would no longer make a psychological appraisal of the facts and circumstances involved in the interrogation . . . but . . . determine whether or not the interrogation had a coercive effect on the particular person making the confession. . . ." *Id.* at 153.

in this manner, *on their facts,* the *decided* cases can be viewed as an application of two "reliability" standards: First, taking into account the personal characteristics of the defendant and his particular powers of resistance, did the police methods create too substantial a danger of falsity? Second, without regard to the particular defendant, are the interrogation methods utilized in this case, *e.g.,* physical violence, "relay questioning," or stripping a suspect naked, sufficiently likely to cause a significant number of innocent persons to confess falsely, that the police should not be permitted to proceed in this manner?[(148)]

Is this two-step "reliability" approach as good as, if not better than, the "voluntariness" formula? Once again, this question evokes another one. Does the "involuntariness" test turn on the effect the challenged police methods have on the *particular* defendant's "mind" or will?

Talk about "overbearing and breaking the defendant's will" suggests, and detailed attention to the personal characteristics of the particular confessor seems to confirm, that it does. If so, Reliability Test (ii) may be *more liberal* than the "voluntariness" test, *e.g.,* it will operate to exclude confessions elicited from tough, hardened individuals which the "voluntariness" test would admit. For if the Court means what it has said on a number of occasions, the "voluntariness" test causes constitutionally permissible police interrogation to vary widely, according to the particular defendant concerned.[(149)] "Criminal experience," it seems, opens up a person to police methods from which the ordinary citizen is legally protected. Certain police conduct, taboo so far as the average man is concerned, becomes perfectly acceptable when addressed to the "criminal classes."[27]

"Ameliorative hopes of modern penology and prison administration strongly counsel against such a view."[(150)] Moreover, the notion seems incompatible with the ideal of equality before the law. Finally, this approach seriously undermines the deterrent effect of the confession law. Police interrogators are not furnished much guidance when the constitutionality of their conduct turns on a retrospective appraisal of how "weak" or "strong" of will and mind their quarry, how soft or tough, how timid or brazen. Resort to questionable tactics is sorely tempting if, though the "sheep" may be freed as a consequence, the "wolves," in whom the police have a greater interest, will nevertheless be punished.

Yet, if in dealing with "criminal classes" and other hardened individuals, something more goes, it is quite clear that not *anything* does. It is "common

---

27. At this point, and in the discussion which follows, I am reasoning by analogy from Mr. Justice Frankfurter's powerful concurring opinion in the famous entrapment case of Sherman v. United States, *supra* footnote 26, and from the MODEL PENAL CODE § 2.10(1), comment (Tent. Draft No. 9, 1959) (favoring Justice Frankfurter's approach). The American Law Institute adopted Justice Frankfurter's formulation of the entrapment defense. MODEL PENAL CODE *supra* footnote 26.

ground" that "one truncheon blow on the head of petitioner," *any* petitioner, I take it, and "a confession following such a blow would be inadmissible because of the Due Process Clause."[151] The same, I think, can be said for the "psychology" of stripping a suspect naked and throwing a blanket on him for a few hours,[152] or for protracted "relay questioning" with little or no respite.[153]

Tired, traditional language can be invoked to explain the consequences of such police methods. It can be said that no matter how tough or savvy the suspect, any form of physical violence (or "relay questioning" for protracted periods, or stripping a person naked and keeping him in that state for hours, or other forbidden conduct) renders a resulting confession "unreliable" or "too untrustworthy to be received."[154] It can be said, too, that such methods make any resulting confession "involuntary," *i.e.*, "overbear" *anybody's* mind, even a Capone's, or "break" *everybody's* will, even a Lepke's. But this is neither true as a matter of fact,[155] nor especially helpful as a matter of legal analysis.

The Court does dwell on the particular character and background of the person confessing, but in recent years at least, has almost always underscored petitioner's subnormal powers of resistance to exclude, not admit, the confessions. Thus, we are told that Fikes was "an uneducated Negro, certainly of low mentality, if not mentally ill";[156] Payne was "a mentally dull 19-year-old youth";[157] Spano was "a foreign-born young man of 25 with no past history of law violation or subjection to official interrogation" who "had progressed only one-half year into high school" and "had a history of emotional instability";[158] Blackburn was "insane and incompetent at the time he allegedly confessed";[159] Reck "had dropped out of school at the age of 16, never having completed the 7th grade, and was found to have the intelligence of a child between 10 and 11 years of age at the time of his trial";[160] Culombe was a "wholly illiterate," "mental defective of the moron class with a mental age of nine to nine and a half";[161] Gallegos was a "child of 14";[162] and Lynumn a widow who "had no previous experience with the criminal law and . . . no reason not to believe that the police had ample power to carry out their threats" to take her infant children away from her.[163]

In finding not "decisive" the fact that there is a "greater possibility" for "coercion" in state denial of a specific request for counsel than from state failure to provide one,[28] the Court did point out in *Crooker v. California* that "while in law school" petitioner "had studied criminal law" and "the manner of his refusal to answer indicates full awareness of the right to be silent."[164] But the same day, in *Cicenia v. Lagay,*[165] the Supreme Court sustained a confession elicited from a petitioner who lacked Crooker's superior intelligence and education, even though he, too, had met rebuff in his efforts to

---

28. Crooker v. California, 357 U.S. 433, 438 (1958).

confer with counsel during detention. It seems more accurate to say, then, that Crooker's conviction was upheld not so much for the reason that he possessed *supernormal* powers of resistance, as for the reason that *he did not lack normal or average powers.*

The same may be said for the affirmance in *Stein v. New York.* [29] Indeed, the character and background of the petitioners are described negatively: "These men were not young, soft, ignorant or timid. They were not inexperienced in the ways of crime or its detection, nor were they dumb as to their rights."[(166)] However, for these petitioners, as well as for others less equipped to resist, "physical violence or threat of it . . . invalidates confessions that otherwise would be convincing. . . . When present, there is no need to weigh or measure its effects on the will of the individual victim."[(167)]

Constitutionally permissible interrogation methods, then, do not vary as freely as first appeared. It is somewhat misleading to say, then, as the Court does in *Stein,* that "the limits in any case depend upon a weighing of the circumstances of pressure against the power of resistance of the person confessing."[(168)]

As *Stein* itself elsewhere recognizes, there are occasions when the "circumstances of pressure" invalidate the confession *regardless* of the suspect's "power of resistance." Certain police methods, even those which *may* be directed at a suspect of average intelligence and background, cannot be invoked against one with subnormal powers of resistance. But other methods, those which may not be employed against a man of average intelligence and background, probably cannot be meted out to a "wolf" or "tiger" either.

In short, much more often than not, if not always, when the Court considers the peculiar, individual characteristics of the person confessing, it is only applying a rule of *inadmissibility.* "Strong" personal characteristics rarely, if ever, "cure" forbidden police methods; but "weak" ones may invalidate what are generally permissible methods. [30]

If this is the case, it would be helpful for the Court to say so without employing the "voluntariness" language. Indeed, as is no secret to the reader

---

29. 346 U.S. 156 (1953).

30. I consider this point subsumed in Haynes v. Washington, *supra* footnote 21, handed down since this commentary was written. There, the Court struck down a confession obtained from petitioner after he was held "incommunicado" for sixteen hours, during which time requests to call his wife were denied and such outside contact conditioned upon his making a statement. Since there was no claim of (i) physical abuse, (ii) deprivation of food or rest, or (iii) stretches of protracted questioning, and since petitioner had made an incriminating oral admission enroute to the police station, if ever "a weighing of the circumstances of pressure against the power of resistance" (*see* text accompanying note 167 *supra*) were appropriate, it would seem to have been so in this case. Yet other than to note in passing that "the petitioner's prior contacts with the authorities" do not "negative the existence and effectiveness of the coercive tactics," (*Id.* at 514), the majority opinion nowhere alludes to Haynes's particular character and background.

The failure to do so evoked an illuminating dissent by Mr. Justice Clark, joined by Justices

who has come with me this far, I think we could survive quite nicely if we were to scrap the "voluntariness" terminology altogether.

Looking back, it may be said that the very vagueness of the "voluntary" terminology has been beneficial in a most significant way, that is, making it easier to broaden the grounds for excluding confessions obtained by objectionable means. Here, as elsewhere, troublesome old phrases may have served their era well in the evolution of the law.[169] But here, as elsewhere, their era is past.

The real reasons for excluding confessions have too long been obscured by traditional language. The time has come to unmask them and to build from there. "It is fatuous, to be sure, to suppose that there will ever be a vocabulary free of all ambiguity. . . . But there are some words which, owing to their history, needlessly obstruct clear thinking,"[170] and "voluntary," "involuntary," et al., are surely among them.

The due process confession cases have too often been characterized by Indians-attacking-the-covered-wagon tactics, *i.e.,* circling around and around the problem and taking pot shots at it. The time has come for a more direct approach.

Harlan, Stewart and White. After dwelling on Haynes's long criminal record, Justice Clark contends (*Id.* at 522):

> [Petitioner] cannot, therefore, be placed in the category of those types of people with whom the Court's cases in this area have ordinarily dealt, such as the mentally subnormal . . . the youthful offender . . . or the naive and impressionable defendant. On the contrary, he is a mature adult who appears . . . to be of at least average intelligence and who is neither a stranger to police techniques and custodial procedures nor unaware of his rights on arrest. Thus the Court's reliance on Lynumn v. Illinois [*see* text *supra* at note 163] is completely misplaced.

Equal Justice in the Gatehouses and Mansions of American Criminal Procedure

October, 1965

Too often we conceive of an idea as being like the baton that is handed from runner to runner in a relay race. But an idea as a transmissible thing is rather like the sentence that in the parlor game is whispered about in a circle; the point of the game is the amusement that comes when the last version is compared with the original.

—Lionel Trilling

The Show in the Gatehouse versus the Show in the Mansion

Back in the early 1940s—and that is the stone age as far as the history of American constitutional-criminal procedure is concerned—even as far back as then, the Supreme Court of the United States was finding support for its "involuntary" confession rule in the image of the accusatorial, adversary trial:

The concept of due process would void a trial in which by threats or promises in the presence of court and jury, a defendant was induced to testify against himself. The case can stand no better if, by resort to the same means, the defendant is induced to confess and his confession is given in evidence. [1]

In another case the Court said:

It is inconceivable that any court of justice in the land, conducted as our courts are, open to the public, would permit prosecutors serving in relays to keep a defendant witness under continuous cross-examination for thirty-six hours without rest or sleep in an effort to extract a "voluntary" confession. Nor can we, consistently with Constitutional due process of law, hold voluntary a confession where prosecutors do the same thing away from the restraining influences of a public trial in an open court room. [2]

Measuring the performance in the "interrogation" room against the standard of a public trial may be a stylish way to write an opinion once the matter

1. Lisenba v. California, 314 U.S. 219, 237 (1941).
2. Ashcraft v. Tennessee, 322 U.S. 143, 154 (1944).

has been resolved in favor of the defendant, but until now, at any rate, it has not been the way to resolve the matter.[1] If it were, if the image of the accusatorial, adversary trial were the basis for judgment, not merely the language of decision, then all the due process confession cases which have reached the Court would have been reversed *per curiam*. For amid all the sound and fury one point is plain: in the absence of judge and jury, law enforcement officers can—and without hesitation do—resort to methods they would never consider utilizing at the trial; the case for the prosecution is stronger—much stronger—if what was done to the defendant was done away from the restraining influence of a public trial in an open courtroom.

The police and the prosecutors (and evidently the public) like it this way. They insist that they *need* it this way. Some people—perhaps a majority of the present Supreme Court—do not agree. This, in a word, is what the shouting is all about.

In the courtroom, the conflict of interest between the accused and the state is mediated by an impartial judge; in the police station, although the same conflict exists in more aggravated form, "the law" passes it by. In the courtroom, a reporter takes down everything; in the police station, there is usually no objective recordation of the events, leading to inevitable disputes over what the police did, or what the suspect said, or both.[2] In the courtroom, the defendant is presumed innocent; in the police station, the proceedings usually begin: "All right—we know you're guilty; come through and it'll be easier for you."

In the courtroom, now that *Gideon v. Wainright* is on the books, if and when the defendant takes the stand, his lawyer is at his side, not only to shield him from oppressive or tricky cross-examination which angers, upsets, or confuses him,[3] but to guide him on direct examination; in the police station the suspect neither has nor (usually) is advised of his right to get counsel. Indeed, leading police manuals emphasize that generally it is unnecessary for an interrogator to warn an offender of his constitutional rights before obtaining his confession.[4]

In the courtroom, not only need the accused answer no questions, he may not be asked any (unless he chooses to take the stand); in the police station, even if the suspect is that rare and troublesome type who *knows of* (he is not likely to be told) and *insists on* his right to remain silent,[3] his interrogators simply will not let him: "The problem . . . is to get him to talk, to convert him

---

3. Escobedo v. Illinois, 378 U.S. 478 (1964) refers to a suspect's "absolute right to remain silent" (at 485) and to his "absolute constitutional right" to do so (at 491). It is unclear whether this "right" attaches the moment a person is taken into custody or only when the investigation has ceased to be a general one and begun to "focus" on him "in particular," or whether the Court merely means that in the absence of counsel the only practical way a suspect can avoid incriminating himself is to remain completely silent. Until *Escobedo* was handed down, at any rate, it seemed that the Constitution only enabled a suspect to refrain from incriminating himself and that his "right" to remain absolutely silent in the face of police interrogation—perhaps more aptly

into a willing subject . . . to find the reason for his reluctance or inability [to talk] and overcome that reason."[4] One technique is to pretend to concede him the right to remain silent and then, after some "psychological conditioning" and after pointing out "the incriminating significance of his refusal to talk," to ask him "innocuous questions that have no bearing whatever on the matter under investigation. . . . As a rule the subject will answer such questions, and then gradually the examiner may start in with questions pertaining to the offense."[(5)]

In the courtroom, we are much concerned about the inability of the accused—going it alone—to tell his story effectively; in the police station, evidently we are untroubled that the "subject" may never be given a real chance to tell his story, albeit in his own fumbling way; his adversaries are trained to allude to a particular piece of incriminating evidence, then "cut off immediately any explanation the subject may start to offer at that time . . . for [otherwise the subject] is putting the interrogator on the defensive and this should never be permitted to occur."[(6)]

In the courtroom, to prevent a defendant's lawyer from guiding him on direct examination constitutes a per se violation of "fundamental fairness." Why? "The tensions of a trial" may make him "unfit to give his explanation properly and completely" without the aid of counsel.[5] Even though he has consulted with counsel *before* he takes the stand, even though his lawyer and family and friends are present, "when the average defendant is placed in the witness chair and told . . . that nobody can ask him any questions, and that he may make such statement to the jury as he sees proper in his own defense, he has been set adrift in an uncharted sea with nothing to guide him"; he may be "overwhelmed by his situation, and embarrassed"; "it will not be surprising if his explanation is incoherent, or if it overlooks important circumstances."[6]

---

characterized as his "immunity" from being required to answer any question—stemmed not from the Constitution as such, but from the police department's lack of legislative authorization to compel an answer. That is to say, until *Escobedo* was decided, at any rate, the Constitution did not appear to prohibit legislatures from investing police with the power to compel nonincriminating answers, although the legislatures had not seen fit to do so.

However, even if the police could be, and were, granted such power, how could an *uncounseled* suspect determine when his answers would be incriminating or when they would constitute a waiver of his privilege not to answer other questions? In short, absent the advice of counsel, if a suspect chose not to incriminate himself, would not remaining completely silent be the only practical way he could assure that he would not do so?

4. W. DIENSTEIN, TECHNICS FOR THE CRIME INVESTIGATOR 98 (1952). This paper makes frequent resort to police interrogation manuals on the premise that they evidence the *best* current standards of professional police work. An indication that the best may not be good enough was Illinois's acknowledgment in the *Escobedo* case that "some [of these recommended interrogation techniques] are patently illegal and coercive" and "others may, in some instances, and in combination with other factors, be open to question in view of recent decisions of this Court." Brief for Respondent at 34, Escobedo v. Illinois, 378 U.S. 478 (1964).

5. Ferguson v. Georgia, 365 U.S. 570, 594 (1961).

6. *Id.* at 593-96.

In the police station, to prevent a "subject's" lawyer from guiding him on "direct examination"—to say nothing of protecting him from improper cross-examination—is not to violate "fundamental fairness." Why not? Torn from his home, his friends, and his neighbors, feeling himself "at the mercy of . . . custodians [who] have strong incentives for seeking a quick solution of probative problems by pressing [him] to acknowledge his guilt,"[7] never allowed to "bolster his confidence,"[8] advised that his interrogators have "all the time in the world,"[9] warned that he "can't win,"[10] the tensions are surely no less, incomplete and incoherent explanations hardly more surprising.

Indeed, as the late Justice Jackson (unsuccessfully seeking to sustain the products of a thirty-six-hour interrogation) readily admitted, "of course" custody and detention of a prisoner—even "for an hour"—is "'inherently coercive.'. . . Arrest itself is inherently coercive, and so is detention. . . . Of course such acts put pressure upon the prisoner to answer questions . . . and to confess if guilty."[7]

For a long time, too long, we have operated on the premise that, as Professor Arthur E. Sutherland recently put it, "a man with his life at stake should be able to surrender an ancient constitutional right to remain silent, under compulsions which in a surrender of a little property would obviously make the transaction void."[11] Asks Professor Sutherland:

Suppose a well-to-do testatrix who says she intends to will her property to Elizabeth. John and James want her to bequeath it to them instead. They capture the proposed testatrix, put her in a carefully designed room, out of touch with everyone but themselves and their convenient "witnesses," keep her secluded there for hours while they make insistent demands, continual or intermittent, weary her with contradictions of her assertions that she wants to leave her money to Elizabeth, and finally get her to execute the will in their favor. Assume, further, that John and James are deeply and correctly convinced that Elizabeth is unworthy and will make base use of the property if she gets her hands on it, whereas John and James have the noblest and most righteous intentions. Would any judge of probate accept the will so procured as the "voluntary" act of the testatrix?[12]

Writing for the majority in a famous confession case some fifteen years ago, Justice Frankfurter assured us:

Ours is the accusatorial as opposed to the inquisitorial system. Such has been the characteristic of Anglo-American criminal justice since it freed itself from practices borrowed by the Star Chamber. . . . Under our system society carries the burden of proving its charge against the accused not out of his own mouth. It must establish its

7. Ashcraft v. Tennessee, *supra* footnote 2, at 161.

case, not by interrogation of the accused even under judicial safeguards, but by evidence independently secured through skillful investigation.[8]

"Under our system society carries the burden of proving its charge against the accused not out of his own mouth." This is "the law" that students eagerly take down in their notebooks—those students, that is, "who do not wish to be confronted with the confused picture of what is actually going on."[13] "[N]ot by interrogation of the accused, *even* under judicial safeguards...." This connotes, and logic (if not justice) would seem to dictate, a fortiori, not by interrogation of the accused without judicial safeguards. But this is not, and long has not been, the case.

Police interrogators may now hurl "jolting questions"[14] where once they swung telephone books,[15] may now "play on the emotions" where once they resorted to physical violence,[16] but it is no less true today than it was thirty years ago that

[i]n every city our police hold what can only be called outlaw tribunals,—informal and secret inquisitions of arrested persons,—which are, terminology aside, actual and very vigorous trials for crime.... Centering all upon the confession, proud of it, staking everything upon it, the major canon of American police work is based upon the nullification of the most truly libertarian clause of the Fifth Amendment.... The legal courts come into operation only after the police are through; they are reduced to the position of merely ratifying the plea of guilt which the police have obtained, or else holding trials over the minor percentage of arrested persons about whom the police could reach no conclusion.... The inquisition held by the police before trial is the outstanding feature of American criminal justice, though no statute recognizes its existence.[9]

The courtroom is a splendid place where defense attorneys bellow and strut and prosecuting attorneys are hemmed in at many turns. But what happens before an accused reaches the safety and enjoys the comfort of this veritable mansion? Ah, there's the rub. Typically he must first pass through a much less pretentious edifice, a police station with bare back rooms and locked doors.

In this "gatehouse" of American criminal procedure[17]—through which most defendants journey and beyond which many never get—the enemy of the state is a depersonalized "subject" to be "sized up" and subjected to "interrogation tactics and techniques most appropriate for the occasion";[18] he is "game" to be stalked and cornered.[10] Here ideals are checked at the door,

---

8. Watts v. Indiana, 338 U.S. 49, 54 (1949).

9. Hopkins, *The Lawless Arm of the Law*, ATLANTIC MONTHLY, Sept. 1931, at 279, 280–81.

10. "[T]he interrogator's task is somewhat akin to that of a hunter stalking his game. Each must patiently maneuver himself or his quarry into a position from which the desired objective may be attained; and in the same manner that the hunter may lose his game by a noisy dash through the bush, so can the interrogator fail in his efforts by not exercising the proper degree of patience." F.

"realities" faced, and the prestige of law enforcement vindicated. Once he leaves the "gatehouse" and enters the "mansion"—if he ever gets there—the enemy of the state is repersonalized, even dignified, the public invited, and a stirring ceremony in honor of individual freedom from law enforcement celebrated.

I suspect it is not so much that society knows and approves of the show in the gatehouse, but that society does not know or care.

[S]ociety, by its insouciance, has divested itself of a moral responsibility and unloaded it on to the police. Society doesn't want to know about criminals, but it does want them put away, and it is incurious how this can be done provided it is done. Thus society, in giving the policeman power and wishing to ignore what his techniques must be, has made over to him part of its own conscience. [11]

True, the man in the street would have considerable difficulty explaining why the Constitution requires so much in the courtroom and means so little in the police station, but that is not his affair. "The task of keeping the two shows going at the same time without losing the patronage or the support of the Constitution for either," as Thurman Arnold once observed, is "left to the legal scholar."[19] Perhaps this is only fitting and proper, for as Thomas Reed Powell used to say, if you can think about something that is related to something else without thinking about the thing to which it is related, then you have the legal mind.[20]

That the legal mind passes by or shuts out the de facto inquisitorial system which has characterized our criminal procedure for so long is bad enough. What is worse is that such an attitude leads many—perhaps requires many—to recoil with horror and dismay at any proposal which recognizes the grim facts of the criminal process and seeks to do something about them.

For example, back in the late 1920s, only a short time before the Wickersham Commission was to document the alarming extent to which the de facto system bred coerciveness and downright brutality,[21] suggestions were made that—rather than a police officer—a magistrate, or prosecuting attorney in the presence of a magistrate, do the interrogation.[22] How did such a proposal fare in the American Law Institute? It was beaten down to the accompaniment of cries that

    (a) it would "violate fundamental principles of personal liberty";
    (b) it would be "opposed to our traditions of fair play";
    (c) it would "result in the unjust conviction of innocent persons";

INBAU & J. REID, LIE DETECTION AND CRIMINAL INTERROGATION 185 (3d ed. 1953). The authors have dropped this graphic language from their later work.

11. MacInnes, *The Criminal Society,* in THE POLICE AND THE PUBLIC 101 (C. Rolph ed. 1962).

(d) "even if the necessary constitutional changes were made and the system adopted by the legislatures... the great body of public opinion would be against it."[12]

As to (a), it is difficult to see why the unregulated and unscrutinized prevalent police station practices do not pose a deeper threat to personal liberty; as to (b), the short retort seems to be "traditions" of fair play, no; "mythology," yes; as to (c), why is an innocent man more likely to answer confusedly or incorrectly when officially questioned by, or in the presence of, a magistrate than when interrogated unofficially and secretly by "a wheedling detective or incredulous policeman?"[23] Finally, as to (d), why was no amendment to the privilege against self-incrimination necessary to authorize existing police interrogation practices, and why are our people not against such practices? Or would they be, if they ever took time out to think about them?

Back in the early 1940s, a member of the Advisory Committee on the Federal Rules of Criminal Procedure proposed that a commissioner do the interrogation at preliminary hearings only after informing the suspect "of his right to the advice of counsel, that he is under no obligation to answer any question, that any answer he chooses to give may possibly be used against him, and that his refusal to answer cannot be used against him."[24] Even today, after more than twenty years of court decisions, legislative hearings, bar group studies, and law review writings, such a proposal offers an arrestee significantly more protection than does the typical police interrogation, but the Advisory Committee rejected it

as being contrary to the basic traditions of Anglo-American criminal procedure, and as probably violative of the constitutional guarantee against self-incrimination. This guarantee is understood to comprise not merely the right to refuse to answer questions, but also the right not to be questioned in a judicial proceeding and before a judicial officer, unless the defendant by voluntarily taking the stand in his own behalf submits to examination.[25]

Evidently, so long as neither the proceeding nor the presiding officer is "judicial," basic traditions are honored and self-incrimination problems avoided.

As a Judge of the Supreme Court of South Africa recently observed, despite "a great deal of emotional writing which elevates the privilege against self-incrimination to 'one of the great landmarks in man's struggle to make himself

---

12. ALI CODE OF CRIMINAL PROCEDURE 26–27 (Tent. Draft No. 1, 1928). I do not mean to suggest these were the only reasons the proposal was defeated. It was also said, for example, that "in this country the magistrates are not equipped for such work, in many instances being laymen." *Id*. at 27.

civilized,'"[13] "the most abundant proof" that it does not prohibit pretrial interrogation

> is to be found in the United States. There the privilege is in the Federal Constitution and in some form or other in the constitutions of all but two of the fifty states . . . . But in none of the forty-nine jurisdictions does it apply to what happens in the police station. The police interrogate freely, sometimes for seven to eight hours on end. The statements thus extracted are given in evidence. There is the provision that only statements made voluntarily may be given in evidence, but that seems to be interpreted rather liberally, judged by our standards.[26]

Four score years ago, Sir James Fitzjames Stephen noted with pride that the fact that "the prisoner is absolutely protected against all judicial questioning before or at the trial . . . contributes greatly to the dignity and apparent humanity of a criminal trial. It effectually avoids the appearance of harshness, not to say cruelty, which often shocks an English spectator in a French court of justice."[27] Whatever the case then, one would have to underscore "apparent" and "appearance" in that statement today. Stephen also told us that "the fact that the prisoner cannot be questioned stimulates the search for independent evidence."[28] Whatever the case then, one cannot but wonder today how often the only thing "stimulated" by the inability of *judicial* officers to question a prisoner is questioning by *police* officers. One cannot but wonder how often the availability of the privilege (or, perhaps more aptly, the inability of the State to undermine the privilege), once the accused reaches the safety and comfort of the mansion, only furnishes the State with an additional incentive for proving the charge against him out of his own mouth before he leaves the gatehouse.

Is the Privilege Checked at the Gatehouse Door?

Those who would not narrow the gap between the nobility of the principles we purport to cherish and the meanness of the station house proceedings we permit to continue may:

(a) Cite the language in the fifth amendment which forbids compelling any person "to be a witness against himself" "in any criminal case" and contend that in the police station the "criminal case" has not yet commenced. But it is hornbook law that the privilege extends to all judicial or official hearings

---

13. Hiemstra, *Abolition of the Right Not to Be Questioned*, S. AFR. L.J. 187, 194 (1963). The reference is to E. GRISWOLD, THE FIFTH AMENDMENT TODAY 7 (1955), which, read in its entirety, strikes me as singularly *unemotional*.

where persons may be called upon to give testimony, even to civil proceedings. [14]

(b) Find some comfort in the assertion by the greatest master of the law of evidence, Wigmore, that the privilege against self-incrimination "covers only statements made in court under process as a witness."[29] As other masters of the subject have pointed out, however, this is an "obviously inaccurate" statement;[30] indeed it is in direct conflict with Wigmore's earlier declaration that the privilege applies "in investigations by a *grand jury,* in investigations by a *legislature* or a body having legislative functions, and in investigations by *administrative* officials."[31]

(c) Remind us (i) that the histories of the privilege and of the rule excluding "involuntary" confessions are "wide apart, differing by one hundred years in origin, and derived through separate lines of precedents"; "if the privilege, fully established by 1680, had sufficed for both classes of cases, there would have been no need for creating the distinct rule about confessions";[32] (ii) that until recently, at any rate, the privilege has never been applicable to police interrogation and "all of the decisions admitting coerced statements of incriminating facts not amounting to a confession assume that the privilege is inapplicable, as does the constant recognition of the accepted police practice which, in the absence of statute, does not require that the accused be warned he need not answer."[15]

Here, as elsewhere, to look to "history" is to see "through a screen of human values that gives importance to some antecedents and relegates others to obscurity"; it is to be less impressed with historical facts "which do not fit into our theories . . . than [with] those that do."[33]

For example, one who would apply the privilege to the police station may select, from the vast conglomerate of determinants which form its history, the fact that the maxim "no man shall be compelled to accuse himself" first meant (and until the seventeenth century probably only meant) that no man shall be compelled to make the *first charge* against himself, to submit to a "fishing" interrogation about his crimes, to furnish his own indictment from his own lips. Until the 1600s all parties concerned seemed to have operated on the

14. "This is a question which was raised and answered long ago, so long ago in fact that lawyers tend to take it for granted. But early courts saw that the protection of the amendment itself would be an empty gesture if it was literally applied." E. GRISWOLD, *supra* footnote 13, at 54–55. *See generally* C. McCORMICK, EVIDENCE 259 (1954); J. MAGUIRE, EVIDENCE OF GUILT § 2.03 (1959); E. MORGAN, BASIC PROBLEMS OF EVIDENCE 145–48 (1962).

15. Morgan, *The Privilege against Self-Incrimination,* 34 MINN. L. REV. 1, 28 (1949). Professor Morgan goes on to point out, however, that "all the authorities dealing with the validity of statutes requiring reports to the police and the keeping of records of various occupational activities, as well as those passing upon the admissibility of evidence obtained by physical and mental examination of an accused by the police or under their direction, proceed upon the theory that the constitutional privilege furnishes protection against inquiries by the police." He urges that the privilege should apply to "inquisitions by the police."

premise that *after* pleading to the indictment, the accused could be compelled to incriminate himself.[34]

Recent studies have disclosed that in Washington, D.C., in 1960, of 1,356 persons "arrested for investigation" and held for eight hours or more, only 1.2 percent were ever formally charged;[35] and that in Chicago in 1956, "50 per cent of the police prisoners produced in Felony Court [were] held without charge for 17 hours or longer"[36] and "another 30 per cent could not be accounted for in terms of pre-booking detention because of police failure to complete the arrest slip." When we apply the privilege to "arrests for investigation" or "routine pickups,"[16] do we disguise a revolutionary idea in the garb of the past or do we restore the privilege to its primordial state?

Nor should it be forgotten that for many centuries there were simply no "police interrogators" to whom the privilege could be applied. Although what Dean Wigmore calls "the first part" of the history of the privilege, the opposition to the ex-officio oath of the ecclesiastical courts, began in the 1200s,[37] "criminal investigation by the police, with its concomitant of police interrogation, is a product of the late nineteenth century";[38] in eighteenth-century America as in eighteenth-century England "there were no police [in the modern sense] and, though some states seem to have had prosecutors, private prosecution was the rule rather than the exception."[39] In fact as well as in theory, observes Professor Edmund M. Morgan, "there can be little question that the modern American police have taken over the functions performed originally by the English committing magistrates [and at least by some colonial magistrates];[40] they are in a real sense administrative officers and their questioning of the person under arrest is an investigative proceeding in which testimony is taken."[41] If modern police are permitted to interrogate under the coercive influence of arrest and secret detention, then, insists Professor Albert R. Beisel, "they are doing the very same acts which historically the judiciary was doing in the seventeenth century but which the privilege against self-incrimination abolished."[42]

I do not contend that "the implication[s] of a tangled and obscure history"[43] dictate that the privilege apply to the police station, only that they permit it. I do not claim that this long and involved history displaces judgment, only that it liberates it.[44] I do not say that the distinct origins of the

---

16. A Chicago police officer defined a "routine pickup" as follows: "Well, as you well know, there has always been supposedly a list of men that they care to question to ascertain if they would have any information as to the case of these various killings. . . ." ILL. DIV., ACLU, SECRET DETENTION BY THE CHICAGO POLICE 20 (1959). *Cf.* Dooley, *Line-Up Line: "You Got Nutt'n on Me,"* Boston Globe, Jan. 27, 1965, at 2, reporting how the Boston police (declaring "open warfare" against the city's "underworld" as a result of 18 "gang-type" slayings) "picked up" 25 "known criminals," put 18 of them "before the lights," and asked each of them: "What did you do that caused you to be arrested?" According to one detective, "If we drag them in often enough, someone is going to spill something."

confession and self-incrimination rules are irrelevant, only that it is more important (if we share Dean Charles T. McCormick's views) that "the kinship of the two rules is too apparent for denial"[45] and that "such policy as modern writers are able to discover as a basis for the self-crimination privilege... pales to a flicker beside the flaming demands of justice and humanity for protection against extorted confessions."[46]

Those who applaud the show in the mansion without hissing the show in the gatehouse may also:

(d) Find refuge in the notion that compulsion to testify means *legal* compulsion. Since he is threatened neither with perjury for testifying falsely nor contempt for refusing to testify at all, it cannot be said, runs the argument, that the man in the back room of the police station is being "compelled" to be a "witness against himself" within the meaning of the privilege. Since the police have no legal right to make him answer, "there is no legal obligation to which a privilege in the technical sense can apply."[47]

Can we accept this analysis without forgetting as lawyers and judges what we know as men?[48] Without permitting logic to triumph over life?[49] So long as "what on their face are merely words of request take on color from the officer's uniform, badge, gun and demeanor";[50] so long as his interrogators neither advise him of his rights nor permit him to consult with a lawyer who will; can there be any doubt that many a "subject" will *assume* that the police have a legal right to an answer?[17] That many an incriminating statement will be extracted under "color" of law?[51] So long as the interrogator is instructed to "get the idea across ... that [he] has 'all the time in the world'";[52] so long as "the power [legal or otherwise] to extract answers begets a forgetfulness of the just limitations of the power" and "the simple and peaceful process of questioning breeds a readiness to resort to bullying and to physical force";[53] can there be any doubt that many a subject will assume that there is an *extralegal* sanction for contumacy?

If these inferences are unfair, if very few "subjects" are misled to believe that there is either a legal obligation to talk or unlimited time and extralegal means available to make them do so—if, in short, they know they can "shut up"—why are the police so bent on preventing counsel from telling them what they already know? Why, at least, don't the officers themselves tell their "subjects" plainly and emphatically that they need not and cannot be made to answer? That they will be permitted to consult with counsel or be brought before a magistrate in short order? And why is the "subject" questioned in

---

17. *Cf.* P. DEVLIN, THE CRIMINAL PROSECUTION IN ENGLAND 26-27 (1960): "[T]he policeman has no power or privilege [to make a suspect answer]; in the eye of the law he is only an interested questioner seeking for information. But in practice he is of course treated very differently. It is probable that even to-day, when there is much less ignorance about these matters than formerly, there is still a general belief that you must answer all questions put to you by a policeman, or at least that it will be the worse for you if you do not."

secret? Why does the modest proposal that a suspect be interrogated by or before an impartial functionary immediately after arrest "meet with scant favor in police circles, even from the most high-minded and highly respected elements in those circles?"[54]

Finally, those who have learned to live with the widespread practices in the gatehouse may take the "waiver" tack. They may:

(e) Concede that the privilege against self-incrimination exists in the police station, but maintain that when (instead of exercising his right to remain silent or to make only self-serving remarks) a suspect "volunteers" damaging statements he has *waived* his rights. This is not much of a concession, for "if the privilege is easily waived, there is really no privilege at all."[55] However, if, "when the state is putting questions, the answers to which will disclose criminal activities by the witness, there is likely to be an especially high insistence checked by an especially high reluctance,"[56] then there is likely to be an especially low incidence of valid waiving of the privilege.

So long as "the classic definition of waiver enumerated in *Johnson v. Zerbst* [1938] . . . — 'an intelligent relinquishment or abandonment of a known right or privilege'—furnishes the controlling standard,"[57] so long as the courts "indulge every reasonable presumption against [such] waiver,"[58] it is difficult to see how the contention that an unadvised suspect waives the privilege simply by talking even presents a substantial question. "The Fourteenth Amendment," announced the Supreme Court only last Term, "secures against state invasion the same privilege that the Fifth Amendment guarantees against federal infringement—the right of a person to remain silent unless he chooses to speak in the unfettered exercise of his own will."[18] Can it seriously be said of the routine police interrogation that the suspect so speaks? Again, only last Term the Court pointed out that "no system of criminal justice can, or should, survive if it comes to depend for its continued effectiveness on the citizens' abdication through unawareness of their constitutional rights."[19] On what else does the existing system depend?[20]

True, the Court did note that "the accused may, of course, *intelligently and knowingly* waive his privilege against self-incrimination and his right to coun-

18. Malloy v. Hogan, 378 U.S. 1, 8 (1964).

19. Escobedo v. Illinois, *supra* footnote 3, at 490.

20. *Cf. Letter from English Policeman on Use of Judges' Rules,* in SELECTED WRITINGS ON LAW OF EVIDENCE AND TRIAL 846 (W. Fryer ed. 1957): "When I said to you that prisoners always opened their mouths too much, I meant it, but what they usually do is to make a statement which they think, in their ignorance of the law, excuses them, e.g., they will frequently say something to this effect: 'I didn't break into the house. It was Smith that did it. I only went with him.' Or: 'I didn't steal the money. Smith took it and gave me some of it.' Frequently they will apologise thinking that then we will let them go, e.g.: 'I'm sorry I did it. I don't know what made me, and I won't do it again.' This may all sound fantastic to you, but it is literally true. The ignorance of the Great British Public neutralises the Judges' Rules. When we deal with an educated man who knows his rights, we have had it, unless we have outside evidence enough."

sel either at a pretrial stage or at the trial,"[21] but generally that presupposes an effective warning.[(59)] Is it likely that the suspect's captors—who are hidden from the gaze of disinterested observors and "who naturally share the purposes and outlook of the prosecutor"[22]—will furnish such warning?

The trouble with both the "waiver" and "no legal compulsion" rationalizations of the existing de facto inquisitorial system is this: when we expect the police dutifully to notify a suspect of the very means he may utilize to frustrate them—when we rely on them to advise a suspect unbegrudgingly and unequivocally of the very rights he is being counted on *not* to assert—we demand too much of even our best officers. As Dean Edward L. Barrett has asked: "[I]s it the duty of the police to persuade the suspect to talk or persuade him not to talk? They cannot be expected to do both."[(60)]

Suspects there are who feel in a "pleading guilty" mood, for some of the many reasons most defendants do plead guilty. Suspects there are who would intentionally relinquish their rights for some hoped-for favor from the state. I do not deny this. I do deny that such suspects do not need a lawyer.

Surely the man who, in effect, is pleading guilty in the gatehouse needs a lawyer no less than one who arrives at the same decision only after surviving the perilous journey through that structure. Both needs are substantial:

An attorney is in a better position than the defendant to evaluate and discuss any plea agreement. Moreover, the attorney will want to inquire about the court's sentencing practice and thus better assess the value of any proposition made by the prosecuting attorney. Under these circumstances, a defendant will have a sympathetic legal expert helping him analyze all relevant factors in arriving at the ultimate conclusion of whether to plead guilty.
. . . .

One can seriously question whether a defendant who pleads guilty should ever be permitted to waive counsel. The need for an attorney may be more dramatically perceived in the trial context, but at least in that situation there may be some tactical advantage for a defendant to be unrepresented—the court and the jury may be more sympathetically disposed toward a layman contending with an accomplished legal expert. In the guilty plea context, however, there is nothing for a defendant to gain by being unrepresented—in fact, the very decision to plead guilty and waive the right to trial requires an evaluation of the prosecution's case, something at which a layman is inept.[23]

---

21. Escobedo v. Illinois, *supra* footnote 3, at 490 n. 14.

22. Weisberg, *Police Interrogation of Arrested Persons: A Skeptical View,* in POLICE POWER AND INDIVIDUAL FREEDOM 153, 154 (C. Sowle ed. 1962). *Cf.* Von Moltke v. Gillies, 332 U.S. 708, 725 (1948): "The right to counsel guaranteed by the Constitution contemplates the services of an attorney devoted solely to the interests of his client.... The Constitution does not contemplate that prisoners shall be dependent upon government agents for legal counsel and aid, however conscientious and able those agents may be."

23. Note, 112 U. PA. L. REV. 888–89 (1964).

It may be argued that putting defense counsel in the interrogation room "merely removes the moral and legal dilemma of plea bargaining from the district attorney's office back to the police station and renders such bargaining even less subject to judicial control than it is today."[24] But a good deal of "plea bargaining" *without* defense counsel takes place in the police station right now. So long as this is the case, why is it more "immoral" and "illegal" for a suspect to bargain with the advice of counsel than without it? After all, it is not uncommon for the police to enjoy the benefit of counsel at such bargaining sessions. Nor is it apparent why the presence of defense counsel, who is presumably better equipped than his client to appreciate, remember, and recreate the nature and scope of the "bargaining," renders such proceedings less subject to judicial control.

It may well be true that

counsel would gain no advantage for his client by advising him to confess to the police which he could not gain later on in his negotiations with the prosecutor. If anything, he would be giving up his one bargaining point without any assurance that the police can deliver on their promise. And if the police failed to deliver, counsel would have no assurance that the confession would be excluded from evidence at the trial. Counsel can always get his client as good a deal, and usually better, from the district attorney without running these risks.[25]

Won't defense counsel realize this? At least isn't he much more likely to do so than an untrained and unadvised suspect? The presence of defense counsel in the police station, then, will not remove plea bargaining from the district attorney's office to the police station, but take it out of the police station— where so often it now is.

24. Enker & Elsen, *Counsel for the Suspect:* Massiah v. United States *and* Escobedo v. Illinois, 49 MINN. L. REV. 47, 68 (1964). It should be noted that Messrs. Enker and Elsen do not make this point in criticism of *Escobedo* but in reply to the argument that even with defense counsel in the interrogation room some suspects will still confess.
25. *Id.*

A Dissent from the *Miranda* Dissents: Some Comments on the "New" Fifth Amendment and the Old "Voluntariness" Test

November, 1966

The world and the books are so accustomed to use, and over-use, the word "new" in connection with our country, that we early get and permanently retain the impression that there is nothing old about it.

—Mark Twain (1883)

[F]or the very reason that those in authority have no right to require a disclosure, those without authority feel justified in seeking to worm it out by threats, by fraud, by holding out false hopes, by putting forward false pretenses. . . . Unwilling to allow a magistrate to institute, as a matter of course, a formal examination, and place the result on record, we leave the same information to be fished for by the sheriff who makes the arrest, by the jailer, by the fellow-prisoner turned informer or by the detective in disguise, and only require the witness who proves it to add perhaps perjury to fraud in swearing that no undue means were used to elicit the confession.

—Simeon E. Baldwin (1883)

IF THE SEVERAL conferences and workshops (and many lunch conversations) on police interrogation and confessions in which I have participated this past summer[1] are any indication, *Miranda v. Arizona*[1] has evoked much anger and spread much sorrow among judges, lawyers and professors. In the months and years ahead, such reaction is likely to be translated into microscopic analyses and relentless, probing criticism of the majority opinion. During this

---

1. 384 U.S. 436 (1966) (Warren, C.J.). Actually, "the *Miranda* opinion" is an opinion for four cases: *Miranda*, No. 759; *Vignera v. New York*, No. 760; *Westover v. United States*, No. 761; and *California v. Stewart*, No. 584. Justices Harlan, Stewart and White dissented in all four cases, joining in separate dissenting opinions written by Justices Harlan and White. Justice Clark, who would continue to follow the "totality of circumstances" rule but assign increased weight to whether the appropriate warnings were given, *see* 384 U.S. at 499, 503, 504, dissented in three of the four cases but concurred in the result in *California v. Stewart* "if the merits are to be reached," *id.* at 504. (He preferred to dismiss the writ of certiorari in *Stewart* for want of a final judgment.)

period of agonizing appraisal and reappraisal, I think it important that various assumptions and assertions in the *dissenting* opinions do not escape attention.

I must agree with Justice Harlan that "the fine points of this [the *Miranda* majority's] scheme are far less clear than the Court admits,"[(2)] but that is a subject worthy of a separate article. I do not deny that some aspects of the majority opinion are questionable, for example, its defining "custodial questioning"[(3)]—which must be preceded by warning the suspect that "he has a right to remain silent, that any statement he does make may be used as evidence against him, and that he has a right to the presence of an attorney, either retained or appointed"[(4)]—to include stopping and questioning on the street.[2] I take it, however, that one may sharply dissent from portions of the

2. Thus, although, as Judge Breitel had pointed out on the eve of *Miranda,* the controversy had centered on what rights the suspect enjoyed and what rights he was entitled to *after* he was brought to the police station, Breitel, *Criminal Law and Equal Justice,* 1966 UTAH L. REV. 1, 8–9, the Court manifested its willingness to enter a thicket "largely ignored by commentators and dealt with ambiguously by most courts." Remington, *The Law Relating to "On the Street" Detention, Questioning and Frisking of Suspected Persons and Police Arrest Privileges in General,* in POLICE POWER AND INDIVIDUAL FREEDOM 11, 15 (C. Sowle ed. 1962).

The Court has had much experience with police station interrogation (if anything, too much), but so far as I know it has never had occasion to consider the admissibility of a statement produced by "on the street" or "on the spot" questioning. I am convinced that the persistent, resourceful, skillful police interrogator is no bogeyman, but he operates within the confines of the stationhouse, not on the streets or even in the squad car. The average patrolman is of a different breed. I am readily persuaded by what the Court has to say about the substantial pressures generated by the isolation, secrecy and unfamiliarity of the "interrogation room," but the Court has virtually nothing to say about the inherently compulsive and menacing nature of "on the street" questioning.

I agree that the privilege protects an individual from being compelled to incriminate himself even though the compulsion be "informal" and "subtle" and that the privilege "does not distinguish degrees of incrimination," 384 U.S. at 476—once a certain degree is reached. Distinguishing degrees, after all, is inherent in the process of defining "compel" within the meaning of the privilege. That the requisite degree will sometimes be reached in the course of "field interrogation" I have no doubt. But always? Necessarily? Typically? Of course *any* questioning by a police officer *anywhere* generates *some* pressures and anxieties—"what on their face are merely words of request take on color from the officer's uniform, badge, gun and demeanor." Foote, *The Fourth Amendment; Obstacle or Necessity in the Law of Arrest?,* in POLICE POWER AND INDIVIDUAL FREEDOM 29, 30 (C. Sowle ed. 1962). This is also true, however, of "general on-the-scene questioning" and of police visits at a suspect's home or place of business, situations where, the Court tells us, the requisite warnings need not (or, at least, need not always) be given, because "the compelling atmosphere inherent in the process of in-custody interrogation is not necessarily present." 384 U.S. at 478.

Finally, if the police must issue the *Miranda* warnings to one detained "on the spot," they are more likely to resort to the more drastic alternative of taking him down to the stationhouse. A stop may well be an "arrest" for some purposes, but it does not stigmatize a man the way a formal "arrest" for a felony does.

On the other hand, this is surely one of those "damned if it did" (cover field interrogation) and "damned if it didn't" issues which sometimes confront the Court. As the Court must have been well aware, confining the *Miranda* rules to stationhouse proceedings—which would have suf-

Miranda dissents without warmly endorsing every aspect of the majority opinion. I take it that here, as elsewhere, one may spot the bad without committing himself to, or knowing, the perfectly good.[5]

Dissenting Justice Harlan, joined by Justices White and Stewart, utters a couple of "hurrahs" for the old test—"a workable and effective means of dealing with confessions in a judicial manner"[6] and "an elaborate, sophisticated and sensitive approach to admissibility of confessions."[7] The aim of the majority, he protests, "is toward 'voluntariness' in a utopian sense."[8] I submit that it is the dissenters who are the dreamers, not the majority. I venture to say that only one with an extravagant faith in the actual operation of the "totality of the circumstances" test could fail to see that the safeguards provided by the old test were largely "illusory."[9] Justice Harlan is distressed that the majority requires the police to show "voluntariness with a vengeance,"[10] but I submit that, as his vote to uphold the confession in *Davis v. North Carolina*[3] well illustrates, he would require the defendant to establish restraint, coercion, and a breaking of the will "with a vengeance."

---

ficed to dispose of all the cases before it—would have put enormous pressure on the police to intensify and widen the less visible "on the street" detention and to slow down or make more circuitous the ride to headquarters. *See* MODEL CODE OF PRE-ARRAIGNMENT PROCEDURE § 5.01, comment at 174 (Tent. Draft No. 1, 1966); *Developments in the Law—Confessions*, 79 HARV. L. REV. 935, 945 (1966). By defining "custodial questioning" to cover "field" and "squad car" questioning, the Court was understandably reaching out (albeit most gingerly) to protect its flanks. For drama and glamor it is hard to beat the "interrogation room" confession, but the "more humdrum" common practice of stopping and questioning raises "far more basic" issues. *See* Packer, *Who Can Police the Police?*, The New York Review of Books, Sept. 8, 1966, at 10, 12.

True, the Court might have taken a "middle ground" on this troublesome cluster of issues and indicated that whether questioning of a person "deprived of his freedom in any significant way" is to be preceded by the requisite warnings should turn on the particular circumstances attending each incident, but to do so might have largely defeated its central purpose, which was to displace the unsatisfactory case-by-case approach in this field with a set of firm, specific, "automatic" guidelines. (The effects of its apparent exceptions for "general on-the-scene questioning" and police visits at a suspect's home remain to be seen.)

If the distinctions between "field interrogation" and "police station" questioning are without a difference for purposes of the requisite warnings, are they nevertheless significant for purposes of "waiver"? Is the "heavy burden" resting on the government to demonstrate that the suspect knowingly and intelligently waived his rights, 384 U.S. at 475, appreciably lighter *outside* the relatively controlled environment of the stationhouse? Considering the greater confusion and higher incidence of "emergency situations" on the street, the substantially greater pressures usually operating in the police station, and the much more extensive means of corroborating evidence of warnings available there, much can be said for an affirmative answer. However, I do not find the answer in *Miranda*. Although I doubt that all those reading the *Miranda* opinion with a magnifying glass can be restrained from expounding in the meantime, this aspect of *Miranda*, above all others, will be brought into focus only by "new prodding of the new facts." *Cf.* K. LLEWELLYN, THE COMMON LAW TRADITION 293 (1960).

3. 384 U.S. 737 (1966) (on federal habeas corpus). Since, in another case handed down the same day, the Court declined to give the new rules retroactive effect, Johnson v. New Jersey, 384

A victim of objectionable interrogation practices could only satisfy this test with some regularity in a utopian judicial world. This was not Davis's world. He could produce a specific notation on the arrest sheet to the effect that he was to be held incommunicado. He could also point to the undisputed fact that no one other than the police had seen him during the sixteen days of detention and interrogation that preceded his confessions. Moreover, on the basis of these confessions he was sentenced to death, which, however painful otherwise, does not "hurt" one who is seeking to gain close appellate court scrutiny and reversal. Nevertheless, Davis lost in the state courts and, on habeas corpus, in the two lower federal courts.[4] True, *Davis* is only one case, but most alleged victims of impermissible police interrogation enter the "swearing contest" with many fewer weapons.

The dissenters are startled at how the majority manages to leap over high historical and linguistic barriers to bring the privilege against self-incrimination into the interrogation room. "A *trompe l'oeil*,"[11] proclaims Justice Harlan. "At odds with American and English legal history,"[12] reports Justice White, joined by Justices Harlan and Stewart. "Decisions like these," warns Justice White, "cannot rest alone on syllogism, metaphysics or some ill-defined notions of natural justice."[13]

Miranda may leave something to be desired, but it deserves a better reception than this. True, it amounts to a substantial jump from *Escobedo*,[5] which, in turn, marked a jump from *Haynes*.[6] But *Miranda* is hardly a thunderbolt from the blue. It is unquestionably a sharp departure from the *recent past,* but if one travels back far enough—"Oh, no!" many a reader will exclaim at this point. "Not another 'we but return to old principle' discourse."[14] I sympathize with these readers.

Police-prosecution-minded critics of the courts can be exasperating; at least they have often exasperated me.[15] But champions of liberty and privacy can also be exasperating; at least they have even exasperated me. Every year I teach *Adamson v. California*,[16] and though I never fail to pummel the majority opinion, I never fail to gag at Justice Murphy's dissent: "Much can be said pro and con as to the desirability of allowing comment on the failure of the accused to testify. But policy arguments are to no avail in the face of a clear constitutional command."[17] I joined in the general rejoicing when *Gideon v. Wainwright*[18] was handed down, but I winced at Justice Black's assertion that "the Court in *Betts v. Brady* made an abrupt break with its own

---

U.S. 719 (1966), it applied the traditional confession rules to strike down the *Davis* confessions, Justices Clark and Harlan dissenting.

4. *See* the discussion at notes 131–48 *infra*.

5. 378 U.S. 478 (1964).

6. 373 U.S. 503 (1963). But this was not nearly as long a jump as the many who were thunderstruck by *Escobedo* seemed to think. *See* Herman, *The Supreme Court and Restrictions on Police Interrogation*, 25 OHIO STATE L.J. 449, 454–56 (1964).

well-considered precedents "[19] and at his assurance that "in returning to these old precedents . . . we but restore constitutional principles. . . . "[20]

I am well aware that for what I am about to say, I, too, shall be accused of finding refuge in constitutional language whose specificity and immutability is largely illusory, of "returning" to a mythical past, or at least of being less impressed with historical facts which do not fit my theories than with those which do. I adhere to the view that whether or not the Court's reading of the privilege against self-incrimination in *Malloy v. Hogan*[21] "makes good sense, . . . it constitutes bad history—*modern* history, that is. "[22] I still maintain that although "the old *Bram* case might well have furnished a steppingstone to the standard advanced in *Malloy*, . . . until *Escobedo*, at any rate, it only amounted to an early excursion from the prevailing multifactor approach. "[23] I claim only this:

(a) The linguistic and historical barriers, whatever they were, which lay in the path of *Miranda's* application of the privilege to "custodial questioning" were considerably less formidable than those surmounted when the privilege was applied to legislative investigations and civil proceedings. Yet long before *Brown v. Mississippi*, [24] the Court's first fourteenth amendment due process confession case, it was settled, rightly or wrongly, that the privilege did apply to these latter proceedings. Given *Counselman v. Hitchcock*[7] and

---

7. 142 U.S. 547 (1892). The Court held that appellant need not answer questions asked in a grand jury investigation which would tend to incriminate him because the "protection of § 860 [of the Revised Statutes] is not coextensive with the constitutional provision. " *Id.* at 565. The statute protected appellant against direct use of his testimony in a criminal proceeding, but "could not, and would not, prevent the use of his testimony to search out other testimony to be used in evidence against him. . . . " *Id.* at 564. Appellee argued that:

> An investigation before a grand jury is in no sense "a criminal case. " The inquiry is for the purpose of finding whether a crime has been committed and whether any one shall be accused of an offense. The inquiry is secret; there is no accuser, no parties, plaintiff or defendant. The whole proceeding is *ex parte*.

Id. at 554. The Court retorted that:

> It is impossible that the meaning of the constitutional provision can only be, that a person shall not be compelled to be a witness against himself in a criminal prosecution against himself. . . . The object was to insure that a person should not be compelled, when acting as a witness in any investigation, to give testimony which might tend to show that he himself had committed a crime. The privilege is limited to criminal matters, but it is as broad as the mischief against which it seeks to guard.

Id. at 562.

In Emspak v. United States, 349 U.S. 190 (1955) and Quinn v. United States, 349 U.S. 155 (1955), the privilege against self-incrimination was successfully invoked by petitioners who refused to answer certain questions asked of them by the Committee on Un-American Activities of the House of Representatives. Members of the Court differed only as to whether petitioners had properly claimed the privilege for themselves; not even the dissenting justices paused to consider whether a congressional investigation is "a criminal case. "

McCarthy v. Arndstein,[8] *Miranda* appears to be an a fortiori case; that is, unless one is prepared to rekindle the *Twining-Adamson-Malloy* debate.

(b) The prize for ingenuity goes not to the Supreme Court for finally applying the privilege to the police station but to those who managed to devise rationales for excluding it from the stationhouse all these years. Dwell for a moment on the reasoning that because police officers have no legal authority to compel statements of any kind, there is nothing to counteract, there is no legal obligation to which a privilege can apply, and hence the police can elicit statements from suspects who are likely to assume or be led to believe that there *are* legal (or extralegal) sanctions for contumacy.[9] Is it unduly harsh to say, as those who do not use strong words lightly have, that such reasoning is "casuistic"[25]—"a quibble"?[26]

(c) Assuming a "first amendment privilege" which would relieve the fifth amendment of its burden in "belief probes,"[27] most, if not all, that can be said for the privilege applies in spades to police interrogation. One would do well to start with what Professor John McNaughton, no warm friend of the privilege, concluded some six years ago after a painstaking analysis of the problem:

The significant purposes of the privilege remaining after the First Amendment alba-tross has been cut free . . . are two: [1] The first is to remove the right to an answer in the hard cores of instances where compulsion might lead to inhumanity, the principal inhumanity being abusive tactics by a zealous questioner. [2] The second is to comply with the prevailing ethic that the individual is sovereign and that proper rules of battle between government and individual require that the individual not be bothered for less than good reason and not be conscripted by his opponents to defeat himself.
. . . .
. . . Both policies of the privilege which I accept, as well as most of those which I reject, apply with full force to insure that police in informal interrogations not have the right to compel self-incriminatory answers. Whether the result is reached by pointing out the elementary fact that police have not been given the authority to compel disclo-sures of any kind or whether the result is put on the ground that the person questioned

---

8. 266 U.S. 34 (1924). Rejecting the government's broad contention that the privilege "does not apply in any civil proceeding," *id.* at 40, as well as its narrow contention that the privilege "does not relieve a bankrupt from the duty to give information which is sought for the purpose of discovering his estate," *id.* at 41, a unanimous Court observed, per Justice Brandeis:

The privilege is not ordinarily dependent upon the nature of the proceeding in which the testimony is sought or is to be used. It applies alike to civil and criminal proceedings, wherever the answer might tend to subject to criminal responsibility him who gives it.

Id. at 40.

9. It is hoped this contention was made for the last time in the *Miranda* oral arguments. Unofficial Transcript of Oral Argument at 101 (Mr. Siegel on behalf of respondent in *Vignera v. New York*), on file in University of Michigan Law Library.

is "privileged" not to answer makes little difference. Answers should not be compelled by police. . . .[28]

(d) There is nothing very new or unusual about the problem which confronted the Court in *Miranda;* there is nothing really startling or inventive about the solution. I think it may fairly be said that the police station is the *third* field on which the basic issue in *Miranda* has been fought. The force of the privilege, or radiations from it, led (in the seventeenth century) to the abolition of judicial interrogation at the trial itself, and (in the nineteenth century) to the disappearance of interrogation at the preliminary examination as well. These developments occurred at a time when "local prosecuting officials were almost unknown"[29] and a "primitive constabulary . . . , consisting of watchmen rather than police officers and wanting in any detective personnel, attempted little in the way of interrogation of the persons they apprehended."[30] Eventually, "but *wholly without express legal authorization,*"[31] interrogation became the function of the emerging organized police and prosecuting forces. Moreover, I think it plain that the last stand will not be made in the stationhouse. By defining "custodial questioning" to mean "questioning initiated by law enforcement officers after a person has been taken into custody or otherwise deprived of his freedom of action in any significant way,"[32] the *Miranda* Court seemed to anticipate still other battlefields—the squad car, the streets, public places, and even homes.

That over the centuries this problem has been popping up in different settings strongly indicates that the *Miranda* Court did not, and did not *need* to, invoke a "new" fifth amendment. This history, however, is also consistent with the view that we cannot, never could for very long, and never will be able to live with the "old" one. It may be that in this area of the law we cannot do what we have done with respect to *Brown v. Board of Education*[33] and *Baker v. Carr,*[34] namely, take our ideals down from the walls where we have kept them framed "to be pointed at with pride on ceremonial occasions,"[10] and "put flesh and blood" on them and "look them in the teeth."[11] But this goes to *Miranda's* hope of posterity, not to its pride of ancestry.

10. Schaefer, *Comments* [on Kamisar, *Has the Court Left the Attorney General Behind?,* 54 KY. L.J. 464 (1966)], 54 KY. L.J. 521, 524 (1966). This symposium was held six months before *Miranda* was handed down.

11. *Id.*

Justice Schaefer also said, it should be noted, that "if the ideals are too broadly stated to meet essential practical objectives then I would suggest that the *ideals* must be modified and that we ought to be frank." *Id.* at 524. He indicated, further, that this might well be the case with respect to police interrogation:

When it is suggested that the right to counsel be projected into the station house, there is an immediate response. Many voices answered—some stridently, but I think none more eloquently than [fellow-panelist] Mr. Kuh answered this morning—saying that it is not possible to enforce criminal law unless station house interrogation in the absence of counsel is permit-

"No Significant Support in . . . History . . . or . . . Language"

The *Miranda* majority's application of the privilege against self-incrimination to police interrogation, insists dissenting Justice White, "has no significant support in the history of the privilege or in the language of the Fifth Amendment."[35] The first authority he cites is the late Professor Edmund M. Morgan, who said that "there is nothing in the reports to suggest that [the rule

---

ted. I think I share that view, but I don't know. . . . There just isn't anything very worthwhile to indicate what has happened and what would happen if station house interrogation were not permitted save in the presence of counsel. It scares me, but I don't know.

Id. at 523.

Miranda, however, does not "fully project" counsel into the stationhouse—at least not to the degree desired by some ACLU spokesmen. On learning of the *Miranda* decision, the executive director of the national group, John de J. Pemberton, Jr., tempered his enthusiasm by voicing "regret that the Court did not take the final step of stating that the privilege cannot be fully assured unless a suspect's lawyer is present during police station interrogation." N.Y. Times, June 14, 1966, at 25, col. 1. Similarly, the director of the New York chapter (Aryeh Neier) commented: "[*Miranda*] doesn't go far enough in protecting those who most need protection. We do believe that a person must have the advice of counsel in order to intelligently waive the assistance of counsel." *Id.*

To say that *Miranda does* permit some stationhouse questioning in the absence of counsel—if a duly advised suspect intelligently waives his right to the assistance of counsel—is not to quibble. Not if, as Los Angeles District Attorney Evelle Younger concluded (after surveying more than 1,000 post-*Miranda* cases, in fully half of which the defendant had made an incriminating statement): "Large or small, . . . conscience usually, or at least often, drives a guilty person to confess. If an individual wants to confess, a warning from a police officer, acting as required by recent decisions, is not likely to discourage him." OFFICE OF THE DISTRICT ATTORNEY, COUNTY OF LOS ANGELES, RESULTS OF SURVEY CONDUCTED IN THE DISTRICT ATTORNEY'S OFFICE OF LOS ANGELES COUNTY REGARDING THE EFFECTS OF THE DORADO AND MIRANDA DECISIONS UPON THE PROSECUTION OF FELONY CASES 4 (Aug. 4, 1966) (copy on file in the University of Michigan Law Library). *See also* Brief for United States, at 30 n.20, Westover v. United States, 384 U.S. 436 (1966): "[T]he great majority of clear admissions or confessions are prompted either by conscience, by a desire to get the matter over with, or by a calculated design to secure more favorable treatment."

But see Kuh, *Some Views on* Miranda v. Arizona, 35 FORDHAM L. REV. 233, 235 (1966):

If we are to be logical and intellectually honest, we must recognize there is rarely such a thing as *Miranda* contemplates—an intelligent, voluntary waiver of the Fifth Amendment privileges . . . . Had the United States Supreme Court recognized what I think is clear—at least the improbability, if not the impossibility, of an intelligent waiver of the Fifth Amendment privilege—the judges might have squarely wrestled with the issue and said: "Confessions are *no longer usable* in our adversary system."

To the same effect is Nedrud, *The New Fifth Amendment Concept: Self-Incrimination Redefined,* 2 NAT'L DIST. ATT'YS ASS'N J. 112, 113 (1966), maintaining that "certainly, under the requirements of the [*Miranda*] Court, no one in his 'right mind' would waive such rights."

Whether suspects are continuing to confess because they don't understand the whole "formula" or because the police are "stretching the truth" when they claim they give the full warning, or because the promptings of conscience and the desire to get it over with are indeed overriding the

excluding coerced confessions] . . . has its roots in the privilege against self-incrimination. And so far as the cases reveal, the privilege, as such, seems to have been given effect only in judicial proceedings, including the preliminary examinations by authorized magistrates."[36]

For Justice White to lead with Morgan is a bit puzzling, since further along in this same article Professor Morgan points out:

The function which the police have assumed in interrogating an accused is exactly that of the early committing magistrates, and the opportunities for imposition and abuse are fraught with much greater danger. . . . Investigation by the police is not judicial, but when it consists of an examination of an accused, it is quite as much an official proceeding as the early English preliminary hearing before a magistrate, and it has none of the safeguards of a judicial proceeding. If the historical confines of the privilege are to be broadened, this surely is an area that needs inclusion for reasons infinitely more compelling than those applicable to the arraignment.
. . . .

---

impact of the warning, the fact remains that they *are* continuing to confess with great frequency—which would not have been the case if the Court had adopted the position taken by the aforementioned ACLU spokesman. Even Brooklyn District Attorney Aaron Koota, who has charged that the new rulings have "shackled" law enforcement, N.Y. Times, Aug. 13, 1966, at 1, col. 2, claims that only forty percent of major felony suspects have refused to make statements after being warned of their rights. N.Y. Times, Sept. 5, 1966, at 17, col. 1. Mr. Koota reported a sharp increase of refusals to talk after *Miranda,* but the commanding officer of one Manhattan detective squad reported that "by and large, they [suspects] readily admit what they've been doing even after they've been told of their rights." N.Y. Times, June 25, 1966, at 1, col. 3. And Mr. Younger disclosed that "the percentage of cases in which confessions or admissions were made has not decreased, as might have been anticipated, because of the increased scope of the admonitions required by *Miranda.*" Los Angeles Survey, *supra,* at 3.

The *Miranda* Court required enough things "at one gulp," for me at any rate, *cf.* 384 U.S. at 502 (Clark, J., dissenting), but a rule that a suspect needs counsel to waive counsel is by no means unthinkable. The "waiver" standards are designed for judicial proceedings; no judge presides in the stationhouse. In oral argument, Justice Stewart raised the possibility that a suspect could not waive his constitutional rights without the advice of counsel and petitioner agreed "that this is the worst place for waiver" because "the party alleging waiver has control of the party alleged to have waived." Unofficial Transcript of Oral Argument in *Miranda* and Companion Cases, at 84 (oral argument of Mr. Earle for petitioner in *Vignera v. New York*), on file in University of Michigan Law Library. *See also id.* at 73. However, the *Miranda* opinion does not explicitly consider this possibility. The ACLU amicus brief, on the other hand, does not explicitly consider any other possibility. Rather, as I read it at any rate, the ACLU contends that effectuation of the privilege requires the *"presence* of counsel" (emphasis added), a phrase it employs a dozen times, Brief for ACLU as Amicus Curiae, at 3, 4, 9, 22–25, 27–28, 33, not merely *advice* as to the immediate availability of counsel, a reading which finds support in the post-*Miranda* comments of the ACLU spokesmen, N.Y. Times, June 14, 1966, at 25, col. 1. The failure of the Court to deal explicitly with (if only to reject) the ACLU contention is surprising, for in all other respects the ACLU amicus brief presents "a conceptual, legal and structural formulation that is practically identical to the majority opinion—even as to use of language in various passages of the opinion." Dash, *Foreword* to Medalie, From Escobedo to Miranda: The Anatomy of a Supreme Court Decision xvii (1966).

Mr. Wigmore himself declares that the protection of the privilege "extends to *all manner of proceedings* in which testimony is to be taken, whether litigious or not, and whether 'ex parte' or otherwise. It therefore applies in . . . investigations by a *legislature* or a body having legislative functions, and in investigations by *administrative* officials." If so, how can testimony taken by the police be excluded?[37]

Continues Justice White:

Our own constitutional provision provides that no person "shall be compelled in any criminal case to be a witness against himself." These words, when "[c]onsidered in the light to be shed by grammar and the dictionary appear to signify simply that nobody shall be compelled to give oral testimony against himself in a criminal proceeding under way in which he is a defendant." Corwin, The Supreme Court's Construction of the Self-Incrimination Clause, 29 Mich. L. Rev. 1, 2. And there is very little in the surrounding circumstances of the adoption of the Fifth Amendment or in the then existing state constitutions or in state practice which would give the constitutional provision any broader meaning. Mayers, The Federal Witness' Privilege Against Self-Incrimination: Constitutional or Common-Law?, 4 American Journal of Legal History 107 (1960).[38]

However, the Corwin article relied upon by Justice White does call attention to a circumstance surrounding the adoption of the fifth amendment which suggests that the constitutional provision is entitled to a broader meaning:

The result [in late seventeenth-century England of the extension from civil to criminal cases of the rule that a party is not a competent witness on account of interest] was that henceforth the mouth of an accused . . . was closed whether *for* or *against* himself; and it is in this form that the immunity of accused persons passed to the American colonies balanced, that is, by the corresponding disability. Not until 1878, following a similar reform in several of the states, was the right to testify in their own behalf, under oath, accorded defendants in the national courts.

. . . .

. . . [S]ince the [federal and early state] constitutional provisions . . . did not overrule the common law in excluding an accused from the witness stand, their stipulation for his immunity taken by itself becomes pointless. If only, therefore, to save the framers of these provisions from having loaded them with a meaningless tautology, their language had to be given other than its literal significance. . . .[39]

What does this immunity of the accused at that time signify? "Therefore," Dean Griswold argues, "the *importance* of the privilege against self-incrimination [at that time] . . . was in investigations, in inquiries, and with respect to questioning of the defendant by the judge in criminal cases, such as had been made notorious by Judge Jeffries."[40] According to Professor Mayers, however, the implications from the accused's incompetence to testify need not and should not carry us so far. He maintains that the privilege is not available to a mere witness, but only to an "accused," and that the privilege is given sufficient content and meaning if it is viewed as protecting an accused *not sworn as a witness* from interrogation by prosecutor or judge at the trial (a practice which continued in England into the eighteenth century and in New York, at least, as late as the Revolution), or as protecting an accused from questioning *before trial*.[41] In the same article invoked by Justice White, Professor Mayers makes these points:

The possibility that Madison and Ellsworth (the latter the chairman of the Senate committee responsible for these changes in arrangement) may have had chiefly in mind the protection of the accused (and of the suspect not yet charged) from *pre*-trial questioning, rather than from questioning at the trial, is enhanced by the fact that the accused was not at that time (or for nearly a century thereafter) a competent witness at his trial. . . . [I]f one concedes, *arguendo,* that the protection of the accused *on trial* was not the object, it does not follow, as seems to be assumed, that the purpose of the provision must have been to protect the *witness*. It could just as well have been intended to protect the accused or the suspect *before trial*. It is perhaps relevant that Madison's own state had had experience with oppressive questioning of suspects by the royal governor just before the Revolution.[42]

. . . .

In 1833 appeared Story's monumental treatise [apparently the *first* treatise on the Constitution which discusses the privilege]. . . . His discussion of the self-incrimination clause of the Fifth Amendment discloses a complete unawareness of its application to the witness, and seems indeed to confine the intention of the provision to the accused in the pretrial stage—to stress the protection against *executive* oppression of the accused.[43]

Professor Mayers, one may fairly conclude, is bent on overruling *Counselman v. Hitchcock,* not on precluding *Miranda v. Arizona.* Professor Mayers, I think it fair to say, regards the application of the privilege to legislative investigations as a much sharper departure from the understanding of the draftsmen who framed the self-incrimination provision, the Congress which proposed it, and the state legislatures which ratified it, than the application of the privilege to police interrogation.

If for no other reason than that there were no professional police either in England or America when the privilege was drafted and ratified, or at least the police had not yet assumed the functions of criminal investigation, the extent to which *Miranda* marks a departure from the "original understanding" will probably never be fully settled. This is not to say, however, that a sketch of the history of pre-police interrogation is unilluminating.

To begin at what should be a sufficient starting point for our purposes, justices of the peace in England were empowered by the middle of the fourteenth century "to take and arrest all those that they may find by indictment, or by suspicion and to put them in prison."[44] Two centuries later, the emergent practice of making some kind of examination of suspects before committing them for formal accusation was legalized by the Statutes of Philip and Mary (1554–55).[45] The "object" of these statutes was "to expose and detect a man assumed to be guilty";[46] pursuant to them "a justice of the peace really acted as police, constable, detective, prosecuting attorney, examining magistrate and complaining witness."[47] By the beginning of the eighteenth century, writes Professor Kauper, "the spirit" of the now fully established rule against self-incrimination "must have been carried over to the preliminary examination, for in this examination there was evident a gradual abandonment of judicial interrogation of the accused. The practice developed of taking only a voluntary statement by the accused after cautioning him as to his rights . . . [The] practice was developing of permitting the accused to have counsel at this examination."[48] The Statutes of Philip and Mary were formally repealed in 1848,[49] but "long before" that, the "inquisitional preliminary examination . . . had sunk into oblivion and a purely judicial inquiry had supplanted it."[50]

In America, the history of preliminary examination ran a parallel course. Colonial magistrates "rigorously examined persons suspected of crime . . . after the manner of the English justice of the peace."[51] In 1641, "when the [Massachusetts] colony was troubled by a wave of vicious criminality [when *wasn't* there a "crime crisis"?], Governor Bellingham consulted the elders of the New England churches on the question 'how far a magistrate might exact a confession from a delinquent in capital cases?' "[52] In their study of colonial New York, Goebel and Naughton, citing examples largely from the early and middle eighteenth century, reported "numerous cases where the minutes reveal the reading at the trial of a prisoner's confession. It had to be proved by the magistrate who took it, but otherwise no further formalities were observed."[53] They point out that "although a confession could only be introduced if not made under oath, it would serve to convict without corroborating evidence, if the defendant had pleaded not guilty in open court."[54] Since the felony defendant conducted his own defense and was thus

directly vulnerable to questioning from the bench . . . the most dangerous juncture at a trial for the defendant-counsel was the moment when the Crown introduced a confession taken by a justice at a preliminary hearing. . . . Obviously if a defendant had any remarks to make about his earlier words, he would likely find himself answering questions from the bench [and] . . . where he had made more than one preliminary statement and had contradicted himself, the introduction of all the "confessions" would tempt him to unguarded speech, or he might be asked to explain.[55]

Although the transference of criminal investigation functions from magistrates to police did not occur as sharply in this country as it did in England,[56] and there were forces other than the use of the privilege which were inimical to a magistrate's exercise of police functions in America,[57] it may be said that "the establishment of the rule against self-incrimination, with its significant reaction in England resulting in abolition of the practice of interrogating the accused, had the same effect in the American colonies. Formal constitutional recognition of the rule contributed to the tradition already accumulating against exercise of inquisitorial powers by the magistrate or justice of the peace."[58] It may also be said that "if the police are permitted to interrogate an accused under the pressure of compulsory detention to secure a confession . . . they are doing the very same acts which historically the judiciary was doing in the seventeenth century but which the privilege against self-incrimination abolished."[59] In this connection it is quite instructive, I believe, to turn to mid-nineteenth-century criticism of judicial "examination" in New York, where that practice survived, relatively late, until that time. Indeed, the analysis of the alleged evils in and suggested remedies for the "examination" as spelled out by the Commissioners on Practice and Pleading[60] in the course of submitting their proposed Code of Criminal Procedure to the New York Legislature *in the year 1849* so strikingly parallels the *Miranda* discussion—if we but substitute "interrogation" for "examination" and "police" for "magistrate"—that I cannot resist the temptation to quote from that remarkable report at length:[61]

. . . [I]n the early stages of the accusation,—when he is hurried before a magistrate upon a charge of which he may be innocent, and of which, even if it be otherwise, the law has not yet adjudged him guilty,—the first dictate of duty seems to be, to inform [the accused] . . . of his rights and to afford him every opportunity to throw around himself the protection of the law. And yet, according to the existing system of practice, upon the idle fiction that every man is presumed to know the law, he is supposed to be informed of the first right secured to him by the Constitution,—that of appearing and defending himself by counsel. If he happens to be ignorant of this, the examination of the case proceeds, and testimony is taken against him which may be illegal in its character, or which, without the substantial opportunity for a cross examination, may in some contingencies be used against him on his trial.

Against this prejudice the Commissioners propose to guard, by requiring the magistrate to inform the defendant of his right to the aid of counsel in every stage of the proceedings, and before any further proceedings are had,—to allow the defendant a reasonable time to procure counsel,—and to send for such counsel in the city or town, as the defendant may name. (Sec. 180, 181.)

. . . .

In this proceeding [the "examination" by the magistrate], the Commissioners have discovered principles which they deem at war with the rights of the accused. The very term "examination," which is used in the statute, and the proceedings pointed out as the mode of taking it, all seem to be a departure from the spirit of the constitutional declaration, which provides that "no person shall be compelled, in any criminal case, to be a witness against himself." The object of the examination, as it was originally instituted, was, not to place the defendant in the hands of a cross-examining magistrate, who might, according to the principles of the French practice, by the exercise of ingenuity, extract from the defendant evidence of his guilt. But it was designed, in the humane and benign spirit of the common law, to give the defendant an opportunity, by a voluntary explanation, to exculpate himself from the charge. . . .

Instead of his being informed, as the fact is, that [the "examination"] is furnished to him as a shield and is not to be used against him as a sword, he is by a loose course of practice, if no other motive be imputable, led to believe that it is one of the ordinary proceedings against him, having in view the establishment of his guilt. He is accordingly examined by a series of searching questions, oftentimes proceeding upon the assumption of his guilt, and is driven to the alternative of equivocating as to the facts, or of denying circumstances plainly true, or of what is occasionally his resort, declining to answer. Those who are in the slightest degree conversant with criminal trials, can well attest how successfully the adoption of either of these alternatives, can be used against the defendant on his trial. . . .

[T]he Commissioners have proposed to dispense entirely with this examination, and to substitute in its place, what the law designed should alone be furnished, an opportunity to the defendant to make a statement in his exculpation. They accordingly provide, that when the examination of the witnesses on the part of the people is closed, the magistrate shall inform the defendant that it is his right to make a statement in relation to the charge against him; that the statement is designed to enable him, if he sees fit, to answer the charge, and to explain the facts alleged against him:—that he is at liberty to waive it,—and that his waiver cannot be used against him on the trial. (Sec. 188.) If he elect to make the statement, it is then to be taken by the magistrate, who, instead of being left at liberty to put every form of question which his ingenuity may suggest, is restricted to asking the defendant general questions as to his age and residence and the like, and to asking him to give any explanation he may think proper, of the circumstances appearing against him, and to state any facts which he thinks will tend to his exculpation. (Sec. 190.) . . .

On the other side of the Atlantic, but a year earlier—1848, the very year the Statutes of Philip and Mary were formally repealed—a Royal Commission appointed to inquire into the state of the criminal law in the Channel Islands found "objectionable" "the preliminary examinations *'au secret,'* and the consequent interrogatoire of the accused,"[62] *despite* the fact that "the present practice . . . requires that [the prisoner] be told that he cannot be compelled to answer the questions of the Court, and that what he says will be used against him at the trial."[63] Again, the Commissioners' comments on the relationship between the "right of silence" and the right to counsel have obvious application to the *Miranda* controversy:[64]

[The prisoner] is not allowed the assistance of Counsel, who would probably advise him not to answer. Such a privilege would amount to the abolition of the interrogatoire. In truth, a voluntary interrogatoire is a contradiction; and the compulsion of the process, once physical but still moral, is not the least objectionable part of the system. The caution to abstain from answering, if the party thinks fit, is always given in words; but a prisoner, acting without counsel, will almost always, in practice, feel himself bound to answer. Then the questions put are those which arise from evidence which has been so arranged (and quite properly) as to give the fullest effect to the *prima facie* case of accusation. The answers given to such questions are given at a great disadvantage; and, probably, this disadvantage is even exaggerated by the prisoner, who is pressed with the circumstances of suspicion marshalled in their most formidable order. Hence arises a temptation to evade and deceive, by which an ignorant person would be seduced, however innocent of the offence charged. Another very dangerous feature in this practice appears to be that its tendency is to engage the Court, which conducts the examination, in a contest with the prisoner. . . .

"It is impossible to deny the efficacy of the present practice as an instrument for the occasional detection of crime," conceded the Commissioners, "but it is equally clear that the practice is liable to mislead, even when administered with the purest intentions."[65] "We have no doubt," they hastened to add, "that the members of the Royal Court were perfectly sincere in assuring us that it is often of the greatest use to a prisoner, and that they never knew an innocent man condemned in consequence of it. But it appears to us dangerous to make legal guilt depend upon anything short of proof from extrinsic evidence or the voluntary confession of the accused."[66]

"Trained Incapacity" and Those Who Lacked It

Why did the fictions exposed in the 1840s have to be exposed anew in the 1960s? Why did the old abuses in new forms so persist and flourish?

For one thing, as I indicated at the outset, the "legal mind" (unhappily) was equal to the task of seeming to reconcile the grim facts with lofty principles: police interrogation—indeed, the "third degree"—did not violate the privilege because the questioning did not involve any kind of judicial process for the taking of testimony.[67] This "trained incapacity" (to use Veblen's phrase) to see the problem in the round was long utilized by those who possessed it not only to shut from their minds the de facto inquisitorial system, but also to thwart attempts to mitigate such a system by "formalizing" or "judicializing" it. For example, when, in the early 1940s, a member of the Advisory Committee on the Federal Rules of Criminal Procedure advocated as a cure for the abuses of secret police interrogation a system whereby a *judicial officer* would question a suspect only after informing the suspect "of his right to the advice of counsel, that he is under no obligation to answer any question, that any answer he chooses to give may possibly be used against him, and that his refusal to answer cannot be used against him,"[68] *the recommendation was rejected "as being contrary to the basic traditions of Anglo-American criminal procedure, and as probably violative of the constitutional guarantee against self-incrimination."* [69] Why basic traditions were honored and self-incrimination problems avoided in the absence of these important safeguards was not made clear. Perhaps this is what Mr. Dooley meant when he told us that he "knowed a society wanst to vote a monyment to a man an' refuse to help his fam'ly, all in wan night."

Some men are brash enough to write books about the law without adequate "legal conditioning." One such man was Ernest J. Hopkins, an official investigator employed by the Wickersham Commission. According to Zechariah Chafee, Hopkins showed "notable skill and enterprise in breaking through the barriers of silence which surround official lawlessness."[12] However, being a newspaperman by profession rather than a lawyer, Mr. Hopkins showed a notable lack of skill and enterprise in grasping why the privilege against self-incrimination meant so much in the courtroom but so little in the police station. Thus, five years before *Brown v. Mississippi* and thirty-five years before *Miranda v. Arizona,* this "untrained observer" said of the prevailing definitions of the "third degree" (*e.g.,* "rigid and severe examination," "oppressive methods," infliction of "suffering"):[13]

[T]hese definitions convey no hint as to the legality or illegality of the basic process or the methods used therein. There is a fundamental right possessed by the American citizen . . . set forth in the Fifth Amendment in the following words:

Nor shall any person . . . be compelled in a criminal case to be a witness against himself.

This strikes directly at the heart of the situation; I do not see why one should seek farther than the Constitution for a clear definition of the third degree. The gross unlawfulness of the practice is thus stated by implication:

The third degree is the compelling of a person in a criminal case to be a witness against himself.

The use of the more objective concept of *compulsion,* borrowed from the Constitution . . . gets us down to the central question, *the legitimacy of the pre-trial inquisition itself.*

There are a thousand forms of compulsion; our police show great ingenuity in the variety employed. But any and all forms of compulsion, with the object of securing confessions, must violate the constitutional guarantee. . . . Our police, from the moment a man falls into their hands in an important case, hound him with the persistent demand "Confess." They may use violence and torture or they may not; but in either case the secret police-held grilling or sweating violates the time-honored and peculiarly important restraint by which Americans, and the English before them, have sought to protect themselves against official tyranny.

For those troubled by the spectacle of a man so unfamiliar with prevailing legal reasoning writing a book about the law, it should be pointed out by way of mitigating circumstances that even eminent lawyers have (happily) demonstrated a surprising lack of "trained incapacity" to see the fairly obvious in

---

12. E. HOPKINS, OUR LAWLESS POLICE vii (1931) (Preface).
13. *Id.* at 193–95 (emphasis in the original).

this area. Take Zechariah Chafee, for example. Chafee knew better. In the early 1930s he had recognized, albeit not been impressed by, the legal reasoning which led to the checking of the privilege at the door of the interrogation room.[70] However, he forgot this a generation later. Indeed, this oversight permeated his defense of the privilege in the 1950s:

There are at least three reasons for the privilege against self-incrimination. In the first place, although it plainly interferes with short-time efficiency by making it harder to discover facts through questioning, the privilege is likely to promote long-time efficiency.

If prosecutors and police could count on grilling a suspect as much as they pleased, they might not take the trouble to build up a solid case from objective proofs. . . .

. . . .

The second reason for stoutly maintaining the right of every man not to be "compelled . . . to be a witness against himself" is that it protects us from something far worse than answering questions. *Nothing else in the Constitution prevents government officials and policemen from extorting confessions. . . .*[14]

Similarly, Dean Erwin Griswold, who wrote a famous little book on the subject, displayed what some might regard as a woeful lack of the requisite special "training":

We may better understand the importance of the Fifth Amendment by considering what not having it would mean. . . . *If we are not willing to let the Amendment be invoked, where, over time, are we going to stop when police, prosecutors,* or chairmen want to get people to talk?[15]

Somewhat surprisingly, in a book billed as "challenging much of the legal folklore which abounds in the discussion of the subject by E. N. Griswold,"[71] Professor Sidney Hook challenged Griswold (and Chafee) only obliquely on this point. Evidently Professor Hook's abundant "common sense" and wide reading in the law failed to compensate for his lack of "formal legal training." Hook took a dim view of the privilege generally. But he, too, seemed to take for granted its applicability to police interrogation

---

14. Z. CHAFEE, THE BLESSINGS OF LIBERTY 186, 188 (1956) (emphasis added). Chafee maintained that "the partial incorporation of [the self-incrimination] clause in the Fourteenth Amendment has made it possible for the Supreme Court to reverse several state convictions based on coerced confessions. . . ." *Id.* at 189. The Court, per Brennan, J., did so look back on the "coerced confession" cases in Malloy v. Hogan, 378 U.S. 1 (1964). *See also* Justice Black, joined by the Chief Justice, dissenting in Cohen v. Hurley, 366 U.S. 117, 131 (1961). But it is not easy to see how, under any concept of "hard-core" self-incrimination implicit in due process, the Court could have sustained some of the state confessions it did. *See* Kamisar, *Equal Justice in the Gatehouses and Mansions of American Criminal Procedure,* in CRIMINAL JUSTICE IN OUR TIME 47–49 (A. Howard ed. 1965) [reprinted in part in this volume].

15. E. GRISWOLD, THE FIFTH AMENDMENT TODAY 75 (1955) (emphasis added). •

(although, quite understandably, he belittled the protection it had in fact provided up to that time for the person subjected to police questioning):

> The use of third degree methods against suspects has always been widespread despite the recognition of the privilege against self-incrimination. . . . This may be granted and the assertion made that the situation would be much worse if the privilege were not recognized. There seems good reason to doubt this. . . . Whatever Constitutional protection the privilege against self-incrimination gives in safeguarding [a person] from lawless police officers is given just as effectively by the due process clause of the Fifth and Fourteenth Amendments. Further, even if it were retained to reinforce bulwarks against illegal practices of arresting authorities, its meaning could be so modified as to permit the invocation of the privilege to be cited explicitly by counsel in pleading before bench or jury as relevant evidence in the case.
>
> . . . .
>
> Dean Griswold insinuates several times that the Fifth Amendment is the most important, if not the only, bar to torture, and that its retention prevents the introduction of police state methods of medieval techniques brought up to date. . . . [I]n general, as we have seen in commenting on Professor Chafee, *all that would be required,* even in the complete absence of the Fifth Amendment, *would be the right to be questioned only in the presence of counsel,* to cut the ground from under the objection.[16]

There goes Professor Hook, showing his lack of "formal legal training" again. "Common sense" *would* suggest, as Chafee put it, that "a person accused of crime needs a lawyer right after his arrest probably more than at any other time."[72] At the time Hook made these remarks, however, the right to the assistance of counsel was deemed inapplicable to police interrogation because the "criminal prosecution" had not yet begun.

In a sense, conditioning police questioning on the presence of counsel— of course, the police would see little or no point in questioning a suspect in the presence, and under the protective eye, of his lawyer—does dispense with the need for the privilege against self-incrimination at this stage—in the same way that conditioning police "encouragement" on the presence of counsel would dispense with the need for the entrapment defense. But *why* should the presence of counsel be required and *why* should we "effectively preclude police questioning—fair as well as unfair—until the accused [is] afforded opportunity to call his attorney"[73]—*in the complete absence of the fifth amendment?*

As is evidenced by the easy assumptions made years ago by those who (fortunately) never acquired the "trained incapacity" to see the problem, the application of the privilege to police interrogation can be defended as either a logical deduction from the constitutional provision or a practical condition upon its successful operation. Moreover, this approach finds much historical

16. S. Hook, Common Sense and the Fifth Amendment 45–46, 58 (1957) (emphasis added).

support in the Anglo-American experience with prototypes of modern police interrogation (much more support than can be produced to warrant the application of the privilege to legislative investigations and civil proceedings).[74] Assuming, arguendo, that in order to give the privilege a reading "as broad as the mischief against which it seeks to guard,"[75] the Court did violence to language and history, the assault occurred, in aggravated form, long ago:

> Is it not clear that a legislative investigation is not a "criminal case"? What application, then, does the constitutional provision have in such proceedings—or in civil trials, or elsewhere, where persons may be subjected to questioning? This is a question which was raised and answered long ago, so long ago in fact that lawyers tend to take it for granted. But early courts saw that the protection of the amendment itself would be an empty gesture if it was literally applied. For example, if the witness is required to answer self-incriminating questions in a civil trial, or in a legislative investigation, the prosecuting officer can use his answers to provide evidence on which he can be prosecuted or convicted. Even if the prosecuting officer cannot use his testimony itself, he can, from that testimony, learn other facts which he could use in the prosecution. . . .
>
> For this reason, courts long ago concluded that if the privilege is to be effective at all it must be given a comprehensive application, and thus must prevent compulsory self-incrimination in *any* proceeding. This is, indeed, a broad construction of the constitutional language, but it is a construction which has seemed to be required if the basic objective of that language is to be realized.[76]

"Necessity" and Other Forces

What would we say of the argument that the fourth amendment does not apply to arrests and searches made *without warrants altogether,* but only prohibits the use of evidence seized pursuant to *defective warrants?*[77] Does it make any more sense to argue that the fifth amendment does not apply to questioning by agents of the state who lack any kind of judicial process for the taking of testimony, but only governs proceedings involving such process? Moreover, it so happened that the Supreme Court frequently advanced the privilege against self-incrimination as *the constitutional basis* for the federal exclusionary rule in search and seizure cases during most of the period the privilege was deemed inapplicable to police questioning.[78] If absent legal process the privilege was not supposed to apply, why wasn't the federal government allowed all these years to use evidence obtained by officers who did not bother to get any warrant at all?[79]

The view that police interrogation is not limited or affected by the privilege against self-incrimination because it does not involve any kind of judicial process for the taking of testimony had a great deal more to commend it than merely the inherent force of its "logic" or the self-restraint and tenderness of the exempted class of interrogators. It must have had, in order for it to have been taken so seriously for so long.

Among the forces at work was one of society's most effective analgesics— "necessity," real or apparent.[80] Its influence may be seen in numerous opinions. Although Justice Jackson recognized, in his much-quoted concurring opinion in *Watts v. Indiana* (1949), that "if the State may . . . interrogate without counsel, there is no denying the fact that it largely negates the benefits of the constitutional guaranty,"[81] he was willing to let this "negation" occur for otherwise "the people of this country must discipline themselves to seeing their police stand by helplessly while those suspected of murder prowl about unmolested."[82] Again, the first axiom of Justice Frankfurter's dissertation on police interrogation and confessions in *Culombe v. Connecticut* (1961) is: "Questioning suspects is indispensable in law enforcement."[83] "Questioning," as Justice Frankfurter and many others used the term, is a "shorthand" for questioning *without* advising the suspect of his rights *or* permitting defense counsel, friends, or relatives to be present.[84]

For the police to persist in interrogating a suspect after denying his specific request to contact his lawyer is unfair and coercive, and any resulting confession should be excluded, contended petitioner in *Crooker v. California*.[17] Such a rule, retorted a 5–4 majority of the Court, per Clark, J., "would have a . . . devastating effect on enforcement of criminal law, for it would effectively preclude police questioning—fair as well as unfair—until the accused was afforded opportunity to call his attorney."[85] Had issue been joined? The Court seemed to think so. What the *Crooker* majority meant to say, I believe, was: We are convinced that precluding (or postponing) police questioning until a suspect's specific request to consult with his lawyer is honored would have a devastating effect on law enforcement (on the eve of *Miranda*, law enforcement would have been delighted to settle for this);[18] we must conclude, therefore, that absent additional coercive factors, such questioning is "fair."

Other significant factors operating over many decades to freeze the status

---

17. 357 U.S. 433 (1958).

18. It now appears that (in a number of jurisdictions, at least) recognition of a right to *retained* counsel *per request* in *Crooker* would not have affected then-existing practice very much. Three years ago, Major Robert Murray, then chief of the District of Columbia Police Department, testified that "over the years if a man was arrested and said 'I want a lawyer' he was given an opportunity to call a lawyer," *Hearings on S. 486 and H.R. 7525 Before the Senate Committee on the District of Columbia*, 88th Cong., 1st Sess. 462 (1963), and that the long-established practice was that when a person said "'I want a lawyer,'" why there is no use wasting time with him. Just get him a lawyer." *Id.* at 470. Reporting on the practice in midwestern cities in the late 1950s, Professor Wayne LaFave disclosed:

[R]etained counsel often do enter a case shortly after arrest and immediately confer with their clients or are present when the case reaches the district attorney's office. In Milwaukee, they may actually sit in on the police interrogation. Indigent suspects are not afforded counsel at

quo were the invisibility of the process—"no other case comes to mind in which an administrative official is permitted the broad discretionary power assumed by the police interrogator, together with the power to prevent objective recordation of the facts"[86]—and the failure of influential groups to identify with those segments of our society which furnish most of the raw material for the process. "One of the most powerful features of the Due Process Model," Professor Herbert Packer recently observed, "is that it thrives on visibility. People are willing to be complacent about what goes on in the criminal process as long as they are not too often or too explicitly reminded of the gory details."[87] Society, one might add, does not *want* to be reminded, does not "want to know about criminals, but it does want them put away, and it is incurious how this can be done provided it is done."[88] It stings too much to say it now, for we are too close to it, but someday it will be said of the first two-thirds of the twentieth century: Too many people, good people, viewed the typical police suspect and his interrogator as garbage and garbage collector, respectively. (This is every bit as unfortunate for the officer as it is for the suspect.) Moreover, with the inadvertent exception of those

---

these early stages. . . . Actually turning away counsel who appears at the station to talk with his client is not a common occurrence.

W. LaFave, Arrest: The Decision To Take a Suspect Into Custody 393–94 (F. Remington ed. 1965).

On the eve of *Miranda,* law enforcement officers also would have been happy to settle for the four-hour "preliminary screening" period proposed by the Reporters for the Model Code of Pre-Arraignment Procedure. *See* Model Code of Pre-Arraignment Procedure § 4.04 (Tent. Draft No. 1, 1966). Less than a decade ago, however, the "dean" of American prosecutors had maintained that "frequently, even forty-eight to seventy-two hours is not enough." Coakley, *Restrictions in the Law of Arrest,* 52 Nw. U.L. Rev. 2, 9 (1957). More recently, a spokesman for the National Sheriff's Association thought forty-eight hours was "reasonable," *Hearings on S. 486 and H.R. 7525, supra,* at 300 (Sheriff Canlis), and the head of the International Association of Chiefs of Police plumped for "at least twenty-four hours, excluding days when courts are not in session," *id.* at 293 (Chief Schrotel).

In the 1963 Senate Hearings, David Acheson, then United States Attorney for the District of Columbia, departed from what might be called "the police-prosecution party line" by testifying that "in some very high percentage of the cases a confession is made if it is going to be made at all, within an hour or two, perhaps three hours after arrest. . . . In the great majority of cases a confession is made fairly promptly after arrest." *Hearings on S. 486 and H.R. 7525, supra,* at 443. In March of this year, on the eve of the oral argument in *Miranda,* Chief John B. Layton of the District of Columbia Police Department termed his department's current policy of "limited stationhouse testimony—with an upper limit of three hours"—"helpful." He disclosed that "admissions or statements" from suspects had been obtained in "about half" the criminal cases involving questioning and that "about seventy-five per cent" of these were obtained in one hour or less. Washington Post, March 4, 1966, at B-2, col. 1. Two days after *Miranda* was handed down, however, in a statement which "appeared to contradict" his earlier views, Chief Layton pointed to the three-hour maximum on stationhouse questioning as one reason why his department had "closed what he believes to be an all-time low number of cases for Washington." Washington Post, June 15, 1966, at A-22, col. 1.

who wrote the interrogation manuals (each, I suspect, equal to a dozen law review articles in its impact on the Court),[19] most law enforcement members and their spokesmen did their best to *keep* society comfortable and blissfully ignorant. Not too surprisingly, they were much more interested in "sanitizing" the proceedings in the interrogation room than in disseminating the life-size details. As long ago as 1910 (when, everybody *now* agrees, things were in a terrible state), the President of the International Association of Chiefs of Police assured us:

> When the prisoner is taken into private quarters and there interrogated as to his goings and comings, or asked to explain what he may be doing with Mr. Brown's broken and dismantled jewelry in his possession, to take off a rubber-heeled shoe he may be wearing in order to compare it with a footprint in a burglarized premises, or even to explain the blood stains on his hands and clothing, that, hypothetically illustrates what would be called the "Third Degree." . . . If a confession, preceded by the customary caution, obtained through remorse or a desire to make reparation for a crime, is advanced by a prisoner, it surely should not be regarded as unfair. . . . Volunteer confessions and admissions made after a prisoner has been cautioned that what he states may be used against him, are all there is to the so-called "Third Degree." . . .[89]

19. The American Civil Liberties Union briefs amicus curiae in *Escobedo* and *Miranda* quote extensively from these manuals. Indeed, the *Miranda* brief reprints a full chapter from C. O'HARA, FUNDAMENTALS OF CRIMINAL INVESTIGATION (1956). In turn, the majority opinion in *Miranda* devotes six full pages, 384 U.S. at 449–54, to extracts from various police manuals and texts "which document procedures employed with success in the past, and which recommend various other effective tactics," *id*. at 448.

Although such manuals had been available for many years, *e.g.*, W. KIDD, POLICE INTERROGATION (1940) and H. MULBAR, INTERROGATION (1951), so far as I can tell neither law review articles nor Supreme Court briefs made much use of them until quite recently. As late as 1964 most of these manuals were not to be found in the libraries of at least two of our greatest law schools. Perhaps the first law review writer to make extensive use of these texts was Bernard Weisberg of the Chicago bar (*see* note 86 *infra*), who later turned up as one of the ACLU lawyers in the *Escobedo* case.

Two weeks after *Miranda* was handed down, Thomas C. Lynch, the Attorney General of California, in Washington for a meeting of the National Crime Commission of which he is a member, reported that a preliminary survey indicated "wide use" in his state of the police interrogation manuals criticized by the Court. He disclosed that he was considering a "purge" of all such manuals. Washington Post, June 30, 1966, at E-2, col. 3. Professor Philip Zimbardo, who made the strong charge that "it is my professional opinion as a psychologist who has been concerned with the experimental modification of attitudes and behavior that these techniques [those illustrated in the manuals] represent a highly sophisticated application of psychological principles which for many people are more compelling and coercive than physical torture" (Zimbardo, "An Analysis of Pre-Arraignment Interrogation Techniques and Their Psychological Implications," at 26, paper read at American Psychological Association Meeting, Sept. 3, 1966), reported that he had "verified that these manuals are used in training interrogators by calling several police academies," *id*. at 10.

As recently as July of this year, the veteran special agent of the Kansas Bureau of Investigation, Alvin A. Dewey, of *In Cold Blood* fame, told the Senate Subcommittee on Constitutional Amendments:

> What is wrong with an officer exercising persistence and patience or showing confidence? Isn't that what any good salesman demonstrates in selling insurance or a car? And a law enforcement officer should be a good salesman in selling a suspect on telling the truth, proving his innocence or guilt. But a salesman cannot do his job if a competitor is standing by, and that is the situation for the law enforcement officer with the presence of an attorney while interrogating a suspect.
>
> . . . .
>
> As to the description of an interrogation room, I wish to define it as a room where people can talk in privacy which is nothing more than an attorney desires in talking to his client or a doctor in talking to his patient. . . . [These rooms] bear no resemblance to torture chambers as some may wish to think, and in fact some are equipped with air conditioning, carpeting, and upholstered furniture.[90]

What I have said so far does not fully account for the persistence of the de facto inquisitorial system. In the late 1920s and early 1930s, complacency about the system was shaken—at least for a while—by the notorious cases of *Ziang Sun Wan v. United States*[91] and *People v. Doran*[92] and by the shocking disclosure of the Wickersham Commission.[93] Still the system survived. Why? Probably because, in addition to the factors I have already mentioned, the practice had become so widespread and entrenched by this time that even most of its critics despaired of completely uprooting it in the foreseeable future. A broad, fundamental attack on the system might well have failed completely; elimination of the more aggravated forms of coercion commanded a high priority and alone appeared feasible. In this regard, the pessimistic views of Zechariah Chafee, co-author of the famous report to the Wickersham Commission on "the third degree,"[94] are instructive:[20]

> Big jumps in policy may be unattainable or undesirable. [What would Chafee have said of *Escobedo* and *Miranda?*] *Bad as the third degree is, we should be very cautious about disrupting the police department and the courts in the hope of abolishing it.*
>
> Let us begin by considering two simple remedies which are free from the foregoing objections.
>
> The first is to shorten this danger period by obtaining the prompt production of the prisoner before a magistrate, after which he should be out of the hands of the police. This is the situation in Boston, and appears to contribute to the virtual nonexistence of the third degree in that city. . . . There is no opportunity for protracted interrogations

20. Chafee, *Remedies for the Third Degree,* Atlantic Monthly, Nov. 1931, at 621, 625–26, 630 (emphasis added). *See also* Warner, *How Can the Third Degree Be Eliminated?,* 1 BILL OF RIGHTS REV. 24 (1940), and the extract from it in footnote 25 *infra.*

lasting over several days and nights, which are common in cities where production in court is illegally delayed. Violence is less probable when scars will not have time to heal before the magistrate sees the prisoner next day. This remedy involves no new law; practically all states require prompt production in court. In introduces no startling innovation in police methods, but merely hastens an act which the police are accustomed to perform. Of course, enforcement of this law will not always be an easy matter. The same motives which cause the police in many cities to investigate brutally also lead them to prolong the time of investigation illegally. However, excessive length of confinement is an offense which the judges can discover and correct more easily than secret coercion. . . .

Secondly, official records should be kept of the exact time of arrest and of detention; of the transfers of prisoners and the places to which they are taken; of interviews by the police with prisoners and the time interrogations begin and end; and (as in Boston) of injuries to prisoners found visible during a daily examination. Facts of this nature fit naturally into the records customarily kept in police stations and jails.
. . . .

The two remedies just recommended have the advantage of forming a natural part of the existing routine of police stations and magistrates courts. . . .

In England, the police are forbidden to interrogate a suspect after his arrest or involuntary detention; thus there is no danger of their using brutality or other pressure to obtain the desired answers. . . . However, it is doubtful if this remedy could be successfully transferred to the United States, at least in the near future. . . . American police officials . . . attach extreme importance to the questioning of arrested persons. They would consider the adoption of the English rule a serious crippling of their activities, and until they feel otherwise it would only be one more law which they would be tempted to violate. How could they be forced to obey it? *It is hard enough to prevent policemen from using physical violence on suspects; it would be far harder to prevent them from asking a few questions. We had better get rid of the rubber hose and twenty-four hour grillings before we undertake to compel or persuade the police to give up questioning altogether.*
. . . .

. . . [The remedies recommended in this article] require no constitutional amendments and no legislation, so that their adoption involves no long delay. *But immediate success must not be expected. The third degree is deeply rooted in official habits in many cities,* and is not likely to disappear entirely until the officials have been persuaded that it is bad and unnecessary.

The *McNabb-Anderson* Briefs: The Government Agrees
That the Privilege Applies to Police Interrogation, But . . .

Until *Miranda* at least, very few of our states adopted the "simple" and relatively modest remedy of "shortening the danger period" by obtaining the prompt production of the prisoner before a magistrate.[95] However, a dozen years after Professor Chafee wrote the aforementioned article the Supreme Court did resort to this remedy, as is well known, in the exercise of its supervisory powers over the administration of federal criminal justice.[21] Neither the opinion of the Court nor the briefs of counsel contain citations to the Chafee article, but the *McNabb* opinion reads as if its author, Justice Frankfurter, had perused the writings of his former colleague more than once.

One would never know it in the midst of all the beating of breasts and gnashing of teeth[96] which greeted both *McNabb* and the *Mallory* case[22] which reaffirmed it, but (as the Chafee article plainly indicates) the new federal rule marked a "compromise" between the objectionable existing practice and the "drastic proposals" then being advanced. That *McNabb* was a "compromise" became quite apparent[23] in the wake of *Escobedo,* but it had not escaped the government lawyers who argued *McNabb* and the companion case of *Anderson v. United States.*[24] Although they had urged the Court not to "hold inadmissible a confession made during the subsistence of any unlawful practice regardless of whether the confession was voluntary,"[97] the government lawyers devoted more space in their brief to "an even more extreme" possibility:

We submit also that the Court should not adopt an even more extreme rule requiring the exclusion of confessions obtained during cross-examination of persons in the custody of the police. The shocking conditions revealed by appellate court decisions and by the researches of investigators naturally give rise to the suggestion that the evils must be ended by abolishing the system of police examination which lies at the root of the evils. The ability to use as evidence confessions obtained by cross-examination is said to lead a lax policy force to rely upon confessions and not upon sound investigatory techniques in tracing clues and uncovering evidence. Similarly it is suggested that proper interrogation too easily becomes bullying and bullying becomes brutality. The evil effects of the resulting "third degree" upon the whole system of law observance and law enforcement can scarcely be exaggerated. Finally, proponents of this view point to the low rate of crime and high rate of crime detection in Great Britain where, apparently, the police are not permitted to interrogate a prisoner except to clarify a volunteered statement.[98]

Some of the reasons advanced by the government to stay the Court's hand in *McNabb* and *Anderson* sound very much like the reasons urged by the federal and state governments a quarter-century later in *Miranda:*[99]

If a remedy is needed in addition to existing sanctions, the remedy should be

21. McNabb v. United States, 318 U.S. 332 (1943).

22. Mallory v. United States, 354 U.S. 449 (1957).

23. Shortly after *Escobedo* was decided, two former federal prosecutors proposed a combination of the *McNabb-Mallory* rule and objective recording of all questioning at places controlled by the police as a "more workable and less drastic means" of controlling interrogation abuses than the presence of counsel at these sessions. Enker & Elsen, *Counsel for the Suspect:* Massiah v. United States *and* Escobedo v. Illinois, 49 MINN. L. REV. 47, 85 (1964).

24. 318 U.S. 350 (1943). Although today *McNabb* is the much more famous case, the government used its brief in *Anderson* as the vehicle for extended treatment of the problem.

administrative or legislative but not judicial. Two reasons support this conclusion. First, the courts are ill equipped to make the investigation necessary before the settled principles may be overturned. Second, the courts have no discretion in the choice of a remedy. The administrative officials may prescribe and enforce regulations designed to protect prisoners against the "third degree." If the legislative branch determined to forbid interrogation by the police and to exclude extrajudicial confessions thus obtained from evidence, it might meet the demands of law enforcement by providing a substitute such as an immediate examination by the prosecuting attorney in the presence of the counsel for the accused, or perhaps some system of quasi-judicial examination accompanied by a limitation, by constitutional amendment where necessary, of the privilege against self-incrimination.[100]

How an "immediate examination by the prosecuting attorney *in the presence of the counsel for the accused"* could possibly "meet the demands of law enforcement"—as law enforcement conceived those demands—is not made clear. Nor is it explained *why* a quasi-judicial examination of the accused might require a modification of the privilege although nonjudicial examination did not. For, and this is perhaps the most extraordinary feature of this extraordinary brief, *the government agreed that the privilege against self-incrimination controlled the admissibility of confessions* (as I read the brief, with some blinking, in *state* as well as federal cases), although, for one thing, it had to "sanitize" police interrogation in order to meet this standard:

[T]he guarantees of the privilege against self-incrimination and of due process of law are limitations put upon the state in protection of the individual against invasions of "his indefeasible right" of personal security, personal liberty, and the privacies of life, where the right has not been forfeited by a conviction for crime. *See Boyd v. United States,* 116 U.S. 616, 630. But the constitutional prohibition is not laid upon only the most obnoxious practices. Even a restrained secret interrogation may gradually turn to mental or physical torture. . . . Therefore, *the accused is given the privilege, which he may choose to exercise or not as he pleases, to check the danger at the outset* by refusing to answer any incriminating questions; if he refuses, the state must not use "physical or moral compulsion to extort communications from him."

The Constitution grants this privilege specifically by the provision in the Fifth Amendment that no man "shall be compelled in any criminal case to be a witness against himself," and it grants the privilege impliedly in the due process clause of the Fifth and Fourteenth Amendments.

. . . .

An accused person feels compulsion to speak, at the outset, in the hope of establishing his innocence and, at the end, when that is gone, in the weight of his conscience, or in the hope of obtaining leniency. But in such a case, the state cannot be said to have coerced the answers. The state has not invaded any right of personal security or privacy against the will of the accused, or exerted moral or physical compulsion to extort the communication. Such a confession, therefore, is admissible.

. . . .

. . .[A] confession made in answer to interrogation by the police may be admitted in evidence without infringement of any constitutional right, *provided that the accused is left free to end the examination* into his guilt or innocence by a refusal to answer, and provided that his will is respected and not subjugated to the will of his accusers.[101]

If there has ever been an alleged "coerced confession" case worth litigating where the defendant was given either the privilege against self-incrimination to exercise "as he pleases" or the freedom to "end the examination" by a simple refusal to answer, I am unaware of it. At any rate, not until *Miranda* did the Court strive to check "the danger [of secret interrogation] at the outset" by requiring that the suspect be fully and fairly advised that he has a "right of silence" which he may "choose to exercise . . . as he pleases." This, as I understand it, is what much of the shouting is about. Not until *Miranda* did the Court make plain that even though the suspect may have answered some questions or volunteered some statements he is "free to end the examination" by indicating that he does not wish to be interrogated further. Again, this, I take it, is what much of the shouting is about.

It is no mean feat to put beyond the reach of the privilege those proceedings in which a man is being "compelled"—in almost pristine form—to testify against himself. But it takes real dexterity to do what the government did in *McNabb* and *Anderson, i.e.,* purport to apply the privilege to a phase of the criminal process which had grown up more or less accidentally and extralegally, yet conclude that this application of the constitutional provision does not change things very much. In order to accomplish such an extraordinary feat, the government not only had to tidy up the facts to suit the standard, but also had to loosen the standard to suit the facts. As the government perceived the matter, the privilege against self-incrimination turned out to be little, if anything, more than the "voluntary" test masquerading under a different label. Whether the route taken in arriving at this result is viewed as augmenting the common law and due process standards a bit or as diluting the force of the privilege (at least as it had been construed in more formal settings) a good deal, all the tests, even the one based on "trustworthiness" wound up in a single ball of wax:

It is familiar and settled law that a "voluntary" confession should be admitted into evidence, and that a "coerced" confession should be excluded. Whatever the logic of the criticisms, this test is applicable whether the due process clauses of the Fifth and Fourteenth Amendments, the constitutional privilege against self-incrimination, or the law of evidence be invoked as ground for the objection.
. . . .

The privilege is not to be "compelled" to give evidence against oneself. And in the leading cases setting aside convictions based upon confessions because due process was denied, the Court carefully pointed out that "the undisputed facts showed that compulsion was applied." *Chambers v. Florida.* . . . Coercion and compulsion exist in this sense when the accused is deprived "of his free choice, to admit, to deny, or to

refuse to answer," when his will is broken so that he will make whatever statement his inquisitors may desire. . . . A confession obtained from a Chinese suffering physical pain who was held *incommunicado* and questioned for seven days and all of one night is obtained by compulsion. *Wan v. United States,* 266 U.S. 1. [Is this example supposed to illuminate the meaning of "compelled" to be a witness against oneself?]
. . . .

Comparison of the constitutional requirement with the criterion of testimonial worth shows that they are essentially the same both in abstract statement and in practical application. Both are summarized in the words "voluntary" and "compulsion". . . . In theory, it may be that a man is less ready to accuse himself falsely than he is to surrender his will to remain silent, but it is doubtful that so fine a line can be drawn in practice. The two aims, to admit true confessions and to abolish abuses, are overlapping; the ultimate test in each case is whether the confession is what the accused was willing to say or what the accusers wished him to tell them.[102]

As the government's approach in *McNabb* and *Anderson* well illustrates, excluding the privilege from the interrogation room is not the only way to reconcile the proceedings inside with the fifth amendment. One may also let the privilege in, but "balance" it. "Outside" the interrogation room, unlike first amendment rights whose assertion "to bar governmental interrogation . . . always involves a balancing by the courts of the competing private and public interests at stake in the particular circumstances shown,"[103] "a proper claim of the privilege against self-incrimination . . . afford[s] a witness the right to resist inquiry in all circumstances."[104] "Outside," the most pressing demands of national security cannot override the privilege; "inside," evidently, routine law enforcement needs may, and often should, prevail. That, at least, is how I view the government's plea of a quarter-century ago to maintain the status quo, to stick with the old "voluntariness" test (alias the privilege against self-incrimination):

If all extrajudicial confessions were excluded from evidence, there would be less aggression against these liberties because the incentive would be largely removed. On the other hand, it is essential that crime be detected and important that all data having testimonial worth be used to establish the guilt or innocence of the accused. Thus, there is a conflict between the demands of individual liberty and the public interest in efficient law enforcement. The test of voluntariness seems to us to resolve this conflict at the line marked by the Constitution. It should not, we submit, be modified by the courts to be more stringent.[25]

As late as 1966, the dissenters in *Miranda* seemed to agree.

25. Brief for United States, at 38, Anderson v. United States, *supra* footnote 24.

A short time earlier, Sam Bass Warner, principal draftsman of the Uniform Arrest Act, who was said to be one of the few professors who had "accompanied the police on their tours of duty in order to learn and report the true facts," Wilson, *Police Arrest Privileges in a Free Society: A Plea for Modernization,* in POLICE POWER AND INDIVIDUAL FREEDOM 21, 26 (C. Sowle ed.

The "Voluntariness" Test: "A Workable and Effective Means of Dealing with Confessions in a Judicial Manner"

Although Justice Clark would modify the old test,[105] he looks back on it as one "which we are accustomed to administering and which we know from our cases are effective instruments in protecting persons in police custody."[106] For Justice Harlan, the pre-*Escobedo-Miranda* cases "show that there exists a workable and effective means of dealing with confessions in a judicial manner"[107] and that "the Court has developed an elaborate, sophisticated, and sensitive approach to admissibility," one "ever more familiar to the lower courts."[108]

Justice Clark's enthusiasm for the pre-*Escobedo* test was not always so abundant. Only five years earlier he had referred to "the elusive, measureless standard of psychological coercion heretofore developed in this Court by accretion on almost an *ad hoc,* case-by-case basis."[109] And long before that (in a search and seizure setting) he had scored the "uncertainty" and "unpredictability" generated by "a case by case approach to due process in which inchoate notions of propriety concerning local police conduct guide our decisions," maintaining that by such an approach "we do not shape the conduct of local police one whit; unpredictable reversals on dissimilar fact situations are not likely to curb the zeal of those police and prosecutors who may be intent on racking up a high percentage of successful prosecutions."[110] As for Justice Harlan, in stressing that the late, lamented test gave *"ample recognition to society's interest* in suspect questioning as an instrument of law enforcement,"[111] he succeeded, it seems to me, in violently shaking the

---

1962), had articulated "the conflict" and the need to strike "a proper balance" much more crisply:

> The difficulties confronting a defendant who desires to reserve his story until trial are well-known. When he is arrested, the police will endeavor to make him "come across." Whether they will violate the Fifth Amendment by compelling him to be a witness against himself, depends upon what is meant by "compelling." If the term "compel" includes a two or three hour examination during which several police officers urge him to confess and do their best to confuse and entrap him into a confession, then the Fifth Amendment is violated in every city in the United States.
>
> . . . .
>
> If in their effort to break down the suspect, our police stopped after giving him a severe grilling for a few hours, we might believe that the Fifth Amendment was being violated and regret that the liberty of the individual was not better respected, but we should have no serious ground for complaint. In fact, it may well be that a proper balance between the individual interest in freedom from compulsory self-incrimination and the social interest in the discovery of crime requires that suspects be subjected to such a cross-examination. The situation becomes serious only when the police go further and indulge in what is popularly known as the "third degree."

Warner, *supra* footnote 20, at 25. *See also* notes 114–16 *infra* and accompanying text *infra*.

aforementioned assurance by Justice Clark that the pre-*Escobedo-Miranda* test was "an effective instrument *in protecting* persons in police custody":

> Cases countenancing quite significant pressures can be cited without difficulty, and the lower courts may often have been yet more tolerant.[112]
>
> One not too distant example is *Stroble v. California*, 343 U.S. 181 [1952], in which the suspect was kicked and threatened after his arrest, questioned a little later for two hours, and isolated from a lawyer trying to see him; the resulting confession was held admissible.[113]

The *Miranda* majority contended that "the absurdity" of denying that a confession obtained under typical "interrogation room" circumstances "is compelled" is "aptly portrayed" by Professor Arthur Sutherland's hypothetical of a well-to-do testatrix who is "captured" by the would-be heirs who "put her in a carefully designed room, out of touch with everyone but themselves . . . [and] keep her secluded there for hours while they make insistent demands, weary her with contradictions of her assertions that she wants to leave her money to [someone else], and finally induce her to execute the will in their favor."[114]

Justice Harlan's retort was that the need of law enforcement "is, of course, what makes so misleading the Court's comparison of a probate judge readily setting aside as involuntary the will of an old lady badgered and beleagured by the new heirs."[115] However, after posing his hypothetical, Professor Sutherland had commented:

> At once one will hear the response that the testatrix is not a criminal; that obtaining a surrender of rights from a criminal is different; that the interest of the state demands that criminals be not coddled. That is to say we are told that a man with his life at stake should be able to surrender an ancient constitutional right to remain silent, under compulsions which in a surrender of a little property would obviously make the transaction void.[116]

This is precisely what Justice Harlan seems to be telling us.

The view that the "voluntariness test" effectively protected suspects seems questionable, in large part because Justice Harlan's sanguine attitude about the "workability" of the "voluntariness" test and the test's growing familiarity to the lower courts seems unwarranted. His attitude hardly finds support in his own recognition that the Court "never pinned [the "voluntariness rubric"] . . . down to a single meaning, but on the contrary infused it with a number of different values"[117] or in his acknowledgment that "apart from direct physical coercion . . . no single default or fixed combination of them guaranteed exclusion and synopses of the cases would serve little use because the overall gauge has been steadily changing, usually in the direction of restricting admissibility."[118] Nor does the touted workability, effectiveness, sophistication, and sensitivity of the old test find support in the Bator-Vorenberg article (which Justice Harlan quotes with approval):

> In fact, the concept of involuntariness seems to be used by the courts as a shorthand to refer to practices which are repellent to civilized standards of decency or which, under the circumstances, are thought to apply a degree of pressure to an individual which unfairly impairs his capacity to make a rational choice. [26]

Nor can the defenders of the old test gain much comfort from the paragraph (which the dissenting Justices do not quote) immediately preceding the one quoted above:

> Judicial decisions speak in terms of the "voluntariness" of a confession, but the term itself provides little guidance. To the extent "voluntariness" has made a determination of the state of an individual's will the crucial question, it has not assisted analysis. Except where a person is unconscious or drugged or otherwise lacks capacity for conscious choice, all incriminating statements—even those made under brutal treatment—are "voluntary" in the sense of representing a choice of alternatives. On the other hand, if "voluntariness" incorporates notions of "but-for" cause, the question should be whether the statement would have been made even absent inquiry or other official action. Under such a test, virtually no statement would be voluntary because very few people give incriminating statements in the absence of official action of some kind. [27]

Justice Harlan did not pause to document his assertion that the pre-*Escobedo* approach to the admissibility of confessions—which was undergoing "a continuing re-evaluation on the facts of each case of *how much* pressure on the subject was permissible"[(119)]—was growing "ever more familiar to the lower courts." Similarly, although Professors Bator and Vorenberg talk about "*the courts*" using the voluntary-involuntary terminology as a "shorthand," they do not cite a single lower court case—only a host of United States

---

26. Bator & Vorenberg, *Arrest, Detention, Interrogation and the Right to Counsel,* 66 COLUM. L. REV. 62, 73 (1966), quoted with approval, 384 U.S. at 507 n.4; *cf.* Kamisar, *What Is An "Involuntary" Confession?,* 17 RUTGERS L. REV. 728, 745–46 (1963) [reprinted in this volume]:

> There is much talk in *Culombe* [v. Connecticut, 367 U.S. 568 (1961)] of "involuntariness" and the "suction process"; of "draining" the "capacity for freedom of choice"; of "overreaching," "overbearing" or "breaking" the "will." But are these words and phrases any more illuminating than, say, the talk of yesteryear about "affected with a public interest," "subject to the exercise of the police power," or "devoted to the public use?" Is "involuntariness" or "coercion" or "breaking the will" (or its synonyms) little more than a fiction intended to vilify certain "effective" interrogation methods? Is "voluntariness" or "mental freedom" or "self-determination" (or its equivalents) little more than a fiction designed to beautify certain other interrogation techniques?

27. Bator & Vorenberg, *supra* footnote 26, at 72–73.

Supreme Court cases and one secondary authority (this writer's *Rutgers Law Review* article) whose complaint, *inter alia,* is that by continuing to define the "voluntariness" required by due process in terms of the old threadbare generalities and empty abstractions (*e.g.,* "made . . . freely and voluntarily and without fear of punishment or hope of reward") and by failing to advise juries of specific types of police misconduct relevant to the issue, the state trial courts were permitting the term to continue to be used in its ordinary, everyday (and unhelpful) sense.[28] Indeed, in *Haynes v. Washington,*[29] which marks the "end of the line" for the old test, the jury was instructed, in effect, to *preclude from its consideration* of the "voluntariness" issue that the accused was not reminded he was under arrest, was not cautioned he could remain silent, nor warned that his answers could be used against him, nor advised of his right to counsel.[120] True, although not relied on as a separate ground of reversal, these instructions were regarded by the 5–4 *Haynes* majority as raising "a serious and substantial question whether a proper constitutional standard was applied by the jury."[121] There seems to be a significant difference, however, between forbidding a trial court from precluding consideration of these factors and requiring the court to instruct affirmatively that they must be taken into account.

The most ambitious attempt to bring order, coherence, and clarity to the "involuntary" or "coerced" confession field, the most arduous effort to develop "a set of principles [in terms of the old test] which could be easily applied in any coerced-confession situation,"[122] was the late Justice Frankfurter's sixty-seven-page "treatise"[123] in *Culombe v. Connecticut.*[30] What was the result of these herculean labors? Justice Harlan, joined by Justices Clark and Whittaker, "agreed to what my Brother Frankfurter has written in delineation of the general principles governing police interrogation . . . and as to the factors which should guide federal judicial review of state action in this field"[124]—but reached the opposite result.[125] Justice Douglas, joined by Justice Black, took a different route than did Justice Frankfurter, but reached the same result.[126] The Chief Justice, in the course of joining the separate concurring opinion of Justice Brennan, would only say of the general princi-

---

28. *See* Kamisar, *supra* footnote 26, at 752–53.

Actually, as Professors Bator and Vorenberg point out in the opening footnote, since their article is "an informal working paper, designed to be used as a basis for discussion," it "contains no documentation of any sort." However, the authors are the principal draftsmen of the American Law Institute's Model Code of Pre-Arraignment Procedure, and, understandably, the commentary to the proposed code, written at about the same time as the article, follows it closely. The passage quoted by Justice Harlan appears verbatim in the commentary, MODEL CODE OF PRE-ARRAIGNMENT PROCEDURE 167 (Tent. Draft No. 1, 1966), and when I refer to Professors Bator and Vorenberg's documentation for this passage I mean that which is contained in the commentary to the code.

29. 373 U.S. 503 (1963).

30. 367 U.S. 568 (1961).

ples enunciated by Justice Frankfurter: "On an abstract level, I find myself in agreement with some portions of the opinion and in disagreement with other portions."[127] Only one member of the Court, Justice Stewart, joined in Justice Frankfurter's dissertation.

Two years after *Culombe* and only a year before *Escobedo,* the Court split 5-4 in *Haynes.* [128] Justice Clark, joined by Harlan, Stewart, and White, JJ., regarded "the Court's reversal . . . [as] an abrupt departure from the rule laid down in the cases of this Court and an enlargement of the requirements heretofore visited upon state courts in confession cases."[129] For the majority's determination that the Haynes confession was "involuntary" the four dissenters could "find no support in any of the thirty-three cases decided on the question by this Court."[130] Does this sound like the Supreme Court, let alone the lower courts, had grown "accustomed to administering" the "voluntariness" test?

For me, the strongest evidence of the *in*effectiveness and the *un*workability of the old test was yet to come. It came *one week after* the *Miranda* case, when, having declined to give retroactive effect to *Escobedo* and *Miranda,*[31] the Court applied the old test (on collateral attack) in *Davis v. North Carolina.*[32]

As indicated earlier,[131] in challenging the admissibility of his confessions, Elmer Davis, Jr., was more fortunate than most in his predicament. He could point to a specific notation on the arrest sheet: "Do not allow anyone to see

---

31. Johnson v. New Jersey, 384 U.S. 719 (1966).

Johnson recalls Judge Qua's observation a decade ago: "Practical considerations may impinge heavily and divert the development of theory from its straight logical course. We all know this occurs from time to time in our own courts and sometimes to the great advantage of the law and the community. Similar forces operate in Washington." Qua, *Griffin v. Illinois,* 25 U. CHI. L. REV. 143, 147 (1957). Although "the advantages" to "the community" of declining to apply *Escobedo* and *Miranda* retroactively are considerable, I think *Johnson* was wrongly decided, for reasons suggested by a series of leading questions in L. HALL & Y. KAMISAR, MODERN CRIMINAL PROCEDURE 503 (2d ed. 1966). How can the Court say that "while *Escobedo* and *Miranda* provide *important new safeguards* against the use of *unreliable* statements at trial, the nonretroactivity of these decisions will not preclude persons whose trials have already been completed from invoking the *same safeguards* as part of an involuntariness claim"? 384 U.S. at 730 (emphasis added). If, as seems plain, *Escobedo* and *Miranda* indicate dissatisfaction with—and lack of confidence in—the actual operation of the old "voluntariness" and "totality of circumstances" tests, just as Gideon v. Wainwright, 372 U.S. 335 (1963) manifests dissatisfaction with and lack of confidence in the old *Betts* "prejudice" and "special circumstances" standards, how can it be sufficient that "our law on coerced confessions is available for persons whose trials have already been completed"? 384 U.S. at 730.

I hasten to add, however, that here again, *compare* footnote 2 *supra,* the Court was faced with a "damned if it did and damned if it didn't" issue. If the Court had given the new confession rulings retroactive effect, I venture to say the roar of disapproval would have been deafening. Not only would many law enforcement officers have proclaimed "chaos" and "catastrophe," but not a few law professors would have chided the Court for "pretending the Constitution is now what it always was" and for "inhibiting judicial creativity."

32. 384 U.S. 737 (1966).

Davis. Or allow him to use the telephone."[132] As Chief Judge Sobeloff pointed out, "rarely do police officials make a written declaration, as they did here, of a design to deny their prisoner's right to counsel and his other constitutional rights."[133] Davis could also point to the uncontested fact that no one other than the police had spoken to him during the sixteen days of detention and interrogation that preceded his confessions. The Supreme Court had "never sustained the use of a confession obtained after such a lengthy period of detention and interrogation as was involved in this case."[134] However, this did not suffice in the Superior and Supreme Courts of North Carolina in 1960.[135] Nor did it impress the federal district court, which first denied him an evidentiary hearing,[136], and then, when reversed on this point,[137] found his confessions to have been "voluntary."[138] Nor, in 1964, was it quite enough for the United States Court of Appeals for the Fourth Circuit, which upheld denial of the writ by a 3-2 vote.[139]

The readiness with which the state and lower federal courts, passing on the admissibility of Davis's confessions, accepted dubious police claims, and the looseness with which they stated (or, more accurately, failed to state) "the facts," is hardly calculated to inspire confidence in the workability and effectiveness of the test—from the defendant's point of view, at any rate. In affirming Davis's conviction, a unanimous Supreme Court of North Carolina observed:

[T]he prisoner was advised he need not make a statement; that if he did it might be used against him.

. . . .

The prisoner asked to see his sister, whom the officers searched for, after some difficulty found, and delivered the prisoner's message. She appeared at the jail and Captain McCall admitted her to a private conference with the prisoner.[140]

The prisoner's sister was admitted to a private conference with him, but, the state court neglected to point out, not until he had already confessed after having been interrogated "forty-five minutes or an hour or maybe a little more" each day for sixteen days.[141] Similarly, the state court failed to note that there was no indication in the record that the prisoner was advised of his rights until the sixteenth day—*after* he had confessed orally but before he had signed the written confession.[142]

After holding a habeas corpus hearing, the federal district court had little difficulty concluding "from the totality of circumstances in this case that the confession was the product of a rational intellect and a free will."[143] How did it deal with the tell-tale notation on the police blotter directing that Davis be held *incommunicado?* It made no reference whatever to this incongruous item in its five-page opinion, four of which are devoted to the "historical facts." Moreover, although the head of the detective division admitted that Charlotte police sought and received permission from the warden of the state prison to keep Davis "temporarily" in their custody, primarily for the reason that they suspected him of the rape-murder to which he later confessed,[144] they managed to convince the federal district court that, for the first twelve of the sixteen days he was their prisoner, they had refrained from asking Davis any questions about the murder, but rather confined their questions to thefts and unlawful entries committed by him after his escape.[145]

"The notation on the arrest record creates suspicions," conceded the 3–2 majority of the Fourth Circuit, "but such suspicions cannot overcome the positive evidence that the notation had no practical effect or influence upon what was done and that help rather than hindrance was offered to [Davis] in his one effort to contact someone outside the prison walls."[146] This is the police version. The Fourth Circuit opinion pointed out elsewhere that Davis's sister had testified at the habeas corpus hearing that "she twice went to see her brother in the Charlotte City Jail, but each time was turned away."[147] The district court, however, "did not believe her, finding, as the officers testified, that neither she nor anyone else was turned away...."[148]

What, if anything, one might ask, does the foregoing discussion prove? The United States Supreme Court reversed (Clark and Harlan, JJ., dissenting), did it not? Yes, indeed, but it should never be forgotten that in the thirty years since *Brown v. Mississippi*,[149] the Supreme Court has taken an average of about one state confession case per year.[150] How fared the many defendants all these years who, in the midst of the confusion and conflict so characteristic of "factual litigation" in this area, could not fall back on extraordinarily helpful "objective facts," as could Davis? How fared the many defendants whose cases did not receive the meticulous attention each Justice gives "death penalty" cases marked in red,[151] as was Davis's case and *two-thirds* of the confession cases the Court has chosen to review these past thirty years?

Analyzing a recent Supreme Court Term, a careful student of that institution's work reported that the Court was asked to review over two thousand cases, of which forty-two involved the death penalty. Although "all of the allegations in these capital cases were so serious that the Supreme Court might have felt compelled to decide each and every one of them" only one condemned man out of four received a hearing, and only one out of eight obtained a reversal.[152] How many garden-variety criminal defendants who cried "coerced confession" but lost the "swearing contest" below were likely to survive the winnowing process above? As Justice Black put it in the *Miranda* oral arguments, "if you are going to determine it [the admissibility of the confession] each time on the circumstances... [if] this Court will take them one by one... it is more than we are capable of doing."[153]

Immediately prior to *Escobedo* and *Miranda*, could we afford to be proud of the progress we had made since the 1924 *Ziang Sun Wan* case? On that occasion two lower federal courts *upheld* a confession obtained from a seriously ill Chinese who had been held *incommunicado* for over a week, most of the time in a secluded hotel room where he was questioned "morning, afternoon and evening (and at least on one occasion after midnight)."[33] (The Government met a much cooler reception in the Supreme Court than it had enjoyed in the lower courts when it depicted the case as one in which the defendant "had voluntarily acquiesced in going to the hotel; he had never complained of the presence of officers there with him... he had been in a good humor all the time about the matter.")[154]

Had we made forty years worth of progress since the 1927 *Doran* case where, despite a powerful dissent by Judge Lehman, joined by Chief Judge Cardozo, what was probably the finest state court in the land *affirmed* a murder conviction based on a confession elicited from a man who had admittedly fainted during the "questioning," who had needed to be revived with whiskey and who admittedly had been "talked to" by an officer wearing a boxing glove on his hand?[34] (A majority of the New York Court of Appeals, per Crane, J., had speculated that "realization of the horrible deed which had been committed and that at last he had been discovered" might have caused the defendant to faint.[155] As for the boxing glove, the majority conceded "this surely was a foolish thing for [the officer] to do, but it was to be considered by the jury with all the other testimony in determining the truth or falsity of Doran's statement about the use of violence.")[156]

True, this was a long time ago, but the lower federal courts in *Ziang Sun Wan* and the state courts in *Doran* utilized a "voluntariness" test not much different from the one still being employed at least by the lower courts in the 1960s.[157] Could we confidently assert that confessions obtained on *Wan*- and *Doran*-type facts would never have passed muster in the lower courts in the sixties?

A short week after they paid their respects to the late "voluntariness" test, Justices Clark and Harlan would have applied it to sustain Davis's confessions. The Court's reversal, they protested, "goes against the grain of our prior decisions."[158] "[T]he sporadic interrogation of Davis," as they saw it, "can hardly be denominated as sustained or overbearing pressure. From the record it appears that he was simply questioned for about an hour each day [for sixteen days] by a couple of detectives. There was no protracted grilling. Nor did the police operate in relays."[159]

"Disagreement," Justice Harlan had said of the "voluntariness" test in his *Miranda* dissent, "is usually confined to that borderland of close cases where it matters least."[160] After three decades and thirty-odd "coerced" confession cases which saw "the overall gauge... steadily changing, usually in the direction of restricting admissibility," as Harlan described the situation in his *Miranda* dissent,[161] was *Davis* still a "close case"? If so, was the need to scrap the "voluntariness" test still a close question?

33. 266 U.S. 1, 11 (1924).
34. 246 N.Y. 409, 422-23, 159 N.E. 379, 384 (1927).

Kauper's "Judicial Examination of the Accused"* Forty Years Later—Some Comments on a Remarkable Article

November, 1974

FOR A LONG TIME before Professor Paul Kauper wrote "Judicial Examination of the Accused" in 1932, and for a long time thereafter, the "legal mind" shut out the de facto inquisitorial system that characterized American criminal procedure. Paul Kauper could not look away. He recognized the "naked, ugly facts" (p. 1224) and was determined to do something about them—more than thirty years before *Escobedo v. Illinois*[1] or *Miranda v. Arizona*.[2]

Kauper proposed that a suspect be brought before a judicial officer immediately upon arrest, without assistance of counsel; that the suspect be allowed to elect whether or not to speak at this appearance; but that (as he would be forewarned), if he chose to remain silent, his silence would be the subject of inference and comment at trial.[1] The original, unexpurgated

---

*Kauper, *Judicial Examination of the Accused—A Remedy for the Third Degree*, 30 MICH. L. REV. 1224 (1932) [hereinafter cited by page].

1. As Kauper pointed out, he was hardly the first to advocate judicial or judicially supervised interrogation as a remedy for the third degree. *See* authorities collected at p. 1240 n.81. The other proposals, however, differed significantly from Kauper's. For example, Judge Simeon Baldwin urged, "let there be no caution [by the magistrate] that [the suspect] need not answer, and no warning that he may be making evidence against himself." 6 A.B.A. Rep. 225, 238 (1883). Baldwin's proposal would in effect have substituted the "inherent pressures," Miranda v. Arizona, 384 U.S. 436, 468 (1966), of judicial interrogation for those of police interrogation. Similarly, the plan briefly considered by the American Law Institute in the 1920s would have authorized a magistrate to interrogate a suspect without advising him that he had a right to remain silent or that anything he said might be used against him, and would have provided further that if the suspect refused to answer any questions, "the magistrate in his discretion may commit him for contempt." ALI CODE OF CRIMINAL PROCEDURE 92, 101 (Prelim. Draft No. 5, 1927), *abandoned in* ALI CODE OF CRIMINAL PROCEDURE 26-27 (Tent. Draft No. 1, 1928). On the other hand, Chafee suggested vaguely that "perhaps even an examination before trial might be permitted if conducted by a responsible magistrate," without specifying how, if at all, the suspect could be made to talk and without indicating what advice, if any, the suspect should be given at this examination. *See* Chafee, *Compulsory Confessions*, 40 NEW REPUBLIC 266, 267 (1924). Others proposed simply that a suspect be afforded a prompt "opportunity" to make his statement before a magistrate "if he is willing to make one," but provided no sanction if the suspect chose to remain silent. *See* 2 J. WIGMORE, EVIDENCE § 851, at 199 (2d ed. 1923); *Outline of Code of Criminal Procedure*, 12 A.B.A.J. 690, 692 (1926). Still others suggested changing the law so that a

Kauper proposal would not, of course, pass constitutional muster today.[2] But Kauper's failure to foresee the direction the Supreme Court would take in the 1960s is hardly surprising. What is surprising is that in the "stone age" of American criminal procedure—some four months before *Powell v. Alabama*,[3] the first great right-to-counsel case, was argued in the Supreme Court, and some four years before *Brown v. Mississippi*,[4] the first fourteenth amendment due process "coerced" confession case, was handed down— Kauper saw the issues so clearly, discussed them so cleanly, and resolved them so honestly.

An eloquent voice protested in the 1960s that "reasonable men could hardly foresee that the provinces would be deemed delinquent in their due process for failing to take one great leap from the right to counsel at trial to a right to counsel before arraignment."[3] But Kauper recognized that "another possible check on arbitrariness which suggests itself is to allow the prisoner the right to counsel during interrogation" (p. 1247), and conceded that "it may be questioned whether legislation would be valid which deprived the prisoner of the right to counsel at the interrogation before a magistrate" (p. 1249). Yet he concluded:

If time must be allowed until counsel is procured, the preliminary interrogation will lose its effectiveness. Its value depends upon interrogation immediately upon arrest. There is the additional objection that the attorney's mere physical presence will give the prisoner a moral support which will interfere with that physhic state which guarantees the effectiveness of the proposed interrogation. And the attorney will discourage

---

defendant may be "forced" to testify *at his trial. See, e.g.,* Chafee, *supra,* at 267; Irvine, *The Third Degree and the Privilege Against Self Crimination,* 13 CORNELL L.Q. 211, 216–17 (1928).

Moreover, in marked contrast to Kauper's elaborate consideration of the relevant issues, most of the other proposals were presented very summarily. This may even be said of the unembellished Wickersham Commission proposal. *See* NAT'L COMM. ON LAW OBSERVANCE AND ENFORCEMENT, REPORT ON LAWLESSNESS IN LAW ENFORCEMENT (1931) [hereinafter WICKERSHAM REPORT]. Not infrequently the proposals were simply "tossed out" in the course of a general diatribe against allegedly unrealistic courts. *See, e.g.,* the quotations collected in ALI CODE OF CRIMINAL PROCEDURE 92–95 (Prelim. Draft No. 5, 1927).

Kauper's article, so far as I can tell, was the first systematic treatment of the problems raised by a judicially supervised interrogation procedure. Apparently Kauper was not only the first to articulate at considerable length the need for, desirability of, and historical support for such a procedure, but also the first to marshal, and to evaluate with any degree of thoroughness, the policy and constitutional arguments against such a procedure.

2. Constitutional deficiencies are absence of counsel and disclosure of the accused's silence at trial. However, provision of counsel would not necessarily destroy the effectiveness of Kauper's procedure if the suspect's refusal to answer questions at the judicial examination could be disclosed at trial. *See* text at notes 35–36 *infra.* Whether such disclosure would be constitutional is at first glance very doubtful, but on a second look, considering the many protective features a modernized version of Kauper's plan would offer, it is certainly arguable. *See* footnote 12 *infra.*

3. Traynor, *The Devils of Due Process in Criminal Detection, Detention, and Trial,* 33 U. CHI. L. REV. 657, 669 (1966).

spontaneity of responses by his client, urge him to be guarded in his replies, encourage him to fabricate a denial or alibi, and make vexatious objections to questions put by the magistrate, so that the procedure will be throttled at this point. It is submitted, therefore, that to grant to the prisoner the right to counsel during the interrogation will defeat the very purpose of the plan. [P. 1247.]

"Square recognition . . . of a privilege against self-incrimination at the pre-arraignment stage" did not occur until 1964,[5] when the Court performed "what might have seemed to some a shotgun wedding of the privilege to the confessions rule";[6] comment on a defendant's refusal to take the stand was not constitutionally banned until the following year.[7] But Kauper conceded in 1932 that "there is good authority for the opinion that [his proposed plan] would violate the privilege" (pp. 1251-52). He recognized, too, "that the possibility of . . . comment [on the accused's refusal to speak at the judicial examination] brings a psychic pressure to bear on [him] impelling him to speak . . . ; in fact this pressure is the very object of the provision" (p. 1251). But he took the position, as have distinguished commentators in our time,[4] that "considering the purpose of the privilege and its history, . . . a threat of comment on the refusal of the accused to answer questions [should not] be deemed compulsion so as to vitiate a statute providing for magisterial interrogation" (p. 1255):

Under the proposed plan for interrogation the accused still has his election to speak or keep silent; he is not—as any other witness would be in the circumstances—committed for contempt for his refusal to speak. To use the constitutional language—he is not compelled to be a witness against himself. Insofar as his silence exposes him to an inference of guilt, he is merely subject to the effect of an ordinary rule of evidence applied in all other instances where appropriate. Drawing such an inference from a refusal to answer questions which a person would naturally answer if innocent is an inevitable logical process based on human experience and common sense. [P. 1252.]

Although the conventional wisdom of his time, and a long time thereafter, was that "the fact that the prisoner cannot be [judicially] questioned stimulates [police and prosecutors to] search for independent evidence,"[8] Kauper understood that often the only thing stimulated by the inability of judicial officers to question a prisoner was questioning by police and prosecutors before the proceedings became judicial, and that often the availability of the privilege

4. *See, e.g.,* W. SCHAEFER, THE SUSPECT AND SOCIETY 60, 63-71, 80 (1967); Friendly, *The Fifth Amendment Tomorrow: The Case for Constitutional Change,* 37 U. CIN. L. REV. 671, 700, 714 (1968). *Cf.* Traynor, *supra* footnote 3, at 676. *See also* Griffin v. California, 380 U.S. 609, 622 (1965) (Stewart & White, JJ., dissenting): "The Model Code of Evidence, and Uniform Rules of Evidence both sanction [comment on the defendant's failure to testify]. The practice has been endorsed by resolution of the American Bar Association and the American Law Institute and has the support of the weight of scholarly opinion."

once the prisoner reached the safety of the courtroom only furnished his captors with an additional incentive to prove the charges against him by introducing statements he made before he left the stationhouse:

[N]o *legal* means is available for confronting the accused with the charge against him, challenging him to explain the evidence pointing to his guilt, interrogating him as to incriminating circumstances, and producing in evidence against him at the trial his refusal to explain or answer.[5] . . . It is not strange that judges are reluctant to compel the police, whose coercive methods are productive of confessions, to observe the rule requiring prompt presentment before a magistrate in whose presence the prisoner can bask in privileged silence.

. . . .

. . . From the viewpoint of police psychology it appears that inauguration of a scheme of magisterial interrogation will greatly weaken the police motive for private interrogation since that motive will find vicarious expression in a substituted device. Viewing the problem historically, Dean Pound ascribes the extra-legal development of the "unhappy system of police examination" in the United States to the sloughing off by justices of the peace of their police powers, including examination of the accused, thereby leaving "a gap which in practice had to be filled outside of the law." The proposed plan would fill the gap which resulted from the differentiation in function between magistrate and police with the effect of forcing the police to adopt the system of extra-legal interrogations. It would vest the power of interrogation in officers who are better qualified to exercise the power of interrogation fairly and effectively. [Pp. 1238–39, 1241.]

5. Kauper noted that the Wickersham Commission had concluded, without elaboration, that "the best remedy" for the third degree "would be *enforcement of the rule* that every person arrested charged with crime should be forthwith taken before a magistrate, advised of the charge against him, given the right to have counsel and then *interrogated by the magistrate*" (p. 1238, quoting WICKERSHAM REPORT, *supra* footnote 1, at 5 (emphasis by Kauper)). But he viewed the Commission's conclusion as a misstatement of existing law with respect to preliminary examination, for at that stage "no judicial pressure of any kind can be brought to bear on the accused to make him speak" (p. 1238).

See also the reaction of Kauper's teacher and future colleague, John Barker Waite: "Unfortunately for the helpfulness of [the Commission's] suggestion, there is no such rule to be enforced. . . . [T]he Commission seems to have forgotten that [the examination before the magistrate] is not an interrogation of the accused [but] a mere review of the evidence already accumulated against him to see whether it warrants holding him for further proceedings. . . . [A]fter the evidence against the accused has been presented [against him, most state statutes provide that] the accused shall be 'afforded opportunity' to make a statement if he so desires. In not half a dozen states is the magistrate authorized to examine the suspect himself, and in those he must first warn the accused of the danger of answering, and must tell him that he need not answer if he does not wish." Waite, *Report on Lawlessness in Law Enforcement*, 30 MICH. L. REV. 54, 58 (1931).

Kauper recognized the possibility that the Wickersham Commission's conclusion was a suggested *reform* of then prevailing law, not a statement that the *existing rules* be enforced. However, since all of the other requirements mentioned in the Commission's proposal "are generally recognized by rules of law now existent, the coupling of these requirements with a non-existent requirement of interrogation by the magistrate is at best seriously misleading and objectionable on that ground" (p. 1238 n.76).

Kauper discussed the issues and spelled out his remedy with remarkable clarity and candor. These may be great scholarly virtues, but they proved to be fatal "political" weaknesses. So long as interrogations remained unregulated and unscrutinized in the back room of the police station, the "legal mind," which had grown uncritically accustomed to them in that setting, was left unmoved and uninterested.[9] But once Kauper, and others advocating similar plans, "formalized" and "judicialized" the interrogation proceedings, the "legal mind" became aroused. Thus, although Kauper-type remedies offered an arrestee significantly more protection than did the typical police interrogation, at least until the eve of *Miranda,* they were beaten down—several decades before *Miranda*—to the accompaniment of cries that they were "opposed to our traditions of fair play," "contrary to the basic notions of Anglo-American procedure," and violative of the privilege against self-incrimination.[10] No opponent of these proposals, however, satisfactorily answered Kauper, who pointed out:

[E]ven by the most severe critics of modern police methods no claim has been made that private police interrogation of the accused intended to elicit a confession violates his right to counsel. A voluntary confession to the police is always admissible in evidence; where a confession is excluded it is not on the ground that the accused is denied the right to counsel but on the ground that the confession is involuntary. The same principle applies to confessions made to the magistrates. There is no reason why an interrogation aimed at obtaining a confession should be transformed in constitutional character merely by the fact that it is conducted with proper safeguards and by an officer who, on other occasions, exercises strictly judicial powers.

. . . .

. . .[C]ompulsory interrogation is forbidden on all occasions. It matters not whether it be interrogation at the trial, at the preliminary hearing, or at some police or magisterial inquisition prior to either. . . . It is submitted that we must differentiate carefully between interrogation *simpliciter* and interrogation under compulsion, and that the former does not constitute a violation of the constitutional privilege. . . . [N]o one has ever suggested that interrogation by the police of a suspect was unconstitutional, unless it was accompanied by physical violence or other unlawful pressure. It is inconceivable that express statutory authorization of magisterial interrogation designed to eliminate the abuses of police methods should be regarded as constitutionally more objectionable. [Pp. 1250, 1251.]

On the eve of *Miranda,* Chief Justice Traynor observed: "The Fifth Amendment has long been the life of the party in judicial or legislative proceedings, but it has had no life it could call its own in the pre-arraignment stage. Prosecutors seemed disposed to live happily ever after with this double standard. . . . Did we or did we not believe in the privilege against self-incrimination? There was never a real confrontation of the question so long as there was a double standard of the privilege."[11] Kauper's article, of course, was a notable exception. Indeed, he confronted the question so honestly and openly that it hurt too much.

Traynor continued:

Although we took it for granted that suspects did incriminate themselves at the prearraignment stage in fear or ignorance, so that in the courtroom they were already damned by their own admissions, we guarded their privilege in court with great ceremony. There they could keep their golden silence. The gold standard began to appear questionable only when it threatened to become a single standard, applicable at the prearraignment stage as well as in court. One seldom heard, however, that we should give thought to going off the gold standard by revising the Fifth Amendment to permit some degree of self-incrimination in open procedures, whether at the trial or pretrial stage. . . . [However], [s]uch a procedure was suggested by Kauper [in 1932] and Pound [in 1934].[6]

Kauper's article cannot be ripped from the context and the needs of his time. In the spring of 1932 the Court had not yet suggested that defendants in a capital case were denied due process when a state refused them the aid of counsel; had not yet banned "dry run" hangings, beatings, and other crude practices on the part of state officers; had not yet taken the first steps in "a movement toward new rights in a field where none existed before."[12] At the time Kauper advocated his plan he certainly had "reasonable confidence" in its constitutionality.[13] Moreover, Kauper's article was not as ambitious as the American Bar Association's *Standards for Criminal Justice,* the American Law Institute's *Model Code of Pre-Arraignment Procedure,* or even *Miranda.* It was, after all, only a remedy for the "third degree." And, as Kauper put it, "[w]hen the worst has been said about magisterial interrogation, its vices do not equal those of present police third-degree methods" (p. 1245).

The de facto inquisitorial system "had become so widespread and intrenched by [the early 1930s] that even most of its critics despaired of completely uprooting it in the foreseeable future."[14] Thus, Zechariah Chafee,

6. Traynor, *supra* footnote 3, at 674–75 & n.78. One may fairly say, however (and find much support for saying it in this very article by Traynor), that *in his time* Professor Kauper was not asking that the fifth amendment be "revised." *See generally* Breitel, *Criminal Law and Equal Justice,* 1966 UTAH L. REV. 1, 16; Hofstadter & Levittan, *Lest the Constable Blunder: A Remedial Proposal,* 20 RECORD OF N.Y.C.B.A. 629, 638 (1956). *Cf.* text at notes 27–34 *infra.*

As late as 1964 the courts were still divided on the constitutionality of comment upon silence at trial. *See* Note, *Procedural Protections of the Criminal Defendant,* 78 HARV. L. REV. 426, 448 (1964). Moreover, although it is no easy task, one may distinguish between comment on failure to testify at trial, banned by Griffin v. California, 380 U.S. 609 (1965); comment at trial on the defendant's silence during secret, unsupervised police interrogation, apparently condemned by Miranda v. Arizona, 384 U.S. 436, 468 n.37 (1966); and comment at trial on the defendant's refusal to answer questions put to him by a magistrate, or by law enforcement officers in the presence of a magistrate, prior to trial. *See* footnote 12 *infra.*

co-author of the famous report to the Wickersham Commission on "the third degree," warned:

It is hard enough to prevent policemen from using physical violence on suspects; it would be far harder to prevent them from asking a few questions. We had better get rid of the rubber hose and twenty-four-hour grillings before we undertake to compel or persuade the police to give up questioning altogether. . . .

. . . .

. . . The third degree is deeply rooted in official habits in many cities, and is not likely to disappear until the officials have been persuaded that it is bad and unnecessary.[15]

Kauper argued persuasively that "[i]f in the greater number of instances police voluntarily took the prisoner to a magistrate . . . for interrogation, police habits would be formed which would have a cumulative effect in undermining the third degree as a police institution" (p. 1243). Furthermore, "in evaluating the probable effectiveness of a system allowing magisterial interrogation, weight must be attached to the effect of the existence of such procedure on the attitude of prosecutor, judge, and magistrate toward third degree practices" (p. 1243). Moreover, "the proposed plan may be effective in helping to crystallize public opinion against the present system of police interrogation. The failure of the public to become aroused except momentarily [over reports of police lawlessness] may be attributed in part to public acquiescence in police methods as supplying a need which our formal procedure does not satisfy" (p. 1244 n.89).

I hasten to add that even after forty years—and thousands of pages of Supreme Court opinions, law review articles, empirical studies, and model codes—one need not be overly defensive about the Kauper proposal. If one were to revise it in light of subsequent developments and the great dialogue they stimulated, the "modernized" version would present an attractive alternative to the *Miranda* model.

Such revisitation and revision of the old Kauper plan has in fact occurred—most notably by two of the most eminent critics of *Escobedo* and *Miranda*, Justice Walter Schaefer and Judge Henry Friendly.[7] A modernized

7. Although arguably comment at trial upon a suspect's silence during the judicially supervised interrogation might be permitted without amending the privilege against self-incrimination, *see* footnote 12 *infra,* both proponents of the modern plan assume the need for, and propose, a constitutional amendment. *See* W. SCHAEFER, *supra* footnote 4, at 78, 80; Friendly, *supra* footnote 4, at 721–22. Judge Friendly's article (which also treats many other aspects of the fifth amendment) is a self-styled "endorsement" of Justice Schaefer's proposal for judicially supervised interrogation by the police, Friendly, *supra,* at 713, but it also constitutes a valuable clarification and embellishment of the Schaefer proposal. *See also* Hofstadter & Levittan, *supra* footnote 6, at 630, 635–36; Note, *supra* footnote 6. Hofstadter and Levittan propose police questioning in the presence of a magistrate, but would not allow comment at trial upon a suspect's

version, based largely on their writings, might take approximately the form of the five provisions that follow:

(a) *A person taken into custody because of, or charged with, a crime to which an interrogation relates, may be questioned only in the presence of and under the supervision of a judicial officer.* [8]

(b) *The person shall immediately (that is, as soon as humanly possible) be brought before a judicial officer who shall, before questioning begins, determine the existence of the grounds for detention or arrest.* [16]

(c) *The judicial officer shall give the person the familiar* Miranda *warnings and, in addition, inform him that if he is subsequently prosecuted his refusal to answer any questions will be disclosed at the trial.* [9]

"Enough has been disclosed in reported decisions to establish incontrovertibly the necessity for supervision" of police questioning. [17] But *Miranda* is satisfied even if the police conduct the waiver transaction and the subsequent interrogation *in secret.* [10] Putting aside the secrecy point for now, [18] it would

---

refusal to speak in the presence of the magistrate. Apparently the authors are content to rely on the assumption that "suspects frequently have a compulsive need to speak; certainly they would do so before a magistrate as freely as before the police." Hofstadter & Levittan, *supra,* at 636.

8. "An amendment permitting interrogation before a magistrate would not preclude earlier questioning conforming to *Miranda* although a state would be free to choose to prohibit this." Friendly, *supra* footnote 4, at 714 n.185.

The proponents of the plan recognize that "the system would be fully effective only if an adequate supply of magistrates and defenders was provided on a 24-hours-a-day, 7-days-a-week basis," but "failure to achieve perfection is scarcely a sufficient objection unless something better is in sight." Friendly, *supra,* at 714–15. *See also* W. SCHAEFER, *supra* footnote 4, at 78.

9. In order to "heighten the importance of this sanction," Judge Friendly "would leave the law that the court cannot comment on the defendant's failure to take the stand at trial where the Supreme Court has placed it. Otherwise defense counsel, knowing that his client may not testify, may think little would be lost by an additional comment on an earlier refusal to answer." Friendly, *supra* footnote 4, at 714.

10. *Miranda* does state that "[i]f the interrogation continues without the presence of an attorney and a statement is taken, a *heavy burden* rests on the government to demonstrate that the defendant knowingly and intelligently waived his [rights]," and that "[s]ince the State is responsible for establishing the isolated circumstances under which the interrogation takes place and has the only means of making available *corroborated evidence* of warnings given during incommunicado interrogation, the burden is rightly on its shoulders." Miranda v. Arizona, 384 U.S. 436, 475 (1966) (emphasis added). This language strongly suggests that, at least where feasible, law enforcement officers must stenographically or electronically record the warnings given to the suspect, as well as his response, so that they may be played back or shown to the trial court. *See, e.g.,* Thompson, *Detention After Arrest and In-Custody: Some Exclusionary Principles,* 1966 U. ILL. L.F. 390, 421. Nevertheless, although "[i]t is obvious that reliance upon the oral testimony of the officer to establish the conditions of interrogation will often lead to a swearing contest . . . which the suspect will rarely win, whether he is telling the truth or not," MODEL CODE OF PRE-ARRAIGNMENT PROCEDURE, Commentary at 140 (Tent. Draft No. 6, 1974), "most courts have held that the testimony of an officer that he gave the warnings is sufficient, and need not be corroborated." *Id.*

It is too much to expect the present Court to "rescue" *Miranda* from the niggardly interpretations of the lower courts. Although many thought language in *Miranda* resolved the matter the

seem preferable, where practicable, to bring the suspect before a judicial officer, "who can better bring home to him the seriousness of his decision to waive."[19] While the judicial officer's advice is not likely to be as emphatic as the defense lawyer's, it is likely to be clearer and more meaningful than the police officer's.

To the extent that "any lawyer worth his salt"[20] will tell his client to "keep quiet," it is no less true that any police officer "worth his salt" will be sorely tempted to get the suspect to talk. Can we really demand of our police that they unbegrudgingly and unequivocally explain to a suspect the very means he may use to frustrate them? As Dean Edward Barrett once asked: "[I]s it the duty of the police to persuade the suspect to talk or persuade him not to talk? They cannot be expected to do both."[21] Chief Judge Bazelon has put it less kindly: A system that places reliance on police warnings "place[s] a mouse under the protective custody of the cat."[22]

A system based on judicial warnings has obvious practical limitations. But as more and more courts hold, in effect, that police questioning outside the stationhouse is not "custodial,"[23] a system of judicial warnings (and/or electronic or stenographic recordings of these warnings and the ensuing proceedings[24]) becomes increasingly practicable.

A word about the substance of the warnings. Kauper, as we have seen, balked at extending the right to counsel to judicially supervised interrogation. He did so in part because he thought such a requirement would substantially impair—certainly in the eyes of the police and the public—the effectiveness of the substitute he was offering for the prevailing illegal interrogation, and in part because such a requirement seemed neither "fair" nor "feasible" in the light of "then existing values and capabilities."[25] Kauper's concern about the delay until counsel was procured—the first objection he raised to allowing the prisoner the right to counsel during magisterial interrogation[26]—must have been a weighty one in the pre-public defender days. As Chief Judge Haynsworth has said:

As our legal resources grow, there is a correlative growth in our ability to implement basic notions of fairness. Few of the concepts of due process entertained today were

---

other way, the "new" Court has held that statements obtained from a suspect in violation of *Miranda* may be used to impeach him if he subsequently takes the stand in his own defense. Harris v. New York, 401 U.S. 222 (1971), bitterly criticized in Dershowitz & Ely, Harris v. New York: *Some Anxious Observations on the Candor and Logic of the Emerging Nixon Majority*, 80 YALE L.J. 1198 (1971). And the Court may yet hold (but one hopes will not, *see* footnote 12 *infra*) that a suspect's *silence* during police custody may be used for impeachment purposes. *See, e.g.*, United States *ex rel.* Burt v. New Jersey, 475 F.2d 234 (3d Cir.), *cert. denied*, 414 U.S. 938 (1973) (Douglas, Brennan & Marshall, JJ., dissenting). I doubt that *Miranda* will be overruled, *but see* F. INBAU, J. THOMPSON, J. HADDAD, J. ZAGEL & G. STARKMAN, CASES AND COMMENTS ON CRIMINAL PROCEDURE 355 (1974). If *Miranda* does remain on the books, however, it will probably be only because easy waiver and other eroding interpretations have sufficiently soothed its critics on the Court.

born full blown. They grew. The transition from *Betts v. Brady*[27] to *Gideon v. Wainwright*[28] to *Argersinger v. Hamlin*[29] is an example. The Bar is large enough and strong enough now to meet the requirements of *Gideon* and *Argersinger;* it well may not have been even a few years ago.[30]

A close student of the right-to-counsel problem has suggested that the difference between Justices Black and Frankfurter in the 1942 *Betts* case may "have come down to a question of timing."[31] Frankfurter might have felt that "the country was not ready for a universal requirement of counsel in serious criminal cases [not even at the *trial* stage]; the bar was not prepared for such a burden; the states would have resisted, and the decision would have been widely ignored."[32] What, then, might be said of the dark days before *Powell v. Alabama*[33] and *Johnson v. Zerbst?*[34]

The right to counsel at a judicially supervised interrogation is surely "fair" and "feasible" today. And it is unlikely that such a safeguard would defeat the purpose of Kauper's proposal. " '[A]ny lawyer worth his salt' [would] have to reflect on the damage his client might suffer from having his refusal to answer disclosed at the trial."[35] Moreover, a lawyer would have to consider that any story that his client was able to produce immediately after arrest and that the police could not disprove in their investigations would be more convincing than his trial testimony weeks or months later, after he had had ample opportunity to prepare the most plausible defense.[36]

(d) *A complete written record shall be kept of the judicial examination; the information of rights, any waiver thereof, and any questioning shall be recorded upon a sound recording device; and the suspect shall be so informed.*

Kauper made plain that "a complete record should be kept of the interrogation" (p. 1248)[37] and that the suspect should be informed that "the whole record of the interrogation will go to the trial court" (p. 1240). I am confident that if audio or video tape had been available at the time, he would have required that the judicial examination be so recorded. This feature of the Kauper plan underscores a major weakness of *Miranda,* at least as interpreted by the lower courts.[38]

Allowing the police to give legal advice to, and obtain "waivers" from, suspects outside the presence of any judicial officer is troublesome enough. It seems inconsistent with *Miranda*'s reliance on the analogy of the trial[39] and with the police function.[40] The problem is aggravated when, even though feasible, no stenographic transcript (let alone an electronic recording) of the "waiver transaction" need be made; when no disinterested observer (let alone a judicial officer) need be present; when—as most lower courts have held— the police officer's disputed and uncorroborated recollections of the "waiver" event suffice.[41] Thus, a cogent criticism of the old "voluntariness" test applies to *Miranda* as well:

No other case comes to mind in which an administrative official is permitted the broad discretionary power assumed by the police interrogator, together with the power to prevent objective recordation of the facts. . . . It is secrecy, not privacy, which accounts for the absence of a reliable record of interrogation proceedings in a police station. If the need for some pre-judicial questioning is assumed, privacy may be defended on grounds of necessity; secrecy cannot be defended on this or any other ground. [42]

Lack of judicial supervision or objective recordation raises doubts not only about the validity of the waiver, but about the propriety of the post-waiver proceedings as well. Once the suspect agrees to answer questions (as he often will, or at least as the police will often persuade the trier of fact that he did), may the police display apparent sympathy, show the suspect incriminating physical evidence, inform him that an accomplice is also being questioned, pretend that the accomplice has already confessed, or understate the seriousness of the suspect's situation (by, for example, withholding information that the victim of his assault has died)?[43] It is bad enough that the legality of the kinds of cajolery to which the police may resort following warnings and a waiver, is, at this late date, "largely unresolved."[44] Worse—indeed, indefensible—is that the courts still have to evaluate these post-waiver interrogation techniques not in the light of who said *exactly what, precisely how,* but "in the dark of what might or might not have happened."[45]

There are few dissents, if any, from the view that one or more police officers (and there are often more than one) usually fare better in a "swearing contest" than does the lone defendant. But not *all* defendants make poor witnesses. Nor do *all* police officers cut impressive figures in the courtroom, instilling confidence in the trier of fact. I share the view that most trial judges are "functionally and psychologically allied with the police,"[46] but not all judges are fungible. Those who sit on most of our large urban courts come increasingly (albeit still disproportionately) from all social strata and all types of practice—with different predispositions. *Some* are highly skeptical of the police. *Some,* as my prosecutor friends insist, may even be downright hostile. Thus judicial supervision and recording of police interrogations may also redound to the benefit of the police by aborting dishonest claims of police intimidation or deception.[47]

I am aware that the *Miranda* Court was probably affected by cries of powerful voices to "go slow," and troubled by cries of powerful voices that it had already gone too far. Indeed, I suspect that one or two of the Justices who made up the 5–4 *Miranda* majority seriously considered turning back. I realize, too, although one would gain little inkling of it from the hue and cry that greeted that much-maligned case, that *Miranda* marked a "compromise" between the old "voluntariness" test (and the objectionable police interrogation tactics it permitted in fact) and extreme proposals that—as the fear (or hope) was expressed at the time—would have "killed" confessions. On the eve of *Miranda* there may have been reason to believe that "the doctrines converging upon the institution of police interrogation [were] threatening to push on to their logical conclusion—to the point where no questioning of suspects [would] be permitted,"[48] but *Miranda* fell well short of that point.

Miranda did not, and did not try to, "kill" confessions. It left the police free to hear and act upon "volunteered" statements, even though the "volunteer" had been taken into custody and neither knew nor was informed of his rights to counsel and to remain silent;[11] it allowed the police to conduct "[g]eneral on-the-scene questioning"[49] or "other general questioning of citizens,"[50] even though the citizen was both uninformed and unaware of his

11. Not a few of the post-*Miranda* generation may be incredulous that the admissibility of "volunteered" statements was ever in doubt. But it was—until the Court shifted from the "prime suspect"-"focal point"-"accusatory state" test(s) of Escobedo v. Illinois, 378 U.S. 478 (1964), to the "custodial interrogation" standard of *Miranda,* or, to characterize it another way, moved from a right-to-counsel base in *Escobedo* to a self-incrimination base in *Miranda. See generally* Kamisar, *"Custodial Interrogation" Within the Meaning of* Miranda, in CRIMINAL LAW AND THE CONSTITUTION 335, 338-51 (Inst. Cont. Legal Educ. ed. 1968).

Justice White had cause to protest in *Escobedo*:

At the very least the Court holds that once the accused becomes a suspect and, presumably, is arrested, any admission made to the police thereafter is inadmissible in evidence unless the accused has waived his right to counsel. The decision is thus another major step in the direction of the goal which the Court seemingly has in mind—to bar from evidence all admissions obtained from an individual suspected of crime, whether involuntarily made or not.

378 U.S. at 495 (dissenting opinion, joined by Clark & Stewart, JJ.). *See also* the then justified doubts and fears voiced in Enker & Elsen, *Counsel for the Suspect:* Massiah v. United States *and* Escobedo v. Illinois, 49 MINN. L. REV. 47, 60-61, 69, 83 (1964) (Court may be in process of shaping "a novel right not to confess except knowingly and with the tactical assistance of counsel"), and, on the eve of *Miranda,* in Traynor, *supra* footnote 3, at 669-73.

On digesting *Miranda,* James R. Thompson [now Governor of Illinois], who had the distinction of making the losing argument in *Escobedo* (but who, I venture to say, made the best argument any lawyer could have made for the State of Illinois), asked: "While the court holds that the police need not stop the person who volunteers information (and presumably holds that the warnings need not be given to such people), does not this concession, while it assumes the statement to be voluntary, fail to take account of the fact that a statement may be volunteered in ignorance of the privilege against self-incrimination and 'of the consequences of foregoing it'?" Thompson, *supra* footnote 10, at 422 (footnote omitted). The Court's answer, I take it, would be that (at this state of the criminal process, at least) the privilege does not protect a person from *unintentionally* incriminating himself but only from being *compelled* to incriminate himself. *See* Hoffa v. United States, 385 U.S. 293, 303-04 (1966). *Cf.* Graham, *What Is "Custodial Interrogation?": California's Anticipatory Application of* Miranda v. Arizona, 14 UCLA L. REV. 59, 76-77 (1966).

Moreover, absent interrogation the coercion of arrest and dentention does not rise to the level of "compulsion" within the meaning of the privilege. Thus, as Justice White points out in his *Miranda* dissent, a suspect "may blurt out [an admissible] confession despite the fact that he is alone and in custody, without any showing that he had any notion of his right to remain silent or of the consequences of his admission." Miranda v. Arizona, 384 U.S. 436, 533 (1966). *But see* MODEL CODE OF PRE-ARRAIGNMENT PROCEDURE § 120.8 (Proposed Official Draft No. 1, 1972); *id.* § 130.1 (Tent. Draft No. 6, 1974); UNIFORM RULES OF CRIMINAL PROCEDURE 212, 241 (Proposed Final Draft, 1974), recommending that, in order to relieve the suspect of some of the confusion and anxiety he may feel following arrest and arrival at the police station, he should be given certain advice at these stages *whether or not any questioning is attempted.*

rights; and, even when the proceedings moved to the station house, and police interrogators were admittedly bent on eliciting incriminating statements from the prime suspect, it allowed them to obtain waivers of the privilege and the assistance of counsel *without the advice or presence of counsel, without the advice or presence of a judicial officer,* and evidently *without any objective recordation of the proceedings.* [51] And yet one heard the question after *Miranda,* "Are confessions dead?"

It may be that in the midst of the "raging controversial process" of redetermining the conformity of our criminal procedure to our ideals, [52] the *Miranda* Court thought it prudent to reserve amplification and reinforcement of the *Miranda* plan for another day, [53] underestimating the risk that there might not be another day. It may well be that at the time it was impossible to persuade a majority of the Court to go an inch further than it did. Moreover, whether the Court should have explicitly required the police to make either tape or verbatim stenographic recordings of interrogations, thus adding fuel to the criticism that it was "legislating," is surely one of those "damned if it did" and "damned if it didn't" issues.

Nevertheless, I still believe, as I did before *Miranda,* that "[i]n the long run, no statute, court rule, or court decision pertaining to warnings or waivers will suffice—for the same reason that the flood of appellate opinions on 'involuntary' confessions have not sufficed—until police interrogation is stripped of its 'most unique feature . . . its characteristic secrecy.'" [54] The Kauper-Schaefer-Friendly proposal does something about this; *Miranda* does not.

(e) *The questions shall be asked by police officers or prosecuting attorneys rather than the judicial officer, but only in the presence of the judicial officer, who may intervene to prevent abuse.*

While Kauper preferred interrogation by a magistrate (pp. 1246–47), this was not of vital concern to him. His main objective was a procedure for interrogation by or *under the supervision of* a judicial officer. He was aware of the arguments that "the prosecutor would be more adept in questioning prisoners" and that if the prosecutor were assigned this task "the magistrate would have less reason to lose his quality of judicial disinterestedness" (p. 1246). Such an alternative was acceptable to him, "provided that the plan were flexible enough to allow the magistrate to interrogate if the prosecutor were unable to be present . . . , for questioning loses much of its value unless it takes place immediately" (p. 1246). (Evidently Kauper balked at authorizing interrogation by the police of his time even in the presence of a magistrate.)

Today, at least, it seems preferable for law enforcement officers to conduct the inquiry. They are better trained and more practiced; they "will know what information is relevant and what direction that inquiries should take." [55] Moreover, "questioning by a judge tends to lapse into partisanship"; [56] the risk would be much greater that the magistrate "might come to feel responsible for the successful outcome of the interrogation from a police point of view."[57]

If *Miranda*'s denial that the "Constitution necessarily requires adherence to any particular solution for the inherent compulsions of the interrogation process as it is presently conducted"[58] is to be taken seriously, the Kauper-Schaefer-Friendly model presents a real alternative. Although the constitutional problems posed by comment at trial upon the suspect's silence during the judicially supervised examination are formidable, they may not be insurmountable.[12] It would be somewhat ironic if the comment provision cannot

12. One may agree that even so mild a "compulsion" as comment upon failure to testify should not be exerted on a defendant to take the stand at trial "so long as the prosecution may bring out an entire criminal history, including crimes unrelated to that with which he is charged and having no real tendency to reflect on his veracity," Friendly, *supra* footnote 4, at 699, yet find such "compulsion" tolerable at the judicially supervised interrogation, where no jury sits to be prejudiced by "other crimes" evidence. *Cf.* Breitel, *supra* footnote 6, at 6–7. The fears that a defendant's demeanor on the witness stand might do his cause a fatal disservice or that unfair cross-examination might induce an innocent defendant to give an appearance of guilt seem exaggerated. *See, e.g.,* W. SCHAEFER, *supra* footnote 4, at 66–67; Note, *supra* footnote 6, at 447. But in any event, comment on refusal to speak at the judicially supervised interrogation will not pressure a defendant to exhibit his nervousness, confusion, and embarrassment before the ultimate triers of fact. Six years ago [1968] it seemed "unrealistic" to expect "the present Court" to draw a distinction between comment on failure to testify at trial and refusal to respond before a magistrate, Friendly, *supra,* at 713 n.180, but "the present Court" no longer sits. The two *Griffin* dissenters (Stewart and White) still do, along with four new members. *Cf.* Friendly, *Time and Tide in the Supreme Court,* 2 CONN. L. REV. 213, 219–20 (1969).

Presumably, under the Kauper-Schaefer-Friendly plan a defendant would be allowed to take the stand for the limited purpose of explaining away his silence before the magistrate. Opposition to trial comment on a defendant's refusal to respond before the magistrate might be further reduced if the trial judge had to determine the admissibility of the silence as evidence of a feeling of guilt in light of the external circumstances surrounding the alleged guilt and the defendant's personal traits. Opposition might also lessen if the defendant were permitted, prior to the ruling on admissibility, to offer evidence explaining his silence for reasons other than guilt. *Cf. Developments in the Law—Confessions,* 79 HARV. L. REV. 935, 1039 (1966).

If it turns out that comment on refusal to respond before a magistrate is constitutionally barred, another route may be available. "A tremendous proportion of defendants" do testify at trial, especially when they have no criminal records. Friendly, *supra,* at 700, *relying, inter alia, on* H. KALVEN & H. ZEISEL, THE AMERICAN JURY 137, 146 (1966). Sufficient pressure might be exerted on a defendant to speak at the judicial examination if his refusal to speak were to be used for impeachment purposes if and when he took the stand at trial. This route, too, is not clear of constitutional obstacles. Perhaps a more formidable barrier than even *Miranda* or *Griffin* is Grunewald v. United States, 353 U.S. 391 (1957), holding that a defendant's refusal to answer grand jury questions on fifth amendment grounds cannot be used to impeach his later trial testimony. *But cf.* Harris v. New York, 401 U.S. 222 (1971), discussed in footnote 10 *supra.* Although the Court drew upon its supervisory power over the administration of federal criminal justice in *Grunewald,* it felt justified in passing on a question "usually within the discretion of the trial judge" because "such evidentiary matter has grave constitutional overtones." 353 U.S. at 423–24. The Court, however, declined to reexamine Raffel v. United States, 271 U.S. 494

pass constitutional muster, for it is not at all clear that such a provision would put more pressure on a suspect to talk than does the present system.

Miranda recognizes that many suspects will assume that "silence in the face of accusation is itself damning and will bode ill when presented to a jury"[59] (and especially, one might add, when presented to a police officer or prosecutor). It also informs trial judges and prosecutors that a suspect's "[standing]

(1926), permitting the defendant's failure to take the stand at his first trial to be used for impeachment purposes when he testified at his second trial. *Grunewald* distinguished grand jury and other "secret proceedings," where a person testifies without the advice of counsel or other procedural safeguards, from "open court proceedings." 353 U.S. at 422–23. Arguably (although I would not like to have to make the argument), judicially supervised interrogation under the Kauper-Schaefer-Friendly plan might be viewed as more akin to a trial situation than to a grand jury or other "secret proceedings."

Judges Friendly and Schaefer seem resigned to the fact that their plan would require a constitutional amendment. *See* footnote 7 *supra*. Whether or not the arguments suggested above have persuaded anyone else that constitutional amendment is unnecessary, they have not convinced me. But these arguments should not be dismissed lightly. A state statute authorizing comment on refusal to respond before a magistrate (or the use of such refusal for impeachment purposes) in the context of the Kauper-Schaefer-Friendly plan might well pass constitutional muster. "[T]he fully formal action of a state legislature [as opposed to the informal, extralegal practices of the police] has a considerable weight; it represents the best and most authentic judgment of the state as a political body." C. BLACK, STRUCTURE AND RELATIONSHIP IN CONSTITUTIONAL LAW 87–88 (1969). An even stronger case, of course, can be made if the Kauper-Schaefer-Friendly plan is enacted by the Congress under its section five power to enforce the fourteenth amendment. *See* C. BLACK, *supra*, at 88–93 (viewing the complete neglect of the problem by the legislative branch as "what is most fundamentally wrong with such situations as those [*Miranda*] set out to correct," and maintaining that the "Court would very seriously respect and in large measure defer to" a good-faith effort to deal with the problem by Congress under its section five power); Burt, *Miranda and Title II: A Morganatic Marriage,* 1969 SUP. CT. REV. 81, 123–34 (extraordinarily skillful, though at times highly strained, "suggested reading" of Title II of the Crime Control Act of 1968, 18 U.S.C. § 3501 (1970)—a purported "repeal" of *Miranda*—"to fit it into the mold" of Katzenbach v. Morgan, 384 U.S. 641 (1966); Professor Burt's discussion would apply a fortiori to a Congressional enactment under section five of the Kauper-Schaefer-Friendly plan, which—*unlike* Title II, I submit, Professor Burt's heroic undertaking to the contrary notwithstanding—certainly would achieve *Miranda's* "general protective purposes"). *See also* C. BLACK, PERSPECTIVES IN CONSTITUTIONAL LAW 106–07 (rev. ed. 1969); Cox, *Constitutional Adjudications and the Promotion of Human Rights,* 80 HARV. L. REV. 91, 106 n.86, 108 (1966); Kurland, Book Review, 34 U. CHI. L. REV. 704, 709 (1967).

Although the Kauper-Schaefer-Friendly plan merits the most serious consideration, I submit that the same cannot be said for either the constitutionality or the desirability of a rule permitting a suspect's silence during secret, unsupervised police interrogation (evidently allowed by *Miranda*) to be used to impeach his trial testimony. *Compare* United States *ex rel.* Burt v. New Jersey, 475 F.2d 234 (3d Cir.), *cert. denied,* 414 U.S. 938 (1973) (Douglas, Brennan & Marshall, JJ., dissenting), *with* Johnson v. Patterson, 475 F.2d 1066 (10th Cir.), *cert. denied,* 414 U.S. 878 (1973), *and* United States v. Hale, 498 F.2d 1038 (D.C. Cir.), *cert. granted,* 43 U.S.L.W. 3325 (U.S. Dec. 9, 1974) (No. 74-364). For one thing, *Grunewald* would seem to apply a fortiori. *See* 87 HARV. L. REV. 882, 885–86 (1974). For another, even if he were allowed to do so, the suspect's subsequent efforts to explain that his silence was attributable to any one of a variety of causes, ranging from not hearing or misunderstanding the officer to fear of reprisals from others,

mute or claim[ing] his privilege in the face of accusation" may not be used against him at trial.[60] But it nowhere requires that a law enforcement officer *advise a suspect* to this effect.[61] "[W]hat a suspect is going to ask himself most urgently at the police station is: 'How do I get out of this mess and avoid looking guilty?'"[62] How, indeed?

How did he get out of, or try to get out of, every other "mess" in his life? As a child did he remain silent when accused by an angry parent, or did he try to talk his way out of it? As an adult did he remain silent when confronted by a disgruntled employer or a suspicious spouse or did he try to talk his way out of it? Absent adequate assurances on this point, is a suspect going to risk "looking guilty" by standing on his rights, or is he going to proceed on the assumptions and habits of a lifetime?

Supplementing the present warnings might help some, but can any set of

---

see Traynor, *supra* footnote 3, at 26, would trigger still another "swearing contest" (*e.g.*, the suspect insisting that he was frightened and bewildered at the interrogation but the officer maintaining that he looked and acted calm and collected). Moreover, the idea that the accused's silence during police interrogation could be used against him at trial is currently being raised in the context of the familiar *Miranda* warnings; "it would be grossly unfair to advise an accused simply that he had 'a right to remain silent,' and then use his silence against him at trial without at the very least having also informed him that if he chooses to exercise his right he may subsequently be impeached by that fact." United States v. Hale, 498 F.2d 1038, 1044 (D.C. Cir.), *cert. granted*, 43 U.S.L.W. 3325 (U.S. Dec. 9, 1974) (No. 74-364).

The *Miranda* warnings could, of course, be revised prospectively, *cf.* CRIMINAL LAW REVISION COMMITTEE [Gr. Br.], ELEVENTH REPORT, EVIDENCE (GENERAL) 16-34 (1972), proposing that adverse inferences may be drawn from a suspect's silence when interrogated, and that the Judges' Rules be modified accordingly. However, such a revision might only aggravate existing problems. Can a police officer be trusted to explain to a suspect how he can have "a right to remain silent" and still have his silence used against him at trial? And even if an officer does his very best to explain, can the average suspect be expected to understand? The available empirical data indicate that a large number of police officers do not give the silence or counsel warnings at all, and many who do do not give them in a meaningful way; moreover, a significant percentage of suspects either misunderstand the existing warnings or fail to appreciate their significance. *See, e.g.*, Leiken, *Police Interrogation in Colorado: The Implementations of* Miranda, 47 DENVER L.J. 1, 15-16, 33 (1970); Medalie, Zeitz & Alexander, *Custodial Interrogation in Our Nation's Capital: The Attempt To Implement* Miranda, 66 MICH. L. REV. 1347, 1375 (1969); Project, *Interrogations in New Haven: The Impact of* Miranda, 76 YALE L.J. 1519, 1550-54, 1571-72, 1613-15 (1967). In this light, how can anyone seriously suggest that we make the *Miranda* warnings significantly more complicated, yet continue to rely on the uncorroborated oral testimony of the police officer to establish the legality of the questioning?

[*Some months after this article was written, the Court handed down United States v. Hale, 422 U.S. 171 (1975), holding, in the exercise of its supervisory powers over the lower federal courts—and without deciding whether* Miranda *mandated such a result—that under the circumstances of the case it was reversible error to cross-examine defendant about his silence during police interrogation. The following Term, in Doyle v. Ohio, 426 U.S. 610 (1976), the Court ruled that when a suspect has been advised of his rights and chooses to remain silent, the subsequent use of his post-arrest silence to impeach an explanation he offers at his trial deprives him of due process.*]

warnings help enough? If, as *Miranda* assumes with good reason, "a once-stated warning [that a suspect has a right to remain silent], delivered by those who will conduct the interrogation, cannot itself suffice" to guarantee that "the individual's right to choose between silence and speech remains unfettered throughout the interrogation process,"[63] it is not readily apparent why a "once-stated warning" that a suspect has a right to remain silent *and* a right to the presence of counsel is supposed to suffice. It is unclear why this or any other series of warnings cannot also "be swiftly overcome by the secret interrogation process."[64] For, "if a choice made with respect to the question of whether or not to cooperate with the police cannot be voluntary if one is confronted with it by the police without the guidance of counsel, how can the choice to dispense with counsel be voluntary in the same circumstances? And won't it be precisely the persons who are most likely to be 'compelled' to cooperate by the subtle coercion of custody who will be 'compelled' by the same subtle coercion to waive the right to counsel itself?"[13]

Police-issued warnings may mitigate—but cannot be expected to dispel fully—"the compulsion inherent in custodial surroundings,"[65] certainly not when, as apparently is often the case, such warnings are delivered in a tone and manner that geld them of much of their meaning or are accompanied by "hedging" that undermines their purpose.[66] Thus, borrowing language from *Miranda,* one may forcefully contend that "as a practical matter, the compulsion to speak in the isolated setting of a police station," even when supposedly offset by warnings, may still be "greater than in courts or other official investigations"—or at a judicially supervised interrogation—where there are "impartial observers to guard against intimidation or trickery."[67]

Assuming arguendo that the comment on the suspect's silence authorized by the Kauper-Schaefer-Friendly plan exerts significantly greater "compulsion" to speak than that allowed to operate under *Miranda*—the informal pressure to "avoid looking guilty" when confronted by anyone in authority under any circumstances and the additional "compulsion" inherent in police custodial surroundings—the comment feature should not be judged and condemned in a vacuum. It is only a small part of an attractive package whose provisions for judicial warnings, judicial supervision of any ensuing interrogation, and objective recording of the entire proceeding seem inherently stronger than the *Miranda* requirements, at least as the latter have generally been applied. Not only does the Kauper-Schaefer-Friendly model go a considerable distance toward investing the interrogation proceedings with the "protective openness and formalities of a court trial,"[68] but it "tend[s] to promote the speedy production of the suspect before a magistrate,"[69] offers "the most efficient way of providing legal counsel upon arrest,"[70] and "meets the equal

13. MODEL CODE OF PRE-ARRAIGNMENT PROCEDURE, Commentary at 40 (Study Draft No. 1, 1968).

protection argument; the rich man and the professional criminal could no longer remain silent without adverse consequences."[71]

For purposes of these remarks, however, the relative merits of the Kauper and *Miranda* models are really beside the point. The point is that two of the most thoughtful judges and legal commentators of our time—two of the leading participants in "a massive re-examination of criminal law enforcement procedures on a scale never before witnessed"[14]—in effect returned to and built upon the Kauper proposal. What more can one say about a forty-year-old article, written in the most explosive field of the law before the first explosion was heard? What more can one say of the man who wrote it as a third-year law student?

14. Miranda v. Arizona, 384 U.S. 436, 523 (1966) (Harlan, Stewart & White, JJ., dissenting) (referring, *inter alia*, to the American Bar Association's project on *Standards for Criminal Justice* and the American Law Institute's *Model Code of Pre-Arraignment Procedure* project).

Judge Friendly and Justice Schaefer played major roles in the Model Code project, as members of the project's Advisory Committee and the Institute's Council, ever since the project was launched in the spring of 1965. Justice Schaefer was also Chairman of the ABA project's Advisory Committee on the Criminal Trial, which prepared four reports between 1964 and 1968. Judge Friendly's *The Bill of Rights as a Code of Criminal Procedure*, 53 CALIF. L. REV. 929 (1965), not only served as a rallying point for critics of the Warren Court's work in the criminal procedure field, but shook (or should have shaken) the Court's warmest admirers.

Fred E. Inbau:
"The Importance of Being Guilty"*

July, 1977

*"The scholar may lose himself in schools, in words
and become a pedant; but when he comprehends his
duties, he above all men is a realist."*

—Ralph Waldo Emerson

AS FATE WOULD HAVE IT, Fred Inbau graduated from law school in 1932, the
very year that "for practical purposes the modern law of constitutional criminal procedure [began] with the decision in the great case of *Powell v.
Alabama.*" [1] In "the 'stone age' of American criminal procedure," [2] Inbau
began his long fight to shape or to retain rules that "make sense in the light of
a policeman's task," [3] more aware than most that so long as the rules do so,
"we will be in a stronger position to insist that [the officer] obey them." [4]

Inbau was a pioneer in American constitutional criminal procedure and
something of a prophet. He discerned events in their beginnings, he foresaw
what was coming, and he forewarned others.

*[Another] general trend has been the Burger Court's concern with what I call the importance
of being guilty.... From the defense point of view this means that in the argument of a case at
the appellate level it is extraordinarily important today, as it really was not in the 1960's, to try
to establish for the client a tolerable claim of innocence. Looking at the same litigation from the
State's point of view, the State representative in appellate litigation today should be clear in
arguing that regardless of what occurred in the proceedings, the individual defendant before the
court is a guilty individual.... That kind of argument is likely to be persuasive with the Burger
Court in a way that it clearly would not have been with the Warren Court.

Whitebread, *Trends in Constitutional Law: A Forecast,* in CONSTITUTIONAL LAW DESKBOOK 9-1
(National College of District Attorneys ed. 1977). *See also* Friendly, *Is Innocence Irrelevant?
Collateral Attack on Criminal Judgments,* 38 U. CHI. L. REV. 142 (1970).

The argument that "the individual defendant before the court is a guilty individual" can carry
only so far. That it did not prevail in the recent case of Brewer v. Williams, 430 U.S. 387 (1977),
hardly refutes Professor Whitebread's point. If anything, the fact that "Williams is guilty of the
savage murder of a small child; no member of the Court contends that he is not,"*id.* at 416
(Burger, C.J., dissenting), persuaded, or helped persuade, four Justices to uphold the admissibility of the confession in the face of "so clear a violation of the Sixth and Fourteenth Amendments
as here occurred," *id.* at 406 (Stewart, J., majority opinion), tends to support Whitebread's view.

Inbau, of course, would have no trouble at all upholding Williams's confession. Indeed, the
detective's "Christian burial speech" ("[Y]ou yourself are the only person that knows where this
little girl's body is ... I feel [that the parents] should be entitled to a Christian burial for [their]
little girl [and that] we should stop and locate it on the way ... ") reads like an Inbau hypothetical. The "speech" would only get results if Williams were guilty; it "did not, and was not likely
to, jeopardize the fairness of [Williams's] trial or in any way risk the conviction of an innocent

This is evident in his 1942 book, *Lie Detection and Criminal Interrogation,* [5] where he sought to to classify the kinds of cajolery and deception to which the police interrogator might and must not resort—and to explain why—an issue which at this late date is still "largely unresolved." [1] It is evident, too, in Inbau's famous 1948 article, "The Confession Dilemma in the United States Supreme Court," [6] where, drawing upon his rich law enforce-

---

man," 430 U.S. at 437 (White, J., joined by Blackmun and Rehnquist, JJ., dissenting). And Inbau's "test of confession admissibility" has long been:

> *"Is what I am about to do or say apt to make an innocent person confess?"*
> If the answer to the above question is "No," the interrogator should go ahead and do or say whatever was contemplated. . . .
> In our judgment this is the only understandable test of confession admissibility. . . . Moreover, it is also the only test that is fair both to the public and to the accused. . . .

F. INBAU & J. REID, CRIMINAL INTERROGATION AND CONFESSIONS 157 (1st ed. 1962). Although this was the original meaning of the "voluntariness" test, it cannot be squared, I submit, with what the Court had been doing in the fifteen years preceding Escobedo v. Illinois, 378 U.S. 478 (1964), nor even, perhaps, what it did as early as Ashcraft v. Tennessee, 322 U.S. 143 (1944). *See* A. BEISEL, CONTROL OVER ILLEGAL ENFORCEMENT OF THE CRIMINAL LAW: ROLE OF THE SUPREME COURT 70-86 (1955); Allen, *Due Process and State Criminal Procedures: Another Look,* 48 Nw. U.L. REV. 16, 20-25 (1953); Allen, *The Supreme Court, Federalism and State Systems of Criminal Justice,* 8 DE PAUL L. REV. 213, 233-40 (1959); Meltzer, *Involuntary Confessions: The Allocation of Responsibility Between Judge and Jury,* 21 U. CHI. L. REV. 317, 326-29, 343, 347-49 (1954); Paulsen, *The Fourteenth Amendment and the Third Degree,* 6 STAN L. REV. 411, 417-23 (1954). *See generally* Kamisar, *What Is an "Involuntary" Confession?* 17 RUTGERS L. REV. 728 (1963) [reprinted in this volume]. *See also* Kamisar, *A Confession's Trustworthiness, It is Argued, Isn't Enough,* N.Y. Times, May 14, 1977, at 19, col. 2.

[*A few months later, after reading the newspaper reports of Williams's second trial, I realized that when I had likened the police tactics in* Brewer v. Williams *to "an Inbau hypothetical" because "the 'speech' would only get results of Williams were guilty," I had spoken too quickly. For Williams's contentions at his second trial (see p. 113 fn. 2 infra of this volume), whether or not true, illustrate how one may dispose of a murder victim's body without necessarily being guilty of the underlying murder.*]

1. H. UVILLER, THE PROCESS OF CRIMINAL JUSTICE: INVESTIGATION 569 (1974). "Oddly," notes Professor Uviller, "the few [post-*Miranda*] lower court decisions addressing deception in interrogation seem reluctant to forbid all forms of misrepresentation, particularly [when] neither shocking nor of the sort which creates the hazard that the innocent suspect might be induced to confess falsely." *Id. See* Frazier v. Cupp, 394 U.S. 731 (1969) (admitting a confession in a pre-*Miranda* case although the police had falsely told the defendant that another had confessed and had also "sympathetically" suggested that the victim's homosexual advances may have started the fight). *See also* Oregon v. Mathiason, 429 U.S. 492 (1977) (per curiam) (holding that *Miranda* warnings need not have been given under the circumstances). "Whatever relevance [the interrogator's false statement to defendant that his fingerprints had been discovered at the scene] may have to other issues in the case, it has nothing to do with whether [defendant] was in custody for purposes of the *Miranda* rule." *Id.* at 714.

[*Two years after this article was written, Professor Welsh White made a major effort to bring order to the chaos in this area, focusing on the kinds of police interrogation techniques, if any, that ought not to be allowed even after a suspect has "waived" his constitutional rights.* White, Police Trickery in Inducing Confessions, *127 U. PA. L. REV. 581 (1979). Professor White con-*

ment background, he roundly condemned the *McNabb* decision[7] on the very grounds upon which the *Mallory* case[8] was criticized fourteen years later and for the very reasons that the so-called *McNabb-Mallory* rule was repealed, more or less, some twenty-five years later. [9]

Inbau's pioneering spirit was also evident in his very first classes at the Northwestern University School of Law. So one of his most illustrious students, Frank Allen, himself a great explorer and early pathfinder in this field, has often told me. Inbau wrung dry the relatively few Supreme Court cases then on the books, perceiving and fretting over all their "dangerous" implications. Long before there were any courses or casebooks bearing that title, Inbau taught criminal procedure and its constitutional dimensions—all the while he yearned for, and fought for, the day when criminal procedure would have no (or at least very few) constitutional dimensions.

How did his students receive him? How did the world receive him? Inbau is—well, Inbau. In the classroom, no less than outside, he was (depending upon your point of view), amusing or exasperating, sensible or outrageous, inspiring or infuriating. Whatever the various reactions he engenders, however, I doubt that any of his students could forget him or his subject matter or how deeply he cared about it. Many of his students, hopefully, were less impressed than he with "the importance of being guilty," but (long before this could be said of most law faculties) all of his students, happily, were bound to be impressed with the importance of constitutional criminal procedure.

McNabb (1943) and *Ashcraft* (1944)[10] greatly worried Inbau. Although the *McNabb-Mallory* rule, which held inadmissible in federal courts incriminating statements made during unlawful detentions, was fashioned "quite apart from the Constitution"[11] and in the exercise of the Court's "supervisory authority over the administration of [federal] criminal justice,"[12] Inbau feared that some day the Court would find it mandated by the "minimal historical safeguards . . . summarized as 'due process of law,'"[13] and thus binding on state courts as well as federal. *Ashcraft* alarmed him no less than *McNabb*. The *Ashcraft* Court had branded thirty-six hours of continuous police interrogation "inherently" or "conclusively" coercive, and Inbau feared that some day the Court would regard all extended police questioning—maybe even any police questioning—"inherently coercive." To Inbau, then, *McNabb* and *Ashcraft* were unexploded grenades rolling around in the interrogation room—and he reacted accordingly. Inbau thought, as did I (arriving on the scene much later), that *McNabb* would explode first,[14] but

---

cludes, inter alia, *that because they are "inherently unfair" or tend to "render the resulting confession involuntary" or to "negate the effect of protections provided by the fifth and sixth amendments," several widely used interrogation techniques (such as the "Mutt and Jeff" routine, recommended by the Inbau-Reid and other manuals) should be "absolutely prohibited."* See especially id. *at 581–86, 608–11, 624–29.*]

we now know that it only fizzled. The live bomb, and the bigger one, turned out to be that contained in *Ashcraft*.[15]

The only thing I have ever found surprising about the *Ashcraft* case is that three Justices dissented.[16] I wish a tape recording of this long stretch of questioning had been available and that the Justices had listened to it, much as they view "dirty movies" in a screening room set up for that purpose. Whether or not a Justice can intelligibly define "coercive questioning," I think he would "know it" when he heard it.[17]

I have often played portions of the tape-recorded six-hour interrogation in the *Biron* murder case[2] to my students. The interrogators neither engaged in nor threatened any violence, but their urging, beseeching, wheedling, nagging Biron to confess is so repetitious and so unrelenting[3] that *two hours of*

---

2. State v. Biron, 266 Minn. 272, 123 N.W.2d 392 (1963), *noted in* 48 Minn. L. Rev. 160 (1963).

Biron was questioned by members of the homicide division of the Minneapolis police department. The decision to tape record the questioning was not made with the intent to offer the tape in evidence (or with any expectation that it would wind up in evidence), but on the premise that the suspect would "crack" quickly and that the playing of Biron's taped confession to his accomplices would lead them to do likewise. But Biron "held out" longer than expected and various detectives took turns questioning him, some of whom did *not* know they were on tape.

Biron's defense lawyer somehow learned that a tape of his client's police interrogation existed and when a member of the homicide division so admitted, the tape was put into evidence. Copies are on file in the University of Minnesota and University of Michigan law libraries.

The five detectives who questioned Biron at one time or another were veteran interrogators. Shortly thereafter, one of them became head of the police department. Some of their tactics, such as those the Minnesota Supreme Court held invalidated Biron's confession, would be sharply condemned by Inbau, *e.g.*, the misrepresentation that despite the fact Biron was slightly "overage" he might be treated as a juvenile offender if he "cooperates." As the extracts in the next footnote illustrate, however, many of their interrogation techniques were recommended by the standard manuals, *e.g.*, keeping the "subject" on the defensive, displaying an air of confidence in the "subject's" guilt, stressing the futility of resistance, sympathizing with the offender, and minimizing the moral seriousness of his offense. *See* the discussion in Miranda v. Arizona, 384 U.S. 436, 449-55 (1966). *See also* Kamisar, *What is an "Involuntary" Confession?*, 17 Rutgers L. Rev. 728, 729-32 (1963) [reprinted in this volume]; Weisberg, *Police Interrogation of Arrested Persons: A Skeptical View*, 52 J. Crim. L.C. & P.S. 21, 23-26 (1961), *reprinted in* Police Power and Individual Freedom 153, 155-58 (C. Sowle ed. 1962).

There is no reason to think that the tactics employed by Biron's experienced interrogators were any different than those they had utilized in scores of other cases over the years. So far as I know, this was the only "confession" they ever lost (at least up to that point), and it was also the only time a tape of their interrogation appeared in the record.

3. A representative sampling follows:

All we're interested in is the truth, John.... We'll *know* when you're lying.... *You* don't know *what we* know, do you? You don't know *one bit*.... Now, we know you didn't *intend* to kill this woman.... You ain't the *only* guy who ever made a mistake.... All we want is *the truth*, John.... Well, were you drinking? You didn't *deliberately* set out to kill a woman. You aren't that kind of a kid. We know that.... You're in trouble, John; let us help you.... Just *listening* is about all most students can stand. Thirty-six hours? Breathes there a police interrogator who can *question* anyone for that length of time? Small wonder that Ashcraft's interrogators questioned him "in relays"; that "*they* became so tired they were compelled to rest."[18] I venture to say that if there had been a tape recording of the Ashcraft interrogation and the Justices had listened to it in a "hearing room" set up for that purpose, long before the tape had ended they would have rushed out the door aghast—or staggered out, in a near-catatonic state.

Maybe not. Maybe Justice Jackson, for one, would have stayed there, to the bitter end, pondering: "Did Ashcraft do it? Did he kill his wife?"

There is reason to think Ashcraft did. The man he named as his wife's killer reminded him that he did not intend to take the entire blame, promptly admitted the killing, and accused Ashcraft of hiring him to do the job. After the interrogation, when examined by his family physician, Ashcraft neither complained of his treatment nor avowed his innocence. Instead he made what this friendly doctor described as an "entirely voluntary" statement *explaining why* he had killed his wife.[19]

Ashcraft is a great case only because Jackson's dissent made it so. The dissent is worth quoting at length. No piece of writing by Jackson better illustrates this self-described "country lawyer's" famed powers of advocacy and his "extraordinary quality of freshness and directness of approach."[20]

---

get it off your chest. We know you didn't *mean* to kill her. . . . You've already told us part of the story. You've gone part way, now go all the way. . . . All we're interested in is the truth. . . . Why, you've got to lie to cover a lie, *you know that*. . . . You've gone part way, why not go all the way? Help yourself for a change. . . . Make it easy on yourself, make it easy on everybody. . . . *Everybody* makes mistakes. This isn't John the Baptist you're talking to, you know. . . . Quit lying. We know when you're lying. . . . This is *your opportunity* to help yourself. We don't have to waste our time with you. We *know* you did it. You're in the crap—right up to your ears. This is your opportunity. We've got you—we've got you *good*. . . . Quit lying. . . . If you're not lying, how come you're so nervous? . . . You just can't bring yourself to admit it. . . . It takes a lot of guts to tell the truth. . . . You'll feel a lot better when you get if off your chest. You're not stupid. You know *that*. . . . Were you drinking? All it takes is a couple of drinks and your mind gets woozy. Is that how it happened? . . . It's not unusual for a kid like you to get into trouble. You're *in trouble,* my friend; this is your chance to get out of it. . . . This has happened before; you're not the first kid to get into trouble. . . . Look, I've heard everything in this business. There isn't *anything* you can tell me which will shock me. . . . Now, we know you're not a killer. You aren't that kind of a kid. We know you didn't *deliberately* kill this woman. . . . Help yourself for a change. *Let us* help you. . . . All we're interested in is the truth. . . .

The Minnesota Supreme Court reversed Biron's conviction on the ground that false legal advice vitiated the confession. The court never suggested that the gnawing police questioning might be inherently coercive or inherently violative of Biron's right to counsel or the privilege against self-incrimination; indeed it repeatedly referred to the interrogation sessions as "interviews." On this latter point, *see* footnote 4 *infra.*

And no opinion by any judge, I think, better captures both the style and substance of Inbau's views on police interrogation and confessions:

> Interrogation *per se* is not, while violence *per se* is, an outlaw. Questioning is an indispensable instrumentality of justice. It may be abused, of course, as cross-examination in court may be abused, but the principles by which we may adjudge when it passes constitutional limits are quite different from those that condemn police brutality, and are far more difficult to apply. And they call for a more responsible and cautious exercise of our office. For . . . we cannot read an undiscriminating hostility to mere interrogation into the Constitution without unduly fettering the States in protecting society from the criminal.
>
> It probably is the normal instinct to deny and conceal any shameful or guilty act. Even a "voluntary confession" is not likely to be the product of the same motives with which one may volunteer information that does not incriminate or concern him. The term "voluntary" confession does not mean voluntary in the sense of a confession to a priest merely to rid one's soul of a sense of guilt. "Voluntary confessions" in criminal law are the product of calculations of a different order, and usually proceed from a belief that further denial is useless and perhaps prejudicial. To speak of any confessions of crime made after arrest as being "voluntary" or "uncoerced" is somewhat inaccurate, although traditional.
>
> A confession is wholly and uncontestably voluntary only if a guilty person gives himself up to the law and becomes his own accuser. The Court bases its decision on the premise that custody and examination of a prisoner for thirty-six hours is "inherently coercive." Of course it is. And so is custody and examination for one hour. Arrest itself is inherently coercive, and so is detention. . . .
>
> But does the Constitution prohibit use of all confessions made after arrest because questioning, while one is deprived of freedom, is "inherently coercive"? . . .
>
> That the inquiry was prolonged and persistent is a factor that in any calculation of its effect on Ashcraft would count heavily against the confession. But some men would withstand for days pressures that would destroy the will of others in hours. Always heretofore the ultimate question has been whether the confessor was in possession of his own will and self-control at the time of confession. . . .
>
> This evidence shows that despite the "inherent coerciveness" of the circumstances of his examination, the confession when made was deliberate, free, and voluntary in the sense in which that term is used in criminal law. This Court could not, in our opinion, hold this confession an involuntary one except by substituting its presumption in place of analysis of the evidence and refusing to weigh the evidence even in rebuttal of its presumption.
>
> . . . .
>
> I am not sure whether the Court denies the State all right to arrest and question the husband of the slain woman. No investigation worthy of the name could fail to examine him. Of all persons, he was most likely to know whether she had enemies or rivals. . . .
>
> Could the State not confront Ashcraft with his false statements and ask his explanation? He did not throw himself at any time on his rights, refuse to answer, and demand counsel, even according to his own testimony. The strategy of the officers evidently was to keep him talking, to give him plenty of rope and see if he would not hang

himself. He does not claim to have made objection to this. Instead he relied on his wits. The time came when it dawned on him that his own story brought him under suspicion, and that he could not meet it. Must the officers stop at this point because he was coming to appreciate the uselessness of deception?

Then he became desperate and accused [Ware]. Certainly from this point the State was justified in holding and questioning him as a witness, for he claimed to know the killer. That accusation backfired and only turned up a witness against him. He had run out of expedients and invention; he knew he had lost the battle of wits. After all, honesty seemed to be the best, even if the last, policy. He confessed in detail.

At what point in all this investigation does the Court hold that the Constitution commands these officers to send Ashcraft on his way and give up the murder as insoluble? If the State is denied the right to apply any pressure to him which is "inherently coercive" it could hardly deprive him of his freedom at all. [4]

---

4. 322 U.S. at 160-69. *See also* Watts v. Indiana 338 U.S. 49, 57, 60-62 (1949) (Jackson, J., concurring). *See generally* Inbau, *Restrictions in the Law of Interrogation and Confessions*, 52 Nw. U.L. REV. 77 (1957); Inbau, *Police Interrogation—A Practical Necessity*, 52 J. CRIM. L.C. & P.S. 16 (1961), *reprinted in* POLICE POWER AND INDIVIDUAL FREEDOM 147 (C. Sowle ed. 1962). Inbau, *Law Enforcement, the Courts and Civil Liberties*, in CRIMINAL JUSTICE IN OUR TIME 97 (A. Howard ed. 1965).

Inbau, I am certain, also applauded Justice Jackson's criticism of the *Ashcraft* Court's use of emotive words: "This questioning is characterized as a 'secret inquisition,' involving all of the horrendous historical associations of those words. . . . [A]ny questioning may be characterized as an 'inquisition,' but the use of such characterizations is no substitute for . . . detached and judicial consideration. . . . " 322 U.S. at 168. *Cf. Hearings on H.R. 7525 and S. 486 Before the Senate Comm. on the District of Columbia*, 88th Cong., 1st Sess. 323, 329-30 (1963) (statement of Fred E. Inbau distinguishing between "persuad[ing]" a person to confess or "play[ing]" upon his sympathies to get him to tell you the truth" and "extracting" a confession or "put[ting] [someone] through the wringer to get it") [hereinafter cited as *1963 Senate Hearings*].

Of course, few advocates of *any* position are able to eschew emotive language. *See, e.g.*, THE MEDIA AND THE LAW 2-3 (H. Simmons & J. Califano ed. 1976) ("gag" orders vs. "protective" orders; "national security" vs. "the right of the public to know"). Critics of police interrogation do use threatening and pejorative terms, but defenders of the system are no slouches themselves in the art of wordsmanship. The veteran special agent of the Kansas Bureau of Investigation, Alvin A. Dewey of *In Cold Blood* fame, likened a police interrogator to a "good salesman . . . selling insurance or a car [who] cannot do his job if a competitor is standing by, and that is the situation for the [interrogator] with the presence of an attorney." Statement before the Subcommittee on Constitutional Amendments of the Senate Committee on the Judiciary, July 21, 1966, at 2 (mimeo) (on file in the University of Michigan Law Library). He also defined the "interrogation room" as a place "where people can talk in privacy which is nothing more than an attorney desires in talking to his client or a doctor in talking to his patient." *Id.* Similarly, Chief Stanley Schrotel of the Cincinnati Police Department, then the immediate past president of the International Association of Chiefs of Police, told a Senate committee that "in the interrogation room . . . you have something akin to a lawyer-client relationship, a doctor-patient relationship." *1963 Senate Hearings, supra*, at 286, 294. He also pointed out that "it takes a very skillful kind of interview, a proper kind of environment, in order to establish the rapport" necessary to get a heinous offender to confess. *Id.* at 293. Inbau himself has likened effective police interrogation to an "unhurried interview" and sought legislative authority "for a reasonable period of police detention" for the interrogation of suspects "not unwilling to be interviewed." Inbau, *Police*

Justice Black, who wrote the opinion for the Court in *Ashcraft*, no less than Justice Jackson, who authored the ringing dissent, knew full well that in 1944 neither the Court nor "the country" was "ready"[21] for an affirmative answer to the question, "[D]oes the Constitution prohibit use of all confessions made after arrest because questioning, while one is deprived of freedom, is 'inherently coercive'?" As we now know, it was not until 1966 that the Court, if not "the country," grew "ready."[22] There is cause to wonder whether "the country" will *ever* grow "ready." And there is reason to think that the present Court is growing weary.[23]

*

It is well known, and it is quite understandable, that the forthright and occasionally irreverent Inbau is greatly admired—adored may not be too strong a word—by the thousands of law enforcement officials who flock to his "short courses" or applaud his hard-hitting speeches at their conferences and conventions. And it is also no secret, and again not surprising, that many of his fellow law professors do not hold him in the same regard.

Inbau is an expert, make no mistake about that, but he is an expert with a maverick strain. He was, and always will be, the spokesman for the plain man, no less than for the police officer and the prosecutor. But the typical expert does not understand the plain man. "What he knows, he knows so thoroughly that he is impatient with men to whom it has to be explained."[24] The typical expert "lacks contact with the plain man. He not only does not know what the plain man is thinking; he rarely knows how to discover his thoughts. He has dwelt so austerely in his laboratory or his study that the content of the average mind is a closed book to him."[25]

Inbau can, and does, stir the multitudes. His writing and speaking is "blood-warm";[26] his words are "loaded with life."[27] One of his weapons is "the homely illustration which makes its way and sinks deep by its appeal to everyday experience."[28] This, written on the eve of the "stop and frisk" cases,[29] is typical Inbau:

> Several months ago I received a notice from the Internal Revenue Service to come to its Chicago office to explain a couple of business expense deductions. One related to a deduction for "an office in home." That referred to a deduction I listed for 1/6 of my apartment rent—for a sizeable den used exclusively for my book writings and various other writings, which, incidentally, account for a third of my total income.

Interrogation—A Practical Necessity, 52 J. Crim. L. C. & P. S. 16, 18–21 (1961), *reprinted in* Police Power and Individual Freedom 147, 149–52 (C. Sowle ed. 1962).

Do not those who use such clean, soft words to describe what typically must be a grim, unpleasant (frightening? cruel?) experience contribute to "linguistic pollution, upsetting the ecological balance between words and their environment"? *See* Schlesinger, *Politics and the American Language,* 43 American Scholar 553, 556 (1974).

It seemed odd that there should be any question about this. It also seemed odd that any question would be raised as to the other modest items of expense charged against these extracurricular income producing activities.

Anyway, I spent several hours locating checks and records to substantiate these deductions—time I would have preferred to use in writing new books or articles. I also appeared in the IRS office at the designated time of 9:30 A.M. I sat in a waiting room for my name to be called—all the while feeling like a charity patient in a health clinic. At 10:05 my name was called, and as I walked by some of the other assembled suspects, one of them—whom I did not know but who obviously knew me—exclaimed: "Inbau; you too!"

This was not an exhilarating experience, I assure you. Nor did I enjoy baring my financial soul to the young lady who grilled me for about twenty minutes.

I hasten to relieve you of any concern over my future; I was "exonerated"; my return was approved.

The various tax reports and various other kinds of reports which a business man has to make to the Federal and State Governments require many disclosures of a private nature and a failure to disclose may incur severe penalties or even a discontinuance of the business itself. Safety and health inspectors of businesses call for privacy intrusions. In the labor relations area, a company has to subject itself to a lot of disclosures, and to the demands of labor unions—privacy invasions, they may be fairly called.

Those of you who have travelled abroad and have had to submit to a customs inspection of your luggage know what it is to have your privacy invaded.

Now don't misunderstand me. I am not saying, or even intimating, that it is wrong for the Internal Revenue Service to ask me to explain my return. Spot checks, or checks based upon suspicion of a false return, are necessary and in the public interest. The same holds true for the disclosures and inspections required of businesses and travellers. *The point I want to make, however, is that if we so-called law abiding citizens have to submit to these indignities and invasions of our privacy—all in the interest and welfare of the public at large—I find it hard to understand why anyone, or any group, should complain so vociferously when a police officer, acting upon reasonable suspicion and in a reasonable manner, requests the identity of, or an explanation from, a person on a dark street at 3 A.M. in a neighborhood which has been experiencing a high incidence of serious crimes.* And why, once the officer does this, should he not be permitted, for his own protection, to frisk the detained person in order to be sure he is not armed with a dangerous weapon. [30]

Yes, Inbau could stir the multitudes (or at least "Middle Americans"). He wrote (horrors) for the *Reader's Digest* [31] as well as the *Police Digest,* [32] the *Police Journal,* [33] and the *Police-Law Review.* [34] He addressed not only the Conference of Chief Justices [35] and various annual conventions of the National District Attorneys Association, [36] but also the National Association of Independent Insurers, [37] the Chicago Association of Commerce and Industry, [38] and a gathering of college alumni at "homecoming." [39] (How many law professors could hold that audience?) But the typical expert "mistrusts his fellow-specialist when the latter can reach [the] multitude. For [the typical expert] the gift of popular explanation is a proof of failure in the grasp of the discipline. His intensity of gaze makes him suspect the man who can state the elements of his mystery in general terms."[40]

Inbau takes strong positions and is given to strong words. On occasion, he is even known to have voiced rage and indignation. These qualities are not calculated to enhance his status in the law teaching ranks. Professors, it seems, are supposed to tiptoe, not crash. They are supposed to be troubled and tentative, not take very strong and very clear positions on anything (except, perhaps, right down the middle). Their stock in trade is not supplying answers but asking questions (and criticizing *others* who have the audacity to propose solutions). They earn points, it seems, by showing how *agonizingly subtle and complex* an issue or a problem actually is, not by suggesting how *simple* it might really be.[41]

The safe course for a law professor, it seems, is to set forth all imaginable arguments (or, better yet, some unimaginable ones, too) on both sides (or better yet, on four or five sides), lament the lack of sufficient data, deplore the "single-minded thinking" which has characterized the field (and probably add that it has generated "much heat but little light"), recognize that valid principles are "in collision," stress that there are no "absolutes," and wind up troubled (or, better yet, tortured and paralyzed) by doubts and uncertainties. The preferred model, in short, is Tevye the dairyman of *Fiddler on the Roof* fame:

> . . . On the other hand, what kind of match would that be, with a poor tailor? On the other hand, he's an honest, hard worker. On the other hand, he has absolutely nothing. On the other hand, things could never get worse for him, they could only get better.[42]

Although Inbau is well aware that his views, and his colorful manner of expressing them, might irritate, even infuriate, his fellow law professors, this has not swayed him from his course.[43] Indeed, one of his missions, as he sees it, is to straighten out "the mess" the law professors, ex-law professors on the bench, and other "sensitive souls" have gotten us into.[44]

Inbau came to the podium from the crime lab, the interrogation room and the trial courts,[45] not the library. Not only was he a pioneer in the development of the polygraph and in the "psychology" of obtaining confessions, but in his younger days he had been the premier lie-detector examiner and just about the craftiest interrogator around. In the course of obtaining hundreds of confessions, he had been known to spill over with such "sympathy" for a murder suspect that he had had to "pause to wipe away a tear."[46] He prefers to represent himself (and perhaps think of himself) as a "practical man" rather than a "law professor."[47] Most professors (and too many judges), I think he would say, are "too naive and otherworldly to intervene in a brass-knuckle world."[48]

If Inbau much cared about how his brethren in the law teaching ranks regard him, however, I think he would be puzzled by the "chilling" effect of his strong positions and strong words. After all, John Henry Wigmore, his idol, mentor, friend, associate, and ideological ally,[49] was known for his "sharp and uncompromising" criticisms.[50] Although a person of elegant manners, when he thought the occasion demanded it, "the Colonel" could strike with the force of an army mule (or the "bite" of a first sergeant),[51] yet this did not prevent him from being acclaimed as "our first legal scholar."[52] Indeed, Wigmore's *Treatise on Evidence,* "unrivaled as the greatest treatise on any single subject of the law,"[53] contains a generous amount of scathing, colorful criticism of the courts—often *for the very reasons* that Inbau has never stopped reproaching them:

Does the *illegal source* of a piece of evidence taint it so as to exclude it, when offered by the party who has shared in the illegality?

... An employer may perhaps suitably interrupt the course of his business to deliver a homily to his office-boy on the evils of gambling or the rewards of industry. But a judge does not hold court in a streetcar to do summary justice upon a fellow-passenger who fraudulently evades payment of his fare; and, upon the same principle, he does not attempt, in the course of a specific litigation, to investigate and punish all offences which incidentally cross the path of that litigation. Such a practice might be consistent with the primitive system of justice under an Arabian sheikh; but it does not comport with our own system of law.[54]

. . . .

[T]he heretical influence of Weeks v. United States, 232 U.S. 383 (1914), [establishing the exclusionary rule in federal search and seizure cases] spread, and evoked a contagion of sentimentality in some of the State Courts, inducing them to break loose from long-settled fundamentals.

... After the enactment of the Eighteenth Amendment and its auxiliary legislation, prohibiting the sale of intoxicating liquors, a new and popular occasion was afforded for the misplaced invocation of this principle; and the judicial excesses of many Courts in sanctioning its use give an impression of easy complaisance which would be ludicrous if it were not so dangerous to the general respect for law and order in the community.[55]

. . . .

... If the officials, illegally searching, came across an infernal machine, planned for the city's destruction, and impounded it, shall we say that the diabolical owner of it may appear in court, brazenly demand process for its return, and be supinely accorded by the Court a writ of restitution, with perhaps an apology for the "outrage"? Such is the logical consequence of the doctrine of Weeks v. U.S. . . .

[T]he essential fallacy of [*Weeks*] and its successors is that it virtually creates a novel exception, where the Fourth Amendment is involved, to the fundamental principle . . . that *an illegality in the mode of procuring evidence is no ground for excluding it.* The doctrine of such an exception rests on a reverence for the Fourth Amendment so deep and cogent that its violation will be taken notice of, at any cost of other justice, and even in the most indirect way. . . .

[This view] puts Supreme Courts in the position of assisting to undermine the foundations of the very institutions they are set there to protect. It regards the over-zealous officer of the law as a greater danger to the community than the unpunished murderer or embezzler or panderer.[56]

. . . .

. . . Holmes, J., in his dissent [in *Olmstead v. United States*, 277 U.S. 438 (1928)] refers to this act of wiretapping as "dirty business." But so is likely to be all apprehension of malefactors. Kicking a man in the stomach is "dirty business," normally viewed. But if a gunman assails you, and you know enough of the French art of "savatage" to kick him in the stomach and thus save your life, is that "dirty business" for *you*? . . . [57]

*

In March, 1962, Fred Inbau published one of his many "prosecutors' convention" speeches, *Public Safety v. Individual Civil Liberties: The Prosecutor's Stand*, [58] but one whose criticism of the Warren Court struck me as especially bitter and scathing—even for Inbau. I regarded it, and I think it may be fairly termed, an "intemperate" piece. I expressed my sense of outrage to Claude Sowle, then editor-in-chief of the *Journal*, who encouraged me to respond. I then dashed off what may fairly be called an "intemperate" reply. [59] I was furious. Inbau had ripped into the Court I loved and my thinking was that "[t]o war against the Court was to war against the Constitution itself." [60] Up to that time, I had never met Inbau, and it would hardly have surprised me if, after reading my biting reply, Inbau had vowed to keep it that way. Instead, he invited me to attend the next Northwestern University School of Law Conference on Criminal Justice.

The Conference (held in November, 1962) turned out to be a memorable occasion. It was there that I first made contact with many law enforcement officers. It was there, too, that I first met James R. Thompson, Claude R. Sowle, and Bernard Weisberg, as well as Inbau.

I expected Thompson, then a very recent graduate of Northwestern and a lecturer in Inbau's Short Course for Prosecutors, to be very much under the influence of his mentor, but that was not at all the case. Thompson even had some nice things to say about the *McNabb-Mallory* rule and thought there was much to be said for the Supreme Court of Illinois adopting such a rule.[61] Inbau didn't seem to mind at all. If anything, he seemed to be proud of the fact that Thompson was his "own man."

Claude Sowle, another former Inbau student and then Inbau's junior colleague on the Northwestern law faculty, gave a stirring talk, striking at the heart of Inbau's position on police interrogation and confessions. He attacked the hypocrisy pervading the criminal justice system; measured the proceedings in the "interrogation" room against the standard of a public trial and found the former sorely wanting—indeed, based upon nullification of the privilege against self-incrimination and the right to the assistance of counsel—and spelled out how all too often the "legal courts" are reduced to the position of merely ratifying the verdict obtained by the police-conducted "outlaw tribunals." Sowle's remarks had a stunning impact on the audience and inspired me, some years later, to write my "Gatehouses and Mansions" paper.[62]

While Sowle was speaking, I studied Inbau closely. I half expected him to shout, "That's enough, Claude!" Instead, Inbau seemed to be basking in the brilliance and independence of his junior colleague. He seemed pleased that Sowle had the rapt attention of the audience, especially the many police officers in attendance.

Another speaker, Bernard Weisberg, also attacked the Inbau position. The contention that all statements made after a suspect's request to contact counsel has been denied should be barred on that ground alone had been rejected in *Crooker,* the Court maintaining that such a rule "would effectively preclude police questioning—*fair as well as unfair*—until the accused was afforded opportunity to call his attorney."[63] Inbau, of course, applauded this stand. But Weisberg argued most persuasively that in the real world "fair" or "proper" or "reasonable" police questioning was virtually nonexistent—and he quoted extensively from Inbau's interrogation manual to make his point. Moreover, pointed out Weisberg, even if the courts could decide when "reasonable" interrogation had come to an end (which he doubted), they could not hope to do so unless full records of these essentially unsupervised proceedings were available for review—and they almost never were.

Weisberg's remarks infuriated many of the police in attendance. One captain leaped to his feet and growled at Weisberg that someone who had never conducted an interrogation himself had no business talking about the subject—and couldn't have anything worthwhile to say. Inbau rushed to the microphone. A good argument could be made, he smiled, that only someone who had been on the *receiving end* of a police interrogation was qualified to talk about the subject. He had neglected to invite such a person, but Weisberg, he suggested, was the next best thing. Weisberg was a thoughtful, articulate spokesman for the accused. True, evidently Weisberg believed that the established practice of police questioning was fundamentally and hopelessly irreconcilable with the adversary system of justice and the Constitution, but so did some members of the Supreme Court. Some day—and not in the too distant future—Weisberg's views might command a majority of the Court. A major purpose of the conference, Inbau reminded the many police officers in the audience, was not just to entertain them with speakers they liked to hear, but to present speakers who would tell them what they ought to know and had to think about. (*This,* I asked myself, was the zealous, pugilistic Fred Inbau? *This* was the fabled "Freddy the Cop"?)[64]

Weisberg was indeed a thoughtful, articulate spokesman. Two years earlier, again in the setting of a conference conceived and planned by Inbau, he had delivered what I consider the most probing and most useful paper ever written on the subject, "Police Interrogation of Arrested Persons: A Skeptical View".[5] Of all the contributors to this "International Conference on Criminal Law," Weisberg's criminal justice credentials were the least impressive. He had no law enforcement background. He was a general practitioner, engaged mostly in corporate and business law. But Inbau had "discovered" Weisberg when the latter had co-authored a 1959 report by the Illinois Division of the ACLU, *Secret Detention by Chicago Police*—and he had given him a wide stage.

Weisberg had the advantages of the amateur—"the freedom from traditional limitations and perspectives, the ability to raise fundamental questions which professionals in the field have long since forgotten to consider."[65] When he came to examine police interrogation, Weisberg was astounded by the virtually unbridled discretionary powers wielded by the "administrative agencies" (police departments) and "administrative officials" (police officers) in this field and by their ability "to prevent objective recordation of the facts":

> The modern police function of preliminary criminal investigation and interrogation of suspects is an unusual instance of discretionary administrative power over persons unregulated by judicial standards. . . . In large measure police station questioning . . . is governed only by the self-imposed restraints of the police and by limited judicial action in the small number of cases in which police conduct becomes a litigated issue.
>
> Whatever the reasons for their circumspection, the failure of the courts to assume supervisory powers over police interrogation practices remains an anomaly. It is sometimes grounded on the American separation of judicial and executive powers. But this doctrine has not prevented the courts from developing judicial standards for other administrative agencies.
>
> Measured by legal standards, the most unique feature of the police station questioning is its characteristic secrecy. It is secrecy which creates the risk of abuses, which by keeping the record incomplete makes the rules about coercion vague and difficult to apply, which inhibits the development of clear rules to govern police interrogation and which contributes to public distrust of the police. Secrecy is not the same as the privacy which interrogation specialists insist is necessary for effective questioning. Inconspicuous recording equipment or concealed observers would not detract from the intimacy between the interrogator and his subject which is said to increase the likelihood of confession.
>
> No other case comes to mind in which an administrative official is permitted the broad discretionary power assumed by the police interrogator, together with the power to prevent objective recordation of the facts. . . . It is secrecy, not privacy, which

5. 52 J. Crim. L.C. & P.S. 21 (1961), in Police Power and Individual Freedom 153 (C. Sowle ed. 1962). This article reproduces a paper Weisberg delivered at Northwestern University School of Law on Feb. 19, 1960.

accounts for the absence of a reliable record of interrogation proceedings in a police station. If the need for some pre-judicial questioning is assumed, privacy may be defended on grounds of necessity; secrecy cannot be defended on this or any other ground.[66]

Weisberg deemed it important to "give some content to the generalities [one might say "euphemisms"] in which the subject [of police questioning] is usually discussed."[67] He thought it "playing Hamlet without the ghost to discuss police questioning without knowing what such questioning is really like."[68] So he turned to "the leading police manual by Professor Fred Inbau and John Reid" to supply the content.[69]

So far as I know, Weisberg was the first law review writer to make extensive use of the interrogation manuals. And, as I have suggested elsewhere, each of these manuals may have been "equal to a dozen law review articles in its impact on the Court."[70] For "one of the most powerful features of the Due Process Model," as the late Herbert Packer observed, "is that it thrives on visibility. People are willing to be complacent about what goes on in the criminal process as long as they are not too often or too explicitly reminded of the gory details."[71]

As fate would have it, Inbau's former student, Jim Thompson, was to argue the *Escobedo* case for the State of Illinois, and Inbau's "adopted" student, Bernie Weisberg, was to argue the case for the ACLU, as amicus curiae.[72] In his *Escobedo* brief, Weisberg maintained that since police interrogation of arrested persons is characteristically conducted in privacy and without a record being made, "the best sources" for understanding police questioning "are the published manuals."[73] Weisberg

urge[d] the Court to examine these books [which he extracted at considerable length in his brief]. They are not exhibits in a museum of third degree horrors. Indeed they carefully advise the police interrogator to avoid tactics which are clearly coercive under prevailing law. They are invaluable because they vividly describe the kind of interrogation practices which are accepted as lawful and proper under the best current standards of professional police work.[74]

Weisberg's great paper on confessions and his powerful *Escobedo* brief set the fashion for civil libertarians. The ACLU brief in *Miranda* (a magnificent performance by Professors Anthony Amsterdam, Paul Mishkin, et al.) reprinted a full chapter from O'Hara's *Fundamentals of Criminal Investigations* (1956). In turn, the majority opinion in *Miranda* devoted six full pages to extracts from various police manuals and texts[75] "document[ing] procedures employed with success in the past, and . . . recommend[ing] various other effective tactics."[76] Many of the examples selected by the Court are the same ones Weisberg used in his 1960 article and in his 1964 *Escobedo* brief.

The curious thing about Weisberg's important contribution to the law of confessions is that, as he readily admits, he never would have pursued his interest in this field *but for Inbau's encouragement*. It is a delicious irony that when Inbau urged Weisberg to think more deeply about the vexing problems of police interrogation and confessions—when back in 1960 he invited this relatively obscure general practitioner to deliver a major paper articulating his "skeptical views" on the subject—Inbau did what some think the privilege against self-incrimination is supposed to prevent—he pulled the lever which sprung the trap on which he stood.[77]

The *Miranda* opinion quotes from or cites the 1953 and 1962 Inbau-Reid manuals no less than ten times—and never with approval.[78] It is plain that these publications "vented Chief Justice Warren's judicial ire."[79] The day after *Miranda* was handed down, Inbau should have been a beaten man. But he wasn't.[6]

He knew, no less than did our most brilliant civil liberties lawyer, that "the judgments" that these issues require "are too large, too ungoverned by a commanding text or clear institutional dictates, to be laid solidly to rest."[7] He knew, too, that "[p]recedents upon such issues are particularly fragile under the buffeting of rapid historical developments that incessantly place unprecedented strains upon the Court."[8] As it turned out, a period of "social upheaval, violence in the ghettos, and disorder on the campuses"[80] had already begun. The political assassinations and near-assassinations of the late 1960s; more urban "riots"; the presidential campaign of 1968; the "obviously retaliatory" provisions of the Crime Control Act of 1968 and other political exploitation of the "law and order" issue; the ever-soaring crime statistics;[81] and the ever-spreading fears of the breakdown of public order soon "combined to create an atmosphere that, to say the least, was unfavorable to the continued vitality of the Warren Court's mission in criminal cases."[82]

I was one of those who implored the Court to "exercise leadership," to be "bold" and "innovative." Yet I was outraged when "its decisions arouse[d], as they must, resentment and political attack."[83] At this point, I became a lawyer "marching behind the solemn, sacrosanct banner of the law. [I] want[ed] it both ways."[84] It seems much clearer to me today than it was fifteen years ago, or even ten, that—although he was wrong on the merits—

---

6. Indeed, a year after *Miranda*, the irrepressible Inbau-Reid team published a new edition of their interrogation manual, retaining, after the prescribed warnings have been given, many of the tactics and techniques that seem to have chagrined the author of the *Miranda* opinion. *See* Broderick, Book Review, 53 CORNELL L. REV. 737 (1968). But *Miranda* "did not condemn any specific techniques or hold that evidence obtained by use of them would be inadmissible. Reliance was placed on warning and counsel to protect the suspect." Elsen & Rosett, *Protections for the Suspect under* Miranda v. Arizona, 76 COLUM. L. REV. 645, 667 (1967). *See also* footnote 1 *supra*.

7. Amsterdam, *Perspectives on the Fourth Amendment*, 58 MINN. L. REV. 349, 353 (1974).

8. *Id.*

Inbau was perfectly within his rights in deploring, and arguing against, *McNabb, Mallory, Mapp,* and *Miranda.*

Although I happen to think that most of Inbau's ideas deserve to be rejected, he nevertheless furthered, or should have furthered, the thinking of all of us. As one of the "Crime Control model's" "few full-fledged academic defenders,"[9] Inbau not only presents the policeman's view of recent cases, but articulates the officer's critical needs and deep concerns. Too many of us are content to point out what the policeman *cannot* or *must not* do. Inbau, on the other hand, will pepper you with hypothetical fact situations and ask: "*You* are the policeman; *what would you do* in this case?" More times than I like to admit, I have felt that the price of remaining faithful to the "Due Process model"[85] was to appear rather foolish. What *can* the policeman do? What *should* he be able to do? How can the legislature be *of assistance* to him? I don't think I am the only law professor who finds it more exhilarating to confine himself to what the policeman *cannot* or *must not* do. But the time has long since passed when we can afford that luxury.

Most people know Inbau only from the rousing talks he gave at the local Rotary Club or from the fighting speeches he delivered at countless prosecutor and police conventions, exhorting the troops to victory in the great "war against crime." But there is more than one Inbau. There is also the Inbau who, in the privacy of his office or over a drink, can dispassionately and masterfully dissect the latest Supreme Court opinions; who can laugh as hard at himself as he does at the "law professors" on and off the bench. There is also the Inbau whose goal at each of the many conferences he conceives and directs is to bring to bear upon problem areas "the greatest possible breadth of viewpoint and depth of insight"[86] and to have all in attendance leave with their swords and banners lowered and their sensitivities raised. As an "expert in controversy," this iconoclastic law professor, no less than the "iconoclast from Baltimore," "welcomed attacks on himself, partly because they showed that his thrusts had gone home, partly because he defended everyone's right to

---

9. The late Alexander Bickel so described Inbau. *See* Bickel, *The Role of the Supreme Court of the United States,* 44 TEX. L. REV. 954, 962 (1966).

When Bickel used the "Crime Control model" term he was, of course, referring to Professor Packer's famous article, *Two Models of the Criminal Process,* 113 U. PA. L. REV. 1 (1964). Packer subsequently rather summarily described the "polar extremes" which represent "competing value choices" as follows:

> The Crime Control model sees the efficient, expeditious and reliable screening and disposition of persons as the central value to be served by the criminal process. The Due Process model sees that function as limited by and subordinate to the maintenance of the dignity and autonomy of the individual. The Crime Control model is administrative and managerial; the Due Process model is adversary and judicial. The Crime Control model may be analogized to an assembly line, the Due Process model to an obstacle course.

Packer, *The Courts, The Police and the Rest of Us,* 57 J. CRIM. L.C. & P.S. 238, 239 (1966).

have his say, and partly because he felt that destructive criticism, even of his own work, was much more stimulating than acclaim. "[87]

Fred would be quick to deny that he is "the professor." If anything, he sees himself as the "anti-professor"—or so he says. Methinks he does protest too much. *One* of the Inbaus, at least, is more "the professor" than a considerable number who profess to be, more "the professor" than any of the Inbaus would ever care to admit.

Brewer v. Williams—
A Hard Look at
a Discomfiting Record

December, 1977

Resistance to the disclosure of [incriminating] information is considerably increased . . . if something is not done to establish a friendly and trusting attitude on the part of the subject. Once rapport is established, you have begun the "yes" attitude. The following devices are recommended: . . . Establish confidence and friendliness by talking for a period about everday subjects. In other words, have a "friendly visit."

—R. Royal and S. Schutt, *The Gentle Art of Interviewing
 and Interrogation*

I told [Mr. Williams his rights]. I further added [that] you and I both know that you are represented by counsel here [in Davenport and] in Des Moines. . . .

I then further advised him that I wanted him to be sure to remember what I had just told him because it was a long ride back to Des Moines and he and I would be visiting.

—Captain Leaming, chief of detectives, Des Moines Police Department[1]

IN RECENT DECADES, few matters have split the Supreme Court, troubled the legal profession, and agitated the public as much as the police interrogation-confession cases. The recent case of *Brewer v. Williams*[1] is as provocative as any, because the Supreme Court there reversed the defendant's conviction for the "savage murder of a small child" even though no Justice denied his guilt,[2]

---

1. 430 U.S. 387 (1977). Although *Williams* raises questions that will long be debated, one issue has already been resolved. Chief Justice Burger doubted that a successful retrial of Williams "is realistically possible." *Id.* at 416 n.1 (Burger, C.J., dissenting). On the other hand, Justice Marshall "doubted very much that there is any chance a dangerous criminal will be loosed on the streets, the bloodcurdling cries of the dissents notwithstanding." *Id.* at 408-09 (Marshall, J., concurring). Williams has since been retried and reconvicted of first-degree murder. Des Moines Register, July 16, 1977, § A, at 1, col. 1. He was resentenced to life imprisonment. *Id.*, Aug. 20, 1977, § B, at 12, col. 4. In a ruling prior to Williams's second trial, the court held that evidence of the discovery of the girl's body was admissible because of the likelihood that the body would have been discovered even without Williams's statements. Y. KAMISAR, W. LaFAVE & J. ISRAEL, MODERN CRIMINAL PROCEDURE 170 (Supp. 1978).

2. 430 U.S. 387, 416 (1977) (Burger, C.J., dissenting). Williams never confessed to the sexual molestation or slaying of the child. Des Moines Register, July 6, 1977, § A, at 4,

he was warned of his rights no fewer than five times,[2] and any "interrogation" that might have occurred seemed quite mild.[3]

On Christmas Eve, 1968, a ten-year-old girl, Pamela Powers, disappeared while with her family at the Des Moines, Iowa, YMCA.[4] It later turned out, as feared, that she had been raped and murdered.[5] Suspicion soon focused on defendant Williams, an escapee from a mental institution and a deeply religious person or, to put it more aptly, "a young man with quixotic religious convictions."[6] A warrant was issued for his arrest on a charge of "child-stealing."[7] Williams, who had fled the state, telephoned a Des Moines lawyer named McKnight and on the attorney's advice surrendered himself to the Davenport, Iowa, police.

Two Des Moines detectives—Captain Leaming, chief of detectives and a nineteen-year veteran of the Des Moines Police Department, and Detective Nelson, a member of the homicide squad and a fifteen-year veteran of the force—arranged to drive the 160 miles to Davenport, pick up Williams, and return him directly to Des Moines.[8] Before being driven back to Des Moines, Williams was advised of his right to remain silent many times: by a Davenport police officer, Lieutenant Ackerman; by the Davenport judge who arraigned him on the child-stealing warrant; by McKnight; by Captain Leaming himself; and by a local Davenport attorney named Kelly.[9] Williams also asserted his rights many times: he requested and was granted a "private audience" with the Davenport judge;[10] after his first meeting with his Davenport lawyer, the lawyer informed the Davenport police that his client

---

col. 1. At his second trial the defense admitted that Williams had carried the body out of the YMCA building and had disposed of it but contended that the child had been sexually assaulted and killed by someone else before being placed in Williams's room in the YMCA. *Id.*, § A, at 1, col. 3. The defense claimed that because Williams was an escapee from a mental institution and had previously molested children, he panicked when he found the body in his room and decided to get rid of it immediately, hoping not to be implicated. *Id.*, July 10, 1977, § A, at 2, col. 1.

Because discovery rules had been liberalized since the first trial, defense lawyers received all investigative reports on the murder, some of which indicated that the police had considered the possibility that the rapist-killer was sterile because the medical examiner who performed the autopsy found semen, but no sperm, in the girl's body. *Id.*, July 14, 1977, § A, at 3, col. 1. These police reports had not been available to the defense at the first trial. *Id.* The defense maintained that Williams was not sterile and that the child's killer had been, but medical experts disagreed sharply over whether the frozen state of the little girl's body would have preserved any sperm present in the body at the time of the murder. *Id.*, July 12, 1977, § A, at 4, col. 5-6.

Although never mentioning his name at the trial (perhaps because the defense could produce no evidence that he was sterile), *id.*, July 9, 1977, § A, at 3, col. 3, the defense raised questions concerning the possibility that the killer might have been Albert Bowers, a former janitor of the building assigned to clean the YMCA washrooms on the day the child apparently was abducted from a washroom. Bowers was killed in a car accident some three years after the first trial and six years before the second. *Id.*, July 6, 1977, § A, at 11, col. 3. According to the defense, Bowers had a history of sexual molestations.

did not want to talk to the police until he met with his Des Moines lawyer;[11] after Leaming advised him of his rights, Williams asked to meet alone with the Davenport lawyer and was allowed to do so;[12] when Leaming was about to put handcuffs on him and start the journey back, Williams again asked to confer alone with his lawyer and again his request was granted;[13] and on the trip back to Des Moines he told Captain Leaming several times that he would tell him "the whole story *after* I see McKnight" back in Des Moines.[14]

Captain Leaming "theorized"[3] that the child's body was buried in the Mitchellville area, a suburb of Des Moines that he and his prisoner would pass on the drive back. Because of bad weather and various stops, the return trip to Des Moines took between five and six hours,[15] and given the freezing rain, slippery roads, and some stops along the way, the drive to the Mitchellville area probably took three or four hours—plenty of time for a skilled interrogator to obtain a confession.[16]

Both the trial court[17] and the federal district court[18] found, despite Captain Leaming's testimony to the contrary, that defense attorney McKnight and the Des Moines police agreed that Williams would not be "questioned" until after he returned to Des Moines and conferred with his lawyer.[4] The federal

---

3. Captain Leaming knew that Williams had headed east and that some of the little girl's clothing had been found in the Grinnell area about 50 miles east of Des Moines. The captain "figured" that Williams "had probably got rid of the body as soon as he possibly could after he left Des Moines." *Id.* at 65. That made Mitchellville, a town 10–15 miles east of Des Moines, a strong possibility. Moreover, a search party had examined both the entire Grinnell area and the Newton area (30 miles east of Des Moines) without finding the girl's body. So the captain "theorized" or "figured Mitchellville." *Id.* at 61, 65, 93–94.

4. Brief for Petitioner, Joint App. at 54, 78, 90. According to the record, in the course of a long-distance phone conversation with Williams, McKnight told his client, in the presence of Leaming and his superior, Chief Nichols, that Williams would not be questioned about, and should not reveal anything about, the case until he returned to Des Moines and conferred with his lawyer. *Id.* at 38–40. Apparently both the trial court and federal district court concluded that *by their silence* the Des Moines police "agreed" to "go along" with McKnight on this matter. The *Williams* majority opinion, however, states that "[a]s a result of these [phone] conversations, it was agreed between McKnight and the Des Moines police officials that Detective[s] Leaming and [Nelson] . . . would not question [Williams] during the trip [back to Des Moines]." 430 U.S. at 391. But there is no indication in the record that after McKnight concluded his phone conversation with Williams *anything* was said by McKnight or by the Des Moines police about not questioning Williams on the return trip. The record does not show an explicit agreement or even that McKnight directly instructed Chief Nichols or Captain Leaming that Williams was not to be questioned on the return trip. *See also* footnote 17 *infra*.

Captain Leaming not only denied that there was any agreement, he also denied *hearing* McKnight *tell* Williams that he would not be questioned on the return trip. Brief for Petitioner, Joint App. at 78, 90. Chief Nichols, however, who listened to McKnight's end of the phone conversation along with Leaming, did testify that he heard McKnight tell Williams that he would not be questioned on the return trip and that Williams should not disclose anything about the case until after he conferred with his lawyer back in Des Moines. *Id.* at 38–40. Presumably, this conflict between the chief and the captain led the trial judge to observe that he was "not entirely convinced" that Captain Leaming "testified with complete candor . . . regarding the 'agreement'

district court found, also over Leaming's denial,[19] that Kelly requested and was refused permission to ride along on the trip back to Des Moines[20] and that Kelly told the Captain that it was his understanding that Williams was not to be questioned about the case until he met with his Des Moines lawyer.[21]

Whether Leaming "questioned" Williams on the long drive back to Des Moines, whether Williams waived his rights, and what other critical events occurred on that long drive turns on the captain's largely uncorroborated testimony.[22] Williams sharply disputed the captain on many points but, as might be expected, none of the courts that passed on the case paid any attention to what he had to say.[5] Yet when the captain got into a controversy

---

with Defendant's attorney." *Id.* at 2. The best interpretation of the record, I believe, is that the chief simply expected or supposed or assumed that Captain Leaming would not try to elicit incrminating information from Williams on the return trip—or that Wiliams would be so "fortified" by advice from both his Davenport and Des Moines lawyers that there would be no point in trying to do so. *Id.* at 40–41.

Kelly, Williams's Davenport lawyer, testified that he told the captain that "it was my understanding that Mr. Williams was to be returned to . . . Des Moines and after his return . . . that [McKnight] would talk to Williams in Leaming's office, and at that time he would reveal where the body [child?] was." *Id.* at 107. According to Kelly, Leaming replied, "'This isn't quite the way I understand it,'" and Kelly retorted that he thought *his* understanding of the arrangements "should be carried out." *Id.* There is no indication in Kelly's testimony that Leaming made any response. *Id.* Because there is no indication in the record that Kelly had any communication with McKnight, whatever Kelly knew about the agreement presumably came from Williams. Thus, if any agreement had been struck between McKnight and the police after the Williams-McKnight phone conversation, Kelly would have known no more about it than Williams.

Dissenting from the Eighth Circuit's ruling that Williams was entitled to a new trial, Judge [now FBI director] Webster commented, "I cannot but assume that the alleged 'broken promise' of Captain Leaming is at the root of the result reached in this case." Williams v. Brewer, 509 F.2d 227, 237 (8th Cir. 1974). But "whatever its subliminal influence on the majority, the [Supreme Court's] decision in *Williams* did not seem to turn on the police agreement." Y. KAMISAR, J. GRANO, & J. HADDAD, CRIMINAL PROCEDURE § 6.4550 (1977). Rather, it seemed to turn on the following: Before Williams started for Des Moines, judicial proceedings had been initiated against him and his right to the assistance of counsel had attached; he repeatedly asserted and exercised this right and the Government failed to establish that he intentionally relinquished it during the drive. 430 U.S. at 401. 404–06.

In his separate concurrence, however, Justice Stevens talked about the defendant "plac[ing] his trust" in a lawyer who "in turn trusted the Iowa law enforcement authorities to honor a commitment made during negotiations which led to the apprehension of a potentially dangerous person," and stressed that "if in the long run, we are seriously concerned about the individual's effective representation by counsel, the State cannot be permitted to dishonor its promise to this lawyer." *Id.* at 415. Assuming that the facts were as the state trial court and federal district court findings evidently led Justice Stevens to believe, his viewpoint would be most forceful.

5. But the Model Code of Pre-Arraignment Procedure "directs the court to give weight to the defendant's account in any factual dispute if it finds that the police department has not set up procedures [full written records and sound recordings] to insure compliance with the Code or has not diligently and in good faith sought to comply with the recordkeeping provisions." MODEL CODE OF PRE-ARRAIGNMENT PROCEDURE § 130.4, Commentary at 343 (Official Draft, 1975) [hereinafter cited as MODEL CODE].

with Williams's Des Moines attorney and into two more disputes with Williams's Davenport lawyer, the federal district court disbelieved Leaming all three times.

To ask whether the disclosure made by Williams on the long drive back should have been excluded is to ask not one question, but a range of questions about *Massiah v. United States*, [23] *Miranda v. Arizona*, [24] and even the hoary "voluntariness" test. Yet none of these questions can be answered without a careful examination of the record in *Williams*. Much attention has been devoted to the so-called Christian burial speech that Captain Leaming delivered on the return trip, [25] but this approach focuses attention on a single snapshot rather than a mural. The speech took no more than a minute or two. What happened the rest of the time? What preceded the speech? What did Leaming tell Williams and how often and at what points along the way? How did Williams respond? When? What did Williams ask Leaming? When? How did Leaming respond, if at all? And if he did, when? Everything hangs on the captain's version of the events.

The Record Examined

Captain Leaming's testimony is less clear than it ought to be as to just when he rendered his now famous Christian burial speech. [26] The best reading of the record, and one confirmed by the testimony of Detective Nelson, [27] who drove the car while Leaming and Williams "visited" in the back, [28] is that it occurred only a short time after they left the Davenport area and entered the freeway. By that time, according to Leaming, he and his prisoner had already "discussed religion . . . intelligence of other people . . . police procedures, organizing youth groups, singing . . . playing an organ, and this sort of thing." [29] According to Leaming, Williams "was very talkative" [30] and "a real good talker." [31] He must have also been a fast one to have touched upon so many topics in the relatively few minutes that elapsed between the time the Leaming party left Davenport and the time Leaming made the speech.

And now to the Christian burial speech itself. The United States Supreme Court and four other courts pondered and dissected this speech, [32] yet, curiously, none of them discussed the fact that Captain Leaming offered two—and, in my judgment, two significantly different—versions of it. The captain's first version was given on April 2, 1969, at a pretrial hearing to suppress evidence; [33] his second version, which was the only one quoted and discussed by the Supreme Court and lower federal courts, was given at the trial held four weeks later. [34] Evidently, nobody noticed at the trial that the version Leaming then gave differed in several respects from his earlier version. He was not asked to explain any inconsistencies and did not do so. The two versions, with related testimony, are set out below:

First Version
I said to Mr. Williams, I said, "Reverend, I'm going to tell you something. I don't want you to answer me, but I want you to think about it when we're driving down the road." I said, "I want you to observe the weather. It's raining and it's sleeting and it's freezing. Visibility is very poor. They are predicting snow for tonight. I think that we're going to be going right past where that body is, and if we should stop and find out where it is on the way in, her parents are going to be able to have a good Christian burial for their little daughter. If we don't and it does snow and if you're the only person that knows where this is and if you have only been there once, it's very possible that with snow on the ground you might not be able to find it. Now I just want you to think about that when we're driving down the road." That's all I said.
Q. About where were you when you said that?
A. Well, not very far out of Davenport. This is on the freeway.
Q. And now when you got to Mitchellville [the Mitchellville turnoff was about 145 miles from Davenport and about 10 to 15 miles outside of Des Moines], did you ask him had he thought about it?
A. No. As we were coming towards Mitchellville, we'd still be east of Mitchellville a ways, he said to me, "How do [did?] you know that [the body] would be at Mitchellville?" And I said, "Well, I'm an investigator. This is my job, and I just figured it out." I said, "I don't know exactly where, but I do know it's somewhere in that area." He said, "You're right, and I'm going to show you where it is."[35]

Second Version
Eventually, as we were traveling along there, I said to Mr. Williams that, "I want to give you something to think about while we're traveling down the road." I said, "Number one, I want you to observe the weather conditions, it's raining, it's sleeting, it's freezing, driving is very treacherous, visibility is poor, it's going to be dark early this evening. They are predicting several inches of snow for tonight, and I feel that you yourself are the only person that knows where this little girl's body is, that you yourself have only been there once, and if you get a snow on top of it you yourself may be unable to find it. And, since we will be going right past the area on the way into Des Moines, I feel that we could stop and locate the body, that the parents of this little girl should be entitled to a Christian burial for the little girl who was snatched away from them on Christmas [E]ve and murdered. And I feel we should stop and locate it on the way in rather than waiting until morning and trying to come back out after a snow storm and possibly not being able to find it at all."

At that point Mr. Williams asked me why I should feel that we would be going right by it. I told him that I knew it was somewhere in the Mitchellville area and I didn't know exactly where, but I did know that it was somewhere in the Mitchellville area, and I felt that we should stop and look.

I stated further, "I do not want you to answer me. I don't want to discuss it any further. Just think about it as we're riding down the road." [After testifying that they stopped and got out to look for the child's shoes (when Williams asked whether they had been found) and stopped again to look for the blanket in which the child had been wrapped (when Williams asked whether it had been found), Captain Leaming continued:]

A. Well, we had further discussions about people and religion and intelligence and friends of his, and what people's opinion was of him and so forth. And, oh, some distance still east of the Mitchellville turnoff he said, "I am going to show you where the body is." He said, "How did you know that it was by Mitchellville?" I told him that this was our job to find out such things and I just knew that it was in that area.[36]

Each version of the Christian burial speech has aspects that are more damaging to the prosecution than the other. For example, in the first version Captain Leaming only says: "*I think* that we're going to be going right past where that body is, and *if we should stop* and find out where it is on the way in, her parents *are going to be able* to have a good Christian burial for their little daughter. If we don't and it does snow and *if you [are]* the only person that knows where this is . . . " (emphasis added). The second version, however, is a good deal more powerful and emotional. This time the captain expresses his desires and preference much more emphatically, and puts a heavier burden on Williams: "*I feel that you yourself are* the only person that knows where this little girl's body is. . . . And, since *we will* be going right past the area . . . *I feel that we could stop* and locate the body, that the parents of this little girl *should be entitled* to a Christian burial for the little girl who was snatched away from them on Christmas [E]ve and murdered. And *I feel we should stop* and locate it on the way. . . . " (emphasis added).

What on their face are merely words expressing a strong preference for a certain course of action take on vivid color from the captain's rank, badge, gun, and demeanor,[37] from his standing as "a fine man" (Williams's lawyer told him so)[38] and as a sensitive, religious person (Leaming himself told him so),[6] and from Williams's probable perception of Leaming as his protector and sympathizer.[7] Williams was Leaming's prisoner, and so far Leaming had been nice to him. Williams would want very much to be nice to Leaming.[8]

6. Leaming testified that shortly after they entered the freeway, he advised Williams that "I myself had had religious training and background as a child, and that I would probably come more near praying for him than I would to abuse him or strike him." *Id.* at 80.

7. Attorney McKnight, who had accepted Leaming's offer to bring Williams back personally, tried to reassure an obviously frightened Williams over the phone that Leaming was a "fine man" who "won't let any harm come to you." *Id.* at 96. On the trip back, Williams expressed fear that Leaming wanted to kill him, and also that the state agents, who were following in a second car in case the first vehicle slid off the icy roads, might want to kill him, too. *Id.* at 66, 80 (testimony of Captain Leaming). Leaming assured Williams that he had no intentions of injuring him in any way or "allowing anyone else to molest or abuse him in any manner while he was in [his] custody." *Id.* at 80.

8. Even persons involved in much milder encounters with the police usually "desire to appear courteous and not to offend. [I]nterrogation is a social situation, and suspects respond according to the normal rules of social interaction in such a situation." Griffiths & Ayres, *A Postscript to*

Under the second version of the speech on which all members of the Court relied, Captain Leaming had made his feelings perfectly clear to Williams, and the latter—undoubtedly nervous,[9] possibly terrified,[10] probably ashamed, hands cuffed behind his back,[11] physically close to Leaming[12]— would have shrunk from the prospect of flustering, displeasing, or irritating his captor.[(39)]

---

the Miranda *Project: Interrogation of Draft Protesters,* 77 YALE L.J. 300, 315 (1967). This study was based on detailed interviews with 21 Yale faculty, staff members, and students who turned in their draft cards as part of an antiwar protest and were then questioned by FBI agents. When word spread that some students had been interrogated, a meeting was organized (the Monday meeting) and members of the Yale law faculty "spoke on the legal rights of persons being questioned . . . explained some of the workings of the criminal process, and discussed the possible objectives of the questioning;" the sense of the meeting was "that talking to the FBI could serve no useful purpose and might conceivably be harmful." *Id.* at 303. Nevertheless,

[E]ven after the Monday meeting, in which the nature of the interrogator's job—and in particular the fact that it *is* a job—was discussed, the suspects remained largely unable to treat their encounter as an early stage in a formal, adversary legal process. Instead, they tended to see the interview in personal terms, almost as if they were talking to a new acquaintance. . . .

. . . .

The feeling of being socially obliged to answer *some* questions was mentioned to us by a sizable number of those questioned after Monday. . . . [E]ven with that background [the Monday meeting], many of them reported feeling rude when they repeatedly told the agents that they refused to answer. . . .

. . . [I]n the social situation we have described above, a question demands an answer (*Miranda* states legal, not social, rules). The suspect is thus in a position of having to *decide* whether to answer each question. In making each such decision, he is subject to [various stresses and incapacities], and above all to the disability of ignorance and the pressure of politeness.

Id. at 315-17 (emphasis in original).

A "social situation" had been established in the Des Moines police car by the time Captain Leaming delivered his speech. He and Williams had already engaged in considerable "small talk"—had been "visiting," to use Leaming's term—and Leaming had already emphasized that he had no personal feelings against his prisoner. *See* footnotes 6-7 *supra* and accompanying text.

9. Even those questioned under the much milder conditions described in footnote 8 *supra* "were very nervous, on the whole. . . . The stakes were high and became more immediate by the very fact of interrogation. More important, they were confronting authority directly; as one suspect put it: 'Well, it *was* the FBI, you know.'" Griffiths & Ayers, *supra* footnote 8, at 314-15. Well, it *was* a police captain, it was the chief of detectives of the Des Moines police force, you know.

10. When Williams phoned his Des Moines lawyer from Davenport, he expressed fear that somebody was "going to hit him in the head." Brief for Petitioner, Joint App. at 96. On the drive back to Des Moines the first thing Williams asked Leaming was whether the captain "hated him" and "wanted to kill him." *Id.* at 94-95, 79-80 (testimony of Captain Leaming). He also voiced concern that the state officers following them in another car might want to kill him. *See* footnote 7 *supra.*

11. Brief for Petitioner, Joint App. at 76, 83 (testimony of Captain Leaming).

12. Leaming and Williams had been sitting close together in the back seat, no objects intruding

Even when he had been in the more spacious and less coercive confines of the Davenport courthouse and Lieutenant Ackerman had asked him where the little girl was and whether she was safe—an admission by the lieutenant that was never followed up at the trial nor mentioned by any of the courts that passed on the case[40]—Williams had been careful not to offend, not to refuse firmly to discuss the matter.[41] It is hard to believe that he would have done so on the long ride back to Des Moines. But Captain Leaming made it easy for Williams—for the moment. He told him just to *think about it*. The pressure would build, however, as they approached the Mitchellville turnoff.

The first thing that strikes one about the earlier version of the Christian burial speech is the very first word—"Reverend." *Why* did Leaming call Williams that? *How many times* did he do so on the drive back to Des Moines? These questions were never asked. *No* questions about Williams being addressed as Reverend were ever asked.

When Leaming began his Christian burial speech, he and his prisoner had been discussing religion in the back seat.[42] Had Williams just said something to the effect that he regarded himself as a man of God or someone dedicated to God?[43] Is that why Leaming chose this moment to launch the Christian burial speech? Or did Leaming call his prisoner Reverend simply because it is a standard interrogation technique, "when interrogating persons of low social status," to address them by some title rather than by their first name?[44] Or did he do so simply because he was aware that "[t]he uneducated and under-privileged are more vulnerable to flattery than the educated person or the person in favorable financial or social circumstances"?[45]

The "Reverend" ploy would seem to reinforce another standard interrogation technique that is well illustrated in both versions of Leaming's speech— the appeal to Williams as a religious person, a good Christian. Indeed, the

---

between them, and Williams knew they would be so positioned for the rest of the long trip. *See id.* at 55, 71, 77, 83, 98.

[T]o be physically close is to be psychologically close. The situation has a structure emphasiz-ing to the persons involved the immediacy of their contact: in an encounter [defined by social scientists, the author noted earlier, as a "type of social arrangement that occurs when persons are in one another's immediate physical presence"] there is opportunity for uninterrupted verbal communication, a strong awareness of expressive nonverbal signs, the maintenance of poise and a sense of roles, engrossment in the activity at hand, and an allocation of spatial position. . . .

. . . .

. . . When the norm governing spatial distance is violated, a person's instantaneous and automatic response is to back up, again and again. The suspect, unable to escape, will become even more anxious and unsure.

Driver, *Confessions and the Social Psychology of Coercion*, 82 HARV. L. REV. 42, 44–46 (1968) (footnotes omitted).

leading manual on the subject discusses both stratagems under the same subheading: "Appeal to the Subject's Pride by Well-Selected Flattery or by a Challenge to His Honor."[46] Under that subheading, the manual points out:

It is occasionally helpful to appeal to the subject's loyalty to a group of persons or to an organization whose reputation and honor has been jeopardized by the subject's unlawful behavior. For instance, an appeal may be made in the name of the subject's church, or any other organization or group toward which the subject appears to have some loyalty or allegiance.[13]

The federal district court did not find that Captain Leaming called Williams "Reverend," and Leaming at the trial never said that he did. The attorney general of Iowa, however, did not deny it. Even though he contended that there was "little support *in the record*" for the federal district court's finding "that Williams' statements were obtained only after Detective Leaming's use of psychology on a person whom he knew to be deeply religious and an escapee from a mental hospital,"[47] he recognized that the "Reverend" stratagem constituted some support for the court's finding. Conceding that Leaming suspected that Williams was religious, the attorney general continued: "While Leaming's notions are *outside the record*, he admits he was in fact playing upon William's religious conscience when he made the statements which are of record. And when he addressed Williams as 'Reverend' he says he did so to win his friendship and confidence."[48]

In his opinion for the Court, Justice Stewart describes the Christian burial speech as follows: "Addressing Williams as 'Reverend,' the Detective said...."[49] Justice Stewart then gives the *second* version of the speech and related testimony in its entirety.[50] But Leaming did not address Williams as Reverend in the second version, only in the first.

The attorney general of Iowa was sufficiently troubled by the "Reverend" ploy to go outside the record to explain why Leaming employed it. Justice Stewart also was sufficiently impressed by the significance of the "Reverend" address to call attention to it. But why did Leaming delete it from his trial testimony? Did similar factors move Leaming to leave out other items as well? Or add other? Why is the earlier version, which Leaming more or less volun-

---

13. F. INBAU & J. REID, CRIMINAL INTERROGATION AND CONFESSIONS 76 (2d ed. 1967). Captain Leaming may have buttressed his appeal to Williams in the name of Christianity in still another way. In their very first conversation he told Williams that he himself "had had religious training and background as a child" and would come nearer to praying for him than to abusing him. *See* footnote 6 *supra* and accompanying text. This, in effect, informed Williams that Leaming knew and appreciated what Williams's moral or religious obligations were under the circumstances.

teered to tell,[14] ignored except for the very first word? Why does the second version become the official version?

The very first word of the first version of the Christian burial speech may be jarring, but the most striking thing to me about the first version, when read in its entirety, is that *something has to be missing.* Captain Leaming tells his prisoner that he thinks "we're going to be going right past where the body is," but does not tell him *where* he thinks it is. An hour or two later, as the car approached the Mitchellville turnoff, Leaming tells us that Williams asked him: "How do [did?] you know that it would be *at Mitchellville?*" (emphasis added). Sometime after he delivered the speech and sometime before Williams asked him how he knew the body was in Mitchellville, Leaming must have told Williams that he knew it was buried there. But when? Just before they approached the Mitchellville area? Immediately after Leaming delivered the speech? Somewhere in between? These questions were never asked at the pretrial hearing.[15]

Moreover, the first version begins "I don't want you to answer me" and ends "I just want you to think about that when we're driving down the road." In the second version, *the order is reversed.* The second time around Leaming did fill the gap—he said that he told Williams he "knew" the body "was somewhere in the Mitchellville area" immediately after delivering the speech. Moreover, in the second version Leaming said that he quickly added: "I don't want to discuss it any further." The first time he testified, however, Leaming never said that he told Williams he didn't want to discuss it any further.

The first version of the speech is considerably less solicitous of Williams's rights than the second. According to the first version, Leaming *prefaced* his remarks with "I don't want you to answer me," then jolted, or tried to jolt or at least to agitate Williams with the news that the police knew or thought they knew where the body was. If this is how Leaming made the statement,

14. When Captain Leaming was cross-examined at the pretrial hearing, the following colloquy occurred:

Q. You didn't ask Williams any questions?
A. No, sir, I told him some things.
Q. You told him some things?
A. Yes, sir. Would you like to hear it?
Q. Yes.
A. All right. I said to Mr. Williams, I said, "Reverend, I'm going to tell you something. . . ."

Brief for Petitioner, Joint App. at 62–63.

15. Although the gap in Leaming's testimony passed unnoticed by the defense, it did not escape the prosecutor. His first question on redirect examination was: "Captain Leaming, prior to the defendant showing you where the body was, had you told him you thought it was in the Mitchellville area?" Leaming's answer was, "Yes, sir"—that's all. *Id.* at 65. He did not tell the prosecutor, and he was not asked, *when* he told this to Williams.

whatever the captain told Williams by way of introduction to the speech was probably dissipated by the main thrust of the speech. After all, Leaming made a strong pitch, and evidently a psychologically sound one. He appealed to someone he knew to be deeply religious in the name of religion. He did not ask Williams *whether* the little girl was alive or dead (as had Lieutenant Ackerman earlier in the day).[51] Nor did he ask Williams *whether* he knew where the body was (as had Ackerman).[52] Rather, Leaming's statement under either version *assumed* that the girl was dead and *assumed,* too, that Williams knew where the body was.[53] Moreover, Leaming's statement did more than merely *imply* that the police knew, or had a pretty good idea, where the body was.

If Leaming delivered the Christian burial speech the way he testified he did at the pretrial hearing, then by the time Leaming finished the speech the *prefatory* remark "I don't want you to answer" was surely no longer uppermost in Williams's mind, if it were still in his mind at all. But then, still according to the first version, Leaming left Williams hanging: "I just want you to think about that when we're driving down the road."

What does that mean? I just want you to think about that when we're driving down the road *toward the place where the girl is buried?* I just want you to think about that while we're driving down the road *and I want you to decide whether or not you want to show us the body by the time we reach the turnoff to the area where the body is?* That *is* what Leaming *wanted,* isn't it? It would not be unreasonable for his addressee so to interpret his closing remark, would it?

Why, according to the first version, did the captain preface his speech with "I don't want you to answer me"? Perhaps he did so because Williams already had asserted his rights many times that day.[54] Indeed, the most plausible interpretation of the record is that Williams had already asserted his rights on the drive back to Des Moines; he had informed Leaming, at least for the first time, that he would tell him "the whole story" when he got back to Des Moines and met with his lawyer.[16] Finally, Leaming probably knew that his Davenport counterpart previously had asked Williams where the little girl was and had come up emptyhanded.[55] Under the circumstances, was Leaming's prefatory remark about not wanting Williams to answer him a way of pretending to concede to him his rights? This, we are told by the experts, "usually has

16. Although the record is not as clear as it ought to be on this point, according to Leaming the first time Williams made this statement was "not too long after we got on the freeway, after we had gassed up [in Davenport] and started—got on the highway and started toward Des Moines. He told me that the first time." Brief for Petitioner, Joint App. 1t 65–66. This almost certainly must have occurred before the Christian burial speech, which was preceded by a considerable amount of conversation. *See* Brief for Respondent, at 17 n.9 (elaborate analysis of the record reaching same conclusion).

a very undermining effect" on someone who asserts, or has asserted, his rights.[56]

Did Leaming's prefatory remark enhance, or was it designed to enhance, the effectiveness of the main body of Leaming's speech by impressing Williams at the outset with his captor's apparent fairness?[57] Was this more evidence of Leaming's sympathy and integrity? A further effort to project an image that matched Williams's concept of the "respected figure"?[58]

Up to this point, I have dwelt primarily on what Captain Leaming might have *said*. But the more significant question, I submit, is what Williams might reasonably have *understood* the captain to say. Why did Williams disclose the location of the body? Was he motivated by the Christian burial speech? Or did he spontaneously offer to find the body?

That Williams probably told the captain at least once after the Christian burial speech that he would reveal "the whole story" when he returned to Des Moines and met with his lawyer[59] was deemed significant by both the Supreme Court majority and by dissenting Justice White.[60] I think it more significant, however, that Williams probably told Leaming the same thing at least once *before*, and apparently just before, the speech was delivered.[61] If so, then Williams might well have viewed Leaming's Christian burial speech as a response to his offer to cooperate by revealing the whole story *after* they returned to Des Moines. And Leaming's speech would have sounded like an expression of dissatisfaction with Williams's limited offer to cooperate. If I am right, then what Williams *probably heard* when Leaming delivered the speech, and what any reasonable person sitting in the back seat of the Des Moines car could well have heard was something like this:

Your offer to tell us or show us where the body is *after* we get back to Des Moines (or have your lawyer or you and your lawyer do so) isn't good enough. For one thing, the way the snow is coming down you might not be able to show us where the body is if we wait that long. I want you to think about telling us or showing us where the body is *before* we get back.

Of course, the captain not only told his prisoner what he wanted him to do, but why—to enable the parents to give their little girl a good Christian burial. What did that mean? What was the point of that? What any reasonable listener would hear, even if he weren't religious, even if it weren't the day after Christmas, [62] was: "The only decent and honorable thing for you to do is to show us where that body is on the way back to Des Moines."[63]

The impact on Williams of the Christian burial speech and the surrounding circumstances was probably so profound that at the very least it cast a shadow over anything Leaming *might* have said about not answering him or not wanting to discuss the matter. If Williams had known any Emerson, been calm enough to recall it, and bold enough to recite it, he might have responded: "What you are stands over you the while, and thunders so that I cannot hear what you say to the contrary." [64]

We need not limit ourselves to speculation about what the hypothetical listener would have heard or apprehended Captain Leaming as saying when he gave his now famous speech. We can do a little better than that. There was another listener in the Des Moines police car—Detective Nelson. Although this point was not pursued at trial nor picked up in any of the courts that passed on the case, the following colloquy occurred when Nelson was cross-examined:

Q. [Y]ou weren't interrogating?
A. No.
Q. So everything you testified to, Williams just started talking?
A. He did a lot of talking, yes, sir.
Q. Without anybody asking him anything?
A. Yes, *other than* . . . when we left Davenport, Captain Leaming *asked him to think about telling us* where the body is. [65]

Williams himself, when he testified, complained repeatedly that Leaming told him that he might as well reveal where the body was on the trip back to Des Moines because after Williams got back, he and his lawyer would show the police where the body was anyway; [66] that it "would be a waste of time to go all the way to Des Moines to get [McKnight] and come back, and that's what [they] would have to do, [and if they did they would] probably be on the road all hours of the night"; [67] and that McKnight "had already instructed [the police that] as soon as . . . [Williams] got to Des Moines [they] would come back and show [the police] where the body was." [68] Williams's version of what was said is significantly stronger than either version given by Leaming. There is nothing in the record to indicate whether Williams's testimony is merely *his understanding* of what Leaming admitted to having said or whether Leaming really said more. Although Leaming testified twice, nobody asked him whether he told Williams any of these things. [69] Yet Williams insisted that these were the things that influenced him to show the police where the body was. [70] Putting aside all of Williams's testimony, we are still left with this: Leaming and Chief Nichols both swore under oath that McKnight told Williams over the phone in their presence that Williams or McKnight would reveal the location of the body after Williams returned to Des Moines. [17] Thus, when Leaming told Williams in the course of rendering his Christian burial speech that he felt they should locate the body on the way

17. The long-distance phone conversation between Williams and McKnight is one of the most mystifying features of the record. *See* footnote 4 *supra*. Shortly after Williams surrendered to the Davenport police, they allowed him to phone McKnight, who took the call in Captain Leaming's

to Des Moines rather than on the following morning, he made a powerful argument. Williams had no reason to doubt the captain's implicit assumption that these were his only two options. It reasonably appeared to him that this was indeed the case.

Even if Leaming told Williams no more than the second version indicates, in light of the earlier phone conversation with McKnight what Williams might well have heard Leaming say, and what any *reasonable person* in Williams's plight might well have heard, is what Williams testified *he did hear*—because his only alternative would be to go all the way to Des Moines, get his lawyer, and come back to the same spot later and under more adverse weather conditions, it would be a waste of time not to show the police where the body was now. [18]

I do not deny that Williams also told the captain one or more times *after* he had heard the famous speech that he would tell him the whole story when he

---

office. Williams's lawyer then permitted both Leaming and Des Moines Police Chief Nichols to hear his end of the conversation. Brief for Petitioner, Joint App. at 37-38, 40-43, 54, 64, 88-90, 96.

McKnight did not testify himself as to what he said, but both Captain Leaming and Chief Nichols did. Leaming said that he heard McKnight say to Williams: "'You have to tell the officers where the body is,' and he repeated a second time, 'You have got to tell them where she is'... He then said, 'When you get back here, you tell me and I'll tell them. I am going to tell them the whole story.'" *Id.* at 96.

Chief Nichols more or less supported Leaming. He testified that McKnight told Williams, "We will talk when you get here." *Id.* at 40. When asked by the prosecutor whether McKnight told Williams that he was going to have to tell the police "everything" or "where she is" or "something of that nature," he replied: "Something of that nature." *Id.* at 41.

Finally, Williams's lawyer in Davenport, Kelly, testified that he told Captain Leaming upon his arrival that it was his "understanding" that when Williams was returned to Des Moines, "You [McKnight] would talk to Williams in Leaming's office and at that time he [Williams] would reveal where the body was." *Id.* at 107.

What McKnight had in mind when he spoke to Williams is unclear. Conceivably, he was trying to pacify the police officials he knew were listening to his end of the conversation. Perhaps McKnight thought that by instructing Williams, in earshot of the police officers, that he would have to turn up the body after he returned to Des Moines, he would be removing any incentive on the officers' part to question Williams on the way back. But Williams, of course, would not have known that was his lawyer's motivation.

Quite possibly, as concurring Justice Marshall assumed, McKnight's plan was to learn the whereabouts of the body from his client and then to lead the police to the body himself. 430 U.S. at 408. In this way, as Justice Marshall observed, Williams "would thereby be protected by the attorney-client privilege from incriminating himself by directly demonstrating his knowledge of the body's location, and the unfortunate Powers child could be given a 'Christian burial.'" *Id.* If this was McKnight's plan, however, there is no indication in the record that he explained it, clearly or otherwise, to his client.

In any event, the crucial question is not what McKnight meant, or even what he said, but what his client *understood* him as saying. If the chief of police and the chief of detectives misunderstood McKnight, and if Williams's lawyer in Davenport misunderstood the arrangements, then surely it is reasonable and probable that Williams misunderstood, too.

18. None of the courts that passed on the case discussed this point.

got back to Des Moines and saw his lawyer. But *why?* Did Williams just say it out of the blue, which seems unlikely, or did somebody or something prompt him to say it?

There is nothing in the record about *why* Williams made these statements or *how* Leaming responded when he did. Ignoring, as everyone does, Williams's testimony that the captain "questioned me periodically concerning where the body was . . . [not] in rapid succession . . . [but] as we travelled a few miles at a time,"[71] the most plausible alternative explanation is that the speech had such a powerful impact on Williams that long after it had been delivered he could still "hear" it. And it may well have sounded louder and louder as the Mitchellville turnoff loomed nearer.

If so, then Williams's postspeech statement(s) that he would tell the whole story *after* they completed the trip may not have been, as Justice White suggested in his dissent, "an indication that he knew he was entitled to wait until counsel was present before talking to the police."[72] Nor was it necessarily, as the majority suggests, "the clearest expression . . . that he desired the presence of an attorney before an interrogation took place."[73] Williams's insistence that he would tell the whole story later more likely was a manifestation of the continuing, and perhaps mounting, pressure he felt as the car approached Mitchellville. If so, Williams's postspeech statements were not simply an acknowledgement that he was aware of his rights or an assertion of his right to counsel, but rather a reiteration—in the face of the captain's counterproposal—of his original position. Which inference you draw, however, is dependent upon which version of the facts you believe: Williams's version? Leaming's first version? Leaming's second version?

The foregoing reading of the record is consistent with Captain Leaming's original description of how Williams finally announced that he was going to show the police where the body was, but finds considerably less support in the version Leaming gave at trial. According to the latter, Williams with no warning and without any preliminary discussion or questions about the body simply blurted out that he was going to show Leaming where the body was.[74] If so, one can hardly blame the captain for not covering his ears—or Williams's mouth. Moreover, according to the second version it is only *after* Williams made this long-awaited announcement and while he was already in the process of guiding the police to the dead girl's clothing that he asked Leaming how he knew the body was in the Mitchellville area.[75]

In the original version, however, the order is reversed. According to this version, Williams *led up* to the disclosure of the body by asking the captain how he knew it would be in the Mitchellville area.[76] If so, this indicates that Williams had been thinking about the speech quite a bit, perhaps all the time they were travelling down the road, and that when Mitchellville was only minutes away he began wobbling.

According to the original version, just before making the crucial disclosure

Williams alerted the captain that he was about to do so. Of course, in light of the many times he had asserted his rights that day, both before and after the group had started on the return trip back to Des Moines, Williams was also alerting the captain that he might be assuming "contradictory positions "[77]— that his apparent change of mind might not be a waiver of his rights, but rather the product of the anxiety and confusion generated by the speech and the imminence of the Mitchellville turnoff—or that he might be laboring under the misapprehension that once he got back to Des Moines he would have to show the police where the body was anyway. [78]

The captain, however, did nothing to clear up any possible misunderstanding. Nor at this high-pressure point in the return trip did he advise Williams, as he had done just before they left Davenport, that he wanted him to remember what he told him about his rights. Nor did he say, as he claimed to have when he gave the speech, that he didn't want Williams to answer him or to discuss the matter (if he ever told him that). Quite the contrary. Leaming *did* discuss the matter. He sensed that his patience was about to pay off and he moved in for the kill. At this point, he was more firm and more emphatic about his knowledge of the body's location: "I'm an investigator. This is my job, and I just figured it out. "[79]

All this, of course, is based on the events that led up to Williams's disclosure as they appear in Leaming's original testimony. These events find no counterpart in what the state of Iowa called the "essentially" similar second version. [80]

Some Final Thoughts

Williams raises some nice questions about the meaning, scope of, and interplay between the *Massiah* and *Miranda* principles. But that is the subject of another article. This one is designed to raise some painful questions about the practical application of those principles—or for that matter about the administration of any rules governing the admissibility of confessions. As I trust those who have come this far with me will agree, the various opinions in *Williams* totter on an incomplete, contradictory, and recalcitrant record. The Supreme Court—and all our courts—deserve better and should demand more.

This case does involve some unusual features. Its peculiarities, however, do not detract from but only illuminate the problem posed by the typical confession case—secret proceedings absent any objective recordation of the facts. [81] If either one of Captain Leaming's two versions of the critical events on the drive back to Des Moines had been his only version, it would have been treated, as an officer's testimony usually is, as the gospel truth. But the case happens to involve an "interrogator" (perhaps we should call him an "elicitor") who testified twice and significantly differently each time. So questions *are* raised.

If Leaming's only antagonist had been Williams, no doubts about the captain's credibility would have surfaced. But this case happens to involve an officer who got into swearing contests with the defense lawyers themselves, as well as with a criminal suspect. Because the captain lost every time he tangled with one of the lawyers,[82] some doubts are raised, or ought to be raised, about the swearing contest that he won when he disputed Williams.

Although the special features of the *Williams* case constitute "alerting circumstances," any trial of the issue of waiver,[19] no less than that of

19. *See* MODEL CODE, *supra* footnote 5, § 130.4, Commentary at 341–42.

Much of the opposition to stationhouse interrogation and to making the right to counsel during questioning waivable reflects concern about the danger of police abuse which cannot subsequently be established in court, a concern which has in no way been lessened by the *Miranda* decision. . . . Although [specified procedures] should help prevent misconduct based on uncertainty about the rules, the risk of abuse from a deliberate or careless violation remains. Therefore, the Code requires the making of written records and sound recordings to help a court to reconstruct what took place while an individual is under police control.

Id.; see id. § 130.4 note, at 39.

Subsection (3) [requiring the establishment of procedures providing for a sound recording of the *Miranda* warnings and any subsequent waiver] is designed to help eliminate factual disputes concerning what was said to the arrested person and what prompted any incriminating statements. . . .

In view of the indications in *Miranda* that the prosecution has a heavy burden of proof to show the validity of any waiver it would seem clear that the obligation to tape should include any such waivers.

Id. The recent case of Michigan v. Mosley, 423 U.S. 96 (1975), no less than *Williams,* underscores the need for sound recordings to help the courts determine whether a valid waiver actually occurred. In *Mosley* the Court held that police may renew the questioning of a suspect who has exercised his right to remain silent at an earlier interrogation session, provided the suspect's right to cut off the questioning is "fully respected" or "scrupulously honored." *Id.* at 103–05. The Court apparently deemed it critical, certainly highly significant, that after declining to discuss certain robberies at an initial interrogation Mosley was subsequently questioned about "an unrelated holdup murder." *Id.* at 104. But it is not at all clear that this was so. Professor Geoffrey Stone has pointed out that the Michigan courts never found—indeed the Michigan Court of Appeals expressed skepticism about the contention—that the subject of the robbery-murder was never brought up at the initial interrogation session. Stone, *The* Miranda *Doctrine in the Burger Court,* 1977 SUP. CT. REV. 99, 130. Professor Stone, who has studied the *Mosley* record (I have not), notes that "Detective Cowie initially testified that he discussed '*several* robberies' with Mosley, [but] then *changed his testimony,* and insisted that he questioned Mosley only about the White Tower Restaurant robbery. According to Cowie, however, Mosley declined to say anything 'about the *robberies.*'" *Id.* at 134 (emphasis added). It seems almost incredible that in the 1970s a murder suspect such as Mosley could twice be questioned—the second time after the exercise of his right of silence—in the *departmental headquarters building* (not in a car or on the street) without any police effort to make an objective record of either interrogation session, and that no court passing on the case would so much as raise questions about the need or obligation of the police to make such a record.

coercion[83]—waged by the crude, clumsy method of examination, cross-examination, and redirect—is almost bound to be unsatisfactory. The *Williams* record illustrates this all too painfully.

The record tells us that several times during the long drive back to Des Moines, Williams told Captain Leaming that he would tell him "the whole story" after he returned to Des Moines and conferred with his lawyer.[84] That's about all. Although all sorts of inferences may be drawn from the record, and admittedly I have drawn a few, we do not really know *how often* Williams said it or *when* he said it. Nor do we really know *why* he said it or *how* the captain responded, if at all, any of the times he said it.

The first time Captain Leaming testified, all he said on direct examination about the Christian burial speech was that shortly after they got on the expressway, he and Williams had "had quite a discussion relative to religion."[85] *That's all.* Only on cross-examination did Leaming reveal for the first time—and he more or less volunteered it[86]—that he had made a Christian burial statement. Williams, who had preceded the captain to the witness stand, had never alluded to anything resembling the Christian burial statement.[20] If it had not happened to pop out on Leaming's cross-examination— and it came out more or less accidentally—there never would have been a "Christian burial speech case."

Which of the two versions is the real speech? Is it some combination of the two? Or is it a third and never-to-be-known version? Is it possible that there was more than one Christian burial speech? Recall that Leaming initially described the Christian burial speech simply as "quite a discussion relative to religion." At the other end of the trip, just before Williams announced that he was going to tell the police where the body was, there were, Leaming testified on direct examination, "further discussions about people and religion."[87]

---

20. Williams did recall a statement by Leaming that he had "an idea" or "knowledge" that the body was buried in the Mitchellville area, and this *was* one of the points made in connection with the Christian burial statement. *See* notes 91–92 *infra* and accompanying text. But Williams never mentioned that the captain had told him that the parents deserved, ought to have, or were entitled to a Christian burial for their little girl, or anything to that effect.

One can only speculate about why, in his testimony, Williams did not mention Captain Leaming's "Christian burial" remarks. It may be that this "young man of quixotic religious convictions" (*see* text at note 6 *supra*) found the subject too painful to discuss. It may be that his lawyer McKnight feared that Williams would lose control of himself if he broached the subject and thus instructed him to avoid doing so. It may be that McKnight thought the speech wasn't "interrogation," only an appeal to his client's conscience. It seems fairly clear that McKnight thought he had stronger points to make, *e.g.,* the "broken agreement" between him and the Des Moines police (which McKnight considered his best argument for excluding the confession); Leaming's false statement that the police knew where the body was; Leaming's urging Williams to spare his lawyer (who apparently had a heart condition) the ordeal of searching for the body in bad weather by revealing where it was himself before they returned to Des Moines—a claim McKnight pressed, but Leaming stoutly denied. *See* Brief for Petitioner, Joint App. at 48, 71, 91.

What kinds of discussions? About Christian burials? About confession being good for the soul? We shall never know. Nobody ever asked.

The federal district court found,[88] and members of the Supreme Court operated on the premise,[89] that the captain had told Williams that he "knew" the little girl's body was in the Mitchellville area (which was untrue). But the first time Williams testified on the subject he recalled variously that the captain had told him that the police had "some *speculation* that the body was near Mitchellville"[90] (which was true); that "we have *an idea* it's near Mitchellville"[91] (which was also true); and that the police had "*knowledge* or *good reason* to *believe*" that the body was in Mitchellville[92] (the second half of which was very close to the truth). Moreover, the first time Leaming broached the subject, he said in response to a question by McKnight that "yes, sir," he did tell Williams: "I *theorize* that the body is at Mitchellville"[93] (which was the precise truth). And the second time he brought up the subject, the captain said he told Williams: "I *think* that we're going to be going right past where the body is."[21] Finally, Detective Nelson, who drove the car back to Des Moines, maintained that Captain Leaming did not tell Williams that "he knew" the body was in the Mitchellville area, but "that he *presumed* the body was in the area."[94] How much longer can we go on like this?

I do not share the view of the *Williams* dissenters that analytically *Williams* "is a far cry from *Massiah*,"[95] but in one sense it is. In *Massiah* the critical conversation between petitioner and "secret agent" Colson, who was Massiah's "friend" and partner in crime, also took place in a car. But the conversation not only was transmitted to a nearby agent by means of a radio transmitter hidden under the front seat of the car, it also was tape-recorded over a minifon device concealed in the glove compartment.[96] In arguing for the admissibility of the recording,[97] then Solicitor General Archibald Cox observed:

No less important than its utility in helping law enforcement is the fact that [the recording of such conversations] safeguards defendants from distorted testimony and aids the administration of justice.... Even slight nuances in describing a conversation may be of crucial importance.... Surely, it is preferable that these crucial facts be established by a recording of the conversation itself.... The recording of the conversation in this case (which we have filed with the Clerk) would have given assurance that the agent had correctly testified that petitioner had actually admitted his guilt to Colson, and that he was neither coerced nor improperly induced to make the admissions.[98]

Whatever the objections to a government informer or undercover agent

---

21. Brief for Petitioner, Joint App. at 63 (emphasis added). Of course, Leaming also testified that he told Williams that he had "figured it out" and "knew" that the body was somewhere in the Mitchellville area. *Id.* at 63, 84.

secretly recording a conversation between himself and a suspect or instantaneously transmitting such a conversation to other agents equipped with radio receivers,[99] they are of little force when applied to a situation in which police, known to be such, have isolated a person from the protection of his lawyer for the purpose of "persuading" or "inducing" him to furnish incriminating evidence.[22]

The short answer to the objection that it is not always feasible to utilize tape recordings is that it should only be required when it is. Certainly, the Des Moines police, or the Davenport police, or the State Bureau of Criminal Investigation agents, some of whom followed Leaming and Williams all the way back, could have come up with a recording device. An objective, reliable record of the proceedings in the car not only seems to have been feasible, but also highly advisable.[100] After all, *Williams* was one of the biggest murder cases in the state's history. In all likelihood the use of a recording device, a tiny administrative and financial burden, would have spared the state the need to contest the admissibility of Williams's disclosures in five courts for eight years.

22. "Courts which have considered the question have held that secret recording of police interrogation does not, in itself, affect the admissibility of statements." MODEL CODE, *supra* footnote 5, § 130.4(2), Commentary at 349.

The Model Code provides that an arrestee be informed that a sound recording is being made, but recognizes that this requirement "raises a difficult question." *Id.* at 348. Such a requirement does minimize the possibility that an arrestee will be misled about the seriousness of his situation, but knowledge that they are being recorded may make many reluctant to speak, even those who would not be inhibited by the knowledge that what they were saying was being reduced to writing (although it could lead *some* to talk more freely, secure in the knowledge that they would not be misquoted). *See id.* at 348–49.

Informing the arrestee that what he may say will be recorded is probably preferable, but I do not feel strongly about it. The important thing is that wherever feasible all conversation between the police and a person in custody be tape-recorded, whether or not the person is informed that this is taking place. If the price for a system requiring sound recordings of the warnings, any waivers or other responses, and any subsequent conversation is that the suspect need not be told that a sound recording is being made, I would be quite willing to pay it.

[*About a year after this article was published, Professor Glanville Williams made a strong case for tape-recording police interrogations,* The Authentication of Statements to the Police, [*1979*] CRIM. L. R. *(Brit.) 1. Professor Williams saw no need to "expressly obtain the suspect's consent to be recorded"; he deemed the posting of "[a] notice about the tape-recording . . . in the interview room" sufficient. Id. at 21. He added:*

A suspect who is anxious to give his side of the story and at the same time fears that the police may, when giving evidence, embroider what he says, should welcome the offer of a tape-recording. If the suspect signs a written statement, and if his refusal to have the interview taped is itself recorded on tape, the statement should be admissible.

The police may fear that, although the suspect does not totally refuse to talk while the recorder is running, the presence of the recorder may inhibit his responses. But the experience of solicitors who use tape-recording for interviews with clients is that the client soon forgets the presence of the recorder.

Id. *at 21–22.*]

It is hard to see why the judges, upon whom these *"Finnegans Wake* records" are inflicted, are so apathetic about the apparent unwillingness of police interrogators to use tape recordings.[23] A veteran criminal investigator and leading authority on investigative methods and technology tells us:

One of the characteristics of modern criminal investigation is the extensive use of recording devices for the production of a transcript of interviews and interrogations. Obviously, the best evidence of an interview is the recorded voice. The words themselves are there; the tones and inflection provide the true meaning; . . .

. . . .

. . . Sensitive interviews and interrogations should always be recorded in important cases. . . . If the interview must take place in a room, *automobile,* or restaurant without previous technical preparation, a pocket recorder can be used or one which is concealed in a briefcase. The investigator can be *wired* for the occasion, i.e., a microphone and small recorder can be attached to his person and concealed beneath his clothes.[101]

It was good of Captain Leaming to tell Williams, as they were about to

23. The problem may not be the unwillingness of the police to *use* tape recordings as much as the reluctance to *offer the tapes in evidence.* In an unknown but considerable number of cases the police may tape-record an interrogation for their own purposes, but with no intent to offer it in evidence (as opposed to the resulting confession itself) and with no expectation that it will ever get beyond the confines of the stationhouse. C.E. O'HARA, FUNDAMENTALS OF CRIMINAL INVESTIGATION 154 (4th ed. 1976) recommends that "the room set apart for interrogations or for interviews in the offices of the law enforcement agency should be equipped with a permanent recording installation," pointing out that there may be several purposes in recording an interrogation other than offering it in evidence: if a suspect contradicts himself or falls into inconsistencies, by playing the interrogation back to him "he may be brought to appreciate the futility of deception," *id.* at 155; if a suspect implicates associates or accomplices, "the record can later be played for the associates for the purposes of inducing them to confess," *id.* at 156; if the interrogator is unable to spot weaknesses in the suspect's story or if the interrogation is interrupted, the officer can listen to the tape, "analyze it for consistency and credibility," and, "after determining the weak points, he can then plan the strategy and tactics to be employed in the next interrogation session." *Id.*

In State v. Biron, 266 Minn. 272, 123 N.W.2d 392 (1963), one of the very few reported cases where a tape recording of the entire interrogation—right from the first question asked—became part of the record, the police decision to make a recording was based on the expectation that Biron would confess or make damaging admissions in a relatively short time and that the playing of his taped remarks to his accomplices would cause them to do likewise. But Biron "held out" a good deal longer than expected, and one or more of the five detectives who took turns questioning him were unaware that they were being taped. The tape did wind up in evidence—and it was disastrous for the prosecution when it did—but the police didn't plan it that way. *See* Kamisar, *Fred E. Inbau: "The Importance of Being Guilty,"* 68 J. CRIM. L. & CRIMINOLOGY 182, 185 n.20 (1977) [reprinted in this volume] (representative sampling of police questions). According to Biron's lawyer, Gerald M. Singer, somebody in the police department "tipped him off" that a tape of his client's interrogation existed, he so informed the trial judge, the judge asked a police witness about this, and the officer admitted that this was so. Interview with Gerald M. Singer, University of Minnesota Law School (March 1962).

leave Davenport, to be sure to remember what the captain had told him about his rights and about being represented by counsel,[102] but it would have been even better if procedures had been in effect that would have enabled *the captain* to remember what he had told Williams about his rights. Lengthy police car "visits" with isolated prisoners, such as occurred in *Williams,* should not be permitted unless all the proceedings, both in the car and during stops along the way, are tape-recorded.[103]

True, a recording can be tampered with, but "it is doubtful that many officers would dare tamper with [such] physical evidence [and in any event] it could be required that the record be [promptly] deposited with the court under seal."[104] Of course, the defendant would have the right to cross-examine the officer testifying to its authenticity. "The fact that it is conceivable that an agent may perjure himself no more makes a recording inherently unreliable and inadmissible than any other evidence which likewise may be fabricated."[105]

Although its need and advisability are graphically illustrated by the gaps, inconsistencies, and confusion pervading the *Williams* record, there is nothing new about this proposal. Even before the advent of tape recordings, Roscoe Pound proposed "legal examination" of suspects before a magistrate and "provision . . . for taking down the evidence so as to guarantee accuracy," in large measure because "it is not the least of the abuses of the system of extralegal interrogation that there is a constant conflict of evidence as to what the accused said and as to the circumstances under which he said or was coerced into saying it."[106] But tape recordings have been available for some time now. More than twenty years ago, the author of a well-known investigation manual pointed out: "Important interrogations [and presumably important "visits" as well] and confessions should be recorded."[107]

To aid the resolution of (and hopefully to avoid altogether) disputes about what happened to someone in custody, the use of sound-recording devices is required by both the American Law Institute[108] and by the National Conference of Commissioners on Uniform State Laws.[109] These procedures are deemed central to the Model Code's "attempt to provide clear and enforceable rules governing the period between arrest and judicial appearance."[110] The Court should deem them central to its mission as well.

The Model Code procedures are designed to effectuate a suspect's rights *before* the time that adversary judicial proceedings have begun. But the case for providing clear and enforceable rules governing the period *following* the initiation of judicial proceedings against a person is still stronger. In such a case, and *Williams* is such a case, "the casual and relatively perfunctory invitation to a *Miranda*-style waiver is [or ought to be] insufficient."[111] At the very least, no claim that a waiver has been obtained should be accepted unless all proceedings subsequent to the initiation of judicial proceedings have been tape-recorded.

I do not think that in the bulk of the post-*Massiah,* post-*Miranda* cases the problem is "lying" as that word is normally used—a false statement deliberately presented as being true, a statement meant to deceive.[24] Rather, I think it is "lying" in the sense that lawyers, poets, and historians often "lie"—they do not "reproduce reality" but "illumine some aspect of reality, and it always makes for deceit to pretend that what is thus illumined is the whole of reality."[25] That is why, not too uncommonly, when a neutral observer reads the petitioner's statement of the case and then the respondent's—or the majority and dissenting opinions in the case—he is compelled to wonder whether they are talking about the same case.

What would it be like to argue a case on appeal or to hand down opinions in such a case without any objective, reliable record—with nothing to rest on but each lawyer's own recollection and interpretation of the critical events at the trial?[26]

It is worth noting that the "Statement of the Case" in Iowa's petition for a writ of certiorari summarily describes the Christian burial speech as follows: "While en route to Des Moines one of the officers commented that the weather was beginning to turn bad and that discovery of the body and a decent

24. Although I believe that Captain Leaming's original version of the Christian burial speech is overall more damaging to the prosecution that his second version, the second is clearly more damaging in several respects. This is strong evidence that the second time the captain testified on the subject he was not "lying," as that term is usually defined.

25. F. Cohen, *Field Theory and Judicial Logic,* 59 YALE L.J. 238, 242 (1950).

26. This question probably understates the criminal defendant's problem by a considerable margin. The more apt analogy would seem to be a situation where no trial transcripts are made, but the appellate courts almost invariably adopt *the government lawyer's version* of what occurred below.

Another analogous situation would be one where only one party to an agreement—the government—is allowed to reduce the agreement to writing, with complete freedom to choose language reflecting its interpretation of the terms, and the courts pay no attention to the other party's protestations that much language in the draft is inaccurate or misleading. *Cf.* Meltsner & Schrag, *Negotiating Tactics for Legal Services Lawyers,* 7 CLEARINGHOUSE REV. 259, 263 (Sept. 1973), in H. EDWARDS & J. WHITE, THE LAWYER AS A NEGOTIATOR 133, 140 (1977):

Quite often the terms that have been agreed upon will be subject to differing interpretations. . . . You should, therefore, volunteer to undertake the labor of drafting the agreement. By doing so, you can choose language which reflects your interpretation of the terms agreed upon. . . . If you draft the document, the other side should be given an opportunity to correct it and to discuss any language not faithfully incorporating the agreement that has been reached. But many lawyers are not thorough editors, so the opportunity to write the first draft becomes the power to choose critically important language. If an adversary writes the first draft, you should be prepared to go over it line by line and, if necessary, to rewrite every word.

On the trial of such issues as coercion, trickery, adequate warnings or effective waiver, the police officer, of course, almost always has the opportunity "to write the first draft"—and all others. And the defendant or the defense lawyer is almost never given a meaningful opportunity to correct any draft, let alone rewrite it.

burial for the child might be delayed by snow covering the body. "[112] Has something been lost in the summary of the captain's testimony? One can demonstrate, or at least forcefully argue, that *much* has—much of the tone, color, and meaning of "the speech"—but one can do so only because how the captain described the speech is a matter of record. What, however, if *the captain* had described the speech the way the Iowa attorney general described it in the petition for certiorari? The captain's word would have been the last word. There would have been nowhere else to turn.

It is not because a police officer is more dishonest than the rest of us that we should demand an objective recordation of the critical events. Rather, it is because we are entitled to assume that he is no less human—no less inclined to reconstruct and interpret past events in a light most favorable to himself—that we should not permit him to be "a judge of his own cause."[113]

In one of his early opinions on the Supreme Court, an opinion that undoubtedly drew upon his rich background as a trial lawyer and state court judge,[114] Justice Brennan pointed out:

To experienced lawyers it is commonplace that the outcome of a lawsuit—and hence the vindication of legal rights—depends more often on how the factfinder appraises the facts than on a disputed construction of a statute or interpretation of a line of precedents. Thus the procedures by which the facts of the case are determined assume an importance fully as great as the validity of the substantive rule of law to be applied. And the more important the rights at stake the more important must be the procedural safeguards surrounding those rights.[115]

This theme should dominate our thinking about the confession problem. Otherwise, decades of experience will surely have been wasted. Otherwise, it will be of no great moment whether new stories are added to the temples of constitutional law or old ones removed.[116] For any time an officer unimpeded by any objective record distorts, misinterprets, or overlooks one or more critical events, the temple may fall. For it will be a house built upon sand.

Brewer v. Williams, Massiah, and Miranda: What Is "Interrogation"? When Does It Matter?

October, 1978

I didn't even know what those words ["psychological coercion"] meant,
until I looked them up in the dictionary after I was accused of using it....
Shucks, I was just being a good old-fashioned cop, the only kind I know
how to be....
I have never seen a prisoner physically abused, though I heard about
those things in the early days....
That type of questioning just doesn't work. They'll just resist harder.
You have to butter 'em up, sweet talk 'em, use that—what's the
word?—"psychological coercion."

—Captain Leaming, reminiscing about his
"Christian burial speech" nine years later.[1]

ON CHRISTMAS EVE, 1968, a ten-year-old girl, Pamela Powers, disappeared
while with her family in Des Moines, Iowa.[2] Defendant Williams, an escapee
from a mental institution and a deeply religious person,[(1)] was suspected of
murdering her, and a warrant was issued for his arrest.[(2)] Williams telephoned
a Des Moines lawyer, McKnight, and on his advice surrendered himself to the
Davenport, Iowa, police.[(3)]

Captain Leaming and another Des Moines police officer arranged to drive
the 160 miles to Davenport, pick up Williams, and return him directly to Des
Moines.[(4)] Both the trial court[(5)] and the federal district court[(6)] found that
defense attorney McKnight and the Des Moines police agreed that Williams
would not be "questioned" until after he returned to Des Moines and conferred
with his lawyer.[3] Before being driven back to Des Moines, Williams was

1. Lamberto, *Leaming's "Speech": "I'd do it again,"* Des Moines Register, April 7, 1977, §
B, at 1, col. 1.
2. Brewer v. Williams, 430 U.S. 387, 390 (1977) (Burger, C.J., dissenting). In view of the
extensive discussion of *Williams,* the "Christian burial speech" case, in Kamisar, *Foreword:*
Brewer v. Williams—*A Hard Look at a Discomfiting Record,* 66 GEO. L.J. 209 (1977) [re-
printed in this volume], a brief description of the case should suffice here.
3. Brief for Petitioner, Joint App. at 54, 78, 90, Brewer v. Williams, 430 U.S. 387 (1977). The
record does not indicate, however, that there was an explicit agreement, or even that McKnight
specifically instructed the Des Moines police not to question his client on the return trip. At best
there seems to have been an understanding or assumption that the police would not do so. *See*
generally Kamisar, *supra* footnote 2, at 212 n.23.

advised of his rights many times—by McKnight over the phone, by Kelly (his Davenport attorney), by the Davenport judge who arraigned him on the warrant, by a Davenport police officer, and by Leaming himself.[7]

More important, Williams *asserted* his rights many times. He retained counsel in both Des Moines[8] and Davenport.[9] He requested and was granted a private meeting with the Davenport judge.[10] After Leaming arrived and advised him of his rights, Williams requested and was granted *two* private meetings with attorney Kelly.[11] Kelly, furthermore, told Leaming that Williams was not to be questioned until he met with McKnight.[12] Kelly also requested, but was refused, permission to ride back with his client.[13] Finally, on the trip back, Williams told Leaming several times that he would tell him "the whole story" *after* he saw McKnight in Des Moines.[14]

The Court's reading of the record, and the best reading,[15] is that not long after Captain Leaming and his prisoner left Davenport and entered the freeway, the captain delivered his now famous "Christian burial speech."[16] Although there are two significantly different versions of the speech,[17] I shall proceed, as did the Supreme Court and lower federal courts, on the assumption that there was only one.[18] According to the Court's opinion, the detective addressed Williams as "Reverend" and continued:

> "I want to give you something to think about while we're traveling down the road. . . . Number one, I want you to observe the weather conditions, it's raining, it's sleeting, it's freezing, driving is very treacherous, visibility is poor, it's going to be dark early this evening. They are predicting several inches of snow for tonight, and I feel that you yourself are the only person that knows where this little girl's body is, that you yourself have only been there once, and if you get a snow on top of it you yourself may be unable to find it. And, since we will be going right past the area on the way into Des Moines, I feel that we could stop and locate the body, that the parents of this little girl should be entitled to a Christian burial for the little girl who was snatched away from them on Christmas [E]ve and murdered. And I feel we should stop and locate it on the way in rather than waiting until morning and trying to come back out after a snow storm and possibly not being able to find it at all."

Williams asked Detective Leaming why he thought their route to Des Moines would be taking them past the girl's body, and Leaming responded that he knew the body was in the area of Mitchellville—a town they would be passing on the way to Des Moines. . . . Leaming then stated:"I do not want you to answer me. I don't want to discuss it any further. Just think about it as we're riding down the road."[19]

Was the Christian Burial Speech "Interrogation" within the Meaning of *Miranda*— or "Compulsion" within the Meaning of the Privilege?

Once the *Williams* Court chose the *Massiah* route over a *Miranda* one, once it decided to resolve the case on "Sixth Amendment-*Massiah*,"[20] not "Fifth

Amendment-*Miranda*, "[21] grounds, [4] there was no longer any need to consider whether the speech constituted police "interrogation" (as that term is normally used). At that point, whether the speech constituted "interrogation" became, or should have become, constitutionally irrelevant. [22]

Nevertheless, the *Williams* majority evidently thought it desirable, if not necessary, to classify the Christian burial speech as a form of interrogation or "tantamount to interrogation"[5]—and all four dissenting Justices insisted it

---

4. 430 U.S. at 397–99. In granting habeas corpus relief, the federal district court in *Williams v. Brewer* relied on three independent grounds—that Williams's disclosures were involuntary, that they were obtained in violation of *Miranda*, and that they were secured in violation of his sixth amendment-*Massiah* rights. 375 F. Supp. at 185. The United States Court of Appeals for the Eighth Circuit appears to have affirmed on the second and third grounds. Williams v. Brewer, 509 F.2d 227, 233–34 (8th Cir. 1975). The Supreme Court, in an opinion by Justice Stewart, saw "no need . . . in this case" to review the *Miranda* doctrine, "designed to secure the constitutional privilege against self-incrimination," or to evaluate the district court ruling that Williams's statements were involuntarily made because, inasmuch as judicial proceedings had been initiated against Williams before the start of his return trip to Des Moines, "it is clear that the judgment before us must in any event be affirmed upon the ground that Williams was deprived of a different constitutional right—the right to the assistance of counsel." 430 U.S. at 397–99. The Court then found "the circumstances of this case . . . constitutionally indistinguishable from those presented in Massiah v. United States [377 U.S. 201 (1964)]." 430 U.S. at 400. The *Massiah* case is discussed extensively in the text at footnotes 38–42 *infra*. In brief, after Massiah had been indicted, had retained a lawyer, and had been released on bail, his codefendant, Colson, invited him to discuss the pending case. Unaware that Colson had decided to cooperate with government agents, Massiah talked freely to him and made several damaging admissions that were overheard by a nearby agent equipped with a receiving device. 377 U.S. at 202–03. The *Massiah* Court held, in an opinion authored by Justice Stewart, that the use of these admissions, "which federal agents had deliberately elicited from him after he had been indicted and in the absence of his counsel," violated petitioner's sixth amendment right to counsel. *Id.* at 206. According to the *Williams* Court, "that the incriminating statements were elicited surreptitiously in the *Massiah* case, and otherwise here, is constitutionally irrelevant." 430 U.S. at 400. The *Williams* dissenters sharply disagreed. *See* text at footnotes 38–42 *infra*.

5. *See* 430 U.S. at 399–400. Writing for the Court, Justice Stewart pointed out several factors indicating that interrogation did in fact take place: (1) Leaming "deliberately and designedly set out to elicit information from Williams just as surely as—and perhaps more effectively than—if he had formally interrogated him"; (2) the Iowa courts "proceeded upon the hypothesis that . . . [the] 'speech' had been tantamount to interrogation"; (3) they "recognized that Williams had been entitled to the assistance of counsel at the time he had made the incriminating statements," "[y]et no such constitutional protection would have come into play if there had been no interrogation"; and (4) in the Supreme Court oral argument the State of Iowa had "acknowledged that the 'Christian burial speech' was tantamount to interrogation." *Id.* at 399–400 & 399 n.6.

The lawyers for the State of Iowa arguably acknowledged *four or five times* that Captain Leaming's speech was tantamount to interrogation (depending, of course, on one's definition of "interrogation"). Although he refused to call it interrogation, Iowa's Assistant Attorney General Winders, who spoke for the first seven minutes of the Supreme Court oral argument, agreed with a statement made by one Justice that when Leaming delivered his speech it would "be correct to say that he wanted the defendant to reveal the whereabouts of the child." Transcript of Oral Argument at 9, Brewer v. Williams, 430 U.S. 387 (1977) (copy on file at the *Georgetown Law Journal*). In the opening minutes of his presentation, Attorney General Turner acknowledged that

was not.[23] To the latter, Captain Leaming's remarks were merely "observations and comments"[24] or only "travel conversation"[25] or simply a "statement . . . accompanied by a request that respondent not respond to it."[26]

I find the dissenters' begrudging view of "interrogation" so disturbing that for purposes of discussion I shall assume that *Williams* is a straight *Miranda* case. This entails the triple assumption that, at the time of Leaming's speech, no judicial proceedings had been initiated against Williams, no agreement had been made between the defense attorney and the police, and no lawyer had been retained by, or appointed for, Williams.[6]

Justice Blackmun's Dissent

In his dissent, Justice Blackmun, joined by Justices White and Rehnquist, deemed it "clear there was no interrogation,"[27] but whether he meant simply no interrogation within the meaning of *Miranda* or no interrogation within the meaning of *Massiah* as well is not readily apparent. If Justice Blackmun

---

Leaming made his "Christian burial" remarks—and "even called" Williams "Reverend"—"to induce [Williams] to tell him where Pamela Powers' body was." *Id.* at 11. Then the Attorney General agreed with Justice Powell's comments that Leaming made the statement for the "purpose" of "lead[ing] Williams into stating where the body was located," and that "a lawyer would consider that [Leaming was] pursuing interrogation," but insisted that this interrogation "was very brief." *Id.* at 16–17.

In his concurring opinion, Justice Powell "join[ed] the opinion of the Court which . . . finds that the efforts of Detective Leaming 'to elicit information from Williams,' as conceded by counsel for [Iowa] at oral argument, . . . were a skillful and effective form of interrogation." 430 U.S. at 412. "Moreover," added Powell, "the entire setting was conducive to the psychological coercion that was successfully exploited." *Id.*

It is possible that the *Williams* majority only considered the Christian burial speech, and only deemed it important to consider it, "interrogation" within the meaning of *Massiah*, not *Miranda*. In context, however, I think this highly unlikely. Moreover, considering the facts of *Massiah, see* text at notes 183–89, 209–24, and footnotes 38–42 *infra,* to talk about "interrogating" a person within the meaning of *Massiah* is to stretch the normal meaning of words to the breaking point. Such peculiar use of language seems no more helpful and no less misleading than to talk about, for example, "interviewing" a person within the meaning of Ashcraft v. Tennessee, 322 U.S. 143 (1944), a case involving thirty-six hours of "relay" interrogation. *See* Kamisar, *Fred E. Inbau: "The Importance of Being Guilty,"* 68 J. Crim. L. & Criminology 182, 186–87 n.24 (1977) [reprinted in this volume] (discussion of pejorative and euphemistic terms to characterize police interrogation).

6. In both *Massiah* and *Williams* the challenged statements were obtained at a time when judicial proceedings had been initiated against the accused *and* he had already obtained counsel. It is fairly clear, however, that the commencement of adversary proceedings *alone* activates the right to counsel. *See* text at notes 419–442 and footnote 93 *infra.* Whether representation by counsel *without more* triggers the right to counsel is a good deal less clear, but New York's *Donovan-Arthur-Hobson* rule operates on this premise. *See* footnotes 89–91 and notes 415–17 *infra.* The Supreme Court is likely to so hold, at least when law enforcement officials treat the defense lawyer deceitfully or disdainfully. *See* text at footnotes 94–97 *infra.*

meant that "not every attempt to elicit information should be regarded as 'tantamount to interrogation' "[28] for *Miranda* purposes he is plainly right when—*unlike* the situation in *Williams*—the suspect is unaware that he is in the presence of a government agent. *Hoffa v. United States,* [29] decided only six months after *Miranda,* illustrates this point.

Hoffa incriminated himself by talking to an apparent friend who was actually a paid government informer.[30] Because Hoffa did not know that his court retainer was a secret government agent,[7] he could not claim that his incriminating statements were the product of legal or factual coercion.[8] The facts of *Massiah* would have provided a similar illustration if judicial proceedings had not been initiated against the defendant and if he had not been represented by counsel when he met with his codefendant, Colson.[9]

It is considerably more difficult to envision instances in which, once judicial proceedings have been initiated, successful attempts to elicit information would not be tantamount to a *Massiah* interrogation or, more accurately, "deliberate elicitations" of incriminating statements. But consider the following hypothetical: Suppose Captain Leaming had admitted that one of the reasons he had decided to drive his prisoner back to Des Moines during

---

7. Hoffa v. United States, 385 U.S. 293, 319 (1966) (Warren, C.J., dissenting) (Partin had "worm[ed] his way into Hoffa's hotel suite and [had become] part and parcel of Hoffa's entourage"). At this time Hoffa made the incriminating statements he had not yet been charged with, or even arrested for, endeavoring to bribe members of the Test Fleet jury. Thus, he was compelled to argue that his *Massiah-Escobedo* rights should have come into play once the government had "*sufficient ground*" for taking the petitioner into custody and charging him with endeavors to tamper with the Test Fleet jury." *Id.* at 309 (emphasis added). The Court purported to be stunned by this argument: "Nothing in *Massiah,* in *Escobedo,* or in any other case . . . even remotely suggests this novel and paradoxical constitutional doctrine. . . . There is no constitutional right to be arrested." *Id.* at 310. The Court did note, however, that if the government had taken Hoffa into custody and charged him with attempts to tamper with the Test Fleet jury "it could not have continued to question [him] without observance of his Sixth Amendment right to counsel." *Id.* at 309 (citing Massiah v. United States, 377 U.S. 201 (1964), and Escobedo v. Illinois, 378 U.S. 478 (1964).

8. *Id.* at 304. It seems fairly clear that the result would have been the same even if the secret government agent had asked questions of Hoffa or otherwise actively elicited incriminating statements from him. Such conduct by an apparent friend still would not have been "coercive," inherently or otherwise. *Cf.* Osborn v. United States, 385 U.S. 323 (1966). The Court in *Osborn* affirmed the conviction of one of Hoffa's attorneys for attempting to bribe a prospective federal juror, even though the informer in this case made at least an overture toward crime by mentioning that one of the prospective jurors was his cousin and falsely telling the attorney that he had visited his cousin and found him "susceptible to money for hanging this jury." *See id.* at 326.

9. In fact, Colson had also held separate meetings in his "bugged" car with two of Massiah's confederates, Anfield and Maxwell, *prior to* their eventual arrest and indictment. These conversations, too, had been tape-recorded and "broadcasted" to Agent Murphy. Anfield was tried together with Massiah; although indicted the same day as Massiah and Anfield, Maxwell and other coconspirators were brought to trial five years later. *See* United States v. Maxwell, 383 F.2d 437, 441 (2d Cir. 1967); Brief for United States at 6, 8, Massiah v. United States, 377 U.S. 201 (1964).

daylight hours rather than at night was that he wanted Williams to get a good look at either the filling station where he had hidden the child's shoes or the turnoff he had taken to bury the body. Suppose Leaming also admitted that he had hoped and prayed that on passing these spots Williams would make "spontaneous" incriminating disclosures. Suppose further that in the long drive back Leaming and Williams discussed nothing bearing even remotely on the murder case, but that Williams did make the hoped-for "spontaneous" disclosures at the filling station or the turnoff. Most courts in this case would surely excuse Leaming's course of action as neither "tantamount to interrogation" nor an "attempt to elicit" incriminating statements.

This hypothetical seems to support Justice Blackmun's contention that no interrogation occurred in *Williams*. I think, however, that the disclosure would be admissible not because it was the product of a *permissible attempt* to elicit information but because *no "attempt" occurred at all*. [10] A police officer who returns a prisoner by the most feasible route does not, it seems to me, "attempt to elicit information" merely because he is aware of the possibility that passing some spot along the way might inspire his prisoner to confess. A police officer need not refrain from detaining a traffic offender and from running a license check on the car, as he normally would do under the circumstances, because he *hopes and prays* that such routine procedures will prompt an admission that the car was stolen. Nor, when he takes a person into custody, need he decline to ask routine questions unrelated to the investigation of the case, such as where the arrestee lives and how he spells his last name, because he harbors the secret desire that such standard "booking procedure" will evoke incriminating statements. [11]

These hypotheticals, however, are a far cry from the *Williams* case. Cap-

10. This is a relatively easy hypothetical because the captain also had perfectly good reasons for driving back during daylight hours. For one thing, he was supposed to bring Williams back as soon as possible. For another, weather conditions, bad enough in daylight (freezing rain, slippery roads, poor visibility), might have made nighttime driving all but impossible. Finally, a heavy snowstorm was predicted for that night. *See* 430 U.S. at 392. Even if an "ulterior motive" theoretically undermines an otherwise justified course of police conduct, an impermissible motive test would probably prove to be unworkable.

Suppose, on the other hand, that Captain Leaming had theorized that Williams had hidden the body in some desolate area unapproachable from the freeway and had driven his prisoner many miles over the back road in order to come as near as possible to this out-of-the-way spot. Such a circuitous return trip, taken for the reason stated, would, I think, be an impermissible "attempt to elicit information," and any incriminating disclosures it produced should be excluded on sixth amendment-*Massiah* grounds.

11. There is general agreement that *Miranda* does not apply to "administrative questioning." Smith, *The Threshold Question in Applying* Miranda: *What Constitutes Custodial Interrogation?* 25 S.C.L. REV. 669, 704–05 (1974); *see* C. WHITEBREAD, CONSTITUTIONAL CRIMINAL PROCEDURE 178–79 (1978); Kamisar, *"Custodial Interrogation" Within the Meaning of* Miranda, in INST. OF CONTINUING LEGAL EDUC., CRIMINAL LAW AND THE CONSTITUTION—SOURCES AND COMMENTARIES 335, 358–60 (1968); *cf.* Graham, *What Is "Custodial Interrogation?": California's Anticipatory Application of* Miranda v. Arizona, 14 U.C.L.A. L. REV. 59, 104–06 ("pur-

tain Leaming did not simply decline to depart from standard operating procedure. He did not simply harbor the secret desire that Williams would be moved to reveal the location of the body on the return trip to Des Moines. Captain Leaming relied on more than a hope and a prayer. He invoked the trickery, deception, and "psychology" recommended in the "how-to-do-it interrogation manuals"[31] that so aroused the ire of the *Miranda* majority.[32] He appealed in the name of religion to someone he knew to be deeply religious.[33] In effect, he challenged Williams to display some evidence of honor and decency.[34] He addressed Williams as "Reverend" admittedly to win his friendship and confidence[35] and also probably because someone like Williams would be more vulnerable to such flattery than persons of high social or professional status.[36] In his "speech," Leaming *assumed* that the girl was dead and that Williams knew where the body was.[37] And he falsely told Williams that he "knew" the girl's body was in the Mitchellville area.[12]

These are all standard interrogation techniques.[38] They *are* tantamount to "straight questioning" because they generate similar pressures, anxieties, and intimidation. They are not only calculated to, but likely to, evoke incriminating statements. They "endanger the privilege against self-incrimination"[39] no less than does more readily identifiable "interrogation."[40]

In determining that no interrogation took place in *Williams,* Justice Blackmun pointed out that although Williams was repeatedly advised of his rights, "it was he who started the travel conversations and brought up the subject of the criminal investigation."[41] There are several responses to Justice Blackmun's contention. First, "interrogation is a social situation, and suspects respond according to the normal rules of social interaction in such a situation."[42] It was highly likely, almost inevitable, that sitting close together in the back seat of a car for hours. Leaming and Williams would "visit." Indeed, just before they started out on their journey, the captain told his prisoner they would be "visiting" on the long ride back to Des Moines.[43] It is not readily apparent why a suspect who "desire[s] to appear courteous and not to offend,"[44] as many persons do even when they are involved in much less "psychologically close" encounters with the police,[45] should somehow "waive" or be deprived of his constitutional protection against police questioning or against police "psychological ploys" that amount to the same thing.[46]

Second, although the record indicates that Williams did start the travel

---

pose doctrine" excuses questions asked for information rather than confession). As a general proposition, *Massiah* is equally inapplicable to such "questioning."

12. The federal district court so found, 375 F. Supp. at 175, and members of the Supreme Court proceeded on the same assumption, 430 U.S. at 393, but Leaming's testimony on this matter was inconsistent. At one point Leaming testified that he had said that he "knew" where the body was, and at another that he told Williams that he had "theorized" (which was true) or had "an idea" (which was also true) that the body was in the Mitchellville area. *See* Kamisar, *supra* footnote 2, at 236.

conversation, his opening question was whether the captain "hated him" and "wanted to kill him" or whether some other police officer was desirous of doing so.[47] This question enabled Leaming to get right to work. He responded that he himself "had had religious training and background as a child" and that he "would probably come more near praying for" Williams than abusing or striking him.[48] Thus, it was Leaming who first brought up the subject of religion and who suggested in their very first conversation that he was aware of Williams's moral and religious obligations under the circumstances.

Although, along with "a great deal of conversation not related to the case," Williams did *ask a few questions* about the progress of the murder investigation[49]—is that surprising?—he neither provided any information about the case in the conversation preceding the Christian burial speech nor indicated in any way that he was going to do so.[50] Nor had there been any previous mention of the body when Leaming launched the speech.

Justice Blackmun further maintained that "Leaming's purpose was not solely to obtain incriminating evidence"; he was also "'hoping to find out where that little girl was,' but such motivation does not equate with an intention to evade the Sixth Amendment."[51] It seems to me, as it did to Professor Kenneth Graham a dozen years ago, that so long as the police conduct is likely to elicit incriminating statements and thus endanger the privilege, it is police "interrogation" *regardless of its primary purpose or motivation,* and that if it otherwise qualifies as "interrogation," *it does not become something else* because the interrogator's main purpose is the saving of a life rather than the procuring of incriminating statements, even though self-incrimination may be foreseen as a windfall.[52]

Justice Blackmun may have had something else in mind. He may have been seeking to invoke the so-called rescue or emergency doctrine.[53] If, when he delivered the speech, Captain Leaming had believed the little girl might still be alive and had been motivated by a desire to find her before she froze to death, I venture to say that one or more members of the 5–4 *Williams* majority would have switched their votes. But in light of the factual circumstances in *Williams,* the "rescue" or "emergency" doctrine could not have been properly applied.

When pressed on cross-examination by defense attorney McKnight about whether he was trying to get as much information from Williams as he could before they returned to Des Moines, Leaming did say that he "was sure hoping to find out where that little *girl* was."[54] In light of the entire record, however, it appears that he probably meant the girl's *body,* not the girl. For only a moment or two earlier, during the same cross-examination by McKnight, the following exchange occurred:

Q. Didn't you [make the Christian burial speech] to him to induce him to show you where the *body* was?

A. I was hoping he would....

Q. Well, I said wasn't [the Christian burial speech] for the purposes of getting Mr. Williams to talk?

A. Well, I was hoping he would tell me where the *body* was, Mr. McKnight, absolutely.[55]

This admission, by itself, might not be conclusive. Indeed, one problem with the "rescue" doctrine is that the record almost never establishes that the investigators knew *for sure,* or even that they assumed, that the victim was dead—and the temptation to attribute a lifesaving purpose to the interrogation, at least in retrospect, is great.[13] The record in *Brewer v. Williams,* however, does demonstrate Leaming's knowledge of the girl's death. Immediately after this cross-examination of Leaming, the following occurred:

Redirect Examination

Q. Captain, when Mr. McKnight was in your office [the morning he talked to Williams long-distance], what conversation did you hear from him when he was on the telephone?

A. Well, I heard him say [to Williams] that, "You have to tell the officers where *the body* is," and he repeated a second time, "You have got to tell them where she is."... "When you get back here, you tell me and I'll tell them...."[14]

Recross Examination [by McKnight]

Q. Say, officer... we didn't know whether the girl was dead or alive when you left here, did we?

A. You [McKnight] told me *she was dead.*

Q. You want to say that I told you that?

A. Yes, sir. You said that Williams told you that....

....

You said he said she was dead when he left the YMCA with her.[15]

Justice White's Dissent

Justice White, who was joined in his dissent by Justices Blackmun and Rehnquist, suggested another reason why Williams was "not questioned": the Christian burial speech "was accompanied by a request by [Leaming] that the

13. Thus, nine years after the event, although nothing in the record substantiates the view that a lifesaving purpose motivated his Christian burial statement, *see* footnote 15 *infra* and accompanying text, Captain Leaming defended his action on the ground that "[i]f we had found that girl alive, with even a breath of life remaining because of what Williams told us, I doubt if anyone would have said anything about anything being illegal." Lamberto, *supra* footnote 1.

14. Brief for Petitioner, Joint App. at 96 (emphasis added).

15. *Id.* at 96–97 (emphasis added). Evidently McKnight thought that revealing to Captain Leaming and Chief Nichols (who was also present) that Williams had told him that the little girl was dead was a foolish thing for Williams's lawyer to have done. Thus, McKnight endeavored a

accused make no response."[56] Not quite. The speech was in fact accompanied by the remark: "I do not want you to answer me. I don't want to discuss it any further. Just *think about it as we're riding down the road."* [16]

Think about what? Think about the fact that "you [Williams] are the only person that knows where this little girl's body is"; that you are the only one who can fulfill the desire and the right of the girl's parents to give their

---

cross-examination and recross to get Nichols as well as Leaming to back down on this point. Although Nichols finally conceded that he was unsure whether McKnight actually said Williams said that the girl was dead, *id.* at 108, he did not retract his testimony that McKnight reported the girl was dead after his phone conversation with Williams, *id.* at 108-09.

The important point is that Captain Leaming was convinced McKnight had told him that the girl was dead and that the captain never doubted this was so. At least nothing in the record indicates that he had any doubt. Indeed, Leaming "figured" that Williams

> had probably *got rid of the body* as soon as he possibly could after he left Des Moines. I felt that it wasn't in the Grinnell area [where a search had turned up the girl's clothing, but no body], it wasn't in the Newton area [where a search had produced nothing]. So I then thought probably as quick as he could get out of Des Moines [Williams] would *dispose of the body....*
> ... [S]o I figured Mitchellville.

Id. at 65 (emphasis added).

16. *Id.* at 392-93 (emphasis added).

Captain Leaming's closing remark seems to illustrate what one interrogation expert, Lt. C.H. Van Meter, has called, in his chapter on "closing," a "'soft'-type closing" or "closing with the door open." C. VAN METER, PRINCIPLES OF POLICE INTERROGATION 100-01 (1973). The first two "samples" of this technique offered by Lt. Van Meter are:

> INTERROGATOR: Karl, I want you to know that I don't feel that this whole problem has been straightened out. I want you to think things over and we can get together later, and maybe go over this whole thing again.

or

> INTERROGATOR: Karl, why don't you kick this thing around in your mind awhile and think over what we have been talking about. All you have to do is let your conscience be your guide in all of this, and then, if you need me to talk over anything, just give a whistle.

Id. at 100. Adds Van Meter:

> In all phases of your interrogation, you must make yourself available to receive the confession, and this holds true at the termination of the interrogation as well. By leaving yourself and the suspect an opening to renew your conversation, you'll quite often give yourself a confession that you would not otherwise have gotten. Make yourself available to the suspect and give yourself the break of being able to easily renew any further contact you might have with him.

Id.

When the police car neared the Mitchellville exit, Williams did announce, according to Captain Leaming, that he was going to show the police where the body was. But one cannot help wondering whether, had Williams not done so, Leaming would have renewed the discussion at this point. Consider the following comments by Van Meter regarding the continuing effectiveness of this "closing" technique:

> [By "closing with the door open"] we left ourselves plenty of room to start anew at a later date if necessary, and also we made our interrogator "available" should the suspect feel that he

daughter a Christian burial; that, because of the predicted snowstorm, even you may be unable to bring about a Christian burial if you do not locate the body before we get back to Des Moines; and that we will be going right past the area on the way into Des Moines.

Leaming was not just asking Williams to think about it. He was setting a time limit on how long Williams had to think about it. He was "asking" Williams, it seems plain to me, to think about *telling him,* or showing him, where the body was *by the time* they reached the turnoff to the area where the body was buried. What else could Leaming have meant? That was the whole point of his Christian burial speech. Certainly that was the way the third man in the police car, Detective Nelson, heard it. When Nelson was asked whether he or Leaming had asked Williams anything on the drive back to Des Moines, he replied that they had not, except that "when we left Davenport, Captain Leaming *asked him to think about telling us* where the body is."[57]

That under the circumstances Leaming's request that Williams not "answer" him or "discuss it any further" is an insignificant factor may be demonstrated, I think, by modifying the facts in the famous *Spano* case (1959).[58] The actual facts were as follows: Spano called his childhood friend, Bruno, then a fledgling police officer, and told him that he had shot a man when still dazed by the man's blows and unaware of what he was doing, and that he intended to get a lawyer and give himself up. Bruno relayed this information to his superiors. The next day Spano, accompanied by counsel, did surrender himself to the authorities. His attorney left him in the custody of the police, who subjected him to intensive questioning. But Spano persisted in his refusal to incriminate himself.[59]

At this point Bruno's superiors instructed him to tell Spano that the latter's phone call "had gotten him 'in a lot of trouble' and that he should seek to extract sympathy from [Spano] for Bruno's pregnant wife and three children."[60] Bruno "played [the] part of a worried father, harried by his superiors, in not one but four different acts"[61] before Spano "succumbed to his friend's prevarications and agreed to make a statement."[62]

Suppose Bruno had had only one session with Spano and in that session he had delivered the following "pregnant wife and three children speech":

> Spano, old buddy, I don't mind telling you that your phone call has gotten me into a lot of trouble. A friend of mine told me this morning

---

wants to talk. We tried for the confession and thereby reinforced in the suspect's mind the fact that we are not convinced that he is innocent as he has stated; further, we gave him a number of good reasons to think about as to why he should confess. By leaving the door open to him, we can renew our conversation anytime by just saying, "Well, Karl, did you think over what we talked about last time?"

Id. at 103.

he heard Lieutenant Gannon is going to see to it that I lose my job. I have an appointment to see the lieutenant in two hours. I'm probably going to get the bad news then.

What a time to lose a job! Three children and a fourth on the way. I don't know how we're going to survive. Mary is a wonderful wife. She's entitled to a husband with a decent job. The three kids are darlings. They're entitled to a father with a decent job.

You're my only hope. You're the only one who can prevent this disaster from happening. If you agree to make a statement I'm sure Lieutenant Gannon will calm down. But considering the mood Gannon is in, if you don't do so this afternoon, not even you may be able to help me.

I'm so upset I can't work. I'm just going to sit right outside your door and try to read a magazine until the time for my appointment with Gannon.

I don't want you to answer me. I don't want to discuss it any further. Just think about it as I'm sitting outside trying to read a magazine.

Suppose further that an hour and a half later Spano had made a statement. Would anyone doubt that Bruno's "speech" constituted "interrogation" or was "tantamount to interrogation"? How is Captain Leaming's "speech" different?

Chief Justice Burger's Dissent

In a third dissenting opinion, Chief Justice Burger suggested that Justice Powell had asserted "that the result in this case turns on whether Detective Leaming's remarks constituted 'interrogation,' as [Justice Powell] views them, or whether they were 'statements' intended to prick the conscience of the accused."[63] But Justice Powell neither made nor suggested any such distinction in his concurring opinion. Quite the contrary. Justice Powell seems to be saying—and rightly so—that "'statements' intended to prick the conscience of the accused," in the words of the Chief Justice, at least when they are likely to persuade the accused to incriminate himself, can be, as they were in the *Williams* case, as "skillful and effective" a "form of interrogation" as any set of direct questions.[64]

If a distinction between "questioning" for the purpose of eliciting information and the use of "psychological ploys," such as appeals to conscience, to achieve the same purpose, emerged anywhere in the *Williams* case, such a distinction was drawn only by the Iowa Attorney General[65] or by the Chief Justice himself. Neither the opinion of the Court nor any of the concurring opinions made that distinction. Nor is it to be found in any of the interrogation manuals. Indeed, appeals to conscience and other "psychological ploys" are the very stuff of which "interrogation" is made. [17] On this point, a page from the "how-to-do-it" and the "how-we-have-done-it-ourselves" manuals is worth a volume of semantics. [66]

The Chief Justice also observed that he found "it most remarkable that a murder case should turn on judicial interpretation that a statement becomes a question simply because it is followed by an incriminating disclosure from the suspect." [67] That would indeed have been a startling contention—if anyone had made it. But no one did.

No one suggested that if Captain Leaming had said, "Let's pull off at the next Holiday Inn and get something to eat," or "I hope we can get back to Des Moines without sliding off these icy roads," or had made some other remark *neither calculated nor likely to elicit an incriminating disclosure* that any such remark would have become "interrogation" if Williams were to have chosen that occasion to announce: "I'm going to show you where the body is." The Christian burial speech did not become "interrogation" because it was followed by an incriminating disclosure; it constituted "interrogation" or its equivalent when first delivered because its purpose and its tendency were to elicit an incriminating disclosure.

A Question by Any Other Name

What may have struck Chief Justice Burger as "remarkable" is the notion that a "statement" or "speech" containing no question marks should be regarded as "questioning" or "interrogation." But how could it be otherwise? The techniques that police interrogators are able to use—and for generations have used—are so many and varied that, unless *Miranda* and the privilege against self-incrimination it is designed to effectuate were to become empty gestures in custodial surroundings, the Court could not have intended to limit their applicability to only one form of official "interrogation" or "compulsion"— verbal conduct ending in question marks. Indeed, as I hope to convince the reader, *Miranda* and the privilege against self-incrimination cannot be limited to situations in which the police *directly address* a suspect or even to those occasions on which they engage in *verbal conduct*. [18]

---

17. *See, e.g.,* C. O'HARA, FUNDAMENTALS OF CRIMINAL INVESTIGATION 102–03 (1st ed. 1956). This manual was quoted extensively by the Court in Miranda v. Arizona, 384 U.S. at 453. *See* footnote 19 *infra*. The first two "categories" described by O'Hara when he set forth "some of the techniques practiced by experienced investigators" are: "Emotional Appeals" (subdivisions include "Sympathetic Approach" and "Kindness") and "Friendliness" (subdivisions include "The Helpful Advisor" and "The Sympathetic Brother," each capitalizing on the subject's need "to square things with his own conscience"). C. O'HARA, *supra,* at 102.

18. Because the custody issue has arisen more frequently and has generally been regarded as a more difficult one, a good deal more attention has been paid to what constitutes *custodial*

Eighty years ago, in the famous *Bram* case (1897),[68] the Court held that when a murder suspect was *informed* by the police that a cosuspect had charged him with the crime, this information "produce[d] upon his mind the fear if he remained silent it could be considered an admission of guilt"[69] and thus under the circumstances rendered the resulting incriminating statement a violation of the privilege.[70] But the only one who asked a question in the course of the *Bram* "interrogation" was *the suspect himself:*

Detective Power: Bram, we are trying to unravel this horrible mystery [the murder of the captain of Bram's ship]. Your position is rather an awkward one. I have had [Seaman] Brown in this office and he made a statement that he saw you do the murder [which was true].

Bram: He could not have seen me; where was he?

---

interrogation than to what constitutes custodial *interrogation.* So far as I have been able to ascertain, however, most, if not all, commentators who have addressed the issue have recognized that "[p]olice conduct, though not verbal, may nevertheless be tantamount to interrogation for purposes of requiring *Miranda* warnings." 3 J. WIGMORE, EVIDENCE § 826a, at 383 n.23 (J. Chadbourn rev. ed. 1970). *See also* C. McCORMICK, EVIDENCE 330 (E. Cleary 2d ed. 1972); Graham, *supra* footnote 11, at 107; Rothblatt & Pitler, *Police Interrogation: Warnings and Waivers—Where Do We Go From Here?* 42 NOTRE DAME LAW. 479, 486 (1967).

J.V. Smith does not define "interrogation," but rather points out "the major areas which are generally held not to be interrogation: volunteered statements and responses given to administrative questions" (the routine questions asked of all arrestees who are "booked" or otherwise processed). Smith, *supra* footnote 11, at 702-03. It seems fairly clear that, although pressuring, persuading, or prompting a suspect to confess by showing him incriminating physical evidence, such as a ballistics report or a bank surveillance photograph, or by confronting him with an accusatory accomplice, *see* footnote 21 *infra,* need involve no verbal conduct, such tactics fit neither of the noninterrogation categories discussed by Smith.

Professor Charles Alan Wright's reading of the *Miranda* opinion differs from mine, but it is plain that he is unhappy with his reading. Although "not clear," "the breadth of the exception for volunteered statements," he observes, "seems to include . . . the statement of a person who has not been given the benefits of warnings and counsel so long as he is not interrogated. If so, the police, so long as they ask no questions, could deliberately hold a person in custody without giving him the *Miranda* warnings, and confront him with the victim of the crime, or perhaps other evidence of it, in the hope that he would then spontaneously say something incriminating. If this is what the Court intended to permit, it has left a large gap in the protections otherwise provided by *Miranda....* " 1 C. WRIGHT, FEDERAL PRACTICE AND PROCEDURE (CRIMINAL) § 76, at 112-13 (1969). I cannot believe that the *Miranda* Court did leave such a "large gap" in the protections it otherwise provided that would permit the police, without giving the requisite warnings or (having given the warnings) after a suspect has asserted his rights, to resort to tactics and techniques that generate pressure, tension, and anxiety *above and beyond* that inherent in normal arrest and detention. *See* footnote 20 *infra.* To call a statement prodded or prompted by police revelation of damaging evidence or by police arrangement of a confrontation with the victim (or with an accusatory accomplice) a "volunteered" or "spontaneous" statement strikes me as a peculiar use of language. "Volunteered" connotes offering something on one's own initiative (the Court in *Miranda* seems to define "volunteered" as produced "without any compelling influences," not merely without verbal conduct, 384 U.S. at 478); "spontaneous" is usually defined as self-generated, happening without external cause.

Power: He states he was at the wheel.
Bram: Well, he could not see me from there.[71]

Escobedo did not "crack" until confronted with an alleged accomplice who claimed that Escobedo had fired the fatal shots. In the presence of the police, Escobedo called his accomplice a liar—"I didn't shoot Manuel, you did it"[72]—and "[i]n this way . . . for the first time, admitted to some knowledge of the crime."[73] Ashcraft did not admit that he had hired Ware to kill his wife until a copy of Ware's confession was given or read to Ashcraft.[74] Neither in *Escobedo* nor in *Ashcraft* did any Justice suggest that the police conduct described above constituted something other than "interrogation" because it was accomplished without any questions being asked. Indeed, in each case the "interrogation" might have been carried out without the police engaging in any "verbal conduct."

In *Rogers v. Richmond* (1961),[75] when petitioner persisted in his refusal to admit involvement in a felony-murder, "Chief Eagan pretended, in petitioner's hearing, to place a telephone call to police officers, directing them to stand in readiness to bring in petitioner's wife [who suffered from arthritis] for questioning."[76] Petitioner continued to hold out until the chief indicated that he was about to have petitioner's wife taken into custody.[77] If the feigned phone call had immediately produced the desired result, however, I doubt that the State would have had the audacity to argue that this psychological ploy was not "interrogation" at all because it was not a "question" or because the statements were not *addressed to* petitioner.

Only once in his opinion for the Court in *Rogers* did Justice Frankfurter label Eagan's remarks "questioning" or "interrogation."[78] Both in his general discussion of the standard demanded by fourteenth amendment due process for determining the admissibility of confessions and in his application of the standard to the particular facts of the case, Justice Frankfurter employed such terminology as the following: "confessions which are involuntary, *i.e., the product of coercion, either physical or psychological,* cannot stand";[79] "confessions obtained by impermissible *methods*";[80] subjecting a defendant "to *pressures* to which, under our accusatorial system, an accused should not be subjected";[81] "whether the *behavior* of the State's law enforcement officials was such as [to] bring about confessions not freely self-determined."[82]

It is true that *Miranda* contains much talk about "custodial police interrogation," "in-custody interrogation," "questioning initiated by law enforcement officers," and about the warnings that must be given "prior to any questioning." But it also contains strong criticism and apparent condemnation of (i) many standard interrogation techniques that need not take the form of "questions," such as "posit[ing]" "the guilt of the subject as a fact," "minimiz[ing] the moral seriousness of the offense," and "cast[ing] blame on the victim or on society,"[83] and (ii) various stratagems that do not require any "verbal conduct" on the part of the police at all, such as the "false lineup" and the "reverse lineup."[19]

It was argued long ago that in-custody interrogation *without more* impermissibly compels a person to incriminate himself.[84] But the courts put that issue aside for many years. It was hard enough to prevent the police from resorting to physical violence, "relay questioning," and other crude and oppressive practices.[85] After three decades and thirty-odd "coerced confession" cases that saw "the overall gauge . . . steadily changing, usually in the direction of restricting admissibility,"[86] the Court in *Miranda* finally held that "[e]*ven without employing* brutality, the 'third degree' *or the specific stratagems described* [in the interrogation manuals, from which it had quoted at length earlier in the opinion], the very fact of custodial interrogation exacts a heavy toll on individual liberty and trades on the weaknesses of individuals."[87] Thus, the Court stated:

We are satisfied that all the principles embodied in the privilege [against self-incrimination] apply to *informal compulsion* exerted by law-enforcement officers dur-

---

19. 384 U.S. at 453. In the "false lineup" ploy, "[t]he witness or complainant (previously coached, if necessary) studies the lineup and confidently points out the subject as the guilty party." *Id.* at 453 (quoting C. O'HARA, *supra* footnote 17, at 106). Thus, no police officer *himself* need *say* anything. In the "reverse lineup" variation, the suspect is again placed in a lineup, "but this time he is identifed by several fictitious witnesses or victims who associated him with different offenses. It is expected that the subject will become desperate and confess to the offense under investigation in order to escape from the false accusations." *Id.* (quoting C. O'HARA, *supra* footnote 17, at 106).

Among the other techniques discussed in this edition of the O'Hara manual is a variation of the "bluff on a split pair": A, a cosuspect, is seated in an outer office also occupied by a busy stenographer. B, a cosuspect, is taken into the interrogation room and the stenographer is then ordered to come in, too—with pencil and notebook. "After an appropriate period of time, the stenographer returns and begins to type from his notes [and in various ways suggests that he is typing up B's confession]. Subsequently, A is returned to the interrogation room, which B has now left. He is viewed with a grave silence. The interrogator opens up with: 'I don't think we'll need any confession from you, but if you want to clear up a few points. . . . '" C. O'HARA, *supra* footnote 17, at 106. The interesting thing about this "interrogation technique" for purposes of present discussion is that it may well pressure or persuade A to incriminate himself while he is watching the stenographer type up "B's confession" or while he is being returned to the interrogation room or when he is "viewed with a grave silence" on his return. If A were to make an incriminating statement at any one of these points, the "interrogation technique" would have "worked" without A having been asked a single question—or without anyone even *speaking to him*.

The first edition of the O'Hara manual was not revised until 1970 (two years after Captain Leaming "visited" with Williams), but post-*Miranda* editions have recognized that the techniques described above and similar tactics spelled out in the first edition may "conflict with the spirit of the *Miranda* ruling" and that "although such techniques may have been accepted as legal, their misapplication or misinterpretation might serve to *produce* or *intensify* the inherent pressures of the *interrogation atmosphere* that the Supreme Court's ruling was designed to overcome." C. O'HARA, FUNDAMENTALS OF CRIMINAL INVESTIGATION 121 (4th ed. 1976) (emphasis added).

ing in-custody questioning. An individual swept from familiar surroundings into police custody, surrounded by antagonistic forces, and *subjected to the techniques of persuasion described* [in the interrogation manuals quoted] above cannot be otherwise than under compulsion to speak. As a practical matter, the compulsion to speak in the isolated setting of the police station may well be greater than in courts or other official investigations, where there are often impartial observers to guard against *intimidation* or *trickery*.[88]

The whole point of applying the privilege to custodial surroundings was that it imposed "more exacting restrictions than [did] the Fourteenth Amendment's voluntariness test."[89] It would be standing *Miranda* on its head to say that because the Court was "concern[ed] . . . primarily with [the] interrogation atmosphere and the evils it can bring,"[90] it somehow managed to *lift* restrictions against other forms of compulsion, persuasion, trickery, and cajolery. The aim of the *Miranda* rules, as the dissenters well understood, was to "reinforce the nervous or ignorant suspect"[91] and to "negate all pressures"[92] above and beyond the coercion of arrest and detention itself[20]—"to offset [the] minor pressures and disadvantages intrinsic to any kind of police interrogation"[93] previously allowable under due process precedents that "exert[ed] a tug on the suspect to confess."[94] How, then, can it be said that the Christian burial speech was not "interrogation" within the meaning of *Miranda?*

It think it is plain that the Christian burial speech was in fact a form of "interrogation." It had the same purpose and effect as a question, "[t]he

---

20. "Zero-value pressure condition[s]" are not required by *Miranda,* nor are they possible in custodial surroundings. *Cf.* C. O'HARA, *supra* footnote 17, at 121. The *Miranda* Court might have held that the inherent and unavoidable pressures produced by arrest and detention *without more* are substantial enough to require "neutralizing" warnings, but it did not do so. Thus, in the absence of "questioning," or some other form of prodding or persuasion, the "compulsion" inherent in arrest and detention does not rise to the level of "compulsion" within the meaning of the privilege. As Justice White correctly pointed out in his *Miranda* dissent, a suspect "may blurt out [an admissible] confession despite the fact that he is alone and in custody, without any showing that he had any notion of his right to remain silent or of the consequences of his admission." 384 U.S. at 533 (White, J., with Harlan & Stewart, JJ., dissenting). *But see* MODEL CODE OF PRE-ARRAIGNMENT PROCEDURE § 120.8 (Official Draft 1975) [hereinafter cited as MODEL CODE]; UNIFORM RULES OF CRIMINAL PROCEDURE 212, 241 (Approved Draft 1974) (recommending that in order to relieve some of pressure, confusion, and anxiety likely to be generated by arrest and arrival at police station, suspect should be given certain advice at these stages *whether or not any questioning is attempted*).

At some point, however, *prolonged* detention (albeit in complete silence) for the purpose and with the likely effect of pressuring or prodding a suspect to confess will supply the "something more" that transforms "custody" into custodial interrogation within the meaning of *Miranda.* *See* Rothblatt & Pitler, *supra* footnote 18, at 486. To put it another way, an extended period of detention raises the pressure and anxiety generated by normal arrest and detention to the level of "compulsion" within the meaning of the privilege. *See* text at footnote 23 and notes 112–13 *infra.*

question was implied if not spoken," and "[e]verything was there but a question mark."[21] More generally, "it simply is not enough to mechanically

21. *See* Combs v. Wingo, 465 F.2d 96, 97-99 (6th Cir. 1972). In *Combs* a murder suspect who had been given *Miranda* warnings asserted his right to counsel. The officer responded: "[A]ll right. I want to read you something." He then read the incriminating ballistics report, whereupon the accused broke down and confessed. *Id.* at 97-98. The state appellate court, in Combs v. Commonwealth, 438 S.W.2d 82 (Ky. 1969), held that the reading of the report (the dissenters referred to the "showing" of the report) did not amount to "interrogation" within the meaning of *Miranda,* but merely constituted "furnish[ing]" defendant "information the police had already acquired by their [independent] investigation." *Id.* at 85. Judge Palmore, joined by Judge Milliken, wrote a strong dissent. In a federal habeas corpus proceeding, the Sixth Circuit, in an opinion written by Judge (now Solicitor General) McCree, agreed with the dissenters in the Kentucky Court of Appeals decision:

> The purpose of a question is to get an answer. Anything else that has the same purpose falls in the same category and is susceptible of the same abuses *Miranda* seeks to prevent. The only possible object of showing the ballistics report to the appellant in this case was to break him down and elicit a confession from him. The question was implied if not spoken. Everything was there but a question mark. It was a form of question and got the desired result.

465 F.2d at 99, quoting 438 S.W.2d at 86 (Palmore, J., with Milliken, J., dissenting).

Both state and federal courts are split on whether confronting a suspect with physical evidence or with an accomplice who has confessed constitutes interrogation within the meaning of *Miranda. See* NAT'L DIST. ATTORNEYS ASS'N, CONFESSIONS AND INTERROGATIONS AFTER *Miranda* 34-35 (J. Zagel 5th rev. ed. 1975) (collection of state and federal cases). It is fairly clear, for example, that the Ninth Circuit would have admitted the ballistics report-prompted confession held inadmissible in *Combs. See* United States v. Pheaster, 544 F.2d 353, 365, 366-68 (9th Cir. 1976) (after asserting right to counsel, suspect told that fingerprint found on kidnappers' note had been positively identified as his; resulting confession admissible); United States v. Davis, 527 F.2d 1110, 1111 (9th Cir. 1975) (after asserting right to remain silent, suspect shown bank surveillance photograph of himself participating in bank robbery and asked to reconsider his position; subsequent waiver deemed valid).

The *Pheaster* case might well have fallen within the "rescue" or "emergency" exception to *Miranda. See* note 53 *infra.* As written, however, the opinion seems fatally defective on several counts, including its reliance on Michigan v. Mosley, 423 U.S. 96 (1975). *See* 544 F.2d at 367.

The Supreme Court in *Michigan v. Mosley* held admissible incriminating statements obtained from a suspect during a second "interrogation session," even though he had asserted his right to remain silent at an earlier session. 423 U.S. at 104-06; *see* notes 336-75 and footnotes 74-86 *infra* and accompanying text (full discussion of *Mosley*). The Court deemed it particularly significant that the suspect had been given "full and complete *Miranda* warnings at the outset of the second interrogation," that the second interrogation was "restricted . . . to a crime that had not been the subject of the earlier interrogation," and that the questioning was resumed by a different officer. 423 U.S. at 104-06. None of these factors was present in *Pheaster.* Whether or not the disclosure of Pheaster that his fingerprint implicated him in the kidnapping constituted "interrogation" (though I think it plain that it did), it was undeniably a police effort to convince Pheaster to change his mind. Under the circumstances, it would be unreasonable to assert that Pheaster's "right to cut off questioning" was "scrupulously honored" or "fully respected." *See id.* at 104. Nor can a renewed effort by the *same* police to persuade Pheaster to talk about the *same* crime that had been the subject of the earlier interrogation, *without* giving him a fresh set of warnings, be viewed as "quite consistent with a reasonable interpretation of [the suspect's] earlier refusal to answer any questions about the [kidnapping]." *See id.* at 105.

attempt to ascertain what 'interrogation' means without considering the rationales behind *Miranda* and the fifth and sixth amendments.... The re-

---

Moreover, whereas *Mosley* only dealt with a suspect who invoked his right to remain slient, *Pheaster* involved a suspect who twice asserted his right to counsel, the first time before the warnings were given and the second time while they were being given. *See* 544 F.2d at 364–65. Both the majority opinion in Mosley and Justice White's concurring opinion recognize that the *Miranda* Court apparently created a per se rule against further interrogation (which presumably includes "nonverbal" police efforts to persuade a suspect to reconsider his position) that is effective after assertion of the right to counsel until an attorney is present, but not after a mere claim of the right to remain silent. *See* 423 U.S. at 104 n.10 (quoting Miranda v. Arizona, 384 U.S. at 474); *id.* at 109–10 (White, J., concurring). *See also* footnotes 77–81 and notes 353–64 *infra*.

Putting aside the *Miranda-Mosley* point, the *Pheaster* court's view that no "interrogation" followed the suspect's assertion of his right to counsel represents a triumph of semantics over reality. Once Pheaster was placed in a car, the agent in charge "engaged [him] in a 'firm' 'one-way conversation.'" 544 F.2d at 365. How is this *different from* "interrogation"? Much, if not most "interrogation," constitutes a "one-way conversation." The court noted a "key distinction between questioning [a suspect] and presenting the evidence against him." *Id.* at 366. This distinction is not found in *Miranda*. The sole authority cited by the *Pheaster* court in support of this distinction was *Davis v. United States,* which is even harder to digest than *Pheaster.*

In *Davis,* after asserting his desire not to talk to an investigating agent, the suspect was shown a bank surveillance photograph of himself participating in the robbery and then asked, "Are you sure you don't want to reconsider?" 527 F.2d at 1111. Confronted with this evidence, the suspect concluded that he *did* want to reconsider after all (or, I think it fair to say, that he might as well), and the court called this a valid "waiver." *Id. Davis* seems to say that, after a person asserts his rights, the police may pressure or persuade him to change his position as long as they restrict their efforts to the presentation or recitation of evidence against him, and that any question based on such evidence is not "interrogation," either because it is "cured by" or "auxiliary to" the presentation or recitation of the evidence.

To those who wish *Miranda* were overruled, the *Pheaster-Davis* approach represents the next best thing. It allows police interrogators to do what they have long been advised to do—"display an air of confidence in the subject's guilt," "point out" some of the "circumstantial evidence indicative of a subject's guilt," and "point out the futility of resistance to telling the truth." F. INBAU & J. REID, CRIMINAL INTERROGATION AND CONFESSIONS 26, 31, 77 (2d. ed. 1967). The *Pheaster-Davis* approach permits a police interrogator, as long as he confines his efforts to presentation or recitation of the incriminating evidence against the suspect, and apparently as long as he asks not more than one or two subsidiary questions, to "'talk [a suspect] out of' his refusal to talk" or "his desire for a lawyer." *Id.* at 4. Not even the authors of the leading interrogation manual thought such questioning possible after *Miranda. See id.*

Furthermore, if these tactics may be resorted to after a suspect has asserted his rights, it would seem to follow that they are permissible a fortiori before he has asserted them. To put it another way, if these tactics do not amount to "interrogation" within the meaning of *Miranda,* then why can they not be employed to "talk a suspect into confessing" without ever advising him of his *Miranda* rights?

The Ninth Circuit seems to be under the impression that as long as a police recitation of the evidence against a suspect is "objective" and "undistorted," it does not constitute "interrogation" within the meaning of *Miranda* or "compulsion" within the meaning of the privilege. *See* United States v. Pheaster, 544 F.2d at 368 & n.9. Putting aside the notion that under our system the weight and quality of the government's evidence should be appraised by the defense attorney and

quirement of 'interrogation' is designed to permit the use by the prosecution of a confession that is given by an accused *without any prompting*. . . . "[22]

Admittedly, "as long as the matter to be considered is debated in artificial terms,"[95] there is the danger that a judge will take the words "questioning" and "interrogation" and the dictionary and be "led by a technical definition to apply a certain name, and then to deduce consequences which have no relation to the grounds on which the name was applied."[96] But "the logic of words" need not, and should not, "yield to the logic of realities."[97] If we "think things not words,"[98] as we must, if we "constantly translate our words into facts for which they stand,"[99] as we must, the words "questioning" and "interrogation" will prove to be no insurmountable barrier.

I must add that one *need not* work with the words "questioning" and "interrogation" at all. The courts' extension of first amendment protections to conduct furnishes a useful analogy. Because the Constitution protects freedom

---

not by the suspect, the "objectivity" with which that evidence is presented goes to *another* issue—trickery.

The police "pressured" Escobedo by telling him that an alleged accomplice claimed that he had fired the fatal shots. It is unclear whether the accomplice actually made such an accusation. *See* text *supra* at notes 72–73. If the information were true, Escobedo was not "tricked," but he was still "pressured." Similarly, the police persuaded Combs that further resistance was futile by showing him a ballistics report implicating him in the murder. If the ballistics report was authentic, Combs was not "tricked," but he was still convinced of the "hopelessness of his situation" and thereby "encourage[d] . . . to confess immediately." *See* C. McCORMICK, *supra* footnote 18, at 330 (discussion of Kentucky Court of Appeals decision). *Miranda* does not ban *unfair* "custodial interrogation"; it bans *any* "custodial interrogation." The fifth amendment prohibition is not limited to *deceitful* "compulsion"; it applies to aboveboard "compulsion" as well. Indeed, the latter is sometimes the most compelling kind.

22. Commonwealth v. Simala, 434 Pa. 219, 226, 252 A.2d 575, 578–79 (1969) (Roberts, J.) (emphasis in original).

The Supreme Court of Pennsylvania has been especially alert on the "interrogation" front. In my judgment, with one exception—Commonwealth v. Franklin, 438 Pa. 411, 265 A.2d 361 (1970) (police statement to appellant that statement from him unnecessary because witnesses had already identified him but that they would like to hear his side of the story held not to be "interrogation"; strong dissent by Roberts, J.)—the Pennsylvania Court has properly classified various forms of official prompting and prodding as interrogation within the meaning of *Miranda*. In the *Simala* case itself an official's statement to the suspect, "you look kind of down in the dumps . . . if you want to talk, talk," was viewed as "interrogation"; the court perceived "no difference for constitutional purposes between questioning an accused outright and more subtly suggesting that he incriminate himself without being asked specific questions." 434 Pa. at 226, 252 A.2d at 579. In Commonwealth v. Leaming, 432 Pa. 326, 247 A.2d 590 (1968), a police officer told appellant that his alleged accomplice had been apprehended and was likely to talk, and that if appellant wished to make a statement this was the time to do so because he was liable to end up a "patsy" otherwise. *Id.* at 335, 247 A.2d at 595. This "advice" was held to be "interrogation." *Id.* at 337, 247 A.2d at 596. In Commonwealth v. Hamilton, 445 Pa. 292, 285 A.2d 172 (1971), appellant was confronted, in the presence of several police officers, with an alleged coconspirator who accused him of being the "triggerman" in the crime. *Id.* at 295, 285 A.2d at 174. In regarding the confrontation as a "form" of "interrogation," the court noted that the coconspirator was admittedly "being used in an attempt to pry an incriminating statement

of "speech," the terms "symbolic speech" and "symbolic conduct" have evolved to embrace conduct, such as flag desecration[100] and the wearing of black armbands,[101] that, to employ one suggested definition, "is intended as expression," "in fact . . . communicates," and in context "becomes a comprehensible form of expression."[102] If the Constitution had furnished protection only against "questioning" or "interrogation," the courts would have developed the concept of "symbolic interrogation" or "symbolic questioning" to encompass various kinds of police "remarks," "observations," and "nonverbal" techniques that imply a question or convey a message and are likely to be so understood by a suspect.

Unlike the conduct protected by the "freedom of speech" clause, however, the governmental conduct prohibited by the very language of the self-incrimination clause commonly connotes far more than the mere "wagging the tongue or wielding a pen."[103] The latter clause protects one from being "compelled" to incriminate himself *without limiting the forms or character of the "compulsion."* Thus, there is no need to consider whether placing a pan of the victim's bones in a suspect's lap,[104] or directing police officers disguised as witnesses to identify the suspect in a lineup,[105] or pretending to bring in a suspect's ailing spouse for questioning,[106] or confronting a suspect with his effusive accomplice,[107] or showing him an incriminating ballistics report[108] or a bank surveillance photograph of himself,[109] or "creat[ing] a verbal vacuum," in the belief that after such a vacuum has been created *"he who speaks first is the loser,"*[23] or delivering a "Christian burial speech" consti-

---

from appellant" and that to permit this technique "would be to place a premium on the ingenuity of the police to devise methods of indirect interrogation, rather than to implement the plain mandate of *Miranda*. . . ." *Id.* at 297, 285 A.2d at 175. In Commonwealth v. Mercier, 451 Pa. 211, 302 A.2d 337 (1973), the reading to appellant of a statement by an alleged accomplice implicating him in the crime was held to be "interrogation"; the court refused "to distinguish between confronting the appellant directly with those who implicate him and reading their statement to him, both have the same effect—both are a form of official interrogation." *Id.* at 214–15, 302 A.2d at 340.

The view, reflected in the Pennsylvania cases, that any police conduct designed to or likely to elicit an incriminating statement should be considered "*Miranda* interrogation" assumes, of course, that the suspect *realizes* that he is talking with or being talked to by a law enforcement official, or that he is aware that a confrontation is taking place in the presence of police. None of the aforementioned Pennsylvania cases involved the use of undercover agents or police informants. As to this issue, *see* text at notes 246–329 and footnotes 43–70 *infra*.

23. *See* R. ROYAL & S. SCHUTT, THE GENTLE ART OF INTERVIEWING AND INTERROGATION 145–46 (1976). Among the techniques that the authors have found to be successful in eliciting admissions are the following:

Once the various buy signs appear, how does the investigator capitalize on them? There are two very popular methods: One is by citing all the facts in summary form and diverting the subject's attention from a breakthrough admission by seeking motive. For example: "I know how you did 'X,' 'Y,' and 'Z'—perhaps it would be in your best interest to tell me why." The other method is to create a verbal vacuum: "I know that you did this, and I will not allow you to put

tutes or is tantamount to "interrogation"—"implicit," "constructive," "symbolic," or otherwise.

It has been said that "there are a thousand forms of compulsion" and that "our police show great ingenuity in the variety employed."[110] But "a confession obtained by compulsion must be excluded whatever may have been the character of the compulsion."[111] If the police conduct is designed and likely to pressure or persuade, or even "to exert a tug on,"[112] a suspect to incriminate himself—the obvious purpose and likely effect of the Christian burial speech—then that conduct is "compulsion" as *Miranda* defines the self-incrimination clause. Then it *augments* or *intensifies* the tolerable level of stress, confusion, and anxiety generated by unadulterated arrest and detention to the impermissible level of "compulsion."[113] Then any resulting statement is not "volunteered"[114] or the product of "the unfettered exercise of [the suspect's] own will."[115] Then it is the kind of police conduct that ought to be and was meant to be forbidden in the absence of waiver, and certainly after assertion, of one's *Miranda* rights.[116]

One may, "by way of convenient shorthand,"[117] call such police conduct "interrogation"—and it is, within the meaning of *Miranda*—but one need not do so. One *need only* call it, and it may be more helpful simply to call it, "compulsion" within the meaning of the privilege.

Massiah, Williams, and Variations Thereon

Until the Christian burial speech case was decided a year ago, lasting fame had eluded *Massiah v. United States*.[24] It was apparently lost in the shuffle of fast-moving events that reshaped consitutional-criminal procedure in the 1960s.

---

yourself in the awkward position of lying to me;—If you are not willing to be completely truthful with me, then I advise you to say absolutely nothing." This will be followed by what may seem to be an eternity of silence. The rule is that after a verbal vacuum has been created, usually *he who speaks first is the loser.* Wait your subject out, and he will probably say: "Okay, what do you want to know?"

Id. (emphasis in original).

The Royal-Schutt "professional manual and guide" amply illustrates why a court that takes what an interrogator says literally may, no less than the suspect, be led astray. *See id.* at 147 (telling suspect you "don't want" him "to be nervous about what I am going to say" "in effect, produces the very nervousness [you have] denied wanting to produce"); *id.* at 144–45 (suspect induced to confess by being told initially, "Just sit there and be quiet; I don't believe that you participated in this highjacking anyhow," and then, at "appropriate intervals": "You could not have done it," "You are too stupid to have done it," etc.) (actual "interrogation" conducted by one of authors).

24. 337 U.S. 201 (1964). *Massiah* is discussed at length in text at notes 183–244 and footnotes 34–42 *infra*.

Massiah "extend[ed] the constitutional role of counsel from the traditional function of preparing for and participating in a trial or trial type proceeding to the representation and counseling of persons under police investigation where they are under indictment. . . . "[25] But that same Term, a scant five weeks later, *Escobedo v. Illinois*[(118)] further extended the constitutional role of counsel to the preindictment stage, that is, "when the process shifts from investigatory to accusatory—when its focus is on the accused and its purpose is to elicit a confession"[(119)]—or when the process so shifts *and* one or more of the limiting facts in *Escobedo* are also present.[26]

---

25. Enker & Elsen, *Counsel for the Suspect:* Massiah v. United States *and* Escobedo v. Illinois, 49 MINN. L. REV. 47, 48 (1964). But dissenting in Milton v. Wainwright, 407 U.S. 371 (1972), Justice Stewart maintained:

> The "retroactivity" of the *Massiah* decision is a wholly spurious issue. For *Massiah* marked no new departure in the law. It upset no accepted prosecutorial practice. . . . In no case before *Massiah* had this Court, at least since *Powell v. Alabama,* ever countenanced the kind of post-indictment police interrogation there involved, let alone ever specifically upheld the constitutionality of any such interrogation. . . . [T]he rule in [*Massiah*] has been settled law ever since *Powell v. Alabama.*

Id. at 381–82 (1972) (Stewart, J., with Douglas, Brennan & Marshall, JJ., dissenting) (lower federal courts had declined to apply *Massiah* retroactively; majority of the Court held that any error in admitting postindictment confession was harmless and thus did not reach retroactivity issue).

26. The factors present in *Escobedo* that could place limitations on subsequent applications of that case include situations in which: (1) the investigation has begun to focus on a particular defendant and is no longer a general inquiry into an unsolved crime; (2) the suspect is in police custody; (3) interrogation by the police is aimed at eliciting incriminating statements; (4) the suspect has requested and been denied an opportunity to secure advice from counsel; and (5) the police fail to warn the suspect effectively of his constitutional rights to remain silent. *See id.* at 490–91. It was unclear whether all these factors would have to be present in a later case in which the rule of *Escobedo* would be applicable and, as a result, commentators disagreed widely over the probable meaning of the case and what it ought to mean. *See* W. SCHAEFER, THE SUSPECT AND SOCIETY 19–23 (1967) (written before *Miranda;* comparision of *Escobedo* and *Massiah* could lead to conclusion that no one on whom suspicion has focused can be interrogated without having or intelligently waiving assistance of counsel); Enker & Elsen, *supra* footnote 25, at 58–79 (*Escobedo* transformed investigatory process into adversary one; extension of right to counsel to curb police abuses not least drastic available means); Friendly, *The Bill of Rights as a Code of Criminal Procedure,* 53 CALIF. L. REV. 929, 950–52 (1965) (*Escobedo* right to counsel may apply only when suspect's case is "ripe for presentation to a magistrate"); Herman, *The Supreme Court and Restrictions on Police Interrogation,* 25 OHIO ST. L.J. 449, 471–81, 485–500 (1964) (*Escobedo* restricts admissible confessions to those obtained voluntarily and under circumstances consistent with waiver of effectively conveyed privilege against self-incrimination); Kamisar, *Equal Justice in the Gatehouses and Mansions of American Criminal Procedure,* in CRIMINAL JUSTICE IN OUR TIME 1, 50–95 (A. Howard ed. 1965) [reprinted in part in this volume] (right to counsel during interrogation exists regardless of suspect's request; only individuals aware of this right can waive privilege against self-incrimination); M. Murphy, *The Problems of Compliance by Police Departments,* 44 TEXAS L. REV. 939, 950–52 (1966) (federal circuit courts apply *Escobedo* differently with respect to when assistance of counsel

In constitutional-criminal procedure circles, 1964 was the year of *Escobedo,* and *Massiah* was understandably neglected in the hue and cry raised over the Illinois case. To the extent that *Massiah* was remembered at all, it was not so much for its own sake but as a steppingstone to *Escobedo* [27] and as a case in which Justice Stewart (author of the Court's opinion in *Massiah,* but a dissenter in *Escobedo*), by drawing the line at "the institution of formal, meaningful judicial proceedings, by way of indictment, information, or arraignment," [120] "had painted himself into a corner . . . from which he could extricate himself only by a highly formalistic reading of the sixth amendment." [121]

It was the kind of a reading that the *Escobedo* majority was not about to give the sixth amendment. The interrogation of Escobedo had taken place before "judicial" or "adversary" proceedings had commenced against him, [122] but, as Justice Stewart characterized the majority's reasoning, "[t]he Court disregards this basic difference between the present case and Massiah's with the bland assertion that 'that fact should make no difference.'" [123]

Escobedo may have seized the spotlight from *Massiah,* but *Escobedo* was soon shoved offstage by that blockbuster, *Miranda v. Arizona.* [124] Although *Miranda* did not overrule *Escobedo* as some had feared and others had hoped, it did not simply reaffirm it either. *Miranda* was "not simply a bigger and better (or worse, depending on your viewpoint) *Escobedo.*" [28] By shifting

---

applies); Robinson, Massiah, Escobedo, *and Rationales for the Exclusion of Confessions,* 56 J. CRIM. L.C. & P.S. 412 (1965) (author evaluates rationales that broaden trend toward exclusion of confessions, including deterrence of undesirable police practices, and suggests alternative means to this end); Traynor, *The Devils of Due Process in Criminal Detection, Detention, and Trial,* 33 U. CHI. L. REV. 657, 668–80 (1966) (to determine when focus on individual should require application of *Escobedo* rule, one should balance suspect's privilege to remain silent against community's right to legitimate police investigation). All this speculation ended when *Miranda* and its companion cases were decided. *See also* footnote 94 *infra.*

27. Thus, on the eve of *Miranda,* Chief Justice Roger Traynor referred to "the recent constellation of cases that include the limelighted *Escobedo* case extending the right to counsel to the pretrial stage," and noted that it was against the "background" of *Gideon* and *Massiah* that the *Escobedo* Court "announced a right to counsel before indictment, and held inadmissible a suspect's damaging statement elicited by police interrogation in the absence of counsel." Traynor, *supra* footnote 26, at 657–58, 668; *see* W. SCHAEFER, *supra* footnote 26, at 22 (discussion of possible scope of *Escobedo* through comparison with *Massiah*); Breitel, *Criminal Law and Equal Justice,* 1966 UTAH L. REV. 1 (speech concerning problem of confessions when counsel is absent; not even mentioning *Massiah*). *But see* Robinson, *supra* footnote 26, at 427 (includes *Massiah* in discussion of confession cases).

That Breitel, Schaefer, and Traynor, three of our greatest state judges, would all take to the lecture podium the same month (April, 1966, two months before *Miranda*) to grapple with the cluster of problems relating to police interrogation and confessions is striking evidence of the "raging controversial process" of reevaluating constitutional-criminal procedure, Breitel, *supra,* at 1, in which we were then engaged.

28. Kamisar, Miranda's *Impact on Police Practices (Panel Evaluation),* in A NEW LOOK AT CONFESSIONS 92 (B.J. George ed. 1967).

from the "prime suspect"-"focal point"-"accusatory state" test or tests of *Escobedo* to a "custodial interrogation" standard[125] or, to characterize it another way, by moving from a right to counsel base in *Escobedo* to a self-incrimination base, "*Miranda* [did] not [enlarge] *Escobedo* as much as it . . . *displaced* it."[29]

Assuming that *Escobedo* had not already done so, did *Miranda* also displace *Massiah?* After *Miranda*, was the institution of judicial proceedings, by way of indictment or otherwise, no more constitutionally relevant than whether the investigation had "begun to focus on a particular suspect"? After *Miranda*, did formal indictment or other adversary litigative proceedings no longer "absolutize constitutional rights or inexorably rigidify adversary postures"?[126] Or, regardless of the circumstances surrounding the interrogation —indeed, regardless of whether police efforts to elicit incriminating statements constituted "interrogation" at all—did indictment, or the initiation of other judicial proceedings, remain an "absolute point at which the right to counsel attaches"?[30]

If one searches the *Miranda* opinion for answers to these questions, he discovers that *Massiah* is never mentioned—not once in Chief Justice Warren's sixty-page opinion for the Court, nor in any of the three dissenting

29. Kamisar, *supra* footnote 28, at 93. *See* Beckwith v. United States, 425 U.S. 341, 344-48 (1976) (*Miranda* implicitly redefined "focus" test as individual taken into custody or deprived of liberty in significant way). Although *Beckwith* is sometimes criticized as one of the Burger Court decisions undermining *Miranda*, "the Warren Court might well have accepted [it]." Israel, *Criminal Procedure, the Burger Court, and the Legacy of the Warren Court*, 75 MICH. L. REV. 1320, 1375 n.246 (1977). Indeed, in holding that *Miranda* abandoned the "focus" test (as it had generally been understood at the time of *Escobedo*) and that its use of "custodial interrogation" marked a fresh start in describing the point at which a suspect's constitutional protections begin, the *Beckwith* Court adopted the view of no less staunch a *Miranda* supporter than Chief Judge Bazelon, who authored the lower court opinion in *Beckwith*. *See* 425 U.S. at 348.

30. The amicus curiae brief of the ACLU in *Miranda* and its companion cases (written by Professors Anthony Amsterdam and Paul Mishkin and, in my judgment, indispensable reading for a full understanding of *Miranda*), pointed out that a "straight right to counsel approach," one "directed to an inquiry as to when such right attaches," may "go both too far and not far enough." Brief for Amicus Curiae ACLU at 8 n.2, 10-11. It "may require the provision of counsel under circumstances where counsel is not necessary to the effectuation of a person's right not to be compelled to incriminate himself" and, on the other hand, "may result in not providing adequate protection when it is found that the point in time at which the right to counsel attaches has not yet been reached, although the danger of compelled self-incrimination looms large." *Id.* at 10-11. Thus, the ACLU advocated an approach that would make the providing of counsel "dependent upon the circumstances of interrogation" and would frame the issue not in right-to-counsel terms but in terms of "the effectuation, during the interrogation, of the Fifth Amendment right." *Id.* at 11.

The ACLU brief noted, however, that "[*Massiah*] apparently holds that indictment is an absolute point at which the right to counsel attaches" and that such a view is "supportable on the basis of the theory of an indictment: that the government has prior to that time completed its investigation and made its basic case. Moreover, the accused's need for trial preparation—and the assistance of counsel therein—has then become established." *Id.* at n.4.

opinions, which total another forty-six pages.[127] Yet, *very little else* even remotely bearing on the general subject is left out. There are quotations from or references to scores of confession cases, including such oldtimers as *Wan v. United States,*[128] *Bram v. United States,*[129] and *Hopt v. Utah.*[130] There are, to give but a few other examples, discussions of law pertaining to police interrogation and confessions in England, Scotland, India, and Ceylon;[131] quotations from the seventeenth-century trial of John Lilburn;[132] and references to Maimonides and other thirteenth-century commentators who "found an analogue" to the privilege against self-incrimination "grounded in the Bible."[133] But there is not a single reference to the then two-year-old *Massiah* case.

Similarly, there is no mention of *Massiah* in the lengthy opinion of the Iowa Supreme Court upholding the admissibility of Williams's post-"initiation of judicial adversary proceedings" and "Christian burial speech"-prompted statements.[134] Nor, and this seems still more startling, is there any mention of *Massiah* in Justice Stuart's "soul searching" dissent.[135] It is only in the federal district court, on habeas corpus, that *Massiah* is first remembered and held to be an alternative and independent ground for granting Williams a new trial.[136]

Why Did the Williams *Court Choose the*
Massiah *Route over a* Miranda *One?*

A majority of the Supreme Court in *Williams* saw "no need" to consider the applicability of *Miranda*[137] and affirmed solely on the basis of *Massiah.*[138] Evidently *Massiah* offered a clearer path to affirmance than *Miranda*. But why?

If the Christian burial speech delivered to Williams during the drive back to Des Moines amounted to "custodial *interrogation,*" then the *Miranda* route to affirmance would seem no less inviting than the one *Massiah* provided. Under the circumstances of the case—Williams asserted both his right to remain silent and his right to counsel *many times* earlier that day and the Christian burial speech was not concerned with another crime nor made by a different officer nor preceded by a new set of warnings—the speech, if it can be considered "interrogation," seems to have been delivered in clear violation of *Miranda* as clarified, or qualified, by *Michigan v. Mosley.*[31]

Yet, was the speech a "form of interrogation" or tantamount to "interrogation"? A major attraction of the *Massiah* route, as I shall dwell upon below, seems to be that it provided a means of bypassing the "interrogation" issue completely. Another advantage offered by the *Massiah* approach was the

31. 423 U.S. 96 (1975) (discussed at notes 335–74 and footnotes 74–86 *infra* and accompanying text). *See also* discussion at footnote 21 *supra*.

application of a higher standard of waiver: the *Williams* Court might have held, as had some lower courts, that a "*Massiah* right to counsel" could not be waived in the absence of counsel or without the consent of counsel—whether it could was still a debatable question[139]—or, alternatively, it might have been held that a waiver of *Massiah* rights "require[d] the clearest and most explicit explanation and understanding of what is being given up."[140] Yet it appears that the *Williams* Court chose the *Massiah* route without capitalizing on either of the advantages offered by this approach.

Justice Powell, concurring in *Williams,* maintained that "the opinion of the Court is explicitly clear that the [*Massiah*] right to assistance of counsel may be waived, after it had attached, without notice to or consultation with counsel."[141] In fact, however, the opinion of the Court was not quite so clear. It may be interpreted as holding only that Williams did not waive his "*Massiah* right to counsel" *even assuming* that one in his situation could do so without notice to or consultation with counsel.[142] In any event, for the State to establish a waiver of the "*Massiah* right to counsel"[32] "it [is] incumbent upon [it, according to *Johnson v. Zerbst*[143]] to prove 'an intentional relinquishment of abandonment of a known right or privilege . . . ,'"[144] and "judged by [this standard] the record in this case falls far short of sustaining [the State's] burden."[145] But Williams had asserted his "*Miranda* right to counsel" numerous times. Was not an alleged waiver of *this right* to be judged by the same standard?

According to *Miranda,* a waiver cannot be presumed because a suspect fails to request a lawyer, and an effective waiver of the right to counsel during interrogation can only be recognized after the warnings are given.[146] Even when the suspect does not assert his right to counsel, *Miranda* tells us that "a heavy burden rests on the government to demonstrate that the defendant knowingly and intelligently waived . . . his right to retained or appointed counsel. . . . This Court has always set high standards of proof for the waiver of constitutional rights, . . . and we re-assert these standards as applied to in-custody interrogation."[147] Once a suspect has *asserted* his right to counsel, as Williams did, the strict *Johnson v. Zerbst* standard of waiver would seem to apply a fortiori; indeed, the *Miranda* opinion notes that once "the individual states that he wants an attorney, the interrogation must cease until an attorney is present."[148]

It may be that the *Williams* Court did operate on the premise that a *heavier* burden rests on the Government to establish a waiver of a "*Massiah* right to counsel" than a waiver of *Miranda* rights,[149] but it never said so. Dissenting

---

32. This is my phrase, not the Court's. The *Williams* Court announced in its opinion that it was putting the *Miranda* doctrine aside and affirming "the judgment before us" on *Massiah* grounds. 430 U.S. at 397–98. In light of this statement, its discussion of waiver seems on its face to be a discussion of waiver of *Massiah* rights. *But see* text at notes 154–77 and footnote 33 *infra*.

Justice White invited it to do so by maintaining that "[t]he issue in this case is whether [Williams]—who was entitled not to make any statements to the police without consultation with and/or presence of counsel—validly waived [his] rights"[150] and by adding in a footnote that "[i]t does not matter whether the right not to make statements in the absence of counsel stems from [*Massiah*] or [*Miranda*]. In either case the question is one of waiver."[151]

If it *did* matter whether the right at stake was based on *Massiah* or *Miranda,* one would think that the *Williams* majority would have so indicated. But the majority met Justice White's contention only with silence.

The jettisoning of *Miranda* by the *Williams* majority and its reliance on *Massiah* becomes even more puzzling when one examines the portion of the Court's opinion that addresses the issue whether Williams waived his right to counsel in the course of the drive back to Des Moines.[152] In light of the earlier discussion by the *Williams* Court,[153] this section of the opinion *seems to say* the following: (i) The Iowa courts erred when, relying largely on Williams's failure to express any desire for the aid of counsel immediately before or at the time of his disclosures, they held that he had waived his "*Massiah* right to counsel";[154] (ii) the federal district court rightly pointed out "that it is the *government* which bears a heavy burden [on the waiver issue]. . . . but that is the burden which explicitly was placed on [Williams] by the state courts";[155] (iii) both the district court and the court of appeals were correct in their understanding of the proper standard to be applied (the *Johnson v. Zerbst* standard);[156] and (iv) judged by this standard the Government did not meet its burden of showing waiver because it failed to establish "not merely comprehension but relinquishment" of the right to counsel.[157] When one studies the language of the Iowa courts and the lower federal courts quoted by the *Williams* majority in its *original context,* however, one discovers that all of it was addressed to the issue whether Williams had waived his *Miranda* rights, not his "*Massiah* right to counsel."

The Iowa Supreme Court saw itself as performing its "duty . . . to see that . . . none of the strict rules of proof set out in *Miranda* were violated by the trial court in passing on . . . the issue as to whether the accused waived his right to remain silent and to have the present assistance of counsel."[158] Because it agreed with the trial court that Williams had voluntarily "change[d] his mind about talking to the officers" on the return trip,[159] it concluded that, in finding a valid waiver, the trial court had "followed the approved test for determining compliance with the *Miranda* mandates."[160] Justice Stuart, who wrote the principal dissent from the Iowa Supreme Court's decision, "personally believe[d] there is nothing morally or legally wrong in permitting police officers"[161] to do what Captain Leaming had done in the instant case, but reluctantly concluded that *Miranda* had held otherwise[162] and that "the spirit, if not the letter of *Miranda* and subsequent decisions has been violated here. "[163] As noted earlier,[164] neither the Iowa Supreme Court opinion nor the dissenting opinions ever referred to *Massiah;* nor had the Iowa trial court.

Thus, when the federal district court ruled that the Iowa courts had "applied the wrong constitutional standards" in finding a waiver,[165] it must have meant, and it is plain that it did mean, that the Iowa courts misunderstood and misapplied *Miranda.* Moreover, unlike the Eighth Circuit and the United States Supreme Court,[166] the district court adhered to the view that "given the factual context of this case, . . . [Williams] could not effectively waive his right to counsel for purposes of interrogation in the absence of counsel (or at least notice to his counsel of the interrogation). "[167] The portion of the district court opinion devoted to waiver,[168] the same portion from which the *Williams* majority quoted at length with approval,[169] therefore deals only with the waiver of *Miranda* rights. The "heavy burden rest[ing] on the government to demonstrate that the defendant knowingly and intelligently waived" his rights,[170] which the Iowa courts overlooked and the State failed to satisfy, is plainly the "heavy burden" imposed by *Miranda.*

Similarly, the section of the Eighth Circuit's opinion in *Williams* entitled "Waiver of Constitutional Rights,"[171] which the Supreme Court also referred to and quoted with approval,[172] deals almost entirely with *Miranda* rights.[173] Sharing the district court's view that the record "discloses no facts to support the conclusion of the state court that [Williams] had waived his constitutional rights other than that [he] had made incriminating statements,"[174] the court of appeals noted, referring to *Miranda,* that "waiver of one's rights may not be presumed from a silent record."[175] A moment later, after recalling that Williams had repeatedly asserted his rights, the court of appeals emphasized the following sentence from *Miranda: "If the individual indicates in any manner, at any time prior to or during questioning, that he wishes to remain silent, the interrogation must cease."* [176]

Why the *Williams* opinion, to borrow a phrase from its author, performed such "a remarkable job of plastic surgery"[177] on the language of the lower federal courts it quoted with approval—*omitting all their references* to *Miranda* and to the self-incrimination clause[33]—is unclear. The courts below

33. Thus, in *Williams* the Supreme Court noted with approval that "[t]he [district] court held 'that it is the *government* which bears a heavy burden [on the waiver issue]. . . . '" 430 U.S. at 402 (emphasis in original). But the Court omitted the first part of the district court's sentence, which stated that: "*Miranda* makes it clear that it is the *government* which bears a heavy burden. . . . " 375 F. Supp. at 182. Similarly, the Court in *Williams* noted with approval that "the District Court concluded [that] '[T]here is no affirmative indication . . . that [Williams] did waive his rights . . . '" 430 U.S. at 402. But once again the Supreme Court omitted a key phrase from the district court's opinion, which read: "As noted in the preceding paragraph, there is no affirmative indication . . . that [Williams] did waive his rights." 375 F. Supp. at 182. The "preceding paragraph," indeed the two preceding paragraphs, both quote the same language from *Miranda,* 384 U.S. at 475: "a valid waiver will not be presumed simply from the silence of the

proceeded on the basis that the Christian burial speech constituted "interrogation" within the meaning of *Miranda*. Thus, the transformation of *Williams* from a *Miranda* case to a *Massiah* one would have been a good deal more understandable if the *Williams* Court found not only "no need to review" the *Miranda* doctrine[178] but no need to consider whether the speech constituted "interrogation" either. Yet the Court chose the *Massiah* route and apparently still proceeded to decide (or at least left little doubt that it was ready and willing to decide) that the speech did constitute, or was tantamount to, "interrogation."[179]

"[T]he clear rule of *Massiah*," announced Justice Stewart for the *Williams* majority, "is that once adversary proceedings have commenced against an individual, he has a right to legal representation when the government *interrogates* him."[180] This is the clear rule of *Miranda* when, as was Williams, the individual being interrogated is in "custody"—regardless of whether adversary proceedings have commenced—and especially when, as did Williams, the individual asserts his right to counsel. The clear rule of *Massiah*, as I shall discuss below, is that once adversary proceedings have commenced against an individual, he has a right to legal representation *whether or not* the government "interrogates" him. Dissenting Chief Justice Burger compounded the confusion, I venture to say, by contending that "this is a far cry from *Massiah*"[181] and that "[h]ere there was no interrogation of Williams in the sense that term was used in *Massiah, Escobedo* or *Miranda*."[182] But it is plain that there was no interrogation of Massiah in the sense that term was used in *Escobedo* or *Miranda*. Indeed, *Massiah* involved no police "interro-

---

accused after warnings are given." In the "preceding paragraph" the district court pointed out that the state trial court's "heavy emphasis... on the 'absence... of any assertion of [Williams's] right to desire not to give information absent of the presence of his attorney' conflicts directly" with the aforementioned *Miranda* language. 375 F. Supp. at 182. The *Williams* opinion also quoted with approval the district court's conclusion that "it cannot be said that the State has met its 'heavy burden' of showing a knowing and intelligent waiver of... Sixth Amendment rights." 430 U.S. at 403. But the district court's comment in full read: "[I]t cannot be said that the State has met its 'heavy burden' of showing a knowing and intelligent waiver of Fifth and Sixth Amendment rights." 375 F. Supp. at 183. Moreover, although the district court had earlier quoted the "heavy burden" language from *Miranda,* indeed put it in italics, *id.* at 182, the *Williams* opinion does not indicate that the source of the "heavy burden" language is *Miranda.*

The *Williams* opinion also quoted with approval from the court of appeals decision: "A review of the record here... discloses no facts to support the conclusion of the state court that [Williams] had waived his constitutional rights other than that [he] had made incriminating statements...." 430 U.S. at 403 (quoting from 509 F.2d at 233). The *Williams* Court then skipped two sentences from the court of appeals opinion and resumed: "The District Court here properly concluded that an incorrect constitutional standard had been applied by the state court in determining the issue of waiver...." *Id.* The two sentences omitted by the Supreme Court are: "Although oral or written expression of waiver is not required, waiver of one's rights may not be presumed from a silent record. Miranda v. Arizona..., 384 U.S. at 475; Carnley v. Cochran, 369 U.S. 506, 516 (1962)." 509 F.2d at 233.

gation" at all (as that term is normally used)—certainly none of its "compelling influences," inherent, informal, atmospheric, or otherwise.

A Close Look at Massiah

The various opinions in *Williams* cannot be intelligently appraised, nor can the implication of the case be fully explored, without a firm grasp of the underlying circumstances of, and the Court's reasoning in, *Massiah*. After he had been indicted for federal narcotics violations, Massiah retained a lawyer, pleaded not guilty, and was released on bail.[183] A codefendant, Colson, invited him to discuss the pending case in Colson's car, parked on a city street.[184] Unknown to Massiah, the indictment against Colson, "as is not infrequently the case," "induced" him to cooperate with government agents in their continuing investigation of the case.[185] A radio transmitter was installed under the front seat of Colson's car to enable a nearby agent, equipped with a receiving device, to overhear the Massiah-Colson conversation.[186] As expected, Massiah made several damaging admissions.[187]

At the district court level, the judge and lawyers alike thought they were dealing with a not-too-unusual fourth amendment-"electronic eavesdropping" case,[188] but it turned out to be an oddball sixth amendment-"confession" case—too odd to suit a 2-1 majority of the Second Circuit, which could not bring itself to exclude statements obtained from someone who, at the time, was "speaking freely and without restraint of any kind."[189] Aberrant though the *Massiah* facts may have been for a "confession" case, the Court's holding—that defendant was denied the right to assistance of counsel when his own incriminating statements, "which federal agents had deliberately elicited from him after he had been indicted and in the absence of his counsel," were used against him[190]—was not. Indeed, it had been anticipated for some time.

Five years earlier, the Court seemed on the verge of handing down what, by way of convenient shorthand, may be called the "indictment rule." In two concurring opinions by Justices Douglas and Stewart in *Spano v. New York* (1959),[191] four members of the Court advanced the view that once a person is formally charged or adversary proceedings have otherwise been initiated against him, his right to the assistance of counsel has "begun" or "attached," that is, unless the person voluntarily and knowingly waives that right, the absence of counsel under such circumstances is alone sufficient to exclude any resulting incriminating statements.[192] This view was promptly adopted by the New York courts,[193] and there was reason to think it would soon command— indeed, already commanded—a majority of the Supreme Court. Although a majority of the *Spano* Court did not reach this question, preferring to exclude the confession on straight "coerced confession" grounds,[194] Chief Justice Warren, who wrote the majority opinion, had previously expressed the view that the right to counsel should begin at an even earlier point. [195] It was almost inconceivable that, when the occasion arose, Chief Justice Warren would disagree with Justice Stewart and others that what is true of the trial itself for an accused's right to a lawyer's help is true of the postindictment proceedings as well. For but a year earlier the Chief Justice had joined in Justice Douglas's view that:

[W]hat is true of the trial [for an accused's right to a lawyer's help] is true of the preparation for trial *and of the period commencing with the arrest of the accused.*
. . . .

The demands of our civilization expressed in the Due Process Clause require that the accused who wants a counsel should have one *at any time after the moment of arrest.* [196]

A 6–3 majority, consisting of the four concurring Justices in *Spano,* Chief Justice Warren, and newly appointed Justice Goldberg, chose *Massiah* as the appropriate occasion to announce the new rule. It is hardly surprising, however, that the dissenters deemed the *Massiah* facts a "peculiarly inappropriate" setting for a major breakthrough on the "police interrogation"-"confession" front. [197]

The view advanced by the concurring Justices in *Spano* and adopted by the Court in *Massiah* grew out of the needs to restrain "the coercive power of the police," [198] to minimize both the "temptation" and the "opportunity" to obtain confessions by coercive means, [199] and to bypass the "seldom helpful" (at least from the defendant's viewpoint) "trial of the issue of coercion." [200] Yet, the government elicited incriminating statements from Massiah without resorting to coercive measures. [201] Massiah had no idea that he was being "interrogated" by the police; he assumed that he was simply talking to a friend, his partner in crime, who had also been indicted. Nor was there any dispute as to what was said and done at the Massiah-Colson meeting, [202] only as to whether it was permissible for a government agent to do and say what Colson had under the circumstances.

Why the Supreme Court did not wait for a more normal "police interrogation" case than *Massiah* to promulgate the "indictment rule" is unclear. Perhaps it was stung by the Second Circuit opinion, which brushed off *Spano* as just another "coerced confession" case and did not even mention the *Spano* concurring opinions. [203] Perhaps it was impressed by, and moved to vindicate, Judge Hays's dissent, which gave considerable weight to the *Spano* concurring opinions [204] and quoted at length from a New York Court of Appeals case that had adopted the "indictment rule." [205] Perhaps the Court was moved to act by the sharp disagreement that had already broken out among the federal courts as to the significance of the *Spano* concurring opinions. [206]

Whatever the reason or reasons, the Court was determined to wait no longer to promulgate the "indictment rule," the peculiar facts of *Massiah* notwithstanding. That the case did not involve typical police interrogation, as did *Spano* and all the post-*Spano* New York Court of Appeals cases,[34] that Massiah had not even been aware that he was being "interrogated," was of no great moment to the *Massiah* Court. The decisive factor was that the government had been bent on, and had succeeded in, getting incriminating statements from a person after he was indicted and in the absence of counsel. It did not matter that in *Spano*

the defendant was interrogated in a police station, while [in *Massiah*] the damaging testimony was elicited from the defendant without his knowledge while he was free on bail.... [A]s Judge Hays pointed out in his dissent in the Court of Appeals, "if [the rule advocated by the concurring Justices in *Spano* and adopted by the New York courts] is to have any efficacy it must apply to indirect and surreptitious interrogations as well as those conducted in the jailhouse. In this case, Massiah was more seriously imposed upon . . . because he did not even know that he was under interrogation by a government agent."[207]

Massiah's statements were held to be inadmissible, not *because,* as the dissenters in *Brewer v. Williams* were to suggest,[208] he was unaware that a government agent was talking to him, but *despite* that fact. The Court had to overcome Solicitor General Archibald Cox's persuasive argument for the Government that even if the *Spano* concurring opinions represented the prevailing view, Massiah's incriminating statements should still be admissible because at the time he made them he was neither in "custody," not even in the loosest sense, nor undergoing "police interrogation." Massiah was under no "official pressure"[209] to answer questions or even to engage in conversation; indeed, his conversation with Colson "was not affected by even that degree of constraint which may result from a suspect's knowledge that he is talking to a law enforcement officer."[210] Furthermore, Colson, a layman unskilled in the art of interrogation, did not and probably could not utilize any of the standard

---

34. One lower court New York case did involve a "jail cell plant" who elicited incriminating statements from defendant after the initiation of judicial proceedings and at a time when he was represented by counsel. *See* People v. Robinson, 16 A. D.2d 184, 224 N.Y.2d 705 (1962). In his *Massiah* oral argument, Solicitor General Cox argued that *Robinson* "was not in keeping with anything the New York Court of Appeals has held" and that the "philosophy" of that court "does not go beyond formal interrogation." Transcript of Oral Argument for United States at 28–29 (copy on file at the *Georgetown Law Journal*) [hereinafter cited as *Massiah* Oral Argument].

The *Massiah* opinion cited *Robinson* without calling attention to its special facts or otherwise indicating that it went "beyond formal interrogation." "Ever since this Court's decision in the *Spano* case," noted the *Massiah* Court, "the New York courts have unequivocally followed [the "indictment rule" advanced in the *Spano* concurring opinions]," citing, *inter alia,* the *Robinson* case. *See* 377 U.S. at 204–05 & n.5.

techniques to persuade or otherwise induce Massiah to incriminate himself. As the Government stressed in its brief:

[T]he Justices who would have gone beyond the majority [in *Spano* and *Crooker*[(211)]] reasoned that a confession obtained in the absence of counsel was inadmissible without a showing of actual coercion because [such] interrogation so frequently involves coercion. . . . [(212)]

. . . Whatever the problems incident to interrogation by the police, that kind of interrogation is not involved here. This case does not involve either coercion or the potentiality of coercion . . . [Massiah] was not questioned by anyone who even appeared to be a government agent; rather, his "interrogator" was his own partner in crime, to whom he talked freely. [Massiah] was, of course, under no police control or restraint at the time and was free to come and go as he pleased.[(213)]

[T]his is clearly not a problem of police interrogation in the usual sense. . . . This plainly isn't *Spano*. . . . [T]here is [no] problem of physical or psychological compulsion or the threat of coercion; . . . indeed, and perhaps most important of all, the defendant was not in custody, . . . not . . . even in the loose and inaccurate sense in which one may be in custody when he's in the district attorney's office being questioned even though he's not under arrest.[(214)] He was free to come and go as he chose. . . . [(215)]

. . . .

. . . [T]here was no official questioning, no pressure of any kind either to stay there or to engage in the conversation or answer questions; nor could it be said in any sense to be an interrogation by an expert interrogator. . . . [(216)]

. . . .

. . . [T]he agent was cooperating with the Government. But I shouldn't think this was material where the informer is simply a layman, someone who is inside the ring and is reporting what goes on. I would distinguish it very sharply from the case where the prosecutor himself, say, in some kind of disguise,[(217)] was drawing out the defendant. . . . [T]his isn't likely to be or fairly thought of as a problem of the expert on one side questioning [a layman] on the other, and I think that's another difference from what I understand to be . . . the true theory of the New York cases. Here, this is very similar to the situation that might develop if the Government were investigating an espionage ring, and somebody had been infiltrated into the ring. . . . [The defendant] later goes back to attend meetings with the ring—must the Government now withdraw its counter-espionage agent? . . . [35]

. . . .

. . . [Spano was] quizzed for the purpose . . . simply of getting evidence against him (there was no further investigation because that was a crime of violence) [and he was quizzed] by experts. . . . [But Massiah] was not in custody; he was not being interrogated in the same sense that lawyers or detectives would interrogate, and I would

---

35. *Massiah* Oral Argument, *supra* footnote 34, at 36–37. Solicitor General Cox devoted a considerable part of his oral argument to a point touched upon in the text above—the use of Colson was not "obviously addressed to extracting evidence," not necessarily or even primarily focused upon obtaining evidence against the particular defendant," and not "centered on ferreting

think, therefore, that our position here was consistent with the views expressed in the concurring opinions in *Spano*.[218]

That Massiah, unlike Spano and the defendants in the various New York cases,[219] was *unaware* that he was dealing with a government agent was a distinction without a difference to the *Massiah* Court. Although Massiah was less seriously imposed upon than the defendant in the ordinary "confession" case *in one respect*—he was not even subjected to the "potentiality of coercion"[220]—the decisive feature of his case was that after he had been indicted, "and therefore at a time when he was clearly entitled to a lawyer's help"[221] and at a time when he was awaiting trial "in an orderly courtroom, presided over by a judge, open to the public, and protected by all the pro-

---

information out against this man." *Id.* at 32, 44. Rather, he argued, it was part of a continuing investigation of what appeared to be an ongoing conspiracy:

> [T]he return of an indictment against one member of what may be a conspiracy in the case of organized crime doesn't terminate the need to press forward the investigation. We're not dealing here, and I think it's important to bear this in mind, with a single crime of violence, a murder.... That's been the case which has frequently come before the Court and there any questioning . . . is obviously addressed to extracting evidence. This is not typically true in the kind of case that we're dealing with. There is the rest of the ring to be uncovered; indeed here Aiken, the big man, was identified and found after this took place. Frequently the defendant himself, while out on bail, resumes or continues his criminal activities....
>
> . . . .
>
> If [the Government] is gathering evidence against this man, if that's the center of what it's doing, then it ought to be treated under the [indictment] rule of the New York cases. Whereas, if the Government is proceeding in normal fashion, as it had been before [the indictment], to carry out an investigation . . . [and]if this testimony comes along, then it should be admissible like any other testimony that comes along.

Id. at 31–32, 39.

In this respect, too, the case for admitting the statements in *Massiah* was stronger than the case for doing so in *Williams*. Williams was suspected of committing—and completing—a single crime of violence. The sole purpose of the "visit" in the car was to gather evidence against Williams. There was no ongoing criminal activity about which to worry. There were no confederates to uncover.

If the Des Moines police had had reason to believe Williams's victim were still alive, then they might have argued that their efforts were not "centered on ferreting information out against this man." There is nothing in the record, however, to indicate that they doubted Williams's lawyer's report that the child was dead when Williams left the YMCA building. Indeed, they were proceeding on the assumption that Williams had disposed of the body as soon as he possibly could after he left Des Moines. *See* text at note 55 and footnotes 13–15 *supra;* footnote 15 *supra.*

The *Massiah* Court's response to the Solicitor General's argument was not to "question that in this case, as in many cases, it was entirely proper to continue an investigation of the suspected criminal activities of the defendant and his alleged confederates, even though the defendant had already been indicted." 377 U.S. at 207. Instead, the Court responded: "All that we hold is that the defendant's own incriminating statements, obtained by federal agents under the circumstances here disclosed, could not constitutionally be used by the prosecution as evidence against *him* at his trial." *Id.* (emphasis in original).

cedural safeguards of the law,"[222] he had been subjected to an extrajudicial, police-orchestrated proceeding[223] designed to obtain incriminating statements from him. Besides, if in one respect—the lack of an inherently or potentially "coercive atmosphere"—Massiah had been less seriously imposed upon than the average "confession" defendant, he was more seriously imposed upon in another respect—he did not, and could not be expected to, keep his guard up "because he did not even know that he was under interrogation by a government agent."[224] This was a nice point (or counterpoint), but it was hardly the decisive one.

Massiah did not discard the *Spano* mold; it enlarged its original form or, if you like, produced a companion mold. The "indictment rule" would not be, and was not meant to be, limited to cases of "indirect and surreptitious interrogations"[225] *because,* as the dissenters in *Williams* were to suggest,[226] these happened to be the *Massiah* facts. Rather, the "indictment rule" was to apply *even though* the "interrogation" was "indirect and surreptitious" ("unapprehended" or "unbeknown" might be better descriptions).[36]

Any doubts that the *Massiah* doctrine applies *whether or not* the suspect was aware that he was talking to the police—and it is hard to see how anyone who studies the briefs or oral arguments in the case can entertain any doubts on this score—were resolved a year later in *McLeod v. Ohio*[227] In that case the Ohio courts admitted into evidence statements obtained from a defendant a week after he was indicted.[228] The Supreme Court of the United States vacated the judgment and remanded the cause "for consideration in light of [*Massiah*]."[229] Nevertheless, the Supreme Court of Ohio adhered to its original position, distinguishing *Massiah* on the ground, *inter alia,* that, unlike Massiah, who "had no knowledge that the conversation was being overheard by a government agent,"[230] McLeod made statements "in the known presence of public officers."[37] As two members of the state court warned their brethren would happen,[231] the Supreme Court reversed per curiam.[232]

Massiah would have been an easier case—and, as it turns out, a less significant one—if, after he had been indicted, Massiah had simply been questioned by police in "an atmosphere of official coercion." Under these facts *Massiah* might have been completely displaced by *Miranda,* as I think

36. The *Massiah* Court quoted with approval from Judge Hays's dissenting opinion: if the rule advanced by the *Spano* concurring Justices and adopted by the New York courts "is to have any efficacy it must apply to indirect and surreptitious interrogations *as well as* those conducted in the jailhouse." *See* text *supra* at note 207 (emphasis added). It is clear in context that "interrogations . . . conducted in the jailhouse" means interrogations in the known presence of the police. *See id.*

37. State v. McLeod, 1 Ohio St. 2d 60, 61, 203 N.E.2d 349, 351 (1956). The Ohio Supreme Court also attempted to distinguish *Massiah* on the ground that at the time McLeod incriminated himself he "was not then represented by counsel and had not even requested counsel." *Id.* That the Ohio court was unsuccessful here, too, is demonstrated by the Supreme Court's reversal. *See* notes 434-42 and footnotes 92-93 *infra* and accompanying text.

Escobedo was,[233] instead of becoming a case that furnishes protection separate and distinct from *Miranda*. If *Massiah* had been a normal "interrogation" case, it would not represent the "pure" or "straight" right to counsel approach that it does;[234] it might have become, as I think *Escobedo* did, no more than a point on an unfinished and probably never-to-be-finished highway.

But *Massiah* was not a typical "confession" case. The questioning in that case did *not* occur in an "atmosphere of official coercion." And it seems no more profitable to wonder what the law of confessions would mean today—and how *Williams* would have been decided—if Colson had been a uniformed police interrogator rather than an undercover agent than it is to speculate about how American history would have been affected if the Mississippi River had flowed northwest instead of south.

The Constitutional Irrelevance of "Interrogation" for Massiah *Purposes*

Taking the *Massiah* facts as we find them and reading the Court's opinion the way it was written, *nothing* turns on whether Massiah was "interrogated"—surreptitiously or otherwise. Indeed, there is no indication that Colson did "question" him, surreptitiously or otherwise,[38] or that he was directed to do so.

Colson's instructions, we are told by Chief Judge Lumbard, writing for a majority of the Second Circuit, "were apparently no more than *to induce* Massiah to talk."[235] Colson's assignment, as described by Judge Hays, dissenting from this decision, was to permit a transmitter to be installed in his car and "to invite Massiah to take a ride with him in the car and *to engage* Massiah *in conversation* relating to the alleged crimes."[236] Massiah's contention, as summarized by Chief Judge Lumbard, was that inasmuch as he was already indicted and represented by counsel he "could not legally *be approached* by persons acting on behalf of the government in the absence of his counsel."[237] Dissenting Judge Hays, relying heavily on the *Spano* concurring opinions, would have honored Massiah's claim for the reason that "federal officers must *deal through and not around* an attorney retained by a defendant under indictment."[238]

Similarly, the Supreme Court, in an opinion authored by Justice Stewart, described the *Massiah* case as one in which the government "succeeded by *surreptitious means* in *listening to* incriminating statements"[239] made by an indicted defendant in the absence of his retained counsel. After disclosing at the outset that it was going to put fourth amendment problems to one side and

---

38. We do not even know, and evidently the Supreme Court did not care, what Colson said or how he said it. Colson did not testify himself and the agent who overheard the Colson-Massiah conversation was *not permitted to testify to anything Colson said,* apparently on the basis of the best evidence rule. Brief for Petitioner at 19 (App. A); Brief for United States at 7, 22 n.11. Thus, the record only contained Massiah's half of the conversation.

only decide whether Massiah's constitutional rights were violated "by the use in evidence against him of incriminating statements which government agents had *deliberately elicited* from him"[240] under these circumstances, the Court went on to hold—employing almost identical language—that Massiah was denied the right to counsel when there was used against him "his own incriminating words, which federal agents had *deliberately elicited* from him after he had been indicted and in the absence of his counsel."[241] The use of the term "deliberately elicited" seems to be quite deliberate.

It takes no great stretch of the imagination to see that a government agent, whether a "secret agent," as in *Massiah,* or a known police officer, as in *Williams,* can "deal around" rather than "through" an attorney retained by a defendant under indictment, [242] or "induce" him to talk [243] or "deliberately elicit" statements from him [244] without asking a single question [39]—indeed, without *saying anything.* Consider the following hypotheticals:

• Suppose federal agents had told Colson to arrange a meeting with Massiah, but warned him to be sure *not* to broach the subject of the pending case against them. Suppose they had given him the following instructions:

When Massiah arrives, don't talk about the case. What's more, *don't say anything.* Just look very sad and depressed. Massiah will undoubt-

---

39. To the contrary is Wilson v. Henderson, 584 F.2d 1185 (2d Cir. 1978), a decision handed down when this article was in galleys. After Wilson, a murder suspect, had asserted his *Miranda* rights, been appointed counsel, and apparently been formally charged, he was removed to a detention cell. There he engaged in a number of conversations with his "cellmate" (who had previously agreed to act as a police informant). At first Wilson minimized his involvement in the crime, but his "cellmate" told him that his story did not sound too good. By the end of the third day, Wilson changed his story and admitted his complicity in the murder. Because the "cellmate" had been specifically instructed not to inquire or question, but to "just keep [his] ears open," and had not in fact "interrogated" Wilson, a 2-1 majority held—over a powerful dissent by Judge Oakes—that Wilson's statements to his "cellmate" were not barred by the *Massiah-Williams* rule.

I submit that the facts in *Wilson* are constitutionally indistinguishable from those presented in *Massiah.* There was no finding or any indication that Colson "interrogated" Massiah or asked him a single question. But the *Massiah* Court did not seem to think this mattered at all. *See* footnote 38 *supra.* What did matter was that in *Massiah* (and in *Williams*)—and equally so in *Wilson*—the government "deliberately and designedly set out to elicit information," Brewer v. Williams, 430 U.S. at 399, from one who was then "entitled to the help of a lawyer." *id.* at 398, and "succeeded by surreptitious means in listening to incriminating statements made by him," *id.* at 400. *See generally* text at footnote 38 and notes 235–41 *supra.*

Because the lower federal courts had relied so heavily on *Miranda* in holding the Christian burial speech inadmissible and because various members of the Supreme Court could not resist discussing whether the speech constituted or was tantamount to "interrogation," *Williams* did generate a certain amount of confusion—one factor that led me to write this article. But Justice Stewart wrote the opinions for the Court in both *Massiah* and *Williams.* I think he would be startled to learn that, although when he authored the *Williams* opinion he evidently thought he

edly do one of two things: He will either try to cheer you up by assuring you that your chances are better than you think (or remind you that things could be a lot worse), and in the process mention some incriminating evidence the Government doesn't know about; or he will share in your pessimism, making some reference to the strong case the Government will present, and along the way say something that will strengthen our hand. However Massiah reacts, he is bound to make some damaging admissions—and Agent Murphy will be listening. So remember, just don't say anything.

Suppose further that when Massiah arrived, Colson, following instructions, covered his face with his hands and shook his head in anguish, or, better yet, burst into tears. Suppose finally that in the course of trying to console his friend and fellow defendant, Massiah had made some damaging admissions. Assuming that these hypothetical facts were the *Massiah* facts, and that the defense could establish that they had occurred (which is no small feat), is there any doubt that the result in *Massiah* would have been the same?

• Colson was a busier undercover agent than is generally realized. Pursuant to government instructions, he held other separate meetings in his specially equipped car with two of Massiah's coconspirators, Anfield and Maxwell, and these conversations, too, had been "broadcasted" to Agent Murphy.[40] Suppose Colson's instructions were to arrange *one* meeting in his "bugged" car with both Massiah and Anfield. Suppose government agents had told him:

> We have reason to believe that Anfield and Massiah are blaming each other for the mess they're in. If we can bring them face-to-face, they will undoubtedly do one of two things—either continue to quarrel with each other or try to patch things up. In either event, damaging

---

was revivifying and expanding *Massiah*, he was actually restricting its scope—or so the *Wilson* majority seems to tell us. It is hard to believe that if a fact situation identical to *Massiah* arose today, the outcome would be different because a secret agent may now induce incriminating statements from one who is formally charged and represented by counsel—so long as he does so by "making conversation," not by asking questions. Yet this is what the *Wilson* majority seems to say; this is how it seems to think the *Williams* case qualifies *Massiah*.

[*Shortly after this article was published, another federal court of appeals did apply the* Massiah-Williams *doctrine to exclude statements obtained by a "cellmate" (a paid informant of the FBI) from a defendant "after his indictment, while he was in custody and had not waived his right to counsel," rejecting the government's argument that* "Brewer v. Williams *limited* Massiah *and its progeny to cases involving 'interrogation' [as that term is normally used]."* Henry v. United States, 590 F.2d 544, 546 (4th Cir. 1978) (2-1 majority, per Winter, J.), cert. granted, _____ U.S. _____, 100 S. Ct. 45 (1979).]

40. *See* footnote 9 *supra*.

admissions are bound to be made, and Agent Murphy will be listening. It's conceivable, but not very likely, that Massiah and Anfield won't start talking about the case. In that unlikely event, Colson, you'll have to prod them. But we really don't think that will become necessary. We think that once those two birds are brought together, they'll just naturally, almost inevitably, get to talking about the case.

Suppose further that as soon as Massiah entered Colson's car and spotted Anfield, already sitting in the back seat, he became conciliatory, admitted that he made some mistakes (for example, that after sealing the cocaine packages with tape, to protect the contents from evaporation, he should have gotten rid of what was left of the roll of tape), gently reminded Anfield that he had also made some mistakes, and then urged Anfield to stop fighting with him so that they could start working together to win the case.[41] On these facts, too, I think the result in *Massiah* would have been the same.

If the *Massiah* facts had been those hypothesized above, the government would still have succeeded by surreptitious means in overhearing incriminating statements made in counsel's absence by one already indicted and represented by, or entitled to, counsel. Even if Colson and Massiah had never addressed each other directly, even if the conversation had taken place entirely between Massiah and Anfield, the government would still have induced Massiah to talk about the case by setting up a meeting in circumstances in which damaging admissions were reasonably expected and highly likely to occur.[42]

41. This is close to what Massiah actually told Colson when they met in the latter's car. Brief for Petitioner at 20–21 (App. A); Brief for United States at 7–8.

42. In both hypotheticals, and in *Massiah* itself, the idea of the meeting, at which the defendant made incriminating statements, originated with the government. A forceful argument could be made that if the meeting is suggested by the defendant himself—especially if the defendant's purpose is to "coach" a witness or codefendant, who, unknown to the defendant, is a government agent, or to threaten him with harm if he appears at the trial at all—that the secret agent's willingness to attend the meeting does not constitute inducing or encouraging a defendant to talk or engaging him in conversation within the meaning of *Massiah*. But the Supreme Court's summary reversal of Beatty v. United States, 377 F.2d 181 (5th Cir.), *rev'd per curiam*, 389 U.S. 45 (1967), indicates that *Massiah* reaches even this far.

In *Beatty* a 2–1 majority, in an opinion authored by Judge Gewin, distinguished *Massiah* on the ground that the meeting there was "government sponsored" in its entirety whereas in *Beatty* the government agents had not instructed Sirles, a government informer who purchased a machine gun from defendant, to engage Beatty in conversation or even to associate with him. 377 F.2d at 190. Defendant had contacted Sirles, requested a meeting, and proposed the time and place of the meeting. Sirles agreed to attend the meeting when a government agent, McGinnis, told him to do so. The meeting was held in Sirles's automobile, in which McGinnis hid himself in the trunk.

Variations on Brewer v. Williams:
Massiah *and* Miranda *Compared and Contrasted*

Despite the obvious similarities between *Massiah* and *Miranda,* that each case is "a law unto itself"[(245)] may be seen, I think, by varying the actual facts in *Brewer v. Williams* so that it becomes only a *Miranda* case, and a simple *Miranda* case at that. Suppose that no adversary proceedings had been initiated against Williams and no defense lawyer had entered the picture. Suppose further that Williams had neither asserted nor even been advised of his right to counsel or his right to remain silent. Then suppose one of the following *alternative* hypothetical fact situations occurred:

• *The "Mother Powers" Ploy.* Williams voluntarily surrenders to the Davenport police. A police lieutenant takes Williams into his office,

---

Although McGinnis's tape-recording device failed to work, he did manage to overhear the entire conversation, during which the defendant threatened to kill Sirles if the machine gun turned up in court or if Sirles appeared against him.

The majority maintained that *Massiah* "only renders inadmissible those statements made as a result of the acts of a secret informer [when such informer] . . . actively and deliberately induced the accused to make such admissions," and that "sanctioning the presence of an informer at a meeting called by the accused and even sending an agent to listen in on the conversation cannot be equated with procuring or deliberately eliciting information from an accused." *Id.* at 190–91. Dissenting Judge Ainsworth argued that *Massiah* required exclusion of defendant's statements even though he had originated the idea of the meeting:

Agent McGinnis' presence secretly in the trunk compartment of Sirles' vehicle was not mere chance or accident. Though appellant is said to have initiated the meeting with Sirles, the secret eavesdropping setup was the result of deliberate prearrangement by McGinnis with the secret informer Sirles for possible use at appellant's trial. . . . To deny [appellant his sixth amendment right] by secret post-indictment and before-trial eavesdropping of conversations with a secret informer, and then recount the prejudicial incriminating statements of appellant at his trial, is to deprive [him] of the effective assistance of counsel at a stage when such advice would have helped him . . . . [O]nce a person is indicted in a criminal case he has a right to counsel before and during the trial and his voluntary conversations and admissions made out of court to secret Government informers, overhead surreptitiously by Government agents, are inadmissible in evidence in the absence of an express waiver by the defendant.

Id. at 193–94.

Evidently the Supreme Court agreed with dissenting Judge Ainsworth; it summarily reversed on the authority of *Massiah.* 389 U.S. 45 (1967) (per curiam). The Fifth Circuit now apparently agrees with this interpretation of the Supreme Court reversal. In a footnote it recently recalled that it "drew another irrelevant distinction in *Beatty*" when "[it] declined to apply *Massiah* on the ground that the defendant had initiated the conversation with the government agent." United States v. Anderson, 523 F.2d 1192, 1196 n.3 (5th Cir. 1975) (dictum) (Godbold, J.) (court emphasized that statements here were induced by government). *See also* Dix, *Undercover Investigations and Police Rulemaking,* 53 TEXAS L. REV. 203, 232–34 (1975) (close discussion of *Beatty*).

leaves him there alone, and posts a guard outside the door. After a few minutes, the lieutenant reappears and tells Williams:

> I've been trying to phone Captain Leaming of the Des Moines police to inform him that you've turned yourself in, but so far I have been unable to contact him (which is true). In the meantime I have learned that Mrs. Powers, the mother of the missing little girl, Pamela, is in the building (which is untrue) and is desirous of having a brief private meeting with you. It seems that she drove down here when she heard reports that your car was spotted in this area. Would you mind sparing Mrs. Powers a few minutes while I get back on the phone and try to contact Captain Leaming again?

Williams agrees, without much enthusiasm, to meet briefly with "Mother Powers" (who is actually a policewoman, about the same age as Pamela's mother, equipped with a tape recorder). No sooner are they alone than "Mother Powers" delivers the following Christian burial speech:

> Deep down in my bones, I feel that my little girl is dead. All I want to do for her now is give her a good, decent Christian burial. I don't think that's too much to ask for your daughter, when she was taken away from you on Christmas Eve. I feel that you know where my little girl's body is. But they are predicting that a lot of snow will fall tonight, and I'm afraid that when it snows not even you will be able to locate the body. . . .

At the end of the speech, Williams tells a tear-stained "Mrs. Powers" that Pamela's body is located not far from the Mitchellville exit and assures her that he will show Captain Leaming where it is on the drive back to Des Moines.

• *The "Weather Forecaster" Ploy.*   The operator of a service station located a hundred miles from Des Moines phones Captain Leaming and reports that a man just walked into his station and told him that he is the one the police are looking for in connection with the disappearance of the little Powers girl, that his car has broken down, that he's "tired of running and hiding," that he's afraid that somebody might kill him, and that he wants to surrender to the police. Captain Leaming and Detective Nelson drive immediately to the service station, followed by a second car, occupied by state agents who have been brought in on the case.

Captain Leaming talks to Williams only long enought for Williams to identify himself, and Leaming then orders him into the police car. Leaming and his prisoner head back toward Des Moines. After a few minutes of "small talk" about matters unrelated to the case, Williams reveals that he is very fond of the music broadcasted over a certain radio station and that he listens to that station as often as possible. Leaming responds: "It's a hard, slow drive back to Des Moines in terrible weather. There's no reason why we can't make you as comfortable as possible. We'll let you listen to that station on the drive back."

Leaming's car then stops at a service station to check the oil. Leaming walks back to the state agents' car and tells the agent in charge:

As you know, my theory is that Williams disposed of the body somewhere in the Mitchellville area. The roads are so slippery and the visibility is so poor that we won't reach the Mitchellville exit for another two and a half hours or so. Now here's what I want you to do. Call this radio station and instruct the weather forecaster to make this weather report two hours from now. [He hands the agent a piece of paper containing the Christian burial speech, which the weatherman is supposed to "work into" his report.] Don't worry, we'll be tuned in on that station all the way back to Des Moines.

Some two hours later, as Leaming and his prisoner near the Mitchellville exit, still listening to Williams's favorite station, they hear the following "weather report":

The weather is bad and getting worse, friends. It's twenty-one degrees above zero at the moment, but the temperature is expected to fall five degrees an hour until it drops to zero. The rain and sleet we're getting right now is bad enough, but three to four inches of snow are predicted for tonight. This is bad news for all of us—but especially for Mrs. Powers, the mother of the missing nine-year-old girl, Pamela Powers.

According to law enforcement authorities, Mother Powers has given up all hope that little Pamela is still alive. Her only wish now, and it is surely a modest one, is that she will be able to give her little girl— snatched away from her on Christmas Eve—a good Christian burial. But she is afraid, and the authorities share her fears, that once the predicted heavy snow falls not even the person who knows where poor Pamela is will be able to find her.

At this point a grim-faced Williams turns to an impassive Leaming and murmurs: "Turn off at the next exit; I'm going to show you where the body is."

• *The "Waitress" Ploy.*   Assume the same facts as in the previous situation with these changes: After a few minutes of "small talk" about matters unrelated to the case, Williams asks Leaming whether they can stop "for a bite" before they get back to Des Moines. Leaming promises Williams that they will stop at a "nice place" near the Mitchellville exit. Leaming's car then stops at a service station to replace the windshield wipers. Leaming walks back to the state agents' car and tells the agent in charge:

> We're going to be stopping at Jimmy's Restaurant just before we get to the Mitchellville exit. I want the "waitress" who takes Williams's order to be Jennie Jordan, a Des Moines policewoman who used to be a waitress. I want Jennie to engage in some "small talk" with Williams about the weather and work in these comments. [He hands the agent a piece of paper.] Get Jennie on the police radio. She's a lot closer to Jimmy's Restaurant now than we are. She ought to be able to get into a waitress's uniform and do a little "brushing up" before we get there.

Some two hours later, Captain Leaming spots Jimmy's Restaurant and announces to Williams:

> Detective Nelson and I are pretty well known in these parts. And everybody knows we've been busting our behinds trying to find the kidnapper of the little Powers girl. If either one of us accompanies you into the restaurant, people are liable to figure out who you are. And then there's no telling what might happen. So we're going to give you a break, Williams. We're going to take off your handcuffs, give you five bucks to eat anything you want, and let you go in *alone*. There's only one exit, and we'll be watching it. We'll also be watching you through those big windows. Don't disappoint us. Don't try anything foolish.

When the "waitress" brings Williams his order, she follows instructions and launches into her version of the Christian burial speech:

> Gee, Mister, I feel sorry for guys like you who have to be out on the road on a night like this. It's sleeting and freezing and the roads must be slippery as hell. But I tell you who I *really* feel sorry for tonight— the mother of that little Powers girl.
>
> Y'know, I got a daughter myself—about the same age as Pamela Powers. Imagine having a little girl like that snatched away from you on Christmas Eve—and not even being able to give her a decent Christian burial. If the searching party doesn't find Pamela's body in the next few hours, nobody will be able to find it for a month—if ever. The weatherman's predicting three to four inches of snow tonight, and once that big snow falls, not even the guy who knows where poor Pamela's body is will be able to find her. . . .

Without finishing his meal, Williams rushes out of the restaurant and back to the police car, shouting: "Start the car! I'm going to show you where the body is!"

In all three hypotheticals, it is plain that the police "deliberately elicited"[246] incriminating disclosures from Williams and therefore that *if* judicial proceedings had been initiated against him (by hypothesis they had not),
the use of the disclosures would have been barred by *Massiah*. I submit,
however, that at least in two of the hypotheticals (the "Mother Powers" and
"waitress" ploys) no "custodial police interrogation" occurred within the
meaning of *Miranda*. [247] If I am right, then the disclosures evoked in at least
these two hypotheticals would be admissible despite the absence of *Miranda*
warnings.

Unlike the *Massiah* doctrine, which operates to prevent the government
from "deliberately eliciting" incriminating statements from a suspect or an
accused, the privilege against self-incrimination erects no such legal barrier.
There is no "right not to confess except knowingly and with the tactical
assistance of counsel";[248] there is only a right not be *compelled* to
confess. *Massiah*, to be sure, raised some doubts about the proposition,[249]
but these doubts were soon laid to rest by the *Hoffa* case.[250]

Hoffa argued that his privilege against self-incrimination had somehow
been violated when he *unwittingly* incriminated himself in the presence of one
Partin, whom Hoffa had thought to be a friend, but who was actually a
government informer. The Court, however, dismissed this contention almost
peremptorily:

[S]ince at least as long ago as 1807 . . . all have agreed that a necessary element of
compulsory self-incrimination is some kind of compulsion. Thus, in the *Miranda*
case, . . . the Court predicated its decision upon the conclusion "that without proper
safeguards the process of in-custody interrogation of persons suspected or accused of
crime contains inherently compelling pressures which work to undermine the individual's will to resist and to compel him to speak where he would not otherwise do so
freely. . . ." In the present case no claim has been or could be made that . . . [Hoffa's]
incriminating statements were the product of any sort of coercion, legal or factual.[251]

By the time *United States v. White*[43] was decided in 1971, the self-
incrimination issue lurking in *Massiah*—"whether law-enforcement officials

43. 401 U.S. 745 (1971) (plurality opinion). On numerous occasions a government informer,
carrying a concealed radio transmitter, engaged defendant in conversations that were electronically overheard by federal narcotics agents. *See id.* at 746–47. The admissibility of the eavesdropping agents' testimony was upheld despite fourth amendment challenge. *See id.* at 754. There
was no opinion of the Court, only a plurality opinion written by Justice White, joined by Chief
Justice Burger and Justices Stewart and Blackmun. *Id.* at 746. The dissenters' fourth amendment
objection went not to the fact that the government had used an apparent colleague or friend to
elicit incriminating statements from a suspect, but to the fact that the secret agent was equipped
with an electronic device. *See id.* at 756 (Douglas, J., dissenting), 768 (Harlan, J., dissenting),
795 (Marshall, J., dissenting). Concurring Justice Brennan and dissenting Justices Harlan and
Marshall seemed to have no quarrel with *Hoffa*, in which the government informer operated
without any electronic equipment. *See id.* at 755, 768, 795.

may seek evidence from an accused's own mouth when [he] does not realize that he is talking to such officials and providing them with evidence that will help to convict him"[252]—was so well settled that it no longer called for discussion. Only respondent's fourth amendment claims were considered, and rejected.[253]

Recognizing that "the Fifth Amendment does not forbid the *taking* of statements from a suspect, [but only forbids] *compelling* them,"[44] the *Miranda* Court, as one of its leading critics put it, "endeavored to supply the missing link in its logic by a conclusive presumption":[45] an individual subjected to custodial police interrogation "cannot be otherwise than under a compulsion to speak."[254] One may quarrel with this conclusion and protest, as has Judge Friendly, that "[a] social scientist or logician would never dream of asserting that any such universal could be inductively proved by reciting the facts in four confession cases . . . even when these were supplemented by copious extracts from police manuals."[255] But *Miranda* does recognize that the fifth amendment only protects against some kind of *compulsion*—and not the kind produced by *custody* alone. In the absence of police interrogation, the coercion of arrest and detention does not rise to the level of "compulsion" within the meaning of the privilege and thus does not give rise to the need for the *Miranda* warnings.[256]

It is the suspect's *awareness* that he is talking with, and being talked to by, the police that generates the "inherently compelling pressures" of in-custody interrogation that the *Miranda* warnings are supposed to dispel.[257] But in the "Mother Powers" and "waitress" hypotheticals, Williams was *unaware* that he was dealing with the police.

The *Miranda* warnings are also designed to correct the widespread misconception that "you must answer all questions put to you by a policeman, or at least that it will be the worse for you if you do not."[258] More generally, the warnings are supposed to relieve the suspect's uncertainty and confusion as to what limits his captors are prepared to go to in order to obtain a confession, and his anxiety that his detention will last *until* he confesses.[259] But these anxieties and misconceptions do not operate—and thus need not be dispelled by the warnings—when the suspect is unaware that the police are talking to him.

The "weather forecaster" ploy is the hardest case of the three. For, although no police officer said anything, Williams listened to and thought about the "weather report" *in the presence of the police*. Furthermore, Williams must have known, or assumed, that the police shared the view that the person who knew where Pamela's body was (and Williams knew the police were convinced he was that person) should disclose this information to the authorities

44. H. FRIENDLY, *A Postscript on* Miranda, in BENCHMARKS 266, 271 (1967) (emphasis in original).
45. *Id.*

before the imminent snowfall so that Pamela's parents would be able to give her a good Christian burial.

In a sense the weather forecaster's remarks constituted a challenge for Williams "to display some evidence of decency and honor."[260] Williams knew it, and he must have known, or assumed, that Captain Leaming also knew it. A failure on Williams's part to meet the challenge might incur the wrath of Captain Leaming, who, up to that point, had been nice to him. A forceful argument can be made, therefore, that under the circumstances postulated the weather forecaster's remarks were tantamount to "police interrogation," but not many courts are likely to agree. Indeed, most of the courts addressing the issue have even held that the response of an arrestee to a question put to *another person in his presence* (often the arrestee's wife or a female companion whom he is trying to protect) is not the product of "interrogation," but is a "volunteered" remark.[261]

The "Mother Powers" ploy is an easier case for admissibility because not only is Williams unaware that he is *talking* to the police, he does not even realize the police are *listening*. To be sure, Williams is being subjected to considerable pressure, but it is not "police blue" pressure. It cannot even be argued, as it could in the "weather forecaster" hypothetical, that the pressure generated by the speech takes on the color of "police blue" from Captain Leaming, who was in the suspect's immediate proximity when the "weather report" was broadcasted and who, the suspect must have sensed, was waiting for an appropriate response.

Williams's position in the "Mother Powers" hypothetical is indeed an uncomfortable one, but for purposes of ascertaining whether there exists a compelling atmosphere within the meaning of *Miranda,* as I understand the case, the situation is the same as if the policewoman *were* Mother Powers. Moreover, and more important, for purposes of establishing whether the conditions surrounding the interrogation are coercive, the situation is the same as if the *real* Mother Powers, who Williams *thinks* she is, were making the same Christian burial speech *without any instructions from or prompting by the police.*[46]

46. When the private citizen—whether friend or relative of the victim, friend or relative of the suspect, partner in crime or fellow prison inmate—is not an agent of the government, that is, not an undercover officer or someone who has agreed to act on behalf of or in cooperation with the authorities, the resulting statements would seem to be admissible as long as they pass the "voluntariness" test, which operates, *inter alia,* to bar statements whose trustworthiness is suspect. *See* Procunier v. Atchley, 400 U.S. 446 (1971) (defendant's statement to insurance agent held admissible; agent not cooperating with government when defendant first gave statement); Milani v. Pate, 425 F.2d 6 (7th Cir. 1970) (prison inmate); Paroutian v. United States, 370 F.2d 631 (2d Cir. 1967) (prison inmate); Stowers v. United States, 351 F.2d 301 (9th Cir. 1965) (confederate and prison inmate); State v. Jensen, 111 Ariz. 408, 531 P.2d 531 (1975) (prison inmate); State v. Miranda, 104 Ariz. 174, 450 P.2d 364 (1969) (retrial and reconviction of Miranda) (woman with whom defendant was living); People v. Price, 63 Cal. 2d 370, 406 P.2d

To be sure, a relative of the victim may exert strong pressure on a suspect to confess; but so may a close friend or parent of the suspect.[262] Yet this is not "official" pressure or persuasion, not the kind the *Miranda* warnings are designed to combat. Whether or not the friend or business associate or relative who tries to induce the suspect to confess is doing so on his own initiative or at the instigation of the police, the pressure on the suspect is the same. And *Miranda* focuses on *the impact* of the "surroundings" and "atmosphere" on the suspect. Again, whether or not the mother of the victim is making a spontaneous, unrehearsed appeal or following instructions—or whether or not she really is the mother—the effects on the suspect are the same.

The "waitress" ploy is the easiest case of the three hypotheticals for admissibility. The use of a "waitress" as a police instrumentality will strike most as a good deal less offensive than the use of the victim's "mother," real or pretended. Furthermore, the Christian burial remarks undoubtedly generate less pressure, albeit unofficial pressure, when they come from the mouth of an apparently disinterested waitress rather than from an apparently grief-stricken mother. Unlike the "Mother Powers" ploy, Williams has no reason to think that the "waitress" suspects he had anything to do with the disappearance of Pamela Powers. From Williams's vantage point, the waitress's remarks are not focused on him at all, but spoken to the world at large. Moreover, in the "Mother Powers" hypothetical, Williams might worry that his failure to oblige the "mother" might be reported by her to the police and cause them to think less of him or become angry with him. In the "waitress" hypothetical,

---

55, 46 Cal. Rptr. 775 (1965) (TV news reporter); People v. Holtzer, 25 Cal. App. 3d 456, 102 Cal. Rptr. 11 (2d Dist. 1972) (victim himself); Anglin v. State, 259 So. 2d 752 (Fla. 1972) (mother of defendant); State v. O'Kelly, 181 Neb. 618, 150 N.W.2d 117 (1967) (criminology professor pursuing his own professional interest in murder case); People v. Cardona, 41 N.Y.2d 333, 360 N.E.2d 1306, 392 N.Y.S.2d 606 (1977) (prison inmate); People v. Gunner, 15 N.Y.2d 226, 205 N.E.2d 852, 257 N.Y.S.2d 924 (1965) (airline stewardess); State v. Perry, 276 N.C. 339, 172 S.E.2d 541 (1970) (prison inmate); State v. Knott, 111 R.I. 241, 302 A.2d 64 (1973) (mother of defendant).

When the private citizen is not a "government agent," *Massiah* bars the resulting statements no more than *Miranda*, even though adversary judicial proceedings have already commenced. As Justice White observed in his *Massiah* dissent:

> Had there been no prior arrangements between Colson and the police, had Colson simply gone to the police after the conversation had occurred, his testimony relating Massiah's statements would be readily admissible at the trial, as would a recording which he might have made of the conversation. In such event, it would simply be said that Massiah risked talking to a friend who decided to disclose what he knew of Massiah's criminal activities.

377 U.S. at 211 (White, J., with Clark & Harlan, JJ., dissenting).

Whether or not an "agency relationship" with the government does exist, however, is often a difficult question. *See, e.g., Milani v. Pate,* 425 F.2d 6 (7th Cir. 1970); Stowers v. United States, 351 F.2d 301 (9th Cir. 1965); State v. Ferrari, 122 Ariz. 324, 541 P.2d 921 (1975); People v. Holtzer, 25 Cal. App. 3d 456, 102 Cal. Rptr. 11 (2d Dist. 1972); People v. Cardona, 41 N.Y.2d 333, 360 N.E.2d 1306, 392 N.Y.S.2d 606 (1977).

however, Williams has no reason to think that the officers waiting for him outside Jimmy's Restaurant have any inkling, or will ever find out, that the waitress who took his order made some Christian burial remarks in his presence.[47]

I do not say that, *aside from* the trickery or deception *inherent* in "undercover" work, a "secret agent" is more free to resort to trickery or deception than is any other government agent.[263] Nor do I mean to suggest that an undercover officer or government informer is more free to oppress or coerce a suspect or otherwise employ objectionable tactics than any other government agent.[264] Nor do I deny that some police impersonations may be unduly offensive. If, for example, a suspect asks for a priest, the authorities should not be permitted to dispatch a policeman masquerading as a priest.[265] Nor, if a suspect asks to place a call to his mother or sister, should a policewoman impersonating the mother or sister be allowed to take the call (no doubt complaining about a bad connection in order to explain why her voice sounds so different).

Moreover, there are undoubtedly limits on the amount and kinds of pressure the government may exert on a dear friend or close relative of the suspect who is reluctant to serve as a secret agent, but who may be persuaded to do so, say, by threats to lodge serious charges or by promises to drop existing charges against him. Indeed, the court may well find it "shocking" for the government to use son against father, brother against brother, even in the absence of a showing that the close relative was pressed into service as a secret agent.[48]

My submission is only that the use of secret agents against one "in custody" is not per se violative of the privilege against self-incrimination. It does not *without more* constitute "compulsion" within the meaning of the privilege ("inherent," "constructive," "conclusively presumed," or otherwise), and

---

47. An even easier case for admissibility under *Miranda*—and an even more graphic illustration of how *Massiah* and *Miranda* is each "a law unto itself"—would be presented by shifting the "weather forecaster" ploy from the police car to Jimmy's Restaurant. Suppose that, as in the case of the "waitress" ploy, Williams was permitted to enter the restaurant alone and that when he did so he heard his favorite radio station being played. Suppose further that while Williams was quietly eating his meal the weather forecaster, acting pursuant to Leaming's instructions, broadcasted his Christian burial weather report. Under these circumstances, any resulting incriminating disclosures would surely be admissible under *Miranda*. Yet, because the weather forecaster had been acting as a "police instrumentality" when he made the broadcast, any resulting disclosures would still be barred by *Massiah*—although admittedly this would be carrying the doctrine a long way—if at the time Williams heard the weather report adversary judicial proceedings had already commenced against him.

48. Professor Dix would prohibit the government from soliciting relatives of the suspect to serve as undercover agents. Dix, *supra* footnote 42, at 224. "Relatives include parents, grandparents, children, grandchildren, siblings, and spouses." *Id. See generally* Note, *Eavesdropping, Informers, and the Right of Privacy: A Judicial Tightrope,* 52 CORNELL L.Q. 975, 994–96 (1967) (need for, but difficulty of, imposing some due process limitation on use of informers, based on "degree of closeness between the informer and the informed-upon").

thus no *Miranda* warnings need to be employed to dispel this compulsion. I also submit that neither confinement, nor the "subtle influences" this condition may produce, evokes the *Massiah* doctrine. It is plain that once adversary judicial proceedings have commenced, the *Massiah* doctrine shields an accused from undercover activity designed to obtain incriminating statements from him, regardless of whether he is "in custody" or subjected to "police interrogation" in the *Miranda* sense (and perhaps the *Massiah* doctrine, or a related one, affords a suspect the same protection when he is represented by counsel or when he has asserted his right to counsel). Nevertheless, when none of these events has occurred (and none did in the "Mother Powers," "waitress," and "weather forecaster" hypotheticals), then there is either a "*Miranda* right to counsel" or no right to counsel at all. If the conditions surrounding or inherent in police efforts to obtain incriminating statements from a suspect do not put his privilege against *compelled* self-incrimination in jeopardy—and the Court has told us that the mere fact that the suspect is in custody does not do so—then there is no right to counsel at all.

More on the Use of "Jail Plants" and Other "Secret Agents" against Those "in Custody"

The "custody"-"surreptitious interrogation" issues are not free from difficulty, and they have not been cleanly resolved by the Supreme Court.[49] Some support, but not a great deal, for the view that "custody" per se does not

---

49. An opportunity to shed further light on the use of jail "plants" was lost when, on the last day of the 1967 Term, the Court, with four Justices dissenting, dismissed the writ of certiorari as improvidently granted in People v. Miller, 245 Cal. App. 2d 112, 53 Cal Rptr. 720 (4th Dist. 1966). Miller v. California, 392 U.S. 616, 616 (1968) (per curiam). Petitioner was arrested for murder, booked on that charge, and placed in a cell. *Id*. at 616–17 (Marshall, J., with Warren C.J., Douglas & Brennan, JJ., dissenting from dismissal of certiorari). Not only did defense counsel meet with his client, but in an effort to prevent her from being questioned, he set up a 24-hour-a-day watch of her cell. *Id*. at 617. Nevertheless, an undercover agent was booked into the jail on a fictitious charge and placed in petitioner's cell. *Id*. Although this occurred before any formal charges were filed against petitioner, the undercover agent remained in petitioner's cell, eliciting information from her, for two days after a complaint was filed formally charging her with murder and on which petitioner was later arraigned. *Id*. The state court viewed the government's action as "completely indefensible" and "most inexcusable," but concluded that the admission of petitioner's statements was "harmless error" and that, in any event, objection to it had not been made. 245 Cal. App. 2d at 144, 53 Cal. Rptr. at 740. *See also* Milton v. Wainwright, 407 U.S. 371 (1972) (holding that any error in admitting postindictment confession to jail "plant" was "harmless error"; merits of petitioner's claim not reached). In *Milton* Justice Stewart wrote a forceful dissent, urging that the judgment be reversed. *Id*. (Stewart, J., with Douglas, Brennan & Marshall, JJ., dissenting). But the underlying issue was an easy one, once it was reached, for the officer who entered petitioner's cell, posing as a fellow prisoner, did so only after petitioner had been indicted and had retained counsel.

trigger the *Massiah* doctrine may be gleaned from *Procunier v. Atchley* [1971].[266] The second time he paid respondent a visit in jail, an insurance agent seemed to be acting as a secret government agent by agreeing to the deputy sheriff's request that the conversation be electronically recorded. But the Court, in an opinion by Justice Stewart, dismissed what was arguably a *Massiah* issue with a brief footnote—"No charges had been filed against the respondent at the time of these conversations. *Cf. Massiah.*"[267]—and proceeded to judge the admissibility of respondent's statements by the due process standard of "voluntariness."[268]

On the other hand, there is, or at least at first blush there appears to be, some lower court authority for the view that government efforts to elicit incriminating statements from one "in custody" do bring *Massiah* or *Miranda* into play. When these "custody"-"surreptitious interrogation" cases are read closely, however, none of them needs to be viewed as requiring the exclusion of the statements obtained in the "Mother Powers" and "waitress" hypotheticals, or in the "jail plant" situations; all these cases can be distinguished or explained away.[50]

Several opinions of the lower California courts can be read to stand for the proposition that the right to counsel or the privilege against self-incrimination or both protect one in custody from undercover investigation, regardless of whether adversary judicial proceedings have commenced against him or regardless of whether he is represented by, or has even requested, counsel.[269] But these cases were decided before *Miranda* and they are not on the *Miranda* "track." Rather, they are on a *Massiah-Escobedo-Dorado*[51] "track," one that

---

50. *See* notes 269–71 and footnotes 51–56 *infra* and accompanying text (discussion of California cases); footnote 63 and notes 327–28 *infra* and accompanying text (cases in other jurisdictions).

51. In People v. Dorado, 62 Cal. 2d 338, 398 P.2d 361, 42 Cal. Rptr. 169 (1965), the court held, at a time when many other state courts were giving *Escobedo* a begrudging reception, that the failure of a suspect to retain or request counsel does not justify the application of a rule different from that established in *Escobedo:*

> The accused's request for counsel indicates no more than that he, himself, at that point . . . perceived the need of legal assistance. The request merely constitutes evidence that the accused finds himself in an accusatory predicament. *Escobedo* did not treat the request for counsel as the reason for the establishment of the right; it points out that the right had previously crystallized in the accusatory stage.

Id. at 349, 398 P.2d at 368, 42 Cal. Rptr. at 176.

Quite understandably, *Dorado* relied very heavily on *Escobedo,* then the dominant United States Supreme Court confession case, and viewed *Escobedo* as extending *Massiah* to critical situations arising before the initiation of adversary judicial proceedings. In concluding that the facts of the instant case brought it within the rule of *Escobedo,* the *Dorado* court mentioned, without any elaboration, that defendant was "in custody," but it stressed that the investigation "had ceased to be a general inquiry into an 'unsolved crime' and had begun to focus on defen-

the *Miranda* Court largely abandoned.[52] The underlying premise of these California cases taken together seems to be that the *Massiah* and *Escobedo* cases prohibit any "surreptitious interrogation" of a person once he is formally charged *or* arrested.[270] This reading of *Massiah* and *Escobedo* was tenable before *Miranda*, but not afterwards.[271]

Although these California cases happen to involve "custodial" situations, they do not really seem to turn on "custody" at all, but rather on the fact, if it can be called a fact, that "the process [had] shift[ed] from investigatory to accusatory"[53] and "its focus [was] on the accused."[54] This is to say, they seem to proceed on the basis that—*whether or not* the suspect is "in custody"—once the investigation has ceased to be "a general inquiry of an unsolved crime [and] has begun to focus on a particular suspect,"[55] constitutional rights come into play.[56]

That a court would proceed on such a basis during the turbulent and unstable post-*Massiah-Escobedo* and pre-*Miranda* era (when these California cases were decided) is understandable. But as far as federal constitutional law is concerned,[272] it has since become clear that nothing turns on whether the suspect has "become the accused" or whether the investigation has "begun to focus" on him.

---

dant"; that the weight of the evidence available to the officers "provided reasonable grounds for focusing upon defendant as the particular suspect"; that the officers "did not merely engage in general questioning but subjected defendant to a process of interrogation that lent itself to obtaining incriminating statements"; and that defendant had never been warned of "his 'absolute constitutional right to remain silent.'" *Id.* at 347, 398 P.2d at 367, 42 Cal. Rptr. at 175.

52. *See* footnotes 28–30, 43–45 and notes 125–26, 248–59 *supra* and accompanying text.

53. Escobedo v. Illinois, 378 U.S. 478, 492 (1964).

54. *Id.*

55. *Id.* at 490.

56. *See* People v. Flores, 236 Cal. App. 2d 807, 811, 49 Cal. Rptr. 412, 414 (2d Dist. 1965) ("Except for the absence of an indictment, we have here a defendant under arrest, on whom the suspicion of the police had already fastened . . . "), *cert. denied,* 384 U.S. 1010 (1966); People v. Ludlum, 236 Cal. App. 2d 813, 815, 46 Cal. Rptr. 375, 376 (2d Dist. 1965) ("defendant was under arrest for the crime herein involved; clearly suspicion had 'focused' on him, not only because he had been arrested, but because [the police] knew, of their own knowledge, that defendant had been in possession of [narcotics]"). *See also* note 270 *infra.*

Similar "focal point"-"accusatory stage" language appears in Justice Marshall's dissent from the dismissal of certiorari in Miller v. California, 392 U.S. 616, 624–25 (1968) (Marshall, J., with Warren, C.J., Douglas & Brennan, JJ., dissenting from dismissal of certiorari) (discussed at footnote 49 *supra*). But this language "does not distinguish focused preindictment investigations concerning subjects not in custody." Dix, *supra* footnote 42, at 231. On its facts *Miller* can be readily distinguished from typical "surreptitious interrogation" cases because petitioner had retained and met with counsel before being placed in a cell and her lawyer attempted to prevent questioning of his client by setting up "a 24-hour-a-day watch of her cell." 392 U.S. at 617 (Marshall, J., with Warren, C.J., Douglas & Brennan, JJ., dissenting from dismissal of certiorari). Furthermore, "it is clear on this record that [the undercover agent] was planted in petitioner's cell in order to subvert her right to counsel." *Id.* at 626.

The *Miranda* warnings were designed to combat the coercive conditions surrounding or inherent in "custodial police interrogation" and the mere fact that one has become the "prime suspect" or "focal point" does not necessarily have *any effect* on the conditions surrounding police interrogations. The *Hoffa* Court did not care whether petitioner had already been the "focal point" when he incriminated himself in the presence of his apparent friend, Partin.[273] For even if the investigation had already "focused" on Hoffa, this would not have rendered his statements any less voluntary.

It is hard to believe that the result in *Hoffa* would have been any different, nor is it easy to see why it should be, if (i) petitioner and Partin had been arrested together and petitioner had made incriminating statements to his "friend" while in a police vehicle on the way to the stationhouse[274] or while sharing the same cell with him;[275] or if (ii) Hoffa alone had been arrested and Partin had then visited him in his jail cell, at which time Hoffa had incriminated himself. In these hypothetical variations on the actual case, Hoffa would still have been "relying upon his misplaced confidence that Partin would not reveal his wrongdoing,"[57] even though he would have done so in a police vehicle or a jail cell rather than in his hotel suite.[58] It could not be said in these hypothetical variations on *Hoffa,* no more than it could in the actual case, I submit, that "petitioner's incriminating statements were the product of any sort of coercion, legal or factual."[276]

Professor Dix would surely quarrel with my conclusion. "The subjects' confinement," he has observed, "is likely to bring into play subtle influences that will make them particularly susceptible to undercover investigators' ploys."[277] "Arguably, " he concluded, "these dangers would justify imposing a *Massiah*-like barrier on all undercover activity directed at an incarcerated subject.[278] I hesitate to disagree with one who has made a most useful, massive study of the use of undercover investigations, but I must—and on two fronts.

First, as I have already indicated, in the absence of additional factors, such as the initiation of adversary judicial proceedings and perhaps representation by counsel, I do not think *Massiah* has any bearing on the "custody"-"surreptitious interrogation" problem. As Professor Dix seems to agree, the special dangers involved when secret agents seek incriminating statements from incarcerated subjects, rather than from suspects at large, are "compelled self-incrimination"[279] dangers. If these dangers justify imposing a barrier

---

57. Hoffa v. United States, 385 U.S. 293, 302 (1966).

58. As Professor Dix points out, "insofar as *Massiah* rests on the subject's interest in privacy, it would seem to have less applicability to the custody situation. The state of prison confinement clearly reduces a person's reasonable expectation of privacy." Dix, *supra* footnote 42, at 230. On the other hand, the use of an "old friend" as a secret agent, rather than a mere stranger who happens to share a cell with the defendant, involves a deeper invasion of the defendant's personal privacy. *Id.* at 221.

(fourth amendment considerations aside), it would be a *"Miranda*-like,*"* not a *"Massiah*-like,*"* barrier.

Some support for Professor Dix's position may be found in the language of Supreme Court opinions. In *United States v. Ash*, [280] for example, the Court viewed *Massiah* as a case in which "counsel could have advised his client of the benefits of the Fifth Amendment" and "sheltered him from the overreaching of the prosecution,"[59] and as one in which "the accused was confronted by prosecuting authorities who obtained, by ruse and in the absence of defense counsel, incriminating statements."[281] In the landmark lineup case, *United States v. Wade (1967)*, [282] the Court suggested that the sixth amendment guarantee applies to *any* "critical" pretrial "confrontation" with the government "where the results might well settle the accused's fate and reduce the trial itself to a mere formality."[283]

It is plain, however, that such language cannot be read literally. Hoffa's meeting with Partin was a "critical confrontation" with a government agent that "settled his fate." One of Hoffa's own lawyers, Osborn, was himself involved in a "critical confrontation" with a government agent, even though he did not realize it at the time, when he conferred with one Vick, whom he had hired as an investigator but who was actually working for and reporting back to federal authorities. [284] Moreover, in *United States v. White,* [285] a government informer, carrying a concealed radio transmitter, "confronted" the accused on numerous "critical" occasions, repeatedly enabling "eavesdropping" federal agents to obtain incriminating statements "by ruse and in the absence of defense counsel." [286]

The constitutionally significant difference between the *Massiah* case and the *Hoffa, Osborn,* and *White* cases cannot be the critical nature of the confrontation between the defendant and the government. Nor can it be the measure of the need for the assistance of counsel. The need for a lawyer, at least one with the wit to realize that his client's meeting with an apparent friend or associate might turn out to be a confrontation with a secret government agent, [287] was equally great in all the cases. The critical nature of the confrontations was also equally great in all the cases, at least from the perspective of their impact on each defendant's fate. But one is not entitled to a lawyer's assistance *whenever* a lawyer "could have sheltered him" from government agents bent on obtaining evidence against him or *whenever* a government confrontation is "critical." Self-incrimination considerations aside, one only

59. United States v. Ash, 413 U.S. 300, 312 (1973). But was Massiah entitled to fifth amendment protection? Was he compelled to speak? How would counsel's presence at the Massiah-Colson meeting in Colson's car have provided Massiah with "assistance" at the "confrontation" with the government unless counsel were aware that Colson was a secret agent? And if counsel were so aware, wouldn't he have *prevented* the confrontation from taking place? *See* Grano, Kirby, Biggers *and Ash: Do Any Constitutional Safeguards Remain Against the Danger of Convicting the Innocent?* 72 MICH. L. REV. 717, 762 & n.285 (1974).

has a right to counsel "at any 'critical stage of the *prosecution*.' "[288] And as Justice Stewart has expressed it:

The requirement that there be a "prosecution," means that this constitutional "right to counsel attaches only at or after the time that the adversary judicial proceedings have been initiated against [an accused] . . ." "It is this point . . . that marks the commencement of the 'criminal prosecutions' to which alone the explicit guarantees of the Sixth Amendment are applicable."[60]

The only constitutionally significant difference between *Massiah* and the other "secret agent" cases letting in the surreptitiously obtained statements must be that in *Massiah,* unlike the other cases, the meeting with the agent took place after the initiation of adversary criminal proceedings, and thus "the explicit guarantees of the Sixth Amendment" had "attached."[289] In the other cases, it may be said, the Court declined to "import into a routine police investigation an absolute constitutional guarantee historically and rationally applicable only after the onset of formal prosecutorial proceedings."[290] These other cases may be said to stand for the proposition that, when a person has not been formally charged with a criminal offense, *Miranda*—and *Miranda* alone—strikes the appropriate constitutional balance.[291] If and when the conditions surrounding or inherent in a "pre-formal charge" confrontation are sufficiently coercive, then the "*Miranda* right to counsel" comes into play. The right to counsel as such, what might be called the "*Massiah* right to counsel," does not. At the "pre-charge" stage, at least when the suspect neither has nor has expressed a desire for counsel, the right to counsel is triggered by, and dependent on, forces that "jeopardize" the privilege against compelled self-incrimination;[292] *it has no life it can call its own.*

Even if I am correct in thinking that the influences at work when a person shares a jail cell with an undercover agent do not, *without more,* bring the *Massiah* doctrine into play, do they nevertheless evoke the protection of *Miranda?* This, I think, is the appropriate question; but again, I would answer it in the negative.

To be sure, in a sense the mere presence of an undercover agent in the same cell with an accused, or in an adjoining one, is "itself . . . an inducement to speak, and an inducement by a police agent."[293] But so is the mere presence

60. United States v. Ash, 413 U.S. 300, 321–22 (1973) (Stewart, J., concurring) (quoting from his plurality opinion in Kirby v. Illinois, 406 U.S. 682, 688, 690 (1972)). To the same effect is Justice Powell's opinion for the Court in the recent case of Moore v. Illinois, 434 U.S. 220, 226–27 (1977) (quoting from Justice Stewart's plurality opinion in *Kirby*). *But cf.* Escobedo v. Illinois, 378 U.S. 478, 486–87 (1964); People v. Dorado, 62 Cal. 2d 338, 349, 398 P.2d 361, 368, 42 Cal. Rptr. 169, 176 (1965).

of one or more uniformed police officers while a person is arrested or transported to the stationhouse or brought to the "booking officer." I would be the last to deny that police custody, without more, generates certain anxieties and pressures. But how can it be maintained that these anxieties and pressures are greater when a suspect or an accused is in the presence of a fellow prisoner than when he is in the midst of the police? Yet, as I have discussed,[294] police custody *without more* is not enough to bring the *Miranda* warnings into play.

Again, I do not deny that the anxieties generated by mere confinement may lead a person "to seek discourse with others to relieve this anxiety."[295] But it is by no means self-evident that he is less likely to do so when these others are police officers rather than fellow prisoners. After all, who will a suspect assume knows more about "the law" and "the system" in general—and his predicament in particular—someone who is sharing his cell or the officer who arrested (or is "booking") him?

I do not deny that one in custody is likely to feel considerable pressure to blurt out protests of innocence in the presence of his captors; or, without any prompting, to depict his role in the best possible light; or to protect dear ones; or to seek information and advice from the arresting or "booking" officer— and in the process to incriminate himself unwittingly. ("What's going to happen to me?" "I've never done anything like this before." "My girl friend had nothing to do with this case." "I did it; my brother wasn't involved." "I didn't rob that man; he owed me the money." "Did you find the weapon (or the body)?" "Who put the finger on me?"[296] The temptation to find out more about one's plight, or how the system works generally, is likely to be even stronger when, as often occurs, the police, in the course of transporting or "booking" the suspect, have already engaged him in friendly conversation about matters unrelated to his case. Yet *Miranda* does not protect one "in custody" who turns to an officer for information, advice, or relief—and in the process incriminates himself unwittingly—simply because he was "in custody" when he did so. Why, then, should *Miranda* protect one who turns to an apparent fellow prisoner for the same reasons simply because he was in custody when he did so?

In one respect (but not, of course, in *several others*), the "jail plant" confession poses a stronger case for exclusion than *Massiah:* "unlike the defendant there, who had been released on bail, petitioner [in a "jail plant" confession situation is] in custody without bail, with a consequent lack of freedom to choose [his] companions."[297] Again, however, this argument proves too much. One who is arrested, transported, and "booked" usually lacks freedom to choose his companions—at least during the pressure-packed, anxiety-ridden first few hours.

In the long drive back to Des Moines, Williams was no doubt "seek[ing] discourse with others" to relieve his anxiety. But the only persons with whom he could seek discourse during that five or six hour trip[298] were Captain

Leaming and Detective Nelson. Yet if Williams and the companions he did not choose had ridden in complete silence for 50 or 100 miles and then Williams had blurted out: "Look, I know where the body is, and I'm going to show it to you—but I didn't kill her; she was already dead when I found her in my room"[61]—or even if Williams had said that he did kill her—it can hardly be doubted that these statements would have been admissible.[62] Nor would the admissibility of any incriminating statements by Williams have posed any serious problem if they had been preceded by conversation—as long as the topics had been limited to "intelligence of other people . . . , organizing youth groups, singing . . . , playing an organ, and this sort of thing."[(299)]

The Importance of the "Interplay" between "Police Custody" and "Police Interrogation"

As *Massiah* itself illustrates better than any other case, the sixth amendment guarantee prevents the government from eliciting or inducing incriminating statements from one against whom adversary judicial proceedings have commenced, whether or not he is in custody and whether or not he is aware that he is dealing with a government agent. As I have argued at length, however, even though a person is in custody, "surreptitious interrogation" is insufficient to bring *Miranda* into play. For unless a person *realizes* he is dealing with the police, their efforts to elicit incriminating statements from him do not constitute "police interrogation" within the meaning of *Miranda*. But perhaps the manner in which I have proceeded, up to this point, has been too "one-dimensional." Perhaps I can state my position more effectively, and concomitantly summarize that position, by dwelling on the *interplay* between the two dimensions of *Miranda*—"police custody" *and* "police interrogation."

The inherent or potential impact of government activity on the mind or "will" of the suspect has nothing to do with the application of *Massiah,* but has everything to do with the invocation of *Miranda*. It is the impact on the suspect's mind of the *interplay* between police interrogation and police custody—each condition *reinforcing* the pressures and anxieties produced by the other—that, as the *Miranda* Court correctly discerned, makes "custodial police interrogation" so devastating. It is the suspect's realization that the *same persons* who have cut him off from the outside world, and have him in their power and control, want him to confess, and are determined to get him to do so, that makes the "interrogation" more menacing than it would be without

61. In fact this turned out to be Williams's contention, at least at his second trial. *See* Kamisar, *supra* footnote 2, at 210 n.4.

62. In response to a specific question along these lines by one of the Justices, Williams's able court-appointed counsel, Professor Robert D. Bartels of the University of Iowa College of Law, conceded as much. *See* Transcript of Oral Argument at 35 (copy on file at the *Georgetown Law Journal*).

the custody and the "custody" more intimidating than it would be without the interrogation.

It is this *combination* of "custody" and "interrogation" that creates—and, in the absence of "adequate protective devices,"[300] enables the police to exploit—an "*interrogation* environment" designed to "subjugate the individual to the will of his examiner."[301] It is this *combination*—more awesome, because of the interplay, than the mere sum of the "custody" and "interrogation" components—that produces the "interrogation atmosphere,"[302] "*interrogation* . . . in a *police dominated* atmosphere,"[303] that "carries its own badge of intimidation,"[304] that "exacts a heavy toll in individual liberty and trades on the weakness of individuals,"[305] and that is so "at odds" with the privilege against compelled self-incrimination.[306]

In the "jail plant" or other "undercover" situations, however, there is no *integration* of "custody" and "interrogation," no *interplay* between the two, at least none where it counts—in the suspect's mind. So far as the suspect is aware, he is not "surrounded by antagonistic forces";[307] "[t]he presence of an attorney, and the warnings delivered to the individual" are not needed to "enable [him] under otherwise compelling circumstances to tell his story without fear, effectively, and in a way that eliminates the evils in the interrogation process."[308] He simply is not in the "compelling circumstances" that require *Miranda* warnings to be given; he is not being subjected to the "interrogation process."

So far as the suspect is aware, his fellow prisoner neither controls his fate nor has a professional interest in his case. So far as the suspect is aware, his fellow prisoner does not care whether he confesses, and thus has little cause to become abusive by trying to "bully" him if he does not.[309] Moreover, even if the fellow prisoner did care, and cared a great deal, there is no reason to think that he possesses the power over the suspect or the necessary skills and training to press demands and to weary the suspect with contradictions of his assertions until the case "is brought to a definite conclusion."[310]

A fellow prisoner may, of course, communicate his determination to get answers to his questions by wielding a knife or clenching his fist, but that is a different case. There is nothing *inherently* compelling about talking with, or being talked to by, a prisoner in the same or an adjoining cell. For the suspect thinks he is dealing with *an equal,* not with his captors.

Why would the suspect doubt that he could end the conversation, or at least change the subject, whenever he pleased? Why would he fear that his companion *would not let him* end the "interrogation"? Why would he worry, if he does not answer all questions put to him by his companion, that "it will be the worse for him"?[311]

When a suspect is arrested and brought downtown for police questioning, at least in the case of a major felony, he will often be in "a crisis-laden situation. The stakes for him are high—often his freedom for a few or many years—and his prospects hinge on decisions that must be quickly made: to cooperate and hope for leniency, to try and talk his way out, to stand adamantly on his rights."[312] But why, when he thinks he is merely conversing with a fellow prisoner, when he has no notion that he is confronting the police, would a suspect worry about "how much leniency cooperation may earn, how likely fast talk is to succeed, and how much a steadfast refusal to talk may contribute to a decision by the police, prosecutor or judge to 'throw the book' at him"?[313]

One can deliberately elicit incriminating statements from a person without having him realize it—that is what happened in *Massiah*. But how can one envelop someone in a "police-dominated atmosphere" without having him realize it? How can one produce an "interrogation environment" well-calculated to "subjugate the individual to the will of his examiner" when the individual is not even aware that he is in the presence of "his examiner"? That is why, I submit, whatever may lurk in the heart or mind of the fellow prisoner (or apparent friend or colleague), if it is not "custodial police interrogation" *in the eye of the beholder,* then it is not such interrogation within the meaning of *Miranda.*

May the Government Do Indirectly What It Cannot Do Directly?

I can already hear the howls of protests: "What you are saying is that the government *may do indirectly* what it cannot do directly!"[63] Am I? *What exactly is it* that the government may not do directly?

What Massiah *Allows.* *Massiah,* as clarified by *Williams,* makes clear that once adversary proceedings have commenced against an individual, gov-

---

63. *See* State v. Smith, 107 Ariz. 100, 102, 104, 482 P.2d 863, 865, 867 (1971) ("What the State may not do directly, it cannot do indirectly.") (but when defendant made incriminating disclosures to "jail plant" he had already been appointed counsel); State v. Daugherty, 221 Kan. 612, 618, 623, 562 P.2d 42, 47, 50 (1977) (*McCorgary* statement, *infra,* quoted with approval and applied) (but "bugged" conversation between defendant and codefendant, cooperating with the prosecution, occurred two days before trial and when defendant represented by counsel); State v. McCorgary, 218 Kan. 358, 359, 363, 543 P.2d 952, 955-56, 958 (1975) ("The whole purpose of the state in using a secret informer is to avoid that which is required of a police officer [informing an in-custody suspect of his rights and not proceeding without a valid waiver]. What the state may not do directly to secure evidence, it cannot do indirectly.") (but "jail plant" obtained incriminating statements from defendant after he had appeared before a magistrate and been appointed counsel); State v. Travis, 116 R.I. 678, 679-83, 360 A.2d 548, 549, 551 (1976) ("The police were not allowed to interrogate defendant directly. There is no authority in these circumstances for the police to do indirectly what they may not do directly.") (but the undercover agent became defendant's "cellmate" shortly after defendant had expressed a desire to consult with a lawyer and refused to say anything until he did). *See also* United States v. Brown, 466 F.2d 493, 494, 495 (10th Cir. 1972) (pointing out that when defendant's friend visited him in his cell, with police "permission," and obtained incriminating statements from him, as the police had

ernment efforts to elicit incriminating statements, whether done openly in the police station or "indirectly and surreptitiously,"[314] violate the individual's right to counsel. But when the government attempts to elicit incriminating statements from an individual before adversary proceedings have commenced against him, it is not necessarily violating his right to counsel. For in the absence of other factors, such as an inherently compelling interrogation environment, an individual is not entitled to counsel *whenever* he is subjected to an "interrogation," but *only* when such interrogations take place at or after the commencement of adversary proceedings.[64]

As I have discussed, Colson deceived not only Massiah, but his codefendant, Anfield, as well. He deceived Anfield in the same way—by arranging a meeting in the same specially equipped car, which enabled the same narcotics agent to overhear the conversation.[315] As far as I am aware, nobody argued that Anfield's right to counsel had been violated; nor would such an argument have much prospect for success. For the electronically overheard Colson-Anfield meeting occurred before adversary proceedings had been initiated against Anfield.[65] Thus, it could not be said, as it could in *Massiah,* that the

---

"requested" him to do, "he was functioning as an instrument of the police" and "doing that which the police themselves could not do.") (but defendant had told the police earlier, when given his *Miranda* warnings, that he did not wish to make any statements and that he did want an attorney).

64. *See* Brewer v. Williams, 430 U.S. at 401; Massiah v. United States, 377 U.S. at 204–05; *cf.* United States v. Hayles, 471 F.2d 788, 791 (5th Cir. 1973). In *Hayles* the court stated:

[I]n one important respect [*Massiah*] retains its vitality and stands as a supplement to *Miranda; Massiah* teaches that . . . after [a defendant] *has been indicted* [or, more generally, adversary proceedings have been initiated against him], [the government] may not nullify the protection *Miranda* affords a defendant by using trickery to extract incriminating statements from him that otherwise could not be obtained without first giving him the required warnings. Today *Massiah* simply means that *after indictment* [or the commencement of judicial proceedings] *and* [or?] *counsel has been retained* the Fifth Amendment [the Sixth Amendment?] prevents law enforcement authorities from deliberately eliciting incriminating statements from a defendant by the surreptitious methods used in that case."

Id. (emphasis added).

The initiation of judicial proceedings *without more* probably activated the "*Massiah* right to counsel." *See* text at notes 419–22 and footnotes 92–93 *infra.* Whether representation by counsel *without more* does so as well is a more difficult question. *See* footnotes 94–97 and notes 443–45 *infra* and accompanying text.

65. When the *Massiah* case reached the Second Circuit, all three judges agreed that evidence obtained from the Anfield-Colson meeting was admissible against Anfield; dissenting Judge Hays argued only that the eavesdrop evidence obtained from Massiah should be barred. *See* United States v. Massiah, 307 F.2d 62, 69 (2d Cir. 1962). But Anfield's conviction was reversed on other grounds. *See id.* at 64.

Five years after Anfield and Massiah were tried, other coindictees, including one Maxwell, were brought to trial. Maxwell had also made the mistake of talking with Colson in the latter's "bugged" car, but did so before judicial proceedings had commenced against him. *See* footnote 9 *supra.* On appeal, as the Second Circuit noted, Maxwell did not press his claim that the recording

government had "indirectly" violated Anfield's right to counsel. Anfield was not yet "entitled to a lawyer's help."[316] He *had no "Massiah* right to counsel" that *could be* violated, no more than did Messrs. Hoffa, Osborn, and White.

What Miranda *Allows.* *Miranda* makes clear that the privilege against compulsory self-incrimination applies both to "informal compulsion" exerted during custodial interrogation and to the more formal variety meted out in court proceedings.[317] But when the government employs an undercover agent, rather than a readily identifiable police officer, it is *not doing indirectly* what *Miranda* forbids it to do. It is not compelling an individual to incriminate himself—informally, inherently, or indirectly. It is not dealing with a prisoner under circumstances in which (in the absence of warnings designed to clarify a confusing situation that the police too often have exploited) a person is likely to assume or be led to believe that there is a legal, or at least an extralegal, sanction for contumacy.[318]

When the government employs a secret agent posing as a fellow prisoner, the suspect does not feel "at the mercy of . . . custodians who have strong incentives for seeking a quick solution . . . by pressing him to acknowledge his guilt."[319] Rather, the suspect thinks he is dealing only with someone "in the same boat," as well as the same cell. The government agent's words do not "take on color from [his] uniform, badge, gun and demeanor"[320] when the agent carries neither badge nor gun and wears not "police blue," but the same prison gray as the defendant.

Under *Miranda,* the government may not rely on an "interrogation environment," which "carries its own badge of intimidation" and is "created for no purpose other than to subjugate the individual to the will of his examiner."[321] But when a government agent conceals his true identity—indeed, *because* he does—the government is not relying on an "interrogation environment" at all. Rather, it is relying on the suspect's "misplaced confidence that [his companion will] not reveal his wrongdoing."[322] Under such circumstances, the government is *deceiving* the suspect—as "Agent" Partin deceived Hoffa and as "Agent" Vick deceived Osborn—but such deception "[does] not tend to show either actual coercion or a potentially coercive setting."[323]

---

and broadcasting of his conversation with Colson violated his right to counsel. United States v. Maxwell, 383 F.2d 437, 442 (2d Cir. 1967). "In any event," added the court, this point "is meritless." *Id.* The court cited Molinas v. Mancusi, 370 F.2d 601 (2d Cir.), *cert. denied,* 386 U.S. 984 (1967), in which defendant's claim that his constitutional rights were violated when a secretly tape-recorded conversation between him and a coconspirator, who was cooperating with the government, was rejected on the ground, *inter alia,* that at the time the conversation took place an indictment had not yet been returned against defendant. *Id.* at 603. "Although the state may have had sufficient evidence to indict Molinas, that is immaterial."*Id.*

When the government utilizes a secret agent to induce a prisoner to incriminate himself, it does not necessarily "trick" him into "waiving" his constitutional rights: findings of trickery and waiver depend on the particular circumstances and the particular constitutional right. When adversary judicial criminal proceedings have already commenced, then, under *Massiah*, the government cannot send an undercover agent against the defendant. But the *Massiah* doctrine does not turn on the existence of a "police-dominated atmosphere" or an "interrogation environment." Perhaps when the suspect has already retained counsel,[66] or perhaps even when he has simply *asserted* his *Miranda* rights,[67] the government may not be permitted to approach him, directly or indirectly—under *Massiah* and perhaps under *Miranda* as well. But when adversary proceedings have not yet commenced and the suspect is not yet represented by counsel, and has not even asserted his *Miranda* rights, then—unless and until he is subjected to "custodial police interrogation," that is, interrogation under inherently compelling circumstances—he *has no* fifth or sixth amendment rights to waive: those rights have not yet come into play.

When an arrestee *volunteers* his version of the events, and the police, well aware that the arrestee is unwittingly incriminating himself, let him talk, they do not thereby violate the person's *Miranda* rights or trick him into waiving them *because, under the circumstances, the person does not have any Miranda* rights.[(324)] *Miranda* tells us, in effect, that "a statement may be volunteered in ignorance of the privilege against self-incrimination and 'of the consequences of foregoing it.' "[(325)] Similarly, when the police interview a person in his home or office, especially when they do so in the presence of a relative or friend, *and* the questioning takes place in a context that does not restrict the person's freedom to terminate the meeting, the police are *not doing indirectly* what they may not do directly. Rather, they are doing what *Miranda* permits them to do—indeed, one might say, recommends that they do.[(326)] They are dealing with the suspect in a situation that lacks "the indicia of coercion that motivated the *Miranda* scrutiny" of in-custody interrogation[68] and that lacks "the elements which the *Miranda* Court found so inherently coercive as to require its holding."[69]

The same may be said, I submit, for the "pure" "jail plant" case, that is, one in which an apparent fellow prisoner induces his cellmate to confess when adversary judicial proceedings have not yet been initiated against the individual, when he is not yet represented by counsel, and when he has not even asserted his *Miranda* rights. Except for the California cases,[(327)] I have found

---

66. *See* notes 371-74, 415-16, 443-45 and footnotes 82-86, 89-91, 94-97 *infra* and accompanying text.

67. *See* text at footnotes 82-86 *infra;* footnote 86 *infra.*

68. United States v. Beckwith, 510 F.2d 741, 742 (D.C. Cir. 1975), *aff'd*, 425 U.S. 341 (1976).

69. Beckwith v. United States, 425 U.S. 341, 347 (1976) (Burger, C.J.).

no case excluding statements obtained from a prisoner by a "jail plant" that did not include one or more of the above factors.[328] These factors aside, I submit that in the "jail plant" situation the government has not "create[d] the kind of atmosphere that . . . triggers *Miranda.* "[329]

To be sure, if the suspect had known his cellmate was a government agent, he would not have talked freely in his presence. But then neither would Hoffa, Osborn, or White, if they had realized they were dealing with undercover agents. *In this sense,* the government can do "indirectly" what it would be unable to do "directly" (as a practical matter, not as a matter of law). Put another way, by concealing its agents' true identities the government can gather evidence that it would not be able to acquire if these agents had to go unmasked. But this will necessarily be the case as long as "[a] law enforcement officer performing his official duties cannot be required always to be in uniform or to wear his badge of authority on the lapel of his civilian clothing" or "to proclaim himself an arm of the law."[70]

Some Final Thoughts

Inspector Gregory: Is there any other point to which you wish to draw my attention?
Sherlock Holmes: To the curious incident of the dog in the night-time.
The Inspector: The dog did nothing in the night-time.
Holmes: That was the curious incident. . . .

—Arthur Conan Doyle, *Silver Blaze*

The curious thing about the treatment of *Miranda* in *Brewer v. Williams* is that neither Justice Stewart, who wrote the majority opinion, nor Justices Marshall, Powell, and Stevens, who filed concurring opinions, made any use of it. Unlike most *Miranda* cases, the issue in *Williams* was neither the adequacy of the warnings nor the effectiveness of the suspect's alleged waiver in immediate response to the warnings. Rather, *Williams* involved "second level" *Miranda* safeguards, those "procedures [*Miranda*] had indicated should be followed when a defendant asserts his rights."[71] It is because these "second level" rights seem to have been so utterly disregarded in *Williams*—especially if the Christian burial speech is viewed as "interrogation"—that the

---

70. Hoffa v. United States, 385 U.S. 293, 315 (1966) (Warren, C.J., dissenting). "It blinks the realities of sophisticated, modern-day criminal activity and legitimate law enforcement practices," added Warren, "to argue the contrary." *Id. See also* Lewis v. United States, 385 U.S. 206, 209 (1966) (Warren, C.J.) (companion case to *Hoffa*).

71. People v. Grant, 45 N.Y.2d 366, 371-72, 380 N.E.2d 257, 260, 408 N.Y.S.2d 429, 432 (1978) (Wachtler, J.).

Court's avoidance of *Miranda* is at least puzzling and at worst (for supporters of *Miranda,* at any rate) downright ominous.

If the issue in *Williams* had been simply whether, after being advised of his *Miranda* rights, the defendant had effectively waived them before or at the time he revealed the whereabouts of the body, the considerable pains the Court took to treat *Williams* as a *Massiah,* and not as a *Miranda,* case[330] would have been more understandable. In that event, the *Williams* case could be viewed as one in which the Court chose the *Massiah,* rather than a *Miranda,* route because (as Professor Jerold Israel has suggested) it was ready and willing to "[adopt] a rather rigorous view of waiver as applied to a defendant's sixth amendment right to counsel," but inclined to "grant the prosecution more leeway in establishing waiver of the privilege against self-incrimination."[331]

The trouble with this explanation is that when Williams's alleged waiver occurred he had already asserted his *right to counsel* numerous times.[332] It may be my shortcoming, but I fail to see why an alleged waiver of a specifically and repeatedly asserted "*Miranda* right to counsel" should not be judged by the same strict *Johnson v. Zerbst* standards applicable to a "*Massiah* right to counsel." Indeed, if one must choose, a right to counsel designed to meet a specific need—"dispel[ling] the compelling atmosphere of the interrogation"[72]—would seem more deserving of protection than the more abstract *Massiah* right, which applies whether or not "the privilege against [compelled] self-incrimination is jeopardized."[73]

If, as the *Williams* Court apparently recognized[333]—and considered the

---

72. At one point in its opinion, the *Miranda* Court commented:

> [In *Escobedo*], as in the cases today, we sought a protective device to dispel the compelling atmosphere of the interrogation. . . . The presence of counsel, in all the cases before us today, would be the adequate protective device necessary to make the process of police interrogation conform to the dictates of the privilege.

384 U.S. at 465–66. The Court later added:

> Even preliminary advice given to the accused by his own attorney can be swiftly overcome by the secret interrogation process. . . . Thus, the need for counsel to protect the Fifth Amendment privilege comprehends not merely a right to consult with counsel prior to any questioning, but also to have counsel present during any questioning if the defendant so desires.

Id. at 470.

73. *Miranda,* 384 U.S. at 478 ("when an individual is taken into custody or otherwise deprived of his freedom by the authorities and is subjected to questioning, the privilege against self-incrimination is jeopardized").

Massiah applies whether or not an individual is deprived of his freedom and whether or not he is subjected to the inherently coercive police questioning that must be preceded by *Miranda* warnings. Moreover, although the "*Miranda* right to counsel" was specifically invoked in *Williams,* the "*Massiah* right" need not be. *See* McLeod v.Ohio, 1 Ohio St.2d 60, 62, 203 N.E.2d 349, 351 (1964), *rev'd per curiam,* 381 U.S. 356 (1965); notes 227–32 and footnote 37 *supra* and accompanying text.

State of Iowa to have in effect conceded[334]—Captain Leaming's speech constituted, or was tantamount to, *Miranda* "interrogation," then *Williams* emerges as a relatively easy *Miranda* case. This, I think, may be seen by contrasting the *Williams* facts with those in *Michigan v. Mosley* (1975).[335]

Although language in *Miranda*—that once an in-custody suspect "indicates in any manner, at any time prior to or during questioning, that he wishes to remain silent, the interrogation must cease"[336]—could be read as creating a per se rule against any further questioning of one who has invoked his "right to silence,"[337] *Mosley* held that interrogation may be resumed at least in the following circumstances: (i) the original interrogation is promptly terminated;[338] (ii) the questioning is resumed only "after the passage of a significant period of time";[339] (iii) the suspect is given "full and complete *Miranda* warnings at the outset of the second interrogation";[340] (iv) a different officer resumes the questioning;[341] and (v) the second interrogation is "restricted ... to a crime that had not been the subject of the earlier interrogation."[342]

The *Mosley* Court seems to have assigned considerable weight to the fact that the second interrogation was restricted to a separate and "unrelated" crime, one "different in nature and in time and place of occurrence from the robberies for which Mosley had been ... [earlier] interrogated."[343] Indeed, Professor Geoffrey Stone has forcefully argued that "this fact seems critical, for in its absence one is left only with a renewed effort to question by a different member of the same police force, in a different room in the same building, only two hours after Mosley's assertion of his right not to be questioned."[344] Of course, this fact, significant if not critical in *Mosley*, is missing in *Williams*.

Doubts have been raised whether, once a suspect has asserted his *Miranda* rights, "a fresh set of warnings" at the outset of the second session is "*sufficient* to dissipate the coercion inherent in the continuing custody and the renewed questioning."[345] But surely under such circumstances a fresh set of warnings is a *minimal requirement* for the resumption of questioning. Yet nothing resembling a fresh set of *Miranda* warnings was given between the time Williams last exercised his *Miranda* rights and the time Captain Leaming delivered his Christian burial speech. Upon arriving in Davenport to bring Williams back to Des Moines, Captain Leaming advised Williams of his rights—and Williams asserted them. He asked, and was allowed, to meet alone with his Davenport lawyer.[346] When Leaming was about to handcuff him and start the journey back, Williams again asserted his rights. Again he asked (this time on his own initiative), and was permitted, to confer alone with his lawyer.[347] Less than an hour later, apparently only a short time after they had left the Davenport area and entered the freeway,[348] Leaming launched into his now-famous speech. At no point between Williams's last meeting with his lawyer and the time he became the recipient of Leaming's remarks on Christian burials can it even be argued that Williams was "reminded again that he could remain silent and consult with a lawyer."[349]

Assuming arguendo that the Christian burial speech did not amount to "interrogation," *Miranda* would still seem to prohibit Leaming's tactics. For whether or not the captain engaged in "interrogation," he surely engaged in efforts "calculated 'to persuade [one who had earlier asserted his *Miranda* rights] to reconsider his position,'"[74] and such persuasion is seemingly forbidden by *Miranda* and *Mosley*.[75] Moreover, and more generally, even if the Christian burial speech did not amount to "interrogation" within the meaning of *Miranda,* how can it be said that a detective who "deliberately and designedly set[s] out to elicit information"[350] from one who has exercised his *Miranda* rights is "fully respect[ing]"[351] or "scrupulously honor[ing]"[76] those rights? And if the claim is made that, although Williams had earlier asserted his rights, he somehow waived them somewhere on the road to Des Moines, how can it be maintained that the Christian burial speech does not constitute "any evidence" that he was "tricked or cajoled into a waiver"?[352]

There remains, of course, one significant, or at least potentially significant, distinction between *Mosley* and *Williams:* Mosley only invoked his right to silence, but Williams repeatedly asserted his right to counsel as well. And, as both Justice Stewart, who wrote the majority opinion in *Mosley,*[77] and Justice

74. *See* People v. Grant, 45 N.Y.2d. 366, 373, 380 N.E.2d 257, 262, 408 N.Y.S.2d 429, 434 (1978) (quoting from *Mosley* passage set forth in note 349 *infra*); *cf.* People v. Jackson, 41 N.Y.2d 146, 152, 359 N.E.2d 677, 682, 391 N.Y.S.2d 82, 87 (1976) (once defendant has asserted rights, waiver obtained after continued and unbroken harrassment invalid).

75. Forbidden, that is, at least when, as in *Williams,* the persuasion is: (i) resorted to by the same officer before whom the suspect had earlier asserted his rights; (ii) neither accompanied nor preceded by a fresh set of warnings; and (iii) not restricted to a crime "different in nature" or "in time and place of occurrence" from the crime or crimes for which the suspect had been arrested or earlier interrogated. *See* Michigan v. Mosley, 423 U.S. 96, 105 (1975).

76. *Id.* at 103-04 ("A reasonable and faithful interpretation of the *Miranda* opinion must rest on the [*Miranda* Court's intention] to adopt 'fully effective means . . . to notify the person of his right of silence and to assure that the exercise of the right will be scrupulously honored . . . .' . . . [T]he admissibility of statements obtained after the person in custody has decided to remain silent depends under *Miranda* on whether his 'right to cut off questioning' was 'scrupulously honored.'") (quoting from Miranda v. Arizona, 384 U.S. at 479). *See also* 384 U.S. at 467 ("In order to combat [the inherently compelling pressures of in-custody interrogation] and to permit a full opportunity to exercise the privilege against self-incrimination, the accused must be adequately and effectively apprised of his rights and the exercise of those rights must be fully honored.").

77. Rejecting the dissenters' argument that *Miranda* established a requirement that once a suspect has asserted his right to remain silent, questioning may be resumed only when counsel is present, Justice Stewart observed:

But clearly the Court in *Miranda* imposed no such requirement, for it distinguished between the procedural safeguards triggered by a request to remain silent and a request for an attorney

White, who concurred in the result in that case,[78] recognized, by providing that "[i]f the individual states that he wants an attorney, the interrogation must cease until an attorney is present,"[353] *Miranda* may have created a per se rule against further "interrogation" after assertion of the right to counsel.

Justice White's observation in *Mosley* that "when [the *Miranda* Court] wanted to create a per se rule against further interrogation after assertion of a right, it knew how to do so"[354] (referring to the assertion of the right to counsel) came back to haunt him in *Williams*. He offered two reasons for the inapplicability of the "rigid prophylactic [*Miranda*] rule"[355] (with respect to the assertion of the right to counsel) to the *Williams* case. The first seems quite strained:

[A]t no time did *respondent* indicate a desire not to be asked questions outside the presence of his counsel—notwithstanding the fact that he was told that he and the

---

and directed that "the interrogation must cease until an attorney is present" only "[i]f the individual states that he wants an attorney."

Michigan v. Mosley, 423 U.S. 96, 104 n.10 (1975).

The lower courts are split over whether an in-custody suspect's request for counsel imposes a per se rule prohibiting the resumption of police questioning until an attorney is present. *See* People v. Grant, 45 N.Y.2d 366, 375 n.1, 380 N.E.2d 257, 262 n.1, 408 N.Y.S.2d 429, 434 n.1 (1978) (collecting cases).

78. Justice White agreed with the *Mosley* majority that "the statement in *Miranda*, 384 U.S., at 474, requiring interrogation to *cease* after an assertion of the 'right to silence' tells us nothing because it does not indicate how soon this interrogation may resume." Michigan v. Mosley, 423 U.S. 96, 109 (1975) (White, J., concurring). Justice White added:

The [*Miranda*] Court showed in the very next paragraph, moreover, that when it wanted to create a per se rule against further interrogation after assertion of a right, it knew how to do so. The court there said "[i]f the individual states that he wants an attorney, the interrogation must cease *until an attorney is present.*"

Id. at 109–10 (quoting from 384 U.S. at 474) (emphasis added by Justice White). Justice White then added in a footnote:

The question of the proper procedure following expression by an individual of his desire to consult counsel is not presented in this case. It is sufficient to note that the reasons to keep the lines of communication between the authorities and the accused open when the accused has chosen to make his own decisions are not present when he indicates instead that he wishes legal advice with respect thereto. The authorities may then communicate with him through an attorney. More to the point, the accused having expressed his own view that he is not competent to deal with the authorities without legal advice, a later decision at the authorities' insistence to make a statement without counsel's presence may properly be viewed with skepticism.

Id. at 110 n.2.

officers would be "visiting in the car." . . . [Williams] did [assert his right to counsel], but he never, himself, asserted a right not to be questioned in the absence of counsel. [79]

Although here, as elsewhere, the police testimony is not as clear as it ought to be,[356] the most plausible reading of the record is that shortly after Captain Leaming and his prisoner had begun the return trip to Des Moines—and shortly before the rendering of the Christian burial speech—Williams informed the captain that he would tell him "the whole story" after he got back to Des Moines and met with his lawyer.[80] This was a clear expression by Williams himself that he did not wish to be questioned outside the presence of his Des Moines lawyer, or at least not until he had conferred with him.[357] But this point is not crucial. Assuming arguendo that Williams made no

79. Justice White's reference to Captain Leaming's disclosure that he and Williams would be "visiting" on the return trip to Des Moines is baffling. There is no reason to think that Williams had any idea that "visiting" is a "term of art" for a low-keyed "interrogation." Presumably, he thought Leaming meant that they would engage in "small talk" unrelated to the case. If so, what would Justice White have had Williams do? Reject Leaming's invitation to visit, which he might well have interpreted as an invitation to be nice to him? Insist that they spend the four or five hours driving back in stony silence? Exact a promise from Leaming that while they were "visiting" he would not try to trick Williams into incriminating himself? Williams was in no mood to displease or irritate Leaming. The *first thing* he asked the captain on the drive back was whether Leaming "hated him" and "wished to kill him." Brief for Petitioner, Joint App. at 79, 94 (testimony of Captain Leaming). Earlier, when he had phoned his Des Moines lawyer from Davenport, Williams had expressed fear that somebody was "going to hit him in the head." *Id.* at 96.

80. Detective Nelson, who drove the car on the drive back to Des Moines, testified that the Christian burial speech was delivered only a short time after they left the Davenport area and entered the freeway. Brief for Petitioner, Joint App. at 104. At one point, Captain Leaming testified to the same effect. *Id.* at 63 (testimony of Captain Leaming). But at another point, when Leaming testified more extensively on this subject, he stated that "eventually"—after considerable talk on various topics, such as religion, organizing youth groups, playing an organ, intelligence of other people, police procedures—"as we were travelling along there," he delivered the Christian burial speech. *Id.* at 80–81. The first time Williams told Leaming he would reveal "the whole story" *after* he conferred with his Des Moines lawyer was "not too long after we got on the freeway, after we had gassed up and started—gotten on the freeway and started toward Des Moines." *Id.* at 65–66.

Moreover, Leaming conceded at another point that even though Williams had stated that he would tell him "the whole story after I see [Des Moines lawyer] McKnight," he "kept getting" what he "could get" from Williams before they got back to Des Moines. *Id.* at 60–61. As Williams's able court-appointed counsel, Professor Robert D. Bartels of the University of Iowa College of Law, put it, either this effort by Leaming

to get as much information as he could before they reached Des Moines . . . included the "Christian burial" speech, or Detective Leaming engaged in further efforts to acquire information that he did not divulge in detail during his testimony. Although the former alternative is the more likely one, for purposes of this case it does not matter which is true.

Brief for Respondent at 17 n.9.
The federal district court did not specifically find that Leaming delivered the speech before the

statement immediately prior to the Christian burial speech, the record is clear that after Leaming announced that they would be "visiting" during the ride back to Des Moines, Williams requested, and was permitted, to confer with his Davenport lawyer *two more times*. [358] And the Davenport lawyer, presumably with the concurrence, if not at the urging, of his client, (i) advised Leaming that "it was his understanding that [Williams] was not to be questioned until he got to Des Moines," [359] and (upon Leaming's expression of some reservations) "stated that that understanding should be carried out"; [360] and (ii) requested, but was refused permission, to ride along with his client on the trip back to Des Moines. [361] Presumably the Davenport lawyer made the request to accompany his client on the return trip in Williams's presence. In any event, Williams soon knew that his lawyer's request had been denied.

It is true that Williams *himself* did not—in so many words—assert "a right not to be questioned in the absence of counsel." [362] What of it? Earlier in the same *Miranda* passage that arguably creates a per se rule against further "interrogation" after assertion of the right to counsel, the *Miranda* Court observed: "If the individual *indicates in any manner* . . . that he wishes to remain silent, the interrogation must cease." [363] It is hard to believe that *Miranda* requires that the right to counsel be asserted with a greater degree of clarity than the right to silence, especially when *Miranda* elsewhere states that if an individual "indicates *in any manner* and at any stage of the process that he wishes to consult with an attorney before speaking there can be no questioning." [364] As the Supreme Court of California has observed:

To strictly limit the manner in which a suspect may assert [his *Miranda* rights], or to demand that it be invoked with unmistakable clarity (resolving any ambiguity against the defendant) would subvert *Miranda's* prophylactic intent. Moreover, it would benefit, if anyone, only the experienced criminal who, while most adept at learning effective methods of coping with the police, is least likely to find incarceration and police interrogation unnerving. [81]

Moreover, why does it matter, as Justice White evidently thinks it does, that Williams himself, as opposed to his lawyers, did not specifically assert a

---

first time Williams told Leaming that he would talk to the captain *after* he consulted with his Des Moines lawyer. The court, however, did find:

Petitioner indicated that he did not wish to talk on the trip by stating that he would talk *after* he got back to Des Moines and spoke with Mr. McKnight. . . . Detective Leaming carried on a conversation with Petitioner during the trip concerning religion . . . and various other topics, including . . . the intelligence of other people, police procedures, organizing youth groups. . . .

See Williams v. Brewer, 375 F. Supp. 170, 174 (S.D. Iowa 1974) (finding of fact number 14). As I have discussed, according to Leaming the discussion of these topics *preceded* the Christian burial speech.

81. People v. Randall, 1 Cal. 3d 948, 955, 464 P.2d 114, 118, 83 Cal. Rptr. 658, 662 (1970) (in absence of compelling evidence to contrary, suspect's phone call to his attorney during

right not to be questioned in the absence of counsel?[365] "Williams had effectively asserted his right to counsel by having secured attorneys at both ends of the automobile trip, both of whom, acting as his agents, had made clear to the police that no interrogation was to occur during the journey."[366] Isn't that enough? Why, after retaining two lawyers, and while isolated from them, should an obviously frightened murder suspect—Williams expressed fear on the return trip that the police might kill him[367]—be required to assert his rights himself, and in a particular manner to boot? Wasn't Williams entitled to assume that his lawyers were more adept at asserting legal rights and dealing with the police than he was? Wasn't that why he hired them?

The second reason Justice White gave for not applying the "rigid prophylactic [*Miranda*] rule" concerning assertion of the right to counsel was that Williams had not been "questioned."[368] I have maintained at considerable length that the Christian burial speech should be viewed as "interrogation" within the meaning of *Miranda*,[369] and have pointed out that the *Williams* majority apparently so regarded it.[370] Nevertheless, Williams need not have prevailed on this issue to have had his incriminating disclosures excluded on *Miranda* grounds. Once the suspect has exercised his right to counsel, and thus brought the "second level" *Miranda* safeguards into play,[371] the issue is no longer simply whether "interrogation" then occurred, but whether "the exercise of the right" was "scrupulously honored."[82] When Leaming delivered the Christian burial speech he was admittedly "playing upon Williams' religious conscience."[372] More generally, he was disregarding Williams's

---

"booking process" tantamount to assertion of *Miranda* rights); *see* People v. Buxton, 44 N.Y.2d 33, 37, 374 N.E.2d 384, 386, 403 N.Y.S.2d 487, 489 (1978) (it would be "an absurd formality" to hold that defendant's request, in presence of police, that his employer call his lawyer did not sufficiently indicate to police his desire for counsel).

82. *See* Miranda v. Arizona, 384 U.S. at 479. That Leaming "honored" Williams's exercise of his right earlier, by permitting him to confer with his Davenport lawyer, is insufficient. In *Miranda* the Court observed:

Even preliminary advice given to the accused by his own attorney can be swiftly overcome by the secret interrogation process. . . . Thus, the need for counsel to protect the Fifth Amendment privilege comprehends not merely a right to consult with counsel prior to questioning, but also to have counsel present during any questioning if the defendant so desires.

Id. at 470.

Assuming arguendo that Williams did not reiterate, *just before* the Christian burial speech, that he would tell the police "the whole story" after he met with his Des Moines lawyer, "[a]t no time during the trip"—certainly at no time prior to the delivery of the speech—"did Williams express a willingness to be interrogated in the absence of an attorney." 430 U.S. at 392. *But see* footnote 80 *supra* and accompanying text (most plausible reading of record indicates that Williams reiterated his intent to tell police everything after meeting with his lawyer). Moreover, after "Williams had effectively asserted his right to counsel by having secured attorneys at both ends of the automobile trip," Leaming "made no effort at all to ascertain whether Williams wished to relinquish that right." *Id*. at 405. Finally, although he need not have done so to preserve this right, Williams specifically asserted his right to have counsel present during the return trip; his

decision to remain silent[373] and trying to "con"[83] or "sweet talk"[84] him into changing his position. Whether or not Leaming's efforts to get as much information as he could from his prisoner before they reached Des Moines[374] amounted to "interrogation," such tactics surely "did not honor, scrupulously or otherwise,"[85] Williams's exercise of his right to counsel and his right to cut off questioning.[86]

Davenport attorney, acting as his agent, sought but was denied permission to accompany him on the return trip. *See* Williams v. Brewer, 375 F. Supp. 170, 173 (S.D. Iowa 1974); *id.* at 176; text accompanying note 361 *supra*.

83. *See* Bator & Vorenberg, *Arrest, Detention, Interrogation, and the Right to Counsel*, 66 COLUM. L. REV. 62, 73 (1966) ("Deception in police interrogation... may consist of 'conning'—seeking to offset the suspect's reluctance to incriminate himself by displays of apparent sympathy, friendship, or moral indignation."). Leaming admittedly addressed Williams as "Reverend" "to win his friendship and confidence." Brief for Petitioner at 13. Leaming also led Williams to believe that he was Williams's protector and sympathizer, indicated that he (Leaming) was a sensitive, religious person, and suggested (not very subtly) to Williams that the only decent and honorable thing for him to do was to reveal the whereabouts of the body on the way back to Des Moines. *See* Kamisar, *supra* footnote 2, at 218-19, 228 (discussion of *Williams* record).

84. *See* text at footnote 1 *supra*.

85. Brief for Respondent at 39.

86. A forceful argument can be made that once a suspect has specifically asserted his "*Miranda* right to counsel" he is essentially in the same position as one whose "*Massiah* right to counsel" has attached. For even though attempts to "induce" a suspect to talk or to "elicit" statements from him may not amount to "interrogation" within the meaning of *Miranda*, they may nevertheless constitute a failure to "respect" or "honor" the exercise of *Miranda* rights—or amount to "trick[ing]" or "cajol[ing]" one who has asserted his rights into waiving them. *See* Miranda v. Arizona, 384 U.S. at 476. Thus, the argument would run, once a suspect has asserted his right to counsel, the "second level" *Miranda* safeguards shield him from "secret agent" activity designed to obtain incriminating statements from him, such as the "jail plant," "Mother Powers," and "waitress" ploys, just as much as the *Massiah* doctrine does once adversary judicial proceedings have commenced against a suspect. *See* United States v. Brown, 466 F.2d 493 (10th Cir. 1972) (discussed in footnote 63 *supra*); State v. Travis, 116 R.I. 678, 360 A.2d 548 (1976) (same).

Whether this is so is a nice question, but the Court need not have reached it to have held Williams's incriminating disclosures inadmissible on *Miranda* grounds. Even if we assume arguendo that some compulsion, subtle or otherwise, must be exerted on a suspect before it may be said that the exercise of his rights was not honored or respected, and that such compulsion is lacking when a suspect is *unaware* that he is dealing with a government agent, these were not the factual circumstances in *Williams*. For Williams knew full well that Leaming was a police captain, and Leaming did exert pressure. As previously mentioned, there is ample reason to believe Williams feared that physical harm might come to him before he ever got back to Des Moines. *See* footnote 79 *supra*. Furthermore, Leaming led his prisoner to believe that he was Williams's protector and sympathizer. *See* footnote 83 *supra*. Under the circumstances, Williams would not take lightly the captain's desires and preferences, which the captain expressed quite emphatically: "*I feel that you yourself* are the only person that knows where this little girl's body is. ... I feel ... that the parents of this little girl *should be entitled* to a Christian burial for the little girl who was snatched away from them on Christmas [E]ve. ... *I feel we should stop and locate it on the way*. ..." 430 U.S. at 392-93 (emphasis added).

If the *Williams* Court did not bury *Miranda,* as some had feared and others had hoped, it surely did not honor it either. Indeed, by "studiously avoiding reliance on *Miranda*"[375] in *Williams,* the Court (as Professor Stone has recently pointed out) maintained its record of not holding "a single item of evidence inadmissible on the authority of *Miranda*" since the present Chief Justice assumed his post in June of 1969.[376] But the Court did reaffirm and revivify *Massiah,* which has now emerged as the other major decision by the Warren Court in the area.[377] Should the defendant-minded, disappointed and troubled by the diminution of *Miranda's* vigor and significance,[378] take comfort from the fact that *Massiah* "is 'alive and well' "?[379]

Today, no doubt, the defendant-minded are a good deal more tolerant of—one might even say, grateful for—the *Massiah* doctrine than they used to be. It was easy in the mid-1960s for the defendant-minded to criticize the *Massiah* doctrine as too "formalistic" or "formulistic."[380] Then the momentum was on their side; then "the doctrines converging upon the institution of police interrogation [were] threatening to push on to their logical conclusion—to the point where no questioning of suspects will be permitted."[87] Although it was unclear just how far the Court's momentum would carry, most commentators recognized the *Massiah* and *Escobedo* were only steps along the way to the final destination.[381] But the winds of change have shifted sharply.[382] "*Miranda* has fallen into disfavor with the present majority of the Court"[383] and is in danger of being "dismantle[d] . . . piecemeal"[384]—or worse.[385] Under these circumstances, the defendant-minded are understandably reluctant to find fault with *Massiah,* as resurrected and expanded by *Williams.* For an invigorated *Massiah* doctrine could become the major doctrine—even the only one—standing in the way of a return to the loosely defined and largely illusory "voluntariness"-"totality of the circumstances" test.[386]

---

87. W. SCHAEFER, *supra* footnote 26 (lecture delivered 10 weeks before *Miranda*); *see* Massiah v. United States, 377 U.S. 201, 208 (1964) (White, J., with Clark & Harlan, JJ., dissenting) ("today's rule promises to have wide application well beyond the facts of this case"); Escobedo v. Illinois, 378 U.S. 478, 495 (1964) (White, J., with Clark & Stewart, JJ., dissenting) (today's decision is "another major step in the direction of the goal which the Court has in mind—to bar from evidence all admissions obtained from an individual suspected of crime, whether involuntarily made or not"); Enker & Elsen, *supra* footnote 25, at 60-61, 69, 83 (1964) (Court may be shaping "a novel right not to confess except knowingly and with the tactical assistance of counsel"); Traynor, *supra* footnote 26, at 669 ("Court's reliance on the sixth amendment . . . apparently makes available to any suspect a full-blown right to counsel [assigned or retained] at the incipient accusatory stage when police interrogation shifts from general inquiry to a probe focusing upon him"); Vorenberg, *Police Detention and Interrogation of Uncounselled Suspects: The Supreme Court and the States,* 44 B.U. L. REV. 423, 433-34 (1964) (author would "not be surprised if the Supreme Court should lay down a flat rule barring confessions obtained from suspects—indigent or not—who have not been furnished with an opportunity to talk to a lawyer"; Court may hold that "even a warning is not enough").

Nevertheless, the shortcomings of *Massiah* have not disappeared with the passage of time. If, as Justice Stewart pointed out in *Massiah,* the failure to vouchsafe the aid of counsel to "an indicted defendant under interrogation by the police in a completely extrajudicial proceeding . . . might deny [him] 'effective representation by counsel at the only stage when legal aid and advice would help him,' "[387] how or why is this less true of the unindicted prisoner? Or one against whom judicial proceedings have not yet been initiated? Under our system of justice, an arrest—no less than an indictment or a first appearance before a magistrate—is supposed to be "followed by a trial, 'in an orderly courtroom, presided over by a judge, open to the public . . . ,' "[388] and not by a secret extrajudicial proceeding, presided over by the police. Why is a "kangaroo court procedure whereby the police produce the vital evidence in the form of a confession which is useful or necessary to obtain a conviction [and thus] in effect deny [an individual] effective representation by counsel"[389] any less a "kangaroo court procedure" because the judicial proceedings have not yet commenced against the individual?

The right to counsel should not "turn on a moment arbitrarily fixed as the beginning of judicial proceedings,"[390] a point that can often be manipulated by law enforcement authorities. Rather, it should accommodate both the government's need for evidence[391] and a suspect's need for "a lawyer's help,"[392] which may be as great, or greater, before the commencement of judicial proceedings as afterwards. It should concern itself with the "overall fairness" of the "interrogation"[393] and the inherent coercion or potential for coercion in the situation. The *Massiah-Williams* doctrine is not substantially related to these needs and concerns; it provides only "an unduly tenuous 'fit.' "[394] As Justice Traynor said of the *Massiah* doctrine, even before it had acquired its name:[395]

It is a formalistic assumption that indictment is the point when a defendant particularly needs the advice and protection of counsel. Often a defendant is arrested under highly suspicious circumstances and from the time he is apprehended his guilt is a foregone conclusion in the minds of the police. . . .

In some cases the evidence against the accused may be stronger at the moment of arrest than it may be in other cases when the indictment is returned [or, to update this rule in light of *Brewer v. Williams,* judicial proceedings have commenced]. It is hardly realistic to assume that a defendant is less in need of counsel an hour before indictment [or the initiation of judicial proceedings] than he is an hour after. . . .

. . . .

It may be argued that if [the rule] is adopted, the police will still have time to interrogate and encourage confessions before an indictment is returned [or judicial proceedings have commenced]. In some cases, however, as in [*Spano* and *Di Biasi*], an indictment may be returned in advance of the defendant's apprehension. In such cases there could be no interrogation of the suspect at all, except in the presence of his attorney [or a waiver meeting the rigorous *Johnson v. Zerbst* standards]. Moreover, if the suspect is in custody before indictment [or the initiation of judicial proceedings], the police could easily frustrate the rule by delaying the indictment [or the commencement of judicial proceedings]. Thus, the rule would operate only occasionally and arbitrarily.[88]

The *Massiah* doctrine and its New York counterpart do reflect the view that "'[t]o maintain the integrity of the judicial process in its use of evidence of criminal guilt'... 'congruence' must be maintained throughout the course of a formally instituted criminal action...."[396] But why not maintain "congruence" "between the judicial and the non-judicial, pre-trial processes"?[397] It is difficult to avoid the conclusion that those judges unmoved by "kangaroo court" proceedings in the nonjudicial, pretrial stages, but stirred to action when these same proceedings are held after the formal institution of a criminal action, are responding chiefly to a violation of the symbol of a fair trial[398] and conveying "symbolic reassurance."[399] When the issue is forced into the open, it seems that the rule of law prevails. Then the "psychological need for the appearance of justice" is satisfied[400] and the importance of the right to counsel is dramatized.[401] This is all to the good as far as it goes, but it does not go nearly far enough.

More than a decade ago, Justice Traynor saw "[t]he logical corollary [to the *Massiah* doctrine], to forestall evasion of the rule,... just around the corner. The right to counsel should now logically materialize whenever the accused was not, but should have been, brought before a judicial officer."[402] However logical this development may seem to some, and it does to me, it is not likely to occur. The Court has extended the sixth amendment right to counsel, as opposed to the *Miranda* right, backwards from the trial through the indictment to the initiation of judicial proceedings, presumably the first appearance before a judicial officer. But, as Justice Stewart's fierce resistance to the application of *Massiah* to the *Escobedo* facts demonstrates,[403] the Court is unlikely to extend the right any further.

Moreover, Justice Traynor's "logical corollary" smacks too much of the *McNabb-Mallory* rule[404] to have much prospect. That rule, fashioned "[q]uite apart from the Constitution"[405] and in the exercise of the Court's "supervisory authority over the administration of [federal] criminal justice,"[406] operated to exclude from federal prosecutions all incriminating statements obtained during prolonged, and hence illegal, prearraignment detention. Even before congressional dissatisfaction with the rule culminated in legislation that badly crippled it,[407] the rule met a hostile reception in the lower federal courts.[408] Nor was it warmly received by the states. Although "the need for something like a *McNabb-Mallory* rule to govern state [confession] cases was apparent"[409]—bypassing conflicts over the nature of the

88. People v. Garner, 57 Cal. 2d 135, 160, 164, 367 P.2d 680, 695, 697-98, 18 Cal. Rptr. 40, 55, 57-58 (1961) (Traynor, J., concurring), *cert. denied*, 310 U.S. 929 (1962).

secret interrogation and minimizing both the "temptation" and the "opportunity" to obtain confessions by impermissible means[410]—the Court never imposed such a rule on the states[411] and only a handful of states adopted it or its equivalent on their own initiative.[412] The chance, in the foreseeable future, of the Court traveling down this road again—by finding something akin to this much-criticized and much-resisted rule of procedure for federal courts mandated by the "minimal historical safeguards . . . summarized as 'due process of law'"[413]—appears to be quite small.[414]

The odds are better, if the Supreme Court is inclined to supplement or to complement the *Massiah* doctrine, that it will be attracted to a rule related to but distinct from *Massiah*—New York's *Donovan-Arthur-Hobson* rule,[89] which, regardless of whether judicial proceedings have yet commenced, bars virtually all police interrogation once a defense attorney enters the picture. Judge Scileppi, writing for the New York Court of Appeals in *Arthur* (1968), explained the protection this rule affords the attorney-client relationship:

[I]n [*Donovan* (1963)] . . . Judge Fuld, speaking for the court, stated [that] " . . . quite apart from [the federal Constitution], this State's constitutional and statutory provisions pertaining to the privilege against self-incrimination and the right to counsel . . . , not to mention our own guarantee of due process . . . , require the exclusion of a confession taken from a defendant, during a period of detention, after his attorney had requested and been denied access to him."[415]

. . . [I]n [*Gunner*] . . . it was argued that *Donovan* . . . [was] not applicable because Gunner's attorney had not physically appeared at the police station and asked to see his client as had Donovan's [but had simply phoned the police chief to advise him that he had been retained by defendant's parents to represent him and "didn't want any statements taken from [him]"].[90] The court rejected this contention holding . . . that a defendant's right to counsel is not dependent upon "mechanical" and "arbitrary"

89. People v. Hobson, 39 N.Y.2d 479, 348 N.E.2d 894, 384 N.Y.S.2d 419 (1976); People v. Arthur, 22 N.Y.2d 325, 239 N.E.2d 537, 292 N.Y.S.2d 663 (1968); People v. Donovan, 13 N.Y.2d 148, 193 N.E.2d 628, 243 N.Y.S.2d 841 (1963); *see* People v. Pinzon, 44 N.Y.2d 458, 377 N.E.2d 721, 406 N.Y.S.2d 268 (1978). *See generally* W. RICHARDSON, EVIDENCE §§ 545, 546 (J. Prince 10th ed. 1973); Lewin, Criminal Procedure, 22 SYRACUSE L. REV. 381, 396–400 (1971); Paulsen, *The Winds of Change: Criminal Procedure in New York 1941–1965*, 15 BUF-FALO L. REV. 297, 304–05 (1966); Uviller, *The Judge at the Cop's Elbow*, 71 COLUM. L. REV. 707, 715–18 (1971); 30 BROOKLYN L. REV. 366 (1964); 51 CORNELL L.Q. 356 (1966); 5 FORDHAM URB. L.J. 401 (1977). As a general matter, New York's *Donovan* rule has not received a warm reception elsewhere. *See* State v. Smith, 294 N.C. 365, 376, 241 S.E.2d 674, 680–81 (1978) (collecting cases). Nevertheless, a model code for pre-arraignment procedure has adopted the New York rule, both as matter of policy and because the rule was deemed required by *Escobedo* and *Miranda*. MODEL CODE, *supra* footnote 20, § 140.7(1); *see id.* at 363–66 & n.3 (commentary to § 140.7). *But see* footnote 94 *infra*.

90. People v. Gunner, 15 N.Y.2d 226, 205 N.E.2d 852, 257 N.Y.S.2d 924 (1965). The defense lawyer phoned the Nassau County Chief of Police. There was no point in his physically appearing at the Nassau County police station for at the time his client was in custody thousands of miles away in Los Angeles. The court barred all statements made by the defendant after his

requirements.[91] Thus, the principle which may be derived from [the New York] cases is that, once the police know or have been apprised of the fact that the defendant is represented by counsel or that an attorney has communicated with the police for the purpose of representing the defendant, the accused's right to counsel attaches; and this right is not dependent upon the existence of a formal retainer.

Nor is it significant that [the defense attorney] did not, immediately upon his arrival at Police Headquarters, instruct the police not to take any statements from the defendant.... Once an attorney enters the proceeding, the police may not question the defendant in the absence of counsel unless there is an affirmative waiver, in the presence of the attorney, of the defendant's right to counsel.... There is no requirement that the attorney or the defendant request the police to respect this right of the defendant.[416]

Unlike the New York courts, which have developed two discrete extra-*Miranda* rules—(i) the "postarraignment, postindictment" rule which presaged the *Massiah* doctrine, and (ii) the *Donovan-Arthur-Hobson* rule, which "prohibit[s] the State from interfering with the attorney-client relationship" by questioning the client in the absence of counsel "with respect to matters encompassed by the representation"[417]—the Supreme Court has not isolated the "initiation of judicial proceedings" and "attorney-client relationship" components and dwelt on their independent significance. In *Spano,* which evoked the influential concurring opinions that ultimately prevailed, as well as in *Massiah* and *Williams,* at the time the challenged statements were obtained the defendant had already retained counsel and judicial proceedings had already been initiated against him.[418]

There is ample cause to believe, however, that the commencement of adversary judicial proceedings *without more* is decisive and that what counts is not whether the confession was elicited at a time when the suspect was already represented by counsel, but whether the confession was obtained "at a time when he was *clearly entitled to* a lawyer's help."[419] Noting that "[e]ver since this Court's decision in the *Spano* case, the New York courts have unequivocally followed [the] constitutional rule" advocated by the concurring Justices in *Spano,*[420] the *Massiah* Court then quoted with approval from *People v. Waterman,*[421] an early post-*Spano* New York case: "Any secret interrogation of the defendant, from and after the finding of the indictment,

---

lawyer's phone call to the Nassau County police, including two he made during the plane flight back to New York. *Id.* at 230-31, 205 N.E.2d at 853-54, 257 N.Y.S.2d at 926-27.

91. More recently, a lawyer's phoning the police department central switchboard and informing the civilian operators that he wished to speak to his client and did not want him questioned has been held sufficient to invoke the *Donovan* rule. People v. Pinzon, 44 N.Y.2d 458, 464, 377 N.E.2d 721, 725, 406 N.Y.S.2d 268, 271 (1978). In *Pinzon* the defense attorney was misinformed (but apparently unintentionally) that the police department did not "have" his client, and none of his calls were put through to the police. *Id.* at 460, 462, 377 N.E.2d at 722, 723, 406 N.Y.S.2d at 268, 269.

without the protection afforded by the presence of counsel, contravenes the basic dictates of fairness in the conduct of criminal causes and the fundamental rights of persons charged with crime."[422] First, this statement of the rule tends to support the view that it is *the right* to counsel, not *actual representation by* counsel, that is decisive. Second, and even more important, Waterman had not yet retained or been appointed counsel when the challenged statements were obtained from him,[423] and the New York court had held that this did not matter: the right to counsel is actuated by "the formal commencement of the criminal action"; it is not "limited . . . to the situation where the defendant already has an attorney."[424] Third, the *Massiah* Court also cited with approval another New York case, *People v. Meyer,*[425] in which the suspect neither had nor, when informed of his rights, had he requested any counsel.[426] This, the New York court held, did not matter either: "While an accused may waive a fundamental right, he did not do so here, nor is he estopped because he had made no request when informed of his rights. . . . [A]ny statement made by an accused after arraignment not in the presence of counsel as in *Spano* . . . and *Waterman* is inadmissible."[427]

The *Massiah* Court then stated that the view expressed in *People v. Waterman* "no more than reflects a constitutional principle established as long ago as *Powell v. Alabama,* . . . where the Court noted that ' . . . from the time of their arraignment until the beginning of their trial, . . . the defendants . . . [were] as much *entitled to* such aid [of counsel] during that period as at the trial itself.'"[428] Since *Spano,* added the Court, "the same basic constitutional principle has been broadly reaffirmed . . . [in] *Hamilton v. Alabama* [and] *White v. Maryland.*"[429] But in *Powell,* "from the time of their arraignment until the beginning of their trial, . . . the defendants *did not have* the aid of counsel in any real sense."[430] Nor, of course, did the petitioners in *Hamilton* and *White* have counsel (in any sense at all) at arraignment or the preliminary hearing.[431] Evidentiary use at trial of the guilty plea White entered at the preliminary hearing but subsequently changed—"a problem not greatly different from the use at trial of [a] . . . confession given to the police rather than to a judge"[432]—was barred because he was entitled to, but had not yet procured or been appointed, counsel at the time of the preliminary hearing. If *Massiah* and *Williams* "no more than reflect a constitutional principle established . . . [in] *Powell*" and applied in *Hamilton* and *White,* if *Massiah* and *Williams* only move the time when the right to counsel accrues back from arraignment or preliminary hearing to the initiation of judicial proceedings, then the establishment of (and interference with) an attorney-client relationship would seem to be constitutionally irrelevant.

We need not limit ourselves, however, to close analyses of *Massiah* and earlier Supreme Court precedents. We can do better than speculate about whether *Massiah* and *Williams* would have been decided the same way if the defendants had not been represented by counsel, or whether *Gideon*[433] and the *Griffin-Douglas* "equality" principle[434] would have required the same result if they had not been. We can turn to *McLeod v. Ohio*.[92]

At the time McLeod voluntarily confessed to law enforcement authorities riding with him in a police vehicle, he was under indictment for murder, but he was not represented by, nor had he even requested, counsel.[435] McLeod's confession was admitted into evidence, and he was convicted.[436] The state supreme court dismissed his appeal because it could find "no debatable constitutional question" presented.[437] But the United States Supreme Court, invoking the newly decided *Massiah* case for the first time, vacated the judgment and remanded the cause "for consideration in light of *Massiah*."[438]

On remand, the state supreme court did not take the hint, although two dissenting judges urged it to do so.[439] Instead, the court reaffirmed its judgment, distinguishing the facts in *McLeod* from those in *Massiah*. It pointed out, *inter alia*, that McLeod, unlike Massiah, had confessed before he had procured or been appointed or "even requested counsel."[440] This distinction failed to impress the two dissenting state judges. They recognized the "possibility" of a waiver of the *Massiah* right to counsel in some postindictment cases, but not in this one because McLeod had never been advised of his right to counsel.[441] In their view, the concurring justices in *Spano* would have reversed and *Massiah* required reversal

on the sole and specific ground that the confession had been deliberately elicited by the police *after the defendant had been indicted, and therefore at a time when he was clearly entitled to a lawyer's help.* True, in *Massiah* the defendant had counsel who was absent when defendant made statements against his interest. But if the use of such statements after indictment of an accused whose counsel is absent is, under the Constitution, prohibited, as *Massiah* holds, there can be no question that the plain import of the opinion is that the Constitution prohibits the use of statements against interest by a defendant who has not even been advised of his right to counsel.[442]

Evidently the Supreme Court of the United States agreed with the dissenting state judges. Certiorari was again granted, and this time the Supreme Court summarily reversed on the authority of *Massiah*.[93]

Although I deem it clear that the "beginning" of a "criminal prosecution" activates the right to counsel, regardless of whether the suspect is represented

92. 381 U.S. 356 (1965) (per curiam) (summary reversal of State v. McLeod, 1 Ohio St. 2d 60, 203 N.E.2d 349 (1964), on authority of *Massiah*); *see* text *supra* at notes 227–32 (discussion of other aspects of case).

93. *See* footnote 92 *supra*. *See also* Hancock v. White, 378 F.2d 479 (1st Cir. 1967) (holding, on the basis of *McLeod*, that *Massiah* doctrine required exclusion of statements taken from defendant during automobile trip with New Hampshire officers, which followed indictment and extradition proceedings in Vermont, even though defendant did not have, and had not requested, counsel in criminal proceeding pending against him in New Hampshire).

by counsel at the time, the converse—the legal effect of representation by counsel when the criminal prosecution has not yet begun—is much less clear.[94] But if I am correct in my belief that the *Massiah* doctrine is in no small part a "symbolic response" to the violation of the symbol of a fair trial, then the Court is likely to respond similarly to police interferences with the attorney-client relationship. I do not claim that the Court will adopt the *Dono-*

94. After recalling that by denying Escobedo's request for counsel "the police did not relieve [him] of the anxieties which they had created in the interrogation rooms," the *Miranda* Court dropped a footnote: "The police also prevented [Escobedo's] attorney from consulting with his client. Independent of any other constitutional proscription, this action constitutes a violation of the Sixth Amendment right to the assistance of counsel and excludes any statement obtained in its wake. *See* People v. Donovan...." 384 U.S. at 465, 465–66 n.35.

It has been forcefully argued that this footnote means literally what it says. *See* Breitel, *supra* footnote 27, at 13 & n.25; Rothblatt & Pitler, *supra* footnote 18, at 492–96. *See also* MODEL CODE, *supra* footnote 20, § 140.7(1); *id.* at 363–66, 365 n.3 (commentary to § 140.7). I cannot agree. It is hard to believe that in the course of writing a 60-page opinion *based on the premise* that police-issued warnings can adequately protect a suspect's rights the Court would say in the next breath that such warnings are insufficient when, but only when, a suspect's lawyer is not allowed to consult with him—that even though a suspect has been emphatically and unequivocally advised of his rights and insists on talking, what he says is inadmissible when, as in *Donovan* and several post-*Donovan* cases, a lawyer *whose services he has not requested* has, *unbeknown to him,* entered the picture. *See* notes 457–58 *infra* and accompanying text. Moreover, as the *Donovan* dissenters noted, the *Donovan* rule, which the *Miranda* Court is said to have adopted in footnote 35 of its opinion, "hold[s] that a defendant with a lawyer has greater rights than one not so favored," People v. Donovan, 13 N.Y.2d 148, 158, 193 N.E.2d 628, 633, 243 N.Y.S.2d 841, 849 (1963) (Burke, J., dissenting), and typically operates "only in the cases where the suspect, or his family, have means to employ counsel," *id.* at 162, 193 N.E.2d at 636, 243 N.Y.S.2d at 852 (Foster, J., dissenting). Such a rule seems hard to square with "the equal protection argument, a ground bass that resounds throughout the *Miranda* opinion." Friendly, *The Fifth Amendment Tomorrow: The Case for Constitutional Change,* 37 U. CIN. L. REV. 671, 711 (1968).

Although the police did not advise Escobedo of any of his rights, "he repeatedly asked to speak to his lawyer." Escobedo v. Illinois, 378 U.S. 478, 481 (1964). At one point the *Escobedo* opinion states that "when petitioner requested, and was denied an opportunity to consult with his lawyer, the investigation had ceased to be a general investigation of 'an unsolved crime' [and] [p]etitioner had become the accused." *Id.* at 485. Indeed, the opinion begins: "The critical question in this case is whether, under the circumstances, the refusal by the police to honor petitioner's request to consult with his lawyer during the course of an interrogation constitutes a denial of 'the Assistance of Counsel'...." *Id.* at 479. At another point the opinion suggests that the decisive factor may be simply whether the investigation has "focused" on the suspect or, put another way, whether he has "for all practical purposes" become the "accused" (although this test is anything but simple in application). *Id.* at 486. At still other points the opinion indicates that some combination of factors (such as police failure to advise the suspect of his right to remain silent, "a process of interrogation that lends itself to eliciting incriminating statements") may activate the right to counsel, but a lawyer's attempt, or police denial of that attempt, to confer with his client is not listed as one of these factors. *See id.* at 490–91, 492.

Thus, although the *Escobedo* opinion does quote from *Donovan* at one point, the refusal of the police to allow petitioner's lawyer to meet with him seems to have no bearing on *Escobedo's* rationale. If this factor has any relevance, it is only because Escobedo became *aware of the fact*

van rule "bag and baggage,"[(443)] but I do believe that it will adopt the basic concept of the rule. I think that it, too, will be struck by the "incongruity" of permitting the state's attorney or the state's "badged and uniformed representative[s]"[95] "to extract a confession from the accused while his own lawyer, seeking to speak with him, [is] kept from him by the police."[96]

The Court is even more likely to be offended when law enforcement officials treat the defense lawyer deceitfully or disdainfully, such as when they

---

that the police were preventing his lawyer from talking to him, and this realization may well have underscored the police dominance of the situation and the gravity of his plight. *See id.* at 480 & n.1, 481–82. Escobedo had unsuccessfully argued in the Illinois Supreme Court that his conviction should be reversed on the ground, *inter alia,* that the trial judge had improperly excluded evidence of the effect on him of seeing his lawyer turned away at the police station. *See* Note, *An Historical Argument for the Right to Counsel During Police Interrogation,* 73 YALE L.J. 1000, 1003 n.3 (1964).

I do not deny that at least some members of the *Escobedo* majority may have been greatly offended by the fact that for several hours, and at least on five separate occasions, various police officers denied Escobedo's lawyer permission to see his client. *See id.* at 480–81. Nor do I discount the possibility that even if Escobedo had not asked to see his lawyer, the persistent and systematic way in which the police rebuffed his lawyer may have led the Supreme Court to reverse for that reason alone. Indeed, one thrust of this part of the article is that the Court is likely to do just that if presented with such a question in the near future. I contend only that the issue cannot be regarded as settled either by *Escobedo,* especially when it seems to have been stripped of its sixth amendment dimension, see the extract from *Kirby* in note 403 *infra,* or by a brief footnote to a discussion of *Escobedo* in the *Miranda* opinion, especially when the footnote refers to a New York case that explicitly declined to rely on the federal Constitution, see the extract from *Donovan* in text at note 415 *supra.*

I must add, however, that in Mathies v. United States, 374 F.2d 312 (D.C. Cir. 1967), after expressing concern over police questioning of a suspect who was represented by counsel without notifying the lawyer, "not[ing] that in other cases the United States Attorney has stated a policy to have counsel for accused persons advised of all interrogation sessions," and "assum[ing] that the episode will not arise again in the future," Judge (now Chief Justice) Burger observed for a unanimous panel: "The prospective application of [*Miranda*] plainly will require that such interviews can be conducted only after counsel has been given an opportunity to be present." *Id.* at 316 & n.3 (Judge Burger referred to no page or footnote in *Miranda* opinion).

95. "Of course, it would not be rational, logical, moral or realistic to make any distinction between a lawyer acting for the State who [by seeking a waiver of the right to counsel from a suspect in the absence of, and without notification to, his lawyer] violates [the Code of Professional Responsibility] directly and one who indirectly uses the admissions improperly obtained by a police officer, who is the badged and uniformed representative of the State." People v. Hobson, 39 N.Y.2d 479, 485, 348 N.E.2d 894, 898, 384 N.Y.S.2d 419, 423 (1976) (Breitel, C.J.). *See also* United States v. Springer, 460 F.2d 1344, 1354–55 (7th Cir.) (Stevens, J., dissenting) (FBI agents referred to as "agents of prosecutor," and their attempts to obtain statements from one already represented by counsel without notifying counsel, "unethical and unfair" in civil context, violates due process in criminal context), *cert. denied,* 409 U.S. 873 (1972); People v. Patterson, 39 Mich. App. 467, 478, 198 N.W.2d 175, 181 (Levin, J., dissenting) (police practice of questioning suspect without obtaining consent of his lawyer "so notorious" that prosecutors must be aware of, and "deemed to have authorized," it), *appeal denied,* 387 Mich. 795 (1972). But in *Massiah,* dissenting Justice White stressed that aside from the fact that they "are not of constitutional dimensions," the canons of legal ethics deal with "the conduct of lawyers and not with the

send an undercover agent against the suspect after his lawyer has done his best to prevent him from talking;[444] mislead the defense lawyer as to where his client is being detained or about to be questioned;[445] or "assure" the lawyer, or "agree" with him, that his client will not be questioned, but then do so "under deceptive auspices."[97] Such police tactics are likely to rouse many members of the bench and bar who are normally complacent about

---

conduct of investigators." 377 U.S. at 210-11 (White, J., with Clark & Harlan, JJ., dissenting). *See generally* Note, *Interrogation and the Sixth Amendment: The Case for Restriction of Capacity to Waive the Right to Counsel,* 53 IND. L.J. 313, 320 n.42 (1978).

96. People v. Donovan, 13 N.Y.2d 148, 152, 193 N.E.2d 628, 629, 243 N.Y.S.2d 841, 843 (1963), *quoted in* Escobedo v. Illinois, 378 U.S. 478, 487 (1964).

Even those courts that have permitted it, finding no violation of the sixth amendment, "have denounced the 'practice of talking to a represented defendant behind his attorney's back' as 'suspect,' 'not commendable,' and a source of 'unease' that threatens 'erosion' of the 'relationship between lawyer and client.'" Note, *supra* footnote 95, at 313. *See also* Vorenberg, *supra* footnote 87, at 432-33. In the wake of *Escobedo,* Professor Vorenberg commented:

> I suggest that even the strongest critics of this decision must feel somewhat uneasy at the contrast between the protections with which we surround a defendant in court and the situation in which Danny Escobedo found himself when he made his statement.
>
> . . . .
>
> I think it is hard indeed to justify keeping a lawyer engaged from talking to his client, because we are afraid he will impress on him his right not to talk if that should be in his best interests.

Id.

97. *See* United States v. Wedra, 343 F. Supp. 1183, 1184, 1188 (S.D.N.Y. 1972) (Weinfeld, J.); *cf.* State v. Weedon, 342 So. 2d 642, 644 (La. 1977) (relying on assurance that client would not be questioned about crime during booking procedure, counsel instructed client that he could answer any questions); State v. Johns, 185 Neb. 590, 596, 177 N.W.2d 580, 584 (1970) (county attorney failed to convey promptly defense attorney's request that client not be questioned in his absence). "If it is offensive to permit police to defy attorney instructions, it is even more so to permit them to break an agreement not to question." Note, *supra* footnote 95, at 320 n.42.

Although the record in *Williams* is shaky on this point, the Iowa trial court found (and the other courts passing on the case assumed) that the Des Moines police and Williams's Des Moines attorney had "agreed" that Williams would not be questioned on the return trip. *See* 430 U.S. at 394; Kamisar, *supra* footnote 2, at 212 n.23. As the Supreme Court's opinion is written, there is no reason to think that *Williams* would have been decided differently (nor should it have been) if there had been no "broken agreement." Nevertheless this factor may have exerted a strong emotional or subliminal influence.

Dissenting from the Iowa Supreme Court decision upholding the admissibility of Williams's disclosures, Justice Stuart noted that he "personally would have no objection" to the "psychological campaign" waged by Captain Leaming on the return trip—"[i]f it were not for the agreement made with defendant's counsel." State v. Williams 182 N.W.2d 396, 408 (Iowa 1970) (Stuart, J., with Mason & Becker, JJ., dissenting). "The aspect of the case" that gave Justice Stuart "the most concern was the obvious effort of the police officers to evade the good faith attempt of defendant's counsel to cooperate with the police department." *Id.* Dissenting from the Eighth Circuit ruling that Williams was entitled to a new trial, Judge (now FBI Director) Webster commented: "I cannot but assume that the alleged 'broken promise' of Captain Leaming is at the root of the result reached in this case." Williams v. Brewer, 509 F.2d 227, 237 (8th Cir. 1974). In

stationhouse goings on—not unlike the way the destruction of the Redwoods and the Everglades would stir those with only a passing interest in protecting the environment.

Does the *Donovan-Arthur-Hobson* rule, or something like it, go to the heart of the "police interrogation"-"confession" problem? Or is it more appearance than substance? Are the lines it draws too fine, too mechanical? Does the rule have too much "the quality of a chess tournament"[446] to it?

The defendant-minded are, understandably, inclined to throw bouquets at the New York Court of Appeals. For even "in the best of times"[447] (for defense lawyers and many criminal law professors, at any rate)—at a time when the Warren Court strove "to alter significantly the nature of American criminal justice in the interest of a larger realization of the constitutional ideal of liberty under the law"[448]—the New York Court of Appeals "led the way" in protecting suspects' rights.[449] And after the "revolution" in criminal procedure had lost its impetus, the New York court (along with several other state courts on this and other fronts) demonstrated by its resurrection of the *Donovan* rule[450] "a determination to keep alive the Warren Court's philosophical commitment to protection of the criminal suspect."[451] Nevertheless, criticize the *Donovan* rule I must.

In the *Gunner* and *Arthur* cases, the New York Court of Appeals refused to confine *Donovan* to its facts and emphasized the "mechanical and arbitrary"[452] nature of a rule that would turn on "the existence of a formal retainer"[453] or on whether an attorney "presents himself at the place where the suspect is in physical custody and expressly requests the opportunity to consult with him."[454] Consequently, all an attorney need do to invoke *Donovan* is to apprise the police that he has "enter[ed] the proceeding."[455] I fail to see how this makes the *Donovan* rule in essence any less mechanical or less arbitrary than it was before *Gunner* and *Arthur* were handed down.

There is not even a weak congruence—indeed, there is no congruence at all—between a defense lawyer's entry into the proceeding and a suspect's need for "a lawyer's help" or the government's need for evidence. Whatever its symbolic value, a rule that turns on how soon a defense lawyer appears at the police station or how quickly he "spring[s] to the telephone"[456] hardly seems a rational way of reconciling the interests of the accused with those of society.

The *Donovan* rule might be more understandable, although still vulnerable to criticism,[98] if it turned on a suspect's request for counsel. But it does not.

---

the Supreme Court of the United States, Justice Stevens closed his concurring opinion by stressing that "[i]f in the long run, we are seriously concerned about the individual's effective representation by counsel, the State cannot be permitted to dishonor its promise to this lawyer." 420 U.S. at 415.

98. As pointed out several months before *Miranda*, one possible argument for limiting *Es-*

Even if a suspect asks, and is allowed to contact a lawyer, he may not be able to locate one quickly enough, or for one reason or another his lawyer may not win the race to the station or to the phone. On the other hand, a suspect's failure to ask for a lawyer need not prove fatal. A lawyer who previously represented the client may learn of his former client's plight and come to the rescue on his own initiative.[457] Or a suspect's family may retain a lawyer on his behalf, without his knowledge or even his request for a lawyer, and this lawyer may "enter the proceeding" in the nick of time.[458]

To the extent that this rule favors the suspects who, or whose families, have the money and the connections to bring a lawyer swiftly into the fray, it "runs counter to society's efforts to accord the indigent the same rights and privileges as the affluent."[459] At worst, such a rule would seem to favor the "professional criminal" most of all.[460] At best, it seems "a fortuitous standard upon which to build an exclusionary rule."[461]

Chief Judge Breitel has made a forceful defense of the rule, and in the process launched a strong attack on *Miranda* (or at least on *Miranda* as it has come to be applied):

> Notwithstanding that warnings alone might suffice to protect the privilege against self-incrimination, the presence of counsel is a more effective safeguard against an involuntary waiver of counsel than a mere written or oral warning in the absence of counsel. . . . The rule that once a lawyer has entered the proceedings in connection with the charges under investigation, a person in custody may validly waive the assistance of counsel only in the presence of a lawyer breathes life into the requirement that a waiver of a constitutional right must be competent, intelligent and voluntary. Indeed, it may be said that a right too easily waived is no right at all. . . .
>
> . . . .
>
> [The *Donovan* rule] protect[s] the individual, often ignorant and uneducated, and always in fear, when faced with the coercive police power of the State. The right to the continued advice of a lawyer, already retained or assigned, is his real protection against an abuse of power by the organized State. It is more important than the preinterrogation warnings given to defendants in custody. These warnings often provide only a feeble opportunity to obtain a lawyer, because the suspect or accused is required to determine his need, unadvised by anyone who has his interests at heart. The danger is not only the risk of unwise waivers . . . , but the more significant risk of

---

cobedo to instances in which the suspect has explicitly asked for an attorney was that "such a request may be regarded as a symptom of psychological distress," a condition that would be "heightened" by a denial of the request. *See Developments in the Law—Confessions*, 79 HARV. L. REV. 935, 1002 (1966). "But the factual premise behind this analysis is questionable: a request for a lawyer probably indicates intelligence and presence of mind; the failure to ask for one may be due to ignorance, confusion or intimidation. Besides, to interpret the significance of a request and its denial in terms of intimidation appears to be a reworking of the voluntariness test. . . ." *Id.* at 1002-03.

inaccurate, sometimes false, and inevitably incomplete descriptions of the events described.[99]

This argument proves too much. If all the unkind things Chief Judge Breitel and other defenders of the *Donovan* rule[462] have said about the *Miranda* warnings are true (and there is reason to think they are),[463] the *Donovan* rule is not a sufficient answer. If the *Miranda* warnings often provide only a "feeble opportunity" for the assertion of constitutional rights, if they do not furnish adequate protection against the "risk of inaccurate, sometimes false, and inevitably incomplete descriptions of the events described," if a warning "inevitably invites avoidance"[464] and "can easily become a meaningless ritual," [465] if the warnings will not dispel "[i]nherent intimidation . . . because the usual suspect, especially the illiterate or non-English speaking individual is so frightened and confused that he cannot fully comprehend [them]," [466] then why are these warnings good enough for the suspect who has not, or whose family or friends have not, contacted a lawyer or whose lawyer has not managed to win the race to the stationhouse or telephone? If "life" must be "breathed" into the *Miranda* warnings (and I agree that it must), why should it be done haphazardly, as the *Donovan* rule seems to do? Why not do it across the board?

If the *Miranda* safeguards have turned out to be as feeble in practice as defenders of the *Donovan* rule and as others believe, why not establish a system enabling a member of the public defender's staff to inform the police, as soon as a suspect is brought to the stationhouse, that he represents the individual, at least at this preliminary stage, and that he wishes to advise the individual of his rights or—more bluntly—that he does not want the individual questioned?[467] Such an extension of the *Donovan* rule, I realize, might strain it to the breaking point, but what does this say about the rule itself?[468] Or, alternatively, why not require that an explanation of the nature and importance of the constitutional rights at stake be given by a judicial rather than a police officer and that waiver be made under judicial supervision?[469] Or, at least, why not require that an in-custody suspect be promptly brought before a judicial officer so that "the typically perfunctory reading of *Miranda* warnings by police" can be swiftly reinforced by the "follow-up advice of . . . a neutral officer of the court"?[470] Or, at the very least, why not require that at the stationhouse, and wherever else feasible, all police conversations and "waiver transactions" be electronically recorded for future judicial scrutiny?[471]

99. People v. Hobson, 39 N.Y.2d 479, 484, 485, 348 N.E.2d 894, 898-99, 384 N.Y.S.2d 419, 422 (1976). Chief Judge Breitel also argued, on behalf of the *Donovan* rule, that attempts by a prosecutor to secure a waiver of the right to counsel from one already represented by counsel, without notifying the defense lawyer, or the *use by a prosecutor* of admissions so obtained from a suspect by the police would constitute a violation of professional ethics. *See* footnote 95 *supra*.

Miranda has weaknesses. The principal cluster of its weaknesses (from the suspect's perspective, at any rate) is that it permits the police to obtain waivers of constitutional rights without the advice or presence of counsel, without the advice or presence of a judicial officer, and without any objective recording of the proceedings.[(472)] But these weaknesses, as I have indicated, are not irremediable.

Whatever its shortcomings, *Miranda* tried to take the "police interrogation"-"confession" problem by the throat. *Massiah* does not. Nor does its first cousin, New York's *Donovan* rule. The *Massiah* doctrine and the *Donovan* rule turn on nice distinctions that often will have no more relationship to the suspect's plight than "the kind of electronic equipment employed"[(473)] had to the protection against unreasonable search and seizure. The distinctions drawn by *Massiah* are also conducive to manipulation by law enforcers.

The danger is that the Court will let *Miranda* wither, placing increasing reliance instead on *Massiah* and perhaps on the *Donovan* rule as well (or some variation of it). There is a certain neat logic to these rules. They also strike responsive chords and are readily rationalized.[100]

The danger is that only when the incongruity between the pretrial proceedings and the ideal of a fair trial is flaunted, when an arraignment or indictment is followed by a "kangaroo court" proceeding or a defense lawyer is spurned or deceived by the police, will the constitutional symbols prevail. The added danger posed by the *Donovan* rule or some variation of it is that by accommodating defense lawyers who insist on claiming their clients' rights, law enforcers may gain a freer hand over those who, or whose families, lack the means to summon a lawyer swiftly. To paraphrase Justice Jackson: There is no more effective practical guaranty against police overreaching than to require that the poor and bewildered be subjected to police interrogation in no greater measure than the affluent and sophisticated. Conversely, nothing opens the door to abuse so effectively as to allow the police to pick and choose only the less fortunate to be the subjects of secret interrogation and thus to escape the outcry from the bar (if not the public) that might be visited upon them if all segments of society were so affected.[(474)]

It is not enough to vindicate the prestige of the lawyer when he has entered

---

100. The *Donovan* rule is said to have had "deep roots" in actual practice "for the longest time." Breitel, *supra* footnote 27, at 9. Lawyers, no less than other persons, "are likely to claim as a right what they desire, especially if they are accustomed to having it." *Cf.* R. PERRY, CHARACTERISTICALLY AMERICAN 153 (1949) (talking generally about Americans). *See also* Note, *Reaffirmation of Confessions Inadmissible under* McNabb-Mallory, 72 YALE L.J. 1434, 1454–55 n.106 (1963) (indicating on basis of letters from various United States attorneys in the spring of 1963 that, if suspect has retained or appointed counsel, United States attorney attempts to direct law enforcement agents to question suspect "either in the presence of counsel or, at least, with his consent").

the proceedings, but otherwise to vindicate the prestige of the police officer. Nor, to return to *Massiah,* is it enough to dramatize the ideal of the adversary system when the issue is forced into the open by the commencement of judicial proceedings, but otherwise to look away when in-custody interrogation takes place under conditions undermining a suspect's constitutional rights.

Symbols *are* important, but more is needed. "[I]t is not sufficient to save the Redwoods [and] the Everglades . . . ; it is equally essential to protect the esthetic quality of farmlands and to improve Coney Island. "[475]

Notes

What Is an "Involuntary" Confession?

1. F. INBAU & J. REID, LIE DETECTION AND CRIMINAL INTERROGATION (3d ed. 1953).

2. These include: A. AUBRY & R. CAPUTO, INTERROGATION FOR INVESTIGATORS (1959); W. DIENSTEIN, TECHNICS FOR THE CRIME INVESTIGATOR (1952); W. KIDD, POLICE INTERROGATION (1940); H. MULBAR, INTERROGATION (1951); C. O'HARA, FUNDAMENTALS OF CRIMINAL INVESTIGATION (1956). Numerous extracts from these manuals may be found in Kamisar, *Illegal Searches or Seizures and Contemporaneous Incriminating Statements: A Dialogue on a Neglected Area of Criminal Procedure,* 1961 U. ILL. L.F. 78, 130-32; Weisberg, *Police Interrogation of Arrested Persons: A Skeptical View,* in POLICE POWER AND INDIVIDUAL FREEDOM 155, 156-58 (C. Sowle ed. 1962).

3. *E.g.,* "it is a good practice to purposely arrange for the presence, on each page of the confession, of one or two errors, such as an incorrect name of a person or street which will be subject to later correction by the confessor when the document is read by or to him." F. INBAU & J. REID, CRIMINAL INTERROGATION AND CONFESSIONS 128-29 (1962).

4. It is surprising how effective a well-timed pat on the shoulder or a grip of the hand can be in obtaining a confession. Coming as a climax to a series of sympathetic expressions constituting the basis for the previously employed techniques, a gesture of this sort may expedite a confession of guilt. . . .

   With female offenders, it is most effective for the interrogator to place his hand on top of the subject's hand or hold her hand in the palm of his. If she begins to cry . . . the interrogator may offer her the support of his shoulder, but within a very short time he should have her straighten up and the interrogation should be resumed.

Id. at 55-56.

For the view by a former head of the Criminal Division of the Department of Justice that "law enforcement will be the better as well as the stronger" for abandoning such "spurious approaches," *see* Rogge, Book Review, 76 HARV. L. REV. 1516, 1517 (1963).

5. Lewellen, *How to Make a Killer Confess,* SAT. EVE. POST, Mar. 31, 1956, at 33,100.

At 44-45 of their book, Inbau and Reid in effect describe how Inbau "cracked" the Talmadge murder:

   In view of the normality and prevalence of this victim-blaming characteristic in wrongdoers, what does this suggest . . .? [T]hat the interrogator use it as "bait" in the interrogation of criminal suspects. . . . [T]ake the case of a man suspected of killing his wife, in which the investigation reveals that the wife had treated the suspect very miserably over the years. . . . [M]uch can be gained by the interrogator's adoption of an emotional ("choked-up") feeling about it all as he relates what he knows about the victim's conduct toward her husband.

6. F. INBAU & J. REID, *supra* note 3, at 14.

7. *Id.* at 16.

8. *Id.* at 27.

9. *Id.* at 31.

10. *Id.* at 58–59.

11. *Id.* at 109. The authors have dropped the graphic language appearing at a corresponding place in their earlier work. F. INBAU & J. REID, *supra* note 1, at 185:

[T]he interrogator's task is somewhat akin to that of a hunter stalking his game. Each must patiently maneuver himself or his quarry into a position from which the desired objective may be attained; and in the same manner that the hunter may lose his game by a noisy dash through the bush, so can the interrogator fail in his efforts by not exercising the proper degree of patience.

12. *Id.* at 111–12.

13. *Id.* at 112.

14. *Id.*

15. *Id.*

16. G. Williams, *Questioning by the Police: Some Practical Considerations,* 1960 CRIM. L.R. (Brit.) 325, 337.

17. F. INBAU & J. REID, *supra* note 3, at 208 (emphasis added).

18. G. Williams, *supra* note 16, at 335.

19. *See* note 2 *supra.*

20. REPORT AND RECOMMENDATIONS OF THE COMMISSIONERS' COMMITTEE ON POLICE ARRESTS FOR INVESTIGATION 1 (D. C. 1962). This Report and Chief Robert V. Murray's "answering" memorandum are appraised in Kamisar, Book Review, 76 HARV. L. REV. 1502 (1963).

21. REPORT, *supra* note 20, at 34.

22. *Id.* at 38.

23. *Id.* at 39.

24. *Id.* at 40.

25. NAT'L COMM. ON LAW OBSERVANCE AND ENFORCEMENT, REPORT ON LAW-LESSNESS IN LAW ENFORCEMENT 126 (1931) (Wickersham Report).

26. Lewellen, *supra* note 5, at 99 (emphasis added).

27. F. INBAU & J. REID, *supra* note 3, at 188.

28. *Id.* at 187–88.

29. Spano v. New York, 360 U.S. 315, 323 (1959).

30. *Id.* The authors discuss *Spano* elsewhere, F. INBAU & J. REID, *supra* note 3, at 154–55, but never mention the interrogator's use of petitioner's friend to overbear his will by "sympathy falsely aroused." *Id.*

31. F. INBAU & J. REID, *supra* note 3, at 181.

32. Rogers v. Richmond, 365 U.S. 534, 540–41 (1961).

33. *Id.* at 543. Although the Court reviewed an application for federal habeas corpus by a state prisoner in *Rogers,* as pointed out in Bator, *Finality in Criminal Law and Federal Habeas Corpus for State Prisoners,* 76 HARV. L. REV. 441, 515 (1963), the

Court did "just what it would have done on direct review had it found an improper assumption in the state's adjudication of the confession issue and a record on which it could not itself rule on admissibility"; rather than have the federal court itself decide the question of admissibility on the basis of the state record, it ordered the prisoner's release subject to the state's power to grant him a new trial under proper constitutional standards.

34. "The interrogation tactics and techniques which we discuss comply, in our opinion, with the legal requirements. . . . They all certainly measure up to the fundamental test that not one of them is apt to induce an innocent person to confess." F. INBAU & J. REID, *supra* note 3, at vii.

35. Rogers v. Richmond, *supra* note 32, at 543.

36. *Id.* at 545.

37. A. BEISEL, CONTROL OVER ILLEGAL ENFORCEMENT OF THE CRIMINAL LAW: ROLE OF THE SUPREME COURT 37–86 (1955).

38. J. MAGUIRE, EVIDENCE OF GUILT 107–66 (1959).

39. JOINT COMM. ON CONTINUING LEGAL ED. OF ALI & ABA, THE PROBLEM OF POLICE INTERROGATION (Paulsen ed. 1961).

40. C. MCCORMICK, EVIDENCE 233 (1954).

41. *See, e.g.,* CALIF. DEP'T OF JUSTICE, BUREAU OF CRIMINAL STATISTICS, CRIME IN CALIFORNIA 99 (Table VI-8) (1960); Goldstein, *The State and The Accused: Balance of Advantage in Criminal Procedure,* 69 YALE L.J. 1149, 1163 n.37, 1189 (1960); Rogge, Book Review, *supra* note 4, at 1518.

42. Thomas v. United States, 298 F.2d 696, 697 (9th Cir. 1961), *cert. denied,* 368 U.S. 964 (1962).

43. Alexander v. United States, 290 F.2d 252, 254 (5th Cir.), *cert. denied,* 368 U.S. 891 (1961).

44. It is true that the trial record shows that petitioner told the judge that he was guilty and said "I throw myself at the mercy of the court, Your Honor." . . .[But] it is entirely possible that petitioner's prior confession caused him, in the absence of counsel, to enter the guilty plea.

Pennsylvania *ex rel.* Herman v. Claudy, 350 U.S. 116, 121–22 (1956). *See also* Cicenia v. Lagay, 357 U.S. 504, 508 n.3 (1958). *See generally* Kamisar, *supra* note 2, at 103–04; Kamisar, *The Right to Counsel and the Fourteenth Amendment: A Dialogue on "The Most Pervasive Right" of an Accused,* 30 U. CHI. L. REV. 1, 26–32 (1962).

45. The problem is not obviated by the fact that Gideon v. Wainright, 372 U.S. 335 (1963) appears to require the assignment of counsel, at least for a guilty plea, at the arraignment stage. A defendant may "waive" his right to counsel or be deprived of the "effective assistance" of same.

46. Wong Sun v. United States, 371 U.S. 471, 485–86 (1963). For an exhaustive study of this case, one which unfortunately appeared after this commentary was written and thus can only be noted, see Broeder, Wong Sun v. United States: *A Study in Faith and Hope,* 42 NEB. L. REV. 483 (1963). See also Kamisar, Book Review, *supra* note 20, at 1509 & n.27.

47. 367 U.S. 643 (1961).

48. Wong Sun v. United States, *supra* note 46, at 486.

49. *Id.*

50. Only a few months before *Wong Sun* was handed down, New York, in what purported to be a routine application of *Mapp,* extended the exclusionary rule in search and seizure cases to all fruits, "oral" as well as "real" evidence. People v. Rodriquez, 11 N.Y.2d 279, 183 N.E.2d 651, 229 N.Y.S.2d 353 (1962).

51. 288 F.2d 366 (9th Cir.), *cert. granted,* 368 U.S. 817 (1961), *restored to the calendar for reargument,* 370 U.S. 908 (1962).

52. At 157 n.34a, the authors discuss Gallegos v. Colorado, 370 U.S. 49, decided June 4, 1962. Certiorari was granted in *Wong Sun* on October 9, 1961, and the case was restored to the calendar for reargument on the same day *Gallegos* was handed down.

53. The cases are collected in Kamisar, *supra* note 2, at 78, 81 n.16, 83 nn.21, 22.

54. By contrast, Professor Paulsen devotes a full third of his "police interrogation" monograph (*see* note 39 *supra*) to whether the police may "stop and question" a suspect when grounds for an arrest do not exist and the person does not wish to be detained.

55. *See* Ashcraft v. Tennessee, 322 U.S. 143, 153 (1944); Ward v. Texas, 316 U.S. 547, 552 (1942); Chambers v. Florida, 309 U.S. 227, 229, 238 (1940). *See also* the discussion in Culombe v. Connecticut, 367 U.S. 568, 627–29 (1961).

56. *See, e.g.,* REPORT AND RECOMMENDATIONS OF THE COMMISSIONERS' COMMITTEE ON POLICE ARRESTS FOR INVESTIGATION 3, 59–60 (D.C. 1962).

57. This rule was formulated by the Stone and Vinson Courts. *See* Stroble v. California, 343 U.S. 181, 190 (1952); Haley v. Ohio, 322 U.S. 596, 599 (1948); Malinski v. New York, 324 U.S. 401, 404 (1945); Lyons v. Oklahoma, 322 U.S. 596, 597 n.1 (1944).

58. *See* Meltzer, *Involuntary Confessions: The Allocation of Responsibility Between Judge and Jury,* 21 U. CHI. L. REV. 317, 354 (1954).

59. *See* Ritz, *State Criminal Confession Cases: Subsequent Developments in Cases Reversed by U.S. Supreme Court and Some Current Problems,* 19 WASH. & LEE L. REV. 202, 208–09 (1962).

Since this commentary was written, the Court observed in Haynes v. Washington, 373 U.S. 503, 519 (1963):

> [T]he coercive devices used here were designed to obtain admissions which would incontrovertibly complete a case in which there had already been obtained, by proper investigative efforts, competent evidence sufficient to sustain a conviction. The procedures here are no less constitutionally impermissible, and perhaps more unwarranted because so unnecessary.

60. F. INBAU & J. REID, *supra* note 3, at 153; Stein v. New York, 346 U.S. 146 (1953).

61. 356 U.S. 560 (1958).

62. F. INBAU & J. REID, *supra* note 3, at 154.

63. *See* C. MCCORMICK, *supra* note 40, at 245–46 n.27; Meltzer, *supra* note 58, at 339–54; Miller, *The Supreme Court's Review of Hypothetical Alternatives in a State Confession Case,* 5 SYRACUSE L. REV. 53 (1953); Paulsen, *The Fourteenth Amendment and the Third Degree,* 6 STAN. L. REV. 411, 423–29 (1954). They did so largely for the reason later advanced in *Payne:*

In that case [*Stein*] this Court did not find that the confession was coerced. Indeed it was there recognized that when "the ruling admitting the confession is found on review to be erroneous, the conviction, at least normally, should fall with the confession. . . ."

Payne v. Arkansas, *supra* note 61, at 568 n.15.

64. Spano v. New York, *supra* note 29, at 324.

65. Culombe v. Connecticut, *supra* note 55, at 621.

66. *See* F. INBAU & J. REID, *supra* note 3, at 149–54.

67. F. INBAU & J. REID, *supra* note 3, at 145 n.13.

68. *Id.* at 146 n.15.

69. *Id.* at 142–43.

70. *Id.* at 145.

71. *Id.* at 144.

72. *Id.* at 147 n.17.

73. *See generally* Comment, 68 YALE L.J. 1003 (1959).

74. Douglas, *The Means and the End,* 1959 WASH. U.L.Q. 103, 113–14.

75. Dession, *The New Federal Rules of Criminal Procedure,* 55 YALE L.J. 694, 708 (1946).

76. 322 U.S. 143 (1944).

77. *See, e.g.,* Allen, *The* Wolf *Case: Search and Seizure, Federalism and the Civil Liberties,* 45 ILL. L. REV. 1, 28–29 (1950); Douglas, *supra* note 74, at 107, 113–14, 120; Kamisar, Wolf *and* Lustig *Ten Years Later: Illegal State Evidence in State and Federal Courts,* 43 MINN. L. REV. 1083, 1192–94 (1959) (and language from various Supreme Court cases quoted therein). *But see* Hogan & Snee, *The* McNabb-Mallory *Rule: Its Rise, Rationale and Rescue,* 47 GEO. L.J. 1, 28–29, 32–33 (1958).

78. *See* Hogan & Snee, *supra* note 77, at 22–23, 27; Comment, *supra* note 73, at 1024–25; A MEMORANDUM ON THE DETENTION OF ARRESTED PERSONS AND THEIR PRODUCTION BEFORE A COMMITTING MAGISTRATE WITH THE STATEMENT OF THE BILLS AND RIGHTS COMMITTEE OF THE AMERICAN BAR ASSOCIATION ON H.R. 3690, at 21 (1944), reprinted in *Hearings Before the Subcommittee on Constitutional Rights of the Senate Committee on the Judiciary,* 85th Cong., 2d Sess., 25, 33–41 (1958); Memorandum by Charles Horsky and Charles Reich, *Hearings, supra,* at 475, 477–78; Statement of Yale Kamisar, *Hearings, supra,* at 766–69.

79. F. INBAU & J. REID, *supra* note 3, at 157.

80. *See* text at notes 31–36 and footnote 6 *supra.*

81. Spano v. New York, 360 U.S. 315, 320 (1959).

82. *Id.* at 320–21.

83. F. INBAU & J. REID, *supra* note 3, at 154.

84. That is, at least as early as Ashcraft v. Tennessee, *supra* note 76. *See* Allen, *Due Process and State Criminal Procedures: Another Look,* 48 Nw. U.L. REV. 16, 20–22 (1953); Paulsen, *supra* note 63, at 417–23.

85. Blackburn v. Alabama, 361 U.S. 199, 206 (1960).

86. F. INBAU & J. REID, *supra* note 3, at 155.

87. *Id;* quoting from Rogers v. Richmond, 365 U.S. 534, 544 (1961).

88. F. INBAU & J. REID, *supra* note 3, at 152.

89. *Id. See also* their discussion at 140–41.

90. *See* text at notes 34–36 and footnote 6 *supra*.

91. Culombe v. Connecticut, *supra* note 55, at 602 (emphasis added).

92. C. McCormick, *supra* note 40, at 157 (emphasis added).

93. *See* text at notes 81, 82 *supra*.

94. Blackburn v. Alabama, *supra* note 85, at 207 (emphasis added).

95. *See* 3 J. Wigmore, Evidence § 822 (3d ed. 1940) and cases collected therein.

96. C. McCormick, *supra* note 40, at 226.

97. Hopt v. Utah, 110 U.S. 574, 585 (1884), quoted with approval in Wilson v. United States, 162 U.S. 613, 622 (1896).

98. Lisenba v. California, 314 U.S. 219, 236 (1941). "The aim of the requirement of due process," the Court went on to say, "is not to exclude presumptively false evidence, but to prevent fundamental unfairness." *Id.*

99. F. Inbau & J. Reid, *supra* note 3, at 156 n.33.

100. The concurring Justices, footnote 11 *supra,* do not make clear which portions of Mr. Justice Frankfurter's discussion of the law they agree with, if any. The dissenting Justices, on the other hand, accept the principles propounded by Frankfurter, but not his application of them to the particular facts.

101. F. Inbau & J. Reid, *supra* note 3, at 157.

102. In his concurring opinion, the Chief Justice voiced well-founded doubts whether the lower courts and law enforcement agencies would receive much guidance "from the treatise for which this case seems to have provided a vehicle." Culombe v. Connecticut, *supra* note 55, at 636.

103. *Id.* at 571.

104. *Id.* at 603.

105. *Id.*

106. *Id.* at 578.

107. *Id.* at 579–80.

108. *Id.* at 601.

109. *Id.* at 581–82 (emphasis added).

110. *Id.* at 580.

111. *Id.* at 574.

112. *Id.* at 575.

113. *Id.* at 575–76.

114. Culombe v. Connecticut, *supra* note 55, at 576.

115. *Id.*

116. *Id.* at 581, 584, 602, 622, 634.

117. *See, e.g.,* Nebbia v. New York, 291 U.S. 502, 531–36 (1934).

118. *Cf.* Holmes, J., dissenting in Tyson & Brother v. Banton, 273 U.S. 418, 446 (1927).

119. Culombe v. Connecticut, *supra* note 55, at 604–05.

120. Culombe v. Connecticut, *supra* note 55, at 602.

121. *Cf.* Frankfurter, J., concurring in Illinois *ex rel.* McCullom v. Board of Education, 333 U.S. 203, 212 (1948).

122. *See* Paulsen, *The Fourteenth Amendment and the Third Degree,* 6 Stan. L. Rev. 411, 429–30 (1954).

123. *Cf.* Royal Commission on Capital Punishment, *Report,* Cmd. No. 8932, at 174–75 (1953).

124. *Cf.* Thomas v. Arizona, 356 U.S. 390, 396 (1958).

125. Examine "the dragnet methods of arrest on suspicion" in Chambers v. Florida, 309 U.S. 227, 229–30, 238 (1940).

126. *Cf.* Ward v. Texas, 316 U.S. 547, 552–53 (1942):

> Instead of taking petitioner to the nearest magistrate, they took him away from the nearest magistrate.... [T]he procedure required by law was not observed in making the removal.... [N]o application was made to a magistrate for a committal to a jail in another county.

127. *See* footnote 20 *supra* and note 146 *infra.*

128. *Cf.* Fournier v. People of Puerto Rico, 281 F.2d 888, 892–93 (1st Cir.), *cert. denied,* Sampedro v. People of Puerto Rico, 364 U.S. 915 (1960).

129. *See* footnote 20 *supra.*

130. In approaching these decisions, we may put aside at the outset cases involving ... such convincingly terror-arousing,and otherwise unexplainable, incidents of interrogation as the removal of prisoners from jail at night for questioning in secluded places.... No such obvious, crude devices appear in this record.

Culombe v. Connecticut, *supra* note 55, at 622.

131. Wolf v. Colorado, 338 U.S. 25, 27 (1949).

132. *See* cases cited at note 55 *supra.*

133. J. MAGUIRE, EVIDENCE OF GUILT 109 (1959).

134. Reck v. Pate, 367 U.S. 433, 442 (1961), quoting from Ashcraft v. Tennessee, *supra* note 76, at 154.

135. Culombe v. Connecticut, *supra* note 55, at 574.

136. *Id.* (emphasis added).

137. Rogers v. Richmond, 365 U.S. 534, 546 n.4 (1961), *referring to* Lyons v. Oklahoma, 322 U.S. 596, 601 (1944). *See* note 139 *infra* and accompanying text *supra.*

138. *Cf.* Frankfurter, J., dissenting in Fisher v. United States, 328 U.S. 463, 487 (1946).

139. Lyons v. State, 77 Okla. Crim. 197, 239, 138 P.2d 142, 164 (1943). In affirming the conviction, the Supreme Court observed:

> The question of how specific an instruction in a state court must be upon the involuntary character of a confession is, as a matter of procedure or practice, solely for the courts of the state. When the state-approved instruction fairly raises the question of whether or not the challenged confession was voluntary, *as this instruction did,* the requirements of due process ... are satisfied and this Court will not require a modification of local practice to meet views that it might have as to the advantages of concreteness.

Lyons v. Oklahoma, 322 U.S. 596, 601 (1944) (emphasis added).

140. Ashcraft v. Tennessee, *supra* note 76, at 146. Although the Court reversed on the "undisputed facts," it did not disapprove this instruction.

Haynes v. Washington, 373 U.S. 503 (1963), decided since this commentary was initially written, clouds the continued validity of the *Ashcraft-Lyons* approach. The *Haynes* jury was instructed, in effect, to preclude from its consideration of the "voluntariness" issue the fact that the confessor was not reminded he was under arrest, and that he was not cautioned he could remain silent nor warned that his answers could be used against him, nor advised of his right to counsel. These instructions, *inter alia*, were regarded by a 5–4 majority as raising "a serious and substantial question whether a proper constitutional standard was applied by the jury," but were not relied on as a separate ground of reversal. *Id.* at 518. However, although some language in the opinion can be construed to the contrary ("[T]hese factors . . . are unquestionably attendant circumstances which the accused is entitled to have appropriately considered in determining voluntariness. . . ." *Id.*), there is a significant difference between forbidding a trial court from precluding consideration of these factors and requiring the court to instruct affirmatively that they must be taken into account.

141. Meltzer, *Involuntary Confessions: The Allocation of Responsibility between Judge and Jury,* 21 U. Chi. L. Rev. 317, 328 (1954).

142. 365 U.S. 534, 542–43 (1961).

143. *Id.* at 542.

144. *Id.* at 541–42.

145. *See* text at footnotes 19–25 *supra.*

146. One or two of these factors will be isolated if and when the Court holds that the unconstitutionality of a contemporaneous arrest or search makes a confession obtained by *state* officers inadmissible *per se. See* text accompanying notes 46–50 *supra.* Wong Sun v. United States, 371 U.S. 471 (1963) is likely to be viewed only as an extension of the "fruit of the poisonous tree" doctrine in search and seizure cases, but it may foreshadow the culmination of the "police methods" approach in due process confession cases.

147. Professor Paulsen relies on *Ashcraft, Malinsky, Haley* and *Watts,* for the view that "questioning . . . conducted in a way which [falls] below judge-created standards of decency" bars a confession irrespective of the effect such methods may have had on the mind of the defendant. *See* Paulsen, *The Fourteenth Amendment and the Third Degree,* 6 Stan. L. Rev. 411, 417–21 (1954). But none of these cases, I think, would pass muster under Reliability Test (ii).

148. *Cf.* Judge (later Chief Justice) Vinson in Neuslein v. District of Columbia, 115 F.2d 690, 694 (D.C. Cir. 1940):

> [A] confession does not make good a search illegal at its inception. This is a part of the broader rule that an illegal search cannot be legalized by what it brings to light. . . . Officers should not be encouraged to proceed in an irregular manner on the chance that all will end well.

149. *See, e.g.,* Columbe v. Connecticut, *supra* note 55, at 620–21, 624–30; Reck v. Pate, *supra* note 134, at 440–43; Fikes v. Alabama, 352 U.S. 191, 193, 196–97. *See also* J. Maguire, *supra* note, at 134 n.5.

150. *Cf.* Frankfurter, J., concurring in Sherman v. United States, 365 U.S. 368, 383.

151. Frankfurter, J., concurring in Fikes v. Alabama, *supra* note 149, at 198.

152. Malinski v. New York, 324 U.S. 401, 407 (1945).

153. Ashcraft v. Tennessee, *supra* note 76, at 149, 153.

154. Jackson, J., writing for the majority in Stein v. New York, 346 U.S. 156, 182. *See also* Justice Jackson concurring in Watts v. Indiana, 338 U.S. 49, 60 (1949).

155. Paulsen, *supra* note 147, at 428.

156. Fikes v. Alabama, *supra* note 149, at 196.
157. Payne v. Arkansas, 356 U.S. 560, 567.
158. Spano v. New York, 360 U.S. 315, 321–22 (1959).
159. Blackburn v. Alabama, 361 U.S. 199, 207 (1960).
160. Reck v. Pate, *supra* note 134, at 435.
161. Culombe v. Connecticut, *supra* note 55, at 620.
162. Gallegos v. Colorado, 370 U.S. 49 (1962) (4–3 majority).

Gallegos raises special problems. As pointed out (F. INBAU & J. REID, *supra* note 3, at 158 n.34a), "this decision seems to protect persons of the defendant's age . . . from any interrogation regarding a criminal offense unless they have the benefit of counsel or other 'friendly adult advisors' at the time of the interrogation." It may be that even an "express waiver" of this right will not suffice, "since by hypothesis the accused is unable to protect his own interests." *The Supreme Court, 1961 Term,* 76 HARV. L. REV. 75, 110 (1962).

163. Lynumn v. Illinois, 372 U.S. 528, 534 (1963).
164. Crooker v. California, 357 U.S. 433, 438 (1958).
165. 357 U.S. 504 (1958).
166. Stein v. New York, *supra* note 154, at 185–86.
167. *Id.* at 182.
168. *Id.* at 185.
169. *Cf.* C. MCCORMICK, *supra* note 40, at 587 (discussion of *res gestae*).
170. J. FRANK, FATE AND FREEDOM 139 (1945).

Equal Justice in the Gatehouses and Mansions of American Criminal Procedure

1. *But see* Note, 31 U. CHI. L. REV. 313 (1964), written on the eve of Escobedo v. Illinois, 378 U.S. 478 (1964).

2. "No other case comes to mind in which an administrative official is permitted the broad discretionary power assumed by the police interrogator, together with the power to prevent objective recordation of the facts. The absence of a record makes disputes inevitable about the conduct of the police and, sometimes, about what the prisoner has actually said. It is secrecy, not privacy, which accounts for the absence of a reliable record of interrogation proceedings in a police station. If the need for some pre-judicial questioning is assumed, privacy may be defended on grounds of necessity; secrecy cannot be defended on this or any other ground." Weisberg, *Police Interrogation of Arrested Persons: A Skeptical View,* in POLICE POWER AND INDIVIDUAL FREEDOM 153, 179 (C. Sowle ed. 1962).

3. "Counsel should not be quick to object, even for 'the legitimate purpose of avoiding oppressive or misleading cross-examination . . . if the witness is able to take care of himself' for 'if your adversary is mistreating the witness, the jury probably will be sympathizing with the witness.'" R. KEETON, TRIAL TACTICS AND METHODS 167 (1954). But in the police station there is no lawyer to judge whether "the witness" can "take care of himself" and no "jury"—at least none likely to sympathize with the witness.

4. *See, e.g.,* F. INBAU & J. REID, CRIMINAL INTERROGATION AND CONFESSIONS 162–67 (1962).

5. *Id.* at 111–12.

6. *Id.* at 27.

7. J. MAGUIRE, EVIDENCE OF GUILT 109 (1959).

8. F. INBAU & J. REID, *supra* note 4, at 27.

9. "Not only must the interrogator have patience, but he must also display it. It is well, therefore, to get the idea across, in most case situations, that the interrogator has 'all the time in the world.' He may even express himself in those exact words." *Id.* at 109.

10. W. DIENSTEIN, TECHNICS FOR THE CRIME INVESTIGATOR 112 (1952).

11. Sutherland, *Crime and Confession,* 79 HARV. L. REV. 21, 37 (1965).

12. *Id.*

13. *Cf.* T. ARNOLD, THE SYMBOLS OF GOVERNMENT 53 (Harbinger Books ed. 1962).

14. W. DIENSTEIN, *supra* note 10, at 109–10, 112.

15. *See* Kamisar, *What Is an "Involuntary" Confession?,* 17 RUTGERS L. REV. 728, 733 (1963) [reprinted in this volume].

16. *But see* U.S. COMM. ON CIVIL RIGHTS, 1961 REPORT V ("Justice") 5–28 (1961); A. TREBACH, THE RATIONING OF JUSTICE 32–36, 40–46 (1964).

17. If memory serves, this gatehouse (or was it outhouse?) and mansion terminology, or something like it, was utilized by Dean Claude Sowle in his remarks at a Northwestern University Law School conference on November 15–16, 1962. Unfortunately, on the erroneous premise that these remarks would later be published, I took no notes on the occasion, and when I began to prepare this essay I discovered that Dean Sowle had destroyed his.

18. F. INBAU & J. REID, *supra* note 4, at 20.

19. T. ARNOLD, *supra* note 13, at 156.

20. *See* L. FULLER, THE MORALITY OF LAW 4 (1964).

21. NAT'L COMM. ON LAW OBSERVANCE AND ENFORCEMENT, REPORT ON LAWLESSNESS IN LAW ENFORCEMENT (1931) (Wickersham Report).

22. ALI CODE OF CRIMINAL PROCEDURE 92–101 (Prelim. Draft No. 5, 1927).

23. Simeon E. Baldwin, quoted in ALI CODE OF CRIMINAL PROCEDURE 93 (Prelim. Draft No. 5, 1927).

24. FED. R. CRIM. P. 249 (Prelim. Draft 1943) (Prof. John B. Waite's proposed Additional Rule 6.1). As the comment to Professor Waite's proposal points out (at 250), such a rule in substance, though in varying form, has been frequently advocated as a cure for abuses of secret police interrogation. For a recent proposal that law enforcement authorities be permitted to question a suspect before a magistrate "who could protect the accused from unfair cross-examination," with the sanction of comment at a subsequent trial for a refusal to speak, see the thoughtful Note, 78 HARV. L. REV. 426, 445–49 (1964).

25. FED. R. CRIM. P. 253 (Prelim. Draft 1943) (reply memorandum prepared by Secretary of Advisory Committee). However, until very recently at any rate (*see* footnote 3 *supra*), under the prevailing view, a suspect only had a right to be free from compulsion to answer, not to be free from all interrogation. Only an "accused," viewed in most jurisdictions as one who had been *formally charged,* was entitled to

"stay off the stand" altogether. *See, e.g.,* C. MCCORMICK, EVIDENCE 257–59 (1954); 8 J. WIGMORE, EVIDENCE § 2268 (J. McNaughton ed. 1961); Meltzer, *Required Records, the McCarran Act, and the Privilege against Self-Incrimination,* 18 U. CHI. L. REV. 687, 693–95 (1951).

26. Hiemstra, *Abolition of the Right Not to Be Questioned,* 80 S. AFR. L.J. 187, 194–95 (1963).

27. 1 J. STEPHEN, HISTORY OF THE CRIMINAL LAW OF ENGLAND 441–42 (1883).

28. *Id.* at 442.

29. 8 J. WIGMORE, EVIDENCE § 2266 (3d ed. 1940).

30. J. MAGUIRE, *supra* note 7, at 15 n.2, E. MORGAN, BASIC PROBLEMS OF EVIDENCE 146–47 (1962).

31. 8 J. WIGMORE, *supra* note 29, § 2252(c). "In administrative proceedings other than inquiries directed at suspects by police, applicability of privilege against self-incrimination is rarely challenged." J. MAGUIRE, *supra* note 7, at 16.

32. 8 J. WIGMORE, *supra* note 29, § 2266.

33. M. COHEN, THE MEANING OF HUMAN HISTORY 114 (1947).

34. *See* C. MCCORMICK, *supra* note 25, at 252–57; 8 J. WIGMORE, *supra* note 29, § 2250; Morgan, *The Privilege against Self-Incrimination,* 34 MINN. L. REV. 1, 8–9.

35. REPORT AND RECOMMENDATIONS OF THE COMMISSIONERS' COMMITTEE ON POLICE ARRESTS FOR INVESTIGATION 39 (D.C. 1962). A ban against "arrests for investigations" was finally ordered by the District Commissioners, effective March 15, 1963, *see* Kamisar, Book Review, 76 HARV. L. REV. 1502, 1512 n.48 (1963), but such arrests are commonly made in other jurisdictions. *See, e.g.,* Foote, *Safeguards in the Law of Arrest,* 52 NW. U.L. REV. 16, 20 (1957); Kamisar and Choper, *The Right to Counsel in Minnesota: Some Field Findings and Legal-Policy Observations,* 48 MINN. L. REV. 1, 42–43, 48 (1963); LaFave, *Detention for Investigation by the Police: An Analysis of Current Practices,* 1962 WASH. U.L.Q. 331; Note, 100 U. PA. L. REV. 1182, 1205–06 (1952).

36. ILL. DIV., ACLU, SECRET DETENTION BY THE CHICAGO POLICE 25 (1959) (according to ACLU sample of 334 cases).

37. 8 J. WIGMORE, *supra* note 29, § 2250.

38. Note, *An Historical Argument for the Right to Counsel during Police Interrogation,* 73 YALE L.J. 1000, 1034 (1964).

39. *Id.* at 1041. *See also* Barrett, *Police Practices and the Law—From Arrest to Release or Charge,* 50 CALIF. L. REV. 11, 16–19 (1962); C. Williams, *Questioning by the Police: Some Further Points—2,* 1960 CRIM. L. R. (Brit.) 352, 353.

40. *See* Kauper, *Judicial Examination of the Accused—A Remedy for the Third Degree,* 30 MICH. L. REV. 1224, 1235 (1932).

41. E. MORGAN, BASIC PROBLEMS OF EVIDENCE 147–48 (1962).

42. A. BEISEL, CONTROL OVER ILLEGAL ENFORCEMENT OF THE CRIMINAL LAW: ROLE OF THE SUPREME COURT 104 (1955).

43. Meltzer, *supra* note 25, at 695. *See also* Comment, 31 U. CHI. L. REV. 556, 559 (1964).

44. *Cf.* Bickel, *Applied Politics and the Science of Law: Writings of the Harvard Period,* in FELIX FRANKFURTER: A TRIBUTE 164, 186–87 (W. Mendelson ed. 1964).

45. C. MCCORMICK, *supra* note 25, at 155.

46. *Id.* at 156.

47. *See* L. MAYERS, SHALL WE AMEND THE FIFTH AMENDMENT? 82–83, 223–33 (1959); 8 J. WIGMORE, *supra* note 25, at 329 n.27. But both authors are quick to marshal the contrary arguments.

48. *Cf.* Frankfurter, J., in Watts v. Indiana, 338 U.S. 49, 52 (1949).

49. *Cf.* Rostow, *The Democratic Character of Judicial Review,* in THE SOVEREIGN PREROGATIVE 147, 164 (1962).

50. Foote, *The Fourth Amendment: Obstacle or Necessity in the Law of Arrest?* in POLICE POWER AND INDIVIDUAL FREEDOM 29, 30 (C. Sowle ed. 1962).

51. *Cf.* Screws v. United States, 325 U.S. 91 (1945).

52. *See* note 9 *supra.*

53. 8 J. WIGMORE, *supra* note 29, at 309.

54. L. MAYERS, *supra* note 47, at 90.

55. Note, 5 STAN. L. REV. 459, 477 (1953).

56. 8 J. WIGMORE, *supra* note 25, at 316.

57. Fay v. Noia, 372 U.S. 391, 439 (1963).

58. Johnson v. Zerbst, 304 U.S. 458, 464 (1938), quoted with approval in Carnley v. Cochran, 369 U.S. 506, 514 (1962).

59. *See* Escobedo v. Illinois, 378 U.S. 478, 491 (1964). Prior to *Escobedo* it was unclear whether a "potential defendant" was entitled to be advised of the privilege against self-incrimination before being called by the grand jury, although "one would suppose that, as a matter of ethics or fair play or policy, a prosecutor would in all cases refrain from calling as a witness before a Grand Jury any person who is *de jure* or *de facto* an accused. The absence of appeals to this court involving the problem under discussion would seem to indicate that some such rule or practice is observed in the prosecutor's offices in this circuit." United States v. Scully, 225 F.2d 113, 116 (2d Cir.), *cert. denied,* 350 U.S. 897 (1955). Two commentators who until quite recently were assistant United States Attorneys report that "although traditionally counsel has not been permitted in the grand jury room, it is the practice to allow the witness who has counsel to leave the grand jury room at any time for consultation with his lawyer." Enker & Elsen, *Counsel for the Suspect: Massiah v. United States and Escobedo v. Illinois,* 49 MINN. L. REV. 47, 91 (1964). *Escobedo* may require that a "potential defendant" at least be afforded an opportunity to consult with counsel before a grand jury appearance. *See* Short v. United States, 342 F. 2d 863, 867–72 (D.C. Cir. 1964); Enker & Elsen, *supra,* at 73–75; *The Supreme Court, 1963 Term,* 78 HARV. L. REV. 143, 222–23 (1964).

[*A decade and a half later, the issues raised in this note remain unresolved. In United States v. Mandujano, 425 U.S. 564, 580 (1976) Chief Justice Burger, speaking for himself and three other Justices but not for the Court, maintained that "to extend* [Miranda] *concepts to questioning before a grand jury inquiring into criminal activity under the guidance of a judge is an extravagant expansion never remotely contemplated by this Court in* Miranda." *Added the Chief Justice (*id. *at 581): "Respondent* [a 'putative' or 'virtual' defendant, was] *informed that if he desired he could have the assistance of counsel, but that counsel could not be inside the grand jury room. That statement was plainly a correct recital of the law. No criminal proceedings had been instituted against respondent, hence the Sixth Amendment right to counsel had not come into play." The latter statement may be read as implying (and concurring*

Justice Brennan, joined by Marshall, J., so read it) that "there is a right to have counsel present for consultation outside the grand jury room but that it is not constitutionally derived and therefore may be enjoyed only by those wealthy enough to hire a lawyer." (Id. *at 608, rejecting this implication*.) See generally *Stone*, The *Miranda* Doctrine in the Burger Court, *1977 Sup. Ct. Rev. 99, 154-67.*]

60. Brief of Edward L. Barrett, Jr., as Amicus Curiae, at 9, People v. Dorado, 42 Cal. Rptr. 169, 398 P.2d 361 (1965) (on rehearing).

A Dissent from the *Miranda* Dissents

1. For example, on the basis of four lively workshop sessions, lasting three full hours, with the Chief Justices of the States at the Eighteenth Annual Meeting of the Conference of Chief Justices, August 5, 1966, I would have to say they were overwhelmingly opposed to the recent confession rulings.

2. 384 U.S. at 505. A number of questions about the reach of *Miranda* are raised in L. Hall & Y. Kamisar, Modern Criminal Procedure 450 (2d ed. 1966).

3. *See* note 32 *infra* and accompanying text *supra*.

4. 384 U.S. at 444. This appears in the self-styled summary of the Court's holding. The warnings (and the reasons for them) are discussed in considerable detail at 467-79 of the majority opinion.

5. *Cf*. L. Fuller, The Morality of Law 11-12 (1964).

6. 384 U.S. at 506.

7. *Id*. at 508. Justice Clark, too, although he maintains that "the majority . . . goes too far on too little, while my dissenting brethren do not go quite far enough," *id*. at 499, retains considerable enthusiasm for the old approach:

> Rather than employing the arbitrary Fifth Amendment rule which the Court lays down I would follow the more pliable dictates of the Due Process Clauses of the Fifth and Fourteenth Amendments which we are accustomed to administering and which we know from our cases are effective instruments in protecting persons in police custody.

Id. at 503.

8. 384 U.S. at 505.

9. A close student of the problem so characterized them a full twenty years ago, pointing to the almost insurmountable problems of proof confronting the alleged victim of improper interrogation practices. Dession, *The New Federal Rules of Criminal Procedure*, 55 Yale L.J. 694, 708 (1946).

10. 384 U.S. at 505.

11. *Id*. at 510.

12. *Id*. at 531.

13. *Id*. at 531-32.

14. *See generally* Israel, Gideon v. Wainwright: *The "Art" of Overruling*, in 1963 Sup. Ct. Rev. 211, 234-42.

15. *See, e.g.*, Kamisar, *On the Tactics of Police-Prosecution Oriented Critics of the Courts*, 49 Cornell L.Q. 436 *passim* (1964).

16. 332 U.S. 46 (1947), *overruled in* Malloy v. Hogan, 378 U.S. 1 (1964).

17. 332 U.S. at 125. Eighteen years later the Court did vindicate Justice Murphy's position, although it was not content to rest on a "plain reading" of the Constitution. Griffin v. California, 380 U.S. 609 (1965) (Douglas, J.).

18. 372 U.S. 335 (1963).

19. *Id.* at 344.

20. *Id.*

21. 378 U.S. 1 (1964).

22. Kamisar, *Equal Justice in the Gatehouses and Mansions of American Criminal Procedure,* in CRIMINAL JUSTICE IN OUR TIME 47 (A. Howard ed. 1965) [reprinted in part in this volume].

23. *Id.* The reference is to Bram v. United States, 168 U.S. 532 (1897).

24. 297 U.S. 278 (1936).

25. Traynor, *The Devils of Due Process in Criminal Detection, Detention, and Trial,* 33 U. CHI. L. REV. 657. 674 (1966).

26. McNaughton, *The Privilege Against Self-Incrimination: Its Constitutional Affectation, Raison d'Etre and Miscellaneous Implications,* in POLICE POWER AND INDIVIDUAL FREEDOM 223, 237 (C. Sowle ed. 1962).

27. *Id.* at 241.

28. *Id.* at 237–38.

29. L. MAYERS, SHALL WE AMEND THE FIFTH AMENDMENT? 86 (1959).

30. *Id. See also* Barrett, *Police Practices and the Law—From Arrest to Release or Charge,* 50 CALIF. L. REV. 11, 16 n.29 (1962).

In England, "it was not until 1842, thirteen years after the formation of the Metropolitan Police, that a small body was detached for detective work, and not until 1878 that the Criminal Investigation Department was formally created." P. DEVLIN, THE CRIMINAL PROSECUTION IN ENGLAND 18 (1959).

"In America the history of preliminary examination follows a course parallel to that run by the English institution whence it was derived." Kauper, *Judicial Examination of the Accused—A Remedy for the Third Degree,* 30 MICH. L. REV. 1224, 1235 (1932).

31. L. MAYERS, *supra* note 29, at 87.

32. 384 U.S. at 444. *Id.* at 477, 478.

33. 347 U.S. 483 (1954).

34. 369 U.S. 186 (1962).

35. 384 U.S. 436, 526 (1966).

36. *Id.,* quoting Morgan, *The Privilege Against Self-Incrimination,* 34 MINN. L. REV. 1, 18 (1949).

37. Morgan, *supra* note 36, at 27–28, 29 (emphasis in the original).

38. 384 U.S. at 526–27.

39. Corwin, *The Supreme Court's Construction of the Self-Incrimination Clause,* 29 MICH. L. REV. 1, 11–12 (1930).

40. Griswold, *The Individual and the Fifth Amendment,* The New Leader, Oct. 29, 1956, at 20, 22.

41. 4 AM. J. LEGAL HIST. 114 n.20 (1960).

42. *Id.* (emphasis in the original).

43. *Id.* at 121 (emphasis in the original).

Professor Mayers is referring to 3 J. STORY, COMMENTARIES ON THE CONSTITUTION OF THE UNITED STATES § 1782 (1883):

[The privilege against self-incrimination] also is but an affirmance of a common law privilege. But it is of inestimable value. It is well known, that in some countries, not only are criminals compelled to give evidence against themselves, but are subjected to the rack or torture in order to procure a confession of guilt. And what is worse, it has been (as if in mockery or scorn) attempted to excuse, or justify it, upon the score of mercy and humanity to the accused. It has been contrived, (it is pretended,) that innocence should manifest itself by a stout resistance, or guilt by a plain confession; as if a man's innocence were to be tried by the hardness of his constitution, and his guilt by the sensibility of his nerves.

44. The Justices of the Peace Act, 1360, 34 Edw. 3, c. 1.

45. 1 & 2 Phil. & M., c. 13, § 4 (1554); 2 & 3 Phil. & M., c. 10, § 2 (1555); *see* R. MOLEY, OUR CRIMINAL COURTS 15 (1930).

46. 1 J. STEPHEN, A HISTORY OF THE CRIMINAL LAW OF ENGLAND 221 (1883).

47. Kauper, *Judicial Examination of the Accused—A Remedy for the Third Degree,* 30 MICH L. REV. 1224, 1233 (1932). *See generally* 5 W. HOLDSWORTH, A HISTORY OF ENGLISH LAW 191–92 (1924); Grant, *Our Common Law Constitution,* 40 B.U.L. REV. 1, 10–12 (1960); 1 J. STEPHEN, *supra* note 46, at 221–25.

48. Kauper, *supra* note 47, at 1233–34.

49. 11 & 12 Vict., c. 42, § 18 (1848).

50. Kauper, *supra* note 47, at 1234.

51. G. HASKINS, LAW AND AUTHORITY IN EARLY MASSACHUSETTS 174 (1960).

52. *Id.* at 201.

53. J. GOEBEL & T.R. NAUGHTON, LAW ENFORCEMENT IN COLONIAL NEW YORK 654 (1944).

54. *Id.* at 653.

55. *Id.* at 653–54.

56. *See* Barrett, *Police Practices and the Law—From Arrest to Release or Charge,* 50 CALIF. L. REV. 11, 17 n.39 (1962).

57. Professor Pound points to "the idea of separation of powers, so much insisted on in the American polity," which "judicialized" the preliminary examination "before the institution of a modern police had developed, and so left a gap which in practice had to be filled outside of law." R. POUND, CRIMINAL JUSTICE IN AMERICA 88 (1929). Professor Moley, however, suggests that in many American communities there may not have been much of "a gap," commenting that "the early development of the county prosecutor as an aggressive agent of law enforcement, and the power and prestige of the sheriff in all frontier communities, probably prevented the justice of the peace and the city magistrates from assuming much importance as investigators of crimes and suspected criminals." MOLEY, *supra* note 45, at 20.

58. Kauper, *supra* note 47, at 1236.

59. A. BEISEL, CONTROL OVER ILLEGAL ENFORCEMENT OF THE CRIMINAL LAW: ROLE OF THE SUPREME COURT 104 (1955).

60. The commissioners were David Dudley Field, David Graham and Arphaxed Loomis.

61. COMMISSIONERS ON PRACTICE AND PLEADINGS, REP'T NO. 4—CODE OF CRIMI-
NAL PROCEDURE XXV, xxvii–xxix (1849).

62. COMMISSIONERS ON CRIMINAL LAW IN THE CHANNEL ISLANDS, REP'T NO. 2
(1848), reprinted in 8 Rep. St. Tr. 1210 (N. S. 1850–58) (App. C).

63. *Id.* at 1200. This marked "a departure from the old law in Terrien and the
Approbation, by which the accused in refusing to answer or not answering pertinently,
would be subjected to the torture." *Id.*

64. *Id.* at 1211–12.

65. *Id.* at 1212.

66. *Id.*

67. Even those who pointed out that "the private or secret interrogation of arrested
persons . . . has become . . . in many cases the foundation of scandal, harsh criticism
and judicial condemnation" conceded that the privilege against self-incrimination "is
obviously limited to judicial statements." ALI CODE OF CRIMINAL PROCEDURE § 38,
comment at 182 (Tent. Draft No. 1, 1928).

68. FED. R. CRIM. P. 249 (Prelim. Draft 1943) (Professor Waite's proposed
Additional Rule 6.1).

69. FED. R. CRIM. P. 253 (Prelim. Draft 1943) (reply memorandum prepared by
Secretary of Advisory Committee) (emphasis added).

70. Since the privilege exists during the trial in open court of a person who has been
formally charged with crime, it seems even more applicable to the preliminary
inquisition of a suspect by police or prosecutors before any judicial proceeding or
formal charge. It is true that there is some difference of opinion whether the third
degree violates the privilege against self-incrimination; a few courts say that it does
not because the questioning does not involve any kind of judicial process for the
taking of testimony. This seems a narrow limitation of a constitutional right.

Chafee, Pollak & Stern, *The Third Degree,* in NAT'L COMM. ON LAW OBSERVANCE
AND ENFORCEMENT, REPORT ON LAWLESSNESS IN LAW ENFORCEMENT 26–27 (1931)
(Wickersham Report).

71. *See* inside cover of paperback edition (Henry Regnery Co., 1963).

72. Z. CHAFEE, DOCUMENTS ON FUNDAMENTAL HUMAN RIGHTS 541 (1952),
quoted with approval in Crooker v. California, 357 U.S. 433, 446 (1958) (Douglas, J.,
dissenting).

73. *See* note 85 *infra* and accompanying text *supra.*

74. *See, e.g.,* Mayers, *The Federal Witness' Privilege Against Self-Incrimination:
Constitutional or Common-Law,* 4 AM. J. LEGAL HIST. 107 (1960); Pittman, *The Fifth
Amendment: Yesterday, Today, and Tomorrow,* 42 A.B.A.J. 509 (1956); C.D. Wil-
liams, *Problems of the Fifth Amendment,* 24 FORDHAM L. REV. 19 (1955).

75. Counselman v. Hitchcock, 142 U.S. 547, 562 (1892), quoted with approval in
Miranda v. Arizona, 384 U.S. 436, 459–60 (1966).

76. E. GRISWOLD, THE FIFTH AMENDMENT TODAY 54–55 (1955).

77. The government came close to making this argument in United States v. Lefkowitz, 285 U.S. 452 (1932), when it contended that general, exploratory searches
could be made incident to a lawful arrest, although such power could not be conferred
by a search warrant. Brief for the United States, at 13, 15, 37 n.6 (emphasis added):

[T]he principles crystallized in the Fourth Amendment were not intended to limit the right of search and seizure incident to a lawful arrest. . . . Nor, we submit, was the search conducted by the officers in the present case a "general exploratory search" of the kind which the framers of the Constitution intended to prohibit by the Fourth Amendment. The abuse there aimed at was the practice of *issuing general warrants* without probable cause. The generality prohibited was not primarily the *generality of the search* actually conducted but the *generality of the authority* to search without any reasonable basis for belief that crime had been committed. . . . The Amendment does not consist of two sentences with a break after the word "violated." It is all one sentence, and the provision that no warrants shall issue except upon probable cause illustrates what is meant by the provision that the right of the people to be free of unreasonable searches and seizures shall not be violated. "The term 'unreasonable' in the constitutions of the States [identical with the Fourth Amendment] has allusion to what had been practiced before our revolution, and especially, to general search warrants, on which the person, place, or thing was not described."

The government's views did not prevail in *Lefkowitz,* but there have been occasions when the Court has ruled, in effect, that a search without warrant confers greater authority than a search under warrant. *See generally* J. LANDYNSKI, SEARCH AND SEIZURE AND THE SUPREME COURT ch. iv (1966).

The government's argument in *Lefkowitz* was topped by the opinion of the court in Hall v. Commonwealth, 138 Va. 727 (1924), which stated that evidence obtained by an officer acting *either* without a warrant *or* under a void warrant was admissible in a criminal prosecution because "we believe the framers of the Constitution of the United States, and of this and other States, merely sought to provide against any attempt, by legislation or otherwise, to *authorize, justify* or *declare lawful* any unreasonable search or seizure" and "if an official, or a mere petty agent of the State, exceeds or abuses the authority with which he is clothed, he is to be deemed as acting, not for the State, but for himself only; and therefore he alone, and not the State, should be held accountable for his acts." *Id.* at 740 (emphasis in the original). The grounds advanced in *Hall* for admitting illegally seized evidence were familiar ones at that time. *See* A. CORNELIUS, SEARCH AND SEIZURE § 9 (2d ed. 1930).

78. *See* J. LANDYNSKI, *supra* note 77, at 77. Indeed, Boyd v. United States, 116 U.S. 616 (1886), "the first Fourth Amendment case of real consequence" and, "in the Court's own view [in 1925], the leading case on the subject of search and seizure" (J. LANDYNSKI, *supra,* at 49), regarded the privilege against self-incrimination as the constitutional backbone of the exclusionary rule.

79. I am only talking about "consistency" between the approach to searches and seizures and self-incrimination on the one hand, and the approach to confessions and self-incrimination on the other, not addressing myself to the merits of basing the exclusionary rule on the fifth amendment. On the merits, as I have indicated elsewhere, I think there is little to be said for it. *See* Kamisar, Wolf *and* Lustig *Ten Years Later: Illegal State Evidence in State and Federal Courts,* 43 MINN. L. REV. 1083, 1088–90 n.16 (1959).

80. It appears to be relatively easy, however, for a given generation to see how the dangers which gripped a *previous* generation were "much exaggerated." The point is made in Chafee, *Thirty-Five Years with Freedom of Speech,* 1 KAN. L. REV. 1, 4–6 (1952).

81. 338 U.S. 49, 59 (1949).

82. *Id.* at 61–62.

83. 367 U.S. 568, 578 (1961). There was no majority opinion. *See* text at footnote 30 and notes 124–27 *supra.*

84. Justice Frankfurter went on to say:

> But if it is once admitted that questioning of suspects is permissible, whatever reasonable means are needed to make the questioning effective must also be conceded to the police.... Often the place of questioning will have to be a police interrogation room, [in part] because it is important to assure the proper atmosphere of privacy and non-distraction if questioning is to be made productive.... Legal counsel for the suspect will generally prove a thorough obstruction to the investigation. Indeed, even to inform the suspect of his legal right to keep silent will prove an obstruction.

367 U.S. at 579–80.

85. Crooker v. California, 357 U.S. 433, 441 (1958).

86. Weisberg, *Police Interrogation of Arrested Persons: A Skeptical View,* 52 J. Crim. L.C. & P.S. 21, 44 (1961), reprinted in Police Power and Individual Freedom 180 (C. Sowle ed. 1962).

87. Packer, *Two Models of the Criminal Process,* 113 U. Pa. L. Rev. 1, 64 (1964).

88. MacInnes, *The Criminal Society,* in The Police and the Public 101 (C. Rolph ed. 1962).

89. Major Sylvester's comments are reported in Larson, *Present Police and Legal Methods for the Determination of the Innocence or Guilt of the Suspect,* 16 J. Crim. L. & Criminology 219, 222–25 (1925) and reported in part in 3 J. Wigmore, Evidence 316–17 (3d ed. 1940).

90. Statement of Alvin A. Dewey before the Subcommittee on Constitutional Amendments of the Senate Committee on the Judiciary, July 21, 1966, at 2 (mimeo.) (on file in the University of Michigan Law Library).

91. 266 U.S. 1 (1924). *See* text *supra* at footnote 33 and note 154.

92. 246 N.Y. 409, 159 N.E. 379 (1927). *See* text *supra* at footnote 34 and notes 155–56.

93. Nat'l Comm. on Law Observance and Enforcement, Report on Lawlessness in Law Enforcement (1931) (Wickersham Report).

94. *See* note 70 *supra.*

95. In most instances, the courts have not even discussed whether in-custody investigation by the police is legal, concentrating instead on determining the point at which the police have gone too far in their interrogation practices so that the confessor should be regarded as coerced. In the few cases where the issue of illegality has been pressed, most state courts have refused to follow the federal courts in excluding evidence obtained during periods of illegal delay and hence have not needed to mark out the boundaries of proper police conduct short of that extreme characterized as coercion.

Barrett, *Police Practices and the Law—From Arrest to Release or Charge,* 50 Calif. L. Rev. 11, 22 (1962). *See also* Schaefer, *Comments* [on Kamisar, *Has the Court Left the Attorney General Behind?,* 54 Ky. L.J. 464 (1966)], 54 Ky. L.J. 521–22 (1966).

96. *See generally* Hogan & Snee, *The* McNabb-Mallory *Rule: Its Rise, Rationale and Rescue,* 47 GEO. L.J. 1 (1958); Note, 68 YALE L.J. 1003 (1959).

97. Brief for United States, at 49–50.

98. *Id.* at 52–53.

99. *Cf.* Brief for the State of New York and Twenty-Six other States as Amici Curiae, in *"Miranda* Cases,* "* at 23, 35–38; Brief for United States at 45, Westover v. United States, 384 U.S. 436 (1966).

100. Brief for United States, at 55–56, Anderson v. United States, 318 U.S. 350 (1943).

101. *Id.* at 39–40, 46, 48 (emphasis added).

102. *Id.* at 28, 41–42, 48–49.

103. Barenblatt v. United States, 360 U.S. 109, 126 (1959) (Harlan, J.).

104. *Id.*

105. *See* footnote 1 and note 7 *supra.*

106. 384 U.S. at 503.

107. *Id.* at 506.

108. *Id.* at 508.

109. Reck v. Pate, 367 U.S. 433, 455 (1961) (dissenting opinion).

110. Irvine v. California, 347 U.S. 128, 138–39 (1954) (Clark, J., concurring).

111. 384 U.S. at 509.

112. *Id.,* referring to the cases synopsized in Herman, *The Supreme Court and Restrictions on Police Interrogation,* 25 OHIO ST. L.J. 449, 456 & nn.36–39 (1964). *See also* Haynes v. Washington, 373 U.S. 503, 524 (1963) (Clark, J., joined by Harlan, Stewart and White, JJ., dissenting):

> [Not] even the fact that one is "held incommunicado, is subjected to questioning by officers for long periods, and deprived of the advice of counsel," without a showing that he had "so lost his freedom of action" that the confession was not his own, requires a reversal under the Fourteenth Amendment. *Lisenba v. California* [314 U.S. 219, 240–41 (1941)]. Finally, the fact that police officers violated state statutes in their treatment of the petitioner does "not furnish an answer" to the question whether a confession was voluntarily made. *Id.* at 235; *see Gallegos v. Nebraska,* 342 U.S. 55 (1951).

113. 384 U.S. at 509 n.5. As Justice Harlan recognizes elsewhere, *see* text *supra* at note 118, in the evolution of the "totality of circumstances" test the use of physical violence in obtaining a confession emerged as a per se ground for inadmissibility, but "causation" questions remained. Stroble, sentenced to death for first degree murder, did not prevail in the Supreme Court because circumstances indicated that he had confessed "quite independently of any duress by the police." 343 U.S. at 191 (Clark, J.).

114. 384 U.S. at 457–58 n.26, quoting from Sutherland, *Crime and Confession,* 79 HARV. L. REV. 21, 37 (1965).

115. 384 U.S. at 516 & n.13. *Compare* footnote 25 *supra.*

116. Sutherland, *supra* note 114, at 37.

117. 384 U.S. at 507.

118. *Id.* at 508.

119. *Id.* at 507 (emphasis in the original).

120. Haynes v. Washington, 373 U.S. 503 (1963).

121. *Id.*

122. So described by the Chief Justice in his concurring opinion in Culombe v. Connecticut, 367 U.S. 568, 636 (1961).

123. Again so described by the Chief Justice, 367 U.S. at 636. The *Miranda* dissenters were gracious enough not to elaborate on the Chief Justice's preference in *Culombe* for developing "the law on a case-by-case approach," declaring "legal principles only in the context of specific factual situations," and avoiding "expounding more than is necessary for the decision of a given case." *Id.*

124. *Id.* at 642 (dissenting opinion).

125. *Id.*

126. *Id.* at 637–41.

127. *Id.* at 636.

128. 373 U.S. 503 (1963).

129. *Id.* at 521.

130. *Id.* at 525.

131. *See* footnotes 3–4 *supra* and accompanying text.

132. Davis v. North Carolina, 384 U.S. 737, 744 (1966).

133. 339 F.2d 770, 780 (4th Cir. 1964). Judge Bell joined in Chief Judge Sobeloff's dissenting opinion.

134. 384 U.S. at 752.

135. 253 N.C. 86, 116 S.E.2d 365 (1960).

136. 196 F. Supp. 488 (E.D.N.C. 1961).

137. 310 F.2d 904 (4th Cir. 1962).

138. 221 F. Supp. 494 (E.D.N.C. 1963).

139. 339 F.2d 770 (4th Cir. 1964).

140. 253 N.C. 86, 94, 96, 116 S.E.2d 365, 370, 371 (1960).

141. *See* 384 U.S. at 745–47; 339 F.2d at 783 (dissenting opinion).

142. *See id.* at 739; 339 F.2d at 782 (dissenting opinion).

143. 221 F. Supp. 494, 499 (E.D.N.C. 1963).

144. *See* 384 U.S. at 743 n.3; 339 F.2d at 779, 784 (dissenting opinion).

145. 221 F. Supp. at 496. "Not humanly possible," asserted the dissenting judges in the Fourth Circuit, 339 F.2d at 784.

146. 339 F.2d at 775 (Haynsworth, J.).

147. *Id.*

148. 221 F. Supp. at 496.

149. 297 U.S. 278 (1936).

150. Including *Brown,* the Court decided 35 state confession cases from 1936 through 1965. *See* National Legal Aid and Defender Association, Defender Newsletter, Vol. II, no. 5, Sept. 1965.

151. *See* E.B. PRETTYMAN, JR., DEATH AND THE SUPREME COURT 305 (1961).

152. *Id.* at 297–98.

153. Unofficial Transcript of Oral Argument in *Miranda* and Companion Cases, at 91 (oral argument of Mr. Earle for petitioner in *Vignera v. New York*), on file in University of Michigan Law Library.

154. Brief for the United States at 43, Ziang Sun Wan v. United States, 266 U.S. 1 (1924).

155. People v. Doran, 246 N.Y. 409, 422, 159 N.E. 379, 384 (1927).

156. *Id.* at 423.

157. Since the *Wan* jury was told that "in determining whether or not said confessions or admissions were voluntary" it "may take into consideration" the "the defendant was not warned that the confessions would or might be used against him or that he was not obliged to make any incriminating statement," that "the police repeatedly questioned him and importuned him to talk about the case" and other specific factors (Brief for the United States, p. 51), these instructions seem *superior* to those given in *Haynes,* some forty years later. *See* discussion in text at footnotes 28–29 and note 120 *supra.* I am aware that Jackson v. Denno, 378 U.S. 368 (1964) required the trial court actually to determine the issue of "coercion" or "voluntariness" himself, at least in the first instance, but presumably how a judge instructs a jury on an issue is some evidence of how he himself would go about resolving that issue.

158. 384 U.S. at 753.

159. *Id.* at 754–55.

160. 384 U.S. at 509.

161. *Id.* at 508.

Kauper's "Judicial Examination of the Accused" Forty Years Later: Some Comments on a Remarkable Article

1. 378 U.S. 478 (1964).

2. 384 U.S. 436 (1966).

3. 287 U.S. 45 (1932). Professor Francis Allen notes that *Powell,* which marked "[the beginning of] the modern law of due process relating to criminal procedure," Allen, *The Supreme Court, Federalism, and State Systems of Criminal Justice,* 8 DE PAUL L. REV. 213, 223 (1959), and "the rise of Hitler to power in Germany occurred within the period of a single year. . . . [P]erhaps, in some larger sense the two events may be located in the same current of history. Both occurrences are encompassed in the crisis of individual liberty which has confronted the western world since the first world war." Allen, *The Supreme Court and State Criminal Justice,* 4 WAYNE L. REV. 191–92, 196 (1958).

Although *Powell* came to stand for the proposition that an indigent defendant had an absolute right to assigned counsel in capital cases, *see* Hamilton v. Alabama, 368 U.S. 52, 55 (1961); Bute v. Illinois, 333 U.S. 640, 676 (1948), as Justice Harlan maintained thirty years later, *Powell* could be plausibly read for the narrow proposition that only "under the particular facts there presented—'the ignorance and illiteracy of the defendants, their youth, the circumstances of public hostility [and] that they stood in deadly peril of their lives'—[did a] state court [have] a duty to assign counsel for the trial as a necessary requirement of due process of law." Gideon v. Wainwright, 372 U.S. 335, 349–50 (1963) (concurring opinion), *quoting* Powell v. Alabama, 287 U.S. 45, 71 (1932). *See generally* Allen, 8 DE PAUL L. REV., *supra,* at 223–33.

4. 297 U.S. 278 (1936).

5. Traynor, *The Devils of Due Process in Criminal Detection, Detention, and Trial,* 33 U. CHI. L. REV. 657, 679 (1966), *referring to* Malloy v. Hogan, 378 U.S. 1 (1964).

6. Herman, *The Supreme Court and Restrictions on Police Interrogation,* 25 OHIO ST. L.J. 449, 465 (1964).

7. Griffin v. California, 380 U.S. 609 (1965).

8. 1 J. STEPHEN, HISTORY OF THE CRIMINAL LAW OF ENGLAND 441–42 (1883).

9. Even if the "legal mind" perceived any self-incrimination problems, it found comfort in the notion (which prevailed until the 1960s) that compulsion to testify meant legal compulsion only. Since the "subject" of police interrogation is threatened with neither a perjury charge for testifying falsely nor contempt for refusing to testify at all, he is not being "compelled" to be a "witness against himself" within the meaning of the privilege. *See generally* Kamisar, *A Dissent from the* Miranda *Dissents: Some Comments on the "New" Fifth Amendment and the Old "Voluntariness" Test,* 65 MICH. L. REV. 59, 65, 77–83 (1966) [reprinted in this volume]. One hopes that this contention was made for the last time in the *Miranda* oral arguments. *See* Unofficial Transcript of Oral Arguments in Miranda and Companion Cases, reprinted in Y. KAMISAR, W. LaFAVE & J. ISRAEL, MODERN CRIMINAL PROCEDURE 538 (4th ed. 1974).

10. *See generally* Kamisar, *Equal Justice in the Gatehouses and Mansions of American Criminal Procedure,* in CRIMINAL JUSTICE IN OUR TIME 21–24 (A. Howard ed. 1965) [reprinted in part in this volume].

11. Traynor, *supra* note 5, at 674.

12. Breitel, *Criminal Law and Equal Justice,* 1966 UTAH L. REV. 1, 16.

13. Friendly, *The Fifth Amendment Tomorrow: The Case for Constitutional Change,* 37 U. CIN. L. REV. 671, 713 n.180 (1968).

14. Kamisar, *supra* note 9, at 87.

15. Chafee, *Remedies for the Third Degree,* ATLANTIC MONTHLY, Nov. 1931, at 626, 630.

16. On the need for, and the constitutional right to, a prompt post-arrest judicial determination of probable cause, *see* Y. KAMISAR, W. LaFAVE & J. ISRAEL, *supra* note 9, at 286–88. Unlike French procedure, judicial examination under Kauper's proposal "should be limited to the specific charge for which the accused is under arrest.... [M]uch prolonged interrogation by the police results from the attempt to justify an unwarranted arrest. That motive would be absent in the case of magisterial questioning" (p. 1248).

[*Some months after this article was published, the Court held in Gerstein v. Pugh, 420 U.S. 103 (1975) (Powell, J.) that one arrested without a warrant is entitled, under the fourth amendment, to a timely "judicial determination of probable cause" as a prerequisite to extended restraint on liberty following arrest, but that the determination may be made without an "adversary hearing."* See generally 2 W. LaFAVE, SEARCH AND SEIZURE 244–52 (1978).]

17. W. SCHAEFER, THE SUSPECT AND SOCIETY 38 (1967).

18. *See* text *supra* at notes 41–47.

19. MODEL CODE OF PRE-ARRAIGNMENT PROCEDURE, Commentary at 40 (Study Draft No. 1, 1968).

20. Watts v. Indiana, 338 U.S. 49, 59 (1949) (Jackson, J., concurring and dissenting).

21. Brief of Edward L. Barrett, Jr., as amicus curiae at 9, People v. Dorado, 62 Cal. 2d 338, 398 P.2d 361, 42 Cal. Rptr. 169 (1965) (on rehearing).

22. Letter from Chief Judge David L. Bazelon to Professor Herbert Wechsler, Director of the American Law Institute, Nov. 16, 1965, *quoted in* W. SCHAEFER, *supra* note 17, at 91 n.77.

23. *See* cases collected in F. INBAU, J. THOMPSON, J. HADDAD, J. ZAGEL & G. STARKMAN, CASES AND COMMENTS ON CRIMINAL PROCEDURE 401-04 (1974); Y. KAMISAR, W. LAFAVE & J. ISRAEL, *supra* note 9, at 580–82. Whether or not *Miranda* applies to "street encounters" was once a lively issue. *Compare* LaFave, *"Street Encounters" and the Constitution: Terry, Sibron, Peters, and Beyond,* 67 MICH. L. REV. 39, 95–106 (1968), *with* Kamisar, *"Custodial Interrogation" Within the Meaning of* Miranda, in CRIMINAL LAW AND THE CONSTITUTION 335 (Inst. Cont. Legal Educ. ed. 1968). *See also* Graham, *What Is "Custodial Interrogation?": California's Anticipatory Application of* Miranda v. Arizona, 14 UCLA L. REV. 59, 78–92 (1966); Pye, *Interrogation of Criminal Defendants—Some Views on* Miranda v. Arizona, 35 FORDHAM L. REV. 199, 212 (1966). Today, however, if "custody" within the meaning of *Miranda* exists outside of the stationhouse, it does so only in "special circumstances," such as where the police have resorted to extraordinarily coercive measures (*e.g.,* where they have arrested a suspect at gunpoint or forcibly subdued him) or engaged in plainly evasive tactics (*e.g.,* where the ride to the stationhouse rivals that "supposedly taken by the driver with a gullible foreigner in his cab," Friendly, *supra* note 13, at 715).

That the present Supreme Court will interpret "custody" or "custodial" as have most lower courts is evidenced by its discussion of the "consent search" in Schneckloth v. Bustamonte, 412 U.S. 218 (1973). Justice Stewart observed for a 6–3 majority:

> [I]t would be thoroughly impractical to impose on the normal consent search the detailed requirements of an effective warning. Consent searches are part of the standard investigatory techniques of law enforcement agencies. *They normally occur on the highway, or in a person's home or office, and under informal and unstructured conditions. . . . [T]hese situations are . . . immeasurably far removed from* "custodial interrogation," where, in *Miranda . . . ,* we found that the Constitution required certain now familiar warnings. . . . In this case [the "consented" search of a car stopped by officers for traffic violations], there is no evidence of any inherently coercive tactics—either from the nature of the police questioning or the environment in which it took place. Indeed, *since consent searches will normally occur on a person's own familiar territory, the specter of incommunicado police interrogation in some remote station house is simply inapposite.* There is no reason to believe under circumstances such as are present here, that the response to a policeman's question is presumptively coerced; and there is, therefore, no reason to reject the traditional test for determining the voluntariness of a person's responses. *Miranda,* of course, did not reach investigative questioning of a person not in custody, which is most directly analogous to the situation of a consent search, and it assuredly did not indicate that such questioning ought to be deemed inherently coercive.

412 U.S. at 231–32, 247 (emphasis added).

Justices Stewart and White, the two *Miranda* dissenters still on the Court, have consistently taken the view in dissenting opinions that *Miranda* was designed "to guard against what was thought to be the corrosive influence of practices which station house interrogation makes feasible," Orozco v. Texas, 394 U.S. 324, 329 (1969) (White & Stewart, JJ., dissenting), and that its rationale "has no relevance to inquiries conducted outside the allegedly hostile and forbidding atmosphere surrounding police station interrogation of a criminal suspect." Mathis v. United States, 391 U.S. 1, 8 (1968) (White, Harlan & Stewart, JJ., dissenting).

24. *See* text *supra* at notes 37–47.

25. "Due process cannot be confined to a particular set of existing procedures because due process speaks for the future as well as the present, and at any given time includes those procedures that are fair and feasible in the light of then existing values and capabilities." Schaefer, *Federalism and State Criminal Procedure*, 70 HARV. L. REV. 1, 6 (1956).

26. *See* text preceding note 5 *supra*.

27. 316 U.S. 455 (1942).

28. 372 U.S. 335 (1963).

29. 407 U.S. 25 (1972).

30. Moffitt v. Ross, 483 F.2d 650, 655 (4th Cir. 1973) ("equality" principle requires appointment of counsel for discretionary appeals and applications for review in U.S. Supreme Court), *revd.,* 417 U.S. 600 (1974).

31. A. LEWIS, GIDEON'S TRUMPET 221 (1964). *But see* Kamisar, Book Review, 78 HARV. L. REV. 478, 479 (1964).

32. A. LEWIS, *supra* note 31, at 221.

33. 287 U.S. 45 (1932). *See* note 3 *supra* and accompanying text.

34. 304 U.S. 458 (1938).

35. Friendly, *supra* note 13, at 714, *quoting* Watts v. Indiana, 338 U.S. 49, 59 (1949) (Jackson, J., concurring and dissenting).

36. *See* Note, *Procedural Protections of the Criminal Defendant*, 78 HARV. L. REV. 426, 446, 447 (1964).

37. *See also* Pound, *Legal Interrogation of Persons Accused or Suspected of Crime,* 24 J. CRIM. L. & CRIMINOL. 1014, 1017 (1934), proposing "legal examination" of suspects before a magistrate and "provision . . . for taking down the evidence so as to guarantee accuracy. As things are, it is not the least of the abuses of the system of extralegal interrogation that there is a constant conflict of evidence as to what the accused said and as to the circumstances under which he said or was coerced into saying it."

38. *See* footnote 10 *supra*.

39. *See* MODEL CODE OF PRE-ARRAIGNMENT PROCEDURE, Commentary at 39–40 (Study Draft No. 1, 1968).

40. *See* text at notes 19–22 *supra*.

41. *See* footnote 10 *supra*.

42. Weisberg, *Police Interrogation of Arrested Persons: A Skeptical View,* in POLICE POWER AND INDIVIDUAL FREEDOM 153, 180 (C. Sowle ed. 1962).

43. In F. INBAU & J. REID, CRIMINAL INTERROGATION AND CONFESSIONS 1 (2d ed. 1967), Professor Inbau and Mr. Reid take the position that "all but a very few of the interrogation tactics and techniques presented in our earlier [pre-*Miranda*] publication are still valid if used after the recently prescribed warnings have been given to the suspect under interrogation, and after he has waived his [rights]." Thus, "aside

from . . . a prescription of the steps that must be taken to comply with *Miranda*, the [new Inbau & Reid edition] seems very close to the version that vented Chief Justice Warren's judicial ire. . . ." Broderick, Book Review, 53 CORNELL L. REV. 737, 741 (1968). *Miranda*, however, "did not condemn any specific techniques as such or hold that evidence obtained by use of them would be inadmissible. Reliance was placed on warning and counsel to protect the suspect." Elsen & Rosett, *Protections for the Suspect Under* Miranda v. Arizona, 67 COLUM. L. REV. 645, 667 (1967).

44. H. UVILLER, THE PROCESS OF CRIMINAL JUSTICE: INVESTIGATION 569 (1974). [*Five years after this article was published, Professor Welsh White made a major effort to resolve the problems in this difficult and largely neglected area, considering especially the restrictions, if any, placed on a police interrogator* after *a suspect has waived his fifth and sixth amendment rights. See White,* Police Trickery in Inducing Confessions, *127 U. PA. L. REV. 581 (1979).*]

45. Traynor, *supra* note 5, at 678.

46. Amsterdam, *The Supreme Court and the Rights of Suspects in Criminal Cases,* 45 N.Y.U.L. REV. 785, 792 (1970), in THE RIGHTS OF AMERICANS 401, 408 (N. Dorsen ed. 1971).

47. Hofstadter & Levittan, *Lest the Constable Blunder: A Remedial Proposal,* 20 RECORD OF N.Y.C.B.A. 629, 630 (1956).

48. W. SCHAEFER, *supra* note 17, at 9.

49. Miranda v. Arizona, 384 U.S. 477 (1966).

50. 384 U.S. at 477.

51. *See* footnote 10 *supra.*

52. Breitel, *supra* note 12, at 1.

53. *See, e.g.,* the suggested projection of the *Miranda* rationale in Thompson, *Dentention After Arrest and In-Custody: Some Exclusionary Principles,* 1966 U. ILL. L.F. 390, 421–22.

54. Kamisar, *supra* note 10, at 85–85, *quoting* Weisberg, *supra* note 42, at 179.

55. W. SCHAEFER, *supra* note 17, at 79.

56. Hofstadter & Levittan, *supra* note 47, at 635.

57. W. SCHAEFER, *supra* note 17, at 80. *See also* Note, *supra* note 36, at 446.

58. 384 U.S. at 467.

59. 384 U.S. at 468.

60. 384 U.S. at 468 n.37.

61. It is not at all clear that a law enforcement officer can advise a suspect with perfect honesty that his silence will not be used against him. It is doubtful that police or prosecutors can, or should, eliminate a suspect's silence from their minds. *See* Elsen & Rosett, *supra* note 43, at 655 (both authors are former federal prosecuting attorneys); LaFave, *supra* note 23, at 106–09. At the time of *Miranda,* however, and at least in the immediately succeeding years (complications may now be setting in, *see* footnote 10 *supra*), an officer could with complete honesty inform a suspect that his silence may not be used against him *at trial.* One can only speculate whether *Miranda's* failure to require the police to issue such a warning was a mere oversight or a policy decision not to stiffen further some suspects' resistance to talk.

62. Elsen & Rosett, *supra* note 43, at 654.

63. 384 U.S. at 469.

64. "Prosecutors themselves claim that the admonishment of the right to remain

silent without more 'will benefit only the recidivist and the professional.'... Even preliminary advice given to the accused by his own attorney can be swiftly overcome by the secret interrogation process." 384 U.S. at 470, *quoting* Brief for the Nat'l District Attorneys Ass'n as amicus curiae.

65. "Unless adequate protective devices are employed to dispel the compulsion inherent in custodial surroundings, no statement obtained from the defendant can truly be the product of his free choice." 384 U.S. at 458.

66. Project, *Interrogations in New Haven: The Impact of* Miranda, 76 YALE L.J. 1519, 1551–52, 1571–72, 1614–15 (1967).

67. 384 U.S. at 461.

68. Traynor, *supra* note 5, at 676.

69. Friendly, *supra* note 13, at 713.

70. As a result of the District of Columbia experience, the Junior Bar "recommended 'that the most efficient way of providing legal counsel upon arrest would be in connection with a prompt presentment before a committing magistrate, available at a downtown location on a 24-hour basis.'" Medalie, Zeitz & Alexander, *Custodial Interrogation in Our Nation's Capital: The Attempt to Implement* Miranda, 66 MICH. L. REV. 1347, 1398 (1969).

71. Friendly, *supra* note 13, at 713–14.

Fred E. Inbau: "The Importance of Being Guilty"

1. Allen, *The Judicial Quest for Penal Justice: The Warren Court and the Criminal Cases,* 1975 U. ILL. L.F. 518, 521.

2. Kamisar, *Kauper's "Judicial Examination of the Accused" Forty Years Later— Some Comments on a Remarkable Article,* 73 MICH. L. REV. 15, 16 (1974) [reprinted in this volume].

3. Paulsen, *Safeguards in the Law of Search and Seizure,* 52 Nw. U.L. REV. 65, 66 (1957).

4. *Id.* But Inbau also told the police, very early in his career, that they themselves "must share a large portion of the blame for the unfortunate practical result of decisions such as those in the *McNabb* [case]. Known instances of miscarriages of justice resulting from the use of force and threats in obtaining confessions have rightfully induced the courts to view with caution all criminal confessions. Better interrogation practices on the part of the police profession as a whole would undoubtedly result in sounder and more practical legal decisions involving criminal confessions." Inbau, *The Courts on Confessions,* THE POLICE DIGEST, Dec. 1943, at 13, 15.

5. F. INBAU, LIE DETECTION AND CRIMINAL INTERROGATION 119–33 (1st ed. 1942).

6. 43 ILL. L. REV. 442 (1948).

7. McNabb v. United States, 318 U.S. 332 (1943).

8. Mallory v. United States, 354 U.S. 449 (1957).

9. 18 U.S.C. § 3501(c) (1970).

10. Ashcraft v. Tennessee, 322 U.S. 143 (1944).

11. 318 U.S. at 341.

12. *Id.*

13. "Judicial supervision of the administration of criminal justice in the federal courts implies the duty of establishing and maintaining civilized standards of procedure and evidence. Such standards are not satisfied merely by observance of those minimal historic safeguards for securing trial by reason which are summarized as 'due process of law'. . . " *Id.* at 340 (Frankfurter, J.). Inbau often referred to the *McNabb* case or the *McNabb-Mallory* rule as the "civilized standards" rule. *See* note 44 *infra.*

14. *See, e.g.,* Watts v. Indiana, 338 U.S. 49, 57 (1949) (Douglas, J., concurring): "Detention without arraignment is a time-honored method for keeping an accused under the exclusive control of the police. . . . We should unequivocally condemn the procedure and stand ready to outlaw . . . any confession obtained during the period of the unlawful detention. The procedure breeds coerced confessions. It is the root of the evil."

15. *Cf.* Brief for the State of Illinois, Escobedo v. Illinois, 378 U.S. 478 (1964), reprinted in Y. KAMISAR, W. LaFAVE & J. ISRAEL, MODERN CRIMINAL PROCEDURE 522 (4th ed. 1974):

"To push the right to counsel back to the point of arrest and to exclude all incriminating statements obtained from an uncounselled defendant anytime thereafter as a product of a fourteenth amendment violation would be, in effect, to impose the *McNabb-Mallory* rule on the states." [*quoting* Kamisar, *The Right to Counsel and the Fourteenth Amendment,* 30 U. CHI. L. REV. 1, 9 (1962).] Indeed, it would be to go beyond the *Mallory* rule which forbids the admission in evidence only of those statements taken during a period of unlawful detention which may not, in any given case, begin at the moment of arrest.

16. 322 U.S. at 156 (Jackson, J., joined by Roberts & Frankfurter, JJ., dissenting).

17. *See* Jacobellis v. Ohio, 378 U.S. 184, 197 (1964) (Stewart, J., concurring).

18. 322 U.S. at 149 (emphasis added).

19. *See id.* at 165–67 (Jackson, J., dissenting).

20. John Lord O'Brian, in MR. JUSTICE JACKSON 9 (Legal Studies of the William Nelson Cromwell Foundation, 1969) (introduction to speech by Hon. Charles S. Desmond in honor of Justice Jackson).

21. *Cf.* A. LEWIS, GIDEON'S TRUMPET 221–22 (1964).

22. Miranda v. Arizona, 384 U.S. 436 (1966).

23. It is probably true that today "nobody, 'liberal' or 'conservative,' is happy with *Miranda,*" Frankel, *From Private Fights Toward Public Justices,* 51 N.Y.U.L. REV. 516, 526 (1976), and there is substantial cause for viewing it as "at best a tense, temporary, ragged truce between combatants." *Id.* Nevertheless, I doubt that *Miranda* will be formally overruled. *But see* F. INBAU, J. THOMPSON, J. HADDAD, J. ZAGEL & G. STARKMAN, CASES AND COMMENTS ON CRIMINAL PROCEDURE 355 (1974). If *Miranda,* or some form of it, does survive, however, it will probably be only because niggardly interpretations of it, *e.g.,* Harris v. New York, 401 U.S. 222 (1971); Michigan v. Mosley, 423 U.S. 96 (1975); Oregon v. Mathiason, 429 U.S. 492 (1977), have sufficiently soothed its critics on the Court.

24. Laski, *The Limitations of the Expert,* 162 HARPER'S MONTHLY 101, 104 (1930).

25. *Id.* at 106.

26. Emerson, *The American Scholar,* in THE PORTABLE EMERSON 44 (M. Van Doren ed. 1946).

27. *Id.* at 32.

28. B. CARDOZO, *Law and Literature,* in LAW AND LITERATURE AND OTHER ESSAYS AND ADDRESSES 18 (1931).

29. Terry v. Ohio, 392 U.S. 1 (1968); Sibron v. New York, 392 U.S. 40 (1968); Peters v. New York, 392 U.S. 40 (1968).

30. Unpublished address by Fred E. Inbau, "Misconceptions Regarding Lawlessness and Law Enforcement," Northwestern Law Alumni Annual Luncheon. Chicago, Ill. (Sept. 26, 1967) at 4–6 (on file in the law libraries of Northwestern University and the University of Michigan).

31. Inbau, *Behind Those "Police Brutality" Charges,* 89 READER'S DIGEST 1 (July 1966).

32. *See* note 4 *supra.*

33. Inbau, *Misconceptions Regarding Lawlessness and Law Enforcement,* THE POLICE JOURNAL, Oct. 1969, at 458.

34. Inbau, *Lawlessness Galore,* POLICE-LAW REVIEW, Aug.–Sept. 1965, at 3.

35. Address by Fred E. Inbau, "The Arrestee and Legal Counsel," Annual Conference of Chief Justices, Washington, D.C. (Aug. 9, 1963) (on file in the law libraries of Northwestern University and the University of Michigan).

36. *See, e.g.,* Inbau, *Public Safety v. Individual Civil Liberties: The Prosecutor's Stand,* 53 J. CRIM. L.C. & P.S. 85 (1962). This paper, also discussed at p. 106 *supra,* had been the keynote address at the 1961 Annual Conference of the National District Attorneys Association in Portland, Oregon.

37. Address by Fred E. Inbau, "Misconceptions Regarding Lawlessness and Law Enforcement," 23rd annual meeting of National Association of Independent Insurers, New York, N.Y. (Oct. 29, 1968) (on file in the law libraries of Northwestern University and the University of Michigan).

38. Address by Fred E. Inbau, "Crime in Our Streets—and What Can Be Done About It?", Governmental Affairs Council, Chicago Association of Commerce and Industry, Chicago, Ill. (Jan. 25, 1968) (on file in the law libraries of Northwestern University and the University of Michigan).

39. *See Lawlessness Galore,* THE TULANIAN, Dec. 1966, at 15.

40. Laski, *supra* note 24, at 108.

41. One notable exception is C. Black, *The Lawfulness of the Segregation Decisions,* 69 YALE L.J. 421 (1960). *But see* C. Black, *Civil Rights in Times of Economic Stress—Jurisprudential and Philosophic Aspects,* 1976 U. ILL. L.F. 559.

42. *Fiddler on the Roof,* Act I, Scene VI, in BEST PLAYS OF THE SIXTIES 283 (S. Richards ed. 1970).

It is hoped those who *arrive at* strong conclusions engage in "on the one hand—on the other hand—*but on the other* hand" thinking somewhere along the way. It seems, however, that the preferred style is not to do so *before* the speech is delivered or the article is published, but "out loud" *in* one's speech or article—better yet, perhaps, *in one's conclusions.*

43. In an "editorial," *"Playing God": 5 to 4,* 57 J. CRIM. L.C. & P.S. 377–78 (1966), Inbau, then editor-in-chief of the *Journal,* ripped into "the Court's one man

majority" for continuing to "play God" when the ALI, ABA, various governmental commissions and other groups were

> seeking to find a proximate solution to some very difficult problems. . . . But a one-man majority of the Court in *Miranda* "pulled the rug" from underneath all of these studies and research groups, and effectively foreclosed a final evaluation of their ultimate findings and recommendations. . . . Considering the complexity of the interrogation-confession problem, a summary 5 to 4 nullification of much of the aforementioned group efforts . . . is awesomely inconsistent with fundamental democratic concepts. It's more like "Playing God: 5 to 4."

A year and a half later, Inbau took cognizance of the fact that his "Playing God" editorial had "infuriated many of my colleagues in the law school world," but "[w]hat I said then may be appropriately repeated now, although I regret whatever infuriation it may again arouse among my law professor colleagues who may be in the audience tonight." Unpublished address by Fred. E. Inbau, "Crime and the Supreme Court," Symposium by the Council of Graduate Students, Ohio State University, Columbus, Ohio (April 24, 1968) (on file in the law libraries of Northwestern University and the University of Michigan).

44. In *Hearings Before a Subcomm. of the Senate Committee on the Judiciary,* 85th Cong., 2d Sess., on H.R. 11477, S. 2970, S. 3325 and S. 3355, at 58, 65 (1958) [hereinafter cited as *1958 Senate Hearings*], Inbau (who stressed at the outset that he did not appear "just" in "his capacity" as a law professor, but as one with much "practical experience") "explained" how the *McNabb* innovation came about:

> Unfortunately the United States Supreme Court, and it was made up at that time of some even more sensitive souls than we see, perhaps at the present time—there were some law professors on it, ex-law professors—and they assumed that these practices which were revealed in these [coerced confession] decisions were commonplace, they were universal, and the Court, acting in that feeling of resentment, laid down in the *McNabb* case its so-called civilized standards rule.

45. Immediately after earning a master's in law at Northwestern University in 1933, Inbau became a member of the Scientific Crime Detection Laboratory at the Northwestern University School of Law, the first such laboratory in the country. When the Chicago Police Department took over the laboratory in 1938, he became its first director and served in this capacity until 1941. For the eight years he was associated with the crime detection laboratory, "criminal interrogation" was his "special interest." *See 1958 Senate Hearings, supra* note 44, at 58. From 1941 until 1945, when he returned to Northwestern as a professor of law, Inbau was a trial attorney. At one time or another he was president of the Illinois Academy of Criminology, the American Academy of Forensic Sciences and the American Academy of Polygraph Examiners.

46. *See* Lewellen, *How to Make a Killer Confess,* SAT. EVE. POST, Mar. 31, 1956, at 33.

47. I do not come here to visit with you in my capacity as a criminal-law professor. I know from my own practical experience, both as a trial lawyer and by reason of my work in the police field, that there is an allergy toward professors on the part of

people who are out on the firing line. I prefer to represent myself to you as one who has had experience in this area of interrogation.

Inbau, in *A Forum on the Interrogation of the Accused,* 49 CORNELL L.Q. 382, 387 (1964) (panel discussion sponsored by the District Attorneys Association of the State of New York). *See also 1958 Senate Hearings, supra* note 44, at 58.

48. *See* S. KRISLOV, THE SUPREME COURT AND POLITICAL FREEDOM 2 (1968).

49. Inbau, I am sure, regarded his being named the first John Henry Wigmore Professor at the Northwestern University School of Law as being given the highest honor that could be bestowed on any student of criminal law and evidence. Wigmore was the organizer and founder of the Scientific Crime Detection Laboratory, to which Inbau devoted the first decade of his professional life. Wigmore also launched *The Journal of Criminal Law and Criminology* in 1910 and contributed "a forthright comment . . . upon a recent criminal case" to its first issue. Inbau, *The Innovator (Editorial),* 32 J. CRIM. L.C. & P.S. 263, 264 (1941). Inbau, of course, was deeply devoted, and a frequent contributor, to the *Journal* all of his professional life. He served as its managing director from 1945–65, and then its editor-in-chief until 1971, when student editors took complete charge of the publication.

The last activity in Wigmore's extraordinary career was participation, along with Inbau, in a regular meeting of the Board of Editors of the *Journal* (April 20, 1943). He died a few hours later. Inbau was the last person to talk to Wigmore. He hailed the cab in which Wigmore met his death.

Wigmore's "last words" on the U.S. Supreme Court were words of reproachment for its recent decision in the *McNabb* case: "He shook his head slowly as he said prophetically that he could see neither sense nor reason in it; that it is bound to cause trouble for it makes it almost impossible for either the police or the prosecutor to get anywhere with their cases; and that he did not know what the Supreme Court could have been thinking about when it wrote that opinion." Curran, *Dean Wigmore at His Last Meeting of the Editorial Board,* 34 J. CRIM. L.C. & P.S. 93, 94 (1943).

The decision in Escobedo v. Illinois, 378 U.S. 478 (1964), was hard enough for Inbau to take, but for Justice Goldberg, author of the opinion of the Court, to find support for his viewpoint in the writings of Wigmore was almost more than Inbau could bear. *See* his remarks in *The Supreme Court's Decisions on Defendants' Rights and Criminal Procedures,* 39 F.R.D. 423, 441 (1966) (panel discussion):

I think it is a serious mistake to say that when we ask for an interrogation opportunity on the part of the police we are asking for the abolition of the privilege against self-incrimination. Unfortunately, Justice Goldberg made the same error in his opinion in the *Escobedo* case. If you recall, . . . he quotes Dean Wigmore's reasons in support of the privilege [378 U.S. at 489, quoting from 8 J. WIGMORE, EVIDENCE § 2251, at 309 (3d ed. 1940)] and then equates that with his approval of the exclusionary rule and the present rules with respect to confession admissibility. Justice Goldberg, I think, should have known better. He was a student of Wigmore's. And Wigmore's treatise very clearly indicates his violent opposition to the exclusionary rule and to any rule of confession admissibility other than one based upon the trustworthiness factor.

I not only know that from Wigmore's writings, but I knew the gentleman very well. . . . I am quite sure he would be greatly disturbed to see himself quoted in the *Escobedo* case as though he were supporting that viewpoint.

As I read the 130-page discussion of confessions in volume 3 of the *Treatise on Evidence,* a volume to which the *Escobedo* opinion never refers, Inbau is plainly right about Wigmore. *See* 3 J. WIGMORE §§ 22–24, 826, 841–43, 856–59, 865, 867 (3d. ed. 1940).

50. Roalfe, *John Henry Wigmore—Scholar and Reformer,* 53 J. CRIM. L.C. & P.S. 277, 280 (1962).

51. In addition to the examples furnished by Roalfe, *supra* note 50, *see especially* Wigmore, *Abrams v. U.S.: Freedom of Speech and Freedom of Thuggery in War-Time and Peace-Time,* 14 ILL. L. REV. 539 (1920) (blistering attack on Holmes-Brandeis position). *See also* note 53 *infra* and text *supra* at notes 54–57.

52. Kocourek, *John Henry Wigmore,* 27 AM. JUD. SOC'Y 122, 124 (1943).

53. Frankfurter, *John Henry Wigmore: A Centennial Tribute,* 58 NW. U.L. REV. 443 (1963), *reprinted in* F. FRANKFURTER, OF LAW AND LIFE & OTHER THINGS THAT MATTER 256 (P. Kurland ed. 1965). In the controversy growing out of the Sacco-Vanzetti case, Professor Frankfurter had been a target of Wigmore's biting tongue. "He never referred to Frankfurter by name but called him the 'plausible Pundit' or 'contra-canonical critic' because of his alleged violation of the [canons of ethics]." Roalfe, *supra* note 50, at 280.

54. 8 J. WIGMORE, EVIDENCE § 2183, at 4–5 (3d ed. 1940).

55. *Id.* § 2184, at 32–34.

56. *Id.* at 35–37.

57. *Id.* § 2184*b,* at 50. *Cf.* Inbau, *Police Interrogation—A Practical Necessity,* 52 J. CRIM. L.C. & P.S. 16, 19 (1961), *reprinted in* POLICE POWER AND INDIVIDUAL FREEDOM 147, 151 (C. Sowle ed. 1962):

[T]he interrogation [of the murder suspect in an actual case within Inbau's "own professional experience"] was "unethical" according to the standards usually set for professional, business and social conduct. . . . But, under the circumstances involved in this case, how else would the murderer's guilt have been established? Moreover, . . . [f]rom the criminal's point of view, *any* interrogation of him is objectionable. To *him* it may be a "dirty trick" to be talked into a confession, for surely it was not done for his benefit.

58. *See* note 36 *supra.*

59. Kamisar, *Public Safety v. Individual Liberties: Some "Facts" and "Theories,"* 53 J. CRIM. L.C. & P.S. 171 (1962). We then went another round: Inbau, *More About Public Safety v. Individual Civil Liberties,* 53 J. CRIM. L.C. & P.S. 329 (1962); Kamisar, *Some Reflections on Criticizing the Courts and "Policing the Police,"* 53 J. CRIM. L.C. & P.S. 453 (1962).

60. *Cf.* A. BICKEL, THE LEAST DANGEROUS BRANCH 265 (1962).

61. Some years later, then Assistant Professor Thompson spelled out his views on the subject in *Detention After Arrest and In-Custody Investigation: Some Exclusionary Principles,* 1966 U. ILL. L.F. 390, 402–14.

62. Kamisar, *Equal Justice in the Gatehouses and Mansions of American Criminal Procedure,* in CRIMINAL JUSTICE IN OUR TIME (Howard ed. 1965) [reprinted in part

in this volume]. Unfortunately, on the erroneous assumption that Professor Sowle's remarks would later be published, I took no notes at the time, only to discover later that the speaker had destroyed his. I again acknowledge my large debt to Sowle. *See also id.* at 20 n.53.

63. Crooker v. California, 357 U.S. 433, 441 (1958) (emphasis in original).

64. A few months earlier, although I did not discover this until many years later, Inbau had done more than simply defend the civil libertarian's right to have his say before a police audience. *See* unpublished and untitled address of May 28, 1962 (emphasis added), at Williamette College of Law, Salem, Ore. (on file in the law libraries of Northwestern University and the University of Michigan). He had told a group of police officers:

> Too often there is the tendency on the part of the police to criticize all that the courts do—to label as technicalities the reasons given for any particular case decision that the individual police officer dislikes. There are times, to be sure, when that is true. But there are many times when the reasons are substantial and basically valid. . . .
>
> As a police officer you may feel that the courts should leave you alone in your efforts to enforce the law, to apprehend criminals and to protect the public. Many courts would also like to be left alone to do as they please. Many legislators would also like to be left alone and unchecked. Many members of the executive branch . . . would also like to function as they please. But in a democratic system, no branch of government, can be permitted to exercise unbridled authority and power. . . .
>
> In any democratic society individual rights and liberties must be preserved and we are willing to do so at the expense of efficiency in government itself. To relate this principle to your situation, let me put it this way. We would rather that some criminals escape detection and punishment—even though you, as a police officer, know positively he is guilty—rather than sacrifice or even jeopardize the rights and liberties of the great mass of individuals who make up this democratic society of ours. This concept is essential. *It is different in Russia, of course. There, efficiency is paramount* [emphasis added].

Parts of this speech read as if they came right out of a Hugo Black opinion or Professor Louis B. Schwartz's ringing civil liberties article, *On Current Proposals to Legalize Wire Tapping,* 103 U. Pa. L. Rev. 157 (1954).

65. Rostow, Book Review, 56 Yale L.J. 412, 413 (1947) (referring to Morris R. Cohen).

66. Weisberg, *Police Interrogation of Arrested Persons: A Skeptical View,* 52 J. Crim. L.C. & P.S. 21 (1961), in Police Power and Individual Freedom 153 (C. Sowle ed. 1962).

Of course, Weisberg's criticism of the old "voluntariness" test applies to *Miranda* as well, at least as it has generally been applied. Although language in *Miranda,* 384 U.S. at 475, strongly suggests that, at least where feasible, the police must stenographically or, better yet, electronically record the warnings given to the suspect, as well as his reponse, so that they may be played back or shown to the court, "most courts have held that the testimony of an officer that he gave the warnings is sufficient and need not be corroborated." ALI MODEL CODE OF PRE-ARRAIGNMENT PROCEDURE 140 (commentary) (Tent. Draft No. 6, 1974).

Weisberg's extraordinary 1960 paper also anticipates and voices grave doubts about the efficacy of a system based on *police-issued* cautions or warnings:

> [A]ny rule which requires a caution inevitably invites avoidance. Even if it is tied to an objective event such as the commencement of interrogation or the time of arrest, the probable conflict of testimony about whether a required caution was in fact given makes satisfactory judicial enforcement doubtful. Any rule requiring a warning is also likely to be ineffectual since the significance and effect of a warning depend primarily on the emphasis and the spirit in which it was given. A warning can easily become a meaningless ritual. . . . The notion that [the interrogator] should precede questioning with a caution suggests that the interrogator should act to protect the interests of the suspect at the same time that he is attempting to obtain damaging statements from him. But this cannot effectively substitute for the loyalty of counsel or the disinterestedness of a judge.

Weisberg, *supra* at 40–41.

67. Weisberg, *supra* note 66, at 22.

68. *Id.*

69. *Id.* at 22–23.

70. Kamisar, *A Dissent from the* Miranda *Dissents,* 65 MICH. L. REV. 59, 86 (1966) [reprinted in this volume].

71. Packer, *Two Models of the Criminal Process,* 113 U. PA. L. REV. 1, 64 (1964).

72. Inbau didn't gain a "clean sweep." Barry L. Kroll, a Michigan Law School graduate, argued the case for Danny Escobedo.

73. See the extracts from the brief in Y. KAMISAR, W. LaFAVE & J. ISRAEL, MODERN CRIMINAL PROCEDURE 519 (4th ed. 1974).

74. *Id.*

75. Miranda v. Arizona, 384 U.S. 436, 449–54 (1966).

76. *Id.* at 448. The *Miranda* dissenters criticized the Court for failing to establish that any of the manuals were the "official manuals" of any police department or even that they were widely used by police interrogators, and voiced doubts that they were, 384 U.S. at 499, 532–33. Two weeks after *Miranda* was handed down, however, Thomas C. Lynch, then Attorney General of California, reported that a preliminary survey indicated "wide use" in his state of the criticized manuals and that he was considering a "purge" of all such publications. Professor Philip Zimbardo, a psychologist greatly troubled by various interrogation techniques, also reported that he had "verified that these manuals are used in training [police] interrogators by calling several police academies." *See* Kamisar, *supra* note 70, at 86 n.109.

77. *See, e.g.,* E. GRISWOLD, THE FIFTH AMENDMENT TODAY 7 (1955).

78. *See* 384 U.S. at 449–55. The references are to F. INBAU & J. REID, CRIMINAL INTERROGATION AND CONFESSIONS (1962); F. INBAU & J. REID, LIE DETECTION AND CRIMINAL INTERROGATION (3d ed. 1953).

79. Broderick, Book Review, 53 CORNELL L. REV. 737, 741 (1968).

80. Allen, *The Judicial Quest for Penal Justice: The Warren Court and the Criminal Cases,* 1975 U. ILL. L.F. 518, 539.

81. *But see* Kamisar, *How to Use, Abuse—and Fight Back with—Crime Statistics,* 25 OKLA. L. REV. 239 (1972).

82. Allen, *supra* note 80, at 539.

83. Jaffe, *Impromptu Remarks,* 76 HARV. L. REV. 1111 (1963).

84. *Id.*

85. *See* footnote 9 *supra.*

86. *See* the introduction to the collection of conference papers in POLICE POWER AND INDIVIDUAL FREEDOM (C. Sowle ed. 1962).

87. D. STENERSON, H.L. MENCKEN: ICONCLAST FROM BALTIMORE 226 (1971).

Brewer v. Williams—A Hard Look at a Discomfiting Record

1. Brief for Petitioner, Joint App. at 75, Brewer v. Williams, 430 U.S. 387 (1977).

2. Brewer v. Williams, 430 U.S. 384, 416 (1977) (Burger, C.J. dissenting).

3. *See* text *supra* at notes 35–36.

4. 430 U.S. at 390.

5. Brief for Petitioner at 4, Brewer v. Williams, 430 U.S. 387 (1977).

6. 430 U.S. at 412 (Powell, J., concurring).

7. Brief for Petitioner, Joint App. at 24–25.

8. *Id.* at 25, 37–38, 53, 60, 97.

9. *See id.* at 42 (Lieutenant Ackerman testifying that Williams was warned of his rights when arrested); *id.* at 45 (Lieutenant Ackerman testifying that Williams conferred with Kelly his Davenport lawyer); *id.* at 47 (Williams testifying that McKnight told him over the phone not to answer any questions until he was in McKnight's presence); *id.* at 49–51 (Williams testifying that he was advised of his rights by Lieutenant Ackerman and Judge Metcalf and that he conferred with Kelly on several occasions); *id.* at 52 (Williams testifying that Kelly advised him to do his talking when he got to his lawyer in Des Moines); *id.* at 75 (Captain Leaming testifying that he advised Williams of his rights).

10. *Id.* at 50.

11. *Id.* at 44, 73.

12. *Id.* at 75 (testimony of Captain Leaming).

13. *Id.* at 76 (testimony of Captain Leaming).

14. *Id.* at 58, 61 (emphasis added) (testimony of Captain Leaming); *see id.* at 60, 65 (same).

15. *Id.* at 48, 56, 93, 98.

16. This point is graphically illustrated by the 1963 congressional testimony of David Acheson, then United States attorney for the District of Columbia:

[I]n some very high percentage of the cases a confession is made if it is going to be made at all, within an hour or two, perhaps 3 hours after arrest. In the great majority of cases a confession is made fairly promptly after arrest. . . . At the present time for all practical purposes if [a suspect] can hold out for 2 hours, 2½ hours, he is pretty well in the clear, but very few of them do.

Hearings on H.R. 7525 and S. 486 Before the Senate Comm. on the District of Columbia, 88th Cong., 1st Sess. 443 (1963).

17. Brief for Petitioner, Joint App. at 1–2.

18. Williams v. Brewer, 375 F. Supp. 170, 173, 176 (S.D. Iowa 1974). In the federal district court both sides agreed that the case would be submitted on the trial court record without the taking of further testimony. *Id.* at 172. The federal court, however, made many more findings of fact than had the state court.

19. *See* Brief for Petitioners, Joint App. at 55 (Leaming denying that Kelly requested permission to ride with him to Des Moines); *id.* at 61, 78, 90 (Leaming denying that Kelly told him not to question Williams during the ride back to Des Moines).

20. 375 F. Supp. at 173, 176.

21. *Id.*

22. Detective Nelson, who drove the car on the return trip to Des Moines while Leaming and Williams "visited" in the back seat, was unable to make out "much of the conversation" because Williams "spoke so low." Brief for Petitioner, Joint App. at 101. He did, however, sharply contradict Leaming on one important point. Sometime before Williams announced that he was going to reveal where the little girl's body was, Williams asked the captain whether the police had found "a girl's shoes" or "her shoes." *Id.* at 58, 81. When the captain replied that he did not know, Williams (according to Leaming) pointed to a Skelly station that could be seen from the expressway and said that he had put the shoes there. *Id.* at 58–59, 82. Judge Webster, dissenting from the Eighth Circuit's decision that Williams's disclosures should have been excluded, maintained that Williams's question about the shoes was "triggered . . . by something [he] saw . . . a filling station." Williams v. Brewer, 509 F.2d 227, 237 (8th Cir. 1974); *see* Brewer v. Williams, 430 U.S. 387, 433 (White, J., dissenting) (Williams asked about victim's clothing because he saw gas station where he had concealed her shoes).

According to Detective Nelson, however, when Williams raised the question of the girl's shoes, the filling station just off the Grinnell exit was not yet in view: "We hadn't come to Grinnell. We were quite a ways away yet at that time." And "we asked Williams if the boots were with the other articles and he stated no, they were behind the filling station . . . just off the exit to Grinnell." Brief for Petitioner, Joint App. at 100. According to Nelson, he then asked Williams *which* Grinnell exit to take and when Williams told him and they came upon two filling stations, he then asked Williams which station was the one where he had put the shoes. *Id.* When Williams told him, according to Nelson, he asked Williams where the boots would be if they were there. *Id.* The filling station owner also testified that when Williams and the two detectives drove into his station, one of the dectives asked Williams, "Now where did you put the boots at?" *Id.* at 72.

In short, according to Leaming—whose version seems to have been regarded by the courts as the only version—Williams saw the filling station as they were driving along the freeway and led the police from the freeway to the trash receptacle behind the filling station *without being asked a single question;* Williams just "nodded his head, that station right over there as we were coming along the freeway and at that time you could see it up there." *Id.* at 59. According to Nelson, however, there was no station "right over there," and when Williams brought up the subject of the shoes, the police asked at least *four questions* before Williams looked in the receptacle behind the filling station.

23. 377 U.S. 201 (1964).

24. 384 U.S. 436 (1966).

25. *See* text *supra* at notes 35–36.

26. *Compare* Brief for Petitioner, Joint App. at 63 (not very far out of Davenport on the way to Des Moines) *with id*. at 81 (much discussion preceded the speech).

27. *See id*. at 104 (Nelson testifying that immediately after they got on the freeway, Leaming asked Williams to think about revealing the location of the body).

28. *See id*. at 55, 75 (Captain Leaming testifying that he reminded Williams of his *Miranda* rights and that he was represented by counsel "because we'll be visiting between here and Des Moines").

29. *Id*. at 81.

30. *Id*.

31. *Id*. at 87.

32. *See* Brewer v. Williams, 430 U.S. 387, 392–93 (1977) (quoting only from second version without acknowledging that there is another version); *id*. at 431–32 (White, J., with Blackmun & Rehnquist, JJ., dissenting) (same); Williams v. Brewer, 509 F.2d 227, 230 (8th Cir. 1974) (same); *id*. at 235 (Webster, J., dissenting) (same); Williams v. Brewer, 375 F. Supp. 170, 174–75 (S.D. Iowa 1974) (same); State v. Williams, 182 N.W.2d 396, 403 (Iowa 1971) (quoting briefly from the first version without acknowledging that there is another version); *id*. at 407 (Stuart, J., dissenting) (quoting from second version without acknowledging that he is quoting from different version from that which majority used).

33. Brief for Petitioner, Joint App. at 63.

34. *Id*. at 66, 81, 84.

35. *Id*. at 63.

36. *Id*. at 81–84.

37. *Cf*. Foote, *The Fourth Amendment: Obstacle or Necessity in the Law of Arrest?*, in POLICE POWER AND INDIVIDUAL FREEDOM 29, 30 (C. Sowle ed. 1962) (discussing on-the-street questioning by investigative officers). Professor Foote only deals with a situation in which an officer stops a person on the street and questions him as to his identity and reason for being where he is, a confrontation that falls short of a full-fledged arrest. But Williams was plainly under arrest, plainly in custody, and thus experiencing additional coercion and anxiety.

38. Brief for Petitioner, Joint App. at 96 (testimony of Captain Leaming).

39. *See* footnote 8 *supra*.

40. At the pretrial hearing, Lieutenant Ackerman stated emphatically and repeatedly that he made no effort to question Williams and that the latter said nothing to him at all. Brief for Petitioner, Joint App. at 44–45. At the trial, however, when the lieutenant was cross-examined by Williams's attorney, the following colloquy took place:

Q. Now didn't you yourself want to question this defendant?

A. Yes, sir, I did.

Q. What did he say to you?

A. I only asked him one question, where was the little girl and was she safe. I told him that we were worried about the safety and the health of the little girl, and if she was alive and if she was in the area, we would like to know so that we could get help to her.

Q. Did he tell you that you ask my lawyer anything you want to know?

A. No, sir, he did not.

Q. What did he say?

A. He said, "Don't you know."

Q. Then what did he say?

A. I says, "Know what?" And, "My lawyer knows."

Q. He said his lawyer knows?

A. His lawyer knows, and that's all that was said.

. . . .

Q. Now let's forget about this violation of the constitutional rights. Let me ask you this [moving on to another topic].

Id. at 72–73.

It is hard to believe that when he headed home with Williams, Captain Leaming had not conferred with Lieutenant Ackerman and learned about the latter's attempt to elicit information from Williams and how Williams had responded. There is every indication that Leaming was a competent officer and it would seem that, as such, he would want to compare notes with the lieutenant who had placed Williams under arrest, booked him, and put him in a cell. *Id.* at 42; *see* R. ROYAL & S. SCHUTT, THE GENTLE ART OF INTERVIEWING AND INTERROGATION 53 (1976) (before conducting interview or interrogation, officer should talk to any other investigators who may have preceded him on case). After Leaming arrived in Davenport, his prisoner-to-be was granted two more private meetings with his Davenport lawyer. Brief for Petitioner, Joint App. at 75–76. These two meetings took a total of 30–35 minutes, according to Leaming. *Id.* During this time, Leaming probably conferred with Lieutenant Ackerman. The record is silent on this point, as it is on too many others, but Leaming did state that after Williams's first meeting with his lawyer, which lasted some 20 minutes, he, Detective Nelson, and Lieutenant Ackerman reentered the room together. *Id.* at 76.

41. *See* note 40 *supra.*

42. Brief for Petitioner, Joint App. at 81.

43. *Cf.* F. INBAU & J. REID, CRIMINAL INTERROGATION AND CONFESSIONS 75 (2d ed. 1967) (suggesting that the interrogator appeal to suspect's pride; for example, by complimenting a clergyman accused of taking indecent liberties with a child for his dedication to God and sacrifices as a man of God).

44. *Id.* Interrogators are told that it is usually better to address persons of high social or professional status "by their first name, or by their last name without attaching the 'Mr.,' 'Mrs.,' or 'Miss,'" in order to dispel their "usual feeling of superiority and independence," but they are advised to address those of low status as "'Mr.,' 'Mrs.,' or 'Miss,' rather than by their first name." *Id.* Addressing an escapee from a mental hospital who is black and who had only been a resident of the state for a few months as Reverend would seem to be applying this advice with a vengeance. "The person of low social status is flattered and acquires a feeling of satisfaction and dignity from such unaccustomed courtesy. By according this subject this consideration the interrogator enhances the effectivenes of whatever he says or does thereafter." *Id.*

45. *Id.*

46. *Id.* at 73.

47. Brief for Petitioner at 12 (quoting Williams v. Brewer, 375 F. Supp. 170, 183 (S.D. Iowa 1974)) (emphasis in original).

48. *Id.* at 13 (emphasis in original).

49. 430 U.S. at 392.

50. *Id.* at 392–93.

51. *See* note 40 *supra* and accompanying text.

52. *Id.*

53. *See* text at notes 35–36 *supra*. This is another suggested interrogation technique:

> [W]hen the interrogator has reason to believe that the subject possesses or knows the whereabouts of an instrument or article which might have some connection with the crime, instead of merely asking, "Do you have such-and-such?" or "Do you know where such-and-such is?", *it is much better to assume* in the question that the subject does have, or does know the location of, the object being sought. . . .
>
> [After discussing a case where the interrogator successfully elicited a confession by *assuming* in his question that an alleged sex deviate kept a diary, the manual continues:] There is every reason to believe that in the foregoing case, if the issue of the diary had been brought up in any way other than by the question, "Where is your diary?" the subject probably would not have divulged its existence or its whereabouts. . . . Had the interrogator merely asked, "Do you have a diary?" the subject probably would have inferred that its existence was not already known and therefore denied that he had one. With the question phrased in such a way *as to imply a certainty of its existence,* however, it became difficult for the subject to make a denial—because *for all he knew the interrogator* or other investigators *might already be aware of its existence* or actually have it in their possession.

F. INBAU & J. REID, *supra* note 43, at 83–84 (emphasis added).

True, the manual talks about "questions" by the interrogator that assume the existence of certain information, not "statements" by the interrogator, but the "psychology" is essentially the same.

54. *See* notes 10–14 *supra* and accompanying text.

55. *See* note 40 *supra* and accompanying text. Unfortunately, this point was never explored at the trial.

56. F. INBAU & J. REID, CRIMINAL INTERROGATION AND CONFESSIONS 111 (1st ed. 1962). Specifically, the authors state:

> The most effective way to deal with a subject who refuses to discuss the matter under investigation is to concede him the right to remain silent. This usually has a very undermining effect. First of all, he is disappointed in his expectation of an unfavorable reaction on the part of the interrogator. Secondly, a concession of this right to remain silent impresses the subject with the apparent fairness of his interrogator.

Id. True, Williams had not refused to talk about the case at all. He had asked some questions about fingerprints and police procedures. But he had not yet supplied the police with any information. He had not yet said anything about the little girl's whereabouts, and had refused to do so when Lieutenant Ackerman asked him about that. In this setting, pretending to concede to Williams his rights would seem to amount to essentially the same "psychological conditioning" as discussed above.

57. *See* note 56 *supra*.

58. *Cf.* R. ROYAL & S. SCHUTT, *supra* note 40, at 122, 134 (suggesting methods of interrogation). Specifically, the authors state:

> When a person desires to confide his troubles voluntarily, he does not go to an enemy or confederate, but rather to a parent, clergyman, medical doctor, lawyer, close friend, or some other respected person who he feels will understand, console, and advise him. When a criminal violator confesses, he, in reality, surrenders his very being and his own free will and destiny into the hands of the interrogator, etc. He will find it much easier to submit if he believes in the interrogator's integrity and is sympathetic to his position. He must believe that the interrogator is neither prosecutor, judge, nor jury.
>
> . . . .
>
> . . . [W]hen the interviewer projects an image that matches the subject's concept of the "respected figure," the subject's defenses are reduced and deterrents to deception are established. The subject's concept of the "respected figure" image is obtainable by studying his subjective needs and conscious desires. The subject's concept, once assessed, is then assumed or projected back at him through the interviewer's acting-out process.

Id.

Recall that the captain had already told Williams that he himself "had had religious training and background as a child" and would probably come nearer to "praying for" Williams than injuring him. *See* footnote 6 *supra* and accompanying text. That doesn't sound like the prosecutor, judge, or jury talking.

59. *See* Brief for Petitioner, Joint App. at 58, 60 (Williams told Leaming several times during trip that he would tell the whole story in Des Moines); *id.* at 65–66 (first time Williams said he would tell the whole story later was not too long after car got on freeway leaving Davenport).

60. *Compare* Brewer v. Williams, 430 U.S. 387, 405 (1977) (Williams's statements that he would tell the whole story *after* seeing McKnight were clear expressions that he desired the presence of an attorney before being interrogated) *with id.* at 432 (White, J., with Blackmun & Rehnquist, JJ., dissenting) (Williams's statement that he would tell the whole story after seeing McKnight indicated his knowledge of his right to have counsel present before being interrogated).

61. *See* footnote 16 *supra* and accompanying text.

62. Justice Powell, concurring in *Williams,* recognized the importance of the totality of circumstances surrounding the speech:

> [T]he entire setting was conducive to the psychological coercion that was success- fully exploited. Williams was known by the police to be a young man with quixotic religious convictions and a history of mental disorders. The date was the day after Christmas, the weather was ominous, and the setting appropriate for Detective Leaming's talk of snow concealing the body and preventing a "Christian burial."

430 U.S. at 412.

63. Although he did not say it in so many words, what Leaming did, in effect, was to use another recommended interrogation technique: "The expression, 'It's the only decent and honorable thing to do,' appears to constitute somewhat of a challenge for the offender to display some evidence of decency and honor." F. INBAU & J. REID,

supra note 43, at 61. It was a challenge, Leaming must have figured, that Williams would find hard to resist.

64. R.W. Emerson, Letters and Social Aims 86 (1876).

65. Brief for Petitioner, Joint App. at 104 (emphasis added).

66. *Id.* at 53.

67. *Id.* at 48.

68. *Id.* at 71.

69. At one point the prosecuting attorney asked Leaming, "Did you at any time tell Mr. Williams that Mr. McKnight told you to tell Williams that he was to tell you the whole story on the way back from Davenport?" Leaming denied it. *Id.* at 58. That was all.

70. *Id.* at 71.

71. Brief for Petitioner, Joint App. at 47–48.

72. 430 U.S. at 432 (White, J., with Blackmun & Rehnquist, JJ., dissenting).

73. *Id.* at 405.

74. Brief for Petitioner, Joint App. at 84. This was, however, after Williams had led Leaming to where he had hidden the girl's boots and the blanket he used to carry her, although neither was found. *Id.* at 83–84.

75. *Id.* at 84.

76. *Id.* at 63.

77. *See* United States v. Springer, 460 F.2d 1344, 1349–50 (7th Cir. 1972) (police not required to make further inquiry into waiver because no contradictory positions maintained when suspect surrendered to authorities to exculpate himself, waived his rights, and subsequently implicated himself); United States v. Hopkins, 433 F.2d 1041, 1044 (5th Cir. 1970) (suspect did not manifest inconsistent conduct because of confusion when he refused to sign waiver form but then volunteered further statements when agent ceased questioning and began to leave); Frazier v. United States (Frazier I), 419 F.2d 1161, 1168–69 (D.C. Cir. 1969) (no valid waiver of fifth amendment rights when suspect signed waiver form but then evidenced confusion by asking agent not to record confession); United States v. Nielson, 392 F.2d 849, 853 (7th Cir. 1968) (police should have inquired further to determine if waiver valid when suspect assumed contradictory positions by refusing to sign waiver form but then immediately offering to continue responding to questions). *See generally* Y. Kamisar, W. LaFave & J. Israel, Modern Criminal Procedure 574–77 (4th ed. 1974).

78. *See* notes 66–70 and footnotes 17–18 *supra* and accompanying text.

79. Brief for Petitioner, Joint App. at 63. If this does not amount to "play[ing] the role of the expert," said to be a "common method of building amplification of guilt as it relates to insecurity," it at least constitutes "speak[ing] with an aura of positive knowledge," a method said to renew "the insecurity process the subject formerly experiences." R. Royal & S. Schutt, *supra* note 40, at 137.

80. Brief for Petitioner at 9 n.1.

81. *See* Kamisar, *Equal Justice in the Gatehouses and Mansions of American Criminal Procedure,* in Criminal Justice in Our Time 84–88 (A. Howard ed. 1965) [reprinted in part in this volume] (no statute, court rule, or court decision will suffice until police interrogation is stripped of its secrecy); Weisberg, *Police Interrogation of Arrested Persons: A Skeptical View,* 52 J. Crim. L.C. & P.S. 21, 44–45 (1961), *reprinted in* Police Power and Individual Freedom 153, 179–80 (C.

Sowle ed. 1962) (most unique feature of police station questioning is its characteristic secrecy).

82. *See* notes 17–22 and footnotes 4–5 *supra* and accompanying text.

83. *See* Crooker v. California, 357 U.S. 433, 443–44, 444 n.2 (1958) (Douglas, J., dissenting) (the issue of coercion is difficult to resolve at trial when the defendant has been interrogated out of the presence of counsel and conflicting accounts are given of what took place); *In re* Groban, 352 U.S. 330, 340 (1957) (Black, J., dissenting) (one who has been privately interrogated has little hope of challenging the testimony of his interrogator as to what was said and done).

84. Brief for Petitioner, Joint App. at 58, 61, 65–66.

85. *Id.* at 56.

86. Q. You didn't ask Williams any questions?

A. No, sir, I told him some things.

Q. You told him some things?

A. Yes, sir. Would you like to hear it?

Id. at 62.

87. Williams v. Brewer, 375 F. Supp. 170, 175 (S.D. Iowa 1974); Brief for Petitioner, Joint App. at 84.

88. Williams v. Brewer, 375 F. Supp. 170, 175 (S.D. Iowa 1974).

89. *See* 430 U.S. at 393 (Leaming told Williams that he knew the body was in the Mitchellville area); *id.* at 432 (White, J., with Blackmun & Rehnquist, JJ., dissenting) (same).

90. Brief for Petitioner, Joint App. at 47–48 (emphasis added).

91. *Id.* at 53 (emphasis added).

92. *Id.* at 52 (emphasis added).

93. *Id.* at 61 (emphasis added).

94. *Id.* at 104 (emphasis added).

95. *See* 430 U.S. at 426 n.8 (Burger, C.J., dissenting) (in contrast to admissions made by Williams, Massiah's statements were obtained surreptitiously, without prior warnings, and could not be independently verified as reliable); *id.* at 430 n.1 (White, J., with Blackmun & Rehnquist, JJ., dissenting) (although issue in *Williams* is defendant's waiver of rights, question of waiver never addressed in *Massiah,* as defendant in that case was unaware both of right to counsel and of informant's identity); *id.* at 440 & n.3 (Blackmun, J., with White & Rehnquist, JJ., dissenting) (statements made by Williams, unlike those of Massiah, were the product neither of a ruse nor of an "interrogation"). My reasons for disagreeing with the dissenters will be discussed at length in a future article [the last essay reprinted in this volume].

96. Brief for United States at 8, Massiah v. United States, 377 U.S. 201 (1964).

97. In the district court Massiah successfully objected to admitting these tapes on the grounds that they contained statements relating to other defendants and to privileged matters. *Id.* The Government, however, filed the recording with the Clerk and maintained that the recording confirmed the testimony of its agent that Colson "did not coerce petitioner into making any incriminating statements or even induce him by appeals to talk in the guise of friendship." *Id.* at 21, 27.

98. *Id.* at 20–21.

99. *See* United States v. White, 401 U.S. 745, 787–89 (1971) (Harlan, J., dissent-

ing) (warrantless third-party bugging undermines the confidence and sense of security of individual relationships and might smother the spontaneity that liberates daily life); Lopez v. United States, 373 U.S. 427, 465–66, 470–71 (1963) (Brennan, J., with Douglas & Goldberg, JJ., dissenting) (electronic surveillance gives rise to police omniscience, one of the most effective tools of tyranny, strikes at freedom of communication, and destroys privacy).

100. The same may be said for Lieutenant Ackerman's dealings with Williams in the Davenport courthouse. The lieutenant, it will be recalled, first denied, then admitted, that he had questioned Williams about the girl's whereabouts.

101. C.E. O'HARA, FUNDAMENTALS OF CRIMINAL INVESTIGATION 146–48 (4th ed. 1976) (first emphasis added).

102. Brief for Petitioner, Joint App. at 55, 75.

103. There would be little point in requiring all conversation in the car to be tape-recorded if the police officers were free to engage in unrecorded talks with their prisoners outside the vehicle during various stops along the way. Thus, on extended car "visits," such as occurred in *Williams,* police officers should be equipped with pocket recorders or other devices when they and their prisoners leave the vehicle. *See* text at note 101 *supra.* In the instant case, Leaming and Nelson need only have been equipped with microphones that broadcast to the state agents in the Bureau of Criminal Investigation car that followed their car all the way back to Des Moines. *See* Brief for Petitioner, Joint App. at 66, 80. The state agents could have used equipment in their car to record all out-of-vehicle conversations.

104. Enker & Elsen, *Counsel for the Suspect:* Massiah v. United States *and* Escobedo v. Illinois, 49 MINN. L. REV. 47, 87 (1964).

105. Brief for United States at 21 n.10, Massiah v. United States, 377 U.S. 210 (1964).

106. Pound, *Legal Interrogation of Persons Accused or Suspected of Crime,* 24 J. CRIM. L.C. & P.S. 1014, 1017 (1934); *see* Kamisar, *Kauper's "Judicial Examination of the Accused" Forty Years Later—Some Comments on a Remarkable Article,* 73 MICH. L. REV. 15, 27–32 (1974) [reprinted in this volume] (evaluation of proposal for complete objective record of judicial examination, including information of rights, any responses, and any questioning; Kauper would have recommended audio or video tape-recording of interrogations if techniques had been available when he wrote); Kauper, *Judicial Examination of the Accused—A Remedy for the Third Degree,* 30 MICH. L. REV. 1224, 1240, 1248 (1932).

107. C.E. O'HARA, FUNDAMENTALS OF CRIMINAL INVESTIGATION 101 (1st ed. 1956).

108. MODEL CODE OF PRE-ARRAIGNMENT PROCEDURE § 130.4 note at 39 (Official Draft, 1975) [hereinafter cited as MODEL CODE]. The Model Code requires tape recordings of the warning and waiver procedures at the police station, noting that "mandatory recording of all casual encounters cannot be required without providing that the prisoner remain throughout custody in a room where sound equipment is available or providing for mobile recording units to accompany each person in custody." *Id.* § 130.4, Commentary at 345.

I submit, however, that if the Reporters-Draftsmen of the Model Code had anticipated a *Williams* fact situation, they would have required tape recordings of the proceedings in the police car. A three- or four-hour secret session, albeit in a moving vehicle, with the prime suspect—indeed, the only suspect—in a murder case is hardly a "casual encounter."

Of course, if the Model Code provisions had governed the disposition of the *Williams* case, it would have been resolved in defendant's favor without ever reaching the question whether the proceedings in the car had to be tape-recorded. The Model Code "provides that once a suspect invokes his right to remain silent or to meet with counsel"—and Williams did both several times—"no law enforcement officer shall seek a waiver or interrogate the suspect in any way until the suspect meets with counsel." *Id.* § 140.8(2)(d), Commentary at 371. *But see* Michigan v. Mosley, 423 U.S. 96, 103–05 (1975) (police may renew questioning of suspect who has exercised his right to remain silent provided the suspect's right to cut off questioning is scrupulously honored).

109. UNIFORM RULES OF CRIMINAL PROCEDURE Rule 243 (Approved Draft 1974) ("the information of rights, any waiver thereof, and any questioning shall be recorded upon a sound recording device *whenever feasible* and in any case where questioning occurs at a place of detention") (emphasis added).

110. MODEL CODE, *supra* note 108, § 130.4 note at 39.

111. Lopez v. Zelker, 344 F. Supp. 1050, 1054 (S.D.N.Y.), *aff'd without opinion,* 465 F.2d 1405 (2d Cir.), *cert. denied,* 409 U.S. 1049 (1972). In *Lopez* Judge Frankel noted that after formal judicial proceedings have been initiated, thus

> [r]iveting tightly the critical right to counsel, a waiver of that right requires the clearest and most explicit explanation and understanding of what is being given up. There is no longer the possibility—and the law enforcement justification—that a mere suspect may win his freedom on the spot by "clearing up a few things." Even in the courtroom, where an impartial judicial officer is presumably impelled by no purpose but fairness, that officer must counsel with care and advise against the likely folly of a layman's proceeding without the aid of a lawyer. We cannot settle for less where the waiver has been proposed by a law enforcement officer whose goals are clearly hostile to the interests of the already indicted person in custody.

Id. at 1054; *see* People v. Lopez, 28 N.Y.2d 23, 28–29, 268 N.E.2d 628, 631, 319 N.Y.S.2d 825, 829 (Breitel, J., with Fuld, C.J., & Burke, J., dissenting) (postarraignment or postindictment interrogation "is no longer a general inquiry into an unsolved crime but rather a form of pretrial discovery"; "the preparation for [defendant's] trial has begun"), *cert. denied,* 404 U.S. 840 (1971).

The Uniform Rules of Criminal Procedure provide that after the initial appearance before a magistrate (Williams, it will be recalled, was arraigned before a judge in Davenport on the outstanding arrest warrant, advised of his rights by the judge, and committed by him to jail), no law enforcement officer or his agent may question a defendant "unless the defendant's lawyer consents or is present at the questioning, or the defendant has waived counsel under Rule 711 [which is the rule for accepting a waiver at or during *the trial*]." UNIFORM RULES OF CRIMINAL PROCEDURE rule 331 (Approved Draft 1974).

112. Petition for Certiorari at 4–6.

113. *See* Cohen, *Field Theory and Judicial Logic,* 59 YALE L.J. 238, 242 (1950).

114. *See* Freund, *William J. Brennan, Jr.,* 86 YALE L.J. 1015, 1016–17 (1977).

115. Speisar v. Randall, 357 U.S. 513, 520-21 (1958); *see* Michigan v. Mosley, 423 U.S. 96, 113 (1975) (Brennan, J., dissenting).

116. *Cf.* Miranda v. Arizona, 384 U.S. 436, 526 (1966) (Harlan, J., dissenting).

Brewer v. Williams, Massiah, and *Miranda:* What Is "Interrogation"? When Does It Matter?

1. Brewer v. Williams, 430 U.S. 387, 412 (1977) (Powell, J., concurring).

2. *Id.* at 390.

3. *Id.*

4. Brief for Petitioner, Joint App. at 25, 37-38, 53, 60, 97, Brewer v. Williams, 430 U.S. 387 (1977).

5. *Id.* at 1-2.

6. Williams v. Brewer, 375 F. Supp. 170, 173, 176 (S.D. Iowa 1974).

7. Brief for Petitioner, Joint App. at 41, 47, 49-51, 52, 75.

8. *See* 430 U.S. at 390.

9. *See id.* at 391.

10. Brief for Petitioner, Joint App. at 50.

11. *Id.* at 75, 76.

12. 375 F. Supp. at 173, 176.

13. *Id.*

14. 430 U.S. at 392 (emphasis added). The record indicates that Williams probably told Leaming this at least once before, and just before the latter delivered the "Christian burial speech," *see* Kamisar, *Foreword:* Brewer v. Williams—*A Hard Look at a Discomfiting Record,* 66 Geo. L.J. 209, 226 n.71, 227 (1977) [reprinted in this volume], but the Court did not consider this point.

15. *See* Kamisar, *supra* note 14, at 215.

16. Brief for Petitioner, Joint App. at 63.

17. For an extensive discussion of these versions, *see* Kamisar, *supra* note 14, at 216-33.

18. *See id.* at 215 n.38.

19. 430 U.S. at 392-93.

20. Massiah v. United States, 377 U.S. 201 (1964).

21. Miranda v. Arizona, 384 U.S. 436 (1966).

22. *See* text *supra* at footnotes 38-42.

23. *See* text *supra* at notes 27-29, 41, 51, 56, 63, 67.

24. 430 U.S. at 439 (Blackmun, J., with White & Rehnquist, JJ., dissenting). In deeming it "clear [that] there was no interrogation," Justice Blackmun also noted that "[i]n this respect, I am in full accord with Judge Webster in his vigorous dissent." *Id.* at 440. Judge (now FBI Director) Webster described Leaming's speech as an "observation about the weather" and an "express[ion] [of] hope that Williams would agree to stop and locate the body." Williams v. Brewer, 509 F.2d 227, 235 (8th Cir. 1974).

25. "[I]t was [Williams] who started the travel conversation and brought up the subject of the criminal investigation." 430 U.S. at 440 (Blackmun, J., with White & Rehnquist, JJ., dissenting).

26. *Id.* at 434 (White, J., with Blackmun & Rehnquist, JJ., dissenting). Justice White also noted that Leaming's speech "was delivered hours before respondent

decided to make any statement." *Id*. But this point is only relevant to the issue whether Williams's disclosure was a "product" of Leaming's speech, not to whether the speech was interrogation when made. On what might be called the causation issue, Justice White's point about the substantial time lapse between Leaming's speech and Williams's disclosure would have been more impressive if Leaming had not ended his speech by telling Williams to "[j]ust think about it [stopping and locating the body on the way into Des Moines] as we're riding down the road" and Williams had not made the disclosure while they were still "riding down the road." *See* text *supra* at notes 56–58.

27. *See* note 24 *supra*.

28. 430 U.S. at 439 (Blackmun, J., with White & Rehnquist, JJ., dissenting).

29. 385 U.S. 293 (1966) (Stewart, J.).

30. *Id*. at 296–98.

31. Graham, *What Is "Custodial Interrogation?": California's Anticipatory Application of Miranda* v. Arizona, 14 U.C.L.A. L. Rev. 59, 106 (1966).

32. *See* 384 U.S. at 448–55.

33. Kamisar, *supra* note 14, at 221–23; *see* notes 34–37 *infra*.

34. Kamisar, *supra* note 14, at 228 n.80.

35. *Id*. at 223.

36. *Id*. at 221–22 & n.57.

37. *Id*. at 224–25 & n.69.

38. *See generally* Kamisar, *supra* note 14, at 221–22 & nn.56–60, 225–28 & nn.69–80.

39. Graham, *supra* note 31, at 104.

40. *See generally* Rothblatt & Pitler, *Police Interrogation: Warnings and Waivers—Where Do We Go From Here?* 42 Notre Dame Law. 479, 486 (1967); text *supra* at footnotes 21–23 and notes 95–113.

41. 430 U.S. at 440 (Blackmun, J., with White & Rehnquist, JJ., dissenting).

42. Griffiths & Ayres, *A Postcript to the* Miranda *Project: Interrogation of Draft Protesters*, 77 Yale L.J. 300, 315 (1967).

43. *See* Kamisar, *supra* note 14, at 209, 215 & n.34.

44. *See* Griffiths & Ayres, *supra* note 42, at 315.

45. *See* Driver, *Confessions and the Social Psychology of Coercion*, 82 Harv. L. Rev. 42, 44–46 (1968) ("To be physically close is to be psychologically close. The situation has a structure emphasizing to the persons involved the immediacy of their contact. . . . When the norm governing spatial distance is violated, a person's instantaneous and automatic response is to back up, again and again. The suspect, unable to escape, will become even more anxious and unsure.").

46. The Iowa Attorney General told the Supreme Court:

Leaming . . . did not really ask any questions. He made this Christian burial statement, and he said "I don't want you to answer me." Now, that may be considered to be—that is going to be a question for this Court to decide, whether that constituted interrogation *or* a psychological ploy.

Transcript of Oral Argument at 16 (copy on file at the *Georgetown Law Journal*) (emphasis added). He later admitted, however, that Leaming's statement was an interrogation, but that "it was very brief." *Id*. at 17.

47. Brief for Petitioner, Joint App. at 79, 94–95.

48. *Id.* at 80.

49. *Id.* at 56.

50. *Id.* at 79–81.

51. 430 U.S. at 439 (Blackmun, J., with White & Rehnquist, JJ., dissenting). Justice Blackmun's "hoping to find out where that little girl was" quotation is taken from the majority opinion, *id.* at 399, which refers to Leaming's testimony in Brief for Petitioner, Joint App. at 95.

52. Graham, *supra* note 31, at 104–06, 126–29.

53. The California courts have admitted into evidence statements obtained without giving the suspect the requisite warnings when the police questioning was motivated primarily by a desire to save the victim's life. *See, e.g.,* People v. Modesto, 62 Cal. 2d 436, 398 P.2d 753, 42 Cal. Rptr. 417 (1965); People v. Dean, 39 Cal. App. 3d 875, 114 Cal. Rptr. 555 (1974). *Compare* Graham, *supra* note 31, at 118–22 (criticizing *Modesto* rule) *and* Rothblatt, *Police Interrogation and the Right to Counsel, Post-Escobedo* v. *Illinois: Application* v. *Emasculation,* 17 HASTINGS L.J. 41, 49–50 (1965) (same) *and* Comment, People v. Dean: *Another Swipe at* Miranda, 4 U. SAN FERN. V.L. REV. 85, 94–96 (1974) (criticizing extension of *Modesto* rule in *Dean*) *with* Friendly, *The Bill of Rights as a Code of Criminal Procedure,* 53 CALIF. L. REV. 929, 949 (1965) (suggesting police may properly question suspect about endangered victim's whereabouts) *and* Traynor, *The Devils of Due Process in Criminal Detection, Detention, and Trial,* 33 U. CHI. L. REV. 657, 677–78 n.86 (1966) (defending *Modesto* rule).

54. *See* Brief for Petitioner, Joint App. at 95 (emphasis added).

55. *Id.* at 92–93 (emphasis added).

56. 430 U.S. at 434.

57. Brief for Petitioner, Joint App. at 104 (emphasis added).

58. Spano v. New York, 360 U.S. 315 (1959).

59. *Id.* at 317–18.

60. *Id.* at 319.

61. *Id.* at 323.

62. *Id.* at 319.

63. 430 U.S. at 419 (Burger, C.J., dissenting).

64. *See* text at footnotes 38–42 *supra.*

65. *See* note 46 *supra.*

66. *Cf.* New York Trust Co. v. Eisner, 256 U.S. 345, 349 (1921) (Holmes, J., dissenting) ("a page of history is worth a volume of logic").

67. 430 U.S. at 419–20 (Burger, C.J., dissenting).

68. Bram v. United States, 168 U.S. 532 (1897). In Malloy v. Hogan, 378 U.S. 1 (1964), the Court, in an opinion authored by Justice Brennan, performed "what might have seemed to some a shotgun wedding of the privilege [against self-incrimination] to the confessions rule." Herman, *The Supreme Court and Restrictions on Police Interrogation,* 25 OHIO ST. L.J. 449, 465 (1964). The *Malloy* Court announced:

[T]oday the admissibility of a confession in a state criminal prosecution is tested by the same standard applied in federal prosecutions since 1897, when, in *Bram v. United States,* 168 U.S. at 532, the Court held that "[i]n criminal trials, in the courts of the United States, wherever a question arises whether a confession is incompetent because not voluntary, the issue is controlled by" [the fifth amendment privilege against self-incrimination].

378 U.S. at 7. *See also* Miranda v. Arizona, 384 U.S. at 461 (quoting same *Bram* language with approval). Although "[t]he old *Bram* case might well have furnished a steppingstone to the standard advanced in *Malloy*, . . . until *Escobedo*, at any rate, it only amounted to an early excursion from the prevailing multifactor approach." Kamisar, *Equal Justice in the Gatehouses and Mansions of American Criminal Procedure*, in CRIMINAL JUSTICE IN OUR TIME 1, 47 (A. Howard ed. 1965) [reprinted in part in this volume]; *see* Escobedo v. Illinois, 378 U.S. 479 (1964) (decided same Term as *Bram*).

69. Bram v. United States, 168 U.S. at 562. Moreover, added the Court, "it cannot be conceived that the converse impression could not also have naturally arisen that by denying [the cosuspect's accusation] there was hope of removing the suspicion from himself." *Id.*

70. *Id.* at 562–64. Bram was confronted with this communication while stripped or being stripped by the police. *Id.* at 538, 561, 563.

71. *Id.* at 539, 562.

72. Escobedo v. Illinois, 378 U.S. 478, 483 (1964).

73. *Id.*

74. Ashcraft v. Tennessee, 322 U.S. 143, 151 (1944). The Court, in an opinion by Justice Black, stated that Ware's confession "was read to Ashcraft." *Id.* The dissenters stated that it "was given" to him. *Id.* at 166 (Jackson, J., with Roberts & Frankfurter, JJ., dissenting). Whether Ware's confession was read to Ashcraft or whether the latter read it himself in the presence of the police or, for that matter, whether Ware directly confronted and accused Ashcraft in the presence of the police strikes me as an insignificant distinction. The result should not turn on whether the police asked a question or even whether they engaged in "verbal conduct"; in all three situations the purpose of the police and effect on the suspect are essentially the same. *See* text *supra* at footnotes 21–22 and notes 110–13.

75. 365 U.S. 534 (1961).

76. *Id.* at 535.

77. *Id.* at 535–36.

78. *Id.* at 548 ("[W]e need not, on this record, consider whether the circumstances of the interrogation and the manner in which it was pressed barred admissibility of the confession as a matter of federal law.").

79. *Id.* at 540 (emphasis added).

80. *Id.* at 541 (emphasis added).

81. *Id.* (emphasis added).

82. *Id.* at 544 (emphasis added). Consider also the observation in the last of the pre-*Escobedo-Miranda* cases, Haynes v. Washington, 373 U.S. 503 (1963), that "[t]he line between proper and permissible police *conduct* and *techniques* and *methods* offensive to due process is, at best, a difficult one to draw, particularly in cases such as this where it is necessary to make fine judgments as to the effect of psychologically coercive *pressures* and *inducements* on the mind and will of an accused." *Id.* at 515 (Goldberg, J.) (emphasis added).

83. 384 U.S. at 450.

84. *See* E. HOPKINS, OUR LAWLESS POLICE 193–95 (1931). According to Professor Zechariah Chafee, Ernest Hopkins, an official investigator for the Wickersham Commission, showed "notable skill and enterprise in breaking through the barriers of silence which surround official lawlessness." *Id.* at vii (preface).

85. Chafee, *Remedies for the Third Degree*, ATLANTIC MONTHLY, Nov. 1931, at 621. "It is hard enough to prevent policemen from using physical violence on suspects; it would be far harder to prevent them from asking a few questions. We had better get rid of the rubber hose and twenty-four hour grillings before we undertake to compel or persuade the police to give up questioning altogether." *Id.* at 626. Professor Chafee coauthored the famous report to the Wickersham Commission on the "third degree."

86. Miranda v. Arizona, 384 U.S. at 508 (Harlan, J., with Stewart & White, JJ., dissenting).

87. *Id.* at 455 (emphasis added).

88. *Id.* at 461 (emphasis added).

89. *Id.* at 511 (Harlan, J., with Stewart & White, JJ., dissenting). The *Miranda* opinion may contain some overstatements, but surely the observation that "[i]n these cases, we might not find the defendants' statements to have been involuntary in traditional terms" is not one of them. *Id.* at 457.

90. *Id.* at 456.

91. *Id.* at 505 (Harlan, J., with Stewart & White, JJ., dissenting).

92. *Id.*

93. 384 U.S. at 516 (Harlan, J., with Stewart & White, JJ., dissenting).

94. *Id.* at 515.

95. *See* Guy v. Donald, 203 U.S. 399, 406 (1906) (Holmes, J.).

96. *Id.*

97. De Santo v. Pennsylvania, 273 U.S. 34, 43 (1927) (Brandeis, J., with Holmes, J., dissenting).

98. O.W. HOLMES, *Law in Science and Science in Law,* in COLLECTED LEGAL PAPERS 224, 238 (1920).

99. *Id.*

100. *See* Spence v. Washington, 418 U.S. 405, 410–11 (1974) (intent to convey particularized message in attaching peace symbol to flag; such conduct protected by first amendment); *cf.* Smith v. Goguen, 415 U.S. 566, 574 (1974) (statute that failed to distinguish between criminal, nonceremonial wearing of flag and noncriminal, ceremonial wearing of flag void for vagueness). *See generally* Ely, *Flag Desecration: A Case Study in the Roles of Categorization and Balancing in First Amendment Analysis,* 88 HARV. L. REV. 1482 (1975); Loewy, *Punishing Flag Desecrators: The Ultimate in Flag Desecration,* 49 N.C. L. REV. 48 (1970); Nimmer, *The Meaning of Symbolic Speech Under the First Amendment,* 21 U.C.L.A. L. REV. 29, 46–57 (1973).

101. Tinker v. Des Moines School Dist., 393 U.S. 503, 505–06, 509–11 (1969). *See generally* Denno, *Mary Beth Tinker Takes the Constitution to School,* 38 FORDHAM L. REV. 35 (1968); Nahmod, *Beyond Tinker: The High School as an Educational Public Forum,* 5 HARV. C.R.-C.L. L. REV. 278 (1970); 39 BROOKLYN L. REV. 918 (1973).

102. Henkin, *On Drawing Lines,* 82 HARV. L. REV. 63, 80 (1968). *See generally* W. LOCKHART, Y. KAMISAR & J. CHOPER, CONSTITUTIONAL LAW 1149–54 (4th ed. 1975) and authorities discussed and collected therein.

103. *Cf.* Henkin, *supra* note 102, at 79.

104. *See* Lyons v. Oklahoma, 322 U.S. 596, 599, 604 (1944). As late as 1930, forcing a murder suspect to view the grisly remains of his alleged victim was not an uncommon method of inducing the suspect to talk. *See* E. HOPKINS, *supra* note 84, at 243, 254, 257–58, 260.

105. *See* Caminito v. Murphy, 222 F.2d 698, 700–01 (2d Cir.), *cert. denied*, 350 U.S. 896 (1955). *See also* footnote 19 *supra*.

106. *See* text at notes 75–77 *supra*.

107. In Commonwealth v. Hamilton, 445 Pa. 292, 285 A.2d 172 (1971), as in the *Escobedo* case, *see* text at notes 72–73 *supra*, the defendant, confronted in the presence of police by another arrestee who accused him of being the "triggerman," denied the charge, but in the process admitted involvement in the crime. 445 Pa. at 295, 285 A.2d at 174; *see* footnote 22 *supra*. A Philadelphia police officer disclosed on cross-examination in this case that "such a technique [police arranging confrontations between suspects for the purpose of obtaining incriminating statements] has been used in 'hundreds' of other cases." 445 Pa. at 296, 285 A.2d at 174.

108. *See* Combs v. Wingo, 565 F.2d 96, 97–98 (6th Cir. 1972); footnote 21 *supra*.

109. *See* United States v. Davis, 527 F.2d 1110, 1111 (9th Cir. 1975); footnote 21 *supra*.

110. E. HOPKINS, *supra* note 84, at 194.

111. Wan v. United States, 266 U.S. 1, 14–15 (1924) (Brandeis, J.) (sick man's statements made after being subject to "interrogation" for seven days inadmissible).

112. *See* note 94 *supra* and accompanying text.

113. *See* footnote 20 *supra*. Note also the quotation from the O'Hara manual in the last paragraph of footnote 19 *supra*.

114. *See* Miranda v. Arizona, 384 U.S. at 478 ("Any statement given freely and voluntarily without any compelling influences [other than those inherent in a normal arrest and detention] is, of course, admissible in evidence. The fundamental import of the privilege while an individual is in custody is not whether he is allowed to talk to the police without the benefit of warnings and counsel, but whether he can be interrogated. . . . Volunteered statements of any kind are not barred by the Fifth Amendment and their admissibility is not affected by our holding today.").

115. *See* Malloy v. Hogan, 378 U.S. 1, 8 (1964).

116. *Cf.* Graham, *supra* note 31, at 92–93.

117. *Cf.* Blackburn v. Alabama, 361 U.S. 199, 207 (1960) ("a complex of values underlies the stricture against use by the state of confessions which, by way of convenient shorthand, this Court terms involuntary"). *See also* Bator & Vorenberg, *Arrest, Detention, Interrogation, and the Right to Counsel,* 66 COLUM. L. REV. 62, 73 (1966); Kamisar, *What Is an "Involuntary" Confession?* 17 RUTGERS L. REV. 728, 745–46 (1963) [reprinted in this volume].

118. 378 U.S. 478 (1964).

119. *Id.* at 492.

120. Dissenting in Escobedo v. Illinois, 378 U.S. 478 (1964), Justice Stewart so described the basis for the decision, and his opinion, in *Massiah. Id.* at 493. *See also* Justice Stewart's opinion for the Court in *Williams:*

Whatever else it may mean, the right to counsel granted by the Sixth and Fourteenth Amendments means at least that a person is entitled to the help of a lawyer at or after the time that judicial proceedings have been initiated against him—"whether by way of formal charge, preliminary hearing, indictment, information, or arraignment." Kirby v. Illinois, 406 U.S. 682, 689 (1973) [plurality opinion by Stewart, J.].

430 U.S. at 398.

121. Herman, *supra* note 68, at 491.

122. Dissenting in Escobedo v. Illinois, 378 U.S. 478 (1964), Justice Stewart observed:

Under our system of criminal justice the institution of formal, meaningful judicial proceedings, by way of indictment, information, or arraignment, marks the point at which a criminal investigation has ended and adversary proceedings have commenced. It is at this point that the constitutional guarantees attach which pertain to a criminal trial.

Id. at 493–94.

123. *Id.* at 493.

124. 384 U.S. 436 (1966).

125. The custodial interrogation standard attached primary significance to the conditions surrounding or inherent in the interrogation, not to the evidence of guilt available to the police at the time of questioning.

126. *See* United States v. Crisp, 435 F.2d 354, 358–59 (7th Cir. 1971) (failure of agents to notify defendant's counsel before interviewing defendant does not require reversal when defendant fully warned of rights). In *Crisp* the court commented:

Massiah . . . must be read in light of . . . [*Miranda*], which expressly recognized the validity of a knowing and voluntary waiver of rights during the "critical stage" of custodial interrogation. . . . As *Miranda* and *Escobedo* clearly indicate, formal indictment is no longer the determinative event upon which constitutional safeguards hinge. By the same token, formal indictment does not absolutize constitutional rights or inexorably rigidify adversary postures.

Id. at 358.

127. Justice Harlan, joined by Justices Stewart and White, filed a long dissenting opinion in *Miranda*. 384 U.S. at 504. Justice White, joined by Justices Harlan and Stewart, wrote a separate long dissent. *Id.* at 526. Justice Clark wrote a third dissenting opinion, although he concurred in the result in one companion case to *Miranda*. *Id.* at 499.

128. 266 U.S. 1, 14 (1924) (that confession not induced by promise or threat does not by itself make it voluntary in law; it must be voluntary in fact, given under no compulsion, to be admissible), *quoted in* 384 U.S. at 462.

129. 168 U.S. 532 (1897) (discussed in text at notes 68–71 *supra*), *quoted in* 384 U.S. at 461–62.

130. 110 U.S. 574 (1894) (confession must be viewed in context made to see if voluntary), *cited in* 384 U.S. at 490.

131. *See* 384 U.S. at 478 n.46, 486–90 & n.64.

132. *See id.* at 459 (Lilburn asserted right to remain silent about self in criminal matters before 1637 inquisitorial court, the Star Chamber).

133. *See id.* at 458 n.27.

134. State v. Williams, 182 N.W.2d 396 (Iowa 1971) (5–4 decision).

135. *Id.* at 406 (Stuart, J., with Mason & Becker, JJ., dissenting).

136. *See* footnote 4 *supra.* It was at this stage of the proceedings that Professor Robert D. Bartels of the University of Iowa College of Law, Williams's court-appointed counsel, entered the picture.

137. *See* footnote 4 *supra.*

138. *Id.*

139. Lopez v. Zelker, 344 F. Supp. 1050, 1054 & n.3 (S.D.N.Y.) (Frankel, J.) (collecting cases), *aff'd without opinion,* 465 F.2d 1405 (2d Cir.), *cert. denied,* 409 U.S. 1049 (1972).

140. *Id.* at 1054; *see* United States v. Satterfield, 417 F. Supp. 293 (S.D.N.Y. 1976) (Knapp, J.), *aff'd,* 558 F.2d 655 (2d Cir. 1977). In *Satterfield* Judge Knapp stated: "Under our interpretation of *Massiah,* after indictment the advice of counsel can be waived only after such warnings and explanations as would justify a court in permitting a defendant to proceed *pro se* at trial." *Id.* at 296. *See also* United States v. Miller, 432 F. Supp. 382, 387–88 (E.D.N.Y. 1977) (adopting strict *Satterfield* waiver standard when suspect has retained counsel and indicated that he wished to consult with him prior to answering questions).

Dissenting from the 10–4 decision in United States v. Brown, 569 F.2d 236 (5th Cir. 1978) (en banc), Judge Simpson maintained that the language in *Brewer v. Williams* that the strict standard of waiver " 'applies equally to an alleged waiver of the right to counsel *whether at trial or at a critical stage of pretrial proceedings'* [430 U.S. at 404] . . . assumes telling significance in light of the stringent requirements for an effective waiver of the right to counsel at trial." 569 F.2d at 242 (Simpson, J., with Goldberg, Godbold & Morgan, JJ., dissenting) (emphasis added by Judge Simpson). "Because a defendant's need for the assistance of counsel at critical stages prior to trial is in many ways as great as his need at trial, it makes sense to require a comparable waiver in both situations." *Id.* at 244.

141. 430 U.S. at 413 (Powell, J., concurring).

142. *See id.* at 405–06. "The Court of Appeals did not hold, nor do we, that under the circumstances of this case Williams *could not,* without notice to counsel, have waived his rights under the Sixth and Fourteenth Amendments. It only held, as do we, that he did not." *Id.* (emphasis in original).

143. 304 U.S. 458 (1938).

144. 430 U.S. at 404 (quoting from Johnson v. Zerbst, 304 U.S. 458, 464 (1938)).

145. *Id.*

146. 384 U.S. at 470.

147. *Id.* at 475.

148. *Id.* at 474; *see* notes 335–74 *infra* and footnotes 74–86 *supra* and accompanying text.

149. *See* Israel, *Criminal Procedure, the Burger Court, and the Legacy of the Warren Court,* 75 Mich. L. Rev. 1320, 1385–86 & n.281 (1977) (discussion of waiver aspect of *Miranda* and how much lighter burden could be placed on Government without overturning *Miranda*).

150. 430 U.S. at 430 (White, J., with Blackmun & Rehnquist, JJ., dissenting).

151. *Id.* at 430 n.1.

152. *See* 430 U.S. at 401–06.

153. *See* text at notes 137–38 and footnote 32 *supra*.

154. *See* 430 U.S. at 401–02.

155. *Id.* at 402 (quoting from Williams v. Brewer, 375 F. Supp. 170, 182 (S.D. Iowa 1974)) (emphasis added by district court).

156. 430 U.S. at 404; *see* text at note 144 *supra*.

157. *Id.* (referring to Johnson v. Zerbst, 304 U.S. 458, 464 (1938)).

158. State v. Williams, 182 N.W.2d 396, 401 (Iowa 1971).

159. *Id.* at 402.

160. *Id.*

161. *Id.* at 406 (Stuart, J., with Mason & Becker, JJ., dissenting).

162. *Id.*

163. *Id.*

164. *See* text at notes 134–35 *supra*.

165. Williams v. Brewer, 375 F. Supp. 170, 182 (S.D. Iowa 1974), *quoted with approval in* 430 U.S. at 402.

166. 430 U.S. at 413; *see* note 142 *supra* and accompanying text.

167. 375 F. Supp. at 178; *see id.* at 181.

168. *Id.* at 181–83 (part V).

169. *See* 430 U.S. at 402–03.

170. 375 F. Supp. at 182 (quoting from Miranda v. Arizona, 384 U.S. at 475).

171. Williams v. Brewer, 509 F.2d 227, 231–34 (8th Cir. 1974).

172. *See* 430 U.S. at 403.

173. The Eighth Circuit seemed to concede that an individual "can voluntarily, knowingly, and intelligently waive his right to have counsel present [even] after counsel has been appointed," but quickly added that it agreed with the district court that the state had failed to show such a waiver. 509 F.2d at 233.

174. *Id.*

175. *Id.*

176. *Id.* (quoting from Miranda v. Arizona, 384 U.S. at 473) (emphasis added by court of appeals).

177. *Cf.* Shuttlesworth v. Birmingham, 394 U.S. 147, 153 (1969) (Justice Stewart characterizing performance of lower court).

178. *See* text at note 137 *supra*.

179. *See* text at footnote 5 *supra*.

180. 430 U.S. at 401 (emphasis added).

181. *Id.* at 426 n.8.

182. *Id.*

183. Massiah v. United States, 377 U.S. 201, 201 (1964).

184. *Id.* at 203.

185. Enker & Elsen, *Counsel for the Suspect:* Massiah v. United States *and* Escobedo v. Illinois, 49 MINN. L. REV. 47, 53 (1964). The authors, former assistant United States attorneys, represented the Government when the *Massiah* case was before the Second Circuit.

186. 377 U.S. at 202–03.

187. *Id.* at 203.

188. Enker & Elsen, *supra* note 185, at 56–57 n.32. The authors point out that Massiah's right-to-counsel contentions were not even raised at the trial. *Id.* Judge

(now Chief Judge) J. Skelly Wright once spontaneously confessed at a conference on confessions: "I happened to be the trial judge in *Massiah* and the [electronic eavesdropping] was objected to on *On Lee* grounds. I admitted this tape because under *On Lee* it was admissible. Then, when *Massiah* went to the Court of Appeals, other objections were made with reference to counsel, which were not even in the record." A NEW LOOK AT CONFESSIONS 239 (B.J. George ed. 1967). *See also* On Lee v. United States, 343 U.S. 747 (1952) (testimony of police eavesdropping on conversations of defendant and acquaintance wired for sound that took place in public part of defendant's business held admissible).

189. United States v. Massiah, 307 F.2d 62, 66 (2d Cir. 1962) (Lumbard, C.J.).

190. 377 U.S. at 206.

191. 366 U.S. 315 (1959).

192. *Id.* at 324 (Douglas, J., with Black & Brennan, JJ., concurring); *id.* at 326 (Stewart, J., with Douglas & Brennan, JJ., concurring).

193. *See* People v. Meyer, 11 N.Y.2d 162, 182 N.E.2d 103, 227 N.Y.S.2d 427 (1962) (holding that postarraignment statement should be treated no differently than postindictment statement); People v. Waterman, 9 N.Y.2d 561, 175 N.E.2d 445, 216 N.Y.S.2d 70 (1961) (holding statement obtained during postindictment questioning in absence of counsel inadmissible); People v. Di Biasi, 7 N.Y.2d 544, 166 N.E.2d 825, 200 N.Y.S.2d 21 (1960) (same).

194. Spano v. New York, 366 U.S. 315, 323 (1959). Chief Justice Warren, writing for the majority, did not confine the opinion to these grounds. He also noted that petitioner was already indicted on a charge of first-degree murder and thus the police were not "merely trying to solve a crime, or even absolve a suspect." *Id.*

195. Crooker v. California, 357 U.S. 433, 441, 448 (1958) (Douglas, J., with Warren, C.J., Black & Brennan, JJ., dissenting).

196. *Id.* at 446, 448 (emphasis added).

197. 377 U.S. at 211 (White, J., with Clark & Harlan, JJ., dissenting).

198. Crooker v. California, 357 U.S. 433, 443 (1958) (Douglas, J., with Warren, C.J., Black & Brennan, JJ., dissenting).

199. This was also the main thrust of earlier attempts to grapple with the confession problem—the *McNabb-Mallory* rule and the "inherently coercive" approach to protracted questioning adopted in *Ashcraft*. In federal courts the *McNabb-Mallory* rule excluded confessions obtained during a period of unnecessary delay in bringing a defendant before a judicial officer. Mallory v. United States, 354 U.S. 449 (1957); McNabb v. United States, 318 U.S. 332 (1943). The *Ashcraft* rule was promulgated to deal with those situations under which confessions are obtained that are "inherently coercive" because of such factors as length or type of questioning. Ashcraft v. Tennessee, 322 U.S. 143 (1944). *See generally* Allen, *The* Wolf *Case: Search and Seizure, Federalism, and the Civil Liberties,* 45 ILL. L. REV. 1, 28–29 & n.86 (1950); Amsterdam, *The Supreme Court and the Rights of Suspects in Criminal Cases,* 45 N.Y.U. L. REV. 785, 806–08 (1970); Douglas, *The Means and the End,* 1959 WASH. U.L.Q. 103, 107, 113–14, 120; Kamisar, *supra* note 117, at 739–40; Comment, *Prearraignment Interrogation and the* McNabb-Mallory *Miasma: A Proposed Amendment to the Federal Rules of Criminal Procedure,* 68 YALE L.J. 1003, 1006, 1037 (1959).

200. Crooker v. California, 357 U.S. 433, 443–44 (1958) (Douglas, J., with Warren, C.J., Black & Brennan, JJ., dissenting).

201. 377 U.S. at 211 (White, J., with Clark & Harlan, JJ., dissenting).

202. *Cf. In re* Groban, 352 U.S. 330, 340 (1957) (Black, J., with Warren, C.J., Douglas & Brennan, JJ., dissenting) ("The witness has no effective way to challenge his interrogator's testimony as to what was said and done at the secret inquisition.").

Massiah did not testify or produce witnesses to contradict the officer's testimony about the meeting. United States v. Massiah, 307 F.2d at 65. The Massiah-Colson conversation was not only broadcasted to a nearby federal agent, but secretly tape-recorded by Colson. Massiah successfully objected to the admission of these tapes on the grounds that they implicated other defendants and contained privileged matters. *See* Brief for United States at 21, Massiah v. United States, 377 U.S. 201 (1964). The Government maintained that the recording would demonstrate that the agent's testimony was reliable and filed it with the Clerk of the Court. *Id.* at 21, 23–24.

203. 307 F.2d at 66.

204. *Id.* at 72.

205. *Id.* (quoting from People v. Waterman, 9 N.Y.2d 561, 566, 175 N.E.2d 445, 448, 216 N.Y.S.2d 70, 75 (1961) (rule excluding statements obtained from indicted defendant when not made in presence of counsel)).

206. In Lee v. United States, 322 F.2d 770 (5th Cir. 1963), Judge Wisdom, writing for the majority, "read *Spano* as the New York Court of Appeals [read] *Spano:* the Constitution gives a defendant the absolute right to counsel, starting no later than after indictment." *Id.* at 778. He was referring to the line of cases adopting the indictment rule for the New York courts. *See* People v. Meyer, 11 N.Y.2d. 162, 164–65, 182 N.E.2d 103, 104, 227 N.Y.S.2d 427, 428 (1962) (holding inadmissible any statement made after arraignment in absence of counsel); People v. Waterman, 9 N.Y.2d 561, 565–66, 175 N.E.2d 445, 447–48, 216 N.Y.S.2d 70, 74–75 (1961) (accused has absolute right to counsel after indictment). The Wisdom opinion in *Lee* evoked a bitter dissent from Judge Hutcheson, who characterized the *Spano* concurring opinions as "separate opinions presenting differing personal views of individual judges," and felt compelled to "emphatically condemn and reject the majority's view." *See* 322 F.2d at 780.

207. 377 U.S. at 206.

208. *See* 430 U.S. at 440 n.3 (Blackmun, J., with White & Rehnquist, JJ., dissenting) (disagreeing with majority's view that *Massiah* regards it as constitutionally irrelevant that statements in that case were surreptitiously obtained and regarding *Massiah* as case in which defendant was worse off than typical confession defendant because he was not even aware that he was under police interrogation); *id.* at 426 n.8 (Burger, C.J., dissenting) (instant case "far cry from *Massiah,*" in part because "Massiah was unaware that he was being interrogated by ruse").

209. Transcript of Oral Argument for United States at 30, Massiah v. United States, 377 U.S. 201 (1964) [hereinafter cited as *Massiah* Oral Argument]; *see* text *supra* at notes 213, 216.

210. Brief for United States at 34.

211. *See* notes 192, 195 *supra.*

212. Brief for United States at 29.

213. *Id.* at 30.

214. *Cf.* Oregon v. Mathiason, 429 U.S. 292 (1977).

215. *Massiah* Oral Argument, *supra* note 209, at 26.

216. *Id.* at 31.

217. *See* text *supra* at note 245 and following hypothetical questions.

218. *Massiah* Oral Argument, *supra* note 209, at 41–42.

219. *See* notes 193, 209 *supra*.

220. *See* text at note 213 *supra*.

221. 377 U.S. at 204.

222. *Id.*

223. *Id.*

224. *See* text at note 207 *supra*.

225. *Id.*

226. *See* note 208 *supra*.

227. 381 U.S. 356 (1965) (per curiam).

228. *See* State v. McLeod, 1 Ohio St. 2d 60, 60, 203 N.E.2d 349, 351 (1964) (state supreme court's summary of lower court's findings).

229. McLeod v. Ohio, 378 U.S. 582 (1964) (per curiam).

230. 1 Ohio St. 2d at 61, 203 N.E.2d at 351.

231. 1 Ohio St. 2d at 63, 203 N.E.2d at 352 (Gibson, J., with O'Neill, J., dissenting).

232. 381 U.S. at 356.

233. *See* footnotes 28–29 and note 125 *supra* and accompanying text.

234. *See* footnote 30 *supra*.

235. 307 F.2d at 66 (emphasis added).

236. *Id.* at 72 (emphasis added).

237. *Id.* at 64 (emphasis added).

238. *Id.* at 72 (emphasis added).

239. 377 U.S. at 201 (emphasis added).

240. *Id.* at 204 (emphasis added).

241. *Id.* at 206 (emphasis added).

242. 307 F.2d at 72 (Hays, J., dissenting).

243. *Id.* at 66.

244. 377 U.S. at 204.

245. *Cf.* Kovacs v. Cooper, 336 U.S. 77, 97 (1949) (Jackson, J., concurring) ("The moving picture screen, the radio, the newspaper, the handbill, the sound truck and the street corner orator have differing natures, values, abuses and dangers. Each, in my view, is a law unto itself, and all we are dealing with now is the sound truck.").

246. *See* text at footnote 38 and notes 235–41 *supra*.

247. The *Miranda* opinion begins:

> The cases before us raise questions which go to the roots of our concepts of American criminal jurisprudence. . . . More specifically, we deal with the admissibility of statements obtained from an individual who is *subjected to custodial police interrogation* and the necessity for procedures which assure that the individual is accorded his privilege . . . not to be compelled to incriminate himself.

384 U.S. at 439 (emphasis added). The Court later stated: "The principles announced today deal with the protection which must be given to the privilege against self-incrimination *when the individual is first subjected to police interrogation* while in

custody at the station or otherwise deprived of his freedom of action in any significant way." *Id.* at 477 (emphasis added).

248. *Cf.* Enker & Elsen, *supra* note 185, at 60–61 (suggesting *Escobedo* Court created just such a right).

249. *See id.* at 57, 60–61, 69, 83 (suggesting real issue in *Massiah* was protection of defendant from governmental deceit, not right to counsel).

250. *See* notes 29–30 and footnotes 7–8 *supra* and accompanying text. *See also* Osborn v. United States, 385 U.S. 323 (1966) (discussed at footnote 8 *supra*).

Miranda also confirmed Justice White's observation, dissenting in *Escobedo,* that a suspect or an accused has no "constitutional right not to incriminate himself by making voluntary disclosures." Escobedo v. Illinois, 378 U.S. 478, 497 (1964) (White, J., dissenting). That *Miranda* leaves the police free to hear and act upon volunteered confessions even though the "volunteer" neither knows nor is informed of his rights is clear from the *Miranda* Court's opinion. *See* 384 U.S. 436, 478 (1966). *But cf.* Graham, *supra* note 31, at 76–77; Thompson, *Detention After Arrest and In-Custody Investigation: Some Exclusionary Principles,* 1966 U. ILL. L.F. 390, 422 (by allowing volunteered confessions Court fails to take account of fact that such a statement may be made in ignorance of both privilege and "consequences of foregoing it"). *Miranda* also allows the police to conduct "[g]eneral on-the-scene questioning" or "other general questioning of citizens," even though the citizen is neither informed nor aware of his rights. 384 U.S. at 477.

251. Hoffa v. United States, 385 U.S. 293, 303–04 (Stewart, J.).

252. Enker & Elsen, *supra* note 185, at 57.

253. *See* 401 U.S. at 753. In the principal opinion Justice White observed:

[H]owever strongly a defendant may trust an apparent colleague, his expectations in this respect are not protected by the Fourth Amendment when it turns out that the colleague is a government agent regularly communicating with the authorities. . . .

Concededly a police agent who conceals his police connections may write down for official use his conversations with a defendant and testify concerning them, without a warrant authorizing his encounters with the defendant and without otherwise violating the latter's Fourth Amendment rights. . . . For constitutional purposes, no different result is required if the agent instead of immediately reporting and transcribing his conversations with defendant, either (1) simultaneously records them with electronic equipment which he is carrying on his person . . . (2) or carries radio equipment which simultaneously transmits the conversations. . . .

Id. at 749, 751.

254. 384 U.S. at 461. In United States v. Fioravanti, 412 F.2d 407 (3d. Cir), *cert. denied,* 396 U.S. 837 (1969), Judge Aldisert, writing for the court, stated:

In recent years, the concept of compulsion or coercion has been further refined to delineate circumstances where even absent active, outward forces of coercion, the mere presence of certain conditions gives rise to constructive forces capable of negating the voluntariness of a given utterance.

. . . .

Thus, *Miranda* has created a presumption of coercion by the mere presence of the dual factors of a police-initiated interrogation and the defendant's being in custody.... This presumption ... may be rebutted by the simple expedients of the defendant's having counsel present or perfecting a knowledgeable and intelligent waiver of [his rights]....

[In the instant case, there] is no proof that the admittedly in-custody statement resulted from any police "interrogation" or "questioning" as contemplated by the Court in *Miranda*....

[It] is inconceivable that the defendant could have experienced the coercion-born type of fear and intimidation set forth in *Miranda,* because when he volunteered this incriminatory statement, he thought that he was conversing with a fellow partner in crime, not a policeman.

Id. at 412, 413.

255. H. FRIENDLY, *A Postscript on* Miranda, in BENCHMARKS 266, 272 (1967). *But see generally* Kamisar, *A Dissent from the* Miranda *Dissents: Some Comments on the "New" Fifth Amendment and the Old "Voluntariness" Test,* 65 MICH. L. REV. 59 (1966) [reprinted in this volume].

256. As Justice White pointed out in his *Miranda* dissent:

Although in the Court's view in-custody interrogation is inherently coercive, the Court says that the spontaneous product of the coercion of arrest and detention is still to be deemed voluntary. [A suspect] may blurt out a confession which will be admissible despite the fact that he is alone and in custody, without any showing that he had any notion of his right to remain silent or of the consequences of his admission.

384 U.S. at 533 (White, J., with Harlan & Stewart, JJ., dissenting). *See* note 254 *supra* (quotation from *Fioravanti*).

257. *See* 384 U.S. at 467. The majority opinion in *Miranda* stated:

[W]ithout proper safeguards the process of in-custody interrogation of persons suspected or accused of crime contains inherently compelling pressures which work to undermine the individual's will to resist and to compel him to speak where he would not otherwise do so freely. In order to combat these pressures and to permit a full opportunity to exercise the privilege against self-incrimination, the accused must be adequately and effectively apprised of his rights and the exercise of those rights must be fully honored.

Id. Earlier in its opinion the Court noted:

The entire thrust of police interrogation [in *Escobedo*], as in all the cases today, was to put the defendant in such an emotional state as to impair his capacity for rational judgment.... In [*Escobedo*], as in the cases today, we sought a protective device to dispel the compelling atmosphere of the interrogation.

Id. at 465.

258. P. DEVLIN, THE CRIMINAL PROSECUTION IN ENGLAND 27 (1960) (noting general public's misimpression), *quoted with approval in* Miranda v. Arizona, 384 U.S. at 468 n.37.

259. *See* 384 U.S. at 467-68. "It is not just the subnormal or woefully ignorant who succumb to the interrogator's imprecations, whether implied or expressly stated, that

the interrogation will continue until a confession is obtained or that silence in the face of accusation is itself damning and will bode ill when presented to a jury." *Id.* at 468; *see* Enker & Elsen, *supra* note 185, at 84–85 (written before *Miranda*) ("So far as the defendant [who is subjected to custodial police interrogation] is aware . . . the fear of indefinite detention can be dispelled only by giving the police what they want.").

260. *Cf.* F. INBAU & J. REID, CRIMINAL INTERROGATION AND CONFESSIONS 61 (2d ed. 1967).

261. *See* Y. KAMISAR, W. LaFAVE & J. ISRAEL, MODERN CRIMINAL PROCEDURE 584 (4th ed. 1974).

[*As this volume goes to press the United States Supreme Court is considering a case which may shed much light on when, if ever, "interrogation" occurs within the meaning of* Miranda *when a suspect is not addressed personally. Rhode Island v. Innis, 391 A.2d 1158 (1978), cert. granted, 440 U.S. 934 (1979). After being warned of his rights, and after expressing a desire to see an attorney, Innis, a murder suspect, was placed in the back of a police vehicle for transportation to police headquarters, only a few minutes away. Aware that Innis could hear what they were saying, two officers in the front seat engaged in a conversation* with each other, *noting that the murder had occurred in the vicinity of a school for handicapped children and expressing concern that one of the children might find the shotgun and injure himself. At this point, Innis interrupted the officers and offered to lead them to where the shotgun was hidden.*

[*The state supreme court excluded the shotgun, as well as the testimony of the officers relating to its discovery, viewing the "front seat conversation" "interrogation" within the meaning of* Miranda:

The police officers in the wagon chose not to discuss sports or the weather but the crime for which defendant was arrested. The defendant, alone in a police wagon with three officers [one sitting in the back with him] at 4 *A.M.*, underwent the same psychological pressures which moved [the defendant in Williams] to lead police to the body of his victim. Police officers in such a situation must not be permitted to achieve indirectly, by talking with one another, a result which the Supreme Court has said they may not achieve directly by talking to a suspect. . . .

391 A.2d at 1162. For a stimulating "interchange of perspectives" on the issues raised by the Innis *case, see Grano, Rhode Island v. Innis:* A Need to Reconsider the Constitutional Premises Underlying the Law of Confessions, *17 AM. CRIM. L. REV. 1 (1979); W. White, Rhode Island v. Innis:* The Significance of a Suspect's Assertion of His Right to Counsel, *17 AM. CRIM. L. REV. 53 (1979).*]

262. Sometimes the same "government agent" may be *both* a parent or close relative of the suspect and a parent or close relative of the victim. *See* People v. Hughes, 203 Cal. App. 2d 598, 21 Cal. Rptr. 668 (1962) (defendant accused of incest with daughter; wife and daughter talked with him in room they knew was "bugged"); Commonwealth v. Bordner, 432 Pa. 405, 247 A.2d 612 (1968) (eldest child set fire to family house, killing seven brothers and sisters; both parents used as "police instrumentalities" in interrogation).

263. *Cf.* Hoffa v. United States, 385 U.S. 293, 311 (1966) (secret agents not more free from constitutional restrictions than other government agents).

264. The "jail cell plant" may not threaten defendant with bodily harm. *See* State v. Atkins, 251 Ore. 485, 446 P.2d 660 (1968) (police placed defendant in cell with

reputedly violent codefendant to gain confession). Nor may the "plant" engage in oppressive tactics. *Cf.* Milton v. Wainwright, 407 U.S. 371, 378–79 (1972) (Stewart, J., with Douglas, Brennan & Marshall, JJ., dissenting). Nor may she persuade her cellmate that she would be better off throwing herself on the mercy of the police than putting her trust in a lawyer. *Cf.* Miller v. California, 392 U.S. 616, 626–27 (1968) (Marshall, J., with Warren, C.J., Douglas & Brennan, JJ., dissenting from dismissal of certiorari). Nor, presumably, may a secret agent lead his cellmate to believe that the invariable practice of the local police, when confronted with a suspect unwilling to confess, is to bring in the suspect's wife or girlfriend "for questioning." *Cf.* Rogers v. Richmond, 365 U.S. 534, 535–36 (1961) (discussed in text at notes 75–82 *supra*).

265. *See* Kamisar, *supra* note 117, at 747 (though voluntary, confession to officer impersonating priest constitutionally impermissible). *See generally* Dix, *Undercover Investigations and Police Rulemaking*, 53 TEXAS L. REV. 203, 211–12 (1975).

266. 400 U.S. 446 (1971).

267. *Id.* at 447 n.1.

268. As Justice Stewart, writing for the Court, pointed out, respondent's trial had taken place several years before *Escobedo* and *Miranda,* and those decisions had not been given retroactive effect. *Id.* at 452–53. But *Massiah* could not be disposed of so easily. The Court had not held, and Justice Stewart did not suggest, that *Massiah* was not to be applied retroactively. Indeed, the following Term, protesting the Court's failure to reach the merits in Milton v. Wainwright, 407 U.S. 371 (1972), Justice Stewart called the retroactivity of *Massiah* "a wholly spurious issue," maintaining that "the rule in that case has been settled law ever since *Powell v. Alabama.*" *Id.* at 381–82 (Stewart, J., with Douglas, Brennan & Marshall, JJ., dissenting); *see* footnotes 25, 49 *supra* (discussion of *Milton v. Wainwright*).

269. People v. Bowman, 240 Cal. App. 2d 358, 49 Cal. Rptr. 772 (1st Dist. 1966) (dictum); People v. Flores, 236 Cal. App. 2d 807, 46 Cal. Rptr. 412 (2d Dist. 1965), *cert. denied,* 384 U.S. 1010 (1966); People v. Ludlum, 236 Cal. App. 2d 813, 46 Cal. Rptr. 375 (2d Dist. 1965). *See also* Dix, *supra* note 265, at 227–36.

270. *See* People v. Bowman, 240 Cal. App. 2d 358, 370–72, 49 Cal Rptr. 772, 780–82 (1st Dist. 1966). In *Bowman* the court stated:

> The court [below] . . . did not presage the adoption of the principle enunciated in *People v. Dorado,* [62 Cal. 2d 338, 398 P.2d 361, 42 Cal. Rptr. 169 (1965)] that where an investigation has progressed to the accusatory stage, statements elicited from an accused without informing him of his [rights] . . . should not be admitted against him without proof of waiver of those rights.
>
> . . . [I]t is clear from *Massiah* that once a defendant is formally charged and has counsel, statements which are thereafter surreptitiously obtained may not be used against him. . . . Similar considerations whether predicated on *Dorado* or *Massiah* preclude use of statements obtained by the prosecuting authorities from the accused by subterfuge before charges have been filed but after he has been taken into custody. . . .
>
> . . . It may be assumed that the surreptitious use of [government agents in various pre-1964 California cases] to secure statements from the accused after his arrest is now proscribed, not only because of *Massiah* [and similar cases], but also because

the necessity of advising the defendant of his right to counsel and right to remain silent precludes the concealment of the identity of an interrogator who seemingly is not, but in fact is, an agent of the prosecuting authorities.

240 Cal. App. 2d 370–72, 49 Cal. Rptr. at 780–82.

But if adversary judicial proceedings have not commenced against one in custody and he does not have and has not requested counsel, then *Massiah* rights do not attach. Furthermore, if the efforts of a government agent who "seemingly is not" such an agent to obtain incriminating statements from one in custody do not constitute "custodial police interrogation"—because the agent "seemingly is not" a government agent—then *Miranda* rights do not come into play either. If under the circumstances neither *Massiah* nor *Miranda* rights are called into play, then there are *no "rights"* of which the person in custody need be advised, which means that the State may conceal the agent's identity.

271. *See* footnotes 28–29 and note 125 *supra* and accompanying text.

272. Here, as elsewhere, state courts, in construing a state constitutional provision more expansively than the Supreme Court has interpreted a parallel or even a textually identical provision of the federal Bill of Rights, may afford the accused greater protection under state law than that said to be required by the federal Constitution. *See generally* Brennan, *State Constitutions and the Protection of Individual Rights,* 90 HARV. L. REV. 489 (1977); Howard, *State Courts and Constitutional Rights in the Day of the Burger Court,* 62 VA. L. REV. 873 (1976); Wilkes, *More on the New Federalism in Criminal Procedure,* 63 KY. L.J. 873 (1975); Wilkes, *The New Federalism in Criminal Procedure: State Court Evasion of the Burger Court,* 62 KY. L.J. 421 (1974); *see also* Y. KAMISAR, W. LaFAVE & J. ISRAEL, MODERN CRIMINAL PROCEDURE 2–5 (4th ed. Supp. 1978) (collecting cases).

273. *See* notes 29–30, 250–51 and footnotes 7–8 *supra* and accompanying text.

In Osborn v. United States, 385 U.S. 323 (1966), it is plain that the investigation had "focused" on petitioner by the time two federal judges authorized a tape recorder to be concealed on the undercover agent's person for his November 11 meeting with petitioner. *Id.* at 326. The possibility of bribing a juror had been considered at a November 7 meeting. *Id.* The same may be said of the investigation in United States v. White, 401 U.S. 745 (1971) (plurality opinion), at least by the *second* or *third* time defendant's conversations with a government informer were electronically overheard by federal narcotics agents. *Id* at 746–47.

274. *Cf.* People v. Ludlum, 236 Cal. App. 2d 813, 46 Cal. Rptr. 375 (2d Dist. 1965) (discussed at note 269 *supra*).

275. *Cf.* United States v. Fioravanti, 412 F.2d 407 (3d Cir.), *cert. denied,* 396 U.S. 837 (1969); Stowers v. United States, 351 F.2d 301 (9th Cir. 1965); State v. McCorgary, 218 Kan. 358, 543 P.2d 952 (1975).

276. *See* Hoffa v. United States, 385 U.S. 293, 304 (1966).

277. Dix, *supra* note 265, at 230.

278. *Id.*

279. *Id.* In his discussion of the "jail plant" problem, Professor Dix uses this very phrase, which makes his primary reliance on *Massiah,* rather than *Miranda,* all the more puzzling.

280. 413 U.S. 300 (1973).

281. *Id.* at 311.

282. 388 U.S. 218 (1967).

283. *See id.* at 224 ("[T]oday's law enforcement machinery involves critical confrontations of the accused by the prosecution at pretrial proceedings where the results might well settle the accused's fate and reduce the trial itself to a mere formality. In recognition of these realities of modern criminal prosecution, our cases have construed the Sixth Amendment guarantee to apply to 'critical' stages of the proceedings.")

284. Osborn v. United States, 385 U.S. 323, 326 (1966) (discussed at footnote 8 and note 273 *supra*).

285. 401 U.S. 745 (1971) (plurality opinion) (discussed at footnote 43 and notes 252–53 *supra* and accompanying text).

286. *Id.* at 746–47.

287. *See* note 283 *supra*.

288. Kirby v. Illinois, 406 U.S. 682, 690 (1972) (plurality opinion) (Stewart, J., with Burger, C.J., Blackmun & Rehnquist, JJ.) (emphasis in original). In *Kirby* the Court declined to apply the right to counsel to identification procedures conducted prior to the start of adversary judicial proceedings. Justice Powell noted simply that he "would not extend" the "*per se* exclusionary rule" of the original lineup cases. *See id.* at 691 (Powell, J., concurring). *See also* United States v. Ash, 413 U.S. 300, 321 (1973) (Stewart, J., concurring) ("a defendant is entitled to the assistance of counsel not only at the trial itself, but at all 'critical stages' of his 'prosecution'").

289. *Cf.* Kirby v. Illinois, 406 U.S. 682, 690 (1972) (plurality opinion).

290. *Cf. id.*

291. *Cf. id.* at 690–91. *See also* Moore v. Illinois, 434 U.S. 220, 227 (1977).

292. *See* Miranda v. Arizona, 384 U.S. at 478 (privilege against self-incrimination jeopardized when individual in custody or deprived of freedom in significant way and questioned). *See also id.* at 439, 457–58, 461, 465–67; footnote 30 *supra* (discussion of Brief of Amicus Curiae ACLU in *Miranda*).

293. Miller v. California, 392 U.S. 616, 626 (1968) (Marshall, J., with Warren, C.J., Douglas & Brennan, JJ., dissenting from dismissal of certiorari).

294. *See* footnotes 44–45 and notes 254–59 *supra* and accompanying text.

295. Dix, *supra* note 265, at 230.

296. *See* Kamisar, "*Custodial Interrogation*" *Within the Meaning of* Miranda, in INST. OF CONTINUING LEGAL EDUC., CRIMINAL LAW AND THE CONSTITUTION— SOURCES AND COMMENTARIES 335, 352–56 (1968) (illustrative cases decided within two years after *Miranda*).

Whether, once an arrestee volunteers a statement, the officer may ask some questions in order to clear up some points, or whether such follow-up questions constitute "interrogation" within the meaning of *Miranda,* is a difficult issue. I think follow-up questions seeking to enhance defendant's guilt or raise the offense to a higher degree (for example, by getting at the defendant's state of mind, "*why* did you do it?" or "*how long* did you *think* about it?") do constitute "interrogation," but follow-up questions merely designed to clarify just what the defendant said or meant to say may well not be. *Compare* People v. Sunday, 275 Cal. App. 2d 473, 481, 79 Cal. Rptr. 752, 756 (1969) (original assertion of rights by defendant does not require permanent application of no-interrogation rule when defendant volunteers statement) *with* People v. Mathews, 264 Cal. App. 2d 557, 566, 70 Cal. Rptr. 756, 764 (1968) (interrogation exists when police officer begins questioning). *See generally* Kamisar, *supra*, at 351–54, 379–82.

297. Miller v. California, 392 U.S. 616, 624 (Marshall, J., with Warren, C.J., Douglas & Brennan, JJ., dissenting from dismissal of certiorari).

298. Because of the freezing rain, slippery roads, and various stops along the way, the trip took this long—and the drive to the Mitchellville area, where the body was buried, probably took three or four hours. *See* Kamisar, *supra* note 14, at 210 n.4.

299. Kamisar, *supra* note 14, at 215. According to Captain Leaming's testimony, these in fact were most of the topics covered—before he launched into his famous Christian burial speech. *Id.*

300. *See* Miranda v. Arizona, 384 U.S. at 458, 465 (adequate protective devices dispel compulsion inherent in police custodial questioning).

301. *Id.* at 457.

302. *Id.* at 456.

303. *Id.* at 445 (emphasis added). *See also id.* at 456, 465.

304. *Id.* at 457.

305. *Id.* at 455.

306. *Id.* at 457–58.

307. *Id.* at 461.

308. *Id.* at 466.

309. *Cf.* Project, *Interrogations in New Haven: The Impact of* Miranda, 76 YALE L.J. 1519, 1545 (1967) (observations of tactics actually used by police to interrogate suspects). *See generally* 8 J. WIGMORE, EVIDENCE 309 (3d ed. 1940).

310. *See Hearings Before Subcomm. No. 2 of the House Comm. on the Judiciary*, 78th Cong., 1st Sess. 6 (1943) (hearings on bill to repeal *McNabb* rule) (testimony of Major Edward T. Kelly, then Superintendent of Police of the District of Columbia) ("I believe that every person should be guaranteed [his constitutional rights], but at the same time I believe, and I am confident, that when a person is charged with the commission of a serious crime, there should not be any interference with the police or detectives until such case is brought to a definite conclusion.").

311. *See* text at note 258 *supra*.

312. Project, *supra* note 309, at 1613–14.

313. *See id.* at 1614.

314. *See* footnote 36 *supra*.

315. *See* text at footnote 40 *supra;* footnote 9 *supra*.

316. "[F]our concurring Justices pointed out [in *Spano*] that the Constitution required reversal of the conviction on the sole and specific ground that the confession had been deliberately elicited by the police *after the defendant had been indicted,* and *therefore* at a time when he was clearly entitled to a lawyer's help." Massiah v. United States, 377 U.S. at 204 (emphasis added). "We hold that [Massiah] was denied the basic protections of [the sixth amendment] guarantee when there was used against him at his trial evidence of his own incriminating words, which federal agents had deliberately elicited from him *after he had been indicted and in the absence of his counsel.*" *Id.* at 206 (emphasis added). *See also* Brewer v. Williams, 430 U.S. at 398 ("Whatever else it may mean, the right to counsel . . . means at least that a person is entitled to the help of a lawyer *at or after the time* that judicial proceedings have been initiated against him. . . . ") (emphasis added).

317. "We are satisfied that all the principles embodied in the privilege apply to informal compulsion exerted by law-enforcement officers during in-custody questioning." Miranda v. Arizona, 384 U.S. at 461. *See also id.* at 467 ("there can be no doubt that the Fifth Amendment privilege is available outside of criminal court proceedings and serves to protect persons in all settings in which their freedom of action is curtailed in any significant way from being compelled to incriminate themselves"). *See* text at notes 84–88 *supra.*

318. *See* Kamisar, *supra* note 68, at 31–32.

319. *Cf.* J. MAGUIRE, EVIDENCE OF GUILT 109 (1959) (confessions usually given when speaker feels at mercy of those holding him in custody).

320. *Cf.* Foote, *The Fourth Amendment: Obstacle or Necessity in the Law of Arrest?* in POLICE POWER AND INDIVIDUAL FREEDOM 29, 30 (C. Sowle ed. 1962).

321. *See* text at notes 301–04 *supra.*

322. *See* text at footnote 57 *supra.*

323. *Cf.* Procunier v. Atchley, 400 U.S. 446, 454 (1971) (discussed at notes 266–68 *supra* and accompanying text).

324. *See* Miranda v. Arizona, 384 U.S. at 478 (rights apply to one taken into custody, deprived of freedom in significant way, and questioned).

325. Thompson, *supra* note 250, at 422 (Professor (now Governor) Thompson criticizes *Miranda* Court for failing to take account of this fact). *But see* Kamisar, *Kauper's "Judicial Examination of the Accused" Forty Years Later—Some Comments on a Remarkable Article,* 73 MICH. L. REV. 15, 30–31 n.59 (1974) [reprinted in this volume].

326. *See* Miranda v. Arizona, 384 U.S. at 477–78 & n.46 (police may visit suspect at home or office, but may not subject him to "custodial interrogation").

327. *See* notes 269–71 and footnotes 51–56 *supra* and accompanying text.

328. *See* cases discussed in footnote 63 *supra. See also* United States v. Holmes, 452 F.2d 249, 269 (7th Cir. 1971) (statement, unilluminated by any discussion that *Massiah's* rationale applies to postarrest, as well as postindictment, surveillance, but at time statements obtained defendant represented by counsel and released on bond); People v. Robinson, 16 A.D.2d 184, 224 N.Y.S.2d 705 (1962) (discussed at footnote 34 *supra*).

329. *See* United States v. Hall, 421 F.2d 540, 545 (2d Cir. 1969) (Friendly, J.).

330. *See* text at notes 152–82 *supra.*

331. *See* Israel, *supra* note 149, at 1386 n.281. *See also id.* at 1381–82 n.268; note 140 *supra* and accompanying text (discussion of lower court cases that have adopted very strict standard for effective waiver of *"Massiah* right to counsel").

332. *See* text at notes 8–14 *supra.*

333. *See* footnote 5 *supra.*

334. *See id.*

335. 423 U.S. 96 (1975) (Stewart, J.).

336. 384 U.S. at 473–74.

337. But the *Miranda* language cannot "sensibly" be so read, maintained the *Mosley* majority. Michigan v. Mosley, 423 U.S. 96, 102–03 (1975).

338. *Id.* at 104, 106.

339. *Id.* at 106.

340. *Id.* at 104; *see id.* at 106.

341. *Id.* at 104–05; *see* note 342 *infra*.

342. *Id.* at 106. The *Mosley* Court offered the following reasons for allowing a resumption of questioning in the fifth situation:

> The subsequent questioning [by Detective Hill] did not undercut Mosley's previous decision not to answer Detective Cowie's inquiries [at the first interrogation session]. Detective Hill did not resume the interrogation about [the two robberies that were the subject of the earlier interrogation], but instead focused exclusively on the Leroy Williams homicide [a homicide that had occurred in the course of a third robbery], a crime different in nature and in time and place of occurrence from the robberies for which Mosley had been arrested and interrogated by Detective Cowie. . . . [Hill's] questioning of Mosley about an unrelated homicide was quite consistent with Mosley's earlier refusal to answer any questions about the robberies.

Id. at 105.

I am operating on the premise that the *Mosley* facts were as the Supreme Court perceived them to be; but there is reason to doubt that this is so. Professor Geoffrey Stone, who has studied the *Mosley* record, indicates that the police testimony provides only shaky support for the view that after declining to discuss certain robberies at the initial interrogation Mosley was subsequently questioned about "an unrelated" robbery-murder. *See* Stone, *The* Miranda *Doctrine in the Burger Court*, 1977 SUP. CT. REV. 99, 134. He also points out that the Michigan courts never found—indeed, the Michigan Court of Appeals voiced skepticism—that the initial interrogation did not concern the robbery-murder. *Id.*

343. Michigan v. Mosley, 423 U.S. 96, 105 (1975).

344. Stone, *supra* note 342, at 134. *But see* Note, *Fifth Amendment, Confessions, Self-Incrimination—Does a Request for Counsel Prohibit a Subsequent Waiver of* Miranda *Prior to the Presence of Counsel?* 23 WAYNE L. REV. 1321, 1333–34 (1977). The Supreme Court of California recently held that assuming arguendo that the "circumstances" relied on by the *Mosley* Court "are essentially the same as those of the [instant case]," they are "inadequate to protect defendant's privilege against self-incrimination under the California Constitution." People v. Pettingill, 21 Cal. 3d 231, 247, 578 P.2d 108, 117–18, 145 Cal. Rptr. 861, 870–871 (1978).

345. Chase, *The Burger Court, the Individual, and the Criminal Process: Directions and Misdirections*, 52 N.Y.U. L. REV. 518, 559 (1977) (emphasis added). Concern about the coercion inherent in the continuing custody as well as the renewed questioning contributed to California's decision to reject *Mosley* as a matter of state constitutional law. *See* People v. Pettingill, *supra* note 344.

346. Brief for Petitioner, Joint App. at 75 (testimony of Captain Leaming).

347. *Id.* at 76 (testimony of Captain Leaming).

348. *See id.* at 55, 63, 74–76, 104 (testimony of Captain Leaming and Detective Nelson). *But cf. id.* at 81 (testimony of Captain Leaming) (discussed at footnote 80 *supra*).

349. *Cf.* Michigan v. Mosley, 423 U.S. 96, 104–05 (1975). The *Mosley* Court described the facts in that case as follows:

> A review of the circumstances leading to Mosley's confession reveals that his "right to cut off questioning" was fully respected in this case. . . . When Mosley stated [at

the first interrogation session] that he did not want to discuss the robberies, Detective Cowie immediately ceased the interrogation and did not try either to resume the questioning or in any way to persuade Mosley to reconsider his position. . . . [Mosley] was given full and complete *Miranda* warnings at the outset of the second interrogation. He was thus reminded again that he could remain silent and could consult with a lawyer, and was carefully given a full and fair opportunity to exercise these options.

Id.

350. *See* Brewer v. Williams, 430 U.S. at 399.

351. Michigan v. Mosley, 423 U.S. 96, 105 (1975).

352. *See* Miranda v. Arizona, 384 U.S. at 476.

353. *See* footnote 78 *supra*.

354. *Id.*

355. 430 U.S. at 436 n.6 (White, J., with Blackmun & Rehnquist, JJ., dissenting).

356. *See generally* Kamisar, *supra* note 14.

357. 430 U.S. at 405.

358. Brief for Petitioner, Joint App. at 75–76 (testimony of Captain Leaming).

359. 375 F. Supp. at 173; *see id.* at 176.

360. *Id.* at 173.

361. *Id.; see id.* at 176.

362. 430 U.S. at 436 n.6 (White, J., with Blackmun & Rehnquist, JJ., dissenting); *see* footnote 79 *supra*.

363. 384 U.S. at 473–74 (emphasis added).

364. *Id.* at 444–45 (emphasis added).

365. 430 U.S. at 436 n.6 (White, J., with Blackmun & Rehnquist, JJ., dissenting); *see* footnote 79 *supra*.

366. 430 U.S. at 405.

367. *See* footnote 79 *supra*. Williams was also an escapee from a mental hospital, black, and a resident of the state for only a few months.

368. 430 U.S. at 436 n.6 (White, J., with Blackmun & Rehnquist, JJ., dissenting).

369. *See* text at notes 31–117 *supra*.

370. *See* footnote 5 *supra*.

371. *See* text at footnote 71 and note 330 *supra*.

372. Brief for Petitioner at 13.

373. *See* Miranda v. Arizona, 384 U.S. at 474 (if suspect "indicates that he wants" counsel "before speaking to the police, they must respect his decision to remain silent").

374. *See* footnote 80 *supra*.

375. 430 U.S. at 436 n.6 (White, J., with Blackmun & Rehnquist, JJ., dissenting).

376. *See* Stone, *supra* note 342, at 100–01. Professor Stone noted:

[T]he Court, in the years since Warren Burger assumed the role of Chief Justice, has handed down eleven decisions concerning the scope and application of *Miranda*. In ten of these cases, the Court interpreted *Miranda* so as not to exclude the challenged evidence. In the remaining case [Doyle v. Ohio, 426 U.S. 610 (1976)], the Court avoided a direct ruling on the *Miranda* issue, holding the evidence inadmissible on other grounds [namely, that it is fundamentally unfair to allow an arrestee's silence to be used to impeach his explanation that is subsequently offered at trial].

Id. at 100.

377. When they were first handed down—a mere five weeks apart—in the spring of 1964, *Escobedo* was considered a much more important case than *Massiah,* but *Escobedo* was more or less displaced by *Miranda. See* footnotes 24–29 and notes 118–25 *supra* and accompanying text.

378. *See generally* Stone, *supra* note 342; Chase, *supra* note 345, at 555–60. *But cf.* Israel, *supra* note 149, at 1373–87 (although ramifications of *Miranda* narrowed, Court still adheres to basic premise that right against self-incrimination applies to custodial interrogation).

379. Israel, *supra* note 149, at 1382. As Professor Israel points out, even the *Williams* dissenters "did not question the basic premise of *Massiah.*" *Id.* Dissenting Justices Blackmun, Rehnquist, and White "indicate[d] that they clearly had no difficulty with *Massiah's* recognition of a defendant's right to counsel during interrogation," but "contended only that [Williams] . . . had waived it." *Id.* at 1382 n.269. "Chief Justice Burger's dissent," continues Professor Israel, "concentrated primarily on the point that per se exclusion of evidence should not be required even if there is a constitutional violation, and therefore the Chief Justice presumably would not accept *Massiah* insofar as it automatically requires exclusion of statements obtained in violation of the right to counsel." *Id.*

380. *See* Herman, *supra* note 68, at 490–91; Kamisar, *supra* note 68, at 44–45; Traynor, *supra* note 53, at 673 (lecture delivered seven weeks before *Miranda*); *Developments in the Law—Confessions,* 79 HARV. L. REV. 935, 1006 (1966) (three months before *Miranda*); Note, *The Right to Counsel During Police Interrogation: The Aftermath of* Escobedo, 53 CALIF. L. REV. 337, 349 n.66 (1965). Justice Traynor's criticism and rejection of what came to be known as the *Massiah* doctrine, but was then known as the "New York rule" or the "*Di Biasi* rule" (after People v. Di Biasi, 7 N.Y.2d 544, 166 N.E.2d 825, 200 N.Y.S.2d 21 (1960), which adopted the view of the *Spano* concurring opinions and presaged *Massiah*) is set forth more fully in his concurring opinion in People v. Garner, 57 Cal. 2d 135, 156–66, 367 P.2d 680, 693–99, 18 Cal. Rptr. 40, 53–59 (1961), *cert. denied,* 370 U.S. 929 (1962). *See* text *supra* at note 395 and footnote 88.

381. *See* footnote 87 *supra* and authorities cited therein.

382. *See, e.g.,* Allen, *The Judicial Quest for Penal Justice: The Warren Court and the Criminal Cases,* 1975 U. ILL. L.F. 518, 538–39; Amsterdam, *supra* note 199, at 801–03; Chase, *supra* note 345, at 518–19, 594–95. Both Professors Allen and Amsterdam indicate that the Court's loss of impetus in the criminal procedure field would have occurred without any change in its personnel.

383. Stone, *supra* note 342, at 100.

384. *Id.* at 169.

385. Some foresee the overruling of *Miranda. See* F. INBAU, J. THOMPSON, J. HADDAD, J. ZAGEL & G. STARKMAN, CASES AND COMMENTS ON CRIMINAL PROCEDURE 355 (1974). Others, whose view I share, suggest that this is unlikely to occur. *See* Israel, *supra* note 149, at 1383–87; Stone, *supra* note 342, at 169. The Court has demonstrated its ability to "shrink" and "chip away" at *Miranda* and will probably be quite content to continue to do so.

386. *See* A. BEISEL, CONTROL OVER ILLEGAL ENFORCEMENT OF THE CRIMINAL LAW 70–107 (1955); Amsterdam, *supra* note 199, at 806–08; Dession, *The New Federal Rules of Criminal Procedure: I,* 55 YALE L.J. 694, 708 (1946); Enker & Elsen, *supra* note 185, at 84–85; Kamisar, *supra* note 255, at 94–104; *Developments in the Law—Confessions, supra* note 380, at 954–84; 72 YALE L.J. 1434, 1438 (1963).

387. 377 U.S. at 204.

388. *Cf. id.* "Under our system of justice the most elemental concepts of due process of law contemplate that an indictment be followed by a trial, 'in an orderly courtroom, presided over by a judge, open to the public. . . . '" *Id. See also* Spano v. New York, 360 U.S. 315, 327 (1959) (Stewart, J., with Douglas & Brennan, JJ., concurring) ("Under our system of justice an indictment is supposed to be followed by an arraignment and a trial.").

389. *Id.* at 325 (Douglas, J., with Black & Brennan, JJ., concurring).

390. Traynor, *supra* note 53, at 673.

391. In People v. Waterman, 9 N.Y.2d 561, 175 N.E.2d 445, 216 N.Y.S.2d 70 (1961), Judge Fuld noted:

Since the finding of the indictment presumably imports that the People have legally sufficient evidence of the defendant's guilt of the crime charged, the necessities of appropriate police investigation "to solve a crime, or even to absolve a suspect" cannot be urged as justification for any subsequent questioning of the defendant.

Id. at 565, 175 N.E.2d at 447–48, 216 N.Y.S.2d at 74–75. This is not always so. *See* text at footnote 88 *supra.* But to the extent that it usually is, the "indictment rule" is subject to the criticism that it is tilted too heavily in favor of the government and would have little practical impact on police interrogation practices. *See* Herman, *supra* note 68, at 484–85. *See also Developments in the Law—Confessions, supra* note 380, at 1011 (view that sixth amendment protection comes into play only after crime is "solved" in sense of amassing enough admissible evidence to convict "would trivialize *Escobedo* by bringing its safeguards into play only after conviction had been assured"). *Brewer v. Williams,* however, reemphasizes the *Massiah* rule; the initiation of judicial proceedings—"whether by way of formal charge, preliminary hearing, indictment, information or arraignment"—now triggers the right to counsel. 430 U.S. at 398 (quoting from Kirby v. Illinois, 406 U.S. 682, 689 (1972) (plurality opinion)). Depending on just when judicial proceedings are now deemed to be initiated, the rule may be less responsive to the government's needs.

Brewer v. Williams itself is a good illustration of the problem. Apparently because he surrendered in Davenport and awaited the arrival of the Des Moines police to bring him back, Williams was "arraigned" on the arrest warrant before a Davenport judge and committed by that judge to confinement in a Davenport jail. These proceedings were unrelated to the need of the Des Moines police for information.

392. Under the *Massiah-Williams* rule, a suspect is "entitled to a lawyer's help" when judicial proceedings have been initiated against him. *See* Brewer v. Williams, 430 U.S. at 398–401; Massiah v. United States, 377 U.S. at 204. There is, however, a very weak congruence, if any, between the initiation of judicial proceedings and a suspect's need for a lawyer's help. Not only may there be as strong a need for a lawyer's help before the commencement of judicial proceedings as afterwards, but it may be too late for a lawyer's help afterwards.

393. Traynor, *supra* note 53, at 673.

394. *Cf.* Craig v. Boren, 429 U.S. 190, 202 (1976) (small statistical difference between 18-to-20-year-old male and female drunk driving arrests provides an "unduly tenuous 'fit'" for any drinking age classification based on gender).

395. *See* note 380 *supra*.

396. People v. Waterman, 9 N.Y.2d 561, 567, 175 N.E.2d 445, 448, 216 N.Y.S.2d 70, 76 (1961). Because the defendant confessed under police questioning during the period between the return of the indictment and his arraignment thereon, there was no need for the court to establish "congruence" beyond the course of a formally instituted prosecution, but the court did observe, with apparent approval: "It has been urged that, 'To maintain the integrity of the judicial process in its use of evidence of criminal guilt, congruence must be maintained *between the judicial process and the non-judicial,* pretrial processes with respect to the methods by which evidence of criminal guilt is secured.'" *Id.* (quoting from A. BEISEL, *supra* note 386, at 102) (emphasis added). It is plain that Professor Beisel had urged that congruence be maintained between the proceedings in the courtroom and those in the police station—regardless of whether a "criminal prosecution" has begun. Thus, in the very next paragraph following the one quoted in part in *Waterman,* Professor Beisel continues:

> Should not, therefore, the privilege against self-incrimination control police and prosecutive officers in securing confessions or other incriminating statements at the police station? Should not an accused, or a witness under proper circumstances, have a right to privilege of silence at the police station? Under the principle of congruence which was just explained, the answer would have to be in the affirmative, since there is no accepted principle which would justifiably demarcate the police or prosecutor from other executive or administrative officials to whom the privilege does apply. . . .
>
> Since the doctrine of waiver is interpreted in a manner which gives an accused real protection for his right of silence in the courtroom, should not the Supreme Court maintain congruence between standards of judicial waiver and those which are applied at the police station, so that an accused can have real protection for his right to silence at the police station? Unless the doctrine of waiver at the police station is made congruent with that of the courtroom, extension of the privilege against self-incrimination into the police station loses most of its practical significance. . . .

Id. at 102–14.

397. *See* note 396 *supra*.

398. *Cf.* T. ARNOLD, THE SYMBOLS OF GOVERNMENT 130 (Harbinger Books ed. 1962) (criminal trial overshadows all other ceremonies as dramatization of values of our spiritual government). "[T]he cultural value of the ideal of a fair trial is advanced as much by its failure as it is by its success. Any violation of the symbol of a ceremonial trial rouses persons who would be left unmoved by an ordinary non-ceremonial injustice." *Id.* at 142.

399. *Cf.* M. EDELMAN, THE SYMBOLIC USES OF POLITICS 4 (1964). *See also id.* at 37, 178–79.

400. *See* Arnold, *The Criminal Trial as a Symbol of Public Morality,* in CRIMINAL JUSTICE IN OUR TIME 140 (A. Howard ed. 1965) ("[Procedural] restrictions are unquestionably handicaps in the enforcement of the law. . . . Nevertheless, there is a

tremendous psychological need for the appearance of justice which a fair trial creates in the public mind.").

401. *Cf.* T. ARNOLD, *supra* note 398, at 128–30, 156.

402. Traynor, *supra* note 53, at 673; *cf.* Friendly, *supra* note 53, at 950 (*Escobedo* "can well be read as requiring the assistance of counsel only when the police elicit a confession at the station house from a suspect, already long detained, whose case is ripe for presentation to a magistrate—in other words, that the police, by unduly deferring such presentation, may not postpone the assistance of counsel that would then become available.").

403. The Court in Escobedo v. Illinois, 378 U.S. 478 (1964), in an opinion by Justice Goldberg, maintained that because petitioner had, at the time of interrogation, "for all practical purposes already been charged with murder," "it would exalt form over substance to make the right to counsel, under these circumstances, depend on whether at [this time] the authorities had secured a formal indictment." *Id.* at 486. Thus, the "fact [that] . . . the interrogation here was conducted before petitioner was formally indicted . . . should make no difference." *Id.* at 485. But dissenting Justice Stewart insisted that "'that fact' . . . makes all the difference." *Id.* at 493. Justice Stewart continued:

> [T]he *vital* fact remains that this case does not involve the deliberate interrogation of a defendant after the initiation of judicial proceedings against him. The Court disregards this *basic* difference between the present case and Massiah's. . . .
>
> . . . .
>
> [T]he court today converts a routine police investigation of an unsolved murder into a *distorted analogue* of a judicial trial. It imports into this investigation constitutional concepts historically applicable only after the onset of formal prosecutorial proceedings. By doing so, [it] *perverts* those precious constitutional guarantees, and frustrates the vital interests of society in preserving the legitimate and proper function of honest and purposeful police investigation.

Id. at 493–94 (emphasis added); *see* notes 120–23 *supra* and accompanying text.

In Kirby v. Illinois, 406 U.S. 682 (1972) (plurality opinion), in which the Court held that a suspect is not entitled to counsel at a showup conducted before the initiation of adversary criminal proceedings, Justice Stewart observed:

> In a line of constitutional cases in this Court stemming back to . . . *Powell v. Alabama,* . . . it has been firmly established that a person's . . . right to counsel attaches only at or after the time that adversary judicial proceedings have been initiated against him. . . .
>
> . . . .
>
> The only seeming deviation from this long line of constitutional decisions was *Escobedo* . . . [which] is not apposite here for two distinct reasons. First, the Court in restrospect perceived that the "prime purpose" of *Escobedo* was not to vindicate the constitutional right to counsel as such, but, like *Miranda,* "to guarantee full effectuation of the privilege against self-incrimination. . . . " Secondly, and perhaps even more important for purely practical purposes, the Court has limited the holding of *Escobedo* to its own facts. . . .

Id. at 688–89. *But see* Grano, *Kirby, Biggers and Ash: Do Any Constitutional*

Safeguards Remain Against the Danger of Convicting the Innocent? 72 MICH. L. REV. 717, 726–30 (1974) (powerful criticism of Justice Stewart's views in *Kirby,* especially his retrospective view of *Escobedo*).

404. Mallory v. United States, 354 U.S. 449 (1957); McNabb v. United States, 318 U.S. 332 (1943).

405. McNabb v. United States, 318 U.S. 332, 341 (1943).

406. *Id.*

407. Title II of the Omnibus Crime Control and Safe Streets Act of 1968 provides that a confession "shall not be inadmissible solely because of delay" in bringing an arrestee before a commissioner if such confession is "made voluntarily," if the weight to be given it is left to the jury and if it "was made or given . . . within six hours immediately following [the defendant's] arrest or other detention." 18 U.S.C. § 3501(c) (1976). In Johnson v. State, 282 Md. 314, 384 A.2d 709 (1978), Chief Judge Murphy observed:

> While it is possible to construe this legislation as restricting the *McNabb-Mallory* rule to delays in excess of six hours, the federal courts have generally construed the statute in a more liberal manner, rejecting *McNabb-Mallory* completely, and holding that a delay in arraignment greater than six hours "merely constitutes another factor to be considered by the trial judge in determining voluntariness". . . .

Id at 345, 384 A.2d at 726 (Murphy, C.J., with Smith & Orth, JJ., dissenting). *See also* United States v. Gaines, 555 F.2d 618, 623 (7th Cir. 1977) (that defendant was held 46 hours by city officials before being turned over to federal officials and presented did not invalidate involuntary admission because no evidence of collusive arrangement between federal and city officials); 53 NOTRE DAME LAW. 545 (1978) (criticism of *Gaines*).

408. *See generally* Hogan & Snee, *The* McNabb-Mallory *Rule: Its Rise, Rationale, and Rescue,* 47 GEO. L.J. 1, 5 (1958); *see also* W. Murphy, *Lower Court Checks on Supreme Court Power,* 53 AM. POLITICAL SCI. REV. 1017, 1023–26 (1956); Rothblatt & Rothblatt, *Police Interrogation: The Right to Counsel and to Prompt Arraignment,* 27 BROOKLYN L. REV. 24, 40–42 (1960); *Developments in the Law—Confessions, supra* note 380, at 988–94.

409. Amsterdam, *supra* note 199, at 808; *see* Broeder, Wong Sun v. United States: *A Study in Faith and Hope,* 42 NEB. L. REV. 483, 564–94 (1963) (*McNabb-Mallory* rests, or should be regarded as resting, on constitutional grounds).

410. *See, e.g.,* Allen, *supra* note 199, at 28–29; Douglas, *supra* note 199, at 107, 113–14, 120; *Developments in the Law—Confessions, supra* note 380, at 988–94; Comment, *supra* note 199, at 1021–24 (1959). *See also* People v. Pettingill, 21 Cal.3d 231, 244, 578 P.2d 108, 116, 145 Cal. Rptr. 861, 869 (1978) (discussion of other important functions served by prompt presentment requirement); Johnson v. State, 282 Md. 314, 321–22, 328, 384 A.2d 709, 713–14, 719 (1978) (Levine, J.) (same).

411. Justice Frankfurter, the author of the *McNabb* and *Mallory* opinions, took note of this in Culombe v. Connecticut, 367 U.S. 568 (1961), by calling the *McNabb* case an "innovation which derived from our concern and responsibility for fair modes of criminal proceeding in the federal courts." *Id.* at 600–01.

412. It was not until 1960 that the states' unanimity in refusing to follow the

Supreme Court's lead in the *McNabb-Mallory* line of cases was broken. *See* People v. Hamilton, 359 Mich. 410, 415–17, 102 N.W.2d 738, 741–42 (1960); Rothblatt & Rothblatt, *supra* note 408, at 42–44. On the eve of *Miranda,* Justice Traynor reported that a second state, Connecticut, had adopted by legislation an equivalent of the *McNabb-Mallory* rule. Traynor, *supra* note 53, at 666 & n.44; *see* State v. Vollhardt, 157 Conn. 25, 39, 244 A.2d 601, 607 (1968) (subsequent case construing statute). Justice Traynor was evidently unaware that Delaware had also adopted a *McNabb-Mallory* rule. *See* Webster v. State, 59 Del. 54, 59, 213 A.2d 298, 301 (1965); Vorhauer v. State, 59 Del. 35, 46, 212 A.2d 886, 892 (1965). Since then, at least three more state courts—Maryland, Montana, and Pennsylvania—have adopted some equivalent of the *McNabb-Mallory* rule. *See* Johnson v. State, 282 Md. 314, 323–30, 384 A.2d 709, 714–18 (1978); State v. Benbo, 570 P.2d 894, 899–900 (Mont. 1977); Commonwealth v. Davenport, 471 Pa. 278, 286, 370 A.2d 301, 306 (1977); Commonwealth v. Smith, 463 Pa. 393, 396–98, 344 A.2d 889, 890–91 (1975); Commonwealth v. Tingle, 451 Pa. 241, 246, 301 A.2d 701, 703 (1973); Commonwealth v. Futch, 447 Pa. 389, 391–94, 290 A.2d 417, 418–19 (1972). It is still true, however, as the most recent state court to adopt the rule readily conceded, that "the vast majority of state courts passing on the question have rejected *McNabb-Mallory* outright, opting instead for a traditional due process voluntariness test of the admissibility of confessions." *See* Johnson v. State, 282 Md. at 324, 384 A.2d at 715.

413. McNabb v. United States, 318 U.S. 332, 340 (1943) ("Judicial supervision of the administration of criminal justice in the federal courts implies the duty of establishing and maintaining civilized standards of procedure and evidence. Such standards are not satisfied merely by observance of those minimal historic safeguards for securing trial by reasons which are summarized as 'due process of law'. . . . ").

414. In Gerstein v. Pugh, 420 U.S. 103 (1975), the Court held that "the Fourth Amendment requires a judicial determination of probable cause as a prerequisite to extended restraint of liberty following arrest [without a warrant]." *Id.* at 114. Nevertheless, the majority held that this determination can be and "traditionally has been decided by a magistrate in a nonadversary proceeding on hearsay and written testimony." *Id.* at 120. Although many states are likely to incorporate the "probable cause" determination into some existing procedures, such as the procedure for setting bail or advising a suspect of his right to counsel, the *constitutional need* for such a postarrest judicial determination of probable cause *could be satisfied,* it seems, *without the presence* of the arrestee—as it is when a magistrate issues a warrant on the basis of a complaint or an officer's affidavit. Moreover, it is unclear whether the government must obtain a judicial determination of probable cause as quickly as some courts required the police to bring an arrestee before a judicial officer to satisfy the *McNabb-Mallory* rule. Nor is it clear whether and under what circumstances a failure to comply with the *Gerstein v. Pugh* requirement will lead to the exclusion of an otherwise admissible confession.

The *Gerstein v. Pugh* holding that neither the appointment of counsel nor other "adversary safeguards" are required for the probable cause determination strongly implies that this judicial determination, like the issuance of an arrest warrant, does not mark the initiation of adversary judicial proceedings. *See id.* at 120, 122. There is, however, some authority for the view that the filing of a complaint or the issuance of an arrest warrant does mark the commencement of judicial proceedings within the meaning of Kirby v. Illinois, 406 U.S. 682 (1971) (plurality opinion). *See* Burton v. Cuyler, 439 F. Supp. 1173, 1181 (E.D. Pa. 1977) (issuance of arrest warrant along with circumstances surrounding lineup indicates initiation of judicial proceedings); Commonwealth v. Richman, 458 Pa. 167, 171, 320 A.2d 351, 353 (1974) (initiation of judicial proceedings in Pennsylvania at arrest). But *Richman* relied in part on the views of a divided panel in Robinson v. Zelker, 468 F.2d 159, 163 (2d Cir. 1972) (arrest warrant initiates judicial proceedings), which was later repudiated by another, unanimous panel of the same court in United States v. Duvall, 537 F.2d 15, 22 (2d Cir.), *cert. denied,* 426 U.S. 950 (1976). Indeed, *Richman* goes so far as to say that a *warrantless* arrest marks the initiation of judicial proceedings, an untenable interpretation of *Kirby* in my view, but a position that a state court may take as a matter of state law (and that some members of the *Richman* court explicitly did take). 458 Pa. at 172, 320 A.2d at 353. The views of the federal district court in *Burton v. Cuyler* seem to conflict with two opinions of its own court of appeals. *See* Government of the Virgin Islands v. Navarro, 513 F.2d 11, 18 (3d Cir. 1975) (dictum) (lineup after arrest not initiation of judicial proceedings); United States v. Coades, 468 F.2d 1061, 1063 (3d Cir. 1972) (preliminary hearing initiates judicial proceedings). But the result in *Burton* is quite understandable on its facts. The challenged lineup was not held until three positive photographic identifications had been made, and by the time the lineup was conducted it seemed plain that the government was committed to prosecuting and was simply amassing further evidence for that purpose.

I think it is no accident that in *Burton, Richman,* and *Robinson,* all of which indicate that judicial proceedings are initiated by an arrest warrant, the issue arose in a pretrial identification—not a police interrogation—context. Although the Supreme Court and courts generally seem to have treated the question of when judicial proceedings commence within the meaning of (i) *Massiah* and (ii) *Kirby* as the same question, the different procedural contexts may have at least a strong subliminal impact on some courts. As a policy matter, it seems considerably more difficult to resist the presence of counsel at a lineup than in the interrogation room. When he can do so, a defense lawyer will usually prevent all police questioning, but he is unlikely—indeed, not empowered—to disrupt pretrial identification proceedings. Moreover, unlike the Warren Court "confession" cases, which arguably "furthered societal values not usually related to guilt or innocence," the Warren Court pretrial identification cases "explicitly sought to protect the innocent from wrongful conviction." Grano, *supra* note 403, at 722.

415. People v. Donovan, 13 N.Y.2d 148, 151, 193 N.E.2d 628, 629, 243 N.Y.S.2d 841, 843 (1963).

416. People v. Arthur, 22 N.Y.2d 325, 328–29, 239 N.E.2d 537, 538–39, 292 N.Y.S.2d 663, 666 (1968). In People v. Hobson, 39 N.Y.2d 479, 348 N.E.2d 894, 384 N.Y.S.2d 419 (1976), the court commented:

[T]he rule of the *Arthur* case is not absolute. Thus, the fact that a defendant is represented by counsel in a proceeding unrelated to the charges under investigation is not sufficient to invoke the rule. . . . The rule applies only to a defendant who is in custody. . . . Moreover, the rule . . . does not render inadmissible a defendant's spontaneously volunteered statement.

Id. at 483, 348 N.E.2d at 897, 384 N.Y.S.2d at 421–22.

417. People v. Ramos, 40 N.Y.2d 610, 622–23, 357 N.E.2d 955, 963–64, 389 N.Y.S.2d 299, 307–08 (1976) (Jasen, J., dissenting) (excellent exposition of reasoning behind New York rule with which *Ramos* majority would agree; dissent disagreed with majority on application of rule to facts of case).

418. Spano v. New York, 360 U.S. 315, 317, 319 (1959).

419. Massiah v. United States, 377 U.S. at 204 ("[Four] concurring Justices pointed out [in *Spano*] that the Constitution required reversal of the conviction upon *the sole and specific ground* that the confession had been deliberately elicited by the police *after the defendant had been indicted,* and *therefore at a time when he was clearly entitled to a lawyer's help."*) (emphasis added); *see* Brewer v. Williams, 430 U.S. at 398 ("[T]he right to counsel . . . means at least that a person is *entitled to* the help of a lawyer at or after the time that judicial proceedings have been initiated against him. . . . ") (emphasis added).

420. 377 U.S. at 204–05.

421. 9 N.Y.2d 561, 175 N.E.2d 445, 216 N.Y.S.2d 70 (1961).

422. 377 U.S. at 205 (quoting from People v. Waterman, 9 N.Y.2d 561, 565, 175 N.E.2d 445, 448, 216 N.Y.S.2d 70, 75 (1961)) (emphasis added).

423. *See* People v. Waterman 9 N.Y.2d 561, 564–65, 175 N.E.2d 445, 447, 216 N.Y.S.2d 70, 74 (1961).

424. *Id.*

425. 11 N.Y.2d 162, 182 N.E.2d 103, 227 N.Y.S.2d 427 (1962).

426. *Id.* at 162, 182 N.E.2d at 104, 227 N.Y.S.2d at 428.

427. *Id.*

428. 377 U.S. at 205 (quoting from Powell v. Alabama, 287 U.S. 45, 57 (1932)) (emphasis added). The same passage from *Powell* is quoted with approval in Brewer v. Williams, 430 U.S. at 398.

429. 377 U.S. at 205 (referring to Hamilton v. Alabama, 368 U.S. 52 (1961), and White v. Maryland, 373 U.S. 59 (1963)).

430. Powell v. Alabama, 287 U.S. 45, 57 (1932) (emphasis added).

431. White v. Maryland, 373 U.S. 59, 60 (1963); Hamilton v. Alabama, 368 U.S. 52, 53 (1961).

432. Enker & Elsen, *supra* note 185, at 51.

433. Gideon v. Wainwright, 372 U.S. 335 (1963).

434. *See* Douglas v. California, 372 U.S. 353, 355 (1963) (indigent has right to appointed counsel on appeal of right); Griffin v. Illinois, 351 U.S. 12, 19 (1956) (indigent has right to free transcript on appeal). *See generally* Y. KAMISAR, W. LaFAVE & J. ISRAEL, *supra* note 261, at 68–80 (discussion of applications and implications of *Griffin* and *Douglas*); Gerard, *The Right to Counsel on Appeal in Missouri,* 1965 WASH. U.L.Q. 463, 479–80 (questioning extent to which state must go to comply with *Douglas*); Israel, *supra* note 149, at 1331–39 (Burger Court has not undermined equality theme established by Warren Court); Kamisar & Choper, *The Right to Counsel in Minnesota: Some Field Findings and Legal-Policy Observations,* 48 MINN. L. REV. 1, 4–14 (1963) (discussion of application and limitations of *Douglas* and *Griffin*). There are different views as to the impact on the equality principle of Ross v. Moffit, 417 U.S. 600 (1974), which declined to extend the *Douglas* right to appointed counsel on first appeal to application for discretionary review in state supreme courts. *Compare* Hartman, *The Burger Court—1973 Term: Leaving the Sixties Behind Us,* 65

J. CRIM. L. & CRIMINOLOGY 437, 442–44 (1974) *and* Kamisar, *Poverty, Equality, and Criminal Procedure,* in NAT'L COLLEGE OF DIST. ATTORNEYS, CONSTITUTIONAL LAW DESKBOOK 1-97 to 1-110 (1977) *with* Israel, *supra,* at 1334–39.

435. State v. McLeod, 1 Ohio St. 2d 60, 60, 203 N.E.2d 349, 350 (1964).

436. *Id.* at 60, 203 N.E.2d at 350.

437. 173 Ohio St. 520, 520, 184 N.E.2d 101, 101 (1962).

438. McLeod v. Ohio, 378 U.S. 582 (1964) (per curiam).

439. 1 Ohio St. 2d at 64, 203 N.E.2d at 353 (Gibson, J., with O'Neill, J., dissenting).

440. *Id.* at 62, 203 N.E.2d at 351 (per curiam).

441. *Id.* at 65, 203 N.E.2d at 353.

442. *Id.* (emphasis supplied by dissent).

443. *Cf.* Bloom v. Illinois, 391 U.S. 194, 213 (1968) (Fortas, J., concurring).

444. *See* footnote 63 *supra* (*Smith, Daugherty,* and *McCorgary* cases). People v. Miller, 245 Cal. App. 2d 112, 53 Cal. Rptr. 720 (4th Dist. 1966), is as shocking a case of "jail plant" interference with the attorney-client relationship as one is ever likely to come across. *See* footnote 49 *supra.* I cannot believe the conviction in that case would have been affirmed if the Supreme Court had reached the merits. *See also* Milton v. Wainwright, 407 U.S. 371 (1972) (discussed in footnote 49 *supra*).

445. *See* United States v. Crookston, 379 F. Supp. 487, 488 (W.D. Tex. 1974); Commonwealth v. McKenna, 355 Mass. 313, 319–20, 244 N.E.2d 560, 563 (1969). *See also* People v. Ressler, 17 N.Y.2d 174, 216 N.E.2d 582, 269 N.Y.S.2d 414 (1966). In *Ressler* the court noted:

> The misleading answer given by the Chief of Detectives [when contacted by a law clerk from the firm retained to represent defendant] that there was nothing wrong and no need for a lawyer threw defense counsel off guard, and the consequence is the same as though the police had been instructed by an attorney for defendant that he was not to be interrogated in the absence of counsel.

Id. at 178, 216 N.E.2d at 583–84, 269 N.Y.S.2d at 415.

Consider, too, People v. Pinzon, 44 N.Y.2d 458, 377 N.E.2d 721, 406 N.Y.S.2d 268 (1978), in which police department central switchboard operators misinformed the defense lawyer (but apparently unintentionally) that the department did not "have" his client. *Id.* at 460, 377 N.E.2d at 722, 406 N.Y.S.2d at 268. The *Donovan* rule applied, held the *Pinzon* court, even though the lawyer had not spoken to any police officers. *Id.* at 465, 377 N.E.2d at 725, 406 N.Y.S.2d at 271. "[C]onfusion or lack of communication within the law enforcement agencies cannot impair the defendant's rights." *Id.*

446. *Cf.* H. FRIENDLY, *On Entering the Path of the Law,* in BENCHMARKS 22, 30 (1967).

447. *Cf.* Amsterdam, *supra* note 199, at 810.

448. Allen, *supra* note 382, at 525.

449. *See* Vorenberg, *Police Detention and Interrogation of Uncounselled Suspects: The Supreme Court and the States,* 44 B.U. L. REV. 423, 430 (1964) (*Donovan* first clear and authoritative decision barring confession from defendant denied opportunity to confer with counsel); Uviller, *The Judge at the Cop's Elbow,* 71 COLUM. L. REV. 707, 716 (1971) (*Donovan* foretold reasoning of *Miranda* "with uncanny clair-

voyance"); 5 FORDHAM URB. L.J. 401, 405 (1977) (*Donovan* preceded in time and exceeded in scope *Escobedo* and *Miranda* holdings).

450. The *Donovan* rule had been badly crippled. *See* People v. Lopez, 28 N.Y.2d 23, 26, 268 N.E.2d 628, 629, 319 N.Y.S.2d 825, 826–27 (rule inapplicable when defendant without retained counsel waived all rights without being informed that he was indicted), *cert. denied,* 404 U.S. 840 (1971); Peoples v. Robles, 27 N.Y.2d 155, 159, 263 N.E.2d 304, 305, 314 N.Y.S.2d 793, 795 (1970) (rule applicable only when affirmative acts by police intended to outwit attorney or victim), *cert. denied,* 401 U.S. 945 (1971). The rule was rescued and revivified in 1976. *See* People v. Hobson, 39 N.Y. 2d 479, 484–85, 348 N.E.2d 894, 898–99, 384 N.Y.S.2d 419, 422 (1976) (extracted in text *supra* at footnote 99. *See generally* 5 FORDHAM URB. L.J. 401, 407–11 (1977).

451. Wilkes, *More on the New Federalism in Criminal Procedure,* 63 KY. L.J. 873, 873 (1975). *See generally* Brennan, *supra* note 272; Howard, *supra* note 272, at 891–907; Wilkes, *The New Federalism in Criminal Procedure: State Court Evasion of the Burger Court,* 62 KY. L.J. 421 (1974).

452. People v. Gunner, 15 N.Y.2d 226, 232, 205 N.E.2d 852, 855, 257 N.Y.S.2d 924, 928 (1965), *quoted in* People v. Arthur, 22 N.Y.2d 325, 329, 239 N.E.2d 537, 539, 292 N.Y.S.2d 663, 666 (1968).

453. People v. Arthur, 22 N.Y.2d 325, 329, 239 N.E.2d 537, 539, 292 N.Y.S.2d 663, 666 (1968).

454. People v. Gunner, 15 N.Y.2d 226, 232, 205 N.E.2d 852, 855, 257 N.Y.S.2d 924, 928 (1965).

455. People v. Arthur, 22 N.Y.2d 325, 329, 239 N.E.2d 537, 539, 292 N.Y.S.2d 663, 666 (1968).

456. Uviller, *supra* note 449, at 718.

457. *See* People v. Arthur, 22 N.Y.2d 325, 327, 239 N.E.2d 537, 538, 292 N.Y.S.2d 663, 664 (1968).

458. *See* People v. Pinzon, 44 N.Y.2d 458, 462, 377 N.E.2d 721, 723, 406 N.Y.S.2d 268, 269–70 (1978); People v. Gunner, 15 N.Y.2d 226, 230, 205 N.E.2d 852, 853, 257 N.Y.S.2d 924, 926 (1965); People v. Failla, 14 N.Y.2d 178, 181, 199 N.E.2d 366, 367, 250 N.Y.S.2d 267, 269 (1964); People v. Donovan, 13 N.Y.2d 148, 151, 193 N.E.2d 628, 629, 243 N.Y.S.2d 841, 842 (1963); People v. Ressler, 24 A.D.2d 7, 8, 261 N.Y.S.2d 823, 824 (1965).

459. Rothblatt, *supra* note 53, at 51. *See also* Paulsen, *The Winds of Change: Criminal Procedure in New York 1941-1964,* 15 BUFFALO L. REV. 297, 305–06 (1966) ("[The *Donovan* rule] puts the man of means and the experienced criminal with access to legal assistance in a much better position than the poor and the inexperienced. It may be that we ought not to model out a system of criminal justice on the privileges of the wealthy or on the advantages enjoyed by the professional criminal. Yet we are not long likely to tolerate a system which gives advantages to those least in need of protection and which fails to extend protection to the most vulnerable").

Of course, a year later the Court handed down *Miranda,* which did seek to "extend protection to the most vulnerable," but, as no one has articulated better than the defenders of the *Donovan* rule, *Miranda,* at least as it has been generally applied, falls far short of the protection furnished by *Donovan. See* text *supra* at footnote 99 and notes 462–66.

One may try to defend the *Donovan* rule on the ground that "when the police bar consultation between a suspect and his lawyer they are taking positive action designed solely to increase the likelihood of a confession, in contravention of their constitutional duty to adopt a 'neutral' stance. . . ." *Developments in the Law—Confessions, supra* note 380, at 1002 (describing argument made by Judge Friendly). As the *Miranda* Court saw it, however, the government must do more than "carve the universe at a natural joint." *Cf.* Tussman & tenBroek, *The Equal Protection of the Laws,* 37 CALIF. L. REV. 341, 344–53 (1949). When the government exerts its powers in the criminal area, stated the *Miranda* Court:

> its obligation is surely no less than that of taking reasonable measures to eliminate those factors [such as poverty] that are irrelevant to just administration of the law but which, nevertheless, may occasionally affect determinations of the accused's liability or penalty. While the government may not be required to relieve the accused of his poverty, it may properly be required to minimize the influence of poverty on its administration of justice.

384 U.S. at 472–73 n.41 (quoting with approval from ATTORNEY GENERAL'S COMM., REPORT ON POVERTY AND THE ADMINISTRATION OF FEDERAL CRIMINAL JUSTICE 9 (1963) (Allen Report)). "Denial of counsel to the indigent at the time of interrogation while allowing an attorney to those who can afford one would be no more supportable by reason or logic than the similar situation at trial and on appeal struck down in [*Gideon*] and [*Douglas*]." *Id.* at 472–73.

Moreover, it is hard to see how confronting an individual "often ignorant and uneducated, and always in fear" and "unadvised by anyone who has his interests at heart," *see* text at footnote 99 *supra,* "with the coercive police power of the State" can be called "adopting a neutral stance," *cf. Developments in the Law—Confessions, supra* note 380, at 1002 ("very process of skillful interrogation is designed to, and does, increase the likelihood that a confession will be obtained").

460. The author of a pioneering study observed, a generation ago, that "it is not uncommon in some cities for a 'mouthpiece' to appear at precinct headquarters before [a 'professional criminal' or 'syndicate representative'] is brought in." W. BEANEY, THE RIGHT TO COUNSEL IN AMERICAN COURTS 207 (1955). A decade later, the author of a major study on police practices reported that generally it is only the professional criminal "whose counsel is likely to know when his arrest takes place." W. LaFAVE, ARREST 407 (F. Remington ed. 1965). *See also id.* at 393–94, 398.

Before ascending to the New York Court of Appeals, where he has since reaffirmed and revivified the *Donovan* rule, Justice (now Chief Judge) Breitel defended the rule as "a practical accommodation." Breitel, *Criminal Law and Equal Justice,* 1966 UTAH L. REV. 1, 9–10. He conceded, however, that:

> It is an accepted fact that in almost all cases the most effective protection for the individual is the advice of counsel from the time of initial arrest or interrogation. Accepted also is the fact that, except for the affluent or sophisticated criminal, it is the rare defendant who has a lawyer available on call.

Id. at 14.

461. 51 CORNELL L.Q. 356, 368 (1966).

462. *See* Rothblatt & Pitler, *supra* note 40, at 492–96.

463. *See, e.g.,* Griffiths & Ayres, *supra* note 42; Leiken, *Police Interrogation in Colorado: The Implementation of* Miranda, 47 DEN. L.J. 1 (1970); Medalie, Zeitz & Alexander, *Custodial Police Interrogation in Our Nation's Capital: The Attempt to Implement* Miranda, 66 MICH. L. REV. 1347 (1968); Project, *supra* note 309. These studies and others, including one by Professor Otis Stephens, are discussed in O. STEPHENS, THE SUPREME COURT AND CONFESSIONS OF GUILT 165–200 (1973).

464. Rothblatt & Pitler, *supra* note 40, at 493 (quoting from Weisberg, *Police Interrogation of Arrested Persons: A Skeptical View,* in POLICE POWER AND INDIVIDUAL FREEDOM 153, 175 (C. Sowle ed. 1962)).

465. *Id.*

466. *Id.* at 494.

467. *But see* Breitel, *supra* note 460, at 14 (on eve of *Miranda*). Justice (now Chief Judge) Breitel commented:

> The argument is . . . made by increasingly large numbers of people that the state or voluntary organizations should provide the lawyer at the inception of the process if "inequality" in treatment is to be avoided. The enormity of lawyer resources that such a proposal would entail is only barely conceivable. It may suggest further problems as to how adequate representation would be spread so far and so thinly. But beyond these practical considerations, the proposal poses a serious question of whether this would be an acceptable disposition of social resources. . . .

Id.

It may well be that I have spent too much time on "the high Alpine meadows" and too little "in the dust of the marketplace," *cf.* H. FRIENDLY, BENCHMARKS 1 (1967), but the logistical problems do not strike me as that staggering, at least not in large urban centers—especially in light of the apparent holding by the New York Court of Appeals that a law clerk, presumably a law student, may trigger the *Donovan* rule (whose invocation hardly requires three full years of law school training). *See* People v. Ressler, 17 N.Y.2d 174, 178, 216 N.E.2d 582, 583–84, 269 N.Y.S.2d 414, 415 (1966) (discussed at note 445 *supra*).

No doubt, it would be argued that, unlike the case of the suspect who has retained counsel, or whose family or friends have done so for him, the indigent suspect is not yet the "client" of the public or voluntary defender who takes it upon himself to instruct the police. This argument is hardly overwhelming when, as the New York Court of Appeals held in People v. Arthur, 22 N.Y.2d 325, 239 N.E.2d 537, 292 N.Y.S.2d 663 (1968), the *Donovan* rule "is not dependent upon the existence of a formal retainer" but may be invoked by a lawyer (at least on behalf of his *former* client) on his own initiative. *Id.* at 327, 329, 239 N.E.2d at 538, 539, 292 N.Y.S.2d at 664, 666; *see* text following footnote 91 *supra;* note 55 *supra* and accompanying text.

No doubt, it would also be argued that the proposal I have suggested would give the indigent suspect an advantage over his somewhat wealthier but less than affluent counterpart, for the latter would not often command the services of retained counsel as swiftly as the former would gain the protection of the defender's office. The answer to this may be that a goodly number of persons who are financially capable of retaining counsel *at later stages* of the criminal process may not be at the immediate postarrest stage and thus should be regarded as indigent at, but only at, this early point. *See* ATTORNEY GENERAL'S COMM., *supra* note 459, at 7–8 ("[P]overty must be viewed as a relative concept with the consequence that [it] must be measured in each case by reference to the particular need or service under consideration. . . . A problem of poverty arises for the system of criminal justice when at any stage . . . lack of means in the accused substantially inhibits or prevents the proper assertion of a right or a claim of right. ").

Although the mechanical difficulties raised by this proposal are not insubstantial, neither, it seems, are they insurmountable. A member of the defender's staff might be permitted to communicate immediately with any person brought down to the police station to determine whether that person has counsel and, if not and if he desires the defender's office to represent him, to determine initially whether he is "indigent" at this stage of the process. *See, e.g.,* COLO. REV. STAT. § 16-3-402(3) (1973) (determination of indigency shall be made by public defender subject to review by court). Under this procedure, or under a procedure whereby all suspects are simply *assumed* to be indigent at the immediate postarrest stage, if it subsequently develops (say, at the first appearance) that the suspect was not indigent, reimbursement could be made to the government (or voluntary organization) for the defender's services. *See* Kamisar & Choper, *supra* note 434, at 53–54; *cf.* L. KATZ, JUSTICE IS THE CRIME 129–30 (1972) (booking officer should be required to appoint counsel for indigent being held; spurious claims of indigency can be handled later).

Of course, extending the protection of the *Donovan* rule to the generality of suspects would not contribute to the goal of finding "an acceptable solution for the intermediate area of post-arrest, pre-station house interrogation." Friendly, *The Fifth Amendment Tomorrow: The Case for Constitutional Change,* 37 U. CIN. L. REV. 676, 716 (1968). But neither does the *Donovan* rule in its present form. Wider application of the *Donovan* rule might well lead the police to engage in more "on the street" questioning and "to slow down or make more circuitous the ride to headquarters." *Cf.* Kamisar, *supra* note 255, at 60–61. But in most cases the courts should be able to cope with such attempts at evasion, and the capacity of the police to send resourceful and skillful interrogators "into the field" would seem to be quite limited. Although "by defining 'custodial questioning' to cover 'field' and 'squad car' questioning," *Miranda* understandably sought to "protect its flanks," *id.* at 61 n.8, police station interrogation was "the evil to which [*Miranda*] was primarily addressed," Friendly, *supra,* at 712.

468. Although many might voice opposition to such an extension of the *Donovan* rule on grounds of logistics and mechanics, *see* note 467 *supra,* their underlying objection is probably concern about the adverse impact of such an extension on prevalent police practices—a concern that does not loom large when, as now, the rule is (and can only be) invoked infrequently and sporadically. An expanded *Donovan* rule would, it cannot be denied, upset the "compromise" worked out by *Miranda,* but only in the same respect, if not the same degree, that the rule does now.

469. *See Developments in the Law—Confessions, supra* note 380, at 1007. Another alternative to the *Miranda* model is the Kauper-Schaefer-Friendly proposal, under which a person taken into custody may be questioned only in the presence of and under the supervision of a judicial officer. In addition to being advised of his rights, the suspect is informed that if he is subsequently prosecuted his refusal to answer any questions will be disclosed at the trial. *See* Kamisar, *supra* note 325, at 23–37 (discussion of Kauper-Schaefer-Friendly proposal providing for judicial warnings, judicial supervision over interrogation, and recording of entire proceeding).

470. Johnson v. State, 282 Md. 314, 331–32, 384 A.2d 709, 719 (1978). In *Johnson* the court indicated:

> [O]ne important function of the initial appearance is to advise an arrestee of his right to counsel; to this extent there is a partial overlap with *Miranda*. Even so, it has been convincingly argued that the typically perfunctory reading of *Miranda* warnings by police at the time of arrest may be insufficient to provide the accused with adequate notice of his constitutional rights; and that a need exists for follow-up advice of the basic right to counsel by a neutral officer of the court, such as is provided by [Maryland rules].

Id. See also Enker & Elsen, *supra* note 185, at 85–90 (advocating extension of *McNabb-Mallory* rule to states and recording of interrogation); 51 CORNELL L.Q. 356, 366–68 (1966) (suggesting right to counsel integrated with provisions for promp arraignment as substitute for *Gunner;* all confessions following unduly delayed arraignment would be excluded).

471. *See* MODEL CODE OF PRE-ARRAIGNMENT PROCEDURE § 130.4 (Official Draft 1974) (requires tape recordings of warnings and waiver procedures at police station); UNIFORM RULE OF CRIMINAL PROCEDURE 243 (Approved Draft 1974) (requires that "the information of rights, any waiver thereof, and any questioning shall be [electronically recorded] whenever feasible and in any case where questioning occurs at a place of detention"). *See also* Enker & Elsen, *supra* note 185, at 85–87 (record to include statement of time during which police interview began and ended and could be required that record be deposited with the court under seal at time defendant appears for preliminary arraignment); Kamisar, *supra* note 14, at 233–43 (incomplete, contradictory record in *Williams* case underscores need to utilize tape recordings); Weisberg, *supra* note 464, at 179–80 (classic statement of need to strip police interrogation of its "most unique feature"—"secrecy"—which is not the same thing as "privacy," but the power of police "to prevent objective recordation of the facts").

472. There *is* language in *Miranda*—although the state courts and lower federal courts have disregarded it—strongly suggesting that, at least when feasible, the police must stenographically or electronically record the warnings given to the suspect, as well as his response. *See* 384 U.S. at 475 ("heavy burden rests on the government to demonstrate" valid waiver of *Miranda* rights; Court reasserted "high standards of proof for the waiver of constitutional rights" "as applied to in-custody interrogation"; "since the State is responsible for establishing the isolated circumstances" of interrogation and "has the only means of making available corroborated evidence of warnings given during incommunicado interrogation, the burden is rightly on its shoulders"); Thompson, *supra* note 250, at 421 (language of *Miranda* pointed out by Professor [now Governor] Thompson). Several months before *Miranda* was handed down, one commentator suggested that "[a] determined Supreme Court might attempt to surmount the [secrecy] problem" by declaring that a defendant's claim of involuntariness "must be accepted as true . . . unless the police can produce some reliable evidence such as a tape-recording of the interrogation to refute it," but then suggested why the Court might stop short of promulgating such a doctrine: "[A] rule that in effect required a tape-recording as a precondition of a confession's admissibility might be thought too naked an exercise of control by the Court over state police practices." *Developments in the Law—Confessions, supra* note 380, at 1021.

473. Silverman v. United States, 365 U.S. 505, 513 (1961) (Douglas, J., concurring) ("[T]he command of the Fourth Amendment" should not "be limited by nice distinctions turning on the kind of electronic equipment employed. Rather our sole concern should be whether the privacy of the home was invaded."); *see* Katz v. United States, 389 U.S. 347 (1967) (Justice Douglas's view prevailed).

474. *Cf.* Railway Express Agency, Inc. v. New York, 336 U.S. 106, 112–13 (1949) (Jackson, J., concurring).

475. R. DUBOS, THE GENIUS OF THE PLACE 7 (1970) (H. Albright Conservation Lectureship). I am indebted to my colleague, Joseph L. Sax, for calling this monograph to my attention.

Table of Cases

Adamson v. California, 44
Alexander v. United States, 227 n.43
Anderson v. United States, 65, 67
Anderson, United States v., 179
Anglin v. State, 186
Argersinger v. Hamlin, 86
Arthur, People v., 213, 214, 220, 296
 n.416, 299 nn.452, 453, 455, & 457,
 301 n.467
Ash, United States v., 192, 193, 285
 n.288
Ashcraft v. Tennessee, 9, 15, 21, 27, 30,
 96, 97, 98, 99–101, 102, 153, 228
 n.55, 229 n.84, 231 nn.134 & 140,
 232 n.153, 250 n.10, 271 n.74, 277
 n.199
Atkins, State v., 282 n.264

Baker v. Carr, 47
Barenblatt v. United States, 243
 nn.103–04
Beatty v. United States, 178–79
Beckwith v. United States, 163, 200
Benbo, State v., 295 n.412
Betts v. Brady, 44, 73, 86
Biron, State v., xii–xv, 98–99, 134
Blackburn v. Alabama, 10, 11, 14, 23,
 229 n.85, 230 n.94, 233 n.159, 273
 n.117
Bloom v. Illinois, 298 n.443
Bordner, Commonwealth v., 282 n.262
Bowman, People v., 283 nn.269 & 270
Boyd v. United States, 241 n.78
Bram v. United States, 152–53, 164, 238
 n.23, 270 n.68, 271 nn.69–71
Brewer v. Williams, xvi–xix, 95–96,
 113–304 *passim*
Brown v. Mississippi, 11, 45, 56, 75, 78,
 244 nn.149–50
Brown, United States v., 197–98, 209,
 275 n.140

Burt, United States *ex rel.,* v. New Jer-
 sey, 85, 91
Burton v. Cuyler, 296 n.414
Bute v. Illinois, 245 n.3
Buxton, People v., 208

Caminito v. Murphy, 273 n.105
Cardona, People v., 186
Chambers v. Florida, 228 n.55, 231
 n.125
Cicenia v. Lagay, 23, 227 n.44
City of St. Paul v. Webb, 18
Coades, United States v., 296 n.414
Combs v. Commonwealth, 156
Combs v. Wingo, 156, 158, 273 n.107
Commonwealth v. ___. *See* name of
 opposing party
Counselman v. Hitchcock, 45, 51, 240
 n.75
Craig v. Boren, 292 n.394
Crisp, United States v., 274 n.126
Crooker v. California, 23–24, 60, 107,
 172, 233 n.164, 240 n.72, 242 n.85,
 256 n.63, 265 n.83, 277 nn.195, 196,
 198, & 200
Crookston, United States v., 298 n.445
Culombe v. Connecticut, 6, 8, 10, 11,
 12–15, 16, 18, 20, 23, 60, 71, 72, 73,
 228 n.55, 229 n.65, 230 nn.91, 102–
 116, & 119–20, 231 nn.130 & 135–36,
 232 n.149, 233 n.161, 242 nn.83–84,
 244 nn.122 & 123, 294 n.411

Daugherty, State v., 197, 298 n.444
Davenport, Commonwealth v., 295
 n.412
Davis v. North Carolina, 43–44, 73–75,
 76, 244 nn.132, 134, & 144
Davis, United States v., 156, 157, 273
 n.107
Dean, People v., 270 n.53

De Santo v. Pennsylvania, 272 n.97
Di Biasi, People v., 277 n.193, 290
n.380
Donovan, People v., 213, 214, 217, 218,
219, 220, 221, 222, 223, 296 n.415,
298 nn.445 & 449, 299 nn.450, 458,
& 459, 300 n.460, 301–02 n.467, 302
n.468
Dorado, People v., 189–90, 193, 246
n.21, 283 n.270
Doran, People v., 63, 76, 245 nn.155 &
156
Douglas v. California, 216, 297 n.434,
300 n.459
Doyle v. Ohio, 92, 289 n.376
Duvall, United States v., 296 n.414

Emspak v. United States, 45
Escobedo v. Illinois, xii, xvi, 28–29, 38,
39, 44, 45, 65, 69, 70, 71, 73, 75, 77,
83, 88, 96, 109, 143, 153, 158, 161,
162–63, 168, 175, 189, 190, 193, 202,
210, 212, 213, 217–18, 219, 220–21,
236 n.59, 251 n.15, 254 n.49, 257
n.72, 271 nn.68, 72, 73, & 82, 273
nn.107 & 120, 274 nn.122, 123, &
126, 280 nn.248 & 250, 281 n.257,
283 n.268, 290 n.377, 291 n.391, 293
nn.402 & 403

Failla, People v., 299 n.458
Fay v. Noia, 236 n.57
Ferguson v. Georgia, 29
Ferrari, State v., 186
Fikes v. Alabama, 16, 18, 23, 232
nn.149 & 151, 233 n.156
Fioravanti, United States v., 280 n.254,
281 n.256, 284 n.275
Flores, People v., 190, 283 n.269
Fournier v. People of Puerto Rico,
19–20, 231 n.128
Franklin, Commonwealth v., 158
Frazier v. Cupp, 96
Frazier v. United States (Frazier I), 264
n.77
Frisbie v. Collins, 18

Futch, Commonwealth v., 295 n.412

Gaines, United States v., 294 n.407
Gallegos v. Colorado, 21, 23, 228 n.52,
233 n.162
Garner, People v., 211–12, 290 n.380
Gerstein v. Pugh, 246 n.16, 295 n.414
Gideon v. Wainright, 28, 44, 73, 86,
162, 215–16, 227 n.45, 245 n.3, 297
n.433, 300 n.459
Grant, People v., 201, 204, 205
Griffin v. California, 79, 82, 90, 238
n.17, 246 n.7
Griffin v. Illinois, 216, 297 n.434
Groban, In re, 265 n.83, 278 n.202
Grunewald v. United States, 90, 91
Gunner, People v., 186, 213–14, 220,
299 nn.452, 454, & 458, 303 n.470
Guy v. Donald, 272 n.95

Hale, United States v., 91, 92
Haley v. Ohio, 17, 228 n.57
Hall v. Commonwealth, 241 n.77
Hall, United States v., 287 n.329
Hamilton v. Alabama, 215, 245 n.3, 297
nn.429 & 431
Hamilton, Commonwealth v., 158–59,
273 n.107
Hamilton, People v., 295 n.412
Hancock v. White, 216
Harris v. New York, 85, 90, 251 n.23
Hayles, United States v., 198
Haynes v. Washington, 17, 24–25, 44,
72, 73, 228 n.59, 231 n.140, 243
n.112, 244 nn.120, 121, & 128–30,
245 n.157, 271 n.82
Henry v. United States, 177
Herman, Pennsylvania ex rel., v.
Claudy, 227 n.4
Hobson, People v., 213, 214, 218, 220,
221–22, 296 n.416, 299 n.450
Hoffa v. United States, 88, 143, 183,
191, 192, 199, 201, 280 n.251, 282
n.263, 284 n.276
Hollman v. State, 17
Holmes, United States v., 287 n.328

Holtzer, People v., 186
Hopkins, United States v., 264 n.77
Hopt v. Utah, 164, 230 n.97
Hughes, People v., 282 n.262

Illinois *ex rel.* McCullom v. Board of Ed., 230 n.121
Innis, Rhode Island v., 282 n.261
In re Groban, 265 n.83, 278 n.202
Irvine v. California, 243 n.110

Jackson v. Denno, 245 n.157
Jackson, People v., 204
Jacobellis v. Ohio, 251 n.17
Jensen, State v., 185
Johns, State v., 219
Johnson v. New Jersey, 43–44, 73
Johnson v. Patterson, 91
Johnson v. State, 294 nn.407 & 410, 295 n.412, 303 n.470
Johnson v. Zerbst, 38, 86, 165, 166, 202, 211, 236 n.58, 275 n.144, 276 n.157

Katz v. United States, 304 n.473
Ker v. Illinois, 18
Kirby v. Illinois, 218, 274 n.120, 285 nn.288, 289, 290, & 291, 293 n.403, 296 n.414
Knott, State v., 186
Kovacs v. Cooper, 279 n.245

Leaming, Commonwealth v., 158
Lee v. United States, 278 n.206
Lefkowitz, United States v., 240 n.77
Lewis v. United States, 201
Leyra v. Denno, 15
Lisenba v. California, 10, 27, 230 n.98, 243 n.112
Lopez, People v., 299 n.450
Lopez v. United States, 266 n.99
Lopez v. Zelker, 267 n.111, 275 n.139 & 140
Ludlum, People v., 190, 283 n.269, 284 n.274
Lynumn v. Illinois, 23, 25, 233 n.163
Lyons v. Oklahoma, 228 n.57, 273 n.104
Lyons v. State, 231 n.139

McCarthy v. Arndstein, 46
McCorgary, State v., 197, 284 n.275, 298 n.444
McCullom, Illinois *ex rel.*, v. Board of Ed., 230 n.121
McKenna, Commonwealth v., 298 n.445
McLeod v. Ohio, 174, 216, 298 n.438
McLeod, State v., 174, 202, 279 nn.229–31, 298 n.435, 436, & 439–42
McNabb v. United States, 8–9, 17, 65, 67, 97, 212, 250 nn.4 & 7, 251 nn.13 & 15, 253 n.44, 254 n.49, 277 n.199, 286 n.310, 294 nn.405, 406, 407 & 411, 295 nn.412, 413, & 414, 303 n.470
Mahon v. Justice, 18
Malinski v. New York, 228 n.57, 232 n.152
Mallory v. United States, 8–9, 17, 65, 97, 212, 250 n.8, 251 n.13 & 15, 277 n.199, 294 nn.404, 407, & 411, 295 nn.412 & 414, 303 n.470
Malloy v. Hogan, 38, 45, 237 n.16, 245 n.5, 270 n.68, 273 n.115
Mandujano, United States v., 236 n.59
Mapp v. Ohio, 7, 19, 227 n.47
Massiah v. United States, xvi–xvii, xix, 117, 129, 132, 139–304 *passim*
Mathews, People v., 285 n.296
Mathiason, Oregon v., 96, 251 n.23, 278 n.214
Mathies v. United States, 218
Mathis v. United States, 248 n.23
Maxwell, United States v., 143, 198–99
Mercier, Commonwealth v., 159
Meyer, People v., 215, 277 n.193, 278 n.206, 297 n.425–27
Michigan v. Mosley, 130, 156–57, 164, 203, 204–05, 251 n.23, 267 n.108, 268 n.115, 287 nn.337–40, 288 nn. 341–43, 344, 345, & 349, 289 n.351
Milani v. Pate, 185, 186
Miller v. California, 188, 190, 283 n.264, 285 n.293, 286 n.297
Miller, People v., 188, 298 n.444

Miller, United States v., 275 n.140
Milton v. Wainwright, 161, 188, 283
  nn.264 & 268, 298 n.444
Miranda v. Arizona, xi–xvii, xix, 41–304
  passim
Miranda, State v., 185
Mitchell, United States v., 17
Modesto, People v., 270 n.53
Moffitt v. Ross, 248 n.30
Molinas v. Mancusi, 199
Moore v. Illinois, 193, 285 n.291
Mosley, Michigan v., 130, 156–57, 164,
  203, 204–05, 251 n.23, 267 n.108,
  268 n.115, 287 nn.337–40, 288
  nn.341–43, 344, 345, & 349, 289
  n.351

Navarro, Government of the Virgin Is-
  lands v., 296 n.414
Nebbia v. New York, 230 n.117
Neuslein v. District of Columbia, 232
  n.148
New York Trust Co. v. Eisner, 270 n.66
Nielson, United States v., 264 n.77

O'Kelly, State v., 186
On Lee v. United States, 277 n.188
Oregon v. Mathiason, 96, 251 n.23, 278
  n.214
Orozco v. Texas, 248 n.23
Osborn v. United States, 143, 192, 199,
  201, 280 n.250, 284 n.273, 285 n.284

Paroutian v. United States, 185
Patterson, People v., 218
Payne v. Arkansas, 8, 18, 23, 228 n.63,
  233 n.157
People v. _____. *See* name of opposing
  party
Perry, State v., 186
Peters v. New York, 252 n.29
Pettingill, People v., 288 n.344 & 345,
  294 n.410
Pheaster, United States v., 156–57
Pinzon, People v., 213, 214, 298 n.445,
  299 n.458

Powell v. Alabama, 78, 86, 95, 161,
  215, 245 n.3, 283 n.268, 293 n.403,
  297 nn.428 & 430
Price, People v., 185–86
Procunier v. Atchley, 185, 189, 287
  n.323

Quinn v. United States, 45

Raffel v. United States, 90–91
Railway Express Agency, Inc. v. New
  York, 304 n.474
Ramos, People v., 297 n.417
Randall, People v., 207–08
Reck v. Pate, 23, 231 n.134, 232 n.149,
  233 n.160, 243 n.109
Ressler, People v., 298 n.445, 299
  n.458, 301 n.467
Rhode Island v. Innis, 282 n.261
Richman, Commonwealth v., 296 n.414
Robinson, People v., 171, 287 n.328
Robinson v. Zelker, 296 n.414
Robles, People v., 299 n.450
Rodriguez, People v., 228 n.50
Rogers v. Richmond, 5–6, 10, 11,
  20–21, 153, 226 nn.32 & 33, 227
  nn.35–36, 229 n.87, 231 n.137, 232
  nn.142–44, 283 n.264
Ross v. Moffitt, 297 n.434

Satterfield, United States v., 275 n.140
Schneckloth v. Bustamonte, 247 n.23
Screws v. United States, 236 n.51
Scully, United States v., 236 n.59
Sherman v. United States, 20, 22, 232
  n.150
Shuttlesworth v. Birmingham, 276 n.177
Sibron v. New York, 252 n.29
Silverman v. United States, 304 n.473
Simala, Commonwealth v., 158
Smith, Commonwealth v., 295 n.412
Smith v. Goguen, 272 n.100
Smith, State v. (Ariz.), 197, 298 n.444
Smith, State v. (N.C.), 213
Sobell, United States v., 18
Springer, United States v., 218, 264 n.77

Spano v. New York, 5, 8, 10, 11, 14, 23, 149–50, 169–71, 172–73, 174, 175, 211, 214, 215, 216, 226 nn.29 & 30, 229 nn.64 & 81–82, 233 n.158, 270 nn.58–62, 277 n.194, 278 n.206, 286 n.316, 290 n.380, 291 n.388, 297 nn.418 & 419

Speiser v. Randall, 268 n.115

Spence v. Washington, 272 n.100

State v. ____. *See* name of opposing party

Stein v. New York, 7, 15, 21, 24, 228 n.60, 232 n.154, 233 nn.166–68

Stowers v. United States, 185, 186, 284 n.275

Stroble v. California, 70, 228 n.57, 243 n.113

Sunday, People v., 285 n.296

Sutton v. United States, 18

Terry v. Ohio, 252 n.29

Thomas v. Arizona, 231 n.124

Thomas v. United States, 227 n.42

Tingle, Commonwealth v., 295 n.412

Tinker v. Des Moines School Dist., 272 n.101

Travis, State v., 197, 209

United States v. ____. *See* name of opposing party

United States *ex rel.* ____. *See* name of individual party

Vollhardt, State v., 295 n.412

Von Moltke v. Gillies, 39

Vorhauer v. State, 295 n.412

Wade, United States v., 192, 285 nn.282–83

Ward v. Texas, 16, 228 n.55, 231 n.126

Waterman, People v., 214–15, 277 n.193, 278 nn.205 & 206, 291 n.391, 292 n.396, 297 nn.422, 423, & 424

Watts v. Indiana, xiii, 30–31, 60, 101, 232 n.154, 236 n.48, 246 n.20, 248 n.35, 251 n.14

Webb, City of St. Paul v., 18

Webster v. State, 295 n.412

Wedra, United States v., 219

Weedon, State v., 219

Weeks v. United States, 105

White v. Maryland, 215, 297 nn.429 & 431

White, United States v., 183, 192, 201, 280 n.253, 284 n.273, 285 nn.285–86

Williams, Brewer v., xiv–xvii, 95–96, 113–304 *passim*

Wilson v. Henderson, 176

Wolf v. Colorado, 231 n.131

Wong Sun v. United States, 6–7, 19, 227 nn.46 & 48, 228 nn.49 & 52, 232 n.146

Ziang Sun Wan v. United States, 63, 75–76, 164, 244 n.154, 245 n.157, 273 n.111

Table of Authorities

Interrogation and Law Enforcement Manuals

A. AUBRY & R. CAPUTO, INTERROGATION FOR INVESTIGATORS (1959), 225 n.2

R. CAPUTO. *See* A. AUBRY & R. CAPUTO

W. DIENSTEIN, TECHNICS FOR THE CRIME INVESTIGATOR (1952), 29, 225 n.2, 234 nn.10 & 14

F. INBAU & J. REID, CRIMINAL INTERROGATION AND CONFESSIONS (1st ed. 1962), 1–12 *passim,* 21, 96, 225 nn.2 & 5, 226 nn.6–15, 17, 27–28, 30–31, & 34, 228 nn.52, 60, & 62, 229 nn.66–72, 79, 83, & 86–89, 230 nn.99 & 101, 234 nn.4–6, 8, 9, & 18, 257 n.78; (2d ed. 1967), 122, 157, 248 n.43, 261 nn.43–46, 262 nn.53 & 56, 263 n.63, 282 n.260

F. INBAU & J. REID, LIE DETECTION AND CRIMINAL INTERROGATION (1st ed. 1942), 250 n.5; (3d ed. 1953), 31–32, 225 n.1, 226 n.11, 257 n.78

W. KIDD, POLICE INTERROGATION (1940), 62, 225 n.2

H. MULBAR, INTERROGATION (1951), 62, 225 n.2

C. O'HARA, FUNDAMENTALS OF CRIMINAL INVESTIGATION (1956), 62, 109, 151, 154, 155, 225 n.2, 266 n.107, 273 n.113; (4th ed. 1976), 134, 154, 266 n.101

J. REID. *See* F. INBAU & J. REID
R. ROYAL & S. SCHUTT, THE GENTLE ART OF INTERVIEWING AND INTERROGATION (1976), 113, 159–60, 261 n.40, 263 n.58, 264 n.79

S. SCHUTT. *See* R. ROYAL & S. SCHUTT

C. VAN METER, PRINCIPLES OF POLICE INTERROGATION (1973), 148

Books

T. ARNOLD, THE SYMBOLS OF GOVERNMENT (Harbinger Books ed. 1962), 234 nn.13 & 19, 292 n.398, 293 n.401

W. BEANEY, THE RIGHT TO COUNSEL IN AMERICAN COURTS (1955), 300 n.460
A. BEISEL, CONTROL OVER ILLEGAL ENFORCEMENT OF THE CRIMINAL LAW: ROLE OF THE SUPREME COURT (1955), 14, 36, 96, 227 n.37, 235 n.42, 239 n.59, 291 n.386, 292 n.396
A. BICKEL, THE LEAST DANGEROUS BRANCH (1962), 255 n.60
C. BLACK, PERSPECTIVES IN CONSTITUTIONAL LAW (rev. ed. 1969), 91
C. BLACK, STRUCTURE AND RELATIONSHIP IN CONSTITUTIONAL LAW (1969), 91

J. Califano. *See* THE MEDIA AND THE LAW
Z. CHAFEE, THE BLESSINGS OF LIBERTY (1956), 56–57
Z. CHAFEE, DOCUMENTS ON FUNDAMENTAL HUMAN RIGHTS (1952), 240 n.72
J. CHOPER. *See* W. LOCKHART, Y. KAMISAR, & J. CHOPER
M. COHEN, THE MEANING OF HUMAN HISTORY (1947), 235 n.33

A. Cornelius, Search and Seizure (2nd ed. 1930), 241 n.77

Criminal Justice in Our Time (A. Howard ed. 1965), xii, 101, 292 n.400

P. Devlin, The Criminal Prosecution in England (1960), 37, 238 n.30, 281 n.258

R. Dubos, The Genius of the Place (1970), 304 n.475

M. Edelman, The Symbolic Uses of Politics (1964), 292 n.399

R. W. Emerson, Letters and Social Aims (1876), 264 n.64

J. Frank, Fate and Freedom (1945), 233 n.170

H. Friendly, Benchmarks (1967), 184, 281 n.255, 298 n.446, 301 n.467

L. Fuller, The Morality of Law (1964), 234 n.20, 237 n.5

B.J. George. See A New Look at Confessions

J. Goebel & T.R. Naughton, Law Enforcement in Colonial New York (1944), 52, 239 nn.53–55

J. Grano. See Y. Kamisar, J. Grano, & J. Haddad

E. Griswold, The Fifth Amendment Today (1955), 34, 35, 57, 240 n.76, 257 n.77

J. Haddad. See F. Inbau, J. Thompson, J. Haddad, J. Zagel, & G. Starkman; Y. Kamisar, J. Grano, & J. Haddad

L. Hall & Y. Kamisar, Modern Criminal Procedure (2d ed. 1966), 73, 237 n.2

G. Haskins, Law and Authority in Early Massachusetts (1960), 239 n.51

5 W. Holdsworth, A History of English Law (1924), 239 n.47

S. Hook, Common Sense and the Fifth Amendment (1957), 57–58

E. Hopkins, Our Lawless Police (1931), 56, 272 n.84, 273 nn.104 & 110

A. Howard. See Criminal Justice in Our Time

Ill. Div., ACLU, Secret Detention by the Chicago Police (1959), 36, 235 n.36

F. Inbau, J. Thompson, J. Haddad, J. Zagel, & G. Starkman, Cases and Comments on Criminal Procedure (1974), 85, 247 n.23, 251 n.23, 290 n.385

J. Israel. See Y. Kamisar, W. La Fave, & J. Israel

H. Kalven & H. Zeisel, The American Jury (1966), 90

Y. Kamisar, J. Grano, & J. Haddad, Criminal Procedure (1977), 116

Y. Kamisar, W. La Fave, & J. Israel, Modern Criminal Procedure (4th ed. 1974), xiii, 246 n.16, 247 n.23, 251 n.15, 257 nn.73 & 74, 264 n.77, 282 n.261, 297 n.434; (Supp. 1978), 113, 284 n.272

Y. Kamisar. See L. Hall & Y. Kamisar; W. Lockhart, Y. Kamisar, & J. Choper

L. Katz, Justice Is the Crime (1972), 302 n.467

R. Keeton, Trial Tactics and Methods (1954), 233 n.3

S. Krislov, The Supreme Court and Political Freedom (1968), 254 n. 48

W. La Fave, Arrest: The Decision to Take a Suspect into Custody (F. Remington ed. 1965), 60–61, 300 n.460

2 W. La Fave, Search and Seizure (1978), 246 n.16

W. LA FAVE. *See* Y. KAMISAR, W. LA
FAVE, & J. ISRAEL

J. LANDYNSKI, SEARCH AND SEIZURE
AND THE SUPREME COURT (1966), 241
nn.77 & 78

A. LEWIS, GIDEON'S TRUMPET (1964),
248 nn.31 & 32, 251 n.21

K. LLEWELLYN, THE COMMON LAW
TRADITION (1960), 43

W. LOCKHART, Y. KAMISAR, & J.
CHOPER, CONSTITUTIONAL LAW (4th
ed. 1975), 272 n.102

C. McCORMICK, EVIDENCE (1954), 11,
12, 35, 37, 227 n.40, 228 n.63, 230
nn.92 & 96, 233 n.169, 235 nn.25, 34,
& 45, 236 n.46; (E. Cleary 2d ed.
1972), 152, 158

J. MAGUIRE, EVIDENCE OF GUILT
(1959), 35, 227 n.38, 231 n.133, 232
n.149, 235 nn.30 & 31, 287 n.319

L. MAYERS, SHALL WE AMEND THE
FIFTH AMENDMENT? (1959), 236
nn.47 & 54, 238 nn.29, 30, & 31

THE MEDIA AND THE LAW (H. Simmons
& J. Califano ed. 1976), 101

R. MOLEY, OUR CRIMINAL COURTS
(1930), 239 nn.45 & 57

E. MORGAN, BASIC PROBLEMS OF EVI-
DENCE (1962), 35, 36, 235 nn.30 & 41

NAT'L DIST. ATT'YS ASS'N, CONFES-
SIONS AND INTERROGATIONS AFTER
MIRANDA (J. Zagel 5th rev. ed. 1975),
156

T.R. NAUGHTON. *See* J. GOEBEL &
T.R. NAUGHTON

A NEW LOOK AT CONFESSIONS (B.J.
George ed. 1967), 277 n.188

R. PERRY, CHARACTERISTICALLY AMERI-
CAN (1949), 223

POLICE POWER AND INDIVIDUAL FREEDOM
(C. Sowle ed. 1962), 1, 39, 42, 46–47,
68, 98, 101, 102, 108–09, 225 n.2,
233 n.2, 236 n.50, 238 nn.26–28, 242

n.86, 248 n.42, 249 n.54, 255 n.57,
256 n.66, 257 nn.67–69, 258 n.86,
260 n.37, 264 n.81, 287 n.320, 301
n.464, 303 n.471

R. POUND, CRIMINAL JUSTICE IN
AMERICA (1929), 239 n.57

E. B. PRETTYMAN, JR., DEATH AND THE
SUPREME COURT (1961), 244 nn.151
& 152

W. RICHARDSON, EVIDENCE (J. Prince
10th ed. 1973), 213

W. SCHAEFER, THE SUSPECT AND SOCI-
ETY (1967), 79, 83, 84, 90, 91, 161,
162, 210, 246 n.17, 247 n.22, 249
nn.48, 55, & 57

H. SIMMONS. *See* THE MEDIA AND THE
LAW

C. SOWLE. *See* POLICE POWER AND IN-
DIVIDUAL FREEDOM

G. STARKMAN. *See* F. INBAU, J.
THOMPSON, J. HADDAD, J. ZAGEL, &
G. STARKMAN

D. STENERSON, H. L. MENCKEN:
ICONOCLAST FROM BALTIMORE (1971),
258 n.87

1 J. STEPHEN, HISTORY OF THE CRIMI-
NAL LAW OF ENGLAND (1883), 235
n.27, 239 nn.46 & 47, 246 n.8

O. STEPHENS, THE SUPREME COURT AND
CONFESSIONS OF GUILT (1973), 301
n.463

3 J. STORY, COMMENTARIES ON THE
CONSTITUTION OF THE UNITED STATES
(1883), 239 n.43

J. THOMPSON. *See* F. INBAU, J.
THOMPSON, J. HADDAD, J. ZAGEL, &
G. STARKMAN

A. TREBACH, THE RATIONING OF JUS-
TICE (1964), 234 n.16

H. UVILLER, THE PROCESS OF CRIMINAL
JUSTICE: INVESTIGATION (1974), 96,
249 n.44

C. WHITEBREAD, CONSTITUTIONAL
CRIMINAL PROCEDURE (1978), 144

2 J. WIGMORE, EVIDENCE (2d ed. 1923),
77; (3d ed. 1940), 9, 11, 15, 20, 230
n.95, 242 n.89, 225 n.49; (J. Chadbourn rev. ed. 1970), 151–52

8 J. WIGMORE, EVIDENCE (3d ed. 1940),
35, 36, 105–06, 235 nn.29, 31, 32, 34,
& 37, 236 nn.47, 53, & 56, 254 n.49,
255 nn.54–57, 286 n.309; (J. Mc-
Naughton ed. 1961), 235 n.25

C. WRIGHT, FEDERAL PRACTICE AND
PROCEDURE (Criminal) (1969), 152

J. ZAGEL. See F. INBAU, J. THOMPSON,
J. HADDAD, J. ZAGEL, & G. STARK-
MAN

H. ZEISEL. See H. KALVEN & H. ZEISEL

**Hearings, Proposed Standards,
Reports, and Statutes**

Allen Report. See ATTORNEY GENERAL'S
COMM.

AMERICAN BAR ASSOCIATION. See JOINT
COMM. ON CONTINUING LEGAL ED.; A
MEMORANDUM ON THE DETENTION OF
ARRESTED PERSONS; STANDARDS FOR
CRIMINAL JUSTICE

AMERICAN LAW INSTITUTE. See CODE OF
CRIMINAL PROCEDURE; JOINT COMM.
ON CONTINUING LEGAL ED.; MODEL
CODE OF PRE-ARRAIGNMENT PROCE-
DURE; MODEL PENAL CODE

ATTORNEY GENERAL'S COMM., REPORT
ON POVERTY AND THE ADMINISTRA-
TION OF FEDERAL CRIMINAL JUSTICE
(1963) (Allen Report), 300 n.459, 301
n.467

CALIF. DEP'T OF JUSTICE, BUREAU OF
CRIMINAL STATISTICS, CRIME IN
CALIFORNIA 99 (1960), 227 n.41

CODE OF CRIMINAL PROCEDURE (ALI)
(Prelim. Draft No. 5, 1927), 77, 78,
234 nn.22 & 23; (Tent. Draft No. 1,
1928), 32–33, 77, 240 n.67

COMMISSIONERS ON CRIMINAL LAW IN
THE CHANNEL ISLANDS, Rep't No. 2
(1848), 54–55, 240 nn.62–66

COMMISSIONERS ON PRACTICE AND
PLEADINGS, REP'T NO. 4—CODE OF
CRIMINAL PROCEDURE (1849), 53–54,
240 n.61

CRIMINAL LAW REVISION COMMITTEE
[Gr. Br.], ELEVENTH REPORT, EVI-
DENCE (GENERAL) (1972), 92

FED. R. CRIM. P. 249 (Prelim. Draft
1943), 55, 234 n.24, 240 n.68

FED. R. CRIM. P. 253 (Prelim. Draft
1943), 33, 234 n.25, 240 n.69

*Hearings Before Subcomm. No. 2 of the
House Comm. on the Judiciary,* 78th
Cong., 1st Sess. 6 (1943), 286 n.310

*Hearings Before a Subcomm. of the Sen-
ate Committee on the Judiciary,* 85th
Cong., 2d Sess., on H.R. 11477, S.
2970, S. 3325, and S. 3355 (1958),
253 nn.44 & 45, 254 n.47

*Hearings Before the Subcommittee on
Constitutional Rights of the Senate
Committee on the Judiciary,* 85th
Cong., 2d Sess. (1958), 229 n.78

*Hearings on S. 486 and H.R. 7525 Be-
fore the Senate Committee on the District of Columbia,* 88th Cong., 1st
Sess. 462 (1963), 60, 61, 101, 258
n.16

JOINT COMM. ON CONTINUING LEGAL
ED. OF ALI & ABA, THE PROBLEM OF
POLICE INTERROGATION (Paulsen ed.
1961), 227 n.39, 228 n.54

The Justices of the Peace Act, 1360, 34
Edw. 3, c. 1, p. 239 n.44

A MEMORANDUM ON THE DETENTION OF
ARRESTED PERSONS AND THEIR PRO-
DUCTION BEFORE A COMMITTING
MAGISTRATE WITH THE STATEMENT

OF THE BILLS AND RIGHTS COMMITTEE OF THE ABA ON H.R. 3690 (1944), 229 n.78

MODEL CODE OF PRE-ARRAIGNMENT PROCEDURE (ALI), xiv, 94; (Tent. Draft No. 1, 1966), 43, 61, 72, 82; (Study Draft No. 1, 1968), 93, 246 n.19, 248 n.39; (Proposed Official Draft No. 1, 1972), 88; Commentary (Tent. Draft No. 6, 1974), 84, 88, 257 n.66; (Official Draft, 1974), 303 n.471; Commentary (Official Draft, 1975), 116, 130, 155, 213, 217, 266 n.108, 267 n.110

MODEL PENAL CODE (ALI) (Tent. Draft No. 9, 1959), 22; (Proposed Official Draft, 1962), 20, 22

NAT'L COMM. ON LAW OBSERVANCE AND ENFORCEMENT, REPORT ON LAWLESSNESS IN LAW ENFORCEMENT (1931) (Wickersham Report), 78, 80, 226 n.25, 234 n.21, 240 n.70, 242 n.93

OFFICE OF THE DISTRICT ATTORNEY, COUNTY OF LOS ANGELES, RESULTS OF SURVEY CONDUCTED IN THE DISTRICT ATTORNEY'S OFFICE OF LOS ANGELES COUNTY REGARDING THE EFFECTS OF THE *DORADO* AND *MIRANDA* DECISIONS UPON THE PROSECUTION OF FELONY CASES (Aug. 4, 1977), 48, 49

Omnibus Crime Control and Safe Streets Act of 1968, 18 U.S.C. § 3501(c) (1976), 294 n.407

REPORT AND RECOMMENDATIONS OF THE COMMISSIONERS' COMMITTEE ON POLICE ARRESTS FOR INVESTIGATION (D.C. 1962), 226 nn.20–24, 228 n.56, 231 nn.127 & 129, 232 n.146, 235 n.35

ROYAL COMM'N ON CAPITAL PUNISHMENT, *Report,* Cmd. No. 8932 (1953), 230 n.123

STANDARDS FOR CRIMINAL JUSTICE (ABA), 82, 94

UNIFORM RULES OF CRIMINAL PROCEDURE (Proposed Final Draft, 1974), xiii, 88; (Approved Draft, 1974), 155, 267 nn.109 & 111, 303 n.471

U.S. COMM. ON CIVIL RIGHTS, 1961 Report V ("Justice") (1961), 234 n.16

Wickersham Report. *See* NAT'L COMM. ON LAW OBSERVANCE AND ENFORCEMENT

Articles and Essays

Alexander. *See* Medalie, Zeitz, & Alexander

F. Allen, *Due Process and State Criminal Procedures: Another Look,* 48 NW. U.L. REV 16 (1953), 18, 96, 229 n.84

F. Allen, *The Judicial Quest for Penal Justice: The Warren Court and the Criminal Cases,* 1975 U. ILL. L.F. 518, pp. 250 n.1, 257 n.80, 258 n.82, 290 n.382, 298 n.448

F. ALLEN, *On Winning and Losing,* in LAW, INTELLECT, AND EDUCATION 16 (1979), xx

F. Allen, *The Supreme Court and State Criminal Justice,* 4 WAYNE L. REV. 191 (1958), 245 n.3

F. Allen, *The Supreme Court, Federalism, and State Systems of Criminal Justice,* 8 DE PAUL L. REV. 213 (1959), 245 n.3

F. Allen, *The* Wolf *Case: Search and Seizure, Federalism and the Civil Liberties,* 45 ILL. L. REV. 1 (1950), 229 n.77, 277 n.199, 294 n.410

Amsterdam, *Perspectives on the Fourth Amendment,* 58 MINN. L. REV. 349 (1974), 110

Amsterdam, *The Supreme Court and the Rights of Suspects in Criminal Cases,* 45 N.Y.U. L. REV. 785 (1970), xx,

249 n.46, 277 n.199, 290 n.382, 291 n.386, 294 n.409, 298 n.447

Arnold, *The Criminal Trial as a Symbol of Public Morality*, in CRIMINAL JUSTICE IN OUR TIME (A. Howard ed. 1965), 292 n.400

Ayres. *See* Griffith & Ayres

Barrett, *Police Practices and the Law—From Arrest to Release or Charge*, 50 CALIF. L. REV. 11 (1962), 235 n.39, 238 n.30, 239 n.56, 242 n.95

Bator, *Finality in Criminal Law and Federal Habeas Corpus for State Prisoners*, 76 HARV. L. REV. 441 (1963), 226 n.33

Bator & Vorenberg, *Arrest, Detention, Interrogation and the Right to Counsel*, 66 COLUM. L. REV. 62 (1966), 71, 209, 273 n.117

Bickel, *Applied Politics and the Science of Law: Writings of the Harvard Period*, in FELIX FRANKFURTER: A TRIBUTE (W. Mendelson ed. 1964), 235 n.44

Bickel, *The Role of the Supreme Court of the United States*, 44 TEX. L. REV. 954 (1966), 111

C. Black, *Civil Rights in Times of Economic Stress—Jurisprudential and Philosophic Aspects*, 1976 U. ILL. L.F. 559, p. 252 n.41

C. Black, *The Lawfulness of the Segregation Decisions*, 69 YALE L.J. 421 (1960), 252 n.41

Breitel, *Criminal Law and Equal Justice*, 1966 UTAH L. REV. 1, pp. 42, 82, 90, 162, 217, 223, 246 n.12, 249 n.52, 300 n.460, 301 n.467

Brennan, *State Constitutions and the Protection of Individual Rights*, 90 HARV. L. REV. 489 (1977), 284 n.272, 299 n.451

Broderick, Book Review, 53 CORNELL L. REV. 737 (1968), 110

Broeder, *The Decline and Fall of* Wolf v. Colorado, 41 NEB. L. REV. 185 (1961), 18

Broeder, Wong Sun v. United States: *A Study in Faith and Hope*, 42 NEB. L. REV. 483 (1963), 227 n.46, 294 n.409

Burt, Miranda *and Title II: A Morganatic Marriage*, 1969 SUP. CT. REV. 81, p. 91

B. CARDOZO, *Law and Literature*, in LAW AND LITERATURE AND OTHER ESSAYS (1931), 252 n.28

Chaffee, Pollak, & Stern, *The Third Degree*, in NAT'L COMM. ON LAW OBSERVANCE AND ENFORCEMENT, REP'T ON LAWLESSNESS IN LAW ENFORCEMENT (1931) (Wickersham Report), 240 n.70

Chafee, *Compulsory Confessions*, 40 NEW REPUBLIC 266 (1924), 77, 78

Chafee, *Remedies for the Third Degree*, ATLANTIC MONTHLY, Nov. 1931, 63–64, 83, 246 n.15, 272 n.85

Chafee, *Thirty-Five Years with Freedom of Speech*, 1 KAN. L. REV. 1 (1952), 241 n.80

Chase, *The Burger Court, the Individual, and the Criminal Process: Directions and Misdirections*, 52 N.Y.U. L. REV. 518 (1977), 288 n.345, 290 nn.378 & 382

Choper. *See* Kamisar & Choper

Coakley, *Restrictions in the Law of Arrest*, 52 NW. U.L. REV. 2 (1957), 61

F. Cohen, *Field Theory and Judicial Logic*, 59 YALE L.J. 238 (1950), 136, 267 n.113

Comment, People v. Dean: *Another Swipe at* Miranda, 4 U. SAN FERN. V.L. REV. 85 (1974), 270 n.53

Comment, *Prearraignment Interrogation and the* McNabb-Mallory *Miasma: A Proposed Amendment to the Federal Rules of Criminal Procedure*, 68 YALE L.J. 1003 (1959), 277 n.199, 294 n.410

Corwin, *The Supreme Court's Construction of the Self-Incrimination Clause,* 29 MICH. L. REV. 1 (1930), 50, 238 n.39

Cox, *Constitutional Adjudications and the Promotion of Human Rights,* 80 HARV. L. REV. 91 (1966), 91

Curran, *Dean Wigmore at His Last Meeting of the Editorial Board,* 34 J. CRIM. L.C. & P.S. 93 (1943), 254 n.49

Dash, *Foreword* to MEDALIE, FROM ESCOBEDO TO *MIRANDA:* THE ANATOMY OF A SUPREME COURT DECISION (1966), 49

Denno, *Mary Beth Tinker Takes the Constitution to School,* 38 FORDHAM L. REV. 35 (1968), 272 n.101

Dershowitz & Ely, Harris v. New York: *Some Anxious Observations on the Candor and Logic of the Emerging Nixon Majority,* 80 YALE L.J. 1198 (1971), 85

Dession, *The New Federal Rules of Criminal Procedure,* 55 YALE L.J. 694 (1946), 229 n.75, 237 n.9, 291 n.386

Developments in the Law — Confessions, 79 HARV. L. REV. 935 (1966), 43, 90, 221, 290 n.380, 291 n.386, 291 n.391, 294 nn.408 & 410, 300 n.459, 302 n.469, 303 n.472

Dix, *Undercover Investigations and Police Rulemaking,* 53 TEXAS L. REV. 203 (1975), 179, 187, 191, 283 nn.265 & 269, 284 nn.277–79, 285 n.295

Dooley, *Line-Up Line: "You Got Nutt'n on Me,"* Boston Globe, Jan. 27, 1965, 36

Douglas, *The Means and the End,* 1959 WASH. U.L.Q. 103, pp. 229 nn.74 & 77, 277 n.199, 294 n.410

Driver, *Confessions and the Social Psychology of Coercion,* 82 HARV. L. REV. 42 (1968), 121, 269 n.45

G. Edwards, *Interrogation of Criminal Defendants—Some Views on* Miranda v. Arizona, 35 FORDHAM L. REV. 181 (1966), xv

Elsen. *See* Enker & Elsen

Elsen & Rosett, *Protections for the Suspect Under* Miranda v. Arizona, 76 COLUM. L. REV. 645 (1967), 110, 249 nn.43, 61, & 62

Ely, *Flag Desecration: A Case Study in the Roles of Categorization and Balancing in First Amendment Analysis,* 88 HARV. L. REV. 1482 (1975), 272 n.100

Ely. *See* Dershowitz & Ely

Emerson, *The American Scholar,* in THE PORTABLE EMERSON (M. Van Doren ed. 1946), 252 nn.26–27

Enker & Elsen, *Counsel for the Suspect:* Massiah v. United States *and* Escobedo v. Illinois, 49 MINN. L. REV. 47 (1964), 40, 65, 88, 161, 210, 236 n.59, 266 n.104, 276 nn.185 & 188, 280 nn.248, 249, & 252, 282 n.259, 291 n.386, 297 n.432, 303 nn.470 & 471

Foote, *The Fourth Amendment: Obstacle or Necessity in the Law of Arrest?,* in POLICE POWER AND INDIVIDUAL FREEDOM (C. Sowle ed. 1962), 42, 236 n.50, 260 n.37, 287 n.320

Foote, *Safeguards in the Law of Arrest,* 52 NW. U.L. REV. 16 (1957), 235 n.35

Foreword, J. CRIM. L. & CRIMINOLOGY (June 1977), xv

A Forum on the Interrogation of the Accused, 49 CORNELL L.Q. 382 (1964), 254 n.47

Frankel, *From Private Fights Toward Public Justices,* 51 N.Y.U. L. REV. 516 (1976), 251 n.23

Frankfurter, *John Henry Wigmore: A Centennial Tribute,* 58 NW. U.L. REV. 443(1963), 255 n.53

Freund, *William J. Brennan, Jr.,* 86
YALE L.J. 1015 (1977), 267 n.114

Friendly, *The Bill of Rights as a Code of
Criminal Procedure,* 53 CALIF. L.
REV. 929 (1965), 94, 161, 270 n.53,
293 n.402

Friendly, *The Fifth Amendment Tomorrow: The Case for Constitutional
Change,* 37 U. CIN. L. REV. 671
(1968), 79, 83, 84, 90, 91, 217, 246
n.13, 247 n.23, 248 n.35, 250 nn.69 &
71, 302 n.467

Friendly, *Is Innocence Irrelevant? Collateral Attack on Criminal Judgments,*
38 CHI. L. REV. (1970), 95

H. FRIENDLY, *On Entering the Path of
the Law,* in BENCHMARKS (1967), 298
n.446

H. FRIENDLY, *A Postscript on* Miranda,
in BENCHMARKS (1967), 184, 281
n.255

Friendly, *Time and Tide in the Supreme
Court,* 2 CONN. L. REV. 213 (1969),
90

J. Gardner, *Hazard and Hope,* in No
EASY VICTORIES (H. Rowan ed. 1968),
xx

Gerard, *The Right to Counsel on Appeal
in Missouri,* 1965 WASH. U.L.Q. 463,
p. 297 n.434

A. Goldstein, *The State and The Accused:
Balance of Advantage in Criminal
Procedure,* 69 YALE L.J. 1149 (1960),
227 n.41

Graham, *What Is "Custodial Interrogation"?: California's Anticipatory Application of* Miranda v. Arizona, 14
U.C.L.A. L. REV. 59 (1966), 88, 144,
152, 247 n.23, 269 nn.31 & 39, 270
nn.52 & 53, 273 n.116

Grano, Kirby, Biggers, *and* Ash: *Do Any
Constitutional Safeguards Remain
Against the Danger of Convicting the
Innocent?* 72 MICH. L. REV. 717
(1974), 192, 293 n.403, 296 n.414

Grano, Rhode Island v. Innis: *A Need to*

*Reconsider the Constitutional Prem-
ises Underlying the Law of Confessions,* 17 AM. CRIM. L. REV. 1 (1979),
282 n.261

Grano, *Voluntariness, Free Will, and the
Law of Confessions,* 65 VA. L. REV.
859 (1979), xi

Grant, *Our Common Law Constitution,*
40 B.U.L. REV. 1 (1960), 239 n.47

Griffith & Ayres, *A Postscript to the*
Miranda *Project: Interrogation of
Draft Protesters,* 77 YALE L.J. 300
(1967), 119–20, 269 nn.42 & 44, 301
n.463

Griswold, *The Individual and the Fifth
Amendment,* The New Leader, Oct.
29, 1956, 238 n.40

Hartman, *The Burger Court—1973
Term: Leaving the Sixties Behind Us,*
65 J. CRIM. L. & CRIMINOLOGY 437
(1974), 297 n.434

Henkin, *On Drawing Lines,* 82 HARV. L.
REV. 63 (1968), 272 n.102, 273 n.103

Herman, *The Supreme Court and Restrictions on Police Interrogation,* 25 OHIO
STATE L.J. 449 (1964), 44, 161, 243
n.112, 246 n.6, 270 n.68, 274 n.121,
290 n.380, 291 n.391

Hiemstra, *Abolition of the Right Not to be
Questioned,* S. AFR. L.J. 187 (1963),
34, 235 n.26

Hofstadter & Levittan, *Lest the Constable Blunder: A Remedial Proposal,* 20
RECORD OF N.Y.C.B.A. 629 (1956),
82, 83–84, 249 nn.47 & 56

Hogan & Snee, *The* McNabb-Mallory
Rule: Its Rise, Rationale, and Rescue,
47 GEO. L.J. 1 (1958), 229 nn.77 &
78, 243 n.96, 294 n.408

O.W. HOLMES, *Law in Science and Science in Law,* in COLLECTED LEGAL
PAPERS (1920), 272 nn.98 & 99

Hopkins, *The Lawless Arm of the Law,*
ATLANTIC MONTHLY, Sept. 1931, 31

Howard, *State Courts and Constitutional
Rights in the Day of the Burger Court,*

62 VA. L. REV. 873 (1976), 284 n.272, 299 n.451

Inbau, *Behind Those "Police Brutality" Charges,* 89 READER'S DIGEST (July 1966), 252 n.31

Inbau, *The Courts on Confessions,* THE POLICE DIGEST, Dec. 1943, 250 n.4

Inbau, *The Innovator* (Editorial), 32 J. CRIM. L.C. & P.S. 263 (1941), 254 n.49

Inbau, *Law Enforcement, the Courts and Civil Liberties,* in CRIMINAL JUSTICE IN OUR TIME (A. Howard ed. 1965), 101

Inbau, *Lawlessness Galore,* POLICE-LAW REVIEW, Aug.–Sept. 1965, 252 n.34

Inbau, *Lawlessness Galore,* THE TULANIAN, Dec. 1966, 252 n.39

Inbau, *Misconceptions Regarding Lawlessness and Law Enforcement,* THE POLICE JOURNAL, Oct. 1969, 252 n.33

Inbau, *More About Public Safety v. Individual Civil Liberties,* 53 J. CRIM. L.C. & P.S. 329 (1962), 255 n.59

Inbau, *"Playing God": 5 to 4,* 57 J. CRIM. L.C. & P.S. 377 (1966), 252 n.43

Inbau, *Police Interrogation—A Practical Necessity,* in POLICE POWER AND INDIVIDUAL FREEDOM (C. Sowle ed. 1962), 101, 102, 255 n.57

Inbau, *Public Safety v. Individual Civil Liberties: The Prosecutor's Stand,* 53 J. CRIM. L.C. & P.S. 85 (1962), 106, 252 n.36

Inbau, *Restrictions in the Law of Interrogation and Confessions,* 52 NW. U.L. REV. 77 (1957), 101

Introduction, POLICE POWER AND INDIVIDUAL FREEDOM (C. Sowle ed. 1962), 258 n.86

Irvine, *The Third Degree and the Privilege Against Self Crimination,* 13 CORNELL L.Q. 211 (1928), 78

Israel, *Criminal Procedure, the Burger Court, and the Legacy of the Warren Court,* 75 MICH. L. REV. 1319 (1977), xvii, 163, 275 n.149, 287 n.331, 290 nn.379 & 385, 298 n.434

Israel, Gideon v. Wainwright: *The "Art" of Overruling,* in 1963 SUP. CT. REV. 211, p. 237 n.14

Jaffe, *Impromptu Remarks,* 76 HARV. L. REV. 1111 (1963), 258 nn.83 & 84

Kamisar, Book Review, 76 HARV. L. REV. 1502 (1963), 226 n.20, 235 n.35

Kamisar, Book Review, 78 HARV. L. REV. 478 (1964), 248 n.31

Kamisar, *A Confession's Trustworthiness, It Is Argued, Isn't Enough,* N.Y. Times, May 14, 1977, 96

Kamisar, *"Custodial Interrogation" Within the Meaning of* Miranda, in CRIMINAL LAW AND THE CONSTITUTION (Inst. Cont. Legal Educ. ed. 1968), 88, 144, 247 n.23, 285 n.296

Kamisar, *How to Use, Abuse—and Fight Back with—Crime Statistics,* 25 OKLA. L. REV. 239 (1972), 258 n.81

Kamisar, *Illegal Searches or Seizures and Contemporaneous Incriminating Statements: A Dialogue on a Neglected Area of Criminal Procedure,* 1961 U. ILL. L.F. 78, pp. 225 n.2, 227 n.44, 228 n.53

Kamisar, Miranda's *Impact on Police Practices (Panel Evaluation),* in A NEW LOOK AT CONFESSIONS 92 (B.J. George ed. 1967), 162, 163

Kamisar, *On the Tactics of Police-Prosecution Oriented Critics of the Courts,* 49 CORNELL L.Q. 436 (1964), 237 n.15

Kamisar, *Poverty, Equality, and Criminal Procedure,* in NAT'L COLLEGE OF DIST. ATTORNEYS, CONSTITUTIONAL LAW DESKBOOK (1977), 298 n.434

Kamisar, *Public Safety v. Individual Liberties: Some "Facts" and "Theories",* 53 J. CRIM. L.C. & P.S. 171 (1962), 255 n.59

Kamisar, *The Right to Counsel and the Fourteenth Amendment: A Dialogue on "The Most Pervasive Right" of an Accused,* 30 U. CHI. L. REV. 1 (1962), 227 n.44, 251 n.15

Kamisar, *Some Reflections on Criticizing the Courts and "Policing the Police,"* 53 J. CRIM. L.C. & P.S. 453 (1962), 255 n.59

Kamisar, Wolf *and* Lustig *Ten Years Later: Illegal State Evidence in State and Federal Courts,* 43 MINN. L. REV. 1083 (1959), 229 n.77, 241 n.79

Kamisar & Choper, *The Right to Counsel in Minnesota: Some Field Findings and Legal-Policy Observations,* 48 MINN. L. REV. 1 (1963), 235 n.35, 297 n.434, 302 n.467

Kauper, *Judicial Examination of the Accused—A Remedy for the Third Degree,* 30 MICH. L. REV. 1224 (1932), 77–94 *passim,* 235 n.40, 238 n.30, 239 nn.47, 48, 50, & 58, 266 n.106

Kocourek, *John Henry Wigmore,* 27 AM. JUD. SOC'Y 122 (1943), 255 n.52

Kuh, *Some Views on* Miranda v. Arizona, 35 FORDHAM L. REV. 233 (1966), 48

Kurland, Book Review, 34 U. CHI. L. REV. 704 (1967), 91

La Fave, *Detention for Investigation by the Police: An Analysis of Current Practices,* 1962 WASH. U.L.Q. 331, pp. 19, 235 n.35

La Fave, *"Street Encounters" and the Constitution: Terry, Sibron, Peters, and Beyond,* 67 MICH. L. REV. 39 (1968), 247 n.23, 249 n.61

Lamberto, *Leaming's "Speech": "I'd do it again,"* Des Moines Register, April 7, 1977, § B, 139, 147

Larson, *Present Police and Legal Methods for the Determination of the Innocence or Guilt of the Suspect,* 16 J. CRIM. L. & CRIMINOLOGY 219 (1925), 242 n.89

Laski, *The Limitations of the Expert,* 162 HARPER'S MONTHLY 101 (1930), 251 nn.24–25, 252 n.40

Leiken, *Police Interrogation in Colorado: The Implementations of* Miranda, 47 DENVER L.J. 1 (1970), 92, 301 n.463

Letter from English Policeman on Use of Judges' Rules, in SELECTED WRITINGS ON LAW OF EVIDENCE AND TRIAL (W. Fryer ed. 1957), 38

Levittan. *See* Hofstadter & Levittan

Lewellen, *How to Make a Killer Confess,* SAT. EVE. POST, Mar. 31, 1956, 225 n.5, 226 n.26, 253 n.46

Lewin, *Criminal Procedure,* 22 SYRACUSE L. REV. 381 (1971), 213

Loewy, *Punishing Flag Desecrators: The Ultimate in Flag Desecration,* 49 N.C.L. REV. 48 (1970), 272 n.100

McCormick, *The Scope of Privilege in the Law of Evidence,* 16 TEXAS L. REV. 447 (1938), 11

MacInnes, *The Criminal Society,* in THE POLICE AND THE PUBLIC (C. Rolph ed. 1962), 32, 242 n.88

McNaughton, *The Privilege Against Self-Incrimination: Its Constitutional Affectation, Raison d'Etre and Miscellaneous Implications,* in POLICE POWER AND INDIVIDUAL FREEDOM (C. Sowle ed. 1962), 46–47, 238 nn.26–28

Mayers, *The Federal Witness' Privilege Against Self-Incrimination: Constitutional or Common-Law?,* 4 AM. J. LEGAL HIST. 107 (1960), 50–51, 238 nn.41–43, 240 n.74

Medalie, Zeitz, & Alexander, *Custodial Interrogation in Our Nation's Capital: The Attempt to Implement* Miranda, 76 YALE L.J. 1519 (1967), 92, 250 n.70, 301 n.463

Meltsner & Schrag, *Negotiating Tactics for Legal Services Lawyers,* 7 CLEARINGHOUSE REV. 259 (Sept. 1973), in H. EDWARDS & J. WHITE,

THE LAWYER AS A NEGOTIATOR (1977), 136

Meltzer, *Involuntary Confessions: The Allocation of Responsibility Between Judge and Jury*, 21 U. CHI. L. REV. 317 (1954), 96, 228 nn.58 & 63, 232 n.141

Meltzer, *Required Records, the McCarran Act, and the Privilege against Self-Incrimination*, 18 U. CHI. L. REV. 687 (1951), 235 nn.25 & 43

Miller, *The Supreme Court's Review of Hypothetical Alternatives in a State Confession Case*, 5 SYRACUSE L. REV. 53 (1953), 228 n.63

Morgan, *The Privilege Against Self-Incrimination*, 34 MINN. L. REV. 1 (1949), 35, 48–50, 235 n.34, 238 nn.36 & 37

M. Murphy, *The Problems of Compliance by Police Departments*, 44 TEXAS L. REV. 939 (1966), 161

W. Murphy, *Lower Court Checks on Supreme Court Power*, 53 AM. POLITICAL SCI. REV. 1017 (1956), 294 n.408

Nahmod, *Beyond Tinker: The High School as an Educational Public Forum*, 5 HARV. C.R.-C.L.L. REV. 278 (1970), 272 n.101

Nedrud, *The New Fifth Amendment Concept: Self-Incrimination Redefined*, 2 NAT'L DIST. ATT'YS ASS'N J. 112 (1966), 48

Nimmer, *The Meaning of Symbolic Speech Under the First Amendment*, 21 U.C.L.A. L. REV. 29 (1973), 272 n.100

Note, 100 U. PA. L. REV. 1182 (1952), 18

Note, 112 U. PA. L. REV. 888 (1964), 39

Note, *Eavesdropping, Informers, and the Right of Privacy: A Judicial Tightrope*, 52 CORNELL L.Q. 975 (1967), 187

Note, *Fifth Amendment, Confessions, Self-Incrimination—Does a Request for Counsel Prohibit a Subsequent*

Waiver of Miranda *Prior to the Presence of Counsel?*, 23 WAYNE L. REV. 1321 (1977), 288 n.344

Note, *An Historical Argument for the Right to Counsel During Police Interrogation*, 73 YALE L.J. 1000 (1964), 218, 235 nn.38 & 39

Note, *Interrogation and the Sixth Amendment: The Case for Restriction of Capacity to Waive the Right to Counsel*, 53 IND. L.J. 313 (1978), 219

Note, *Procedural Protections of the Criminal Defendant*, 78 HARV. L. REV. 426 (1964), 82, 248 n.36

Note, *Reaffirmation of Confessions Inadmissible under* McNabb-Mallory, 72 YALE L.J. 1434 (1963), 223

Note, *The Right to Counsel During Police Interrogation: The Aftermath of* Escobedo, 53 CALIF. L. REV. 337 (1965), 290 n.380

Outline of Code of Criminal Procedure, 12 A.B.A.J. 690 (1926), 77

Packer, *The Courts, The Police and the Rest of Us*, 57 J. CRIM. L.C. & P.S. 238 (1966), 111

Packer, *Two Models of the Criminal Process*, 113 U. PA. L. REV. 1 (1964), 111, 242 n.87, 257 n.71

Packer, *Who Can Police the Police?*, The New York Review of Books, Sept. 8, 1966, 43

Paulsen, *The Fourteenth Amendment and the Third Degree*, 6 STAN. L. REV. 411 (1954), 96, 228 n.63, 229 n.84, 230 n.122, 232 nn.147 & 155

Paulsen, *Safeguards in the Law of Search and Seizure*, 52 NW. U.L. REV. 65 (1957), 250 nn.3 & 4

Paulsen, *The Winds of Change: Criminal Procedure in New York 1941–1965*, 15 BUFFALO L. REV. 297 (1966), 213, 299 n.459

Pitler. *See* Rothblatt & Pitler

Pittman, *The Fifth Amendment: Yesterday, Today, and Tomorrow,* 42 A.B.A.J. 509 (1956), 240 n.74

Pollak. *See* Chafee, Pollak & Stern

Pound, *Legal Interrogation of Persons Accused or Suspected of Crime,* 24 J. CRIM. L. & CRIMINOL. 1014 (1934), 248 n.37, 266 n.106

Project, *Interrogations in New Haven: The Impact of* Miranda, 76 YALE L.J. 1519 (1967), 250 n.66, 286 nn.309, 312, & 313, 301 n.463

Pye, *Interrogation of Criminal Defendants—Some Views on* Miranda v. Arizona, 35 FORDHAM L. REV. 199 (1966), 247 n.23

Qua, *Griffin v. Illinois,* 25 U. CHI. L. REV. 143 (1957), 73

Remington, *The Law Relating to "On the Street" Detention. Questioning and Frisking of Suspected Persons and Police Arrest Privileges in General,* in POLICE POWER AND INDIVIDUAL FREEDOM (C. Sowle ed. 1962), 42

Ritz, *State Criminal Confession Cases: Subsequent Developments in Cases Reversed by U.S. Supreme Court and Some Current Problems,* 19 WASH. & LEE L. REV. 202 (1962), 228 n.59

Roalfe, *John Henry Wigmore—Scholar and Reformer,* 53 J. CRIM. L.C. & P.S. 277 (1962), 255 n.50

Robinson, Massiah, Escobedo, *and Rationales for the Exclusion of Confessions,* 56 J. CRIM. L.C. & P.S. 412 (1965), 162

Rogge, Book Review, 76 HARV. L. REV. 1516 (1963), 225 n.4, 227 n.41

Rosett. *See* Elsen & Rosett

Rostow, Book Review, 56 YALE L.J. 412 (1947), 256 n.65

Rostow, *The Democratic Character of Judicial Review,* in THE SOVEREIGN PREROGATIVE (1962), 236 n.49

Rothblatt, *Police Interrogation and the Right to Counsel, Post-Escobedo v. Illinois: Application v. Emasculation,* 17 HASTINGS L.J. 41 (1965), 270 n.53, 299 n.459

Rothblatt & Pitler, *Police Interrogation: Warnings and Waivers—Where Do We Go From Here?,* 42 NOTRE DAME LAW. 479 (1967), 152, 155, 217, 269 n.40, 300 n.462, 301 nn.464-66

Rothblatt & Rothblatt, *Police Interrogation: The Right to Counsel and to Prompt Arraignment,* 27 BROOKLYN L. REV. 24 (1960), 294 n.408, 295 n.412

Schaefer, *Comments* [on Kamisar, *Has the Court Left the Attorney General Behind?,* 54 KY. L.J. 464 (1966)], 54 KY. L.J. 521 (1966), 47-48, 242 n.95

Schaefer, *Federalism and State Criminal Procedure,* 70 HARV. L. REV. 1 (1956), 248 n.25

Schlesinger, *Politics and the American Language,* 43 AMERICAN SCHOLAR 553 (1974), 102

Schrag. *See* Meltsner & Schrag

L.B. Schwartz, *On Current Proposals to Legalize Wire Tapping,* 103 U. PA. L. REV. 157 (1954), 256 n.64

Scott, *Criminal Jurisdiction of a State over a Defendant Based Upon Presence Secured by Force or Fraud,* 37 MINN. L. REV. 91 (1953), 18

Smith, *The Threshold Question in Applying Miranda: What Constitutes Custodial Interrogation?,* 25 S.C.L. REV. 669 (1974), 144, 152

Snee. *See* Hogan & Snee

Stone, *The* Miranda *Doctrine in the Burger Court*, 1977 SUP. CT. REV. 99, pp. 130, 237 n.59, 288 nn.342 & 344, 289 n.376, 290 nn.378, 383, 384, & 385

The Supreme Court, 1961 Term, 76 HARV. L. REV. 75 (1962), 233 n.162

The Supreme Court, 1963 Term, 78 HARV. L. REV. 143 (1964), 236 n.59

*The Supreme Court's Decisions on De-
fendants' Rights and Criminal Procedures,* 39 F.R.D. 423 (1966), 254 n.49

Sutherland, *Crime and Confession,* 79
HARV. L. REV. 21 (1965), 30, 234
nn.11–12, 243 nn.114 & 116

tenBroek. *See* Tussman & tenBroek

Thompson, *Detention After Arrest and
In-Custody: Some Exclusionary Principles,* 1966 U. ILL. L.F. 390, pp. 84,
88, 249 n.53, 255 n.61, 280 n.250,
287 n.325, 303 n.472

Traynor, *The Devils of Due Process in
Criminal Detection, Detention, and
Trial,* 33 U. CHI. L. REV. 657 (1966),
78, 79, 81–82, 88, 92, 162, 210, 238
n.25, 245 n.5, 246 n.11, 249 n.45, 250
n.68, 270 n.53, 290 n.380, 291
n.390, 292 n.393, 293 n.402, 295
n.412

Tussman & tenBroek, *The Equal Protection of the Laws,* 37 CALIF. L. REV.
341 (1949), 300 n.459

Uviller, *The Judge at the Cop's Elbow,*
71 COLUM. L. REV. 707 (1971), 213,
298 n.449, 299 n.456

Vorenberg, *Police Detention and Interrogation of Uncounselled Suspects:
The Supreme Court and the States,* 44
B.U.L. REV. 423 (1964), 210, 219,
298 n.449

Vorenberg. *See* Bator & Vorenberg

Waite, *Report on Lawlessness in Law Enforcement,* 30 MICH. L. REV. 54
(1931), 80

Warner, *How Can the Third Degree Be
Eliminated?,* 1 BILL OF RIGHTS REV.
24 (1940), 63, 68–69

Weisberg, *Police Interrogation of Ar-
rested Persons: A Skeptical View,* in
POLICE POWER AND INDIVIDUAL
FREEDOM (C. Sowle ed. 1962), 1, 39,

98, 108–09, 225 n.2, 233 n.2, 242
n.86, 248 n.42, 249 n.54, 256 n.66,
257 nn.67–69, 264 n.81, 301 n.464,
303 n.471

Wilkes, *More on the New Federalism in
Criminal Procedure,* 63 KY. L.J. 873
(1975), 284 n.273, 299 n.451

Wilkes, *The New Federalism in Criminal
Procedure: State Court Evasion of the
Burger Court,* 62 KY. L.J. 421 (1974),
284 n.272, 299 n.451

W. White, *Police Trickery in Inducing
Confessions,* 127 U. PA. L. REV. 581
(1979), xii, 96–97, 249 n.44

W. White, Rhode Island v. Innis: *The
Significance of a Suspect's Assertion
of His Right to Counsel,* 17 AM. CRIM.
L. REV. 53 (1979), 282 n.261

Whitebread, *Trends in Constitutional
Law: A Forecast,* in CONSTITUTIONAL
LAW DESKBOOK (National College of
District Attorneys ed. 1977), 95

Wigmore, Abrams v. U.S.: *Freedom of
Speech and Freedom of Thuggery in
War-Time and Peace-Time,* 14 ILL. L.
REV. 539 (1920), 255 n.51

C.D. Williams, *Problems of the Fifth
Amendment,* 24 FORDHAM L. REV. 19
(1955), 240 n.74

C. Williams, *Questioning by the Police:
Some Further Points—2,* 1960 CRIM.
L.R. (Brit.) 352, p. 235 n.39

G. Williams, *The Authentication of
Statements to the Police,* 1979 CRIM.
L.R. (Brit.) 1, pp. xviii, 133

G. Williams, *Questioning by the Police:
Some Practical Considerations,* 1960
CRIM. L.R. (Brit.) 325, p. 226 nn.16
& 18

Wilson, *Police Arrest Privileges in a
Free Society: A Plea for Modernization,* in POLICE POWER AND INDI-
VIDUAL FREEDOM (C. Sowle ed.
1962), 68

Zeitz. *See* Medalie, Zeitz, & Alexander